FOUR
SOFTWARE
TOOLS
PLUS

WADSWORTH SERIES IN COMPUTER INFORMATION SYSTEMS

Understanding Database Management Systems, Second Edition, Joseph A. Vasta

The COBOL Handbook, Linda Belcher

A Complete Course in Structured COBOL Programming, John C. Molluzzo

Information Systems in Management, Third Edition, James A. Senn

Four Software Tools, Tim Duffy

Four Software Tools (with Lotus 1-2-3, WordPerfect, and dBASE III Plus), Tim Duffy

Four Software Tools (with WordPerfect, VP-Planner, and dBASE III Plus), Tim Duffy

Four Software Tools, Alternate Edition (with VP-Planner, WordStar, and dBASE III), Tim Duffy

Hands-On Lotus 1-2-3 (with an introduction to IBM PC DOS), Tim Duffy

A Casebook: Four Software Tools, Tim Duffy and Wendy Duffy

Structured COBOL Programming, John C. Molluzzo

Big Blue BASIC, Second Edition, Peter Rob

Contemporary Systems Analysis and Design, Raymond T. Clarke and Charles A. Prins

Applied Structured BASIC, Roy Ageloff and Richard Mojena

IBM PC BASIC, Peter Rob

Essentials of Structured BASIC, Roy Ageloff and Richard Mojena

Programming in dBASE II and dBASE III, Peter Rob

Introduction to Microcomputer Programming, Peter Rob

FOUR
SOFTWARE
TOOLS
PLUS

Applications and Concepts

Tim Duffy
Illinois State University

Wadsworth Publishing Company
Belmont, California
A Division of Wadsworth, Inc.

Computer Science Editor: Frank Ruggirello
Editorial Assistant: Carol Carreon
Production Editor: Sandra Craig
Managing Designer: Carolyn Deacy
Print Buyer: Karen Hunt
Interior and Cover Design: Vargas/Williams/Design
Copy Editor: Betty Duncan-Todd
Art Editor: Edie Williams
Photo Researcher: Monica Suder and Associates
Compositor: Thompson Type, San Diego

IBM is a registered trademark of the International Business Machines Corporation.

dBASE III, dBASE III Plus, and Ashton-Tate are trademarks of Ashton-Tate. The dBASE III Plus Command Summary in Appendix B is copyright Ashton-Tate 1985. All rights reserved. Used by permission.
10159 West Jefferson Boulevard
Culver City, CA 90230
(213) 204-5570

WordPerfect is a registered trademark of WordPerfect Corporation.

VP-Planner Plus is a trademark and Paperback Software is a registered trademark of Paperback Software International, Berkeley, CA, U.S.A.

Lotus and 1-2-3 are trademarks of Lotus Development Corporation.

Lotus charts adapted from Arthur Andersen & Co. materials.

Printed in the United States of America   48
    3 4 5 6 7 8 9 10—93 92 91 90

Library of Congress Cataloging-in-Publication Data

Duffy, Tim.
    Four software tools plus.

    (Wadsworth series in computer information systems)
    Includes index.
    1. Microcomputers—Programming. 2. Computer programs.
I. Title. II. Series.
QA76.6.D82 1989   004.16   88-33858
ISBN 0-534-10164-X

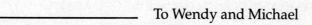 To Wendy and Michael

Important: Please read this page before using the dBASE III Plus program, a copy of which is being made available to you for use in conjunction with the Textbook pursuant to the terms of this Agreement for educational training and/or demonstration purposes. By using the dBASE III Plus program, you show your agreement to the terms of this license.

EXCLUSIONS OF WARRANTIES AND LIMITATIONS OF LIABILITY

The copy of the dBASE III Plus program made available for use with this textbook is a limited functionality version of dBASE III Plus, and is intended solely for educational, training and demonstration purposes. Accordingly, this copy of dBASE III Plus is provided "as is," without warranty of any kind from Ashton-Tate or Wadsworth Publishing Co. Ashton-Tate and Wadsworth Publishing Co. hereby disclaim all warranties of any kind with respect to this limited functionality copy of dBASE III Plus, including without limitation the implied warranties of merchantability and fitness for a particular purpose. Neither Ashton-Tate nor Wadsworth Publishing Co. shall be liable under any circumstances for consequential, incidental, special or exemplary damages arising out of the use of this limited functionality copy of dBASE III Plus, even if Ashton-Tate or Wadsworth Publishing Co. has been apprised of the likelihood of such damages occurring. In no event will Ashton-Tate's or Wadsworth Publishing Co.'s liability (whether based on an action or claim in contract, tort or otherwise) arising out of the use of this limited functionality copy of dBASE III Plus exceed the amount paid for this textbook.

LIMITED USE SOFTWARE LICENSE AGREEMENT

DEFINITIONS
The term "Software" as used in this agreement means the Limited Use version of dBASE III Plus which is made available for use in conjunction with this textbook solely for educational, training and/or demonstration purposes. The term "Software Copies" means the actual copies of all or any portion of the Software, including back-ups, update, merged or partial copies permitted hereunder.

PERMITTED USES
You may:
— Load into RAM and use the Software on a single terminal or a single workstation of a computer (or its replacement).
— Install the Software onto a permanent storage device (a hard disk drive).
— Make and maintain up to three back-up copies provided they are used only for back-up purposes, and you keep possession of the back-ups. In addition, all the information appearing on the original disk labels (including copyright notice) must be copied onto the back-up labels.
    This license gives you certain limited rights to use the Software and Software Copies for educational, training and/or demonstration purposes. You do not become the owner of and Ashton-Tate retains title to, all the Software and Software Copies. In addtion, you agree to use reasonable efforts to protect the Software from unauthorized use, reproduction, distribution or publication.
    All rights not specifically granted in this license are reserved by Ashton-Tate.

USES NOT PERMITTED
You may not:
— Make copies of the Software, except as permitted above.
— Rent, lease, sublicense, time-share, lend or transfer the Software, Software Copies or your rights under this license except that transfers may be made with Ashton-Tate's prior written authorization.
— Alter, decompile, disassemble, or reverse-engineer the Software.
— Remove or obscure the Ashton-Tate copyright and trademark notices.
— Use the Software or Software Copies outside the United States or Canada.

DURATION
This agreement is effective from the day you first use the Software. Your license continues for fifty years or until you return to Ashton-Tate the original disks and any back-up copies, whichever comes first.
    If you breach this agreement, Ashton-Tate can terminate this license upon notifying you in writing. You will be required to return all Software Copies. Ashton-Tate can also enforce our other legal rights.

GENERAL
This agreement represents the entire understanding and agreement regarding the Software and Software Copies and supersedes any prior purchase order, communication, advertising or representation.
    This license may only be modified in a written amendment signed by an authorized Ashton-Tate officer. If any provision of this agreement shall be unlawful, void, or for any reason unenforceable, it shall be deemed severable from, and shall in no way affect the validity or enforceability of the remaining provisions of this agreement. This agreement will be governed by California law.

CONTENTS IN BRIEF

PART ONE | **INTRODUCTORY MICROCOMPUTER CONCEPTS** | **1**

Chapter 1 | **The Computer**   2
Chapter 2 | **Microcomputer Hardware**   24
Chapter 3 | **Microcomputer Software**   56
Chapter 4 | **Introduction to DOS**   88

PART TWO | **HANDS-ON APPLICATIONS** | **109**

Chapter 5 | **Advanced DOS Concepts**   110
Chapter 6 | **Beginning Word Processing with WordPerfect**   132
Chapter 7 | **Intermediate Word Processing with WordPerfect**   160
Chapter 8 | **Advanced Word Processing with WordPerfect**   198
Chapter 9 | **Beginning Spreadsheet with Lotus 1-2-3**   220
Chapter 10 | **Intermediate Spreadsheet with Lotus 1-2-3**   258
Chapter 11 | **Advanced Spreadsheet with Lotus 1-2-3**   290
Chapter 12 | **Introduction to Data Base Management**   348
Chapter 13 | **Beginning Data Base Management with dBASE III Plus**   374
Chapter 14 | **Intermediate Data Base Management with dBASE III Plus**   400
Chapter 15 | **Advanced Data Base Management with dBASE III Plus**   432

PART THREE | **APPLIED CONCEPTS** | **455**

Chapter 16 | **Graphics**   456
Chapter 17 | **Graphing with 1-2-3**   478
Chapter 18 | **Telecommunications**   514
Chapter 19 | **Integrated Software Systems**   536
Chapter 20 | **Management Information Systems and System Analysis**   568
Chapter 21 | **Ethics, Social Issues, and Computer Security**   600
Chapter 22 | **Desktop Publishing**   618
Chapter 23 | **Future Trends**   634

Appendix A | **Instructions for Using Educational Versions of Software**   A-1
Appendix B | **Software Command Summaries**   A-10
Appendix C | **WordPerfect 5.0**   A-37
Appendix D | **BASIC**   A-68
Appendix E | **Purchasing a Home Computer**   A-109
| **Glossary**   A-114
| **Index**   A-148

CONTENTS

Preface   *xxiii*

PART ONE · **INTRODUCTORY MICROCOMPUTER CONCEPTS**   **1**

Chapter 1

The Computer   2

Chapter Objectives   3
What Is a Computer?   4
What Is a Computer System?   5
History of the Electronic Computer   6
Computer Generations   8
Classifications of Today's Computers   9
Data and Computers   13
Data and Information   13
Data Storage and the Hierarchy of Data   13
How a Computer Locates Data   15
How a Computer Processes Data   15
Chapter Review   16
Key Terms and Concepts   19
Chapter Quiz   20
Questions for Thought   22

Chapter 2

Microcomputer Hardware   24

Chapter Objectives   25
Hardware Components   26
Input   26
Processing   30
Microprocessor Chips and Computer Design   36
Output   38
Secondary Storage   44
Diskette Dos and Don'ts   46
Other Disks   49
Chapter Review   51
Key Terms and Concepts   52
Chapter Quiz   52
Questions for Thought   55

Chapter 3

Microcomputer Software   56

Chapter Objectives   57
Software Menus   58
Horizontal Menus   58
Vertical Menus   60

Software Categories   62

Programming Languages   62

Application Programs   64

Integrated Software   69

Special-Use Application Software   69

Productivity Software   71

Operating Systems: IBM PC DOS and MS DOS   72

Chapter Review   82

Key Terms and Concepts   82

Chapter Quiz   83

Computer Exercises   86

Questions for Thought   86

Chapter 4   **Introduction to DOS   88**

Chapter Objectives   89

Disk Commands   90

File Commands   90

Time Commands   91

Internal and External Commands   91

Format Notation   91

Rules Common to All DOS Commands   91

Information About Specific DOS Commands   92

Disk Commands   93

CHKDSK (Check Disk) Command   93

DISKCOPY (Copy Disk) Command   94

FORMAT Command   96

File Commands   98

COPY Command   98

DIR (Directory) Command   99

ERASE Command   101

RENAME (or REN) Command   102

TYPE Command   102

Time Commands   103

DATE Command   103

TIME Command   103

DOS Command Summary   104

DOS Commands by Function and Type   104

Chapter Review   105

Key Terms and Concepts   105

Chapter Quiz   105

Computer Exercises   107

PART TWO   **HANDS-ON APPLICATIONS**   **109**

Chapter 5   **Advanced DOS Concepts   110**

Chapter Objectives   111

Batch Files: The DOS Automator   112

How Batch Files Work   112

Rules for Creating Simple Batch Files   113

Creating Batch Files   113

Executing a Batch File   114

Substituting Data in Batch File Execution   115

Sample Batch Files   115

Introduction to Disk Directories   116

Directories and Directory Commands   116

The Active (Current) Directory   119

PATH: Executing Commands Without Changing Directories   121

DOS Directory Commands   122

Configuring Your System   124

Chapter Review   127

Key Terms and Concepts   127

Chapter Quiz   127

Computer Exercises   130

Chapter 6   ***Beginning Word Processing with WordPerfect   132***

Chapter Objectives   133

Overview of WordPerfect   136

Word Processing   136

Merge Feature   136

Speller and Thesaurus   137

Additional Features   137

Starting WordPerfect   137

Diskette Systems   137

Hard Disk Systems   138

WordPerfect Screen   138

Text Window   140

Entering and Canceling Commands   140

Help Feature   140

Operating WordPerfect   140

Entering a Document   140

Saving a Document (File) to Disk   142

Save   142

Exit   142

Retrieving the File   143

List Files   143

Moving Around the Document   144

Cursor Movement Commands   145

Page Breaks   146

Re-forming a Paragraph   146

Editing Text   147

Inserting Text   147

Deleting Text   148

Summary of Delete Commands   *151*
Restoring Deleted Text   *152*
Line Spacing   *152*
Printing the Document   *153*
Chapter Review   153
Key Terms and Concepts   155
Chapter Quiz   155
Computer Exercises   157

Chapter 7   **Intermediate Word Processing with WordPerfect   160**

Chapter Objectives   161
Saving Files   162
Backup Feature of WordPerfect   162
How WordPerfect Handles Files with the Backup   162
The Original File   *163*
Backup Files   *163*
Temporary Files   *163*
How WordPerfect Handles Files   163
Creating Files   *163*
Editing Files   *163*
Using Files Subsequently   *164*
WordPerfect Codes   164
Printing Files   165
Special Text Entry Commands   167
Center Command   *167*
Boldface Command   *168*
Underline Command   *168*
Flush Right Command   *168*
Overstrike Command   *168*
Combining Commands   *169*
Date Command   *169*
Margin Commands   170
Indent   *171*
L/R Indent   *172*
Margin Release   *172*
Tabs and Resetting Tabs   173
Block Command   174
Marking a Block of Text   *174*
Using Blocks with Previously Covered WordPerfect Commands   *174*
New WordPerfect Commands That Use the Block Feature   *176*
Disk Full Errors   179
Search and Replace Commands   180
Search   *180*
Replace   *180*
Chapter Review   181
Key Terms and Concepts   183

Contents

Chapter Quiz   183
Computer Exercises   186

Chapter 8

Advanced Word Processing with WordPerfect   198

Chapter Objectives   199
Speller   200
Page Format   203
Page Number Position   203
New Page Number   204
Center Page Top to Bottom   205
Page Length   205
Top Margin   206
Headers or Footers   206
Page Number Column Position   207
Suppress for Current Page Only   207
Conditional End of Page   208
Widow/Orphan   208
***Print Format   209**
Pitch   209
Lines per Inch   210
Right Justification   210
Underline Style   210
Sheet Feeder Bin Number   212
Insert Printer Command   212
Line Numbering   212
Chapter Review   212
Key Terms and Concepts   213
Chapter Quiz   213
Computer Exercises   215

Chapter 9

Beginning Spreadsheet with Lotus 1-2-3   220

Chapter Objectives   221
Introduction to Spreadsheets   222
Why Use Spreadsheet Software?   222
Spreadsheet Syntax   225
Problem-Solving Steps Using Spreadsheets   227
Introduction to Lotus 1-2-3   227
Parts of 1-2-3   227
Starting Lotus 1-2-3   229
Lotus 1-2-3 Screen   230
Navigating Around the 1-2-3 Worksheet   231
How Lotus 1-2-3 Uses Other Keys   232
Data Entry   234
Entering Formulas   235

Circular References   236
Built-in Functions   236
Correcting Errors on the Worksheet   237
Getting Help   238
Entering a Sample Lotus 1-2-3 Worksheet   238
Step-by-Step Instructions for 1-2-3 Sample Worksheet—COMPSALS   240
Saving and Retrieving Worksheet Files   245
Chapter Review   248
Key Terms and Concepts   248
Chapter Quiz   249
Computer Exercises   252

Chapter 10   ***Intermediate Spreadsheet with Lotus 1-2-3   258***

Chapter Objectives   259
Range   260
The Copy Command   261
Formatting   263
Adding and Deleting Rows and Columns   265
Moving Cell Contents   266
The Print Command   267
Print Menu   268
Print Default Settings   271
1-2-3 and the Print Line Counter   271
Forced Page Breaks   272
1-2-3 Functions   272
More on Data Entry   274
1-2-3 Sample `FUNCTION` Worksheet   275
1-2-3 Sample `FUNCTION` Spreadsheet   277
Chapter Review   283
Key Terms and Concepts   284
Chapter Quiz   284
Computer Exercises   286

Chapter 11   ***Advanced Spreadsheet with Lotus 1-2-3   290***

Chapter Objectives   291
Controlling Your Worksheet Environment   292
Worksheet Zero Command   292
GoTo Command   292
System Command   292
Changing the Directory   292
Column Hide   293
Finding Circular References and Status Commands   295
Password Protecting Your Worksheets   296
Range Transpose   297

Range Names 298
Name Menu 299
Naming Instructions 300
More Range Name Examples 300
Use of Dummy Columns or Rows in Expanding Ranges 304
Sorting 306
Sort Menu 306
Worksheet Practice with the Sort Command 308
Titles 311
Titles Menu 311
Titles Instructions 312
Relative and Absolute Addressing 312
Automatic Versus Manual Worksheet Recalculation 315
More on Functions 315
@IF and Logical Operators 315
@DATE and Arithmetic 317
Worksheet Practice 317
Loan Amortization Worksheet 317
Car Loan Evaluation Worksheet 324
Cell Contents Listing for Amortization Worksheet 326
Cell Contents Listing for Car Loan Worksheet 327
Chapter Review 328
Key Terms and Concepts 328
Chapter Quiz 329
Computer Exercises 331

Chapter 12

Introduction to Data Base Management 348

Chapter Objectives 349
Traditional Approach to Information Processing 350
Problems of the Traditional Approach 350
Role of the Data Base Management System 352
Data Base Management System Example 352
Advantages of Data Base Management Systems 354
Parts of a Data Base Management System 355
Query Language 355
Report Generator 356
Data-Definition Language 356
Data-Manipulation Language 359
Role of the Data Base Administrator 359
Data Dictionary 359
Transaction Log 359
Configuration Control 360
Security 360
Backup and Recovery 360
Data Base Organization Methods 360
List Structures 361

Hierarchical (Tree) Structures   362
Network Structures   363
Relational Structures   363
Indexing   363
Sequential (Traditional) File Data Processing Versus Relational Data
  Base   367
Building a Data Base   367
Chapter Review   369
Key Terms and Concepts   370
Chapter Quiz   370

Chapter 13

Beginning Data Base Management with dBASE III Plus   374

Chapter Objectives   375
Introduction to dBASE III Plus   376
Limitations of dBASE III Plus   376
Modes of dBASE III Plus   377
Starting dBASE III Plus   377
The Assistant Menu Screen   377
The Help Facility   380
Leaving dBASE III Plus   381
Communicating with dBASE III Plus   382
Setting the Default Drive   382
Full-Screen Cursor Menus   383
Creating a dBASE III Plus File   383
Activating the Data Base   388
Adding Records to the File   391
Editing Records in the File   393
dBASE III Plus File Types   394
Data Base Files   394
Chapter Review   395
Key Terms and Concepts   395
Chapter Quiz   395
Computer Exercises   398

Chapter 14

Intermediate Data Base Management with dBASE III Plus   400

Chapter Objectives   401
Access and Display Commands   402
Command Execution from the Assist Menu   402
DISPLAY   409
DIR   410
Access and Display Commands Entered from the Dot Prompt   410
? and RECNO( ) Commands   414
Pointer Position Commands   414
GO and GOTO   414

SKIP   415
GOTO TOP   415
GOTO BOTTOM   416
Other Commands and Functions   416
DATE   416
End of File (EOF)   416
Beginning of File (BOF)   416
SUM   416
Record Alteration Commands   418
REPLACE   418
DELETE, PACK, and RECALL   419
Report Template and the CREATE REPORT Command   422
Printing a Report   426
Chapter Review   427
Key Terms and Concepts   428
Chapter Quiz   428
Computer Exercises   430

Chapter 15   ***Advanced Data Base Management with dBASE III Plus   432***

Chapter Objectives   433
Arrangement Commands   434
SORT   434
INDEX   437
Location Commands   444
LOCATE   445
SEEK   445
BROWSE   448
Chapter Review   449
Key Terms and Concepts   450
Chapter Quiz   451
Computer Exercises   453

PART THREE   ***Applied Concepts***   ***455***

Chapter 16   ***Graphics   456***

Chapter Objectives   457
Graphics Hardware   458
Graphics Output   459
Types of Computer Graphics Applications   460
Presentation Graphics   460
Graphics Editors/Paint Programs   466
Design Graphics   472
Chapter Review   474
Key Terms and Concepts   474
Chapter Quiz   474
Computer Exercises   475

Chapter 17   **Graphing with 1-2-3   478**

Chapter Objectives   479
Steps in Building a Graph and Printing the Graph   480
Graph Menu   480
Type   481
ABCDEF   482
Reset   482
View   482
Save   483
Options   483
Name   485
Quit   485
Generating Graphs   485
Simple Bar Graphs   485
Entering Titles   488
Changing Data Ranges   490
Side-by-Side Bar Graphs   490
Converting to Line Graphs   492
Entering Legends   493
Reconverting to Bar Graphs   494
Pie Charts   494
Exploded Pie Chart   495
Stacked-Bar Charts   496
XY Graphs   498
Formatting the X and Y Numeric Scaling   500
Labeling Graph Data Points   501
Graph Printing   502
PrintGraph Menu   504
Step-by-Step PrintGraph Instructions   506
Chapter Review   507
Key Terms and Concepts   509
Chapter Quiz   509
Computer Exercises   512

Chapter 18   **Telecommunications   514**

Chapter Objectives   515
Computer Communications   516
Data Transmission   516
Data Conversion   516
Transmission Speed   518
Direction of Data Transmission   519
Communications Protocol Modes   520
Communications Software   521
Networks   522
Distributed Data Processing   522
Data Transmission Considerations   522

Communication Media   523
Multiplexors and Concentrators   524
Front-End Processor   526
Network Topologies   526
Local Area Networks   530
Chapter Review   531
Key Terms and Concepts   532
Chapter Quiz   532
Questions for Thought   535

Chapter 19   ***Integrated Software Systems   536***

Chapter Objectives   537
Introduction to PC Works   539
Starting Works   539
Help Feature   541
Exiting Works   541
Word Processing   541
Word Processing Command Summary   545
Commands Using Extend   546
Spreadsheet   546
Pointer Movement Commands   548
Works and Ranges   548
Clear/Erase Command   549
Copy Command   549
Format Command   551
Printing the Worksheet   552
Charting   553
Data Base   555
Querying the Data Base   558
Sorting   558
Reporting   559
Integration   561
Chapter Review   563
Key Terms and Concepts   565
Chapter Quiz   565
Questions for Thought   567

Chapter 20   ***Management Information Systems and System Analysis   568***

Chapter Objectives   569
Management Information Systems   570
Decision-Making Levels   570
Types of Decisions   571
Reporting Methods   572
MIS Versus Transaction Processing Systems   573

Decision Support Systems and MIS   *573*
What Is a System?   **574**
System Characteristics   *575*
System Analysis   **577**
System Development Life Cycle   *578*
Data Gathering   *580*
The System Analysis Report   *583*
System Design   *588*
Hardware Evaluation and Selection   *588*
System Development (Module Design)   *588*
System Implementation   *592*
Chapter Review   **594**
Key Terms and Concepts   **595**
Chapter Quiz   **596**
Questions for Thought   **599**

Chapter 21   ***Ethics, Social Issues, and Computer Security***   ***600***

Chapter Objectives   **601**
Education and Computer Literacy   **602**
Computers in the Workplace   **602**
Job Security   *602*
Privacy and Job Monitoring   *603*
Health Considerations   *603*
Computer Crime   **604**
Examples of Computer Crime   *604*
Characteristics of a Computer Criminal   *606*
Federal Law Dealing with Computer Crime   *608*
Software Development   **608**
Individual Privacy and Computers   **608**
Computer Security and Controls   **610**
General Controls   *610*
Program Controls   *612*
Documentation   *613*
Chapter Review   **613**
Key Terms and Concepts   **614**
Chapter Quiz   **614**
Questions for Thought   **616**

Chapter 22   ***Desktop Publishing***   ***618***

Chapter Objectives   **619**
Desktop Publishing Defined   **620**
Hardware for Desktop Publishing   **620**
Laser Printers   *621*
Scanners   *623*

Software for Desktop Publishing   625
Document Design   626
Chapter Review   628
Key Terms and Concepts   630
Chapter Quiz   630
Questions for Thought   632

Chapter 23   *Future Trends   634*

Chapter Objectives   635
Artificial Intelligence   636
Natural Language   636
Robotics   636
Vision and Sensing Systems   636
Expert Systems   638
Applications   639
Obtaining an Expert System   640
Fifth-Generation Computers   641
Communications Technology   641
Impact of Fiber Optics   642
Changes in Government Regulation   642
Impact on the Individual   642
Impact on Hardware   642
Chapter Review   643
Key Terms and Concepts   643
Chapter Quiz   643
Questions for Thought   645

Appendix A   *Instructions for Using Educational Versions of Software   A-1*

Introduction   A-1
Starting WordPerfect 4.2   A-1
Steps for Using VP-Planner Plus   A-2
Steps for Using dBASE III Plus   A-3
Spreadsheet Compatibility   A-4
Features of VP-Planner Plus to Avoid   A-4
Features of Release 2(.10) to Avoid   A-4
VP-Planner Plus Incompatibilities with Text   A-4
Backup Feature of WordPerfect 4.2   A-5
WordPerfect 4.2 Set-up Menu   A-5
Backup Feature of WordPerfect 5.0   A-5
WordPerfect 5.0 Set-up Menu   A-7

Appendix B   *Software Command Summaries   A-10*

                     WordPerfect 4.2 Command Summary   A-11

Contents

WordPerfect 5.0 Command Summary   *A-15*

dBASE III Plus Command Summary   *A-19*

Conventions   A-20
Operators   A-20
Functions   A-21
Selected dBASE Commands   A-21
Selected SET Commands   A-23
Full-Screen Cursor Movement Codes   A-23
**Control Key Strokes Operable When dBASE Is Not in Full-Screen
     Mode   A-24**

Lotus 1-2-3 Command Menus   *A-25*

Lotus 1-2-3 Command Structure Charts   A-26
1-2-3 Function Summary   A-30
Data Base Functions   A-30
Date and Time Functions   A-30
Financial Functions   A-31
Mathematical Functions   A-34
Special Functions   A-35
Statistical Functions   A-35
String Functions   A-35

Appendix C   ***WordPerfect 5.0***   *A-37*

WordPerfect Screen (p. 138)   A-38
Line Spacing (p. 152)   A-38
Printing the Document (p. 153)   A-39
WordPerfect Codes (p. 164)   A-40
Printing Files (p. 165)   A-41
Print Option of Print Menu   A-41
Options Portion of Print Menu   A-43
Date Command (p. 169)   A-43
Margin Commands (p. 170)   A-44
Tabs and Resetting Tabs (p. 173)   A-45
Block Command (p. 174)   A-48
New WordPerfect Commands That Use the Block Feature (p. 176)   A-48
Format (p. 199)   A-52
Line   A-53
Page   A-54
Document   A-58
Other   A-60
Font   A-61
Appendix Review   A-63
Key Terms and Concepts   A-64

Appendix Quiz   A-64
Computer Exercises   A-66

Appendix D

BASIC   A-68

Starting BASIC   A-69
Leaving BASIC   A-70
Writing Programs in BASIC   A-70
Session 1: Entering a Simple Program   A-70
More on Listing a Program   A-73
Exercises   A-76
Session 2: File Commands and Program Editing   A-77
Other Useful Commands   A-81
Exercises   A-82
Session 3: Constants and Variable Names   A-82
Exercises   A-86
Session 4: The IF Statement and Looping   A-87
Exercises   A-89
Session 5: READ, DATA, and RESTORE Statements   A-90
Exercises   A-92
Session 6: Advanced Topics   A-93
Reserved Words   A-98
Selected BASIC Command Summary   A-99

Appendix E

Purchasing a Home Computer   A-109

Typical Computer System Components   A-110
The Issue of Compatibility   A-110
Special Requirements   A-111
Where to Purchase the Machine   A-111
Software Considerations   A-112
Hidden Costs   A-112
Summary   A-113

Glossary   A-114

Index   A-148

PREFACE

Almost as soon as the original *Four Software Tools* was introduced to the marketplace, I received requests from instructors and users of the text to include computer concepts and literacy topics. The majority of these individuals emphasized that the "hands-on" flavor of the text should be maintained but that important subjects related to all classes of computer systems should also be included in the book. *Four Software Tools Plus: Applications and Concepts* is a response to those requests. The goal of this book is to introduce students to the wide range of computers found in the business world, to develop hands-on skills with several important software packages, and to present important concepts related to computers.

The first chapter provides an overview of the different types of computers, a brief history of computing, an introduction to the way computers process data, and an introduction to data storage techniques. Chapters 2 and 3 introduce students to the basic hardware and software that is typically found in a business computer environment.

Part Two contains the hands-on chapters: advanced DOS topics, word processing, spreadsheets, and data base management. Each of the hands-on subjects (with the exception of advanced DOS) is divided into introductory, intermediate, and advanced coverage. Because this text is not meant to replace the original *Four Software Tools* text in its entirety, a number of advanced topics not relevant to software novices have been omitted. Since this text has a new goal, Chapter 12 now defines the term *data base*, emphasizes the advantages of data base management, and describes the role of data base management in an organization, the management of the data base, and the organization of the data base itself. Again, Chapter 12 emphasizes all classes of data base management systems, while the hands-on chapters, Chapters 13–15, emphasize the role of microcomputer-based DBMSs.

The two chapters on graphics, Chapters 16 and 17, are included to introduce students to the uses of graphics in the business world and also to give students some first-hand experience using Lotus 1-2-3 to generate graphs of their own. Presentation graphics packages, paint/editor packages, and CAD/CAM applications are also described.

Chapter 18, Telecommunications, was included because of the impact that the interconnection of computers is having on today's society. Students are introduced to elementary telecommunications terminology relevant to microcomputers as well as to larger computers. Various methods that can be used to connect computers to networks are also described. Finally, the local area network, the vehicle most frequently used for connecting multiple microcomputers, is covered.

Chapter 19, Integrated Software Systems, features the Works package by Microsoft to illustrate how data can be created in one software application and then used in that application or passed to another application for use. While it is not necessary for students to have access to the Works package, students who do have access to it can follow along with the discussion.

All students taking introductory computer courses need at least a brief introduction to the topic of management information systems and system analysis. It is this area of the organizational use of computer technology that has impacted all sizes of organizations by providing timely information needed by managers to make decisions and solve problems. The goal of Chapter 20 is to give students the flavor of management information systems as well as to walk them through the steps involved in selecting and developing new hardware/ software systems for solving organizational problems.

In an era of much abuse of individuals' rights to data privacy as well as the wanton destruction of data via software viruses, a chapter on computer ethics, social issues, and computer security is a necessity. Problem areas discussed in Chapter 21 include software piracy, viruses, privacy, health concerns, and computer security.

No computer textbook would be complete without a discussion of the important area of desktop publishing. This productivity tool is having an enormous impact on all aspects of society because it allows the quick generation of typeset-quality text. The hardware and software requirements of desktop publishing are covered in Chapter 22, along with a discussion of the PageMaker desktop publishing package produced by Adobe Systems Incorporated.

Chapter 23 contains a brief introduction to the area of artificial intelligence and a look at trends in computer technology that will continue to have an impact on our daily lives.

Objectives of the Textbook

The primary goal of most introductory computer courses is to bring students to the point where they feel comfortable using the computer to solve problems. The objective of this text is thus to teach students both computer concepts and to solve realistic problems using the most readily available "off-the-shelf" general applications software. The book does not go into extreme detail about each package but rather provides a general introduction that will familiarize students with the commonly used aspects of each general applications package.

The general applications software packages covered in this textbook are WordPerfect 4.2 and 5.0 (word processing), Lotus 1-2-3 Release 2.01 (spreadsheets), and dBASE III Plus (data base management). Coverage of the IBM Personal Computer Disk Operating System (PC DOS) is also included. After completing this textbook, students will have the conceptual and hands-on microcomputer skills necessary to solve numerous problems using these software packages.

Applications Software

Three packages have emerged as de facto standards in each of the general applications software areas just discussed. WordPerfect, developed by the WordPerfect Corporation, is now the best-selling word processing package for business use. dBASE III Plus, developed by Ashton-Tate, is typically used as the data base management standard. Lotus 1-2-3 is still without doubt the standard against which all other spreadsheet packages are measured. In spite of the many clones that have entered the marketplace, Lotus 1-2-3 remains the best-selling spreadsheet package for business. Many employers now expect their newly hired college graduates to have at least a working knowledge of this important business tool.

One problem that faces educators today is how to acquire inexpensive, well-written software that represents programs students will be expected to use in the business world. Two of the companies just mentioned (WordPerfect and Ashton-Tate) have entered into an agreement with Wadsworth Publishing Company to solve this problem of acquiring quality software by making available through Wadsworth educational versions of their software packages for use in the classroom.

Coverage of WordPerfect in this book did prove to be a challenge, however. WordPerfect Corporation is now supporting only the Release 4.2 educational version of its software, and the company has no plans to provide an educational version of Release 5.0. The fact that some schools will use only the educational version, while other schools will prefer to use the most recent version, WordPerfect 5.0, creates the problem of which version to cover. We solved this problem by describing Release 4.2 in the main text and noting in the margin those features that change in Release 5.0. Appendix C then covers the new material in WordPerfect 5.0.

Providing spreadsheet software for a book that covers Lotus 1-2-3 is also not without problems. The full Lotus 1-2-3 package retails for $495, a price unaffordable for most students. While the student version costs less than $50, its files can be read only by that student version. To solve this problem and make inexpensive spreadsheet software available to students, the VP-Planner Plus software package is provided by the publisher to adopters of the text. VP-Planner Plus, distributed by Paperback Software, is a 1-2-3 Release 2.01 work-alike. This means that most of the topics and assignments covered in the text can be done with VP-Planner Plus. Any incompatibilities are discussed in Appendix A. Please note that VP-Planner Plus has been included with students in mind. We believe that students will greatly appreciate the ability to do about 98 percent of the assignments on a computer outside the official computer lab without a large outlay of cash for spreadsheet software.

Note that Appendix A contains specific information for students about characteristics of educational software that differ from the complete packages. For example, the instructional version of dBASE III Plus limits file size to 31 records.

Hardware Rationale

The introduction of the IBM Personal Computer revolutionized the world of third-party applications software for microcomputers. The IBM PC included much more memory than previous microcomputers and was therefore capable of running programs that could more effectively address much larger problems. This is especially true in the area of spreadsheets. Many existing packages were rewritten to take advantage of the additional memory available on the IBM PC. The IBM has so changed the microcomputer world that it has emerged as a de facto standard by which other microcomputers are judged.

Hardware Requirements

An IBM PC or compatible computer with two disk drives and 256K of RAM memory (320K if WordPerfect 5.0 is used) is required. You will also need a color monitor/graphics adapter board to properly display the 1-2-3 graphics on the screen. A printer (with graphics capabilities if you wish to print 1-2-3 graphs) is also required for printing documents, reports, graphs, and worksheets.

The hard (fixed) disk is a piece of equipment that has resulted in many changes in the way computer concepts are covered in the classroom. During the last few years the prices of hard disk technology have plummeted. Because hard disk technology is now affordable for most colleges and universities, such hard disk topics as directories as well as instructions for running software from a fixed disk are covered in this text.

Structure of the Text

Four Software Tools Plus works best in a hands-on environment—that is, the step-by-step exercises in the text make most sense when an individual is sitting at a computer so that he or she can immediately see the results of his or her actions. A symbol like the one in the margin indicates hands-on material.

Each of the software packages described previously is covered in enough detail to satisfy the requirements of a computer novice. However, the text assumes that each package has already been configured for use by the student.

If a package has not been configured for a specific machine, please refer to the documentation for that package.

The software packages can be covered in any order. However, you are encouraged to cover at least the first three chapters before going on to one of the specific packages.

Learning Aids and Sample Files

Exercises are provided at the end of each chapter to give students quick feedback on their progress. In addition to the written exercises, hands-on computer exercises are included at the end of appropriate chapters to provide feedback through challenging applications of material covered in the chapter. A number of sample diskette files—including sample worksheets, text files, and data base files—have been provided for use with text lessons and exercises.

Appendix A, Instructions for Using Educational Versions of Software, and Appendix C, WordPerfect 5.0, have already been mentioned. Appendix B presents command summaries for WordPerfect 4.2 and 5.0 and for dBASE III Plus, as well as graphic depictions of the various menus used by Lotus 1-2-3 and a summary of commonly used 1-2-3 functions. Appendix D offers an introduction to the BASIC programming language using Microsoft's BASICA. Appendix E discusses the subject of buying a microcomputer.

An extensive Glossary of computer terms used in the text appears after the appendixes (defined terms appear in boldface type where they are defined in the text), and keyboard templates for each of the software tools (WordPerfect 4.2 and 5.0, Lotus 1-2-3, and dBASE III Plus) appear at the end of the book.

In-depth Projects

The appropriate chapters of the book contain in-depth projects using WordPerfect and Lotus 1-2-3. These projects pull together key aspects of the various software packages, with an emphasis on interpackage communication. Please note, though, that the WordPerfect projects require the full version of the software.

CAI Study Guide

Assistant Instructor: CAI Study Guide for Four Software Tools Plus, prepared by Wayne E. Thomsen, uses both text-based and computer-assisted techniques to help students review material covered in the textbook. Text and graphic material on the disk allows students to review the concepts and techniques and then tests students' knowledge of the topics covered in each chapter. We believe that the use of CAI materials will make the learning task more enjoyable for students enrolled in their first computer course.

This concept of student support via computer-assisted instruction techniques is an important example of using computers to teach computer concepts in a structured educational environment. Only a text with such support can claim to be a state-of-the-art instructional package.

Teaching Aids

An Instructor's Manual is provided without charge to each adopter of the text. The manual contains a lecture outline and transparency masters for each chapter. A disk containing all of the finished worksheets at the end of each spreadsheet chapter is also included. As a bonus, the disk also contains a Lotus 1-2-3 GRADBOOK template instructors can use for tracking students' grades. The GRADBOOK template, which is completely macro-driven, makes the tedious process of tracking grades much easier.

A computerized test generator is also available to adopters of *Four Software Tools Plus*. The test generator, which includes true-false, multiple-choice, fill-in-the-blank, and short-answer test questions, makes the process of creating tests easy. Contact your Wadsworth representative or call Sales Service at (415) 595-2350 for a copy.

Acknowledgments

When I first started writing the original textbook, *Four Software Tools*, I did not realize what a tremendous effort such an endeavor entailed. I soon learned that a multitude of people are needed to make a textbook a success. These individuals include family, friends, colleagues, and many people in the publishing business. I am deeply indebted to my wife, Wendy, who initially encouraged me to start on the first version of this text. Without her encouragement, the original text might never have been finished.

I would also like to thank the reviewers of this manuscript: Linda Bowen, Western Illinois University; David Burgett, McLennan Community College; Ron Goodman, Quincy Junior College; Donald L. Hall, Manatee Community College; Peter Irwin, Richland College; Tomislav Mandakovic, Florida International University; Mike Michaelson, Palomar College; Jeff Mock, Diablo Valley College; Leonard Presby, William Paterson State College; Jan Truscott, San Joaquin Delta College; David Van Over, University of Georgia; and Mary Allyn Webster, University of Florida.

Thanks, too, to the reviewers of other versions of the manuscript: Julia Bradley, Mount San Antonio College; Margaret "Kit" Ellis, Seattle Central Community College; Mike Goul, Arizona State University; Richard Hatch, San Diego State University; Stephen Johnson, Linn-Benton Community College; Judith Scheeraen, Westmoreland County Community College; Robert Schuerman, California Polytechnic State University, San Luis Obispo; John Turchek, Robert Morris College; and Christopher Wolfe, Texas A&M University.

The efforts of the individuals at Wadsworth Publishing Company must also be acknowledged because they are responsible for turning a dog-eared manuscript into professional final copy. Frank Ruggirello, senior computer science editor, is without equal in the publishing business. Frank is always a joy to talk with or to visit. His judicious use of Giants game tickets, great restaurants, excellent brown sauce, and peaceful drives along the ocean will always be remembered with fondness. Sandra Craig did a phenomenal job of completing this project. There were times when it appeared to be an impossible task to get the book finished, but her expert management of the project brought it to a successful conclusion.

A frequently overlooked ingredient in the success of a textbook is the sales staff of a publishing company. Without their marketing efforts, any text, no matter how good, would fail. There is no doubt in my mind that the Wadsworth corporation has one of the finest, most professional staffs in the country. The efforts of individuals like Ragu Raghavan, Peggy Hopp, and Gerry Levine, along with many others, will always be greatly appreciated. I also consider many of these people friends.

Finally, I would like to dedicate this book to my wife, Wendy, and our son, Michael. These are the two most important people in my life. Michael, especially, made this project a challenge. His efforts to get Dad to play chase—which included pressing the Reset button of Dad's computer and grabbing Daddy's diskettes and running merrily down the hallway—all made this project more interesting.

MEMO

TO: Users of the Limited-Use version of WordPerfect 4.2
FROM: WordPerfect Corporation
RE: The limitations of Limited-Use WordPerfect 4.2
DATE: June 30, 1987

The Limited-Use introductory version of WordPerfect 4.2 (L-WP) is intended to allow one to learn the features of WordPerfect 4.2; however, the L-WP is not intended to allow one to print usable academic or professional documents.[1]

Certain limitations *(which should not deter learning WordPerfect through the L-WP)* have been encrypted into L-WP to guard against productive use, and are as follows:

I.   One may work with as large a document on screen as desired, but one may only save to disk a data file no larger than 50,000k (appx. 25–30 regular pages).

      1. A data file created with the L-WP cannot be imported into regular WordPerfect, nor can a file created in regular WordPerfect be imported into L-WP.

II.   Data files of any size may be printed through parallel printer port "1" without defining a printer, but font changes and extended ASCII characters are not allowed. Also, "*WPC" will be printed after each paragraph.

III. One will be able to learn all the functions of WordPerfect 4.2's speller and thesaurus by calling up the "readme.wp" file and following the step-by-step directions; however, one cannot use the L-WP speller and thesaurus with any of one's own documents because there are only a limited number of words in the L-WP speller and thesaurus. (The regular speller has 115,000 words, and the regular thesaurus has approximately 150,000 words.)

IV.   The help file of L-WP allows the user to retrieve the function-key template, but similar to the speller and the thesaurus described above, space will not allow the full help files on the L-WP disk.

L-WP is designed to be used for introductory, word processing courses, and thus far has been well received in these types of environments. Notwithstanding the broad abilities provided in the L-WP, presumably the L-WP will not satisfactorily substitute for regular WordPerfect 4.2, and therefore the full feature version may be obtained directly from WordPerfect Corporation at a 75% educational discount.

---

[1]"*WPC" will be automatically printed after each paragraph of text to discourage academic or professional use of the L-WP. *See* paragraph II above.

PART ONE

INTRODUCTORY MICROCOMPUTER CONCEPTS

The Computer

Chapter Objectives

After completing this chapter, you should be able to:

Define a computer

List the parts of a computer

Describe the four generations of computers

Define the stored-program concept

Describe the types of computers

Describe the hierarchy of data

Describe how a computer accesses data

Describe how a computer processes data

The computer has had a greater impact on our society than has any other device invented in the second half of the twentieth century. As late as the mid-1970s, computers were used by relatively few people. For many people today, computers are as much a part of a daily life as automobiles, telephones, and electric lights.

In business, computers track and process inventory, accounts receivable, accounts payable, and payroll. They are used in education to schedule classes, train students, and record grades. In the medical professions, computers diagnose and monitor patients. Scientists use computers to analyze our solar system, forecast weather patterns, and conduct experiments.

Of all the computer types, the microcomputer has been the most helpful in improving our ability to control information and solve problems. The microcomputer is used by Fortune 500 companies and small businesses alike to file information, produce documents and correspondence, and perform time-consuming financial calculations and projections. It has boosted the productivity of workers at all organizational levels, from the mail room to the board room. Because it has a tireless capacity to perform practice exercises and simulations, the microcomputer is also an excellent teaching tool for primary and secondary school students.

This chapter looks at computers and the computing process in general, as well as the microcomputer you'll be using throughout this book. We'll see how computers have evolved to meet our changing needs to manage and process information. The chapter also examines how humans transfer data to computers and how, in turn, computers interpret, locate, and process that data.

What Is a Computer?

A **computer** is a general-purpose electronic device that performs high-speed arithmetic and logical operations according to internal instructions, which are executed without human intervention.

The key terms and implications of this definition are examined below:

Electronic. Electricity is the computer's lifeblood. In a high-speed computer, electricity pulses at half the speed of light through the intricate silicon-chip circuits that serve as the machine's brain cells.

Arithmetic Operations. Computers can perform the **arithmetic operations** of addition, subtraction, multiplication, and division.

Logical Operations. Computers can perform such **logical operations** as comparing one datum with another. This allows the computer operator to determine if the datum is less than, equal to, or greater than another datum.

Instructions Contained Internally. Computers can store instructions used to manipulate data. A complete set of instructions for performing some type of operation is called a **program**. For example, a payroll program enables a computer to calculate an organization's payroll, taking into account a variety of factors such as salary levels, overtime hours, and part-time employment.

Internal Storage. A program requires some **internal storage** capability in order to manipulate data. Like its human counterpart, this storage system is called memory. **Memory** holds the computer's operating system, the program being executed, the data operated on, and any intermediate results that are created by the program.

General Purpose. By retrieving a variety of programs from memory and executing them, a computer can perform an almost limitless number of

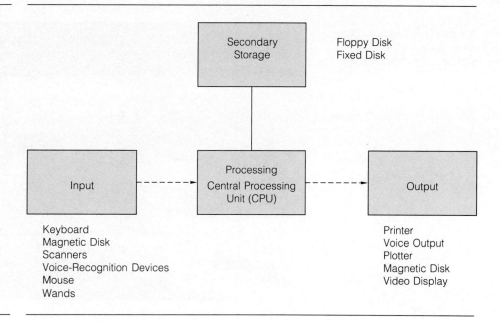

Figure 1.1
The four functional parts of a
computer system.

tasks—from calculating a business's monthly expenses to drawing
architectural blueprints.

What Is a
Computer System?

A **computer system** has four functional parts: input, processing, storage, and
output (Figures 1.1 and 1.2). The input portion of a computer system permits
the user to enter instructions or data into the computer, just as the five senses
allow people to receive information about the world. Numerous **input devices**
are used, the most popular being the keyboard.

The computer's processing or "thinking" unit is called the **central processing unit (CPU)**. The CPU processes data and performs arithmetic and
logical calculations. It is divided into three parts: primary storage (or memory),
the control unit, and the arithmetic/logic unit (Figure 1.3).

The **primary storage** holds the executing program's instructions, the data
being processed, and intermediate calculations generated by the program. This
memory is short-term and retains data only while the program is running; the
memory is lost when the computer's power is turned off. The control unit
directs the computer's actions by holding each instruction as it is being executed, decoding that instruction, and then directing the other CPU components on what actions to take. The arithmetic/logic unit performs the arithmetic
operations of addition, subtraction, multiplication, and division, and any comparisons required by the program.

In contrast to primary storage, **secondary storage** is separate from the
CPU and can store data indefinitely (the memory is not lost when the power is
turned off). Specific secondary memory can be inputted into the computer
anytime the operator needs that information for some task. Just as a student
can open a particular reference book whenever necessary, an accountant can
access a client's billing history by putting the proper magnetic disk into his or
her computer.

Today, the magnetic disk is the most popular form of secondary storage.
The bulk of data processed by a computer resides in secondary storage and is
moved into primary storage only when needed for processing. This means that
data are constantly being transferred from secondary storage to primary storage and back again. The process of transferring data into a computer is known

Figure 1.3
The three parts of the CPU
are the control unit, the arith-
metic/logic unit, and primary
storage.

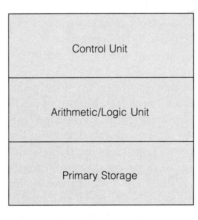

Control Unit	• Decodes program instructions • Directs computer on how to process an instruction
Arithmetic/Logic Unit	• Adds, subtracts, multiplies, and divides • Performs any comparisons
Primary Storage	• Holds current program instructions • Holds data to be processed by program • Holds intermediate results created by executing program instructions

as the **read process**. The process of transferring data out of a computer back to secondary storage is known as the **write process**. Data not required by the CPU for processing are stored in secondary storage.

   Output devices store and present data in forms that can be read by either humans or machines. In short, they "communicate" processed information in ways comparable to our use of speech, writing, and mathematical notation to communicate information and ideas. Commonly used humanly readable devices are the monitor, printer, and plotter. A common machine-readable device is the magnetic disk, which stores data as magnetic charges. When needed, these data are read by the computer and processed by a program, then displayed on a screen or printed.

History of the Electronic Computer

Prior to the mid-twentieth century, people used mechanical computers to perform calculations, tabulate large numbers, and control a variety of large machines such as industrial weaving looms. Electronic computers were first developed during the 1930s and 1940s. From 1939–1942, John V. Atanasoff, an Iowa State College physics professor, and his graduate-student assistant Clifford E. Berry developed a computing device that performed mathematical

(a)   *(b)*

Figure 1.4
The first computers. (a) The ABC computer—the first electronic computer designed.
(b) The ENIAC computer. [Courtesy of (a) Iowa State University and (b) IBM]

calculations (Figure 1.4a). Called the Atanasoff–Berry Computer (ABC), it used vacuum tubes to process data, making it the first entirely electrical computer. Although Atanasoff and Berry never completed their computer, it served as a model for many future computer designs.

The first electronic computer completed was the ENIAC (Electronic Numerical Integrator and Computer) (Figure 1.4b). Financed by the U.S. Army for use in World War II, the ENIAC was designed by University of Pennsylvania professors John W. Mauchly and J. Presper Eckert, Jr., to compute artillery ballistic tables. The thirty-ton ENIAC filled a twenty-foot by forty-foot room, contained 18,000 vacuum tubes, and could perform mathematical computations 1,000 times faster than did the adding machines of the time. Although fast at computing, this mammoth computer had to be programmed by manually wiring it to three walls of plug-boards containing more than 6,000 switches. Entering a new program was a tedious process requiring several days or weeks.

In 1945, John Von Neumann, who had worked with Eckert and Mauchly at the University of Pennsylvania and later went to Princeton, published a paper on the stored-program concept. The **stored-program concept** permitted the reading of a program into a computer's memory and then executing the program instructions without rewiring the computer. Programs were fed and stored into the computer in **binary notation**, which uses only the values 1 and 0. Computers read the binary code electronically to perform logical operations, interpreting 1 to mean on and 0 as off. The first computer to use the stored-program concept was the EDVAC (Electronic Discrete Variable Automatic Computer), developed by Von Neumann, Eckert, and Mauchly at the University of Pennsylvania.

Stored programs give computers tremendous flexibility and reliability and are far faster and less error-prone than are manually wired programs. A computer with a stored-program capacity can be used for numerous applications by loading and executing the appropriate program.

The next major computer-design breakthrough was the development of translators that allowed people to communicate with computers by means other than binary numbers. In 1952 Grace Murray Hopper developed the first compiler, a program that can translate English-like statements into machine-readable binary code. Hopper, a U.S. Navy officer, also developed the COBOL (Common Business Oriented Language) compiler, a project jointly sponsored by private business, education, and the federal government during the late 1950s. COBOL allowed, for the first time, a computer program that had been written for one manufacturer's computer to be run on another manufacturer's computer without being rewritten. Suddenly, programs were easily transported, and the business world started accepting computers with enthusiasm.

Computer Generations

Four generations of computers are differentiated by their electronic components. Vacuum tubes were used for the first generation of computers, transistors for the second, integrated circuit chips for the third, and large-scale and very large-scale integrated chips for the fourth (Figure 1.5a).

The First Generation, 1951–1958. First-generation computers used vacuum tubes for processing information. Operators inputted data and programs in a special code on punched cards (Figure 1.5b). Internal storage was provided by a rapidly rotating drum on which a reader/recorder device placed magnetic spots. Like their radio counterparts, vacuum-tube computers were far bulkier and generated far more heat than do contemporary models.

Eckert and Mauchly helped usher in the first-generation era by forming a private computer company and building UNIVAC I, which the Census Bureau used to tabulate the 1950 census (Figure 1.5c).

International Business Machines (IBM), which was selling punched-card equipment and had unsuccessfully competed for the 1950 census contract, started manufacturing electronic computers and quickly became a strong contender in the market (Figure 1.5d).

Although expensive and of limited use, computers soon gained acceptance by business and government. By the mid-1950s, IBM and Remington Rand, which had purchased Eckert's and Mauchly's company, had emerged as the dominant computer manufacturers. Their clients included Sylvania, General Electric, and the federal government. In 1956 IBM usurped Remington Rand's early leadership in the industry and became the world's largest manufacturer of computers, a position the company maintains to this day.

The Second Generation, 1958–1964. In 1947 three Bell Laboratories scientists developed a transistor that was faster, more reliable, 200 times smaller, and required less electricity than did the vacuum tube. The transistor earned its inventors the Nobel Prize and made possible a new generation of faster, more compact computers. Compare a vacuum-tube radio and a transistorized radio to get an idea of how this new technology similarly reduced computer size.

Second-generation computers also used magnetic cores instead of magnetic drums for internal storage. These cores comprised tiny, wired rings of magnetic material on which instructions and data could be stored (Figure 1.5e).

Computer programs, or software, also improved. COBOL, developed during the first-generation era, became commercially available. Programs written for one computer now could be transferred to another computer with minimal effort. Writing a program no longer required a thorough understanding of computer hardware.

Second-generation computers were substantially smaller and faster than were their vacuum-tube predecessors and were used for a variety of new applications, such as airline-reservation systems, air-traffic control, and general-purpose simulations. The U.S. Navy used second-generation computers to construct the world's first flight simulator, Whirlwind I.

The Third Generation, 1965–1970. Third-generation computers emerged with the development of integrated circuits—silicon chips on which hundreds of electric components have been placed together, or integrated. Silicon chips are smaller, faster, and cooler, and they consume less energy than do transistors. Consequently, computers again became smaller, faster, and more energy-efficient.

Before the advent of integrated circuits, computers were designed for either mathematical or business application but not both. Integrated circuits enabled computer manufacturers to increase program flexibility and to standardize their model lines. IBM's 360 (Figure 1.5f), one of the first commercial computers to use integrated circuitry, could perform both file processing and mathematical analysis. Customers could upgrade their 360 to a larger IBM model and still run their existing programs.

With the introduction of the 360, IBM captured 70 percent of the market, driving RCA, General Electric, and Xerox out of the large-computer field. However, the 360's standardization permitted the growth of storage-device manufacturers, whose competitively priced peripheral equipment was compatible with the IBM series.

To avoid competing directly with IBM, Digital Equipment Corporation (DEC) redirected its efforts toward small computers. Far less costly to buy and operate than large computers, minicomputers were first developed during the second-generation computer era and came into widespread use in the 1960s and 1970s. DEC introduced its first minicomputer, the PDP-1, in 1960 (Figure 1.5g) and by 1969 had a line of best-selling minicomputers.

Integrated-circuit technology also prompted the emergence of the software industry. Standard programs were rewritten to work in contemporary integrated-circuit computers and in hardware still on the drawing boards. This upward compatibility enabled firms to continue using their existing software after they upgraded their computer hardware.

The Fourth Generation, 1971 to Today. Two improvements in computer technology mark the beginning of fourth-generation computers. One was the replacement of magnetic-core memory by silicon-chip memory. The other was the placing of much more circuitry on each chip. Intel Corporation took this idea to its logical conclusion by creating the microprocessor, a single chip containing all the circuitry required to make it programmable.

The microprocessor chip made the compact size and resultant popularity of personal computers possible. A single chip could now contain two of the CPU components, the control and arithmetic/logic units. Primary memory, the third component, is performed by other chips.

Today, LSI (large-scale integration) and VLSI (very large-scale integration) technology enables hundreds of thousands of electronic components to be stored on one chip (Figure 1.5h). Using VLSI, a manufacturer can make a small computer that rivals the power of a room-sized first-generation computer.

Classifications of Today's Computers

Today's computers can be roughly divided into microcomputers, minicomputers, mainframes, and supercomputers, with each group characterized by size, price, speed of operation, and memory/processing capabilities.

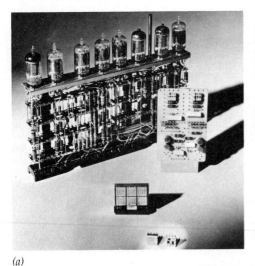
(a)

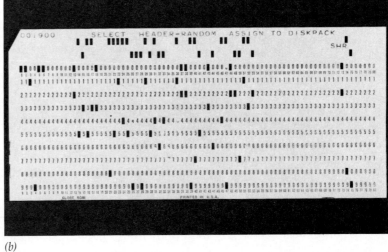
(b)

(c)

(d)

Figure 1.5
(a) The electronic components of the four computer generations. Left to right: A vacuum tube, a transistor, an integrated chip, and a VLSI chip. (b) A punched card inputted data into first-generation computers. (c) UNIVAC I tabulated the 1950 census. (d) IBM's 650 computer, introduced in 1953. [Courtesy of (a, b, d) IBM; (c) Unisys Archives]

Microcomputers are the smallest, least costly, and most popular computers on the market (Figure 1.6a). Microcomputers range from around $100 to several thousand dollars and vary as widely in power, with some models rivaling minicomputers and older mainframes in capabilities. Businesses use microcomputers for everything from preparing spreadsheets to performing desktop publishing.

Thanks to the microprocessors' compactness, microcomputers are small enough to fit on top of a desk or, in some cases, in a briefcase. In business applications, the microcomputer may function as a stand-alone unit or be hooked up with other microcomputers or a mainframe to expand their capabilities. Because of their low price, microcomputers are sold like appliances in department, discount, and computer-specialty stores. The availability of low-cost, easy-to-use programs plays a major role in consumer acceptance of microcomputer brands.

Figure 1.5 (continued)
(e) Magnetic core used as internal storage for second- and third-generation computers.
(f) An example of an IBM 360 mainframe computer. (g) DEC PDP-1, one of the most
popular early minicomputers. (h) A VLSI circuit. [Courtesy of (e, f) IBM; (g) Digital
Equipment Corporation; (h) NCR Corporation]

Minicomputers were first developed during the 1960s to perform specialized tasks such as handling data communications (Figure 1.6b). Today's minicomputers rival some mainframes in power and are used in word processing, industrial automation, and multioperator applications.

Minicomputers are smaller, cheaper, and easier to maintain and install than are mainframes but are in declining demand because of the increasing power of microcomputers. However, several operators linked to the same minicomputer can still access resources such as printers and disk storage faster than a network of microcomputer operators can. Minicomputer prices range from around $50,000 to several hundred thousand dollars.

Mainframe computers are large, fast systems capable of supporting several hundred input and output devices such as keyboards and monitor screens. Large businesses, universities, banks, and hospitals rely on mainframe computers for their tremendous operational speed and processing capacity. For

(a)

(b)

(c)

(d)

Figure 1.6
Today's computers. (a) A typical microcomputer system—a Compaq. (b) A Prime
minicomputer and peripherals. (c) A typical mainframe computer room. (d) A Cray-2
supercomputer. [Courtesy of (a) Compaq Computer Corporation; (b) Prime Computer,
Inc.; (c) NCR Corporation; and (d) Cray Research Inc.]

example, minicomputers could not possibly handle the thousands of reservation orders that travel agents make each day with an airline, but mainframe
computers can and do. Mainframe computers range in price from several
hundred thousand dollars to several million dollars.

A mainframe computer produces considerable heat so its environmental
temperature and humidity must be controlled by special systems. Besides the
environmental costs, mainframe computers require large support staffs. Typically, the computer vendor (seller) trains the user's staff and provides maintenance support. In turn, the staff operates and programs the mainframe
computer.

Supercomputers are the fastest, most expensive computers manufactured (Figure 1.6d). They can run numerous different calculations simultaneously, thereby processing in a minute what would take a personal computer

several weeks or months. Scientists at Sandia National Laboratory in New Mexico built a supercomputer consisting of 1,024 processors. Each processor has the computing capability of a computer and is assigned a separate part of one massive problem, which is worked by all the processors simultaneously. Called the "hypercube," this supercomputer solves problems 1,000 times faster than does a typical mainframe computer.

Most supercomputers are used for scientific work, particularly for creating mathematical models of the real world. Called **simulation**, this process is especially useful in seismology, oil exploration, weather forecasting, and predicting the spread of pollution. Supercomputers cost millions of dollars and only a few are produced each year.

Data and Computers

To understand how a computer solves problems, it is important to understand the difference between data and information, the various data levels, and how the computer accesses data.

Data and Information

Data are raw facts that have not been processed or manipulated. Hours worked, employee name, and Social Security number are all examples of data. **Information** is data that has been processed or manipulated. Gross pay (calculated by multiplying hours worked by pay rate) is an example of information. What constitutes data or information depends on who is requesting the information—one person's information may be another person's data.

For example, suppose an individual needs to book a flight that will arrive in San Francisco on a particular day and time. A travel agent will use the destination, time constraints, and flight availability as data to figure out what flight to book. The reservation that fulfills all the requirements constitutes the information the travel agent needs. At the airline's corporate headquarters, that reservation may become part of booking data that help the airline to compute what flights should be scheduled to San Francisco.

Data Storage and the Hierarchy of Data

Listed below is the data-storage hierarchy, beginning with the smallest information piece and ascending to the largest.

1. Bit
2. Byte, or character
3. Field, or item
4. Record
5. File
6. Data base

As noted earlier, computers store information in binary code—1 meaning on, 0 meaning off—which parallels the on-off nature of electronic components. Sequences of these bits (short for binary digit) make up a byte, and each byte represents a different alphabetic, numeric, or other character used to communicate. Chapter 2 examines this topic in more detail.

A **field**, or **item**, contains one or more related bytes that describe an attribute of an entity for which data are being stored. For example, an entity of an accounts-receivable system may be a particular customer (subject), while

Figure 1.7
Hierarchy of data items in a
manual filing system.

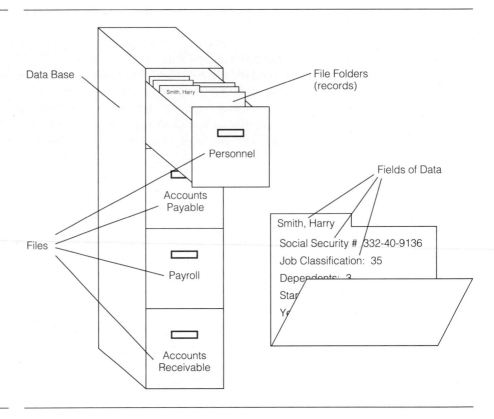

the entity's attributes might be described by such data fields as customer name,
address, current balance, and so on.

A **record** is a grouping of related fields (attributes) dealing with one entity.
In our accounts-receivable example, a record might contain the following fields:

  Customer number

  Customer name

  Customer address

  Credit limit

  High historical balance

  Current accounts-receivable balance

  Date customer record established

  Date of last activity

A computer record is analogous to a file folder in a manual filing system.

Logically related records are collected in a **file**. The collection of all
accounts-receivable records in a computer is the accounts-receivable file (Figure 1.7), just as the collection of all manual-system file folders in a filing cabinet is the manual file.

A **data base** comprises all of the organization's files that have been cross-
indexed and structured for updating and data retrieval. A corporation's data
base may include payroll, accounts-receivable, and accounts-payable files (Figure 1.7). A computer data base is comparable to one or more manual filing
cabinets.

How a Computer Locates Data

There are two basic ways to organize data within a file: the sequential-access method and the direct-access method.

The **sequential-access method** stores records in ascending or descending order by **record key**, data that identify one record from others. Student Social Security numbers serve as record keys in many colleges' sequential files. The file must be searched in sequence; if the desired record is passed, the operator must return to the start of the file and search again.

Sequential filing's big disadvantage is the time delay created by accessing all intervening records before the proper data are found. For example, a computer searching for seat availability on Flight 225 to San Francisco will have to read flight numbers 1–224. However, sequential filing is very suitable for processing many records at once, such as preparing payroll checks on payday, on magnetic tapes or disks, which are among the most affordable computer storage media.

The **direct-access method** uses algorithms or indexes to locate a record. An **algorithm** is a series of steps that manipulates the record key to find a record. An **index** lists key fields, which in turn contain all the file's records and their locations.

Using direct access, a computer operator could find out about seat availability on Flight 225 by directly accessing that particular flight. This makes direct access particularly useful for applications where information is required as questions occur. For example, someone who wanted to book a seat on Flight 225 could telephone a travel agent and find out the flight's booking status while speaking with the agent.

How a Computer Processes Data

Computers process data by batch or real-time methods, both of which require a master file and a transaction file. A **master file** holds semipermanent summary data about an entity. Master files contain records containing unique key contents. For example, the contents of each Social Security field must differ from one record to the next. Some data fields will change and some will remain the same when the master record is updated by information from a transaction file.

A **transaction file** contains data about some business action and is by nature transitory. After its information is inputted and used to update the appropriate master file records, the transaction file is discarded. Transaction record keys do not have to be unique, so several transactions can be stored for each master file record.

In the early days of computing, most processing was done by batch mode, whereby records are grouped together and processed all at once. With **batch processing**, a specific file update or information request (query) is processed only when needed or as a regular schedule dictates.

In business applications, batch processing starts with a preprinted form called the **source document** on which information about a business occurrence or transaction is recorded. A source document used for computing payroll is the time card, which lists an employee's Social Security number, name, regular hours worked, and overtime hours worked (Figure 1.8). Source documents are gathered at the end of the day or some other predetermined time and then transcribed (keyed) into machine-readable form by data-entry operators.

The transcribed information is fed into the computer and examined by an **edit program** to ensure that it is properly recorded. If an entered transaction is

Figure 1.8
A time card record summary
form for reporting hours
worked.

XYZ Corporation Time-Card Summary Form

Employee ID Number	Employee Name	Total Regular Hours	Total Overtime Hours
333-23-1098	Fred Tuerk	40	0

a time card, the edit program will check to see if the record is for a valid employee and if the numbers entered in the hours-worked and overtime fields are reasonable amounts. Transactions deemed to be in error by the edit program are returned to the payroll department for correction, then reentered into the transaction file. Finally, the entire batch of payroll records is processed, and the checks are printed (Figures 1.9 and 1.10).

Batch processing has two major drawbacks: The transcription step is both time-consuming and error-prone, and the files are only as current as the last processing run. For these reasons, the batch method is now used when intermittent processing of a large number of records against a file offers a distinct advantage.

Real-time processing updates or processes each transaction as it is entered into a computer and transmits the resultant information back to the operator (Figure 1.11). Thus, at any given time, a real-time file will be as current as the last entered information. Real-time processing's up-to-date nature requires that files be stored on a direct-access median, the most popular being magnetic disks. Most travel agents use real-time processing to make airline reservations (the transactions) because flight prices and space availability are constantly changing and must be continually updated.

Unlike transcribers of batch systems, people who use real-time systems are usually familiar with the files being processed and are therefore less likely to make errors when inputting new information. Moreover, real-time edit programs are at the beginning (front end) of the processing, so errors can be caught and corrected as they are made. Due to real-time processing's numerous advantages, many batch-processing systems have been converted to real-time systems.

Chapter Review

The computer has had a greater impact on our daily lives than has any other device invented in the second half of the twentieth century. A computer is electronic, performs arithmetic and logical operations, contains a stored program, and has internal storage. The stored-program concept imparts general-purpose capability to computers by enabling them to execute any program that can be loaded into their memories.

Computer history is marked by four technological generations. First-generation computers used vacuum tubes as the primary electronic components. Second-generation computers were made of transistors, and some

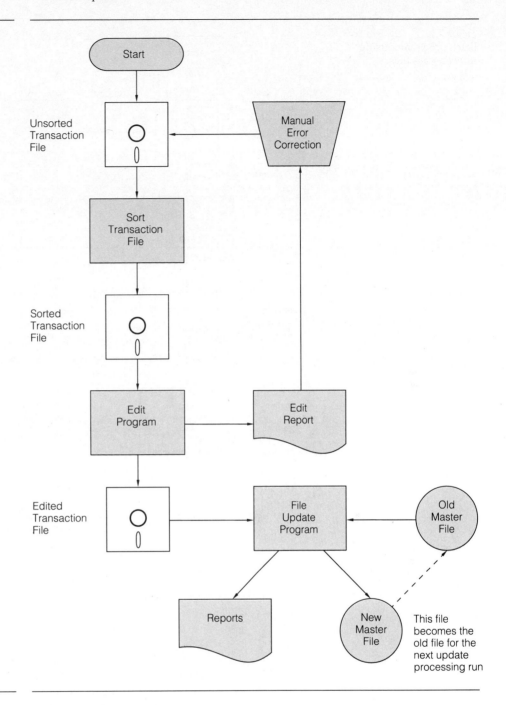

Figure 1.9
Batch processing using magnetic tape.

commercial models featured compilers. Third-generation computers were composed of integrated circuits and featured standardized architecture, which permitted upward compatibility of software. Fourth-generation computers rely on large-scale and very large-scale integrated circuits and process by real-time systems.

A computer system comprises input, processing, output, and storage portions. The processing portion, or CPU, is divided into the control unit, the arithmetic/logic unit, and the main memory. The control unit decodes and executes instructions; the arithmetic/logic unit performs calculations and com-

Figure 1.10
Batch processing using
direct-access files.

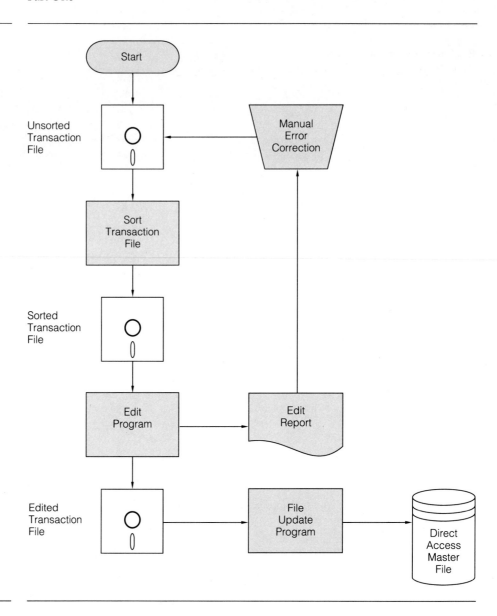

Figure 1.10
Batch processing using direct-access files.

parisons; the main memory provides temporary storage and holds the operating system, program instructions, data, and intermediate results.

How we use facts in a computer program determines whether the facts are data or information. Data are raw facts that computers process; information is processed data.

A computer operator enters data or instructions through an input device. Secondary storage devices provide long-term storage. While main memory is volatile, secondary storage is not. Output devices display information in either humanly readable or machine-readable form.

The four computer categories are microcomputer, minicomputer, mainframe computer, and supercomputer. Microcomputers are desktop size or smaller and provide general-purpose functions. Minicomputers can support multiple users but for many purposes are being replaced by microcomputers.

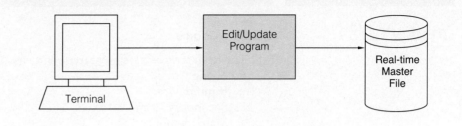

Figure 1.11
Real-time processing using direct-access files.

Mainframe computers are very large, support hundreds of users, and require a controlled-temperature environment. Supercomputers are the largest, fastest computers and are used for extremely complex modeling and problem solving.

Data are stored by the computer in an ascending hierarchy of information forms that includes bits; bytes, or characters; fields, or items; records; files; and data bases. Any record must be identified by a unique record key. Stored data can be accessed by the sequential-access or direct-access method. Sequential access requires that all intervening records be read until the desired record key is located. Direct-access methods use either an algorithm or an index to locate and access a record.

Two modes for processing data are batch and real-time. In batch processing, records are grouped and then processed all at once, whereas real-time systems process transactions as they occur. Batch processing can use either a sequential-access or direct-access filing system, but real-time processing requires direct-access filing.

Key Terms and Concepts

algorithm	master file
arithmetic operations	memory
batch processing	microcomputer
binary notation	minicomputer
computer	output devices
computer system	primary storage
CPU (central processing unit)	program
data	read process
data base	real-time processing
direct-access method	record
edit program	record key
field, or item	secondary storage
file	sequential-access method
index	simulation
information	source document
input devices	stored-program concept
internal storage	supercomputer
logical operations	transaction file
mainframe computer	write process

Chapter Quiz

Multiple Choice

1. The term *permanent* is most frequently associated with which of the following?
   a. Input device
   b. Secondary storage
   c. Main memory
   d. Control unit
   e. None of the above

2. Which of the following is responsible for decoding and executing instructions?
   a. Arithmetic/logic unit
   b. Control unit
   c. Main memory
   d. CPU
   e. All of the above

3. Which of the following cannot be in main memory?
   a. Program instructions
   b. Data
   c. Intermediate results
   d. All of the above can be stored in main memory.

4. Which of the following computers could be small enough to fit in a briefcase?
   a. Microcomputer
   b. Minicomputer
   c. Mainframe computer
   d. Supercomputer
   e. None of the above

5. Which of the following computers is used for large, complex simulations?
   a. Microcomputer
   b. Minicomputer
   c. Mainframe computer
   d. Supercomputer
   e. None of the above

True/False

6. The process of manually transferring information from a source document to a machine-readable form is known as transportation.

7. The most popular form of secondary storage is magnetic tape.

8. Batch processing operates on a group of transactions and processes them at the same time.

9. Mainframe computers are being used to replace supercomputers.

10. Real-time processing requires direct-access files.

Answers

1. b 2. b 3. d 4. a 5. d 6. f 7. f 8. t 9. f 10. t

Exercises

1. Define the following terms:
   a. Computer
   b. Stored-program concept
   c. Transcription
   d. Direct-access method
   e. Batch processing
   f. Master file

2. _____ operations involve comparing two data items.

3. The _____ concept requires program instructions to be stored within the computer.

4. The term _____ refers to processed data.

5. The major benefit of a stored program is that it provides a tremendous flexibility and _____ to the user.

6. The _____ portion of a computer system allows you to enter instructions of data.

7. Memory that automatically erases when the power is turned off is referred to as _____ memory.

8. The _____ is the most popular secondary storage device.

9. List and describe the three parts of the CPU:
   a.

   b.

   c.

10. The _____ of the CPU decodes and executes instructions.

11. The act of transferring data from secondary storage to main memory is referred to as the _____ process.

12. The _____ of the CPU is responsible for making comparisons between two pieces of data.

13. The class of computer that many times is replaced by a microcomputer is the _____.

14. The class of computer that can cost less than $1,000 is the _____.

15. The class of computer that can have hundreds of display terminals attached is the _____.

16. The smallest element in the hierarchy of data is the _____.

17. A method of arranging 0's and 1's to represent a character is referred to as a binary _____.

18. The element in the hierarchy of data that is used to store something related to an attribute is called a _____.

19. The element in the hierarchy of data that is used to store data about an entity is a _____.

20. A collection of logically related records is a _____.

21. The item that identifies a record is called a _____.

22. The _____ access method stores records in order by record key.

23. The _____ access method uses an algorithm or index to store or locate a record.

24. The processing mode that requires grouping of transactions is called _____ processing.

25. Real-time processing mode requires _____ files.

26. List the major components of the four computer generations:
    a.

    b.

    c.

    d.

27. The device that is generally viewed to be the precursor of all computers is called the _____ computer and was designed but not completely developed by _____ and _____.

28. The _____ is generally viewed as the first commercially available computer.

29. _____ is usually credited with developing the stored-program concept.

30. Although the company known as _____ was late in manufacturing computers, it now dominates the market place.

Questions for Thought

1. Examine the enrollment system used for your college/university. Is this a batch or real-time system? Try to imagine what types of manual processes would have to be used if this process were done by hand instead of by computer. Mentally, go through the procedures of how such a manual system would work in allowing students to select their classes while keeping track of the number of students currently enrolled such that the maximum enrollment figure is not exceeded. Imagine doing this for all classes at your institution.

2. Do some library research on early computers. There exist many "family trees" of earlier computers in reference texts. Detail the differences in power between a computer in the IBM 360 family that was marketed during the 1960s and today's modern mainframe computers.

3. How do today's more powerful microcomputers compare with the first computers that were marketed during the 1950s? What are the differences in size, speed, and cost? What differences in programming languages are there between the two types of computers? What differences are there in the requirements of support staff in running the two types of computers?

4. Compare and contrast two computer firms manufacturing computers today. When you select your firms, make certain that they both manu-

facture the same type of computer (supercomputer, mainframe, mini-computer, or microcomputer). One way to start is to examine the annual reports of the two companies that you selected. Some of the differences that you might want to note are what type of market are they appealing to, what is the relative size of the companies, what type of products do they produce, and what are the perceived differences as stated by each company.

5. List on paper the computer-driven applications that you come into contact with each day. What would happen if the computers driving these applications stopped functioning? What would be the impact of such an occurrence on your life and on your ability to function on a day-to-day basis?

Chapter 2

Microcomputer Hardware

Chapter Objectives

After completing this chapter, you should be able to:

List and describe the five parts of a microcomputer-based information system

List and describe the microcomputer's four main hardware parts

Define and discuss basic technical terms related to microcomputers

List and describe the different input devices

Describe the various parts of the processing unit

List and describe the different output devices

Describe the different secondary storage media used for microcomputers

Discuss how to handle diskettes properly

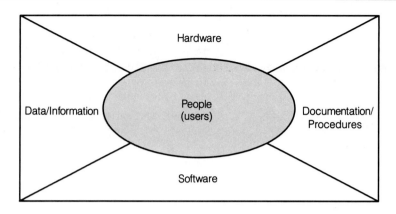

When you use a library to do research for a class paper, you employ a complex information system that includes both tangible and intangible elements. Among the tangible elements are yourself, the card catalog, other files that indicate where to find information, and the source books and papers containing the information you seek. The intangible elements include your research goals, the file information you use to locate your source books, and the information you find in those source books.

A microcomputer also is part of an information system. This system comprises five parts: people (users), hardware, software, procedures (documentation), and data/information (Figure 2.1). The most important of these is people, for it is their information and problem-solving needs that dictate what components are appropriate for the rest of the information system.

Like a library, the **microcomputer information system** has both tangible and intangible parts. The tangible elements include the computer users, the computer's four **hardware** components (input, processing, output, and secondary storage), and the texts that guide the user in operating the system. Computer manufacturers assemble the computer's components in a variety of forms. Some computers have all the hardware housed in one casing, others have them separated. However, all the hardware parts store and process information by using **chips**—silicon wafers containing miniature electronic components called semiconductors.

The intangible elements include all the information the user needs to run the microcomputer system, including data, processed data, software, and procedures. Data and processed data are the primary tools of problem solving. Software is the set of instructions the computer uses to manipulate the data. **Procedures** are written instructions that guide people in the use of software and hardware. A computer operator may refer to a procedures manual when it's time to change the paper in a printer.

Hardware Components

Input

To use a computer, a person must have some means of entering data into the machine. This task is accomplished with input devices. These devices also allow a person to manipulate stored data by issuing commands to the computer.

The standard input device for the microcomputer, or **personal computer (PC)**, is the keyboard. The keyboard has three parts: function keys (in the left-hand part of the keyboard), alphanumeric keys (in the middle), and the numeric key pad (in the right-hand area) (Figure 2.2a).

The **alphanumeric keys** on most computers are arranged in the "QWERTY" configuration, the same as a typewriter. (QWERTY spells out the first six characters of the keyboard's upper alphabetic row.) Alphanumeric keys are used to enter alphabetic, numerical, and punctuation characters.

Function keys (usually labeled F1, F2, and so forth) enable the computer user to answer questions, issue instructions, or select items from a menu of options. The software dictates the specific function of these keys.

The **numeric key pad** permits the operator to quickly enter numbers and numeric symbols, do mathematical calculations, and sometimes perform other special tasks.

Important Keys and Their Functions. The *ESC (escape) key* cancels or interrupts a previous command and is ordinarily used by the user to get out of trouble.

The *Ctrl (control) key* sends commands to the computer or software when it is held down while other keys are pressed. Instructions often use the caret symbol (^) to indicate that the Ctrl key should be pressed. For example, ^PrtSc says to hold down the Ctrl key while the PrtSc key is pressed.

Like the shift key on a typewriter, a computer's *SHIFT key* creates upper-case alphabetic characters and shifts number and symbol keys. The *Caps Lock key* operates like a typewriter's shift lock, except it shifts only letter keys.

The *ENTER key* (also called the *RETURN key*), the large rectangular key above the PrtSc key, is used to tell the computer to accept a command. Pressing ENTER confirms some entry the operator has made.

The *Alt (alternate) key*, like Ctrl, performs special functions by being held down while the other keys are pressed.

The *PrtSc (print/screen) key*, when held down with the SHIFT key, prints information displayed on the computer screen (transference of some graphics may require special procedures).

A newer 101-key keyboard has a top row of function keys, a redesigned numeric key pad, and additional cursor movement keys (Figure 2.2b).

Many microcomputers can handle a variety of input devices in addition to the keyboard. These devices include the mouse, touch pads, touch screens, light pens, voice-recognition units, and bar code–recognition units.

Mouse. After the keyboard, the most popular input device is a hand-held pointer tool called the **mouse**. An operator drags the mouse across a flat surface to maneuver a pointer on the monitor screen. Mice come in a variety of forms, but the most popular are mechanical models that ride on a ¾-inch steel or rubber ball. As the mouse is dragged, the ball's rolling motions are turned into electrical impulses, which the computer uses to move a screen pointer. Buttons on the mouse allow the operator to get the computer's attention and issue commands (Figure 2.3).

For many functions, such as selecting text and graphics, the mouse is far faster than the keyboard. However, mice do not eliminate the need to use the keyboard. Nor can mice be used with all microcomputer software. Apple Macintosh software usually supports mice, whereas IBM and IBM–compatible software sometimes does not. We'll examine the functions of mice more thoroughly in later chapters.

Tablets. A graphics **tablet** consists of a flat drawing surface and a pointing tool that functions like a pencil. The tablet turns the pointer's movements into digitized data that can be read by special computer programs (Figure 2.4). Graphics tablets range from palm- to desktop-size.

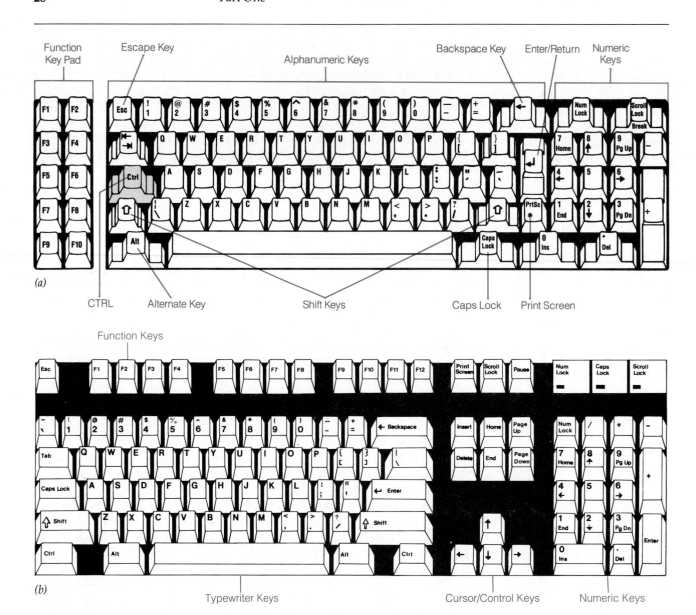

Figure 2.2
(a) An IBM PC keyboard has three parts: function keys, alphanumeric keys, and numeric key pad. (b) A 101-key keyboard. (Courtesy of IBM)

Light Pen. **Light pens** work somewhat like ordinary pens, but they use light and a computer screen instead of ink and paper to record information. By pressing a light pen to the monitor screen, a computer user can select program operations (menu items) or draw images. A light pen looks like an oversized writing pen attached to an electric cord and requires special software support (Figure 2.5).

Light pens are used by large warehouses for order-entry applications, by department stores as point-of-sale tools, and by graphics professionals for applications like computer-aided design.

Scanners. **Scanners** convert text, photographs, and black-and-white graphics into computer-readable form and transfer the information to a computer

(a)

Figure 2.3
(a) A Microsoft mouse.
(b) The internal parts of a mechanical mouse. (Courtesy of
Microsoft Corporation)

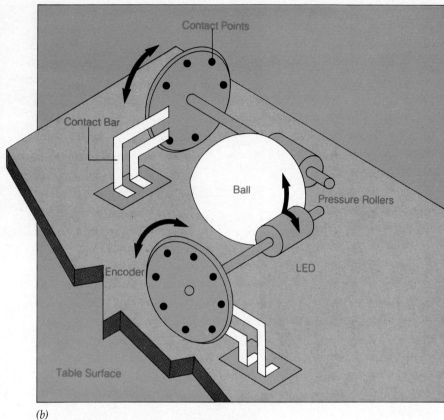

(b)

Figure 2.4
A typical hand-held touch
tablet. (Courtesy of PTI
Industries)

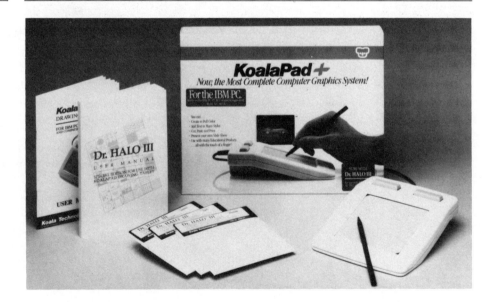

(Figure 2.6). Capable of scanning a page of print and graphics in mere seconds, scanners provide the fastest, easiest, and most accurate means of entering printed information into a computer.

Most scanners are sold with software that controls the scanning device and allows the operator to select output resolution, image size, and image

Figure 2.5
A light pen. (Courtesy of PC
Lite-Pen Company)

Figure 2.6
An HP ScanJet desktop scanner and an example of a
scanned image. (Courtesy of
Hewlett-Packard Company)

brightness and contrast levels. After the image has been scanned and transferred to the computer, it can be modified or saved in secondary storage. We'll
return to scanners when we discuss desktop publishing.

Touch Screens. One of the tools humans use most to impart information and
issue commands is the pointed finger. The **touch screen** takes advantage of
this, allowing the computer operator to use a finger as a pointing device.
Touching the screen executes a command, just like pressing a function key or
moving and clicking a mouse. The major disadvantage of touch screens is that
few software programs can work with them. Also, consumers have complained
that the vertical distance between their touch screens and keyboards makes
rapid inputting difficult. Consequently, touch screens have fallen out of favor
with some computer manufacturers.

Processing

Computers were created to manipulate information. This task is performed
by the processing unit, which includes the microcomputer's "brain" and all of
the devices it needs to receive input and send output. The processor has four
parts: microprocessor, primary memory, buses and boards, and interfaces
(Figure 2.7).

Figure 2.7
Some of the parts included on a typical IBM PC micro-computer system board. (Courtesy of IBM)

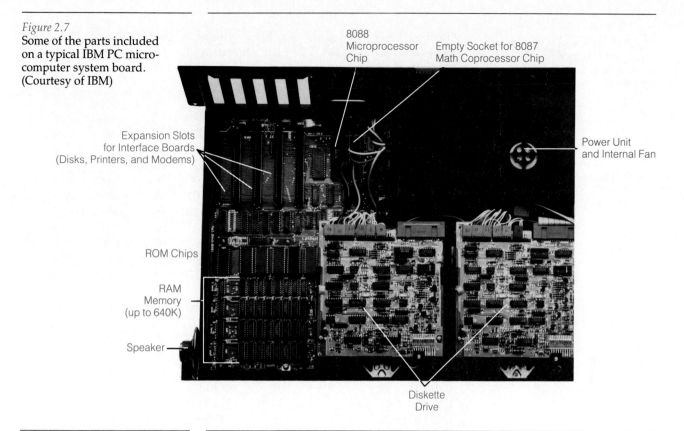

8088
Microprocessor
Chip

Empty Socket for 8087
Math Coprocessor Chip

Expansion Slots
for Interface Boards
(Disks, Printers, and Modems)

Power Unit
and Internal Fan

ROM Chips

RAM
Memory
(up to 640K)

Speaker

Diskette
Drive

Figure 2.8
Decimal numbers and their binary equivalents.

Decimal	Binary
0	0
1	1
2	10
3	11
4	100
5	101
6	110
7	111
8	1000
9	1001
10	1010

Microprocessors. The brain of a microcomputer system is the **microprocessor**, typically called the *central processing unit (CPU)*. The CPU is responsible for controlling data flow and executing program instructions on the data. It can perform adding, subtracting, multiplying, and dividing and compare numbers and characters.

As noted in Chapter 1, a computer performs all operations in binary notation. In this language, every character (letter, numeral, or symbol) entered on the keyboard is instantly translated into a combination of 1's and 0's, called a binary equivalent. Figure 2.8 displays some examples of decimal numbers and their binary equivalents.

Information storage is figured in bits, bytes, and kilobytes. A **bit** (short for binary digit) is the smallest binary unit; it can be a 1 or a 0. Computers use groups of bits as information chunks, somewhat like the way people use words to send and receive messages. The smallest of these groups contains 8 bits and is called a byte. A **byte** can hold any of 256 different values, depending on how the bits are ordered. Individual bytes represent specific numerals or characters. To store the letters *CPU* in memory, a computer would need 3 bytes—one for each character.

A **kilobyte (K)** of storage represents 1,024 bytes. To make it easier to calculate a CPU's storage capacity, most computer users think of a K as being 1,000 bytes. A 256K system, for instance, is popularly thought of as being able to store 256,000 bytes, but it actually can hold 262,144 (1,024 × 256) bytes.

A computer system's binary code determines how any specific character is represented in binary digits. Most microcomputers use the **American Standard Code for Information Interchange (ASCII)** to represent data (Figure 2.9).

Binary	Hex	Decimal	Symbol	Binary	Hex	Decimal	Symbol
0110000	30	48	0	1010110	56	86	V
0110001	31	49	1	1010111	57	87	W
0110010	32	50	2	1011000	58	88	X
0110011	33	51	3	1011001	59	89	Y
0110100	34	52	4	1011010	5A	90	Z
0110101	35	53	5	1100001	61	97	a
0110110	36	54	6	1100010	62	98	b
0110111	37	55	7	1100011	63	99	c
0111000	38	56	8	1100100	64	100	d
0111001	39	57	9	1100101	65	101	e
1000001	41	65	A	1100110	66	102	f
1000010	42	66	B	1100111	67	103	g
1000011	43	67	C	1101000	68	104	h
1000010	44	68	D	1101001	69	105	i
1000101	45	69	E	1101010	6A	106	j
1000110	46	70	F	1101011	6B	107	k
1000111	47	71	G	1101100	6C	108	l
1001000	48	72	H	1101101	6D	109	m
1001001	49	73	I	1101110	6E	110	n
1001010	4A	74	J	1101111	6F	111	o
1001011	4B	75	K	1110000	70	112	p
1001100	4C	76	L	1110001	71	113	q
1001101	4D	77	M	1110010	72	114	r
1001110	4E	78	N	1110011	73	115	s
1001111	4F	79	O	1110100	74	116	t
1010000	50	80	P	1110101	75	117	u
1010001	51	81	Q	1110110	76	118	v
1010010	52	82	R	1110111	77	119	w
1010011	53	83	S	1111000	78	120	x
1010100	54	84	T	1111001	79	121	y
1010101	55	85	U	1111010	7A	122	z

Notice that upper- and lower-case letters have different binary codes. For this reason, an operator must be specific about the characters he or she inputs: "a" does not mean the same thing to a computer as "A."

Microcomputers vary widely in their storage capacity, depending on whether the CPU uses 8-bit, 16-bit, or 32-bit chips. An 8-bit microprocessor uses 8 bits (1 byte) at a time, and so forth (Figure 2.10). Eight-bit microprocessors have a maximum usable (addressable) storage of 64K, or 65,536 bytes; 16-bit microprocessors, 1,000K, or 1 million bytes; and 32-bit microprocessors, 16,000K, or 16 million bytes. Some 8-bit computers get around their storage limitation by using **banked memory**. For example, the Apple IIe has two banks of 64K each, giving it a total memory capacity of 128K. However, the IIe can access only one bank at a time.

Microcomputers also vary considerably in their operating speed. Operating speed is a function of the bit size of the CPU chips, the system's clock speed, and the presence of coprocessing units. A CPU's speed increases with bit size, so 16-bit computers are usually much faster than are 8-bit ones.

Clock speed, measured in millions of cycles per second (megahertz, or MHz), indicates how fast a computer can process information and is a function of the ease with which electricity passes through the CPU. Computers perform

(a)

(b)

Figure 2.10
Typical 16-bit computers.
(a) Kaypro 286i, (b) Hewlett-
Packard Touchscreen II, and
(c) NEC Powermate I/SX.
[Courtesy of (a) Ron Powers,
Kaypro Photo Department;
(b) Hewlett-Packard Com-
pany; and (c) NEC Information Systems, Inc.]

(c)

a single processing step in one clock cycle. For example, a computer requires ten clock cycles to compute a problem that calls for ten processing steps. The faster its clock, the quicker a computer can run through its requisite clock cycles. Most microcomputer clocks operate at 4–25 MHz. A computer with a 16-MHz clock performs calculations four times faster than does a computer with a 4-MHz clock.

The **coprocessor** is used primarily for mathematical manipulation, freeing the CPU to concentrate on other tasks. However, the coprocessor will perform its function only if the computer software is programmed to call upon it for mathematical applications. Otherwise, the software will use the slower CPU.

For most computer buyers, the speed of the CPU and the amount of addressable storage are not critical. Usually, consumers first select software that will satisfy their particular processing needs and then buy a computer capable of running that software. (Chapter 3 covers software.)

Primary Memory. A computer's primary memory, or internal storage, holds the operating system, instructions for manipulating data, and "raw" (file) and "refined" (processed) data. Memory capacity determines the length and complexity of programs a computer can handle. In computers with little memory, complex programs have to be broken down into subprograms to fit. Storage capacity also determines how much data can be stored in the computer, thus limiting, for example, the size of a document it can hold. Of course, additional memory can be obtained by purchasing and installing additional memory chips.

Computers use two types of memory: **read-only memory (ROM)** and **random-access memory (RAM)**. ROM stores programs and information needed by the computer. These instructions are permanently "burned" into the ROM chip (**nonvolatile memory**) and cannot be changed by an operator, hence the term *read only*.

Basic instructions needed to start the computer are usually put in ROM memory. Sometimes, utility programs and software packages are also burned into ROM. Examples of ROM-resident programs include the BASIC program found in some IBM PCs and the Lotus 1-2-3 spreadsheet program Hewlett-Packard offers in its portable computer.

Unlike ROM, random-access memory is accessible to the computer user. With RAM, the user can store, change, and erase information. In addition, RAM memory holds data and program instructions vital to the computer's functioning. RAM capacity determines what software programs can be run and how much data can be processed. A spreadsheet package like Lotus 1-2-3 may require every byte of a computer's RAM. The so-called user-friendly programs also require considerable RAM. Generally, the more user-friendly a program is, the more RAM it needs.

RAM has **volatile memory**—unless stored, it is lost when the computer is turned off. Some computers use a nonvolatile RAM called "bubble memory," but this feature is expensive.

Buses. The processing unit constitutes the computer proper. Any hardware connected to the computer proper is known as a peripheral. **Peripherals** include input and output devices that enable the operator to interact with the computer, such as video displays, disk drives, printers, keyboards, and modems. By adding peripherals, the user can adapt his or her computer for a wide variety of applications, from printing letters to monitoring and adjusting a home's temperature.

Buses are processing components that facilitate information transfer between a computer and its peripherals. Suppose a user commands a computer to print a particular document. The CPU sends that command and the document to be printed to the bus system. The bus system holds on to the CPU's message while it alerts the printer that information is forthcoming, then sends the data on to be printed. Without a bus system, a computer operator would have to write a special communication program for each peripheral.

There are two basic types of bus systems—open and closed. On its **main system board** (sometimes called a **mother board**), an **open-bus system** contains expansion slots that allow users to expand the system as needed. The IBM XT, for example, has eight expansion slots. A peripheral is added to the computer system by plugging it into an expansion slot with an interface board (Figure 2.11). The IBM PC, IBM compatibles, and the Apple II computer are all open-bus computers.

Closed-bus systems are equipped with sockets called established ports that accept peripheral connecting cables. To expand a closed-bus system, the

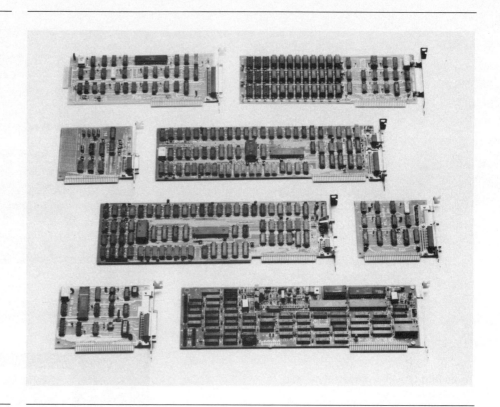

computer operator merely plugs a peripheral into a port. However, the computer can accept only as many peripherals as it has ports to accept them.

Interfaces. **Interfaces**, or adapter boards, are circuit-filled components that act like machine translaters, enabling a computer and its peripherals to communicate. Thus, an interface will translate computer output into a form usable to a printer, or it will turn a scanner's input into a binary code the computer can understand and record.

In open-bus systems, the interface is a separate component that connects the peripheral to the processing unit. In closed-bus systems, the interface is built into the computer.

Interfaces are either parallel or serial. A **parallel interface** transmits all the bits contained in a byte of storage simultaneously. At least eight wires, one for each bit, are needed to carry the information. However, most parallel devices have additional wires to handle a variety of data-checking and message-carrying functions. The standard method of parallel data transmission is called **centronics**.

A **serial interface** transmits a byte one bit at a time. Only two wires are needed, one to send bits and the other to receive them. Other lines accommodate data-checking and message-carrying functions. No real standards for serial transmission have been established in the computer industry, and, consequently, serial interfaces are more difficult to work with than are parallel ones. Parallel transmission is faster, but serial transmission allows information to be transmitted farther (parallel devices usually restrict cable length to under fifteen feet). Disks and printers usually use parallel transmission; printers, terminals, and, in particular, modems usually use serial transmission.

(a)

Figure 2.12
Three IBM PC-AT–compatible computers. (a) Zenith Data Systems A-248, (b) Dell System 220, and (c) Compaq Deskpro. [Courtesy of (a) Zenith Data Systems; (b) Dell Computer Corporation; and (c) Compaq Computer Corporation]

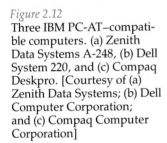

(b)

(c)

Microprocessor Chips and Computer Design

Compatibles. IBM established an industry standard when it introduced its PC in 1981. The PC used Intel's new 8088 (pronounced "eighty eighty-eight") microprocessor as its main chip. For some time, IBM was one of the few manufacturers offering a microcomputer powerful enough to be used for business applications. However, the ready availability of the 8088 chip enabled other manufacturers to begin making inexpensive copies of the IBM PC.

Years later, IBM introduced its PC-AT, which featured the 80286 32-bit microprocessor chip and was powerful enough to support multiple users. Shortly afterward, competitors introduced 80286-chip clones, some of which work two or three times faster than the original AT (Figures 2.12 and 2.13).

(a)

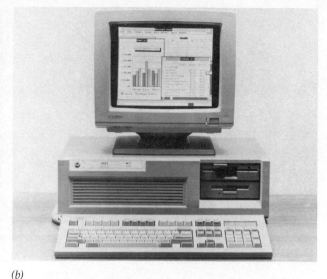

(b)

Figure 2.13
Three 80386 microcomputers.
(a) Compaq Deskpro 386, (b)
Dell System 310, and (c)
Zenith Data Systems Z-386.
[Courtesy of (a) Compaq
Computer Corporation; (b)
Dell Computer Corporation;
and (c) Zenith Data Systems]

(c)

Clones have become an important segment of the computer market, both in terms of their sales and in the technologic advances they inspire. Typically, these computers are copies of IBM or Apple Computer models and incorporate many of the same chips. Clones can run at least some of the original model's software and are described as being compatibles. Thus, IBM clones are said to be "IBM compatibles." Among consumers, clones are very popular because they are usually more affordable than, and just as reliable as, the original models.

In 1977 Apple began publishing its computers' specifications so other companies would manufacture hardware and software that Apple owners could use to upgrade their equipment. This "open-architecture" policy proved to be extremely popular with consumers, and IBM initiated a similar policy. However, the outstanding success of some clone manufacturers later forced IBM and Apple to downplay their open-architecture policy.

(a)   (b)

Figure 2.14
Two full-featured portable microcomputers. (a) Zenith Data Systems Z-181 portable with
an 8088c microprocessor chip and (b) Compaq Portable 386 with an 80386 microprocessor
chip. [Courtesy of (a) Zenith Data Systems and (b) Compaq Computer Corporation]

Portability. Consumers have long sought a computer portable enough to be
carried in a briefcase or placed under an airplane seat. But many early portable
computers turned out to be disappointingly weak compared with desktop
models. However, portable computers are becoming more practical as the
power of microprocessing chips increases.

Manufacturers produce two types of portable computers (Figure 2.14).
One type is battery-powered and has a highly readable **liquid crystal display
(LCD) monitor**, one or more disk drives (usually 3.5-inch drives), and a very
low weight, usually less than twelve pounds. Battery-powered portables provide great flexibility in use; the operator can use them almost anytime
and anywhere. During the flight back home, for example, an executive could
use a battery-powered portable to write a summary of an out-of-town business
meeting.

The second type of portable is bulkier and requires 110-volt service but
offers faster information retrieval and far more secondary storage than do
battery-powered portables. A plug-in portable might have a hard disk capable
of storing twenty million or more characters, a disk drive, an extremely readable screen, and a powerful microprocessor chip such as the 80286. Consumers
who value power over convenience would find a plug-in portable superior to a
battery-operated one.

Output

Output devices convert the information that comes out of a computer into
either images on a screen or on paper. Consumers often evaluate a microcomputer system according to the quality of output it produces, demanding that it
be accurate, easy to read, and rapidly available.

The **monitor**, or video screen, is the primary microcomputer output device. Some monitors are attachable; others are built into the main computer
box (Figure 2.15). Screens display images in two colors, such as black and
white, green and white, or yellow and brown.

(a)

(b)

(c)

(d)

Figure 2.15
Output display devices that
can be attached to a microcomputer. (a) Color monitor,
(b) and (c) Princeton graphic
monitors, (d) Kaypro portable, and (e) Hewlett-Packard
portable. [Courtesy of (a)
IBM; (b, c) Princeton Graphic
Systems, an Intelligent Systems Company; (d) Ron
Powers, Kaypro Photo De-
partment; and (e) Hewlett-
Packard Company]

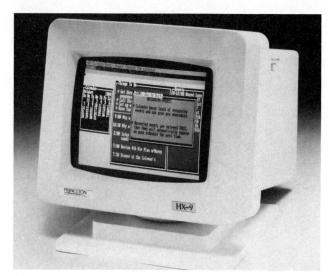

(e)

Figure 2.16
(a) Monochrome and (b) color
CRTs.

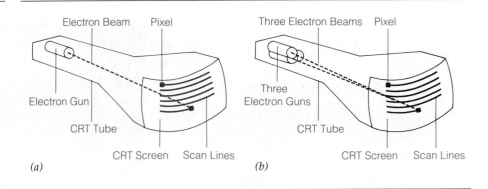

Televisions and monitors create images with a **cathode-ray tube (CRT)**, a vacuum tube that fires electrons at a phosphor-coated screen (Figure 2.16). Thousands of tiny glowing dots of energized phosphor called **pixels** (short for picture elements) form the screen's images. The more pixels a screen contains, the sharper the image. To keep the pixels glowing, the CRT must rebombard the screen fifteen to thirty times a second in a process called refreshing.

There are seven types of video display:

1. Televisions make adequate display screens for games, but their poor, eye-fatiguing resolution is inadequate for some applications such as word processing. To work their best, televisions must be attached to a device called a radio-frequency (rf) modulator.

2. One-color display monitors operate with one active color, say, black on a white or gray background. These monitors provide better resolution than televisions but still cause eye fatigue after extensive viewing. A variety of the one-color display is the **monochrome monitor**, which uses many more pixels per character and produces a crisper display.

3. **Color monitors** are excellent for presenting graphics, depicting graphs, and playing games. However, they are not good for displaying text data found in spreadsheets and word processing because the images frequently tear in the screen and the pixels often appear multicolored.

4. **Flat-screen monitors** were developed for lap computers and use some type of display that does not need a large tube, such as an LCD (liquid crystal display) screen. LCD screens have black characters on a white or gray background, are lightweight, and sometimes suffer from poor readability. Many watches and calculators use LCD screens.

5. **Enhanced graphics adapter (EGA) monitors** offer extraordinary resolution, thanks to their 640×350–dot screens that can display sixty-four or more different colors (Figure 2.17a).

6. **Video graphics array (VGA) monitors** present clearer, more vivid graphics than do any of the contemporary display devices. Their 640×480–dot screens use 262,144 colors, 256 of which can be displayed at the same time. Monochrome VGAs offer up to sixty-four shades of gray. VGA monitors are especially useful in computer-aided design (CAD) applications, business graphics, and video games.

7. **Multipurpose monitors** are fairly new to the marketplace. They can handle color, EGA, and monochrome signals, thereby providing the user with three monitors in one (Figure 2.17b).

By hooking several of the above monitor types to a computer, an operator

(a)

(b)

Figure 2.17
(a) Princeton Graphic Systems SR-12P EGA graphics monitor. (b) Sony multisync CPD-1302 monitor capable of handling both color and EGA graphics. [Courtesy of (a) Princeton Graphic Systems, copyright 1986, used by permission; (b) Sony Corporation of America]

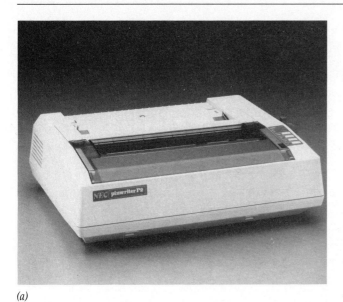

(a)

(b)

Figure 2.18
Two dot-matrix printers. (a) NEC Pinwriter P_2 and (b) IBM Personal Computer Graphics Printer. [Courtesy of (a) NEC Information Systems, Inc.; (b) IBM]

can benefit from the advantages of each. For example, a monochrome monitor can be used for text-related applications, and a color monitor can be used when graphics are needed.

Printers. Monitors are ideal for temporary display, but a printer is needed to preserve the output on paper. **Printers** use dot-matrix, thermal, daisy-wheel, ink-jet, and laser printing methods. **Dot-matrix printers** form characters out of dots and are the most popular microcomputer printers (Figure 2.18). They use

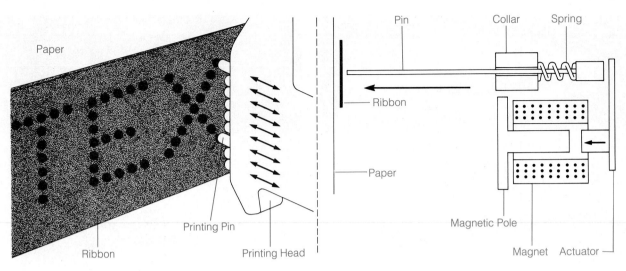

Figure 2.19
The print-head mechanism of a dot-matrix printer has up to twenty-four vertical print pins. These pins strike an inked ribbon as the print head moves horizontally across the page. In this example, capital letters are being printed by a seven-pin print head. Two additional pins are available to create the lower portion (descenders) of lower-case letters.

Figure 2.20
Typical thimble print heads. (Courtesy of NEC Information Systems, Inc.)

a moving print head with seven to twenty-four tiny print pins, which strike an inked ribbon to form dotted characters on paper (Figure 2.19). The more print pins in the print head, the better the quality of type. The speed of these printers varies from 80 characters per second (cps) to about 450 cps.

Thermal printers produce a print style that looks similar to dot matrix, but the characters are formed by burning dots onto special paper. Output speed is about 80 cps.

Letter-quality printers produce typewriter-quality characters and come in two types of print mechanism, the **daisy wheel** and **print thimble** (Figure 2.20). Both print at 10–60 cps.

(a)

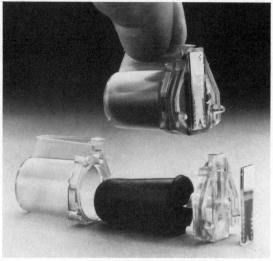

(b)

Figure 2.21
(a) The graphics capability of an ink-jet printer. (b) The disposable ink cartridge used in the Hewlett-Packard ThinkJet printer. (Courtesy of Hewlett-Packard Company)

Figure 2.22
A Hewlett-Packard LaserJet printer. (Courtesy of Hewlett-Packard Company)

Ink-jet printers shoot little jets of ink from disposable cartridges onto paper to form characters (Figure 2.21). These printers vary greatly in the legibility of their output, but the best ones print letter quality characters. Output speed exceeds 200 cps.

Like modern copiers, the **laser printer** employs the photocopying process to create type and graphics. A laser beam traces characters onto a photosensitive drum, then bonds toner (an inklike solution) and paper together with heat to produce a printed page (Figures 2.22 and 2.23). Laser printers can make only one copy at a time, but they are among the fastest printers. They also provide high resolution (about 300 dots per square inch) and are therefore essential to desktop publishing. At first very expensive, laser printers have

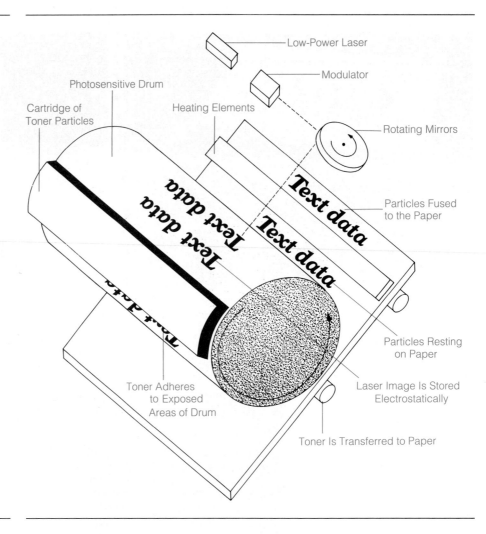

Low-Power Laser

Modulator

Photosensitive Drum

Cartridge of
Toner Particles

Heating Elements

Rotating Mirrors

Particles Fused
to the Paper

Text data

Particles Resting
on Paper

Toner Adheres
to Exposed
Areas of Drum

Laser Image Is Stored
Electrostatically

Toner Is Transferred to Paper

dropped markedly in price, and many computer owners now use them instead of impact printers.

The **plotter** uses a moving pen (sometimes the paper also moves) to create high-quality graphics such as architectural drawings (Figure 2.24). With contemporary plotters, computer users can produce multicolored drawings by changing the machine's pen. Once in high demand, plotters have declined in popularity since the advent of the laser printer.

Secondary Storage

Diskettes. For years, tapes were the only nonvolatile storage medium available. Today, the standard secondary storage device for microcomputers is the **diskette**, also called the **disk** or **floppy disk**. Its chief advantage is the ability to directly access files (see Chapter 1). Tape storage requires a computer to run sequentially through all the files until the proper one is found, just as a stereo owner has to forward or reverse an audio tape to locate a particular song. In contrast, a computer can directly access a disk track, just as a stereo owner can set a turntable's stylus at the beginning of a particular song track on an album. Disks are also more portable and less expensive than tapes.

Figure 2.24
A number of Colorwriter plotters manufactured by Gould Electronics. (Courtesy of Gould Electronics)

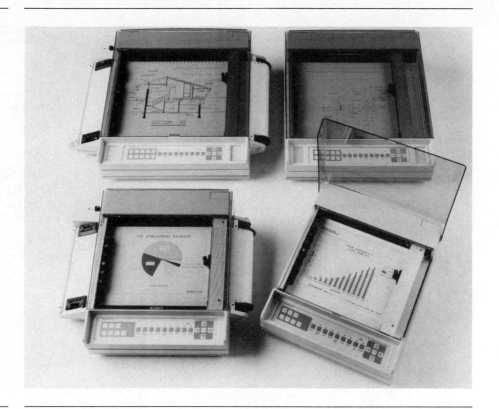

A disk is simply a Mylar plastic circle that has a ferrous oxide coating capable of holding magnetic spots (Figure 2.25). Disks come in different sizes (identified by diameter), but the most common is 5.25 inches. These Mylar circles are encased in flimsy black plastic covers. The term *floppy* alludes to the disk's physical flimsiness and its flexibility in providing storage (Figure 2.26).

Disks provide storage for data, documents, and programs that need to be kept for an extended period. Before a new disk can be used, it must be prepared so that the computer can recognize it and record data on it. This process is called **formatting** because it is performed by the FORMAT command.

Disks bear a printed label that indicates the manufacturer and identifies the top side of the disk. Disks should always be inserted in the disk drive with the label up and your thumb on the label.

Two round holes are visible at the center of the disk. The larger one, called the **centering hole**, is clamped by the disk drive, which then rotates the disk inside its protective cover. On good-quality disks, the centering holes are reinforced by plastic rings. The smaller hole to the right of the centering hole is the **timing hole**. It indicates the beginning of a track or sector and tells the disk drive where to start reading or writing. (If there is only one hole on the disk, the disk is soft-sectored; if there is more than one hole, the disk is hard-sectored.)

Below the centering hole is an oval opening called the **read/write access hole**. Through this hole, read/write heads read from or record to the disk. Information is stored on the disk in concentric circles called **tracks** (Figure 2.26c). Each track is subdivided into **sectors**, each of which can store 512 bytes. There are nine sectors per track, forty tracks per disk side, and two sides per disk, so each 5.25-inch disk has a storage capacity of 368,640 bytes (512 × 9 × 40 × 2). Disk storage is also measured in K—a 5.25-inch disk holds 360K.

(a)   *(b)*

Figure 2.25
(a) Manufacturing line where disks are cut from Mylar plastic and (b) machine producing
the Mylar. [Courtesy of (a) BASF Systems Corporation and (b) Polaroid Corporation]

Soft-sectored disks are divided into sectors by the computer during the formatting process. **Hard-sectored disks** are manufactured with their tracks divided into sectors. IBM computers and IBM compatibles use soft-sectored disks. Hard-sectored disks cannot be used in computers with disk drives designed for soft-sectored disks, nor will soft-sectored disks work in hard-sectored disk drives.

The two small cutouts below the read/write access hole are stress notches which allow the disk to bend without creasing. Along the upper right-hand edge of the disk is a rectangular notch known as the **write-protect notch**. Covering this notch with a piece of tape prevents alteration of the disk's information, but the disk remains readable. Many software program disks don't have a write-protect notch, so their information is permanently safeguarded from alteration or erasure. To protect the Mylar from scratching, manufacturers glue a piece of lubricated fabric inside the protective plastic jacket to trap foreign particles and decrease drag.

Diskette Dos and Don'ts

Dos:

1. Copy (back up) all records! Never trust a single disk with important data or files.

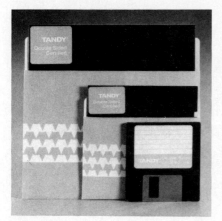

(a)

Figure 2.26
(a) Typical 8-inch, 5.25-inch, and 3.5-inch disks. (b) Various features of a typical 5.25-inch disk. (c) A 5.25-inch disk with tracks and sectors. [Courtesy of (a) Tandy Corporation and (b) BASF Systems Corporation]

(b)

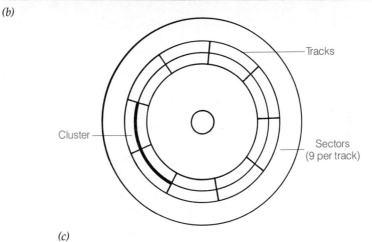

(c)

2. When finished using a disk, place it inside its protective paper envelope to keep out dust, coffee, and other contaminants.

3. Store disks vertically, like record albums. Laying disks flat or at an angle will bend and warp them.

4. Place a label on every disk; this will simplify locating it when needed.

5. Be especially careful when inserting a disk into the disk drive. It's very easy to crease a disk by catching it on a piece of internal machinery. If you do crease a disk, back it up immediately.

6. Close the disk-drive door gently to allow the disk to center properly. Snapping the door shut can catch the disk off center and damage it.

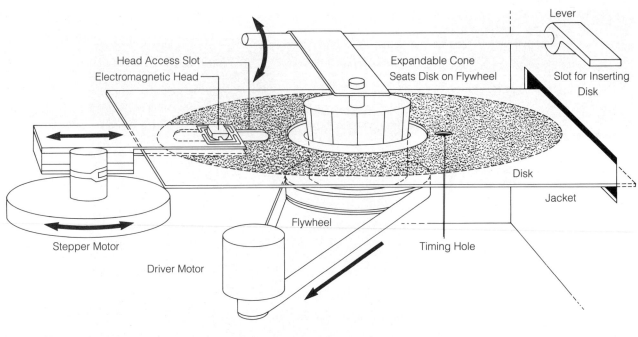

Figure 2.27
A floppy disk drive.

7. Keep disks away from magnetic fields, which are generated by magnets, some color monitors, and older telephones.

8. Handle disks with care; carelessness can destroy hours of computer work in an instant.

Don'ts:

1. Never write on a disk's plastic cover with a pencil or ballpoint pen—doing so could damage the Mylar. Fill in the label prior to affixing it to the disk. If you must write on a label already on the disk, use a felt-tip pen and a light hand.

2. Don't touch the disk surface with fingers, tissue, or solvents or place an unprotected disk on a dusty surface.

3. Don't bend or crease disks. Special protective packages are available for mailing disks.

4. Don't place disks in direct sunlight, on top of radiators, in the trunks of cars, next to cold windowsills, or otherwise expose them to temperature extremes.

5. Don't expose disks to airport X-ray machines or library security devices.

How Floppy Disk Drives Work. Information is both read from and recorded to the disk by the **disk drive** (Figure 2.27). An expandable cone inside the drive clamps the disk onto a flywheel, which then rotates the Mylar disk inside its protective plastic jacket. A system of lights and light sensors enables the computer to locate the beginning of a track containing the data that the user is seeking. After motors position the read/write heads at the appropriate track, the information can be read from or written onto the disk.

Other Disks

Several manufacturers have switched from the 5.25-inch disk to the 3.5-inch disk. Eventually, the 3.5-inch disk may become the preferred microcomputer storage device. Because there are hundreds of millions of 5.25-inch disks in use, many computer owners have added a 3.5-inch disk drive to their systems so that they can use both types of disk. Below is a summary of various disks used in today's microcomputers.

5.25-Inch Disks	3.5-Inch Disks
180K	—
360K	720K
1.2 meg	1.4 meg

Hard Disks. Hard disk systems are becoming an increasingly popular medium for storing microcomputer information because they offer greater storage capacity and provide faster data retrieval than do floppy disks. **Hard disks** contain one or more rigid platters for recording data. Like floppy disks, these platters have a metal oxide coating for holding the magnetic charges that represent characters. Read/write heads hover fourteen-millionths of an inch above the disk surface to read or record data. The platters rotate on a spindle at about 3,600 rpm, twelve times the speed floppy disks do (the faster a disk rotates, the quicker the read/write heads can locate a track of information).

Hard disks are available with either a removable disk **cartridge** or a fixed disk in a sealed housing, commonly known as the Winchester disk (Figure 2.28). The Winchester was first developed by IBM for use on mainframe computers and is the more popular disk system. Some hard disk units use both the removable cartridge and the Winchester disk.

The diameter of the platters varies from 3–5.25 inches, and the amount of data that can be stored on a disk also varies greatly. Rather than being measured in Ks (thousands of bytes), hard disk storage is measured in **megabytes (meg)**, or millions of bytes.

Some precautions must be taken with hard disks. In removable-cartridge disks, contaminants such as hair or dust can collect on a platter, tripping the read/write head and causing it to strike the Mylar disk. Due to their sealed housing, Winchester disks rarely have this problem.

Another difficulty is backing up a hard disk's stored data. Here, removable-cartridge disks offer an advantage. The operator simply copies the stored data onto another cartridge, then shelves the copy for safekeeping. Winchester disks are more difficult to back up. Most can have their data copied onto floppy disks, but this is a lengthy process. It would require twenty-eight 5.25-inch floppies to store all the information contained on a full 10-meg hard disk. However, some hard disk manufacturers now offer ¼-inch tape cartridges that can copy 10–40 meg of data in a few minutes (Figure 2.28d).

Optical Disk (CD ROM). Floppy disks and hard disks record information using magnetic spots. Another, newer form of secondary storage is called the **compact disk (CD)**, which stores data optically. CDs are already a popular form of storing music (Figure 2.29). Lasers burn information into the CD as bubbles, which later can be read by another laser. However, the burned-in information cannot be erased or altered. Accordingly, CD technology is currently used only for ROM and is classified as write-once/read-many-times (WORM) storage. For many applications, this feature is a disadvantage. Future CD ROM may allow a user to erase data and store new data.

One CD ROM can hold 5 billion characters, compared with the 40-million character capacity of a large hard disk. In fact, CD ROM capacity is often

(a)

(b)

(c)

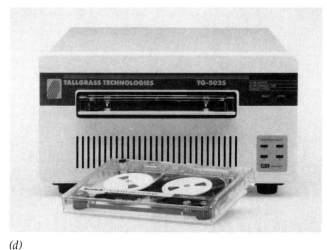

(d)

Figure 2.28
(a) ST4192N-Seagate full-height 5.25-inch high-performance, hard disk drive with embedded controller, SCSI interface, and 160 meg of formatted capacity. The drive has an average access time of 17 msec. (b) ST157R-Seagate 3.5-inch hard disk drive with ST412/RLL interface and 40 meg of formatted capacity. The drive features an average access time of less than 30 msec and only 9 watts of power. (c) Typical half-height Winchester hard disk with tape backup system. (d) A 24-meg external hard disk with magnetic tape backup. [Courtesy of (a, b) Seagate Technology, (c) Alloy Computer Products, and (d) Tallgrass Technologies Corporation © 1985]

figured in 1,000-meg units called gigabytes. This high storage feature and the integrity of its storage method make CD ROM disks ideal for archival and backup and recovery applications. CD ROM is also valuable for storing large data bases of information that do not change frequently, such as the Microsoft Bookshelf reference library (Figure 2.30). This package includes a spelling checker, Roget's II: Electronic Thesaurus, electronic versions of *Bartlett's Familiar Quotations*, the *1987 World Almanac, The American Heritage Dictionary*, and *The Chicago Manual of Style*, a U.S. ZIP Code Directory, a grammar checker, a collection of customizable templates for standard business forms, and the Business Information Sources directory. Other types of data bases that are available include financial data bases, flight-simulation data bases, and bibliography data bases.

Figure 2.29
A typical CD ROM disk.
(Courtesy of 3M)

Figure 2.30
Microsoft Bookshelf reference
for authors contained on a
CD ROM. (Courtesy of
Microsoft Corporation)

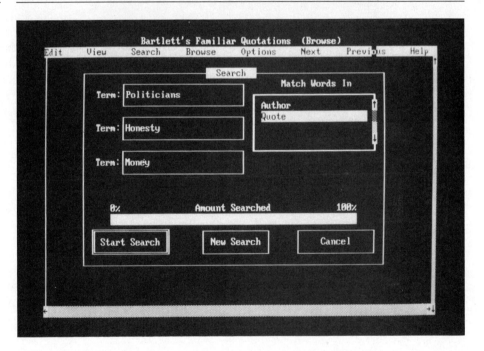

Chapter Review

A microcomputer system comprises five separate parts: people (users), hardware, software, documentation/procedures, and data/information. Of these, the human is most important because it is his or her needs that determine what components are appropriate for the other four parts.

The hardware component comprises input, processing, output, and storage. The microprocessor chip serves as the hardware component's brain.

A number of different types of output devices such as monitors and printers can be attached to a microcomputer system. Information can be stored on a nonvolatile storage medium, the most popular being the disk.

The two basic types of computer memory are RAM and ROM. RAM stores data and program instructions inside the computer. The byte is the smallest piece of RAM storage; it holds one character of storage. Pieces of data are stored in RAM in a special binary code called ASCII. ROM is used primarily by the computer.

Key Terms and Concepts

alphanumeric keys
ASCII (American Standard Code for Information Interchange)
banked memory
bit
bus
byte
cartridge
CD (compact disk)
centering hole
centronics
chip
clock speed
closed-bus system
color monitor
coprocessor
CRT (cathode-ray tube)
daisy wheel
disk drive
diskette, or disk
dot-matrix printer
EGA (enhanced graphics adapter) monitor
flat-screen monitor
floppy disk
formatting
function keys
hard disk
hard-sectored disk
hardware
ink-jet printer
interface
kilobyte (K)
laser printer
LCD (liquid crystal display) monitor
letter-quality printer
light pen

main system board
megabyte (meg)
microcomputer information system
microprocessor
monitor
monochrome monitor
mother board
mouse
multipurpose monitor
nonvolatile memory
numeric key pad
open-bus system
parallel interface
PC (personal computer)
peripheral
pixel
plotter
printer
print thimble
procedures
QWERTY
RAM (random-access memory)
read/write access hole
ROM (read-only memory)
scanner
sectors
serial interface
soft-sectored disk
tablet
thermal printer
timing hole
touch screen
tracks
VGA (video graphics array) monitor
volatile memory
write-protect notch

Chapter Quiz

Multiple Choice

1. Which of the following items is part of the microcomputer?
   a. RAM (random-access memory)
   b. Interface
   c. ROM (read-only memory)
   d. Bus
   e. All of the above are part of a microcomputer.

2. Which of the following is not an output device?
   a. Printer

b. Plotter
c. Monitor
d. Keyboard
e. All of the above are output devices.

3. Which of the following statements is correct?
   a. RAM is the nonvolatile memory.
   b. ROM is the memory used to hold data and instructions.
   c. The bus is used to move data and instructions from one part of the computer to another.
   d. The laser printer uses new technology to make it an input device.

4. Which of the following terms do(es) not apply to a disk?
   a. Sector
   b. Track
   c. Soft-sectored
   d. Byte
   e. All of the above terms apply to a disk.

5. Which of the statements below is false?
   a. About eight "families" or types of microprocessor are currently on the market.
   b. A 32-bit processor will probably be slower than an 8-bit processor.
   c. RAM restrictions will not usually restrict the type of software you are allowed to run on your computer.
   d. b and c.
   e. All of the above are false.

True/False

6. A letter-quality printer is typically faster than a dot-matrix printer.

7. A disk is an example of nonvolatile storage.

8. As a general rule of thumb, the more bits a microprocessor chip can handle at one time, the more memory it can address and the faster it operates.

9. Hard disks are typically faster and more reliable than are floppy disks.

10. Monochrome display monitors are easier to read than are one-color monitors because they use more pixels.

Answers

1. e 2. d 3. c 4. e 5. e 6. f 7. t 8. t 9. t 10. t

Exercises

1. Define or describe each of the following:
   a. microprocessor   h. centronics
   b. bit   i. pixel
   c. byte   j. track
   d. ASCII   k. sector
   e. RAM   l. K
   f. ROM   m. meg
   g. bus

2. List some typical input devices for a microcomputer.
   a.

   b.

c.

d.

3. The standard code used for storing information in microcomputers is the _____ code.

4. Differences among 8-, 16-, and 32-bit microprocessing computer chips limit the amount of addressable _____ memory.

5. Memory that is only capable of 64K functioning at one time but that has a total storage capacity of 128K is called _____ memory.

6. The type of monitor that displays characters with the pixels (dots) close together is the _____ display.

7. _____ memory is available to the user, but _____ memory is used only by the machine.

8. The unit of storage required to hold a numeric digit or character is called a(n) _____.

9. A _____ interface transmits 1 bit at a time, whereas a _____ transmits at least 8 bits at once.

10. The terms *diskette* and _____ *disk* are synonymous.

11. A K of memory is equal to about _____ bytes, and a meg of memory equals about _____ bytes of storage.

12. List some advantages and disadvantages using hard disk storage devices.
Advantages:
a.

b.

Disadvantages:
a.

b.

13. Why is the human element so important in a microcomputer system? Do you know of any examples of individuals not satisfied with their microcomputers because they were inappropriate to the users' particular problem?

14. A printer that prints characters using dot patterns is called a _____ printer.

15. A _____ chip greatly speeds up processing that involves mathematical manipulation.

16. An input device that is moved across the surface of a flat area and that issues instruction by pressing one or more buttons is a(n) _____.

17. An input device that can digitize images contained on a sheet of paper is called a(n) _____.

18. The individual spots on a monitor screen used to generate a character are referred to as _____.

19. A printer that is rated at a speed of pages per minute is the _____ printer.

20. A type of secondary storage that cannot be erased is called _____.

Questions for Thought

You may wish to refer to some recent issues of *PC Magazine, PC World, Infoworld, PC Week,* or *Personal Computing* in researching some of the following questions.

1. Do some research at the library to find the differences among the various families of microcomputers that utilize the various chips (8088, 80286, and 80386). What are the differences in speed, processing power, and cost among the various computers that use these chips? What are types of applications that these various microcomputers are used for?

2. Check the recent literature to find out what advances have been made lately in the fast-changing CD ROM field.

3. What would be the hardware components for a computer system that you feel would meet your needs? What type of computer, printer, and other hardware peripherals would you want for your system? List the various components along with their cost. What motivated your selection of these choices?

4. Research which companies are currently the leaders in the following hardware areas: microcomputers, fixed disks, printers, and monitors.

5. Prepare a report examining the success that IBM has had in getting computer users to support its Micro Channel Bus Architecture. Is IBM currently gaining or losing market share in the microcomputer market?

Chapter 3

Microcomputer Software

Chapter Objectives

After completing this chapter, you should be able to:

Describe various types of menu items

List and describe the three classifications of software

List and describe the five classifications of application software

Describe the role of integrated application software

Describe the function of the IBM disk operating system (DOS)

List and describe the various parts of DOS

List and describe the rules for file names

Describe how to prepare a diskette for use

Describe how to start (boot) the computer system

Describe how DOS uses the prepared disk

Describe how DOS uses "wild cards"

Describe how DOS uses various keys to give commands

Chapter 2 discussed the microcomputer system's hardware—the seeable, touchable components. This chapter covers the **software** components—the set of instructions the computer uses to manipulate and process data. Without software, the computer is a useless collection of hardware. Load software into a computer, and the machine acts as if it has received an instant education; suddenly, it "knows" how to operate and how to think.

Software Menus

Early microcomputer software packages were so complex that consumers often had to spend many hours reading instructions (documentation) before they could run the programs. Consumers complained loudly about the lack of user-friendly software. Software developers responded by adding menus and prompts to packages. Like an index that helps readers locate information in a book, a **menu** tells users where to find information in a program.

Menus greatly improved the "friendliness" of programs by reducing the number of commands an operator had to learn in order to use a software package. A software menu, like its restaurant counterpart, offers a user a list of options from which to select. Selecting an option either executes a command or brings to the screen a submenu of options. Often, prompts are included in the menu to guide the user step-by-step through the operation.

Menus of just about every conceivable type have been incorporated in software. Some software packages require the user to execute a special command to bring a menu onto the screen, whereas others automatically display a menu. There are two basic types of menu structures—horizontal and vertical. Software packages can have either type or both.

Horizontal Menus

Horizontal menus are displayed across the screen in one or two rows of text. An operator can issue a command on the menu in a variety of ways, such as pressing a function key, entering the command's first character, pressing the numeric key that corresponds to the command's selection number, or highlighting the command option with a pointer and pressing the ENTER key.

Figure 3.1
Lotus 1-2-3 Main Menu structure.

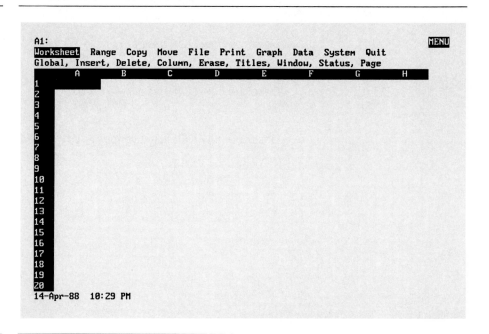

The software package Lotus 1-2-3 displays a two-line menu along the top of the worksheet screen (Figure 3.1). The first line contains various menu selections, and the second contains submenu options or descriptions of what highlighted commands will do if invoked. Note that no two menu selections start with the same first letter. This permits the user to easily select the proper command by entering its first character. Lotus 1-2-3 also allows the operator to select a command by highlighting the proper menu selection and then pressing the ENTER key. Once invoked, the Lotus 1-2-3 Main Menu stays on the screen until the undertaken task has been completed.

Many software packages have more than 100 commands that can be executed via menus and submenus. (See Appendix B for the menu structure of Lotus 1-2-3.) The menu system lists groups of commands under specific menu options. For example, any command dealing with a print operation is found under the Print command of the Lotus 1-2-3 Main Menu. Submenus facilitate the logical progression from one menu to the next.

The series of commands (and their corresponding menus) involved in retrieving the file called COMPSALS from a disk using Lotus 1-2-3 (Figure 3.2) would be as follows:

1.   Start from READY Mode (Figure 3.2a).
2. /   Invoke the Main Menu.
3. F   Select the File command from the Main Menu (Figure 3.2b).

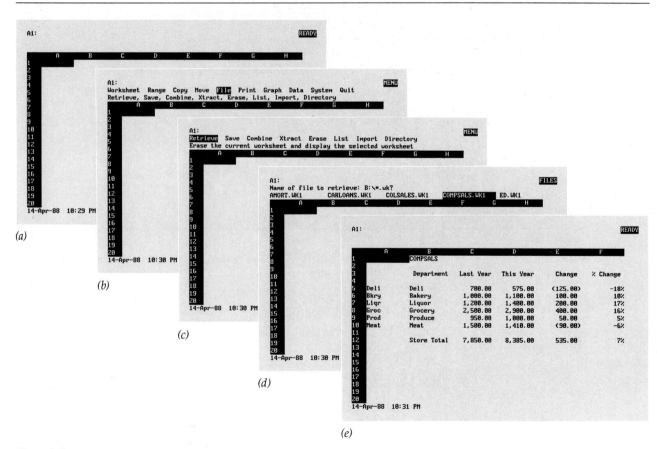

(a)

(b)

(c)

(d)

(e)

Figure 3.2
The graphic steps in retrieving the COMPSALS file.

Figure 3.3
WordStar half-screen vertical
menu.

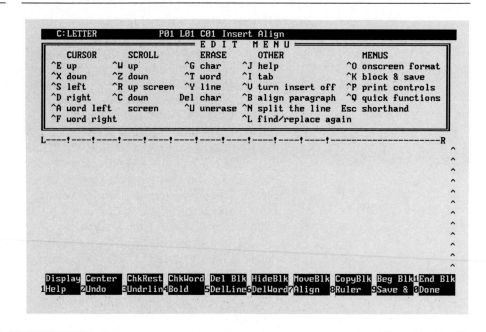

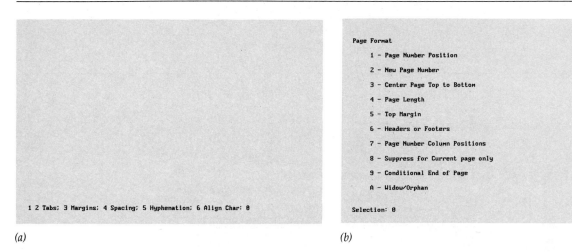

(a)   *(b)*

Figure 3.4
WordPerfect (a) horizontal and (b) vertical menus.

4. R   Select the Retrieve command from the File submenu (Figure 3.2c).

5.   Highlight the COMPSALS command using the right arrow key (Figure 3.2d).

6. ENTER   Press the ENTER key to load the file (Figure 3.2e).

Vertical Menus

Vertical menus occupy more screen area than do horizontal menus. Some vertical menus (like those used in WordStar) occupy only half a screen, while others (like some used in WordPerfect) take up the entire screen. Some packages combine horizontal menus with full-screen vertical menus (Figures 3.3 and 3.4).

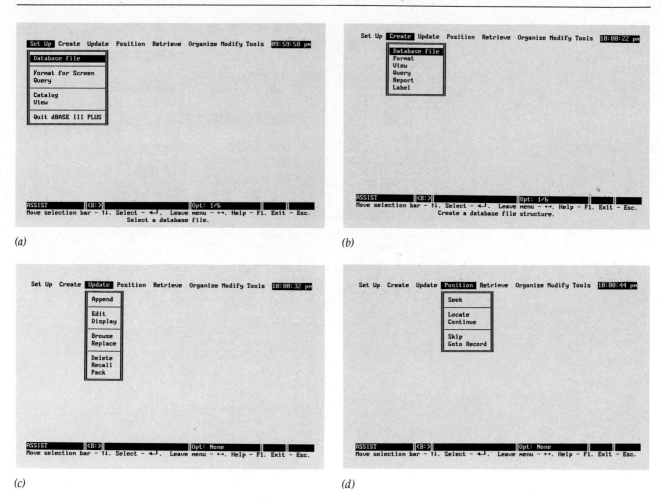

Figure 3.5
Four dBASE III pull-down menus that can be displayed on the screen.

Typically, vertical menus display more selection items and are more informative than are horizontal menus. Vertical menus can be in full-screen, pull-down, or pop-up form. Pull-down and pop-up menus disappear after the user enters a command.

Pull-Down Menus. Like window shades, these menus pull down from a horizontal menu bar located along the top of the monitor screen. The operator uses the Right or Left arrow key to select a menu heading. Underneath the heading, the computer displays a vertical menu. Using Up and Down arrow keys, the operator then selects from this menu and presses the ENTER key to execute the command. The dBASE III Plus uses a pull-down menu (Figure 3.5).

Pop-Up Menus. These menus pop up on the screen. Typically, pop-up menus are **RAM-resident programs**, meaning they are loaded into RAM when the computer is turned on and retained there until the computer is turned off or a special command is issued to purge the program from memory. As such, pop-up menus operate independently of the software application being run. When an operator activates a pop-up menu (using a special keystroke sequence), the computer suspends whatever software it is executing and presents the utility program. After selecting some function from the menu, the operator can then

Figure 3.6
The Sidekick pop-up menu
structure.

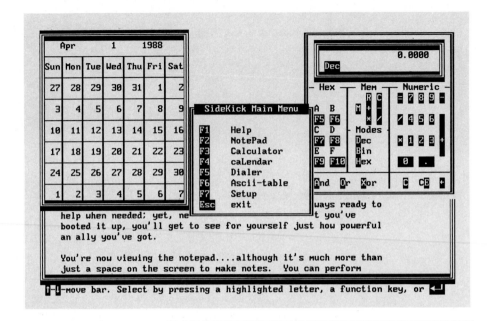

Figure 3.7
Types of software.

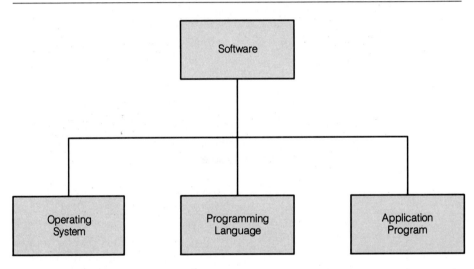

return to the original program. Figure 3.6 shows a popular resident-utility program called Sidekick, which will be discussed in more detail later in the chapter.

Software Categories

The three general categories of software are programming languages, application programs, and operating systems (Figure 3.7). All three software types are needed to make computers usable to the average person.

Programming Languages

Programming languages enable people to write software specially for a particular application or problem that can't be handled by off-the-shelf programs. For example, suppose a clothing manufacturer wants to computerize its payroll system. The manufacturer pays its workers by the number of shirts they sew per hour, not by hourly wage, according to a varying scale. Because most off-the-shelf spreadsheet programs are designed to calculate payroll by hourly wage, they could not help the clothing manufacturer. The manufacturer would have to write, or hire a programmer to write, a software package that would suit its special needs.

Some programming languages are simple enough that laypersons can learn to use them within a few hours; others are used only by well-trained professionals. In either case, the user may require hundreds or thousands of hours to solve a particular problem by writing a tailor-made program. It is not recommended that novice computer users attempt to write their own programs, except as an exercise to learn about the programming process or when a particular application requirement can't be met by existing programs.

To write a computer program, users usually follow a set of procedures called the system-development life cycle, which provides guidance on how to tackle complicated problems through systems analysis. For example, before writing a program for the clothing manufacturer hypothesized above, the programmer would have to analyze the company's payroll system and then tailor the software accordingly. We will cover systems analysis in depth in Chapter 20.

The most common microcomputer programming languages are **BASIC** (Beginner's All-Purpose Symbolic Instruction Code), **FORTRAN** (Formula Translator), **COBOL** (Common Business-Oriented Language) (Figure 3.8), and **Pascal**. Some programming languages, especially BASIC, the most popular of all, have numerous versions. Consequently, a program written on one computer often must be changed before it can be run on another computer. Some data base packages, such as dBASE, have a built-in programming language (Figure 3.9).

Language Processors. Programming languages are necessary because computers only work with binary numbers. While humans can understand this code, it is so excruciatingly slow and difficult for programmers to use that they can easily commit errors. To be more productive, programmers use English and mathematical symbols arranged in a special syntax. This is then converted into binary code by other special-purpose software. Programmers categorize languages in levels according to their readability. **Low-level languages** are difficult to understand and require programmers to code instructions in considerable detail. **High-level languages** use English-like statements, which even novice programmers can master after minimal training.

A high-level programming language must be translated into binary code before a computer can read it. Special software packages called **language processors** translate instructions prepared in a specific programming language (such as BASIC or COBOL) into binary code, much as a diplomatic translator might interpret Swahili into English. The set of program instructions written in a high-level language is called the **source code**. (See Figure 3.8.) The set of translated binary instructions that the computer can execute is called the **object code**.

Language processors are either compilers or interpreters. **Compiler** software translates a complete program into machine language while checking for any errors that have been made by the programmer. A human counterpart to the compiler would listen to an entire speech in Swahili, then repeat it all in English. COBOL uses a compiler to translate source code and generate the object code. The object program, which is the program that performs all actual processing, becomes operative if there are no errors in the source program.

In contrast, an **interpreter** translates a program one instruction at a time. As each instruction is interpreted, the program checks for syntactic errors. It

Figure 3.8
A portion of a COBOL
program.

```
ID DIVISION
PROGRAM-ID. PROG1.
ENVIRONMENT DIVISION.
INPUT-OUTPUT SECTION.
FILE-CONTROL.
        SELECT INVENTORY-FILE ASSIGN TO PFMS.
        SELECT PRINT-FILE ASSIGN TO PFMS
DATA DIVISION.
FILE SECTION.
FD      INVENTORY-FILE
        LABEL RECORDS ARE STANDARD
        RECORD CONTAINS 20 CHARACTERS
        DATA RECORD IS INVENTORY-REC.
01      INVENTORY-REC.
        02   PART-NO            PIC X(5).
        02   DESCRIPTION        PIC X(15).
FD      PRINT-FILE
        LABEL RECORDS ARE STANDARD
        RECORD CONTAINS 133 CHARACTERS
        VALUE OF FILE-ID IS 'PRINTER1'
        DATA RECORD IS PRINT-REC.
01      PRINT-REC.
        02   FILLER             PIC X(5).
        02   PART-NO-OUT         PIC X(5).
        02   FILLER             PIC X(10).
        02   DESCRIPTION-OUT     PIC X(15).
        02   FILLER             PIC X(98).
PROCEDURE DIVISION.
START-HERE.
        OPEN INPUT INVENTORY-FILE OUTPUT PRINT-FILE.
READ-TIME.
        READ INVENTORY-FILE AT END GO TO EOJ.
        MOVE SPACES TO PRINT-REC.
        MOVE PART-NO TO PART-NO-OUT.
        MOVE DESCRIPTION TO DESCRIPTION-OUT.
        WRITE PRINT-REC AFTER ADVANCING 2 LINES.
        GO TO READ-TIME.
EOJ.
        CLOSE INVENTORY-FILE PRINT-FILE.
        STOP RUN.
```

works like a human translator converting into English each sentence of Swahili as it is spoken. BASIC and the dBASE internal programming language typically make use of an interpreter to translate high-level instructions.

Because they need to translate a program only once, compiler programs are generally three to five times faster than interpreter programs.

Application Programs

Most people find it reassuring that they need not know how to program in order to use a microcomputer effectively. For most of their needs, microcomputer users can buy off-the-shelf software called application programs.

Figure 3.9
A portion of a dBASE
program.

```
IF # > 0
   @ 5,0 SAY "Sorry, there are no records in the data base"
   STORE 1 TO count
   DO WHILE count < 50
      STORE count + 1 TO count
   ENDDO
   RELEASE count
   ERASE
   RETURN
ENDIF
SET INDEX TO
GO TOP
DO WHILE T
   STORE " " TO pause

   STORE T TO badans
   STORE " " TO mchoice
   IF *
      @ 1,50 SAY "DELETED"
   ELSE
      @ 1,50 SAY "        "
   ENDIF
   @ 1,72 SAY DATE()
   @ 5,0 SAY "Product Number:"
   @ 5,16 SAY Prd:num
   @ 7,0 SAY "Product Description:"
   @ 7,21 SAY Prd:desc
   @ 9,0 SAY "Product Cost:"
```

Application programs are precoded sets of generalized computer instructions that are designed to resolve particular data-processing needs. The computer operator need only select the right application program for the job, just as you would need to choose the proper tool to tighten a bolt. A general ledger package, a mailing list program, and PacMan are all examples of application programs.

Application software can be divided into five core applications: electronic spreadsheets, word processing, communications, data base management, and graphics (Figure 3.10).

Electronic Spreadsheets. **Electronic spreadsheet** programs allow users to manipulate various data that can be expressed in rows and columns. A *cell* (the point where a row and a column intersect) can contain text, numbers, or formulas, which establish its relationship with other cells. Whenever the user changes the contents of one cell, the spreadsheet automatically recalculates all other cell values. This feature saves an enormous amount of time, for it frees the operator from the tedium of recalculating by hand.

VisiCalc, originally designed for the Apple II computer by Harvard Business School graduate students Dan Flystra and Dan Bricklin, was the first spreadsheet introduced for microcomputers. VisiCalc led many business-

Figure 3.10
Types of application
software.

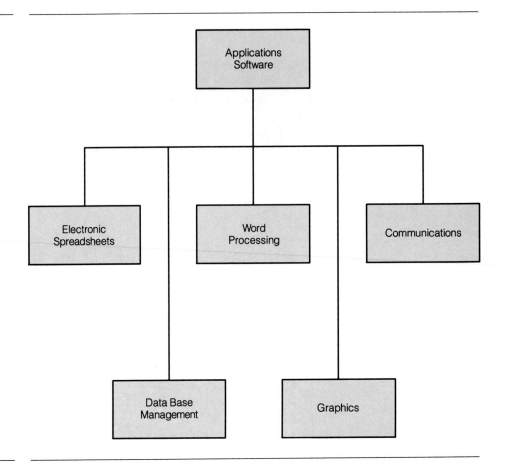

people to view the microcomputer as a useful business tool rather than as a plaything.

Many microcomputer spreadsheet packages now available far surpass the original VisiCalc in power and capability. Just as VisiCalc helped popularize Apple microcomputers, other spreadsheet packages, such as **Lotus 1-2-3**, spurred businesses to purchase the IBM PC. Later, we will study the Lotus 1-2-3 spreadsheet program (Chapters 9–11).

Sophisticated spreadsheet packages can do much more than manipulate rows and columns of numbers. Some have advanced features such as "if-then-else" logic and tests for "less-than-greater-than." These operations could be used in such tasks as calculating payroll. A less-than-greater-than test could pick out those employees who worked more than forty hours in a week. The if-then-else operation could have the computer calculate these employees' wages according to a different rate. In effect, this operation would say to the computer: "If an employee's weekly hours total more than forty, then calculate his or her wages according to an overtime formula." Another advanced feature is the ability to determine the minimum, maximum, or average value in a range of numbers.

Some spreadsheets also allow the importing or exchanging of information with other application programs. This feature enables users to perform additional calculations with data already processed or to print out reports.

The following are only a few of the business and personal applications that spreadsheet programs can be used to accomplish:

Product planning

Production forecasting

Marketing

Materials and labor requirements

Merger and acquisition of real estate

Cash-flow analysis

Checkbook registers

Personal balance sheet

The usefulness of an electronic spreadsheet alone has justified many microcomputer purchases by individuals and businesses.

Word Processing. How often, in drafting a letter or report, have you filled a wastebasket with "reject" paper? How often have you crossed out lines or tried to squeeze additional comments on the sides of the page? How often have you wished you could easily move a paragraph from one place to another?

Word processing simplifies the task of writing, editing, and printing a document. It also improves personal productivity by allowing the user to duplicate a document without retyping it or to recall the document six months later without having to leaf through a ton of paper to find it. Word processing does not necessarily reduce the time it takes to produce an original report from scratch. But it does provide users with the means to generate an almost perfect document without having to spend hours retyping drafts.

Moreover, word processing software enhancements will also check spelling and, at the instruction of the user, automatically correct misspelled words. Later, we will examine WordPerfect, one of today's most commonly used word processing packages.

Communications. **Communications packages** enable businesses to transmit vital information—say, information about an unfolding merger—over telephone lines in only minutes. Many businesses communicate with computers at distant locations through terminal systems. Such a system usually comprises a monitor to receive and a keyboard to transmit information. However, microcomputers are replacing terminals because they can perform the terminal's function and serve as a stand-alone computer system.

Microcomputers communicate long distances by means of a modem—an abbreviation for modulator–demodulator. A **modem** translates the computer's binary signals into audible sounds, which can be sent via telephone lines. The modem at the other end reconverts the sounds into binary code.

A modem can be either internal (placed inside the machine in an expansion slot) or external (connected to a serial interface on the computer) (Figure 3.11). Modems come with a variety of features, such as **auto-answer** capability, which enables the computer to answer the phone, and **auto-dial** capability, which allows the computer (via the modem) to dial a desired number. Such added features increase a modem's cost.

Both internal and external modems translate data at a speed measured as a **baud rate**, or bits per second. Common transmission rates for today's modems are 1,200 to 9,600 baud.

The modem has helped spawn a new industry that provides information to computer owners. Microcomputers owners can receive stock information and buy or sell stocks through the Dow Jones News/Retrieval. The Source allows microcomputer subscribers to book an airline seat, rent a car, reserve a hotel room, and purchase consumer goods.

Several microcomputers can be linked into a **local area network (LAN)** through which users can share resources such as hard disks and printers. Modems are not needed to attach a computer to the network (Figure 3.12).

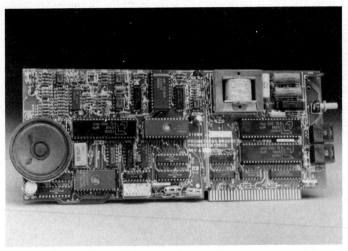

(a)

(b)

Figure 3.11
(a) This internal modem fits neatly on one board, which snaps into a vacant expansion slot inside the computer. (b) An external modem that hooks up to a serial port (expansion card) contained on the computer. (Courtesy of Prometheus Products of Fremont, California)

Data Base Management. **Data base management** programs help users to organize, update, and store records and files in virtually unlimited ways. For example, suppose a large firm has placed information about each employee in a data base file. Let's say the firm gets a request from the government for information on how many of its employees are over fifty-five years of age. Without computer assistance, personnel department workers would have to spend hours searching employee file folders to see who is over fifty-five. However, if employee birth dates were recorded in a computer data base, a personnel worker could simply instruct the computer to search for files containing birth dates of a given year and earlier. Within moments, the computer would produce a list of employees.

A data base management software package permits users to access information from the file quickly, saving vast amounts of time. Later, we will examine the data base management package dBASE III Plus (Chapters 13–15). Its predecessor, dBASE II, was the first relational data base created for microcomputers.

Graphics. It has been estimated that humans can comprehend a well-made graph up to 100,000 times faster than the printed statistics it represents! As a means of imparting information, graphics can offer similar advantages over reading or listening. While word processing has increased the ease of producing reams of printed information, computer graphics have increased the comprehension and speed with which printed information can be absorbed.

Two popular software programs that can convert raw data into **graphic displays** are Chart-Master and Lotus 1-2-3 (Figure 3.13). Plotters and color printers can produce hard copies of graphs created on a computer screen, and there are even devices that make photographic slides of computer-generated graphics. We'll cover the graphics capabilities of Lotus 1-2-3 later in this text.

Figure 3.12
Figure 3.12
The expansion cards, cables, and software necessary for connecting microcomputers together in a local area network. (Courtesy of Novell, Inc., Orem, Utah)

Integrated Software

Microcomputer users can derive great benefits from the five core program applications. However, these applications offer even more advantages when their problem-solving capabilities are combined.

Lotus 1-2-3 is one such **integrated package**. It contains a powerful spreadsheet with low-level data base management and medium-level graphics. An operator writing a business report with Lotus 1-2-3 could exit out of the spreadsheet package and open the graphics package to create an illustrative graph, then return to the spreadsheet at the exact place he or she left off. The resultant report generated using a package like WordPerfect 5.0 could mix graphs, text, and statistics for maximum impact. Since the advent of Lotus 1-2-3, the market has seen several packages (including Framework, Symphony, and Intuit) that combine all five core applications.

Special-Use Application Software

The five core applications represent general software packages that can be used to solve a variety of problems. Besides these, software writers have created many special-purpose application programs, designing each to solve only one type of problem. Examples include

Grading programs for teachers

General ledger

Accounts receivable and payable

Payroll

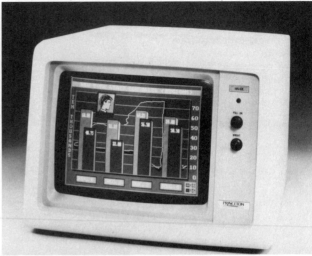

Figure 3.13
Effective use of graphics to present information. (Courtesy of Princeton Graphic System, an Intelligent Systems Company, and Polaroid Corporation)

Mailing lists

Computer games

Educational programs

Personal accounting

Practical software programs have also been written for personal use. Financial programs are available that allow an individual to track checks written, credit charges made, and the tax deductibility of various expenses, as well as to generate monthly income and balance statements. Sophisticated stock-portfolio programs are available that enable users to access the Dow Jones data base and to buy or sell stock from their homes.

Educational software is in plentiful supply, addressing everything from learning the alphabet to preparing for the SAT exam. These programs use such techniques as simulation, drill and practice, and computerized tutorials. Children can learn programming and improve their problem-solving skills with the computer programming language called LOGO.

Educational software offers many advantages. Students can benefit from computer-assisted instruction nearly any time—at night, on weekends, or during regular school hours. With computerized drill and practice programs, students receive instant verification or correction of their answers. Moreover, computerized instruction can be specially programmed to meet the needs of the individual student.

Business software is also abundant. There are packages for nearly every business problem, from general ledger to payroll. Many such programs have proved their soundness by withstanding the scrutiny of public accounting firms. Some software packages address specific industries, such as real estate or the health professions.

These are only a few of the many available software packages designed to solve very specific types of problems. With the wide assortment of general- and special-application packages available, the average user does not need to have programming skills to use the microcomputer's problem-solving capabilities at home and in the workplace.

Productivity Software

Recently, a new type of software has emerged that saves time by performing repetitive tasks quickly. Two examples of **productivity software** are desktop organizers and outliners.

Desktop Organizers. Picture the typical executive's desk. A leaning stack of papers clutters one corner. At another corner is a jumble of gadgets that includes the telephone, clock, and Rolodex. Legal pads and memos form a paper mountain in the center, under which a calendar and calculator lie hidden. The executive is speaking on the telephone, frantically trying to find a scrap of paper with some vital information on it.

Software designers have devised the perfect solution to the cluttered desktop—the desktop organizer. **Desktop organizers** can include such capabilities as calculators, notepads, automatic dialers, and appointment calendars, all neatly tucked away in the computer's memory and ready for instant access. Most desktop organizers are RAM-resident programs, so there is no need to insert a disk in order to call to the screen a calendar, notepad, or other desktop tool. The user simply issues a command.

The first desktop organizer to be marketed was Sidekick, a highly successful RAM-resident program developed by Borland International. It contains all of the desktop tools mentioned above, displaying each in a separate window on the screen (Figures 3.14 and 3.15). An executive can use his or her favorite spreadsheet package to enter formulas, then invoke Sidekick's calculator to check the work without exiting from the application program.

Outliners. **Outliner** software assists users in outlining concepts for a number of tasks, such as preparing a paper, planning a house, developing a sales strategy, or any other project that requires logical step-by-step planning. Some outline processors contain a built-in word processor that enables the user to embed major blocks of text within the outline. Outlining packages contain three basic types of lines: title, headline, and subhead. Both titles and headlines contain only one line of text. The title provides information about the goal of the outline; the headline indicates what information will follow. Below each headline are indented subheads, which may in turn be followed by lower levels of subheads.

One popular outline processor is Think Tank. A user can display the intricate details of a planning step by dividing a subhead into ever more refined

Figure 3.14
Calculator window of Sidekick, which can be invoked from within another software package, such as Lotus 1-2-3.

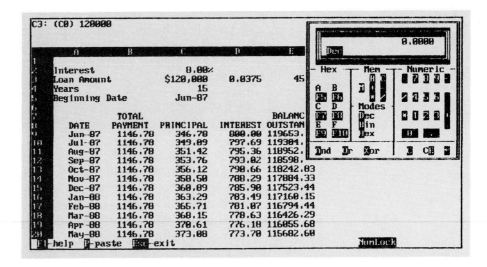

Figure 3.15
Various Sidekick windows active over a Lotus 1-2-3 worksheet.

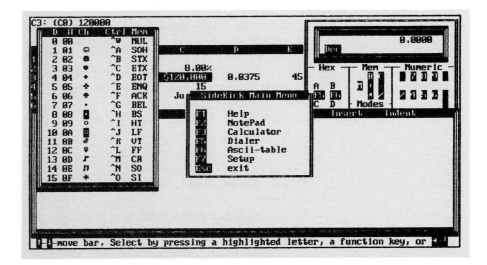

levels. Conversely, the user can display just the "big picture" by commanding the program to show only headlines (Figures 3.16 and 3.17).

Operating Systems: IBM PC DOS and MS DOS

Operating system software coordinates the computer's hardware and supervises the input, output, storage, and processing functions. Operating systems allow the user to issue commands to the computer, such as "open a file," "copy screen to print," or "copy file *x* from this disk to that disk." Without this software, a user would need a degree in computer science to operate a microcomputer effectively.

Every computer has an operating system, which varies with the type of computer (e.g., microcomputer or mainframe, IBM or Apple). The operating system must be activated when the computer is turned on; otherwise the operator cannot interact with the computer. Some operating systems activate automatically; others require the user to insert a diskette containing the operating system.

Figure 3.16
Expanded Think Tank outline with title, headings, and sub-headings.

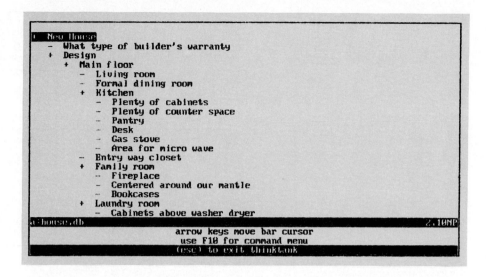

Figure 3.17
Collapsed Think Tank outline.

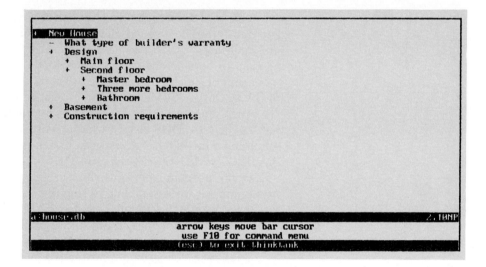

The IBM Personal Computer **disk operating system (DOS)** is a collection of programs designed to make it easy for users to create and manage files, run programs, and use the system devices attached to the computer. This section provides rudimentary information about various DOS commands required for daily use of the IBM PC. (For more information, refer to the Disk Operating System reference manual, written by Microsoft.) Knowledge of DOS is critical because this software dictates how programs are executed on IBM and IBM-compatible microcomputers. The operating system sets many practical limits on a computer's usefulness.

The software firm **Microsoft** developed PC DOS for IBM when the computer manufacturer decided to make a microcomputer. Microsoft markets virtually the same operating system, under the name **MS DOS**, to many of the manufacturers of IBM-compatible computers. The two operating systems are identical for all intents and purposes.

Parts of DOS. PC DOS contains three program parts: the I/O (input/output) handler, the Command Processor, and utility programs (Figure 3.18).

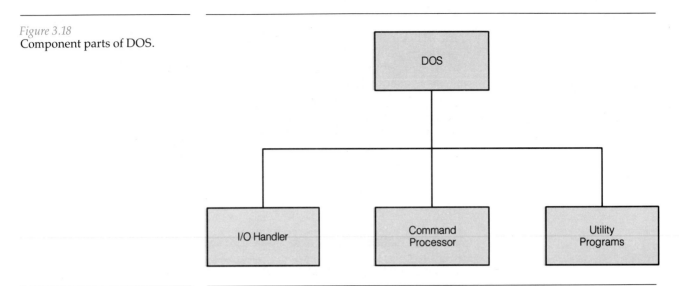

Figure 3.18
Component parts of DOS.

The I/O handler manages input and output, encoding and decoding all data transferred between application programs and peripherals such as monitors, keyboards, disk drives, and printers. It also contains routines for preparing data to be stored on a disk, whether the data consist of a program, a document, or something else. The I/O handler comprises "hidden" files called IBMBIO.COM and IBMDOS.COM, which we will discuss shortly.

The Command Processor has built-in functions (also called subprograms) that handle most DOS tasks, including copying files, running programs, and examining a disk's table of contents to determine what files are stored there. The file COMMAND.COM contains the Command Processor.

Utility programs perform "housekeeping" tasks that don't readily fit in the Command Processor. Utility programs are referred to as external files because they are stored separately on disks. Utilities handle such tasks as formatting disks, comparing files and/or disks, and reporting the available free space on a disk.

The above DOS programs are stored on a disk in four pieces:

1 The **boot record** contains the program responsible for loading the rest of DOS into the PC. The boot record is contained on every formatted disk, regardless of whether it contains DOS.

2. The **IBMBIO.COM** program acts as the I/O handler, managing all input and output to and from the computer.

3. The **IBMDOS.COM** program acts as the DOS file manager and contains file-related functions that can be used by DOS disk-stored files.

4. The **COMMAND.COM** program accepts DOS commands and runs the appropriate programs.

Only the COMMAND.COM program appears in the disk directory. The others are "hidden" program files that reside on the disk but are not shown when the directory command is issued.

When DOS is placed on a disk, it consumes considerable storage space. In fact, DOS requires about 40K of storage space, leaving about 320K of storage available on a typical disk for programs and data. DOS does not have to be placed on data disks, but it should be placed on any disks that will be used to run application programs.

Boot Process. Starting a computer has long been known as the **boot process**, a term derived from the old expression "pulling oneself up by the bootstraps." There are two basic ways to initiate the boot process: the **cold start**, starting the computer when the power is off, and the **system reset**, or **warm start**. To warm start a computer, the user presses the Ctrl and Alt and, while these keys are depressed, presses the Del key.

When a computer is cold or warm started, the CPU executes the bootstrap loader, a small program contained in ROM. The bootstrap executes. It checks the disk directory to ensure that the disk has, in consecutive storage locations, the IBMBIO.COM and IBMDOS.COM programs, which are then loaded in order into RAM.

The IBMBIO.COM program executes next. It checks to see what peripherals are attached to the computer and prepares the units for use. For example, the IBMBIO.COM initializes a printer, signaling it to stand by to receive information. After IBMBIO.COM has finished, the IBMDOS.COM program performs **initialization** work that allows data to be passed to a disk and stored. Next, the COMMAND.COM file is brought in from the disk and placed in RAM, completing the boot process.

After the boot process is completed, DOS checks for an AUTOEXEC.BAT file on the boot disk. **AUTOEXEC.BAT** files are commands that the user wants the computer to execute automatically each time it is started, such as starting an application program. If there is such a file, DOS executes its commands.

If the computer does not find an AUTOEXEC.BAT file, the computer displays a screen prompt requesting the date. The date may be entered using as delimiters (punctuation indicating where one part of a file name ends and the next part begins) either dashes (the mm-dd-yy format) or slashes (the mm/dd/yy format). If a date is not entered and the RETURN key is pressed, the system will default to 1-01-80, and any files saved during this session will have the default date as the creation or change date. Next, the computer asks for the time, which is entered using colons (the hh:mm format) as delimiters. The entry 10:42 indicates that the time is 10:42. After the operator has entered the date and time, the computer displays these three lines at the top of the screen:

```
The IBM Personal Computer DOS
Version 3.10 (c) Copyright IBM Corp 1981, 1982, 1983
A>
```

A> is the DOS prompt. The appearance of A> signals that DOS is waiting for a command to be entered. The date and time entered are recorded in the directory for any files that are created or changed during this session.

Starting DOS. If the computer power is off (cold start):

1. Insert the DOS disk or the program disk with DOS (label side up and thumb on label) in disk drive A (the left-hand disk drive).
2. Close the drive door.
3. If peripherals are attached, turn their power switches to the ON position.
4. Turn the system unit power switch (located on the right-hand side, toward the rear of the machine) to the ON position.

If the computer power is already on (system reset or warm start):

1. Insert the DOS disk or the program disk with DOS (label side up and thumb on label) in disk drive A.
2. Close the drive door.
3. Press and hold down both the Ctrl and Alt keys; then press the Del key. Release the three keys.

Both of these procedures load DOS into memory. Starting the computer and loading DOS takes from three to forty-five seconds, depending on how much memory the PC has.

When first turned on in a cold start, a computer performs a memory check to ensure that all of the RAM locations are capable of storing and retrieving data correctly. This memory check is not performed during a system reset. The memory check consumes most of the computer's start-up time, and the more memory a machine has, the longer the test takes.

Default Drive. The "A" in A> (the DOS prompt) designates the **default disk drive** to DOS, telling it which disk to use to retrieve a file or execute a command. Unless the user specifies another drive, DOS will search only the default-drive disk for file names. The default can be viewed as the drive currently in use.

DOS tries to start a computer by trying to find DOS on drive A. If it cannot find DOS there, it checks to see if there is a hard disk with DOS. If DOS is on the disk in drive A, the default is A>. If DOS is on the hard disk, the default drive is C>. Additional drives attached to the computer are specified by consecutive letters of the alphabet: B for the second disk drive, C for the third, and so on.

The user can change the default drive by keying (entering) the designation letter of the desired drive in either upper- or lower-case letters—DOS always translates the letter into upper case. A colon must be keyed after the letter. For example, to change to disk drive B, the user would change the prompt as follows:

    A>_   [original drive]

    A>B:_   [new drive designation]

    B>_   [new prompt]

B is now the default (current) drive, and henceforth DOS will search only the disk located in disk drive B to execute commands or find file names that are entered, unless the user specifies another drive.

Directory. DOS disk files are kept in a **directory**, which contains file names, file extensions, file size, and the dates and times when the files were created or last updated. The directory of a disk can be listed by using the DIR command. For example, a disk directory might yield the list on the following page:

Figure 3.19
Components of a file name.

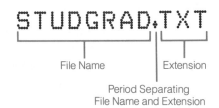

```
A>dir
Volume in drive A has no label
Directory of A:\

COMMAND   COM   17792   10-20-83   12:00p
PROCEDUR        17408   11-23-84   12:03a
INTRNOUT         3968   11-23-84   12:02a
AIS             32256    1-01-80   12:52a
INTRNOUT  BAK    3968   11-22-84    1:01p
AISOUTL          2816   10-24-84   12:09a
ARTICLE         14592   11-01-84   12:02a
INTAUDI         11136   11-15-84    3:26p
INTERN    BAK   12032   12-04-84    5:36p
INTCOVER  BAK     768   12-11-84   12:06a
INTCOVER          768   12-11-84   12:02a
INTERN          12032   12-05-84   12:01a
ISECON    BAK   15488    1-01-80   12:03a
ISECON          15488              12:09a
       14 File(s) 173056 bytes free
```

Notice that the directory listings have one or more spaces between the file name and the file extension. This is because the DOS directory does not show delimiters. To access a file, the user must place the period between the file name and the extension.

Next to the directory is a system area known as the **file allocation table (FAT)**. Its job is to keep track of which sectors store particular files and to inventory available space on the disk so that new files can be created and stored in unused areas. Each disk has one directory and two copies of the FAT. If the system has a problem reading the first copy of the FAT, it reads the second.

File Names. A *file* is a collection of related information that can be data (data file) or instructions for manipulating data (program file). Users keep track of the files on a disk by name. Each file name must be unique. If a disk has a MICRO.1 file name and the user stores a second file named MICRO.1, then the computer will destroy the original MICRO.1 and replace it with the second.

Within space and special character limitations, users can name files anything they wish. Disk **file names** can be one to eight characters in length and can be followed by a one- to three-character **file name extension**, separated by a period. A student data file for grades, for example, might be called STUDGRAD.TXT. The components of this name are labeled in Figure 3.19.

The characters that can be used for file names are

A–Z	!	}
0–9	'	-
$	(	^
&	)	-
#	-	`
@	{	

All other characters are invalid. An invalid character is assumed to be a delimiter, which truncates the file name. Embedded spaces (blanks within the file name or file-name extension) are not allowed.

File names should reflect the data held in the files. For example, a student drafting an English term paper on a computer could title the file ENGTP—an abbreviation for English term paper.

When used, the optional file-name extension should immediately follow the file name. The same character set allowed for file names can be used for file-name extensions. All other characters are invalid. DOS can locate a file with a file-name extension only if the user enters both the file name and its extension. The only exceptions to this rule are the DOS file extensions BAT, EXE, or COM.

Generally, special characters should not be used in file names because some software packages do not accept them. In addition, Microsoft may use special characters as DOS commands in future versions of the operating system program. For example, the %, <, >, and \ characters were allowable in DOS 1.0 and DOS 1.1 but are invalid in all versions of the software from DOS 2.0 on.

A 360K disk can store as many as 112 files. Or a single disk can store a single document of 360K, as long as it is the only file on the entire disk. A hard disk, however, does not have this limitation, and DOS allows a file to be up to 32 billion bytes in size.

Global File-Name Characters, or Wild Cards. **Global file-name characters**, also known as **wild cards**, enable users to execute commands against files whose names have one or more characters in common. The two wild cards used in DOS are **?** and *****. A ? character in a file name or extension indicates that any character can occupy that position. For example, a computer will respond to the command

```
DIR REPORT?.?
```

by listing all directory entries on the default drive having file names of seven characters and beginning with REPORT. The listed entries may have any character in the seventh position. Files that would be listed by the above DIR command include

```
REPORTA
REPORTB
REPORTB.2
```

An * in a file name or extension indicates that any character can occupy that position and any remaining positions in the file name or extension. For example, a computer will respond to the command

```
DIR W*.*
```

by listing all directory entries on the default drive having file names beginning with W and having any or no extension. The file names in this example may be from one to eight characters in length, and the extensions may be one to three characters in length. (The second * in the above command tells DOS to list any files that start with a W with or without a file extension.) Files that would be listed by the above DIR command include

```
WS       COM
WSOVLY1  OVR
WINSTALL COM
WORK01
```

Preparing a Disk. Data are stored on a disk's narrow, concentric recording rings called tracks, which are further divided into sectors. Before a disk can store data, it must be organized. This is done by the formatting (initializing) process, which magnetically marks the boundaries of the tracks and sectors. These magnetic tracks demarcate the information boundaries on the disk, somewhat like traffic lanes dictating the routes and directions of cars.

Every operating system has specific formatting needs. For DOS to recognize a disk and track files on it, the disk must be formatted to DOS standards. The FORMAT utility program that resides on the DOS disk performs this task. An operator only has to FORMAT a disk the first time it is used.

FORMAT verifies the storage integrity of every sector of a disk. It finds and write-protects tracks that have bad (nonrecordable) sectors, sets up the directory, establishes the FAT, and puts the boot record program at the beginning of the disk. It can also create a copy of DOS on a new disk if that option is specified in the original command.

There are two commands to FORMAT a disk. The first, which both formats the disk and places DOS on the disk, must be used if the user wants to store application software to the disk. The second command formats the disk but does not place DOS on it and should be used for disks that will only store data.

```
FORMAT B:/S
FORMAT B:
```

Versions of DOS. Since first creating PC DOS and MS DOS, Microsoft has written several versions of the operating system. These versions include DOS 1.1, 2.0, 2.1, 3.0, 3.1, and 3.2. The digit to the left of the decimal indicates the version of the operating system; the digit to the right of the decimal indicates the release of the operating system. The 1.0, 2.0, and 3.0 versions represent the first releases of their respective versions.

Version 1.X (1.0, 1.1, 1.2, and so on) was the original operating system for the IBM PC computer and compatibles. This operating system truly represents the infancy of the PC. Many of the commands that now appear in the operating system did not even exist in this version. Also, many commands that were in this first version have been significantly altered to perform other tasks in addition to those originally expected of them. This first version of DOS supported only floppy disk drives.

Version 2.X, a major upgrade of version 1.X, was the operating system Microsoft developed specifically for the IBM XT microcomputer. This version of DOS was the first to support a hard disk drive and the first that allowed the creation of directories and subdirectories for storing programs and files in separate areas on a disk. It also allowed operators to reassign the use of disk drives (for example, the operator could designate drive B the default drive).

Version 3.X, the next major DOS improvement, appeared about the same time as the IBM AT microcomputer. Although Version 3.X does not take advantage of the full power of the 80286 microprocessor chip and was not designed specifically for the AT, it still enhanced the power of the new computer. Version 3.X provides a number of advanced features, some of which are creating its own RAM disk; supporting networking, or connection of several computers to share resources (version 3.2); and supporting 3.5-inch disk drives (version 3.2).

Each succeeding DOS version has been able to perform increasingly complex tasks and, consequently, has required a corresponding increase in memory. The following depicts the growth of DOS:

DOS Version	Disk Space (bytes)	Memory (bytes)
1.1	13,663	12,400
2.0	39,660	24,576
2.1	40,320	26,576
3.0	58,926	37,024
3.1	62,122	37,040
3.2	68,668	43,712

How DOS Uses the 5.25-Inch Disk. Most disk drives record 48 tracks per inch (tpi) on diskette, but only a 5/6-inch strip of disk actually holds tracks. With 48-tpi drives, then, only 40 usable tracks are actually created. These tracks are labeled 0 through 39.

Each track is usually divided into eight or nine sectors. An IBM PC, unless told to do otherwise, will automatically divide a track into 9 sectors, creating 720 total sectors on a disk (40 tracks × 9 sectors × 2 sides). Of these 720 sectors, 12 are reserved by the system to be used as follows:

4 sectors to hold the FAT (two copies, with 2 sectors per copy)

7 sectors to hold the directory

1 sector to hold the boot program in the boot record

Therefore, 708 sectors (with a total user storage of 362,496 bytes) remain available on a disk formatted without the operating system.

Space within a track is allocated in increments called **clusters** (Figure 3.20). A cluster on a single-sided disk is 1 sector; a cluster on a double-sided disk consists of 2 adjacent sectors. The operating system will allocate just one cluster to a file, then wait until that cluster is filled before assigning another.

Another important disk concept is the **cylinder** (Figure 3.20). On a floppy disk there are 40 tracks on each side of the disk, each track on the top side lying directly above the corresponding track on the bottom side. All like-numbered tracks on all recording surfaces constitute a cylinder. On floppy disks, 2 tracks make up each cylinder; on a hard disk, there may be up to 10 tracks to a cylinder.

DOS refers to the bottom of the disk as side 0 and the top as side 1. On a double-sided disk, DOS starts storing data on the outermost track (referred to as track 0) of side 0, filling sectors 0 through 8. It then goes to side 1 to use track 0, sectors 0 through 8; then back to side 0 to use track 1, sectors 0 through 8; and so on. This process continues until the entire disk is full. (If the disk is single-sided, of course, DOS does not switch sides.)

The cylinder concept allows the disk drive to access information much faster than would otherwise be possible. The read/write heads need only be activated electronically from one side to another until the cylinder of storage is filled, at which point the read/write head can position itself mechanically to the next cylinder. Mechanical delay is always more time-consuming than is electronic delay.

Control Keys. **Control keys** are used whenever commands or input lines are entered. When two keys are required to convey a command—for example, Ctrl-Break—the first key must be pressed and held down while the second key is pressed. Control keys include the following:

ENTER—makes a line or command available to the computer

Ctrl-Break—stops a program that is executing

Ctrl-S—temporarily stops output to the screen so that it can be examined (restart the output by again pressing Ctrl-S)

SHIFT-PrtSc (or Ctrl-P)—toggles the printer echo either ON or OFF

Esc—cancels the current line (many programs also use this key to stop processing or get out of some difficulty)

Back arrow—moves the cursor back one position

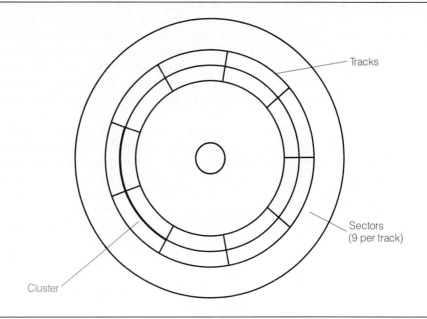

Figure 3.20
Cylinders and clusters on a disk.

Function keys—used by various packages to cut down on the number of keystrokes required to enter a command

Num Lock—activates either the numeric key pad or the arrow keys and other special function keys

DOS Editing Keys. **DOS editing keys** allow the user to make changes to the last DOS command entered, a feature that can save many keystrokes. The instruction buffer, referenced with some of the keys below, is a temporary holding area that retains the user's last command so that it can be quickly executed again.

Del—skip one character in the current line

Esc—cancel the current line without changing the data in the instruction buffer

F1—copy and display one character from the instruction buffer to the cursor position in the current line

F2—copy all characters from the instruction buffer up to a specified character and place them in the current line

F3—copy all remaining characters from the instruction buffer up to the current line

F4—skip all characters in the instruction buffer up to a specified character

F5—place the current line in the instruction buffer for more editing

Ins—insert characters at the current cursor location using this toggle

The F3 key is probably the most important of the keys listed above. Pressing it summarily reissues the prior command held in the instruction buffer.

The three basic types of software for microcomputers are operating systems, programming languages, and application programs. Users do not have to know how to program to make effective use of today's microcomputers.

If a user does decide to program, he or she will probably use a high-level language such as BASIC or Pascal. The instructions of these programming languages must be converted into a machine-understandable format before they can be executed by the computer. The translation process is performed by either a compiler or an interpreter.

Application programs are prewritten programs that are used to solve specific user problems. The five basic problem areas addressed by application software are electronic spreadsheets, word processing, data base management, communications, and graphics. A number of these general applications can be combined in one piece of software by a process known as integration. Integration allows the operator to pass data/information quickly from one application to another and to manipulate or process it without having to leave one application and start another.

The disk operating system (DOS), a critical piece of software that is loaded into the machine at start-up time, allows the user to perform once laborious tasks (formatting a disk, copying files, or listing the directory of a disk) with ease.

Information stored on a disk is contained in files. Each file must have a unique file name. File names follow rather rigid naming conventions.

DOS uses disk drives in executing commands. It also uses information contained on special areas of the disk or in files. Global (wild card) characters can be used to access some of this information if it is file-related.

A> (DOS prompt)
application program
auto-answer
auto-dial
AUTOEXEC.BAT
BASIC
baud rate
boot process
boot record
cluster
COBOL
cold start
COMMAND.COM
communications package
compiler
control keys
cylinder
data base management
default disk drive
desktop organizer
directory
disk operating system (DOS)
DOS editing keys
electronic spreadsheet
file allocation table (FAT)
file name
file-name extension
FORTRAN

global file-name characters
graphic display
high-level language
IBMBIO.COM
IBMDOS.COM
initialization
integrated package
interpreter
language processor
local area network (LAN)
Lotus 1-2-3
low-level language
menu
Microsoft
modem
MS DOS
object code
operating system
outliner
Pascal
productivity software
programming language
RAM-resident program
software
source code
system reset
VisiCalc
warm start

wild cards   ?
word processing   *

Chapter Quiz

Multiple Choice

1. Which of the following is not an example of application software?
   a. WordPerfect
   b. VisiCalc
   c. BASIC
   d. dBASE III Plus
   e. All of the above are examples of application software.

2. Which of the following is not a benefit of word processing?
   a. Easy to make changes
   b. Allows user to move parts of a document to new locations
   c. Increases efficiency
   d. May check your spelling
   e. All of the above are benefits of word processing.

3. Which of the statements below is(are) false?
   a. A modem can only be an input device.
   b. The term *baud* refers to how fast data are transmitted.
   c. Two modems, one at each end, are needed for computers to communicate using telephone lines.
   d. Auto-dial features are not typically found on modems.
   e. a and d are false.

4. Which of the statements below is false?
   a. A file name can have up to eight characters.
   b. A file name must have an extension.
   c. A period must appear between a file name and its extension.
   d. The file-name extension can have one to three characters.
   e. All of the above statements are true.

5. DOS is NOT made up of which of the following parts?
   a. Boot record
   b. IBMBIO.COM
   c. IBMDOS.COM
   d. COMMAND.COM
   e. It is composed of all of the above parts.

True/False

6. You do not have to format a disk before you use it for the first time.

7. The difference between a cold boot and a system reset is that the RAM memory is not checked during the system reset.

8. Only the disk on the default drive is checked during a search for files unless the computer is otherwise instructed.

9. DOS keeps track of where files are stored by using the file allocation table (FAT).

10. Global characters (wild cards) are normally not much help in formulating useful DOS commands.

Answers

1. c 2. e 3. e 4. b 5. e 6. f 7. t 8. t 9. t 10. f

Exercises

1. Define or describe each of the following:

a. software	h. baud
b. compiler	i. data base management
c. interpreter	j. integration
d. application program	k. DOS
e. electronic worksheets	l. cold boot
f. word processing	m. system reset (warm boot)
g. modem	n. default drive

2. A software _____ provides alternatives from which you can make selections.

3. A(n) _____ menu takes up one or more lines on your monitor screen.

4. Some menu systems like Lotus 1-2-3 may require you to pass through several _____ in order to perform an operation.

5. Menus that take up the entire screen are called _____.

6. Menus that are associated with a menu line at the top of a screen are called _____ because they appear as a menu option is selected.

7. A(n) _____ translates a program all at once, whereas a(n) _____ translates a program a statement at a time.

8. The _____ code of a program is written by a programmer.

9. List the five core software applications.

   a.

   b.

   c.

   d.

   e.

10. The device that translates digital signals into audible noises that can be transmitted across telephone lines is called a(n) _____.

11. _____ allows you to pass data quickly from one application to another.

12. The _____ interfaces between the user and the hardware.

13. The company named _____ wrote the DOS for the IBM PC.

14. List and describe the four parts of IBM PC DOS.

    a.

    b.

    c.

    d.

15. List and describe the parts of a file name. Place an * to the left of the required part(s).

    a.

    b.

16. List the pieces of information given by the directory command for each file.

    a.

    b.

    c.

    d

    e.

17. The _____ command is used to prepare a disk for use.

18. A _____ boot requires that the power to the machine be off beforehand.

19. The disk that is automatically searched is the _____ disk.

20. Of the 720 sectors created on the disk, only 702 are available to the user. The remaining sectors are taken up by _____, _____, and _____.

21. Like-numbered tracks from both recording surfaces are called _____.

22. The wild card character _____ is used to identify a variable in only one position.

23. If a file was originally created with a file extension, that extension must be used any time that the file is referenced in the future. The exceptions to this rule are when the extension is

    a.

    b.

    c.

24. Up to _____ files can be stored on a single disk.

25. Two adjacent sectors that are used for storing data in a file are called a(n) _____.

1. Enter the following commands using your DOS system disk. Describe what happens.
   a. DIR *.COM
   b. DIR ?I*.COM
   c. DIR ?I*.*
   d. DIR *.*

2. What happens when you press the F3 key?

3. When are you required to use a period (.) with a file name?

4. List the three keys that are used for a system reset (warm boot) and then perform one.
   a.

   b.

   c.

5. What two pieces of information does DOS automatically prompt you for when the boot process is finished (provided there is no AUTOEXEC.BAT file present)?
   a.

   b.

6. What is the DOS prompt that automatically appears on the screen after the boot process is finished for a disk-based system?

Questions for
Thought

1. Compare and contrast the menu-driven operating environments of the Macintosh and Windows or Presentation Manager for MS DOS machines. What are the strengths and weaknesses of each? How has the MS DOS marketplace responded to the Windows or Presentation Manager packages?

2. Prepare a report on designing software visual interfaces for users. Examine what software developers can do to make their application packages easier for users to operate.

3. Prepare a report that compares and contrasts five of the best-selling word processing packages. What are the relative strengths and weaknesses of each? Which of these packages would you be willing to purchase? Support your decision.

4. Prepare a report that compares and contrasts five of the best-selling spreadsheet packages. What are the relative strengths and weaknesses of each? Which of these packages would you be willing to purchase? Support your decision.

5. Research an application software package that would solve a problem or perform a task that you are interested in. Which packages are its major competitors? What are the relative strengths and weaknesses of the software package that you have selected? Based on your research, would you still purchase this package?

Chapter
4

Introduction to DOS

After completing this chapter, you should be able to:

Distinguish between internal and external DOS commands

Discuss the format notation of DOS commands

Discuss information common to all DOS commands

Discuss each of the commands covered in this chapter

As was indicated in Chapter 3, the disk operating system (DOS) is the vehicle that we use to actually communicate with the computer. It is the DOS that takes care of loading a program in the proper location in RAM, accessing data from the proper file(s), storing data to our secondary storage device, deleting files, and updating the status of which files are stored in which sectors via changes to the file allocation table (FAT)—tasks that are many times referred to as housekeeping. It is the DOS that takes our commands, interprets them, and, when the instruction is correct, passes it to the computer for execution.

Several of the most basic DOS commands were introduced and covered briefly in Chapter 3. This chapter examines those commands from Chapter 3 in more detail and introduces a number of other commands. Again, these commands are those that are most frequently used by novices. Some more advanced commands are covered in Chapter 5. As you progress with your understanding of the microcomputer, you may also want to examine a DOS manual to find other commands that might be of interest to you.

To facilitate coverage of these commands, they have been broken down into three basic families of commands. Each of these families of commands is first discussed briefly. This brief discussion is then followed by a more in-depth discussion of each command. The three families of DOS commands to be discussed are disk commands, file commands, and time commands.

Disk Commands

- The **CHKDSK command** is used to examine the directory and file allocation table (FAT) of a disk as well as produce disk and memory status reports. CHKDSK can also be used to repair errors in the directories or FAT. This is the only command that allows you to verify the amount of RAM that has been installed for the computer (up to 640K).

- The **DISKCOPY command** allows you to copy the entire contents of the disk that is in the specified source drive onto the disk that is in the specified target drive—exactly as the information appears on the source disk.

- The **FORMAT command** is used to initialize the disk in the designated or default drive so that it conforms to a recording format that DOS can use. As it executes, FORMAT analyzes the entire disk for defective sectors, initializes the directory, sets up space for the file allocation table, and records the boot program in the boot record.

File Commands

- The **COPY command** allows you to copy one file or a number of files with the same name characteristics (this is accomplished by the use of wild cards) to another disk. It also allows you to copy one or more files and create a new file with a different name on the same disk. In the latter case, a different name must be given in the new COPY command.

- The **DIR command** allows you to obtain lists of files contained in the directory or of specified files or families of files using wild cards. A line is displayed for each file and includes the file name, extension (if any), file size, and date and time of creation (or updating). Again, this command is used to copy files or families of files and would not typically be used to copy an entire disk of files to another disk.

- The **ERASE command** is used to delete a specific file or group of files from the disk in the designated drive. (If no drive is specified, the default is used.)

• The **RENAME command** allows you to change the name of an existing file to a new name.

• The **TYPE command** is used to display the contents of a file to the screen. It allows you to view a file without first starting another program that might normally be used in processing that file.

Time Commands

• The **DATE command** allows you to change the date that has been stored by DOS (today's date). Ultimately, the date is stored in the directory entry for any records/files that are created or altered and resaved during a session using the computer.

• The **TIME command** is used to change the time that is currently held by DOS. This time is placed in the directory entry for any file that is created or updated and then stored to disk.

Internal and External Commands

DOS has two types of commands: internal and external. An **internal command** is executed immediately because it is built into the command processor COM-MAND.COM. An **external command** resides on disk as a separate file (an external command is also sometimes referred to as a utility) and must be read from the appropriate disk device before it can be executed. This means that if the file is not at the default drive location, you must indicate the location of the file by placing the drive identifier in front of the command/file name so that DOS will be able to find the file and execute the instructions contained in it. For example, if the FORMAT command is used to format a disk in drive B and if the FORMAT.COM file resides in the default drive A, issue the following command:

```
A>FORMAT B:
```

However, if the FORMAT.COM file resides on a disk other than the default drive (for example, on device C), the default drive is A, and if you wish to format the disk in drive B, use the following command:

```
A>C:FORMAT B:
```

Format Notation

Format notation refers to the rules that must be followed when entering commands for DOS. These rules are sometimes referred to as *syntax*. The following rules indicate how DOS commands are to be entered.

Rules Common to All DOS Commands

1. Any words shown in capital letters must be entered exactly as shown. They can, however, be entered as any combination of upper- and lower-case letters because DOS automatically changes all letters to upper case.

2. Supply any items shown in lower-case letters.

3. Items in brackets ([ ]) are optional.

4. Ellipsis points (. . .) indicate that the item they accompany can be repeated as many times as desired.

5. All punctuation (except brackets)—commas, equal signs, question marks, colons, slashes, and so on—must be included where shown.

Commands are usually followed by one or more **parameters**—information of any kind that is entered in addition to the command name. For example, the name of the file to be copied and the destination drive for the copy are parameters for the COPY command.

A **delimiter** is a character that shows where one part of a command ends and another part begins. Common delimiters are the space, comma, semicolon, equal sign, and tab key, although generally only the space (usually represented in instruction manuals as the character *b*) is used. A period is not a delimiter. Commands and parameters must always be separated by delimiters.

Examples:

```
ERASE FILE01
RENAME OLDFILE NEWFILE
```

No part of a file name can be separated by a delimiter.

Examples:

```
B:REPORT.DOC        [correct]
A: REPORT DOC       [incorrect twice]
```

You can end commands while they are running by pressing Ctrl + Break. It may take a while for the command to affect the computer. The Ctrl + C command works in the same fashion.

Operationally, drives can act in either of two roles: A **source drive** is one that data are transferred from, and a **target drive** is one that data are transferred to. Depending on the particular operation involved, a drive may function as either the source drive or the target drive.

NOTE TO NETWORK USERS Some adopters of this textbook may be using a networked device. Such individuals cannot use the following commands. If you do try to use such a command, DOS responds with the following message:

```
Cannot <command> to a network device
```

The <command> entry is the name of the command that you entered at the keyboard. The commands covered in the text that do not work over a network on a shared or attached device are

```
CHKDSK
DISKCOPY
FORMAT
```

Information About Specific DOS Commands

Information about each DOS command described on the following pages is divided into five areas: (1) the command itself is named; (2) the purpose (function) of the command is presented; (3) the syntactical format of the command is detailed, with any optional parameters; (4) the nature of the command is given, identifying whether it is part of DOS (internal) or is a utility (external); and (5) any remarks or explanations about the command are given.

Disk Commands _____   ***CHKDSK (Check Disk) Command***

Function: This command allows you to analyze the directory and the
file allocation table (FAT) disk and produces disk and
memory status reports. CHKDSK can also repair errors in
the directories or FAT.

Format: `CHKDSK [d:][filename][/F][/V]`

Type: External

Remarks
&

Examples: CHKDSK temporarily makes the drive specified in d: the
default drive. If CHKDSK ends prematurely (because, for
example, you replied A to a disk error message), the default
drive changes to the drive that CHKDSK was checking.

CHKDSK will not automatically correct errors found in
the directory or FAT unless you specify the /F parameter. If
the /F parameter is not specified, CHKDSK functions but
does not actually make corrections, allowing you to analyze
the possible consequences of making a correction. It is
generally inadvisable to make corrections unless there is a
major problem; if the error is in the directory or FAT itself, a
large part of the data on the disk can be lost.

If the /V parameter is specified, a series of messages (one
for each file) identifying the status of each file will be
displayed.

CHKDSK FILENAME tells if the file specified (in this case,
FILENAME) has been stored in contiguous sectors on disk.
When a disk has recently been formatted, the 512 individual
byte sectors used to store files store input files contiguously.
After some files have been erased and other files added,
however, DOS still attempts to store any new files or
additions to existing files in the first vacant sector.
Occasionally, a large file ends up being stored in a number of
nonadjacent sectors as a result. Such a file, referred to as a
fragmented file, slows DOS's reading speed because the
read/write heads will have to be moved physically to a
number of different locations on disk.

If the number of noncontiguous locations reported by
CHKDSK is large, re-forming the file by using the COPY
command may improve performance.

CHKDSK does not prompt you to insert a disk in the
specified drive; it automatically assumes that the disks are in
the appropriate drives and begins to execute shortly after the
ENTER key has been pressed.

The status report displayed by CHKDSK contains the
following pieces of information:

    1. Disk Report—

       Total disk space

       Number of bytes used for hidden or system files

       Number of bytes used for user files

       Bytes used by tracks containing bad sectors

       Bytes available for use

2. RAM Report—

   Bytes of total memory (RAM)

   Bytes of available (unused) memory

After the diskette has been checked, error messages (if any) are displayed, and a status report like the following appears:

```
362496 bytes total disk space
 22528 bytes in 2 hidden files
135168 bytes in 1 user files
 (4608 bytes in bad sectors)
204800 bytes available on disk
262144 bytes total memory
249744 bytes free
```

Notice that two hidden files were reported in the above status report. These are the DOS system files IBMBIO.COM and IBMDOS.COM, which are hidden from normal directory searches.

You should run CHKDSK occasionally for each disk to ensure the integrity of the file structures.

Examples of some uses of CHKDSK follow:

1. Run the CHKDSK program that resides on drive A against the disk in drive B.

   ```
   A>CHKDSK B:
   ```

2. Tell CHKDSK to correct any errors in the above example automatically.

   ```
   A>CHKDSK B:/F
   ```

3. Find out if the file REPORT has much fragmentation.

   ```
   A>CHKDSK REPORT
   ```

4. Find out if any of the files on the disk in drive A: are fragmented.

   ```
   A>CHKDSK *.*
   ```

5. With B as the default drive, execute CHKDSK from drive A against the disk in drive B.

   ```
   B>A:CHKDSK
   ```

DISKCOPY (Copy Diskette) Command

Function: This command allows you to copy the contents of the diskette that is in the specified source drive onto the diskette that is in the specified target drive—exactly as the information appears on the source disk.

Format: `DISKCOPY [d:][d:][/1]`

Type: External

Remarks
&
Examples: The first parameter specified is the *source drive*, and the
second is the *target drive*. The /1 parameter causes
DISKCOPY to copy only side 0 (the first side) of the disk,
regardless of whether the disk is single- or double-sided. The
same drives (or different ones) can be specified as source and
target. If the drives are the same, a single-drive copy
operation is performed. At appropriate times, a prompt to
insert the disk is displayed; when this has been done,
DISKCOPY prompts the user to press any key in order to
continue.

The following command causes DOS to load in the
DISKCOPY file from the default disk drive.

```
A>DISKCOPY A: B:
```

The contents of a disk to be placed in drive A are to be
copied to a disk to be placed in drive B. The following
message is displayed:

```
Insert source disk in drive A:
Insert target disk in drive B:
Strike any key when ready:
```

The DISKCOPY program then checks to see if the disk in
drive B is formatted. If it isn't, DISKCOPY formats it. It then
performs the copy process and after copying displays the
following prompt:

```
Copy another (Y/N)?_
```

If Y is depressed, the next copy is done on the originally
specified drives, and DISKCOPY again prompts the user to
insert the source and target disks. If N is depressed, the
command ends.

The following command is different from the one above in
that it expects the source disk to be in drive B and the target
disk to be in drive A:

```
DISKCOPY B: A:
```

Because preexisting files on the target disk are destroyed
when the copy process begins, it is important that you
understand how the command works and that you develop
consistency when using DOS copy commands. This will
result in fewer instances of accidental data destruction.

If both parameters are omitted, a single-drive copy
operation is performed using the default drive. On a single-
drive system, all prompts are for drive A, regardless of any
drive specifiers that have been entered.

Disks subjected to a lot of file creation and deletion activity
become fragmented because disk space is allocated to files

on the basis of where the first available opening is. Because a disk with fragmented files can degrade performance by requiring excessive head movement and rotational delays in finding, reading, or writing a file, the CHKDSK *.* command should be used on busy disks from time to time to identify the extent of fragmentation. If a lot of fragmentation exists, use the COPY command to eliminate it.

The following command, for example, can be used to copy all the files (in unfragmented order) from the disk in drive A to the disk in drive B:

```
COPY A:*.*   B:
```

WARNING It is safest to use preformatted disks when using DISKCOPY. You should also make certain that there are no bad sectors on the target disk. Because the copy generated is a mirror image, good data can end up being placed in a bad sector during a DISKCOPY operation.

FORMAT Command

Function: This command is used to initialize the disk in the designated or default drive so that it conforms to a recording format that DOS can use. FORMAT analyzes the entire disk for defective sectors, initializes the directory, sets up space for the file allocation table, and records the boot program in the boot record.

Format: `FORMAT [d:][/S][/1][/8][/V][/B]`

Type: External

Remarks
   &

Examples: All new disks must be formatted. An unformatted disk is unrecognizable to DOS.

If the /S parameter is specified in the FORMAT command, the operating system files IBMBIO.COM, IBMDOS.COM, and COMMAND.COM are copied from the default disk onto the newly formatted disk. Using the /S parameter creates a system disk, with all the operating system files necessary to boot the system. The external utility programs, however, must be copied from a DOS master disk.

If you specify the /1 parameter, the target disk is formatted for single-sided use.

The /8 parameter tells FORMAT to prepare the disk with eight sectors per track, instead of the default number of nine per track. You should let DOS use the default number so that you gain the additional 40K of disk space.

The /V parameter, which prompts the user for a volume label, cannot be used with the /8 parameter. You will be prompted for the volume name and can enter up to eleven characters. Thereafter, the volume name appears when the DIR and CHKDSK commands are executed, further identifying the disk for you.

The /B parameter creates a disk with eight sectors per track and leaves room for IBMBIO.COM and IBMDOS.COM to be placed on the disk at a later time with the SYS command. Because it does not record these files onto the disk, any version of the IBM operating system can be placed there.

Formatting destroys any previously existing data on the disk. Do *not* format a disk that contains data you will need later, or it will be lost forever.

During the formatting process, discovery of any defective sectors in a track results in the whole track's being marked RESERVED. This prevents any sectors in the **reserved track** from being allocated to a data file.

The DOS system files are marked as hidden files. FORMAT produces a status report that indicates (on separate lines) the following information:

Total disk space

Space currently allocated to system files

Space marked as defective

Amount of space available for future files

The following command causes the disk in drive B to be formatted and the operating system files to be copied:

```
A>FORMAT B:/S
```

The system begins by issuing the following message:

```
Insert new diskette for drive B:
and strike any key when ready
```

After you insert the appropriate disk and strike any key, the system issues the following message while disk formatting is taking place:

```
Formatting...
```

Once the formatting is complete, the system issues this message:

```
Formatting...Format complete
System transferred

362496 bytes total disk space
 40960 bytes used by system
 (4608 bytes in bad sectors)
316928 bytes available on disk

Format another (Y/N)?_
```

Enter Y to format another disk; enter N to end the format program.

The FORMAT B:/S command causes DOS to be placed on a nine-sectored track disk, creating what is known as a **system disk**. This is desirable when the disk is to contain programs for use, and it permits the system to be booted from the disk.

If the disk is to be used only to store data (a so-called **slave disk**), the FORMAT B: command should be selected. This command performs all the tasks mentioned above except placing the files IBMBIO.COM, IBMDOS.COM, and COMMAND.COM on the disk. The system cannot be booted from such a disk; if booting is attempted, DOS will display the message:

```
Non-System disk or disk error
Replace and strike any key when ready
```

File Commands

COPY Command

Function: This command allows you to copy one file or a number of files with the same name characteristics to another disk. It also allows you to copy one or more files and create a new file with a different name on the same disk. In the latter case, a different name must be given to the new copy.

Format:
```
COPY [/A/B]filespec[/A][/B]
        [d:][filename[.ext]][/A][/B]
```
or
```
COPY [/A/B]filespec[/A][/B]
        [d:][filename[.ext]][/A][/B][/V]
```

Type: Internal

Remarks
&

Examples: The parameter `filespec` is the source file. The parameter `[d:][filename[.ext]]` is the target file.

Only the commonly used aspects of the COPY command are discussed here. For more coverage, refer to the DOS manual.

In the following example, the file REPORT is copied onto the disk contained in drive B. Because no name for the new file is specified, it has the same name as the original file. For the same reason, the source drive and the target drive must be different; otherwise, an error message is displayed.

```
A>COPY REPORT B:
```

In the following example, the file FILE01 is copied from the disk in disk drive B onto the disk in default drive A, with no change in the file name.

```
A>COPY B:FILE01
```

In the following example, all files from the disk in the default drive are copied onto the disk in drive B. The file names remain unchanged, and each is displayed as its file is copied. This method is very useful if the files on the default drive disk (drive A) are fragmented.

```
A>COPY *.* B:
```

In the following example, file FILE01 is copied, and the copy is renamed FILE01.BAC. Because a drive is not specified, the default drive is used. Both files now reside on the same disk.

```
A>COPY FILE01 FILE01.BAC
```

In the following example, file FILE01 is copied, and the copy on the disk in drive B is renamed FILE01.BAC. But because a target drive is specified, two copies of the file are made: One resides on the disk in drive A and has the name FILE01; the other resides on the disk in drive B and has the name FILE01.BAC.

```
A>COPY FILE01 B:FILE01.BAC
```

In the following example, file FILE01.ABC is copied from the disk in drive A onto the disk in drive B, and the copy is named FILE01.XXX.

```
A>COPY FILE01.ABC B:*.XXX
```

DIR (Directory) Command

Function: This command allows you to obtain lists of all files contained in the directory or of specified files or families of files. A line is displayed for each file and includes the file name, extension (if any), file size, and date and time of creation (or updating).

Format: `DIR [d:][filename[.ext]][/P][/W]`

Type: Internal

Remarks
&
Examples: The /P parameter causes the display to pause after twenty-three lines have been displayed. The message `Strike a key when ready...` is then displayed.

The /W parameter produces a five-column–wide display of the directory. Only the file name and extension for each file are displayed.

The wildcard characters ? and * can also be used with the file-name and extension parameters.

In the following example, all directory entries on the default drive are listed.

```
DIR
```

In the following example, all directory entries on the disk in drive B are listed.

```
DIR B:
```

A typical directory listing might look like this:

```
A>DIR
Volume in drive A has no label
Directory of A:\

COMMAND     COM     17792     10-20-83     12:00P
WSOVLY1     OVR     41216      6-21-84      3:30P
WSMSGS      OVR     29056      4-12-83
WINSTALL    OVR     38528      3-02-83
WS          INS     43776      3-02-83
WSU         COM     21376      1-01-80     12:04a
WINSTALL    COM      1152      3-02-83
WST         COM     21376      6-21-89      3:29P
INSTALL     EXE     36352      3-28-84      8:00a
AUTOEXEC    BAT        11      1-01-80     12:01a
MM          INS      2816      3-28-84      8:01a
WSD         COM     21376      6-21-89      3:30P
WS          COM     21376      6-21-89      3:28P
MAILMRGE    OVR     13568      3-28-84      8:03a
SYSTEM1              128       1-01-89     12:00a
PISANI               640       1-30-89     12:07a
CHKDSK      COM      6400     10-20-83     12:00P
LETTER               128       1-01-89      4:21a
PRINT                128       1-01-89     12:03a
DIR1                   0       1-01-89     12:52a
        20 File(s) 11264 bytes free
```

The file name, extension, size of the file, creation date, and time of creation are given for each file on the disk. At the end of the directory listing is given the amount of available storage on the disk.

In the following example, all directory entries on the disk in the default drive that start with a W will be listed.

```
A>DIR W*.*
```

The listing elicited by the above instruction might look like this:

```
A>DIR W*.*
Volume in drive A has no label
Directory of A:\

WSOVLY1     OVR     41216      6-21-84      3:30P
WSMSGS      OVR     29056      4-12-83
WINSTALL    OVR     38528      3-02-83
WS          INS     43776      3-02-83
WSU         COM     21376      1-01-80     12:04a
WINSTALL    COM      1152      3-02-83
WST         COM     21376      6-21-84      3:29P
WSD         COM     21376      6-21-84      3:30P
WS          COM     21376      6-21-84      3:28P
         9 File(s) 11264 bytes free
```

Only files that begin with a W are included in this directory listing.

In the following example, all directory entries on the disk in the default drive that have an extension of .COM are listed.

```
A>DIR *.COM
```

The listing elicited by the above instruction might look like this:

```
Volume in drive A has no label
Directory of A:/

COMMAND    COM    17792    10-20-83    12:00P
WSU        COM    21376     1-01-80    12:04P
WINSTALL   COM     1152     3-02-83
WST        COM    21376     6-21-89     3:29P
WSD        COM    21376     6-21-89     3:30P
WS         COM    21376     6-21-89     3:28P
CHKDSK     COM     6400    10-20-83    12:00P
MORE       COM      384    10-20-83    12:00P
        8 File(s) 8192 bytes free
```

The DIR /P command causes a directory listing to be displayed to the screen one page at a time. After the twenty-third line, the following message is displayed at the bottom of the screen:

```
Strike a key when ready ..._
```

The DIR /W command is used to get a display of only the file names and extensions of the disk files. The names are displayed in five columns, and the amount of available storage is also given.

```
               Volume in drive A has no label
               Directory of A:/

COMMAND  COM  WSOVLY1   OVR  WSMSGS   OVR  WINSTALL  OVR  WS
WSU      COM  WINSTALL  COM  WST      COM  INSTALL   EXE  AUTOEXEC BAT
MM       INS  WSD       COM  WS       COM  MAILMRGE  OVR  SYSTEM1
PISANI        CHKDSK    COM  LETTER        PRINT          DIR1
            20 File(s) 11264 bytes free
```

ERASE Command

Function: This command is used to delete a specific file or group of files from the disk in the designated drive. (If no drive is specified, the default drive is used.)

Format: ERASE filespec
or
DEL filespec

Type: Internal

Remarks
&
Examples: The shortened form **DEL** can be used in place of ERASE.

The global characters ? and * can be used in the file name and in the extension. *Global characters should be used with caution*, however, because several files can easily be erased with a single command. If proper care is not taken in using this command, a user may inadvertently delete all of the files on a disk.

To erase all files on a disk, enter

```
ERASE [d:]*.*
```

The system files IBMBIO.COM and IBMDOS.COM cannot be erased because they are hidden files and are not accessible.

If *.* is used to erase all the files on a disk, DOS issues the following message to verify that all files are to be erased:

```
Are you sure (Y/N)?
```

You then enter Y and depress ENTER to erase or enter N and depress ENTER to cancel the command.

In the following example, the file FILE01.PRG is erased from the disk in drive A:

```
A>ERASE FILE01.PRG
```

RENAME (or REN) Command

Function: This command allows you to change the name of an existing file specified in the first parameter to the new name and extension specified in the second parameter.

Format: `REN[AME] filespec filename [.ext]`

Type: Internal

Remarks
&
Examples: The abbreviated form **REN** can be used for the RENAME command. The global characters ? and * can also be used with this command.

In the following example, file FILE03 on drive B is renamed NEWFILE:

```
RENAME B:FILE03 NEWFILE
```

In the following example, file FILE03 on drive B is renamed FILE03.XY:

```
REN B:FILE03 *.XY
```

TYPE Command

Function: This command causes the contents of the requested file to be displayed on the screen.

Format: `TYPE filespec`

Type: Internal

Remarks
&

Examples: Depress Ctrl-PrtSc if you want the contents of a file to be
printed as they are being displayed. Depress Ctrl + S to
cause the output to pause, and then press any other key to
continue scrolling.

   Text files appear in a legible format; other files, however,
such as object program files, may contain nonalphabetic or
nonnumeric characters that render them unreadable.

   In the following example, file FILE03.PRG on the disk in
drive B is displayed on the screen:

```
TYPE B:file03.prg
```

Time Commands

DATE Command

Function: This command allows you to change the date that has been
stored by DOS (today's date). Ultimately, the date is placed in
the directory entry for any files that are created or altered
and resaved during this session.

Format: DATE [mm-dd-yy]

Type: Internal

Remarks
&

Examples: If a valid date is entered with the DATE command, the new
date is accepted by DOS. Otherwise, the DATE command
produces the following prompt:

```
Current date is day mm-dd-yy
Enter new date:_
```

   The system displays the day of the week in the day
location. Don't worry that you have never told it the day of
the week: DOS has a formula for calculating this piece of
information.

   To leave the date unchanged, press ENTER.

   The valid delimiters within the date are hyphens (-) and
slashes (/). This means that the dates 4-23-89 and 4/23/89 are
both correct. DOS also allows you to mix these delimiters, so
the date 4/23-89 also works.

   Any date is acceptable as today's date as long as the digits
are in the correct ranges for each field. This means, for
example, that you can't enter 16 for a month (12 is the
maximum) or 35 for a day (31 is the maximum). DOS also
does not allow you to enter a date prior to 1-1-80.

   If a mistake is made, the error message Invalid date
is displayed.

TIME Command

Function: This command permits you to change or enter a new time for
the system. This date then becomes part of any directory
entry of a new file.

Format: `TIME [hh:mm:ss.xx]`

Type: Internal

Remarks
&

Examples: Upon receiving a valid time entry from the user, DOS stores that information until the system is shut down or until a new time is entered. In the latter case, the system displays the following prompt:

```
Current time is hh:mm:ss.xx
Enter new time:_
```

In this prompt, hh is for hours, mm is for minutes, ss is for seconds, and xx is for hundredths of a second.

To leave the time as currently set, press ENTER.

A twenty-four-hour clock pattern is used. This means that 1:00 P.M. is entered as 13:00. Most people are concerned only with hours and minutes; the seconds and hundredths do not have to be used.

If partial time information (for example, just hours) is entered, the remaining fields are shown as zeros.

The valid delimiters for time fields are colons (:)—separating hours, minutes, and seconds—and the period (.)—separating seconds and hundredths of a second.

If an invalid time or invalid delimiter is entered, the `Invalid time` message will be displayed.

In the following example, when the ENTER key is depressed, the time recorded by the system is changed to 18:25:00.00.

```
A>TIME
Current time is 00:25:16.65
Enter new time:18:25_
```

DOS Command Summary

CHKDSK	Checks the status of a disk and prepares the status report
COPY	Copies one or more files
DATE	Changes the system date
DEL	Deletes one or more files
DIR	Lists the files in the directory
DISKCOPY	Copies a complete disk
ERASE	Deletes one or more files
FORMAT	Prepares a disk for use
RENAME	Renames disk files
TIME	Changes the system time
TYPE	Displays file contents on the monitor screen

DOS Commands by Function and Type

Time: DATE, TIME

File: COPY, DEL, DIR, ERASE, RENAME, TYPE

Disk: CHKDSK, DISKCOPY, FORMAT

Internal Commands	*External Commands (Utilities)*
COPY	CHKDSK
DATE	DISKCOPY
DEL	FORMAT
DIR	
ERASE	
RENAME	
TIME	
TYPE	

Chapter Review

The two basic types of DOS commands are internal and external. Internal commands are part of the DOS file COMMAND.COM. To execute one of these, you need only enter the command from the keyboard. External commands reside on disk as separate, external files. For one of these to be executed, the disk it is on must reside in the default drive or in a drive that you specify with a drive identifier.

Each DOS command has characteristics in common with other DOS commands; DOS also makes use of a common format notation. Disk-oriented commands all have unique features that can only be expressed adequately when discussed in detail.

Key Terms and Concepts

CHKDSK command	internal command
COPY command	parameter
DATE command	REN
DEL (delete) command	RENAME command
delimiter	reserved track
DIR (directory) command	slave disk
DISKCOPY (copy diskette) command	source drive
ERASE command	system disk
external command	target drive
FORMAT command	TIME command
format notation	TYPE command
fragmented file	

Chapter Quiz

Multiple Choice

1. Which of the statements below is false with respect to copying files using IBM PC DOS?
    a. DISKCOPY is the command used to re-form fragmented files.
    b. COPY can create a copy of a file on the same disk, but a different name must then be used.
    c. COPY can be used to create a backup file on another disk.
    d. DISKCOPY creates an exact copy of a disk's contents. It does this sector by sector and track by track.

2. The FORMAT command does all but which of the following tasks?
    a. Divides each track into eight or nine sectors.
    b. Marks any track having a bad sector(s) as reserved.
    c. Builds the directory.

    d. Builds the FAT.

    e. Performs all the above tasks.

3. Which of the following entries might not appear on a report generated by CHKDSK?

    a. The total amount of installed RAM

    b. The total amount of disk storage

    c. The amount of available disk storage

    d. The number of bytes in bad sectors

    e. All of the above can appear.

4. Which of the commands below cannot use the * or ? wild cards?

    a. ERASE

    b. COPY

    c. CHKDSK

    d. DISKCOPY

    e. DIR

    f. All of these commands can use wild cards.

5. Which of these commands will cause the contents of the file FILE1 on a disk in drive A: to be copied to a disk in drive B:?

    a. `A>COPY FILE1 A:`

    b. `B>COPY A:FILE1`

    c. `A>COPY FILE1 A:FILE1.BAK`

    d. Both a and b

    e. All of the above will accomplish the task.

True/False

6. If you do not give a drive specifier in a command, DOS assumes that the command you have just entered is to be executed against the default drive.

7. An external command must reside on the default disk unless a drive specifier is given.

8. The COMMAND.COM file contains the external DOS commands.

9. The ERASE and DEL commands can be used interchangeably.

10. The computer can be booted from a slave disk.

Answers

1. a 2. e 3. e 4. d 5. b 6. t 7. t 8. f 9. t 10. f

Exercises

1. Define or describe each of the following:

    a. internal command   c. COPY versus DISKCOPY

    b. external command   d. system versus slave disk

2. List three internal DOS commands.

    a.

    b.

    c.

3. List three external DOS commands.

    a.

b.

c.

4. Give the following FORMAT commands (assume A as the default):
   a. Format the disk in drive A, placing the operating system on it.
   b. Format the disk in drive A without placing the operating system on it.
   c. Format the disk in drive B, placing the operating system on it.
   d. Format the disk in drive B without placing the operating system on it.

5. Without changing the default drive, give the following COPY commands:
   a. Copy file FILE1 from the default disk A and create file FILE1.BAK on drive A.
   b. Copy file FILE1 from the default disk A onto the disk in drive B.
   c. Copy file FILE1 from disk B and copy it onto the disk in default drive A, using the same name.
   d. Copy file FILE1 from disk B and copy it onto the disk in default drive A, using the name FILE1.BAK.

6. The default drive is A. Enter the command that would erase file FILE1 from the disk in drive B, without changing the default drive.

7. The DOS command that is used to re-form fragmented files is the _____ command.

8. The DOS command that is used to examine the directory and print a table of contents is the _____ command.

9. Two commands that can be used to delete unwanted files are
   a.

   b.

10. The command used to create a "carbon" copy of the disk in drive A onto the disk in drive B is _____.

11. Two commands that can be used to tell you the amount of available space on a disk are
    a.

    b.

12. The format notation [] means that these parameters are _____ when using this command.

13. The copy command that also copies all the files of one disk onto another disk is the COPY _____.

14. What happens when you enter the command ERASE *.*? What prompt do you receive? What happens if you continue?

Computer Exercises

1. Enter the following DIR commands:
   a. Display the directory, one page at a time.
   b. Display the directory using the wide-parameter option.

2. Change the date and time of the system. Use the DATE and TIME commands to verify that the change was properly made.

3. What is the date on the SEMPCINT.DOC file? What command do you have to use to get the date?

4. Run CHKDSK on your diskette. Fill in the following blanks:
_____ bytes total disk space
_____ bytes in _____ hidden files
_____ bytes in _____ user files
_____ bytes in bad sectors
_____ bytes available on disk
_____ bytes total memory
_____ bytes free

5. Make a backup copy of the SEMPCINT.DOC file on your disk, using the COPY command. What did you name it? _____

6. Run CHKDSK again, and fill in the blanks:
_____ bytes total disk space
_____ bytes in _____ hidden files
_____ bytes in _____ user files
_____ bytes in bad sectors
_____ bytes available on disk
_____ bytes total memory
_____ bytes free

7. Make a backup copy of the SEMPCINT.DOC file on your disk, using the COPY command.
   a. Copy it onto another file on your disk.
   b. Copy it onto another disk.

8. Erase the SEMPCINT.DOC file.

9. List (TYPE) the contents of the backup file of SEMPCINT.DOC on your screen. Give the instruction that you used: _____.

PART TWO

HANDS-ON APPLICATIONS

Chapter

5

Advanced

DOS Concepts

Chapter Objectives

After completing this chapter, you should be able to:

Tell what a batch file does

Discuss the types of batch files

Discuss how to create batch files

Discuss how to create batch files with replaceable parameters

Discuss the concept of directories

Discuss common directory commands

Discuss the concept of active directory

Discuss how to use the CONFIG.SYS file to configure your system

Discuss how to set up a RAM disk using the VDISK.SYS file inside the CONFIG.SYS file

Batch Files:
The DOS Automator

The disk operating system (DOS) gives you tremendous power on your computer. DOS allows you to perform tasks on files such as copying, deleting, renaming, listing them as they occur in the directory, and listing them in sorted order. DOS also allows you to customize the operating environment to meet your specific needs. Customization involves placing any number of DOS commands in a file and then executing the commands contained in that file. The file that contains these DOS commands is known as a **batch file**.

A batch file then feeds its DOS commands to DOS. Once DOS receives a command from a batch file, it executes it and tries to access any other commands in that file. A batch file can have any file name but is required to have a .BAT file extension. The .BAT file extension indicates to DOS that the file contains system commands rather than word processing text, machine language, or any other data.

What are the advantages of using a batch file? Batch files can save you large amounts of time. You can tell DOS to execute all DOS commands in the file by typing the batch file's name. Since the commands are already correctly entered into the file, you don't have to worry about making mistakes in any of the DOS commands or file names.

Why is the term *batch* used in referring to a batch file? The term goes back to the early days of data processing when batches of machine-readable documents or system commands were submitted to a computer. The computer's operating system would process a batch of operating system instructions at one time, while a computer program would process a batch of machine-readable documents at one time. With early computers, information could not be entered interactively as it was needed. Instead, information was recorded on punched cards, magnetic disks, or magnetic tapes and then entered into the machine. There was very little interaction between the operator and the machine or between a user and the computer.

Batch files on today's microcomputers contain frequently executed sequences of DOS commands. Such sequences include booting the machine, entering date and time, and then starting a program; copy commands for backup for critical files; and using batch files to make it easier for beginners to use the microcomputer.

How Batch Files Work

There are two types of batch files. The first executes automatically upon booting the system (AUTOEXEC.BAT); the second can be executed only by entering its name from the keyboard. When you are executing the second type of batch file, you do not have to include the .BAT file extension.

When DOS executes the commands in a batch file, it follows the same steps that it uses in executing any DOS command. It checks to see if the command is contained in the COMMAND.COM file (internal command). If the command is not an internal command, it checks to see if the command is contained on the default disk (unless a drive identifier was used). It assumes that such a command contains either a .COM or .EXE file extension. If DOS is unable to find a .COM or .EXE file, it checks to see if there is a file on the indicated disk with an appropriate .BAT file extension. When DOS encounters any one of these circumstances, it starts to execute that command/batch file.

The user does not have to wait for all of the commands in a batch file to be executed before stopping the process. You can stop a batch file at any time by entering a Ctrl + Break command or a Ctrl + C command. Either of these commands bring the following message:

```
Terminate batch job (Y/N)?_
```

If you press the N key, the batch file continues processing. If you press the Y key, DOS returns you to the default disk with the standard DOS prompt (i.e., A>, B>, or C>).

An AUTOEXEC.BAT batch file executes during the boot process immediately after DOS has been loaded into RAM memory. Note that you can have only one AUTOEXEC.BAT file on a disk at any one time. If there happens to be more than one, DOS executes the first AUTOEXEC.BAT file that it finds in the directory. Here is a sample AUTOEXEC.BAT batch file:

```
REM start-up procedure
DATE
WP
```

Notice that the batch file contains only three commands. **REM** displays the message start-up procedure on the screen. The DATE command prompts the user for the date. After the date has been entered, the WP command starts the WordPerfect word processing program. Thus this batch file allows an individual, without much knowledge of a computer, to use a WordPerfect disk that contains DOS and this batch file and, without having to learn any DOS commands, do their word processing. Remember, it does not matter to DOS whether a command is in upper-case letters, lower-case letters, or a combination of the two.

Rules for Creating Simple Batch Files

The following rules are imposed by DOS when you name and create a batch file:

> You can create batch files by using either the DOS COPY command to copy commands to a batch file or by using a word processor in nondocument or programming mode.

> Please note that when you use the COPY option, DOS erases all the data in a file and starts fresh. You cannot modify an existing batch file with the COPY command.

> The file name of a batch file must be entered according to standard DOS procedures; that is, it can have one to eight allowable characters.

> The file extension *must* be .BAT.

> The file name cannot be the same as a DOS internal command or as any file with a .COM or .EXE file extension, because DOS cannot differentiate between such commands and may execute the internal command instead of the .BAT command. If another file residing on the disk has the batch file name but a different file extension, DOS executes the file that it finds first in the directory.

Creating Batch Files

Batch files can be created in a number of ways, two of which are covered here: using the COPY CON: facility of DOS or using the nondocument mode of a word processor. The **COPY CON:** procedure uses the DOS copy feature to copy all commands entered at the keyboard to the batch file. The COPY CON: convention is most appropriate when you are creating a small batch file. If you have to make changes to a large batch file, a word processor is better because you don't want to destroy your existing text and start from the beginning. The following steps would be required to create the AUTOEXEC.BAT file:

```
1. A>COPY CON:AUTOEXEC.BAT
```

```
2. REM start-up procedure
3. DATE
4. TIME
5. ^Z
```

Let's examine each of these steps. The COPY CON: portion of step 1 tells DOS that a file is to be created from entries generated at the keyboard. The AUTOEXEC.BAT tells DOS the name of the file to be created.

Steps 2–4 contain the commands that are to be placed in the file. DOS knows you are finished with a line when you press the ENTER key.

Step 5 contains a ^Z entry. The ^Z indicates the end of the file to DOS. DOS now knows to record all commands in the file to disk. The ^Z is achieved not by entering the characters ^Z but by pressing the F6 function key. When you press the F6 key, DOS stores the file to disk under the name used in the COPY CON: command (AUTOEXEC.BAT).

A frequent problem in using the COPY CON: facility is error correction. Once you press ENTER, you cannot make changes in a line. If you make mistakes, continue entering the various DOS commands and make any changes using the nondocument mode of a word processor.

This batch file could be entered using the nondocument or programming mode of a word processing language. Remember, nondocument mode does not embed any special ASCII control sequences in a file. After the AUTOEXEC.BAT file has been opened, the above commands can be entered exactly as they appear.

There is no difference in how the two files execute. The only difference is in how they are created. Most people, once they are familiar with a word processor, prefer to create batch files with their nondocument mode, because errors are much easier to correct.

Executing a Batch File

The following rules apply when you are ready to tell DOS to execute a batch file:

DOS assumes that the batch file resides on the default drive unless you indicate otherwise by using a drive identifier (for example, C:SAMPLE.BAT).

To start a batch file, simply enter the file name. You do not have to enter the .BAT file extension.

Once the batch file is located by DOS, the operating system begins executing commands residing in the batch file one at a time. When one command has been executed, DOS automatically loads the next command and tries to execute it.

If DOS loads an instruction and is unable to interpret it, a `Syntax error` message is displayed.

Once a batch file has begun execution, you can stop it by entering a Ctrl + Break or Ctrl + C DOS interrupt command. Once one of the above commands is entered, DOS displays the following message:

```
Terminate batch job (Y/N)?_
```

If you answer N, the batch file continues to execute, and the next command is read and executed. If you answer Y, the stream of commands coming from the batch file is interrupted, and you are returned to DOS (a system prompt is displayed to the screen).

If you have removed the disk, DOS will prompt you to reinsert the disk containing the batch file. If you simply want to stop the execution, enter another interrupt command (Ctrl + Break or Ctrl + C); otherwise, reinsert the original disk and press any key to continue.

Substituting Data in Batch File Execution

Most DOS commands require one or more pieces of data (parameters) that tell the operating system exactly how to execute a command and on which files it should be executed. The RENAME command, for example, requires two parameters: The first parameter indicates which file is to be renamed, and the second supplies the new name.

DOS provides you with the ability to substitute parameters for DOS commands that reside in a batch file. This is accomplished by indicating to DOS when and where replaceable parameters are to be used. **Replaceable parameters** are pieces of information in a DOS command that might change from one user to the next. A replaceable parameter is represented by a percent sign (%) followed by a single digit (i.e., %1). This convention allows you to designate ten pieces of information that can be supplied by commands residing in a batch file (%0 through %9).

One application of a replaceable parameter enables you to print a text file quickly and easily without starting up a word processing software package. This is accomplished by a batch file with the single DOS statement:

```
COPY %1 PRN
```

This batch file takes any output and redirects it to the printer. You could name this batch file PRINTIT.BAT. The PRINTIT.BAT name allows DOS to differentiate this file name from the DOS PRINT command. Now, when you want to print a file—for example, MEMO—enter the command

```
PRINTIT MEMO
```

When DOS receives this command, it locates the batch file PRINTIT and passes the parameter MEMO to the COPY command. It then takes the contents of the file MEMO and sends it to the printer.

Sample Batch Files

Many of today's IBM or IBM-compatible computers have expanded memory cards that allow you to add up to 640K of regular RAM to your microcomputer. This extra RAM allows you to turn part of your RAM into an electronic disk that can be used to store program files and pass them, with tremendous speed, to the CPU. If you use programs such as WordStar that require a lot of disk I/O, a RAM disk can give you much faster processing.

The following batch file allows you to create a RAM disk as you boot the system. This particular example makes use of a utility provided by the Quadram Corporation on their multifunction card. Of course, this batch file has to be named AUTOEXEC.BAT and would be stored on the disk containing all of the WordStar program files.

```
QMZ QD=10, QC=0, QS=0, BATCH
COPY *.*C:
C:
WS
a:
```

Let's examine these statements. The first calls the Quadram utility QM2 and tells it, among other things, to create a RAM disk. This becomes device C: (this first statement can be replaced by the VDISK statement in the CON-FIG.SYS file, discussed later in this chapter). The next statement takes all of the files that appear on the disk in drive A and copies them, one at a time, to the RAM disk. The next statement makes the RAM disk (default C>) the default drive. The fourth statement starts WordStar. The last statement changes the default drive to A when you exit WordStar.

The next example of a batch file contains the statements necessary for starting a student version of VP-Planner Plus.

```
DATE
VPP
```

The first command prompts you for the date and then resets the computer's system date from the data that you enter at the keyboard. The second command starts VP-Planner Plus.

Introduction to Disk Directories

Before we look at directories, let's review how DOS prepares a regular double-sided disk via the FORMAT command. When DOS is finished formatting a disk, it prepares the **directory** and places it in seven sectors. This directory can hold up to 112 files. DOS, in essence, limits the number of files that you can place on your disk. DOS also limits the number of files that a directory can hold on other types of disks. Here is a list of the type of disk and its maximum number of files:

Disk Type	Maximum Files
Single-sided	64
Double-sided	112
High-density (AT)	224
Hard disk	512

Although DOS appears to limit the number of files that can be stored on a disk, this is not really the case. Can you imagine that a high-density disk with 1.2 meg of storage or a hard disk with 10 to 20 meg, or more, is able to store only a limited number of files? You can circumvent this apparent limitation on any disk by using subdirectories. Directories can be used on diskettes, but they are most frequently used on hard disks and high-density diskettes.

The main directory is referred to as the **root directory**, and any additional directories are **subdirectories**. Subdirectories allow you to store more information (files) on a disk and to organize your disk more effectively. This means that you can place your word processing programs and files in a subdirectory for word processing or your data base management programs and data base files in a data base subdirectory. Such an organization is shown in Figure 5.1.

Each of the subdirectories depicted here can be divided into other subdirectories. The data base directory might be subdivided into two subdirectories, one to be used for holding business-related data files and the other for personal data files.

Directories and Directory Commands

A subdirectory is like a root directory except that it is itself a file and contains DOS housekeeping entries in a regular directory, but it does not have the size

Figure 5.1
Three subdirectories under
the root directory.

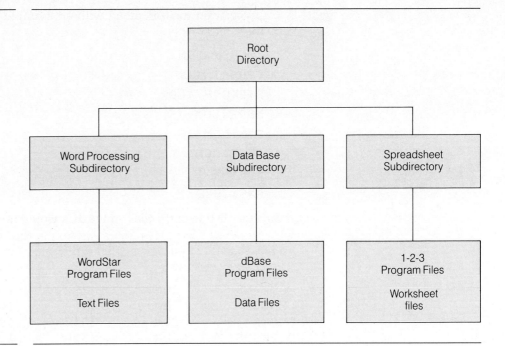

limitation of the root directory. A subdirectory can expand indefinitely (or until there is no more disk space).

Since a subdirectory is a file, it must be named. However, it cannot be built like other files. Rather, the commands used are the following:

Command	Purpose
Make directory (**MKDIR**) [**MD**]	Build a file to contain the new directory entries.
Change directory (**CHDIR**) [**CD**]	Move to another directory and make that the active directory.
Remove directory (**RMDIR**) [**RD**]	Delete the file containing the directory.
TREE	Display all directories on the disk.

The first three directory commands are internal commands. They can be executed either by their complete DOS name (in parentheses) or their abbreviated name [in brackets]. The TREE (found only in PC DOS) is an external command and resides as a separate file on disk. The syntax of these commands is discussed in greater detail at the end of the chapter.

Before you make a subdirectory, you should plan how you want to store data on your disk. You may decide to store programs and information by application type such as depicted in Figure 5.1, or you may plan to store programs and information by project. A third possibility is to combine these two techniques, storing information by project within an application.

The Make Directory (MD) Command. Once you have an idea of how you want to store your information, you can build the subdirectories that will hold the information. This is accomplished via the MKDIR (MD) command.

If you want to work along with an example, format a system disk and copy these files to it:

```
CHKDSK.COM
FORMAT.COM
DISKCOPY.COM
MORE.COM
SYS.COM
TREE.COM
SORT.EXE
ANSI.SYS
```

A directory listing of the files on the disk would now appear as follows:

```
Volume in drive A is TIM DUFFY
Directory of A:\

COMMAND     COM      17792     10-20-83      12:00P
CHKDSK      COM       6400     10-20-83      12:00P
FORMAT      COM       6912     10-20-83      12:00P
DISKCOPY    COM       2576     10-20-83      12:00P
MORE        COM        384     10-20-83      12:00P
SYS         COM       1680     10-20-83      12:00P
TREE        COM       1513     10-20-83      12:00P
SORT        EXE       1408     10-20-83      12:00P
ANSI        SYS       1664     10-20-83      12:00P
        9 File(s) 294912 bytes free
```

You are now ready to build three subdirectories for storing information: for word processing (WP), spreadsheets (SS), and data base management (DB). Each is created by using the MD commands:

```
A>MD WP
A>MD DB
A>MD SS
```

After each command is entered, drive A starts up to record information for that subdirectory's file. You can now issue a DIR command, and the following information will be displayed on your screen:

```
Volume in drive A is TIM DUFFY
Directory of A:\

COMMAND     COM      17792     10-20-83      12:00P
CHKDSK      COM       6400     10-20-83      12:00P
FORMAT      COM       6912     10-20-83      12:00P
DISKCOPY    COM       2576     10-20-83      12:00P
MORE        COM        384     10-20-83      12:00P
SYS         COM       1680     10-20-83      12:00P
TREE        COM       1513     10-20-83      12:00P
SORT        EXE       1408     10-20-83      12:00P
ANSI        SYS       1664     10-20-83      12:00P
WP                  <DIR>                3-29-89      12:05a
DB                  <DIR>                3-29-89      12:05a
SS                  <DIR>                3-29-89      12:05a
       12 File(s) 291840 bytes free
```

Notice that this listing shows that DOS is treating the directories as files. The original listing had nine files but after you created the subdirectories, it has twelve files. You can differentiate a subdirectory from a file by the <DIR> message (abbreviation for directory), which is displayed in place of the extension and file size data. Notice that the date on which the subdirectory was created (the system date stored in the machine at startup time) is also listed.

Also notice that the bytes free entry has changed since the three subdirectories were created. Each subdirectory takes a minimum of 1K, or 1,024, characters of storage.

The Change Directory (CD) Command. Once your subdirectories have been created, you can reach a subdirectory via the CD (change directory) command. To move from the root directory to the data base (DB) subdirectory, you enter the CD DB command. To make sure that you have moved to the right subdirectory, you can issue the DIR command to see where you are. The following output will be displayed on your monitor.

```
Volume in drive A is TIM DUFFY
Directory of A:\DB

.           <DIR>       3-29-89        12:08a
..          <DIR>       3-29-89        12:08a
       2 File(s)  291840 bytes free
```

The output of this DIR command is just a bit different from the output of the root directory. Notice that the second line of this directory listing contains A:\DB. This denotes the subdirectory that is considered by DOS to be active. You can always tell when you are at the root directory because the output of the DIR command will give the default drive followed only by a backslash, for example, A:\.

You can also use the CD command to find out where you are in a subdirectory tree since the CD causes DOS to respond with the current active directory:

```
CD          (command)
A:\DB       (response)
```

If you were at the root directory, the same command would produce a different response:

```
CD

A:\
```

You can also use the CD command to leave the subdirectory and return to the directory above in the hierarchy by entering CD .. or CD\, but if you use the first option, be sure to put a space between the CD and the two periods. Entering one of these commands moves you from the current subdirectory to the directory immediately above it. In this case, if you are at the DB subdirectory, you are taken to the root directory.

The Active (Current) Directory

The active (current) directory concept is especially important in a hard disk or high-density disk environment. After you have moved to a subdirectory in your hard disk, you can switch the default drive to one of your diskette drives, and DOS will remember which is the active subdirectory. If you copy files from the diskette to the hard disk drive that contains the active (current) subdirectory, they will be placed in that subdirectory.

For example, suppose that your current active subdirectory is on drive B. Also suppose that you have changed your default drive from B to A but want to copy a file called MEMO.TXT back to your active subdirectory on drive B. All that is required is to enter the following command:

```
A>COPY MEMO.TXT B:
```

Since DOS remembers which is the active subdirectory, it automatically copies the file to that subdirectory.

When you are copying information from one directory to another, remember that both the directory and the file name must be used. For example, if you want to copy the FORMAT.COM file from the root directory to the DB directory, you enter the following DOS command:

```
A>COPY FORMAT.COM \DB
```

This command translates as: Take the file called FORMAT.COM and copy it to the DB subdirectory; use the existing name. Now, if you want to refer to the FORMAT.COM file as it exists in the DB subdirectory while you are in the root directory, enter \DB\FORMAT.COM. When you refer to files in directories other than the active directory, you must use their full names. The subdirectory is part of that name.

While remaining at the root directory, you can copy the FORMAT.COM file from the DB subdirectory to the WP subdirectory by using the following command:

```
A>COPY \DB\FORMAT.COM \WP
```

Again, you must specify all of the sending information, which in this case is the name of the subdirectory and the name of the file, and all of the receiving information, which (unless you are going to change the name of the file) is only the receiving directory. The complete name for a file, including the complete subdirectory name, is referred to as the **path**.

The TREE Command. You may someday use a microcomputer system that is not familiar to you, in which case you may not know what subdirectories are on a disk or which files are in which subdirectory. Then the PC DOS TREE command will be extremely helpful. The TREE command is an external file that must reside on one of the disks. In this example, it is in the root directory. The TREE command generates the following output:

```
DIRECTORY PATH LISTING FOR VOLUME TIM DUFFY

Path: \SS
Sub-directories: None

Path: \WP
Sub-directories: None

Path: \DB
Sub-directories: None
```

This information might not be enough for you. The TREE command also has a /F parameter that lists any files found in a directory in addition to the directory name. The TREE /F command generates the following display:

```
DIRECTORY PATH LISTING FOR VOLUME TIM DUFFY

Path: \SS
Sub-directories: None

Files:           None

Path: \WP
Sub-directories: None

Files:           FORMAT.COM

Path: \DB
Sub-directories: None

Files:           FORMAT.COM
```

The Remove Directory (RD) Command. Assume that the DB subdirectory is no longer needed. Since you do not want to waste the disk space taken up by this directory and its files, you want to erase it. However, the ERASE command cannot be used to remove a directory. You must use the RMDIR (RD) command. First, all files must be deleted from the directory with the ERASE *.* command. If you forget to remove any file from the subdirectory, DOS will display the error message:

```
Invalid path, not a directory
or directory not empty
```

If you receive this error message, simply go to that directory and erase the rest of the files from it; position back to the directory above; and then issue the RD command to remove the subdirectory.

PATH: Executing Commands Without Changing Directories

Assume that you have a computer system with a hard disk (device C) and two diskette drives (devices A and B). While you are working on drive A, you want to execute the DOS command CHKDSK. This command, however, resides in the subdirectory DOSFILES that you created to hold the external DOS files. (This saves room on the root directory and also provides storage that is easy for you to remember.) The problem is that you must switch to the DOSFILES subdirectory, issue the DOS command CHKDSK, and then switch back to your current drive or directory and resume work. This process takes several change drive (CD) commands, which you would like to avoid.

The **PATH command** provides the capability to automatically search specified drives or directories if the desired file cannot be found in the active disk or directory. It can be used for any file with a .EXE, .COM, or .BAT file extension.

PATH Command.

Function: The PATH command searches specified drives and directories for commands or batch files that are not found on the current drive or directory.

Format: PATH [[d:]path[[;[d:]path...]]
        or
        PATH;

Type: Internal

Remarks
&

Examples: The PATH command allows you to specify a list of drives
and subdirectory names separated by semicolons. When
you now enter a command that is not found in the current
active disk or subdirectory, DOS searches the named drives
and subdirectories in the sequence you entered them; the
current drive or subdirectory is left unchanged.

Entering PATH with no parameters displays the current path. Entering
PATH; (with only a semicolon) resets the search path to the current drive and
subdirectory, which is the DOS default.

A path can be any valid series of subdirectories separated by a backslash.
Each separate path must be separated by semicolons, and the search by DOS
for the program or batch file will be in the order of the drives and subdirectories specified in the PATH command. If the file cannot be found in the current
directory and the designated paths, a Bad command or filename message will appear. If you give a bad drive name or subdirectory, DOS will skip
that parameter without displaying an error message.

If, in the example above, you want to tell DOS to automatically go to the
DOSFILES subdirectory if it is unable to find a specified program or batch file
in the active drive or subdirectory, you should give the following PATH
command:

```
PATH c:\dosfiles
```

Now, when a command is entered, DOS first searches the active disk
and subdirectory; if it is unable to locate the desired program file, it searches
the DOSFILES subdirectory to see if it is located there. If it finds the appropriate file, the command is executed; and if it is unable to locate the file, the
message Bad command or file name appears on the monitor.

You may want DOS to search two subdirectories for command files. For
example, you might want DOS to examine the DOSFILES subdirectory
and the UTILITY subdirectory as well. This is accomplished via the following
command:

```
PATH c:\dosfiles;c:\utility
```

Now when a command is entered, DOS first searches the active disk or
subdirectory. If it is unable to locate the desired program file, it searches the
DOSFILES subdirectory to see if the file is located there; if it is not, it searches
the UTILITY subdirectory. If it finds the file, the command is executed; if it is
unable to locate the file, the message Bad command or file name appears on the monitor.

DOS Directory Commands

CHDIR (or CD) Command.

Function: Changes the current DOS directory or displays the current
directory of the default drive.

Format: CD [d:][path]
or
CHDIR [d:][path]

Type: Internal

Remarks
  &
Examples: The abbreviated form CD can be used for the CHDIR
          command.
              Use the `[d:]` parameter to specify the drive on which
          the subdirectory that you want to change resides or on
          which you want to display the current directory.
              The CD \ command moves you from the current
          subdirectory to the root directory. The CD . . command
          moves you from the current directory to the next higher
          directory.

MKDIR (or MD) Command.

Function: Creates a subdirectory on a specified drive named by the
          characters following the command.

Format: `MD [d:][path]`
          or
          `MKDIR [d:][path]`

Type: Internal

Remarks
  &
Examples: The abbreviated form MD can be used for the MKDIR
          command.
              Use the `[d:]` parameter to specify the drive on which
          you wish to create the subdirectory. If no drive is specified,
          the default drive is assumed.
              DOS specifies no limit to the number of directories that
          you can create. The only limitation is the amount of storage
          available on your default device. Neither is there a limit to
          how many times a file name can appear on a disk as long as
          each occurrence is in a different subdirectory.

RMDIR (or RD) Command.

Function: Removes the subdirectory of the name composed of the
          characters following the command.

Format: `RD [d:][path]`
          or
          `RMDIR [d:][path]`

Type: Internal

Remarks
  &
Examples: The abbreviated form RD can be used for the RMDIR
          command. All files must be erased from the subdirectory
          before it can be removed. If files remain in the subdirectory
          and the RD command is executed, the following error
          message will be displayed on the monitor:

          `Invalid path, not a directory`
          `or directory not empty`

          You cannot remove root directories from a disk.

Part Two

TREE Command.

Function: Displays all of the directories on a disk and, using an optional parameter, lists the files of the root directory and of each subdirectory.

Format: `TREE [d:][/F]`

Type: External

Remarks
&

Examples: Use the `[d:]` and `[path]` optional parameters that appear before the TREE command to tell DOS in what drive and what subdirectory this external file resides. Use the optional `[d:]` following the TREE command to tell DOS against which drive to execute the command. Use the optional `[/F]` parameter to tell DOS to list each file contained in each subdirectory.

Configuring Your System

DOS, beginning with version 2.0, enables you to use commands that customize or configure your computer system. Any time that you start DOS via a boot operation, DOS searches the root directory of the active drive for a file named **CONFIG.SYS**. If the CONFIG.SYS file is found, DOS reads that file and uses the commands in it to customize its environment. If CONFIG.SYS is not found, DOS uses default values.

The CONFIG.SYS file can be created in a number of ways: You can use the COPY command to create it, you can use the EDLIN editor, or you can use your word processing package. This file can contain various commands, but only the commands commonly used to configure your system are covered here: ASSIGN, BREAK, BUFFERS, DEVICE, and FILES.

ASSIGN. The **ASSIGN statement** can be used in a CONFIG.SYS file to reassign device names. You must have the ASSIGN.COM file on your boot disk.

Break. The **Break option** can be either on or off and allows you to instruct DOS to check for a control break (Ctrl + Break) when a program requests DOS to perform any tasks. The default for DOS is off. If you want DOS to search for Ctrl + Break whenever it is requested, use the command BREAK = ON. This is especially useful if you wish to break out of a program compile (such an operation produces few or no standard device operations).

Format: `BREAK = [ON¦OFF]`

Buffers. The **Buffers option** permits you to determine the number of disk buffers that DOS is to allocate in memory when it starts (the default is two for a PC and three for an AT). A buffer is part of RAM that is used by the computer to hold information that has been read, is to be written to disk, or is to be printed.

Format: `BUFFERS = x`

The *x* represents a number between 1 and 99 and is the number of disk buffers that DOS allocates in RAM when it starts. Each of these buffers requires 512 bytes of RAM. Since DOS automatically starts with two buffers, only 1,024 bytes are used for buffers. This 1K of buffer storage may not be enough for such simple operations as looking at the directory of a diskette or a subdirectory of a hard disk, especially if there are many small files. A small number of buffers means that a lot of shifting of data has to occur in this reserved area. Therefore, a directory listing takes much less time when more buffers are allocated in RAM.

Data base applications also require more buffer space. A small number of buffers (for example, the default value 2) means that the response of the data base in retrieving data from disk is going to be slow. Any data base program that makes use of relative addressing (a topic to be covered later in the text) requires a larger number of buffers to increase performance.

How many buffers should you set aside? This is determined by the size of your computer and the types of processing applications that you want to perform. Since each buffer takes up 512 bytes, you probably don't want to specify 50 of them when you have a machine with only 128K of storage. Too many buffers can have a negative effect on the performance of your machine. When you increase the number of buffers too much, DOS spends too much time searching the buffers for data. For most applications about twenty buffers are sufficient.

DEVICE. The **DEVICE command** allows you to specify the name of a file containing a device driver. A number of standard drivers are automatically loaded into memory by DOS. For instance, the standard input, standard output, standard printer, diskette, and fixed disk device drivers are automatically loaded by DOS during the boot process. The DEVICE command allows you to load special drivers that come with DOS (ANSI.SYS or VDISK.SYS) that come with DOS on the DOS Master Disk.

The ANSI.SYS driver file located on disk provides a standard interface for programs, regardless of which manufacturer made them. This driver allows you to program applications that do not have to access the ROM BIOS (which is different in most machines and causes most of the compatibility problems of software) but instead send special instructions using this driver.

Format: `DEVICE = ANSI.SYS`

The **VDISK.SYS** driver file located on the DOS master disk enables you to create a RAM disk using part of your computer's memory. This RAM disk simulates all of the properties of a diskette in a disk drive. RAM disks have a number of advantages: Since their speed is limited only by the speed of RAM, they are fast; more than one RAM disk can be installed; if you have an AT computer with extended memory (more than 1 meg), you can use that memory for one or more RAM disks; you can specify the amount of RAM memory for each disk.

RAM disks also have a few disadvantages. Each one increases the size of DOS by 720 bytes. Most importantly, however, if power is lost or you forget to transfer files to a physical disk, all of the contents of the RAM disk are lost and cannot be recovered.

Format: `DEVICE = vdisk.sys[bbb][sss][ddd][/E[:m]]`

The `[bbb]` parameter is the size of the RAM disk in K and is specified as a decimal number. The default size is 64K. The allowable range is between 1 and the amount of memory actually installed in your machine. It would usually be between 128 and 320K.

The `[sss]` parameter is the sector size in bytes. The sizes that you can use are 128, 256, and 512 (the default value is 128).

The [ddd] parameter is the number of files that are allowed in the directory of the RAM disk (64 is the default). This value, if entered, can be between 2 and 512.

The /E parameter tells DOS to place the RAM disk in extended memory, and the m parameter tells DOS how many sectors of data are to be transferred at one time (the default is 8). This value, if entered, can be between 1 and 8.

The following sample VDISK command installs a 320K RAM disk with 512-byte sectors and 128 directory entries. The VDISK.SYS file is found on the default drive.

```
DEVICE = VDISK.SYS 326 512 128
```

When you start your computer using DOS 3.1, VDISK displays the following message when it executes:

```
VDISK Version 2.0 virtual disk x
```

This message means that DOS has encountered the DEVICE = VDISK.SYS command in the CONFIG.SYS file and is trying to execute it to install the RAM disk with the drive letter *x*.

FILES. The **FILES command** allows you to specify the maximum number of files that can be open at any one time (the default value assigned by DOS is 8).

Format: FILES = x

The *x* can be any number between 8 and 255. The default value is 8, which means that no more than eight files can be open at any one time. What does this mean to you? Any file access, whether it is a read, write, or close, is performed by telling DOS which file such a task is to be performed against.

When a file is opened, DOS reserves a fixed amount of memory called a *control block* to handle I/O for this file. The size of this area depends on the value specified in the FILES = command. A number commonly used for this option is 15. This is especially valid when you are using a program, such as dBASE III Plus, that allows you to have several data files open at any one time.

Creating the CONFIG.SYS File. One of the easiest ways to create a CONFIG.SYS file is to use the COPY command of DOS. This is accomplished by issuing the COPY CON:CONFIG.SYS command. This command places you in the line-by-line editor of DOS, and you can enter any commands that you want. Be sure, however, that the command is correct before you press the ENTER key, since you cannot go back and correct any errors. When you have finished entering the desired commands, depress the F6 key (a ^Z appears) to indicate to DOS that you have finished.

 The following lines represent the commands necessary to create a CONFIG.SYS file that will set the number of buffers to 20 and the number of files to 15, and that will create a 256K-RAM disk with 256-byte sectors and a directory containing 64 entries.

```
COPY CON:CONFIG.SYS
BUFFERS=20
FILES=15
DEVICE=VDISK.SYS 256 256 64^Z
```

Chapter Review

Three advanced topics are covered in this chapter: batch file commands, directory commands, and commands used for configuring the system.

Batch files allow you to save DOS commands to a file with a .BAT file extension and then execute those commands by entering the name of the batch file. The commands in the batch file are executed one at a time by DOS as though you were entering them from the keyboard.

There are two types of batch files: The first type is an AUTOEXEC.BAT, and the second type is a file with a .BAT file extension. The major difference between the two types of files is that an AUTOEXEC.BAT file is automatically executed by DOS when the boot process has finished and a regular batch file must be invoked by entering the name of the file.

Directories and subdirectories are used to divide disk storage space into functional units. This allows you to place all word processing files in one directory, all spreadsheet files in another directory, and all data management files in still another directory. Directories are most appropriate on a hard disk but can be used as easily on diskettes. The major advantage of directories, besides allowing you to group similar files, is that the file number limitations that DOS places on the root directory can be avoided by building a subdirectory.

A number of directory commands are available in DOS. The MKDIR (MD) command allows you to build a directory. The CHDIR (CD) allows you to move in a downward or upward direction from one directory to another. Once all files have been erased from a directory, the RMDIR (RD) command can be used to delete a directory.

The CONFIG.SYS file can be used to configure your system. The CONFIG.SYS file can contain instructions to DOS on how many files to have open at one time. It can also provide information to DOS about how many disk buffers for receiving disk I/O to have active at any one time. The CONFIG.SYS file can also contain the VDISK command used to construct a RAM disk. The instructions contained in the CONFIG.SYS file are used by DOS during the boot process to configure the system.

Key Terms and Concepts

ASSIGN statement	MKDIR (MD)
batch file	path
Break option	PATH command
Buffers option	REM
CHDIR (CD)	RMDIR (RD)
CONFIG.SYS	replaceable parameters
COPY CON:	root directory
DEVICE command	subdirectory
directory	TREE command
FILES command	VDISK.SYS

Chapter Quiz

Multiple Choice

1. Which of the following statements about batch files is true?
   a. Batch files are automatically executed by DOS.
   b. Batch files contain special instructions in binary for DOS.
   c. DOS automatically searches the root directory of the system disk from which the boot process occurred for an AUTOEXEC.BAT file.

    d. A batch file can only be named AUTOEXEC.BAT.

    e. None of the above statements is true.

2. A batch file cannot contain

    a. Frequently executed DOS commands.

    b. Commands needed upon booting the computer.

    c. Commands that are used to configure the system by setting up disk I/O buffers.

    d. Commands used to start a software package.

    e. All of the above commands can be in a batch file.

3. A root directory is

    a. The first directory created to hold a subdirectory's files.

    b. The first directory that you make on disk.

    c. A directory that has subdirectories beneath it.

    d. The directory that is automatically created by DOS when it initializes a disk.

    e. None of the above statements is true.

4. Which of the following directory commands is used to display your location in a subdirectory?

    a. MD

    b. CD

    c. RD

    d. TREE

    e. None of the above

5. Which command is used to create a RAM disk using the CONFIG.SYS file?

    a. RAMDISK

    b. VDISK

    c. BUFFERS

    d. RAMBUFFR

    e. None of the above

True/False

6. The CONFIG.SYS file is located and the commands in it are executed any time that you start a new program.

7. Batch commands are executed one at a time by DOS.

8. The root directory of a disk is always limited by the number of files that can be stored in it.

9. Most of the DOS commands that deal with disk directories are internal commands.

10. Once the standard drivers have been loaded by DOS, DOS searches the boot disk to see if a CONFIG.SYS file resides on it and finishes the start-up process.

Answers

1. c 2. c 3. d 4. b 5. b 6. f 7. t 8. t 9. t 10. t

Exercises

1. Define or describe each of the following:
   root directory
   batch file
   VDISK.SYS

2. The _____ batch file is automatically executed once the boot process has finished.

3. The _____ command is used to build a batch file without invoking a word processor.

4. A batch file can be interrupted by entering the _____ series of keystrokes.

5. The _____ key is depressed once you have finished entering the batch file from DOS.

6. The character that is used to indicate replaceable parameters is
   _____ .

7. The directory created automatically on any disk device during the format process is called the _____ directory.

8. A double-sided 5.25-inch disk can store a maximum of _____ files without using directories.

9. Directories are created by using the _____ DOS command.

10. Directories are erased by using the _____ DOS command.

11. Before a directory can be removed, all files must be removed using the DOS _____ command.

12. The directory command that is part of PC DOS but not MS DOS is the _____ command.

13. A directory is actually viewed by DOS as a _____ of data.

14. When you issue a DIR command, a directory has a _____ entry in place of the file extension and file size entries.

15. The _____ command is used to find out where you are in a series of directories and subdirectories.

16. The file named _____ contains instructions that tell DOS how to configure the system.

17. The _____ command tells DOS how much memory to use for disk I/O operations.

18. The _____ command tells DOS how many files can be open at any one time.

19. The _____ file allows you to build a RAM disk in memory.

20. The file that contains the standard method of accessing devices without going through the ROM BIOS is the _____ file.

Computer Exercises

The following exercises are necessary to create files that are needed later in the text. Any time that you see the ^Z entry you are to depress the F6 function key.

1. For running the student version of VP-Planner, create a batch file called RUNVP.BAT using the following steps:

```
COPY CON:RUNVP.BAT
DATE
VP^Z
```

2. On the system disk that you use to boot your computer, place the following CONFIG.SYS file. This diskette with the CONFIG.SYS file should then be used to boot your computer any time that you want to use dBASE III Plus.

```
COPY CON:CONFIG.SYS
FILES = 15
BUFFERS = 20^Z
```

Chapter

6

Beginning Word

Processing with

WordPerfect

Chapter Objectives

After completing this chapter, you should be able to:

Understand basic concepts of word processing

Define and discuss common word processing terminology

Discuss the steps involved in using word processing packages

Discuss the various parts of the WordPerfect package

Discuss the parts of the status line of the entry screen

Discuss a number of cursor movement commands

Discuss a number of elementary WordPerfect commands necessary
for the novice

Most people must be able to express their thoughts or needs by the written word, at least occasionally. It is usually desirable to clarify what has been committed to paper by refining, rephrasing, and restating. *Word processing* can be defined as the manipulation of text data including creating a document, editing and changing it, storing and retrieving it, and printing it.

Word processing has usually been accomplished using handwritten or typewritten pages, but with either method the process of revising text is difficult and time-consuming. When using a typewriter, for example, you have to retype the entire page even if you want to make only one change. Or if time constraints disallow retyping, you must "cut and paste," using scissors, correction tape, correction fluid, and maybe glue, and then copy the patched document on a copy machine before anything approaching a professional-looking document can be achieved.

Word processing software makes changing a document much easier by automating the process of entering, editing, revising, storing, and printing. One of the most important aspects of computerized word processing (see Figure 6.1) is that you do not have to plan the original document carefully. Rather, you can compose the document while sitting at the keyboard; a rough outline is all that you need at the outset. Composing at the keyboard may require some practice on your part, but you will soon get used to composing documents as you enter them. You may also find that you don't forget to make points that somehow slip your mind when you are handwriting text. You can then print out or review the document and make changes. Thus word processing greatly increases productivity.

Word processing began in the early 1900s with the introduction of the mechanical typewriter. The qwerty keyboard of this device was designed to prevent keys from jamming rather than to increase the speed of data entry by the user. The system was recognized as a vast improvement over handwriting; nonetheless, during the period from 1930 to 1950, various methods of automating the process of producing repetitive documents were attempted.

In the early 1960s IBM introduced the **mag typewriter**, which used a magnetic tape cartridge for sequential access to stored documents. This was hailed as a dramatic advance because it allowed a user not only to store, retrieve, and then type a document but also to make immediate insertions, deletions, and corrections on the original without having to retype the entire document.

Line editors, the original word processors, are software development aids that allow a programmer to make changes in a line of program code. The program must be stored on some type of disk device, and only one line at a time can be changed and formatted in the program because line editors cannot deal with anything larger than one line.

During the late 1960s and early 1970s, many large computer manufacturers decided to enter the word processing market by marketing add-on software packages that could be attached to existing mainframes or by introducing stand-alone word processing machines. Many mainframe word processing packages were too complicated to learn to use without special training, so businesses that originally purchased add-on packages have since shifted to **stand-alone**, or **dedicated, word processors**.

Stand-alone word processors are computers whose sole task is word processing. They are fast, easy to use, and extremely flexible in their ability to produce printed output. The screen usually shows exactly what will appear on the printed page. Most mainframe word processing packages required the user to embed strange control codes in the text to perform specific functions—such as centering a line of text, indenting a paragraph, underlining a block of text,

Figure 6.1
Typical hardware configuration used for word processing. (Courtesy of NEC Information Systems, Inc.)

or setting margins or tabs—and to see the document as it would appear in print, the user had to print it.

Until the early 1980s, the stand-alone word processor appeared to be the answer to most users' needs. Its major drawback was its high cost: A stand-alone word processing device typically cost $15,000 to $20,000, including computer, monitor, disk drives, printer, and software. Only large organizations could assume such an expense for such a tool. In addition, the units were so large that a significant part of a room had to be reserved for each one. Today's models are less bulky than their predecessors, but they still have limited processing versatility.

During the late 1970s, word processing packages were introduced for microcomputers. The first was developed by Bob Barnaby and Seymour Rubinstein for one of the first microcomputers, the IMSAI. Word processing packages for microcomputers are commonly a composite of mainframe and stand-alone word processing programs with some new additions. Examples include Electric Pencil, WordStar, Samna III, Word, WordPerfect, and Scripsit.

At first, word processing on microcomputers suffered many of the same limitations as mainframe software and so did not threaten the stand-alone word processing market. It was not easy to use, and it was less powerful than the software on the dedicated systems. In recent years, however, microcomputer word processing software has succeeded in closely matching the features provided by manufacturers such as CPT and Wang. Because of the versatility of the software, the user can choose from a wide array of computers and printers to optimize the match of software and hardware to the application.

The lower costs of microcomputer word processing have had an impact on large and small organizations alike. Large businesses have been able to expand the word processing function beyond the "pool" concept, placing personal equipment in the hands of individuals. Small businesses have found that they can afford word processing. And now individuals are finding that they too can afford this powerful tool.

One major difference among microcomputer-based word processing packages is how they handle document size. Some packages limit the size of the document to the amount of available RAM, making ten to sixteen pages the effective maximum. In contrast, what can be referred to as **virtual-file allocation** word processing packages contain only about six to twelve pages of a document in RAM at one time, saving the remainder on disk.

A later trend in microcomputer word processing software was the addition of writing aid programs such as spelling and grammar checkers and thesauruses. Some word processing software comes with these options built in, whereas others make them installable at additional cost. Add-on programs compatible with many word processing packages are also available from third-party vendors.

A still later add-on feature has been desktop publishing. **Desktop publishing** gives the user typeset quality such as you see in newspapers and textbooks. It also allows you to combine text with pictures.

One problem that continues to plague vendors of word processing software for microcomputers is that the keyboards on most microcomputers are not arranged very well for the typist. A number of companies now offer a variety of replacement keyboards (Figure 6.2).

Ever since line editors became available to computer programmers for making on-line changes to programs, people have used the computer for editing functions such as moving, copying, inserting, and deleting text. Changes over the past few years, however, have signaled a development beyond using the computer for mere editing and printing.

Overview of WordPerfect

WordPerfect is judged by many software reviewers to be one of the best word processing packages on the market. It provides you with great flexibility. The WordPerfect software package is composed of the word processor, a merge program, Speller, Thesaurus, and other advanced features.

Word Processing

The word processing portion of WordPerfect provides most of the power needed by a typical person. It allows you to type your text (document) into a file in RAM and then later to store the document on disk. You can also make manual corrections of spelling or grammar in the document, rearrange blocks of text or make other changes required by the process known as **revision**, and print your document.

What appears on the screen in WordPerfect is more or less what will appear on the printed page: If you tell WordPerfect to indent a paragraph, the paragraph is indented on the screen; if you want the output to be double-spaced, it is double-spaced on the screen. This feature applies to most commands, except some print commands.

WordPerfect also has the virtual-file feature; so the length of the document is limited only by the size of the file-storage medium in use. WordPerfect requires that only a portion of a long document be in RAM at any one time. Thus, if you have a storage medium capable of holding 1,000 pages of text, you can process a 1,000-page document with WordPerfect. (We'll discuss later why this might not be desirable.)

Merge Feature

The **Merge** feature of WordPerfect allows you to combine (merge) a "boiler plate" or template letter with a list of names and addresses, individualizing the letter for each addressee.

Figure 6.2
Two keyboards that can be used for word processing, replacing the original keyboard.
(Key Tronic KB5151 courtesy of Key Tronic; Computer Smartline Smart-board courtesy of
WICO Corporation)

A Merge application requires two types of data: **constant information** (the unchanging information contained in the template letter) and **variable data** (consisting of parts that change from one letter to another). Merge must be told where to find the variable data—in a data file, for example, or entered from the keyboard—and it must be given a description of the variable data, including the order of the information within each record of the file. Finally, Merge must be told where in the template letter to place the variable data.

Speller and Thesaurus

The WordPerfect **Speller** enables you to proof a document on the screen. This feature not only finds errors but also helps you correct them. The dictionary contains over 100,000 words and allows you to add or delete words. Speller can perform a phonetic analysis of a word and offer its "best guess" about the correct word needed. In addition to performing the spelling check function, Speller provides you with a word count.

Thesaurus contains about 10,000 words, among which you can find antonyms and synonyms for many words, thereby helping you find just the right word. Up to three words and their references are displayed on a screen.

Additional Features

In addition to the preceding features, WordPerfect enables you to manipulate columns of text, perform math within a document, automatically insert footnotes and endnotes, build a table of contents or an index, and make drawings or include figures containing graphics within the body of a document.

Starting WordPerfect

The manner in which you start WordPerfect depends on whether you are using a diskette or hard disk microcomputer.

Diskette Systems

To start WordPerfect on a diskette, you first boot the computer using a DOS system disk (this is probably the disk containing WordPcrfect). You then enter the date and time, if you want this information to appear in the directory entries of the files you create.

With a diskette system, you usually place your WordPerfect program diskette in drive A and the diskette that is to hold your document in drive B. To get WordPerfect to store files in the diskette in drive B, change the default drive to B and then tell DOS to execute the WordPerfect program in drive A. This is accomplished by entering the following commands:

```
A>B:
B>A:WP
```

The first command (B:) changes the default drive to B. The second command (A:WP) tells DOS to go to drive A and execute the file WP.EXE. WordPerfect now is able to automatically save any files to the diskette in drive B.

Hard Disk Systems

To start WordPerfect on a hard disk system, boot the computer and then tell DOS to activate the directory in which your WordPerfect program and data files reside. This is accomplished by using the change directory (CD) DOS command (see Chapter 5); that is, if your WordPerfect directory is named WP, enter CD \WP. After you have activated the directory, you can start Word-Perfect by entering WP at the DOS prompt. Any files that you create will now be saved to this activated directory.

If you have WordPerfect installed on hard disk and try to start it from diskette by using the diskette-based option discussed above, the program will first start executing from drive A. Once it has started, however, it looks on the hard disk for a directory called WP. If it finds a WP subdirectory containing WordPerfect, it will execute from that directory rather than from the diskette drive from which it was started. This ensures the fastest execution speed possible.

Once you issue the WP command to start WordPerfect, the screen depicted in Figure 6.3 is displayed on your monitor.

The NOTE line indicates on which drive the WordPerfect files are located. If you start WordPerfect from a diskette and the files also reside in a directory called WP on the hard disk, this directory will be displayed instead of drive A. The *Please Wait* message informs you that the required WordPerfect files are being loaded by the computer. If you are using the Training version, an information screen appears (Figure 6.4).

WordPerfect Screen

Once the WordPerfect files are loaded from disk, the screen depicted in Figure 6.5 appears on your monitor.

The dash in the upper left-hand corner of the screen is the cursor. The **status line** is the single line of information at the bottom of the screen; it is the twenty-fifth line on your screen. In this example, C:\WP\FILENAME indicates the name of the file that is being manipulated. This entry is absent when you are creating a document. It contains the file name only when you are editing an existing text file.

WordPerfect allows you to open two document files at one time and to manipulate both. The Doc 1 entry of the status line indicates that the first document is on the screen.

5.0   The Pg and Ln entries give the current page number and the line on which the cursor is located. You can see at a glance where you are in a document.

Figure 6.3
The WordPerfect copyright screen.

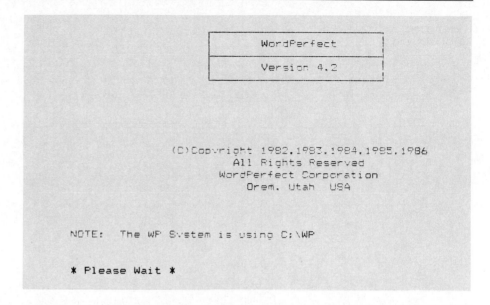

Figure 6.4
Opening screen for the training version of WordPerfect.

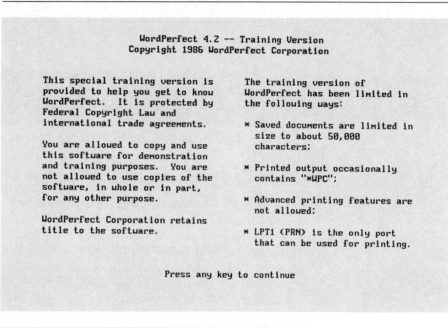

5.0   The position indicator, P o s, tells the position of the cursor in a line of text and also provides other information. Notice that the position indicator contains the value of 16 even though the cursor appears to be in position 1 on the screen. The position displayed on the screen is the position of the line in which this character will appear on the printed document. The various characteristics of the printed document will be covered later in this chapter.

When the position indicator appears as P o s, the Caps Lock key is off; but if it appears as POS, the Caps Lock key is on, and only upper-case characters will appear on the screen. The number that follows P o s also informs you of the status of other features. It tells you whether or not the Boldface or Underline features (to be discussed in detail later) are invoked. If you have invoked Boldface, then the number appears in boldface. If Underline is invoked, then the number appears underlined. If both features are on, the number will be boldface underlined.

Figure 6.5
A clear screen with the status
line at the bottom.

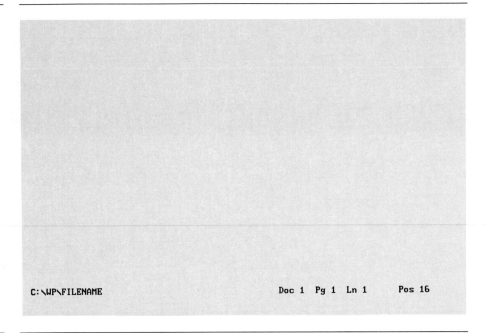

C:\WP\FILENAME   Doc 1 Pg 1 Ln 1   Pos 16

Text Window

The **text window**, or **data entry window**, is composed of the twenty-four blank
lines above the status line. When you first start WordPerfect, these lines are
blank. As you enter text, the window fills with characters, from top down. The
twenty-four displayable lines in the text window are the maximum amount of
text that can be displayed on a standard monitor at any one time.

Entering and Canceling Commands

WordPerfect makes extensive use of the function keys in conjunction with the
Ctrl, SHIFT, and Alt keys to enter commands. To ease the learning process, the
WordPerfect Corporation designed a labeled template that fits over the function
keys of your keyboard (a copy can be found in the back of this textbook).

To make the program as easy to use as possible, recent modifications to
the WordPerfect program enable the user to issue commands in two or more
ways. For example, if a typing error should happen to issue an unexpected
command that results in the appearance of a "strange" screen or menu on
your monitor, you can get out of the difficulty (or any such difficulty) by simply
pressing the F1 (Cancel) key.

Help Feature

WordPerfect contains a built-in Help feature that can be invoked by pressing
the Help key (F3). You can then get information about a command or function
by entering the first letter of the command or by pressing the desired function
key. Figure 6.6 depicts the Help screens that appear when the List Files (F5)
command is issued.

Operating
WordPerfect

Entering a Document

You can type your document without worrying about the approach of the end
of a line (as you would have to on a typewriter), because WordPerfect automatically moves a word that is too long for a line down to the next line via the

Figure 6.6
(a) The first help screen for
the List Files (F5) command.
(b) The second help screen for
the List Files (F5) command.

```
List Files (File Management)

    Lists all files on a disk or in a directory that match the filename
    template given (the default is *.* which means all files).  The free disk
    space and current document size are also shown.

    You can move the block cursor to select any file using the arrow keys,
    Screen up/down, Page up/down or letters.  Typing a letter activates the
    name search feature.  You can type in some (or all) of a filename and the
    closest match will be found.

    Marking files:  Pressing the "*" key marks or unmarks the file you are
    currently on and then moves you to the next entry.  The Mark Text key will
    mark/unmark all the files in the current listing.  All marked files can
    then be deleted, printed, copied or searched.

    Pressing the Print key will print the directory listing through the
    WordPerfect print queue.


              Type 1 for more help on List Files Options
```

(a)

```
List Files Options


    1.  Retrieve:  Bring file into WordPerfect.
    2.  Delete:  Delete all marked files or just the currently selected file.
            Empty directories can also be deleted.
    3.  Rename:  Change a file's name
    4.  Print:  Print all marked files or just the file you are on.
    5.  Text In:  Retrieve a DOS text file.
    6.  Look:  Show contents of a file.  You can scroll down through  the file.
            If the entry is a directory, the files in  that directory will be
            listed.
    7.  Change Directory:  Change default directory or create new directories.
    8.  Copy:  Copy all marked files or just the currently selected  file to
            another disk or directory.
    9.  Word Search:  You list the word(s) to be found, and all the files which
            contain the word(s) will be shown.

        Ex.:  International  or  "WPCORP word*program";HP,LaserJet
              ; = logical AND    ? matches one letter
              , = logical OR     * matches one or more letters
```

(b)

word wrap feature. The only time you have to enter a **hard return** is at the end of a paragraph.

To practice entering text, type in the two paragraphs that follow. Use the TAB key (located above the Ctrl key) to indent. Don't be concerned if the text on your screen does not look like that below, and don't correct errors that you make. We shall discuss how to delete text and correct errors later.

A file is a collection of related information in the form of data or of instructions for manipulating that information. In other words, files can be either data files or program files. You keep track of files on a disk by name. Each file name must be unique; if you try to record a file using a name that already exists on the disk, the content of the previous file will be destroyed and replaced with the content of the new file.

With a few exceptions, you can name your file anything you wish. Disk filenames can be one to eight characters in length and can be followed by a filename extension that is preceded by a period and is one to three characters in length. For example, a student data file for grades might be called STUDGRAD.TXT.

Saving a Document (File) to Disk

There are two methods of saving a file to disk. The first returns you to the document, and the second enables you to start a new document or return to DOS.

Save

The Save (F10) command saves (stores) the current document in a file on disk. If the file is new, you are prompted to enter a file name. If the file is an old one that has been retrieved from disk, the name of the file is first displayed with a prompt. For example:

```
Document to be Saved: C:\WP\EXERCISE
```

Notice that the drive name is displayed along with the subdirectory, if any, and the file name. Press the ENTER key. You will now be asked if you want to overwrite the existing file with the new one:

```
Replace C:\WP\EXERCISE?(Y/N)N
```

Respond with a Y. After the file has been saved, you are returned to the document and can resume editing. This procedure saves any changes that have been made to your document. It is advisable that you do this regularly while working on a file, even though WordPerfect does provide a backup facility (to be discussed later).

Exit

If you want to save a file and then leave WordPerfect or create or edit another document, press the Exit (F7) key. You will then be asked if you want to save the file, to which you respond Y. After the file has been saved on disk, Word-Perfect displays the following prompt:

```
Exit WP? (Y/N)N        (Cancel to return to document)
```

If you respond N, the existing document is erased from RAM, and you receive a blank screen ready for new text; if you answer Y, you are returned to DOS. If you issue the Cancel (F1) command, you are returned to your document.

Save your two-paragraph practice file using the Exit (F7) command and the filename INPUT1; but remain in WordPerfect. After entering the command, you should see a `saving INPUT1` message at the bottom of the screen. You now have a file called INPUT1 on your disk. Be sure to respond N to the prompt to leave WordPerfect.

IMPORTANT When you want to leave WordPerfect, always use the Exit command. Remove the WordPerfect program disk only when the DOS prompt (A>, B>, C>, or D>) appears on the screen. If you remove the program disk while the computer is running, you can destroy the disk.

If you turn off the computer without first properly exiting WordPerfect, unallocated clusters (sectors) are placed on the disk. If you consistently exit WordPerfect improperly, your diskette will eventually fill with these unallocated sectors, and you will receive a `Disk Full` error message.

Retrieving the File

To practice viewing a file in various ways, load the file BOOKEXER from your disk. Use the Retrieve (SHIFT + F10) command to load the file. This file contains the Introduction to Word Processing portion of this chapter. You will be using this file to try out the various WordPerfect commands that control the cursor movement.

List Files

What do you do if you forget the name of the file that you want to retrieve? The List Files (F5) command solves this and other problems. The List Files (F5) command allows you to view a directory of all files on disk; find the files that contain a specific word or phrase; read or scan a document; retrieve a document to the screen; delete, rename, print, or copy a file; and retrieve an ASCII file.

When you first issue the List Files (F5) command, WordPerfect prompts you for the name of the disk and subdirectory to be displayed, with the current disk and subdirectory as the default. At this time you can change the directory by pressing the = key and entering the name of a new directory, or you can press the ENTER key to accept the current one. A screen like Figure 6.7 now appears on your monitor.

The top lines of the screen provide the date, time, disk/directory name, size of the document in memory, and amount of space available on disk. The middle portion contains, for each of the various files on disk, the name, size, date, and time of creation. Use the cursor keys to move the bar from one file to the next. The bottom two lines contain a menu of various tasks that can be performed.

To execute a command, move the bar to the file via the arrow keys and then select a menu option. The various options are as follows:

> *Retrieve.* This command allows you to issue the Retrieve command from the List Files screen rather than having to return to your document before issuing the command. *Never retrieve any WordPerfect program files*

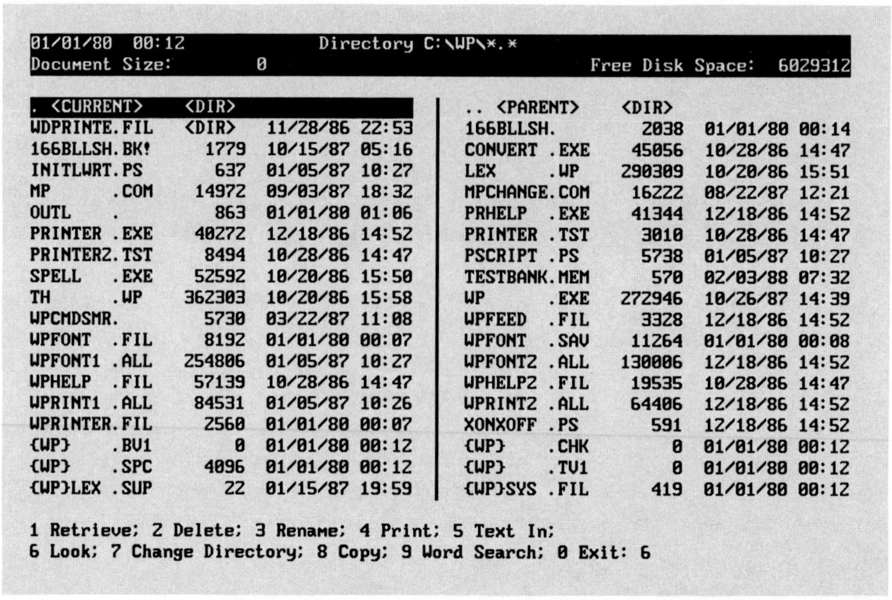

Figure 6.7
The List Files screen.

```
01/01/80  00:12              Directory C:\WP\*.*
Document Size:          0                Free Disk Space:  6029312

. <CURRENT>  <DIR>                    .. <PARENT>   <DIR>
WDPRINTE.FIL <DIR>   11/28/86 22:53   166BLLSH.      2038  01/01/80 00:14
166BLLSH.BK! 1779    10/15/87 05:16   CONVERT  .EXE 45056  10/28/86 14:47
INITLWRT.PS  637     01/05/87 10:27   LEX      .WP  290309 10/20/86 15:51
MP     .COM  14972   09/03/87 18:32   MPCHANGE.COM  16222  08/22/87 12:21
OUTL   .     863     01/01/80 01:06   PRHELP   .EXE 41344  12/18/86 14:52
PRINTER .EXE 40272   12/18/86 14:52   PRINTER  .TST 3010   10/28/86 14:47
PRINTER2.TST 8494    10/28/86 14:47   PSCRIPT  .PS  5738   01/05/87 10:27
SPELL  .EXE  52592   10/20/86 15:50   TESTBANK.MEM  570    02/03/88 07:32
TH     .WP   362303  10/20/86 15:58   WP       .EXE 272946 10/26/87 14:39
WPCMDSMR.    5730    03/22/87 11:08   WPFEED   .FIL 3328   12/18/86 14:52
WPFONT .FIL  8192    01/01/80 00:07   WPFONT   .SAV 11264  01/01/80 00:08
WPFONT1 .ALL 254806  01/05/87 10:27   WPFONT2  .ALL 130006 12/18/86 14:52
WPHELP .FIL  57139   10/28/86 14:47   WPHELP2  .FIL 19535  10/28/86 14:47
WPRINT1 .ALL 84531   01/05/87 10:26   WPRINT2  .ALL 64406  12/18/86 14:52
WPRINTER.FIL 2560    01/01/80 00:07   XONXOFF  .PS  591    12/18/86 14:52
{WP}   .BU1  0       01/01/80 00:12   {WP}     .CHK 0      01/01/80 00:12
{WP}   .SPC  4096    01/01/80 00:12   {WP}     .TV1 0      01/01/80 00:12
{WP}LEX .SUP 22      01/15/87 19:59   {WP}SYS  .FIL 419    01/01/80 00:12

1 Retrieve; 2 Delete; 3 Rename; 4 Print; 5 Text In;
6 Look; 7 Change Directory; 8 Copy; 9 Word Search; 0 Exit: 6
```

(any file that starts with WP or any file with a .COM or .EXE file extension), because you can damage them and ruin your copy of the program.

Delete. This command displays the message `Delete filename?` `Y/N N`. If you depress the Y key, the file is deleted; otherwise, it remains on the disk.

Rename. This command allows you to rename the indicated file. Simply enter the new name at the prompt `New Name:_`.

Print. This command sends the indicated file to the printer.

Text In. This command allows you to load any ASCII (DOS) file at the cursor location.

Look. This command allows you to view a file without loading it into RAM, by displaying it a page at a time to the screen. The message `Press any key to continue _` is displayed at the bottom of your screen (and doing so returns you to the file directory). You can use cursor commands to scroll through the file, but you cannot make changes to the file.

Change Directory. This command allows you to access files from another directory or disk. WordPerfect will then use the indicated directory or disk for saving or retrieving files.

Copy. This command allows you to copy the indicated file to another file, disk, or directory.

Word Search. This command allows you to display all files in the current directory that contain a word or phrase that matches a pattern that you provided.

Moving Around the Document

Cursor movement commands move the cursor over the text in the text window. The cursor movement commands of WordPerfect are executed by using the ten-key numeric key pad (Figure 6.8).

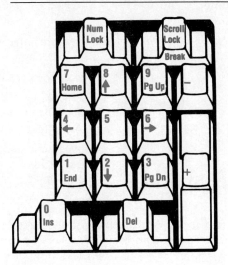

Figure 6.8
Various functions of the numeric key pad that are supported on IBM and IBM-compatible computers.

Pressing the Up-arrow key moves the cursor up one line, and pressing the Down-arrow key moves the cursor down one line. Other commands are not quite so obvious, but with a little practice they, too, become almost second nature.

Cursor Movement Commands

Simple Movement

Up arrow	Moves the cursor up one line
Right arrow	Moves the cursor to the right one position
Left arrow	Moves the cursor to the left one position
Down arrow	Moves the cursor down one line

Horizontal Movement

Ctrl + Right arrow	Moves the cursor to the first character of the next word to the right
Ctrl + Left arrow	Moves the cursor to the first character of the next word to the left
End	Moves the cursor to the end of the line
Home, Right arrow	Moves the cursor to the right edge of the current screen
Home, Left arrow	Moves the cursor to the left edge of the current screen
Home, Home, Right arrow	Moves the cursor to the extreme right edge of the document
Home, Home, Left arrow	Moves the cursor to the extreme left edge of the document

Vertical Movement

Home, Home, Up arrow	Moves the cursor to the beginning of the file

Home, Home, Down arrow	Moves the cursor to the end of the file
PgUp	Moves the cursor to the first line of text on the previous page
PgDn	Moves the cursor to the first line of text on the next page
—	Moves the cursor up one screen (twenty-four lines) of text
+	Moves the cursor down one screen (twenty-four lines) of text
Ctrl + Home #	Moves the cursor to the top of the page having the given number

A feature of WordPerfect's cursor movement is that the cursor stays in the same relative position on a line as you move from one line to the next or from one screen to the next. For example, if your cursor is at position 41 and you begin to move the cursor down the page, the cursor stays in position 41. Should the next line be shorter, the cursor moves to the right-most position of that line. If a blank line intervenes (for example, between paragraphs), the cursor moves to position 10 on the blank line (the first position within your document) and upon reaching the next line moves back to position 41.

The Ctrl + Home # command merits some additional discussion. This command positions the cursor at the top of the indicated page number (#). For example, if you want to move the cursor to the top of page 10, you enter the keystrokes Ctrl + Home (whereupon you receive the prompt Go to _); you then enter 10 and press ENTER. After the repositioning message disappears from the top of the screen, you are at the top of page 10.

Page Breaks

WordPerfect allows you to see where a page break will appear when the file is printed. A **soft page break** occurs when one page is full and another page is about to begin. To indicate a soft page break, WordPerfect places a line of dashes (--------) across the screen. This line appears after the fifty-fourth line of text on the screen, but it does not become part of your document. It is placed on the screen only to mark the breaks between pages and to aid you in keeping "widow" or "orphan" lines out of your document. A **widow** is the first line of a paragraph that appears alone at the bottom of a page. An **orphan** is the last line of a paragraph that appears alone at the top of a page.

A **hard page break**, caused by entering the command Ctrl + ENTER, becomes part of the document. A hard page break occurs on a page at any place you have issued the Ctrl + ENTER command. After this command, the cursor moves to the next page. WordPerfect uses a line of equal signs (= = = = = = = = =) across the screen to indicate a hard page break. A hard page break can be deleted from a document by positioning the cursor to the line immediately above the row of equal signs and depressing the Del key.

Re-forming a Paragraph

When you edit a document, you delete text from some lines and insert text in others. This deletion and insertion of text gives a line a ragged appearance. WordPerfect automatically issues a **re-form** command to realign the text within the left- and right-hand margins whenever you press an Up or Down cursor key.

Editing Text

After text has been entered, you will want to correct spelling and grammatical errors, delete unwanted words, and smooth punctuation. Many times, however, you will detect typing errors as soon as you make them. WordPerfect, because it combines the input and editing modes, makes it easy for you to correct errors while entering text. You simply move the cursor back to the error and correct it. In contrast, some other word processing packages require you to shift manually from input mode to edit mode.

Editing a document can take place in *real time* or *batch mode*. Real-time editing corrects an error as soon as it occurs; batch-mode editing may involve printing out the document and proofreading for errors. For efficiency, word processing experts recommend that, rather than correcting your errors as they occur, you complete the document and then go back and correct errors—in other words, they recommend using the batch mode. If you're not interested in becoming an expert word processor but simply want to have as error-free a document as possible, go ahead and correct the errors as they occur.

Regardless of which editing method you prefer, you will eventually want to print out the rough draft of your document and mark any errors for correction. You should print out the document rather than proofing it on the screen, because you're still too intimately involved with the work on the screen to see even obvious errors. This also can occur with printed output, but less often because you can take more time and review the document away from the computer.

After you have marked the corrections on the document, it is a fairly easy task to make changes using the following WordPerfect commands: cursor movement commands to move through the document, commands to insert new text into the body of the document, and commands to delete unwanted text.

Inserting Text

With WordPerfect, you can insert new text into a document in two ways: with the insert option (the WordPerfect default) or the typeover option.

Insert Option. The **Insert option** of WordPerfect is the default. To insert text into a document, simply place the cursor at the desired location and enter the new characters. These appear to the left of the cursor. Existing text is moved to the right on the same line. If text extends beyond the right-hand margin, it will be re-formed as soon as you issue a vertical cursor movement command.

Assume that you want to insert the word *black* before the word *cat* in the sentence, The cat ran up the tree. Since the Insert option is the WordPerfect default, position your cursor under the *c* of *cat* and enter the word *black* (followed by a space). Here is the way the screen will look, character by character.

```
The bcat ran up the tree.
The blcat ran up the tree.
The blacat ran up the tree.
The blaccat ran up the tree.
The blackcat ran up the tree.
The black cat ran up the tree.
```

You can see that the existing text is moved to the right as you enter each character. If the text overruns the right-hand margin, remember that it will be re-formed when a vertical cursor movement command is used.

ENTER Key and Space Bar in Insert Mode. The ENTER key and the Space Bar both play a role in editing data. When pressed, the ENTER key signals the end of a paragraph by inserting a hard carriage return, and any text to the right of the cursor is moved to the next line. The ENTER key can also be used to insert one blank line—each time it is pressed—between existing lines of text.

The Space Bar can be used to slide existing text to the right in a line. Each time it is pressed, any existing text moves to the right one position.

Typeover Option. Sometimes you want to insert text and don't want any of the existing text to remain on the line. You can accomplish this by pressing the Ins key to turn on the **Typeover option**. WordPerfect now displays the message Typeover on the status line where the filename usually appears. You return to the insert option by pressing the Ins key again. What happens if you change the preceding practice sentence from "up the tree" to "down the street"? (You don't want to keep any of the "old" text in this example.) Shown below is the line *before, during,* and *after* you add the new phrase in typeover mode.

Before:

```
The black cat ran up the tree.
```

During:

```
The black cat ran do the tree.
The black cat ran do the tree.
The black cat ran dowthe tree.
The black cat ran downhe tree.
```

After:

```
The black cat ran down the street._
```

The ENTER key inserts blank lines in a document in either mode. Remember, you can delete hard carriage returns by pressing the Del key when the cursor is positioned on a blank line.

You'll quickly become accustomed to the differences in the two modes and begin to favor one over the other. The option that you use most is a matter of personal choice.

Deleting Text

WordPerfect allows you to delete text one character at a time, one word at a time, part of a word at a time, part of a line at a time, a line at a time, and the rest of a page. Look before you delete. WordPerfect is somewhat forgiving with the Delete commands, because deleted text from only the last three Delete commands can be restored using the Undelete command. The Undelete feature will be discussed after the Delete commands.

Deleting One Character at a Time. WordPerfect provides two commands for deleting material one character at a time. The Del key deletes the character at the cursor position, and the BACKSPACE key deletes the character to the left of the cursor position.

The following example illustrates the use of the Del key. The cursor is placed under the *t* of *cat,* and the Del key is pressed. At once, only the *ca* remains, and the cursor now appears under the blank between *ca* and *ran.*

Before:

```
The black cat ran down the street.
```

After:

```
The black ca_ran down the street.
```

The second example illustrates the use of the BACKSPACE key in deleting text. The cursor is positioned under the *t* of *cat*, the BACKSPACE key is pressed. Only the *ct* remains, and the cursor still appears (as before) beneath the *t*.

Before:

```
The black cat ran down the street.
```

After:

```
The black ct ran down the street.
```

All text is moved to the left automatically as characters are deleted.

Role of Codes When Deleting Characters. As mentioned previously, WordPerfect embeds special codes in text to tell the monitor how to display text, to tell the printer how text is to be printed, and to accomplish any number of other special tasks. When you are deleting text one character at a time and one of these special codes is encountered, WordPerfect responds with a message such as

```
Delete [name of code]? (Y/N)N
```

To delete this code, enter a Y. If you want to leave the embedded code, simply press N or ENTER.

Rejoining a Split Paragraph. The Del command can be used to rejoin a split paragraph. A split paragraph occurs when you inadvertently press ENTER and insert one or more hard carriage returns. In the example below, two hard carriage returns are embedded after the word *for.* To delete them requires that you first position the cursor one space to the right of *for* and then press the Del key twice. The paragraph is now rejoined:

Before:

```
    A file is a collection of related information in
the form of data or of instructions for _


manipulating that information. In other words, files
can be either data files or program files. You keep
track of files
```

After:

```
    A file is a collection of related information in
the form of data or of instructions for manipulating
```

```
that information. In other words, files can be either
data files or program files. You keep track of files
```

Deleting One Word at a Time. WordPerfect allows you to delete one word at a time. Simply position the cursor beneath any character of a word and press Ctrl + BACKSPACE. This deletes the entire word and any trailing space to the next word. WordPerfect automatically closes up the text in the line.

In the example below, the word *ran* is deleted. The cursor is placed beneath the *r*. The Ctrl + BACKSPACE command is issued. The cursor is now located beneath the *d* of *down*.

Before:

```
The black cat ran down the street.
```

After:

```
The black cat down the street.
```

Deleting Part of a Word. WordPerfect also allows you to delete the right- or left-hand portion of a word. The Home, Del command sequence is used to delete any characters in a word to the right of the cursor. In the example that follows, the characters *ack* of the word *black,* along with the trailing blank, are deleted. The cursor is first placed beneath the *a,* and then the Home, Del command is issued.

Before:

```
The black cat ran down the street.
```

After:

```
The blcat ran down the street.
```

The Home, BACKSPACE command sequence deletes any characters in a word to the left of the cursor. In the example that follows, the characters *bl* of the word *black* are deleted. The cursor is first placed beneath the *a,* and then the Home, BACKSPACE command is issued.

Before:

```
The black cat ran down the street.
```

After:

```
The ack cat ran down the street.
```

Deleting a Line or a Portion of a Line. You use the Ctrl + End command to delete the rest of a line (and any embedded codes) to the right of the cursor or to delete an entire line.

The example that follows illustrates the deletion of text from the cursor position to the end of the line via the Ctrl + End command sequence. The portion of the sentence beginning with the word *ran* will be deleted when the cursor is positioned beneath the *r* and the Ctrl + End command is issued.

Before:

```
The black cat ran down the street.
```

After:

```
The black cat _
```

The Ctrl + End command deletes an entire line of text when the cursor is at the beginning of the line. If the line is part of a paragraph and contains a **soft carriage return** (automatically placed within the document by the word wrap feature), the text is moved up one line, replacing the deleted line. When a line that contains a hard carriage return (inserted by pressing ENTER) is deleted, a blank line (holding the carriage return) remains. The carriage return itself must be deleted by pressing the Del key.

In the next example, the second line is to be deleted. The cursor must be placed at the beginning of the second line. Then the Ctrl + End command is issued. Only the first and third lines of text remain, and the second line is now blank (containing only the hard carriage return). After pressing the Del key, the text is re-formed.

Before:

```
The black cat ran down the street.
It was chased by a big dog.
The cat ran up a tree to escape.
```

After:

```
The black cat ran down the street.
The cat ran up a tree to escape.
```

Deleting to the End of the Page. WordPerfect allows you to delete text from the cursor position to the end of the current page by issuing the Ctrl + PgDn key sequence. Both codes and text are deleted. When the Ctrl + PgDn command is issued, the following message appears on the status line of your screen:

```
Delete Remainder of Page (Y/N)N
```

Enter a Y to delete the text, or if you change your mind, choose the default N by pressing ENTER.

Summary of Delete Commands

Del	Deletes character at cursor
BACKSPACE	Deletes character to left of cursor
Ctrl + BACKSPACE	Deletes the word at the cursor location
Home, Del	Deletes portion of a word from cursor location to end of word
Home, BACKSPACE	Deletes portion of a word from cursor location to the beginning of word
Ctrl + End	Deletes to the end of the line
Ctrl + PgDn	Deletes to the end of the page

Restoring Deleted Text

WordPerfect saves the last three pieces of text that have been deleted. A deletion, in this sense, is any group of characters that is erased between two moves of the cursor. There is no limit to the number of characters in any of these three deletions, and any of the delete commands are included.

When you want to retrieve deleted text, you first move the cursor to the location where you want the text reinserted; then press the F1 (Cancel/Undelete) key to display the retrieve menu:

```
Undelete: 1 Restore; 2 Show Previous Deletion: 0
```

The last piece of text deleted is now highlighted in your document at the cursor location. If this is the correct piece of text, press the 1 key; otherwise, press the 2 key to display the previous deleted text, and so on. The 0 cancels the operation.

Remember, the location of your cursor plays an important role in the text restoration process. If you suddenly realize that the cursor is not at the proper location, press the 0 or ENTER key to end this restore session.

Enter the following sentence: *The black cat ran up the street*. Now, delete the word *black* and the word *the*. Position the cursor under the *c* of *cat*. Now press the Cancel/Undelete (F1) key. The undelete menu is displayed:

```
Undelete: 1 Restore; 2 Show Previous Deletion: 0
```

The word *the* (the last word to be deleted) is highlighted. Tell WordPerfect to show the previous deletion by pressing the 2 key. The word *black* (highlighted) now appears in the appropriate location. To restore this word, simply press the 1 key.

Line Spacing

5.0   Up to this point we have used only single spacing. For readability, however, you may want to double- or even triple-space a document. WordPerfect provides this ability through the Line (SHIFT + F8) command. Once you enter this command, the following menu appears in the status line:

```
1 2 Tabs; 3 Margins; 4 Spacing; 5 Hyphenation; 6 Align Char: 0
```

The 4 key indicates the current spacing with a message/prompt such as

```
[Spacing Set]1
```

Enter a new number to change the spacing: 2 for double spacing and 3 for triple spacing. Once you enter the appropriate value and press ENTER, the entire document is re-formed to this new spacing—except for areas in which you have previously entered other Spacing commands.

It is important to note that when you issue the Spacing command, a code is embedded within the text at the cursor location to tell WordPerfect how to display and print the text. Only the text following the cursor is affected by the spacing command; if you want the entire document respaced, be sure to position the cursor at the beginning of the document.

Likewise, once the spacing for the entire document has been changed, a portion (for example, a paragraph) can be spaced differently by moving the cursor to the desired paragraph and resetting the spacing. The rest of the document is now re-formed to the new spacing. You next position the cursor at the beginning of the next paragraph and issue a spacing command to return to the previous spacing. The document now has the first portion and the last portion with one spacing and the middle portion with another.

 Try the Spacing command on the INPUT1 file that you created earlier. Load it into RAM (making certain that the cursor is at the beginning of the document); then issue the Line (SHIFT + F8) command and enter a 2 to switch to double spacing. Below is a partial listing of the file after the Spacing command has been executed. The margins may be different from yours.

```
A file is a collection of related information in the

form of data or of instructions for manipulating that

information. In other words, files can be either data

files or program files. You keep track of files on a
```

Issue the Save (F10) command to save the re-formed INPUT1 file.

Printing the Document

5.0   You are now ready to print your INPUT1 document. WordPerfect enables you to print a file that resides either in RAM or on disk; you are not required to save the file to disk before you can print. The Print command is evoked by the SHIFT + F7 keystrokes. Once the Print command has been given, the following menu is displayed:

```
1 Full Text; 2 Page; 3 Options; 4 Printer Control; 5 Type-through; 6 Preview; 0
```

To begin the print operation depress the 1 key. After the * Please Wait * message is displayed on the screen, your document will be printed. Notice that the text on your screen has a ragged right-hand margin and that the printed text has a smooth right-hand margin (**right-justification**). This smooth right-hand margin is one of the print defaults of WordPerfect. We'll see later how to turn this off.

A printed document (see Figure 6.9) appears as a result of a number of WordPerfect defaults. Some are the following: All margins are one inch, there are fifty-four printable lines of text per page, all documents are single-spaced, and pica pitch (ten characters per inch) is in effect. How to change these print defaults will be discussed in a later chapter.

Chapter Review

Word processing involves entering, saving, changing, and printing documents and written correspondence. Computerized word processing, which greatly eases this process, has undergone a revolution from difficult-to-use programs for mainframe computers, through large, specialized, and expensive dedicated word processing systems using minicomputers, to the inexpensive, adaptable, and easy-to-use word processing software packages for microcomputers that have appeared in the last decade. These systems have made computerized word processing affordable for just about anyone who has the need.

A large number of such packages are on the market. One of the most popular is WordPerfect, which comes with Speller/Thesaurus, Merge, and Math capabilities. These features provide a comprehensive word processing software system.

Figure 6.9
WordPerfect preset print
default.

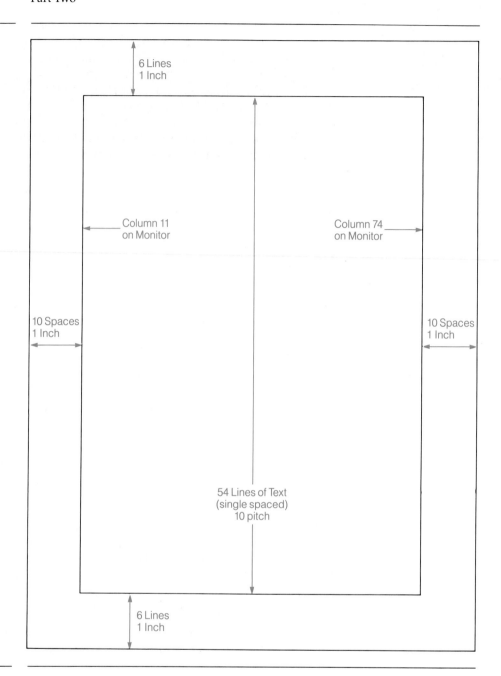

6 Lines
1 Inch

Column 11
on Monitor

Column 74
on Monitor

10 Spaces
1 Inch

10 Spaces
1 Inch

54 Lines of Text
(single spaced)
10 pitch

6 Lines
1 Inch

WordPerfect is a command-driven word processing package. These commands involve using the function keys alone or in conjunction with the Ctrl, SHIFT, and Alt keys. When you start WordPerfect, you first see a clear screen with a status line, which contains information about the location of the cursor and also provides an area for displaying prompts or menus to the user.

The area above this status line is called the entry window. Twenty-four line "chunks" of text that are being entered or edited are displayed in this window.

Cursor movement commands allow you to move the cursor in the document. The simple, horizontal, and vertical cursor movement commands provide you with flexibility in moving around a document.

Editing is the process of making changes to an existing document. Changes can be made in insert or typeover mode. Insert moves existing text to the right. Typeover simply replaces existing characters with new characters. Other editing commands include commands for deleting text, breaking paragraphs, and changing the line spacing.

Key Terms and Concepts

constant information
cursor movement
data entry window
dedicated word processor
deleting text
desktop publishing
hard page break
hard return
Insert option
line editor
line spacing
mag typewriter
Merge
orphan
re-form

revision
right-justification
soft carriage return
soft page break
Speller
stand-alone word processor
status line
text window
Thesaurus
Typeover option
variable data
virtual-file allocation
widow
WordPerfect
word wrap

Chapter Quiz

Multiple Choice

1. Which of the following is not used for word processing?
   a. Line editor
   b. Typewriter
   c. Dedicated word processor
   d. Microcomputer with WordStar
   e. All of these are used for word processing.
   f. None of these is used for word processing.

2. Which of the following statements about WordPerfect is(are) false?
   a. It was originally developed for the CP/M operating system.
   b. It allows a document to be as large as the amount of available RAM.
   c. It is a tremendously popular word processing package.
   d. It requires that you store a document before you can print it.
   e. All of the above statements are true.

3. Which of the following statements is true?
   a. WordPerfect is used for entering, editing, and printing documents.
   b. WordPerfect can be used for generating synonyms.
   c. The Merge allows you to personalize a "form" letter.
   d. All of the above statements are true.

4. Select the following WordPerfect command(s) that affect one word at a time:
   a. Left arrow
   b. —
   c. Ctrl + BACKSPACE
   d. Ctrl + End
   e. Ctrl + Right arrow
   f. Ctrl + Left arrow

5. Which of the following is not typically contained on the status line?
   a. File name
   b. Page number
   c. Amount of available RAM
   d. Line number

True/False

6. Word processing can be accomplished with either a typewriter or a computer.

7. When using word processing software, you must first carefully plan how your document is going to appear.

8. WordPerfect limits document size to the amount of available RAM memory.

9. A command-driven word processing package forces you to have the menu on the screen at all times.

10. The ENTER/RETURN key is pressed at the end of each line in a paragraph.

Answers

1. e 2. b and c 3. d 4. c, e, and f 5. c 6. t 7. f 8. f 9. f 10. f

Exercises

1. Define or describe each of the following:
   a. virtual-file allocation   e. status line
   b. word wrap   f. page break
   c. hard carriage return

2. List the three types (levels) of computers that have had word processing developed for them.
   a.

   b.

   c.

3. A _____ allows you to change only one line at a time.

4. A computerized word processing software package allows you to create a document without much prior planning. This process is called _____ _____ at the keyboard.

5. _____ word processors are minicomputers that perform only word processing.

6. Word processing software for _____ has resulted in much lower priced word processing systems.

7. _____ file word processing packages allow you to have a file as large as the amount of available storage on your disk.

8. The feature that automatically moves a word that will not fit on the current line down to the next line is called _____.

9. The _____ key is pressed only at the end of a paragraph.

10. The line at the bottom of the data entry window is called the _____ _____ line.

11. _____ movement commands move the cursor over the text.

12. The line of dashes (--------) in a document is called a _____ .

13. A(n) _____ line occurs when the first line of a new paragraph appears by itself at the bottom of the page.

14. A(n) _____ line occurs when the last line of a paragraph appears by itself at the top of the page.

15. The WordPerfect command _____ _____ is used to re-form a paragraph so that it will fit in new margins.

16. The WordPerfect command _____ is used to delete one line of text from a document.

17. The WordPerfect command _____ is used to change the line spacing in a document.

18. The _____ command is used to exit WordPerfect properly.

19. WordPerfect uses a line of _____ to indicate hard page break.

20. The Go to a specific page command is _____ .

Computer Exercises

1. Following is a summary of the cursor movement and scrolling commands covered in this chapter. Load the file called BOOKEXER and practice using these commands with that file.

Cursor Movement Commands

Simple Movement Commands

Up arrow	Moves the cursor up one line
Right arrow	Moves the cursor to the right one position
Left arrow	Moves the cursor to the left one position
Down arrow	Moves the cursor down one line

Horizontal Movement Commands

Ctrl + Right arrow	Moves the cursor to the first character of the next word to the right
Ctrl + Left arrow	Moves the cursor to the first character of the next word to the left
End	Moves the cursor to the end of the line
Home, Right arrow	Moves the cursor to the right edge of the current screen
Home, Left arrow	Moves the cursor to the left edge of the current screen
Home, Home, Right arrow	Moves the cursor to the extreme right edge of the document

Home, Home, Left arrow	Moves the cursor to the extreme left edge of the document

Vertical Movement Commands

Home, Home, Up arrow	Moves the cursor to the beginning of the file
Home, Home, Down arrow	Moves the cursor to the end of the file
PgUp	Moves the cursor to the first line of text on the previous page
PgDn	Moves the cursor to the first line of text on the next page
–	Moves the cursor up one screen (twenty-four lines) of text
+	Moves the cursor down one screen (twenty-four lines) of text

 When you have finished experimenting with the commands, change the spacing to double spacing and reform the document. When this is finished, issue a F10 command and save the file.

Other Commands

TAB	Move cursor to the next tab stop.
Save (F10)	Save the file to disk.
Exit (F7)	Leave WordPerfect or clear screen.
Retrieve (SHIFT + F10)	Retrieve a file from disk for editing.
List Files (F5)	List the files in this directory or on this disk.
Hard Page Break (Ctrl + ENTER)	Insert a page break that will always appear at this position.
Typeover (Ins)	Switch between insert or typeover mode.
Undelete/Cancel (F1)	Restore text from the last three delete commands or cancel a command.
Print (SHIFT + F7)	Direct the output to the printer.

2. Below is a summary of delete commands covered in this chapter.

Summary of Delete Commands

Del	Deletes character at cursor
BACKSPACE	Deletes character to left of cursor
Ctrl + BACKSPACE	Deletes the word at the cursor location
Home, Del	Deletes portion of a word from the cursor to the end of the word
Home, BACKSPACE	Deletes portion of a word from the cursor to the beginning of the word
Ctrl + End	Deletes to the end of the line
Ctrl + PgDn	Deletes to the end of the page

Clear the WordPerfect screen and retrieve the file called EXER1B. Delete the underlined words in the paragraphs below that are found in the file. Correct any spelling errors. Notice that as you make changes to the text it automatically re-forms as you use cursor movement commands.

One of the <u>most</u> important aspcts of <u>microcomputer</u> computerized word proacessing is that the original document does not not haav to be carefooly planed. Ruther, wurdprocessing allows yu to compose a dokumint wile sitting ut the keybord.

Line editors were the originul word processors. <u>They wer really grat for secretaries</u> Line editors are software development aids that allow a pgraogrammer to make a change(s) to a line of program code.

From the days that line editurs weere made avaluble to komputer programers for making unline chaunges to pograms, usirs huv been taking adnatage of the kompooter to perform basic editing functions such as <u>making hay while entering data, to perform basic editing functions such moving, copying</u>, inserting, and deleting tixt.

Save the file back to disk using the Save (F10) command.

 3. Clear the WordPerfect screen. Enter the following text and save it in a file called CHGEX3. After you have saved the text, print it out. Once the file is saved, review the printout and make any necessary corrections. Insert a hard page break after the first paragraph. Exit WordPerfect.

One major difference among microcomputer-based word processing packages is how they handle document size. Some packages limit the size of the document to the amount of available RAM, making ten to sixteen pages the effective maximum. In contrast, what could be referred to as a "virtual-file" allocation word processing package contains only about six to twelve pages of a document in RAM at one time, saving the remainder on disk.

A later trend in microcomputer word processing software was the introduction of supplementary writing aid programs such as spelling checkers, grammar checkers, and thesauruses. Some word processing software comes with these options built in, while others make them installable at additional cost. Add-on programs compatible with many word processing packages are also available from third-party vendors.

Chapter
7

Intermediate Word Processing with WordPerfect

After completing this chapter, you should be able to:

Discuss the various ways to save a file

Discuss how WordPerfect creates and saves a file

Discuss the various print options that are available in the Print Options Menu

Discuss the margin commands

Discuss the Center command

Discuss the tab commands

Discuss how to handle blocks of text using Bold, Underline, Center, Redline and Strikeout, Cut, and Copy commands

Discuss how various previously covered commands can be used with marked blocks of text

Discuss some new commands that require the block feature

Discuss the Move command

Discuss the Search command

Discuss the Replace command

In the previous chapter, you were introduced to a number of WordPerfect commands for entering and editing text. This chapter considers how Word-Perfect saves files and how it uses various files. In addition, the Print command and its various options are covered in detail. **(If you are using the student version of WordPerfect, Print features marked in this book with an asterisk are not available.)** Other commands include the margin commands, centering, and tabs.

This chapter also introduces you to the block commands, the Search command, and the rectangle feature of WordPerfect. The Block command enables you to mark off parts of a document and perform various tasks with them, such as move them to another position within the document, perform special formatting, and cut or copy the marked text. The Search command allows you to locate text and replace it with other text.

Saving Files

If you remember, WordPerfect has two methods for **saving files**, the first of which involves simply issuing the **Save command** (F10). This command can be issued any time, and it is especially important that you use the command periodically (every ten minutes or after entering about two pages of text) when you are entering or editing large documents. If you do not save your documents periodically and a power failure occurs, all of your work is lost.

The second way to save a file is to first issue the **Exit** (F7) **command**. Then WordPerfect asks whether or not you want to save the file. You might not want to save a "quick and dirty" document (such as a letter) to disk, or you may have messed up a document to the point that you do not want to save it. In such a situation, all you have to do is respond N to the prompt; WordPerfect then asks if you want to exit WordPerfect. If you respond with an N, the screen, along with RAM memory, is cleared, and you can start a new document.

The reason WordPerfect can exit from a document without affecting the original file is that when you retrieve a document, it is loaded into a temporary file. Thus, when you make changes in the document, you are really entering data and making changes only in that temporary file. When you save your document, this temporary file becomes permanent, replacing the old file on disk.

Backup Feature of WordPerfect

As you might have gleaned from the preceding discussion, saving your file to disk from time to time can save you a tremendous amount of mental distress and work if something goes wrong. WordPerfect provides two *automatic* backup facilities to aid those people who have difficulty in remembering to save documents to disk periodically.

The backup feature of WordPerfect is not a default option. You must specifically tell WordPerfect that you want to use a backup option. Invoking the backup option as well as changing defaults is accomplished by using the WordPerfect **Set-up Menu**. (See Appendix A about how to activate the backup feature of WordPerfect.)

How WordPerfect Handles Files with the Backup

Let's examine how WordPerfect handles these various files when it is performing tasks for you. The three basic files that WordPerfect deals with are (1) your original document file, which is stored on disk; (2) a backup of the file which it automatically creates (after the first file is originally created and then edited and saved); and (3) a temporary file that it creates and to which any changes are made.

The Original File

WordPerfect *never* works directly on a file when you are editing, although it does work directly on a file that you are creating. During editing, WordPerfect creates a temporary file which it uses to store the original file, to enter new text, and to edit the text. When you issue a Save command, WordPerfect stores the edited data from the temporary file in the original file that you retrieved from disk when you started this session.

Backup Files

After telling WordPerfect to create **backup files**, you will find files on your disk with the .BK! extension. These are the backup files that were automatically created for you by WordPerfect. The content of the backup file is identical to the content of your document before the last save command was executed. So the automatic backup is always one generation old. At the end of a session, the backup file is automatically deleted when you save your document and is replaced with the original file. (Refer to Appendix A.)

Because a backup file is not directly available to WordPerfect, it cannot be edited or accessed by a Retrieve command. Instead, the backup file can be copied to another file or renamed, without the .BK! file extension. After that it can be retrieved with the Retrieve command.

Temporary Files

When you open a file to make changes to an existing document, you are not really entering data or making changes to that file; instead, WordPerfect is placing the data and/or copying the data into a **temporary file** in RAM. If there is not enough room in RAM, the extra text is placed in an overflow file on the WordPerfect disk called {WP}.TV1. This explains why you can totally "botch" your file and exit, knowing that your original file remains safe and unbotched.

How WordPerfect Handles Files

It is important that you understand exactly how WordPerfect creates and saves a file and then lets you retrieve and edit it. In the discussion that follows, assume that you want to create a file called REPORT.

Creating Files

To create the file called REPORT, you type the text for the document. This text is actually placed in the temporary file in RAM. After you save the file to disk using the name REPORT, the REPORT file appears in the disk directory.

Editing Files

When you retrieve the REPORT file for editing, WordPerfect opens a temporary file in RAM and copies into it the original file from disk. If there is not enough room in RAM, it places any overflow into the {WP}.TV1 file on the WordPerfect disk. Any changes that you now make to the REPORT text are actually made to the temporary file in RAM.

When you finish the session and issue a Save command, the REPORT file on disk becomes the backup file REPORT.BK!, the temporary RAM file becomes the new REPORT file, and both files are saved.

Using Files Subsequently

You now have two files: REPORT, which is the latest version, and RE-PORT.BK!, which was the version that existed before your latest WordPerfect session.

What happens at your next session? Again, you retrieve REPORT, and a temporary RAM file is created to receive any changes you make. Then, when you save the newly edited file at the end of this session, the (now two-generation-old) REPORT.BK! file is automatically deleted. The old RE-PORT file becomes the new REPORT.BK! file, and the newly edited RAM file becomes the new REPORT file.

Suppose, though, that you somehow manage to destroy seventy percent of your current document, but you discover this before you issue the Save command. What do you do? Since the destruction has occurred only to the temporary RAM file, not to the original, you simply issue the Exit (F7) command without saving. The original file remains unchanged.

However, suppose that you do not realize before you issue the Save command that you have destroyed seventy percent of the file. Then you open the file later to make additional changes and discover the damage. What do you do then? At this point many people panic and destroy everything; the one thing you do not want to do is issue any type of save command, because that will destroy the only remaining good copy of the file—the .BK! file.

To restore the file, issue the Exit (F7) command but do *not* save the file. You get a clear screen. Now, issue the List Files (F5) command, move the bar to REPORT.BK!, take option 8, and copy the REPORT.BK! to a file called TEST. You can now retrieve TEST.

Why not name the REPORT.BK! file REPORT? If you did and you subsequently destroyed this copy of the file, you would no longer have a source of backup. By giving the new copy the name TEST, you still have the file REPORT.BK! as backup if anything happens to the new file.

Even though WordPerfect automatically provides a backup, you should periodically copy important files to another disk. This protects you when you have one of those days when absolutely nothing goes right and you destroy not only your original but also the backup copy in a moment of panic.

When you check to make certain that a disk has enough room for a document, remember that you are possibly dealing with *three* disk files. There must be enough room on the disk for the original file, the temporary file overflow (if needed), and the backup file.

WordPerfect Codes

When you are entering text and issuing commands that tell WordPerfect what to do with that text, WordPerfect is embedding **codes** ("invisible" commands) that tell the monitor how to display text, tell the printer how to print text, or tell WordPerfect the characteristics of the text so that it can properly handle it. These codes are not usually visible to the user but, at times, can make their presence known. For instance, if you press the Right arrow key to move the cursor from one character to the next, but the cursor does not move, then you probably have come across one of these hidden codes. They can be made visible by moving the cursor to the area of the problem and entering the **Reveal Codes command** (Alt + F3). WordPerfect then displays a screen like that in Figure 7.1.

Notice that your screen is divided into two parts. The top portion contains the actual text (three lines above and three lines below the current cursor location); the bottom portion contains the text and any embedded codes. They are separated by the status line and a line of triangles (representing the **tab stops**). The codes are surrounded by brackets [ ].

Figure 7.1
The Reveal Codes screen
used to find embedded codes
within text.

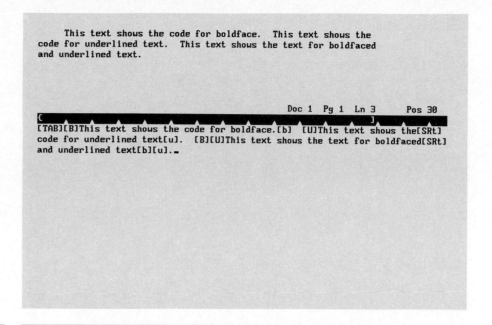

In this example, soft carriage return [SRt] codes can be seen at the ends of two lines on the bottom portion of the screen. The hard carriage return at the end of the paragraph is visible as [HRt]. Finally, there is a [TAB] code at the beginning of the paragraph, used to mark the paragraph indent command.

You can edit the codes in the lower portion of the Reveal Codes screen just as you would edit regular text. For example, assume that you want to get rid of the [TAB] code. First move the cursor one space to the left of [TAB] and then press the Del key. [TAB] disappears, and that line of text moves flush left. The Reveal Codes screen disappears and you are returned to your text when you press the ENTER key.

The Reveal Codes function provides easy editing of the often rather complex instructions that you have issued. You'll be making extensive use of these codes and, no doubt, of the ability that WordPerfect gives you to edit codes and correct errors.

Printing Files

5.0

Chapter 6 shows you how to print a file with what could be termed the "quick and dirty" method, which assumes that fanfold paper is mounted in the printer. However, you may want your output printed on good single-sheet rag bond paper, or you may not want to print the complete document, or you may want to print only "this" page, or you may want to print the page number on every page. The Print (SHIFT + F7) command enables you to give complete printing instructions to WordPerfect.

When WordPerfect prints a file, the character position that is number ten on the screen automatically becomes position number ten on the paper. Thus WordPerfect automatically gives you a ten-character left-hand margin on the printed output. This margin can be expanded simply by positioning the paper farther to the left in the printer.

After the Print (SHIFT + F7) command is issued, the Print Menu appears at the bottom of your screen:

1 Full Text; 2 Page; 3 Options; 4 Printer Control; 5 Type-Thru 6 Preview: 0

Figure 7.2
Print Options Menu.

```
Change Print Options Temporarily

    1 - Printer Number           1

    2 - Number of Copies         1

    3 - Binding Width (1/10 in.)  0












Selection: 0
```

5.0 **NOTE** WordPerfect usually provides the zero (0) entry of a menu as the default. If you press the ENTER key, you are usually returned to the document or to a higher-order menu.

> *Option 1.* This "quick and dirty" method takes note of all print options that you have previously defined and prints the entire document accordingly.
>
> *Option 2.* Only the page on which the cursor resides is printed.
>
> **Option 3.* The Print Options Menu (see Figure 7.2) is displayed. This menu enables you to specify (1) which printer to use and (2) the number of copies you want. The binding width option (3) tells WordPerfect how much space you want it to add (in tenths-of-an-inch) to the left-hand margin for binding the finished document. Any printer changes specified here are temporary and will only affect this print operation.
>
> **Option 4.* The Printer Control Menu (see Figure 7.3) is displayed. The numeric entries of this menu let you select the printer to be used and the font, number of copies, and binding width. The alphabetic commands control the order and priority of print jobs and let you start and stop a print job.

Option 1 of the Printer Control Menu displays the same menu as option 3 of the Print Menu (see Figure 7.2), but the Print Options Menu option is temporary whereas this option remains in effect until you exit WordPerfect.

Option 2 of the Printer Control Menu lists the printers for which Word-Perfect has been configured. Up to six printers can be specified, and the "active" printer (the one to which output is directed) is changed with this option. It is important that you have the correct printer specified; otherwise, strange characters will appear on your paper, or the entire document may (maddeningly) be printed with only one line on a sheet of paper.

*Option 3 of the Printer Control Menu enables you to add or change printers. The library of printer drivers must be present on the WordPerfect program drive before new printers can be added.

Figure 7.3
Printer Control Menu.

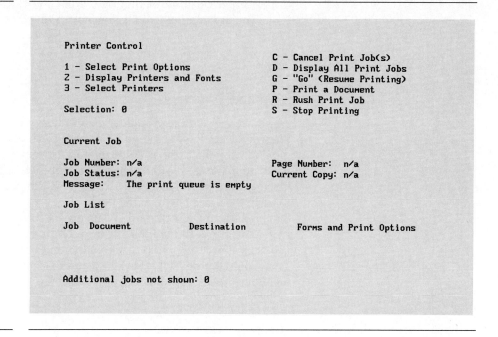

```
Printer Control

                                      C - Cancel Print Job(s)
  1 - Select Print Options            D - Display All Print Jobs
  2 - Display Printers and Fonts      G - "Go" (Resume Printing)
  3 - Select Printers                 P - Print a Document
                                      R - Rush Print Job
  Selection: 0                        S - Stop Printing


Current Job

  Job Number:  n/a                    Page Number:  n/a
  Job Status:  n/a                    Current Copy: n/a
  Message:     The print queue is empty

  Job List

  Job  Document            Destination          Forms and Print Options




  Additional jobs not shown: 0
```

5.0   WordPerfect has its own queuing method for printing files. A **queue** is another word for a waiting line. Many word processing packages can accept printing instructions for only one document at a time, and before instructions for printing another document can be given, the previous document must be finished. WordPerfect creates a queue (waiting line) of documents to be printed. If printing of the current document is not finished, a document for which you issue the Print command is placed at the end of the waiting line. Any documents nearer the front of the line must print before WordPerfect prints the added document.

On the Printer Control Menu, the alphabetic commands, the current job information, and the job list either contain information about print jobs or control how jobs in the queue are handled. Novices with WordPerfect usually need to be concerned only about the Stop Printing and Resume Printing commands.

Printing multiple files requires that you issue multiple Print commands. For each Print command issued, WordPerfect prompts you for the name of the file and adds that to the queue for later printing. After all of the files that you want to print have been added to the queue, simply press the ENTER key.

When you exit this menu, you are returned to the document rather than to the Print Menu. Returning to the Print Menu requires that you again press the ENTER key.

After you have made any changes via the print menu at the bottom of the screen (other than issuing a Print command through option 4), simply press the 1 key to print the document. Provided that the changes made were appropriate, your document should print correctly.

Special Text Entry Commands

Center Command

WordPerfect, like most other word processing packages, automatically centers a line of text via the **Center** (SHIFT + F6) **command**. Assume that you want to center the heading "Section Title" on the screen. Position the cursor to the desired line, enter the Center (SHIFT + F6) command (the cursor now moves to the center position of the line), enter the text, and press the ENTER key when you are finished. You'll then have a line that looks like this:

```
             Section Title
```

Boldface Command

The **Boldface command** results in dark, heavy print like that appearing here in the words "boldface command." Boldface characters are generated in ways that depend on your printer. Letter-quality printers usually type each letter four times to achieve the dark character; dot-matrix printers usually make two, three, or four passes over the text, moving the print head slightly on each pass to fill in the areas between the dots.

Boldfacing is achieved by using the Bold (F6) command: The first F6 command turns the boldface feature on; the second turns it off. To **boldface this text**, enter the Bold (F6) command and type the words **boldface this text**. Then enter another Bold (F6) command to terminate the boldface printing. The text now appears as boldface print on screen.

Underline Command

The **Underline command** underscores every character of text as well as the spaces between words.

Letter-quality printers usually print a letter and then its underscore, without moving the print head. Dot-matrix printers usually make two passes: the first to print the text and the second to print the underscore.

The type of monitor that you have also determines how these characters are displayed to the screen. A monochrome monitor displays the underline, but a color monitor may show "highlighted" text.

Underlining is achieved by using the Underline (F8) command: The first F8 command turns the underline feature on; the second turns it off. To <u>underline this text</u>, enter the Underline (F8) command and type the words <u>underline this text</u>. Then enter another Underline (F8) command to terminate the underlining. The text now appears as underlined print on screen.

Flush Right Command

The **Flush Right command** aligns text against the right-hand margin. It can be used to position dates, headings, and other pieces of data against the right margin. The Flush Right (Alt + F6) command, when issued, jumps the cursor to the right-hand margin. Then type the text and press the ENTER key when you are finished. An example of flush right text follows:

```
                              Fred Chalmer's Grocery Store
```

Overstrike Command

The **Overstrike command** allows you to print one character and then print another character on top of it. This enables you to place diacritical marks—accents (´ or `), circumflexes (ˆ), macrons (¯), and tildes (˜), for example—over words.

This command is achieved by pressing the Super/Subscript (SHIFT + F1) keys and selecting the Overstrike option. Next the overstrike character is entered. Although the first of the two characters does not appear on the screen, it will appear on the printout.

Assume that you want to type the Spanish phrase *Voy a pasar un año en España*, which means *I'm going to spend a year in Spain*. First type *Voy a pasar un an*, which takes the cursor one space past the character over which the tilde is to be placed. Then enter the Super/Subscript (SHIFT + F1) command, select the overstrike option, type the tilde (˜) and the text *o en Espan*, enter the Super/Subscript (SHIFT + F1), select overstrike, and type ˜a.

Your line on the screen should now look like this: `Voy a pasar un a˜o en Espa˜a`. The tildes will print over the appropriate *n*'s, even though they are not visible on the screen. To verify that they are present, issue a Reveal Codes command.

Combining Commands

Any of the commands discussed above can be combined. For example, you can have **boldfaced, underlined text** simply by turning both features on before typing the text and both features off at the desired location. The features do not have to be turned on and off in any particular order; just remember to turn them off. If you do forget, it will be quickly obvious.

You may forget which features you have turned on or off. If your text does not appear the way you want it in your document, use the Reveal Codes (Alt + F3) command. Centering codes are represented by [C] and [c], Boldface codes are [B] and [b], and Underline codes are [U] and [u]. Once the beginning code is deleted, the text on your screen returns to normal.

You can also delete codes with other edit commands. When you are deleting one character at a time and come to an embedded code, WordPerfect displays a message on the status line:

```
Delete [Bold]? N
```

The name of the code is contained between brackets, and the default is no.

Date Command

5.0 The **Date command** accesses the system date information that you entered and changes it so that it is presented in a format such as January 7, 1989. This command requires that you enter the system date manually or have a clock/calendar in your computer. The Date command, invoked via the Date (SHIFT + F5) command, displays the following menu:

```
Date: 1 Insert Text; 2 Format; 3 Insert Function: 0
```

Option 1 inserts the date at the cursor location. Option 2 allows you to build your own date format scheme and, to facilitate this process, displays the Date Format Menu in Figure 7.4. Using the options provided in the Date Format Menu, you can indicate to WordPerfect exactly how you want the date and time displayed in your document. WordPerfect does, however, place a twenty-nine-character limit on the format pattern.

Option 3, the Insert function, enables you to "date stamp" a document. Then, no matter when you print or retrieve the document, the current date and time will be inserted. For example, if you type a document on January 7, 1989 and then print it two days later, the printout will be dated January 9, 1989.

Figure 7.4
Date Format Menu.

```
Date Format

    Character    Meaning
       1         Day of the month
       2         Month (number)
       3         Month (word)
       4         Year (all four digits)
       5         Year (last two digits)
       6         Day of the week (word)
       7         Hour (24-hour clock)
       8         Hour (12-hour clock)
       9         Minute
       0         am / pm
       %         Include leading zero for numbers less than 10
                   (must directly precede number)

    Examples:  3 1, 4      = December 25, 1984
               %2/%1/5 (6) = 01/01/85 (Tuesday)
               8:90        = 10:55am

Date Format: 3 1, 4
```

Margin Commands

5.0

The WordPerfect Line Format (SHIFT + F8) command enables you to reset the right- and left-hand margins. The default margins are a left-hand margin of 10 and a right-hand margin of 74. The values may be 0 through 250. The new margins you set begin at the current cursor location; if the cursor is not at the beginning of a line, a [HRt] is inserted in the text by WordPerfect to place the margins at the beginning of a line. Once you issue the Line Format (SHIFT + F8) command and choose option 3 from the menu, the following prompt is displayed:

`[Margin Set] 10 74 to Left = _`

The first number, 10, is the current setting for the left-hand margin, and the second number, 74, is the current setting for the right-hand margin. To change the left-hand margin, enter a new value and press the ENTER key. A prompt similar to that below will appear.

`[Margin Set] 10 74 to Left = 10 Right = _`

After you enter a new value for the right-hand margin and press the ENTER key, the new margins are in effect. These margins will remain in effect until new ones are entered. To change the margins for another part of your document, position the cursor at the beginning of a new line and repeat the process. Since embedded codes are used, various margins can be used in various parts of the document without interfering with each other.

Assume that the following text (the Input1 file) is part of a document:

```
A file is a collection of related information. This
information can be in the form of data or instructions
for manipulating that information. In other words,
files can be either data files or program files. You
keep track of files on a disk by their names. Each
filename must be unique (different) from any other
filename.
```

5.0 Now suppose that you want the left-hand margin to be in column 20 and the right-hand in column 65. You position the cursor to the beginning of the line, issue the Line Format (SHIFT + F8) command, and set the margins to 20 and 65. You should see the following:

```
A file is a collection of related information.
This information can be in the form of data or
instructions for manipulating that
information. In other words, files can be
either data files or program files. You keep
track of files on a disk by their names. Each
filename must be unique (different) from any
other filename.
```

Indent

From time to time you might want to reset the left-hand margin for only a single paragraph of text. For example, it is a convention to indent a long quote five spaces into the document from the left-hand margin. This is accomplished by using the Left Indent (F4) command. The **Left Indent command** resets the left-hand margin to the next tab stop. The default tab stops occur every five spaces and operate like those on a typewriter. You have already used them in indenting the first line of a paragraph.

Assume that you want to change the left-hand margin for only the following paragraph:

```
A file is a collection of related information. This
information can be in the form of data or instructions for
manipulating that information. In other words, files can be
either data files or program files. You keep track of files
on a disk by their names.
```

To accomplish this you must perform the following tasks: first, position the cursor to the beginning of the line, issue the Left Indent (F4) command, and move the cursor to re-form the paragraph.

```
     A file is a collection of related information.
This information can be in the form of data or
instructions for manipulating that information. In
other words, files can be either data files or program
files. You keep track of files on a disk by their
names.
```

The current left-hand margin for the above paragraph is at the second tab location (column 20). To reset the left-hand margin to column 30 (the fourth tab location) requires entering the Left Indent (F4) command four times. The changed text can be seen below:

```
          A file is a collection of related
     information. This information can be in the
     form of data or instructions for manipulating
     that information. In other words, files can
     be either data files or program files. You
     keep track of files on a disk by their names.
```

L/R Indent

Occasionally, you might want to indent both the left- and right-hand margins for a single paragraph. This task involves using the **L/R Indent** (SHIFT + F4) **command**. Assume that you have the following paragraph:

```
    A file is a collection of related information. This
information can be in the form of data or instructions for
manipulating that information. In other words, files can be
either data files or program files. You keep track of files
on a disk by their names.
```

To indent both margins requires positioning the cursor at the beginning of the first line of the paragraph, issuing the L/R Margin (SHIFT + F4) command, and pressing the cursor key. The finished product can be seen below:

```
        A file is a collection of related
    information. This information can be in the form
    of data or instructions for manipulating that
    information. In other words, files can be either
    data files or program files. You keep track of
    files on a disk by their names.
```

Notice that both the left- and right-hand margins have moved inward five spaces.

Margin Release

The Margin Release (SHIFT + TAB) command moves the cursor one tab stop to the left each time you issue it; it is used to create a **hanging paragraph**, in which the first line begins at the left margin and the remaining lines are indented. It can even move the cursor beyond the current left-hand margin. Each time the command is issued, a code is inserted at the cursor location. You can issue Margin Release (SHIFT + TAB) commands until the left-most tab stop is reached. Assume that you want to edit the following paragraph from the Input1 file:

```
        A file is a collection of related information.
    This information can be in the form of data or
    instructions for manipulating that information. In
    other words, files can be either data files or
    program files. You keep track of files on a disk by
    their names.
```

If you want to create a hanging paragraph (see the following example) in which the first line begins at the current left-hand margin and the remainder of the lines are indented, you must first issue an Indent (F4) command and then issue the Margin Release (SHIFT + TAB) command. The indent ends when you press the ENTER key.

```
A file is a collection of related information. This
    information can be in the form of data or
    instructions for manipulating that information.
    In other words, files can be either data files
    or program files. You keep track of files on a
    disk by their names.
```

Tabs and Resetting Tabs

5.0

Previously, this chapter mentioned that each of the triangles beneath the status line on the Reveal Codes screen represents a tab stop. The tab stops in WordPerfect work the same way on a typewriter, except that the cursor (rather than the entire carriage) is repositioned to the next tab. The cursor is moved from one tab stop to another by pressing the TAB key.

You may want tab stops at only two or three locations, since one tab stop every five positions may be too many for a particular application. You can clear all tab stops from the ruler line below by first entering the Line Format (SHIFT + F8) command. The menu below is then displayed:

```
1 2 Tabs; 3 Margins; 4 Spacing; 5 Hyphenation; 6 Align Char: 0
```

Select option 1 or 2. WordPerfect now displays the following information about the current tab stops:

```
L....L....L....L....L....L....L....L....L....L....L....L....L....L....L....
0123456789012345678901234567890123456789012345678901234567890123456789
      20        30        40        50        60        70        8
Delete EOL (Clear tabs); Enter number (set tab); Del (clear tab);
Left; Center; Right; Decimal; .= Dot leader; Press EXIT when done.
```

Each L represents one tab stop on the ruler line, and as you can see, there is one tab stop every five positions. The menu is the two lines at the bottom. The Exit (F7) command is issued when all changes are finished.

To delete all of the tab stops, enter the Delete EOL (Ctrl + End) command. This command is usually executed before the new tab stops are entered, which cuts down on the number of TAB keystrokes. Once the Delete EOL command has been issued, only periods remain in the ruler line. You can now issue the Cancel (F1) command to return to your document, or you can create new tab stops. To create new tabs, simply move the cursor to the appropriate location and type t (tab). Assume that you have set tab stops at positions 15 and 30. Now, if you enter the two columns of text below, you will see the following:

```
         Men's           125.00
         Women's          35.00
         Boy's             5.00
         Sports          123.50
```

Notice that the columns are oriented toward alphabetic text; that is, the text aligns at the left-hand side of the column, and the numbers do not align on the decimal points.

Aligning columns of numbers is accomplished by using the **Tab Align** (Ctrl + F6) **command**. This command lines up text or numbers vertically on a character such as a decimal point. Once the tab stops have been set, position the cursor to the first line in the document, issue the Line Format (SHIFT + F8) command, and take option 6 (Align Char;). WordPerfect gives you a prompt:

```
Align char = .
```

The decimal point (period) is the default **alignment character** (therefore this command is not needed when you want to align numbers). You can change this character as often as you wish. To realign the preceding example, each line has to be entered again: Enter the information at the first tab, then position

Part Two

5.0 the cursor to the second tab by issuing the Tab Align (Ctrl + F6) command, and then enter the numeric text.

```
Men's              125.00
Women's             35.00
Boy's                5.00
Sports             123.50
```

Notice that the numbers align on the decimal point. You also may have noticed that Align char = . appears on your screen as a reminder. Typed text moves to the left until the alignment character is entered (a . in this case) or until the TAB, Tab Align, or ENTER key is pressed. Text typed after the Tab Align command is inserted normally.

Block Command

Using the Block command involves first marking the text to be included in the block and then issuing a command to tell WordPerfect what to do with the marked text.

Marking a Block of Text

A **block** of text can be any group of characters, words, sentences, paragraphs, or pages of text. Before WordPerfect can execute a command against a block of text, it must know what is contained in the block.

To mark a block, position the cursor at the beginning of the text to be included in the block and issue the Block (Alt + F4) command. The message Block on then flashes on and off in the status line. Now move the cursor to the end of the block. As you move the cursor over the text to be included in the block, the text changes to reverse video on your screen (a process many times referred to as painting).

You can use any of the pointer positioning commands to enlarge the block (or to make it smaller). For instance, the Right arrow extends the block one character at a time to the right, and the Down arrow extends the block one line at a time. After you have defined the block, you can issue any command that can use blocked text (Figure 7.5).

Using Blocks with Previously Covered WordPerfect Commands

A number of commands that have been covered previously can now be used with Block, including Boldface, Underline, Centering, and Overstrike.

Bolding, Underlining, and Centering Blocks. Have you ever forgotten to press the Bold command before you typed the text? You no doubt found that inserting the Bold command after the text was entered had no effect whatsoever. Getting the text boldfaced seemed to require you to retype the text. But there is an easier way: Mark the text as a block and then issue the Bold command.

 For example, how would you boldface the words *Stand-alone word processors* in the following example?

```
    Stand-alone word processors are computers whose
sole task is word processing.
```

You first have to position the cursor under the *S* of *Stand*. Now, issue the Block (Alt + F4) command (Block on now flashes in the status line), paint to the

Figure 7.5
WordPerfect commands with which you can use the block commands.

Bold	Replace
Center	Save
Delete	Sort
Flush Right	Spell
Mark Text	Super/Subscript
Move	Underline
Print	Upper/Lower Case (Switch key)

right four words, and issue the Bold (F6) command. The text now appears as follows:

Stand-alone word processors are computers whose sole task is word processing.

This same sequence of steps is used for underlining or centering text. If you want to both boldface and underline some text, you must first mark the text and issue one of the special feature commands. Then you must issue two GoTo (Ctrl + Home) commands to rehighlight the block of text before you issue the command for the other feature.

If you want to center a block of text, WordPerfect displays the message [Center]? (Y/N) N; simply press Y to **center block**.

Deleting Blocks of Text.   Up to now you have been able to delete text only in a rather rigid format. For instance, you can delete a character, part of a word, a word, part of a line, an entire line, or to the end of the page. With the Block command, however, you can delete any marked text by pressing the Del key. Suppose that you want to delete the last sentence in this paragraph:

In the early 1960s IBM introduced the mag typewriter, which used a magnetic tape cartridge for sequential access to documents that had been stored on the tape. This was hailed as a dramatic advance because it allowed a user not only to store and then retrieve a document, but also to make immediate insertions, deletions, and corrections on the original without having to change the entire document manually.

Performing this task requires you to position the cursor at the *T* of the word *This*, invoke the Block (Alt + F4) command, paint the text to be deleted, press the Del key, and respond Y to the prompt [Delete block]? (Y/N) N. You should see the following text:

In the early 1960s IBM introduced the mag typewriter, which used a magnetic tape cartridge for sequential access to documents that had been stored on the tape.

Save Block. Using the **Save** (F10) command with a **block** saves it to a separate file on disk. It is convenient to place an often used portion of a document on disk and retrieve it at the cursor location whenever it is needed.

Saving a block requires the following steps: (1) marking the text via the Block command; (2) issuing the Save (F10) command, at which time Word-Perfect responds with the Block Name:_ prompt; (3) enter the name you want for the file and press the ENTER key; (if the file already exists, the message Replace (filename)? (Y/N) N̲ appears); and (4) issue another Block (Alt + F4) command to turn off the block feature.

You may want to add a block of text to the end of a disk file via the Append feature of WordPerfect. Issue the Move (Ctrl + F4) command after the text has been marked and select the Append option. When WordPerfect displays the Append to: _ prompt, enter the name of the file to which you want the text added and press the ENTER key. The text is then added to the end of the specified file.

Print Block. The **Print Block command** lets you print a portion of a document that is longer than the current page, while not printing the entire document. To print a block of text, mark the block and then issue the Print (SHIFT + F7) command. WordPerfect now displays the prompt Print Block? (Y/N) N̲. Press the Y key to start printing. Turn off the block feature with another Block (Alt + F4) command.

New WordPerfect Commands That Use the Block Feature

5.0 *Move.* The **Move command** provides you with great flexibility in cutting or copying chunks of text and moving them from one place in a document to another. It also allows you to delete the original text—which can consist of a sentence, paragraph, page, or block of text. Using the Move feature of WordPerfect is a two-step process that first requires you to indicate which text is to be moved or copied and then to indicate where the text is to be copied or moved. The Move command, invoked by pressing the Ctrl + F4 keys, displays the following menu (only the Move part is of interest now):

Move 1 Sentence; 2 Paragraph; 3 Page;Retrieve 4 Column; 5 Text; 6 Rectangle:0̲

The Move (Ctrl + F4) command executes at the current cursor location for a sentence, paragraph, or page of text. After you have indicated to WordPerfect the amount of text that you want moved by pressing the appropriate key, the affected text changes to reverse video on your screen and the following menu is displayed:

1 Cut; 2 Copy; 3 Delete: 0̲

The **Cut option** removes the highlighted text from your document and places it in a temporary file.

The **Copy option** leaves the original text in your document but also copies it to a temporary file. The highlighted text in the document returns to regular video and is left unchanged. The copy feature works much as a duplicating machine might, leaving the original intact.

The **Delete option** removes the marked text from your document without saving it to a temporary file (this text can, however, be restored via the Undelete command).

5.0

After you have indicated a cut or copy operation to WordPerfect, you must now position the cursor to the place in your document that you want to receive the block. You again issue the Move (Ctrl + F4) command and this time use the Retrieve portion of the menu. To perform a regular retrieve, press the 5 key, and the marked text is copied, beginning at the cursor.

The following example shows how the Move command (Cut option) is used to move the second sentence to a new position behind the third sentence. The original order is as follows:

```
    This is the first sentence. This is the second
sentence. This is the third sentence. This is the
fourth sentence.
```

To mark the second sentence, position the cursor anywhere in that sentence. Enter the Move (Ctrl + F4) command, and the Move menu is displayed at the bottom of your screen. Select the *Sentence* option (placing the sentence in reverse video), and then take the *Cut* option. The highlighted text is now deleted from the paragraph and saved to a temporary file, and WordPerfect knows what type of operation is to be performed. After re-forming, the text appears like that below:

```
    This is the first sentence. This is the third
sentence. This is the fourth sentence.
```

You now move the cursor to the *T* at the beginning of the fourth sentence. Issue the Move (Ctrl + F4) command and select the *Text* option from the menu. The text is now moved and should look like the following:

```
    This is the first sentence. This is the third
sentence. This is the second sentence. This is the
fourth sentence.
```

The next example shows the use of the *Copy* option of the move feature. The same sequence of commands are executed except that the *Copy* option instead of *Cut* is selected.

Before:

```
    This is the first sentence. This is the second
sentence. This is the third sentence. This is the
fourth sentence.
```

After:

```
This is the first sentence. This is the second
sentence. This is the third sentence. This is the
second sentence. This is the fourth sentence.
```

Rectangular or Columnar Blocks. You may want to move a **rectangular** or columnar **block** of text in a highlighted area, rather than the entire text. The regular block move transfers all of the text, from the beginning of the marked area to the end of the marked area, no matter how wide the line or lines happen to be. For rectangular blocks, however, you specify the width of the text block to be moved. The beginning and ending locations of the cursor

5.0   determine the upper left-hand and lower right-hand corners of the rectangular block of text.

Position the cursor at the upper left-hand corner of the text to be moved. Enter the Block (Alt + F4) command, paint the text (the entire lines are painted), and place the cursor in the lower right-hand corner. Even though the entire text looks as though it is painted, subsequent commands will reduce the area.

After you have painted the block, issue the Move (Ctrl + F4) command and select the Cut/Copy Rectangle option from the following menu:

```
1 Cut Block; 2 Copy Block; 3 Append; 4 Cut/Copy Column; 5 Cut/Copy Rectangle:0
```

The area of text denoted by the original upper left-hand and lower right-hand cursor positions is now highlighted on the screen, and the following menu is displayed.

```
1 Cut; 2 Copy; 3 Delete: 0
```

Only the highlighted text is affected by your choice of operation. All text outside the highlighted area remains unchanged. When you retrieve the text, be sure to use the Rectangle option; otherwise, the text from the last *regular* Move command will be restored to the cursor location rather than the text from the rectangle just marked. Also make certain that there is enough room in the area that is to receive the block. If there is not enough room, existing text will be moved to the right, and the document will look like a mess.

In the next example, assume that Col1 is to be moved to the right of Col2:

```
Col1       Col2
Col1       Col2
Col1       Col2
Col1       Col2
```

In this case, the cursor must be moved under the C of the first Col1, and the Block (Alt + F4) command is issued. The blocked area is now extended to include the last Col1. Notice that all of the lines in both columns appear in reverse video. Issue the Move (Ctrl + F4) command, and select the Cut/Copy Rectangle option. Now only Col1 is highlighted. Tell WordPerfect to execute a Cut command. Your screen will show the following:

```
Col2
Col2
Col2
Col2
```

Now position your cursor at the location that you want to place the text—in this case, to the right of Col2. Enter the Move (Ctrl + F4) command and select the Rectangle option. The following will then appear on your screen:

```
Col2       Col1
Col2       Col1
Col2       Col1
Col2       Col1
```

5.0 *Superscript/Subscript.* The **superscript** or **subscript** options allow you to print a character or a block of characters ⅓ to ½ line above (superscript) or below (subscript) the current line of text. This WordPerfect feature is useful in both the scientific and the academic environments.

These commands may not be supported (that is, the output cannot always be predicted) on dot-matrix printers, but they are usually supported by most letter-quality printers. The Super/Subscript (SHIFT + F1) command displays the menu:

```
1 Superscript; 2 Subscript; 3 Overstrike; 4 Adv Up; 5 Adv Dn; 6 Adv Ln: 0
```

To subscript or superscript a character, simply make the appropriate selection and enter the character. If you want to subscript or superscript more than one character, first mark the text with the Block (Alt + F4) command; then issue the Super/Subscript (SHIFT + F1) command and tell WordPerfect whether or not the text is a Superscript or Subscript.

Superscripts and subscripts do not appear on the screen. To verify how the text will print, you must issue the Reveal Codes (Alt + F3) command.

Simple subscript:	A_2
Simple superscript:	2^2
Multiple subscript:	$Chromium_{Dioxide}$
Multiple superscript:	A^{23}

Case Conversion. Have you ever entered text only to find later that the characters are all in upper case? The only way to correct this has been to erase the text and retype it. WordPerfect has a **case conversion** feature that allows you to correct such errors. For example, suppose that the following text appears in your document:

```
STAND-ALONE WORD PROCESSORS ARE COMPUTERS WHOSE
SOLE TASK IS WORD PROCESSING.
```

To convert the text to lower case, use the Switch (SHIFT + F3) command, which displays the following menu:

```
Block: 1 Uppercase; 2 Lowercase: 0
```

The steps involved in switching the case of the characters are (1) block the text that you want to change (beginning with the *T* of *STAND*), (2) issue the Switch (SHIFT + F3) command, (3) select the appropriate option (lowercase), and (4) turn off the Block command with another Block (Alt + F4). The text should now appear like the following:

```
Stand-alone word processors are computers whose
sole task is word processing.
```

Disk Full Errors

If you fail to check the status of your diskette, you may receive a `Disk full - Strike any key to continue` message when you try to save a file. This means that there is not enough disk space for both the text and the changes that you've made to the file. If you leave WordPerfect at this point, you lose the entire document and any editing that you have done. The most important thing to remember is not to panic!

If you are using the backup option of WordPerfect, remember that not only is your original file on disk, but the BK! backup file is on disk as well. Use the List Files (F5) command and delete any unwanted files from your disk to make room (BK! files are likely candidates). Then try the Save command again.

Unless your document is extremely large, it resides completely in RAM; so another option is to replace the data diskette with a blank, formatted diskette and save the file. In a hard disk environment, save the file to a diskette in drive A.

If a disk full message appears while you are printing, you must print the file from Printer Control or List Files. You cannot print from the screen via a Print command, since this option creates a separate print file on disk and, as a result, takes up even more disk space.

Search and Replace Commands

The Search and the Replace commands enable you to locate (or to locate and change or delete) a word or phrase wherever it appears in your document. The primary limitation is that the phrase can be no longer than 60 characters.

Search

The **Search** (F2) **command** allows you to locate the first and all subsequent occurrences of a word or phrase. When the command is entered, the cursor moves to the right of the first occurrence of the word or phrase.

First, the Search (F2) command is issued to WordPerfect, which responds with the prompt ⟶ Srch _ in the status line. Then you enter the desired word or phrase (up to sixty characters) and issue the Search (F2) command to initiate the search. The cursor will appear to the right of the first occurrence of the desired text in the file; to find the next occurrence, enter the Search (F2) command twice. The search operation has ended when you see the * Not Found * message displayed in the status line.

The regular search command is a forward search. This means that the search starts at the current cursor location and moves toward the end of the file. You can also use a reverse search, which starts at the current cursor location and moves toward the beginning of the file. The **Reverse Search** (SHIFT + F2) **command** works in the same manner as the forward search.

In addition to finding desired text, the Search command can also find embedded codes. For example, if you are interested in finding the next hard carriage return, simply press the ENTER key to obtain the prompt ⟶Srch_. This time the search string is [HRt].

You can also return the cursor to the position it had before the last Search (F2) command was executed by entering the GoTo (Ctrl + Home) command twice.

Replace

The **Replace** (Alt + F2) **command** is used to find a word or phrase and then replace it with another word or phrase. When the Replace command is initially entered, you receive the prompt w/Confirm? (Y/N) N. If you respond N, every occurrence of the old word or phrase is replaced automatically. If you respond Y, WordPerfect will stop at each occurrence of the found word or phrase and prompt you with Confirm? (Y/N) N. Y replaces and moves to the next occurrence; N leaves the old word or phrase and moves the cursor to the next occurrence.

The search and replace process is as follows. Press Alt + F2. Answer the confirm prompt. Then WordPerfect prompts ⇢ Srch: _. Enter the text that you want to replace and press the F2 key. You are prompted: Replace with: _. Type the replacement text and again press the F2 key. The search and replacement process proceeds as you indicated, either automatically for all of the document that follows the initial cursor location or with confirmation after each find.

The search and replace character strings can also be embedded codes.

Some clarification is needed for special types of operations. If you want to find complete words such as *dog* rather than *dogma* or *dogmatic*, you must enter spaces before and after the word you want. Lower-case characters can be used to search for either upper-case or lower-case characters, whereas upper-case characters can be used to search only for upper-case characters.

Wild Card. The WordPerfect Search/Replace command also enables you to search for special character strings using the so-called **wild-card technique**. For example, assume that you want to locate any word in your document that begins with the character *d* and has *g* as the third character. Such a search would locate words such as dig, dog, dug, dogmatic, and digital. To issue such a Search/Replace command requires that you enter the following criteria at the Search/Replace prompt:

d^V^Xo

The ^V (Ctrl + V) indicates to WordPerfect that it should get ready for a special command. The ^X (Ctrl + X) tells WordPerfect that this character can be any character. Your Search/Replace command can now proceed.

Chapter Review

WordPerfect provides you with two ways to save a file to disk: (1) Save the document to disk and return to the same document and (2) issue the Exit command, which allows you to save the document and either exit Word-Perfect or clear RAM and the screen.

When you are editing a file using WordPerfect, you are not dealing directly with that file but rather with a temporary file that WordPerfect has copied from the original file. Temporary files residing in RAM and, if necessary, an overflow file provide for good error handling. If you really mess up the file that you are editing, all that you have to do is issue the Exit (F7) command. The original file remains intact, and the messed-up file is erased.

Another handy feature provided by WordPerfect is the backup file, identified by its .BK! file extension. The backup file holds the contents of the file that existed on disk before the last save was executed. If you mistakenly erase your original file, you can recreate it by using the Copy command contained in the List Files feature.

The Print command (SHIFT + F7) allows you to print the file currently in memory. This command provides you with tremendous flexibility in how a document is printed. For instance, it allows you to determine which printer to use as well as how many copies of the document to print. You can print only the page where the cursor is located. You also have control over which files to be printed, cancelled, or rushed to printing.

WordPerfect provides the ability to center, boldface, or underline text. A code at the beginning of the text turns the selected feature on, and another code at the end of the text turns it off. Two or more of these codes can be used together.

WordPerfect also provides you with a number of commands that are used for resetting margins. (1) The Line Format (SHIFT + F8) command enables you to reset both the left- and right-hand margins. (2) The Left Indent (F4) command resets the left-hand margin to the next tab stop only for the current paragraph. (3) The L/R Indent (SHIFT + F4) indents both the left- and right-hand margins of a paragraph by one tab stop.

A number of ways to position or rearrange data are provided by Word-Perfect. (1) The Center (SHIFT + F6) command automatically centers any text between the right- and left-hand margins. (2) You can use the TAB (SHIFT + F8, 1) command to set tab stops in a way that is similar to tab stops on a typewriter or for creating columns of data. (3) Tabs can be set for text or numeric data. (4) The Tab Align (Ctrl + F6) command is used to align the decimal points of numerals.

Block commands enable you to mark an area of text in a document and then to move the marked material, copy it to another position in the document, delete it, save it to a file on disk, or change its display characteristics.

Before you can issue block manipulation commands, you must mark the desired text by issuing a Block (Alt + F4) command and paint with cursor movement commands. A block can consist of one or more characters, words, phrases, sentences, paragraphs, or pages.

The Move (Ctrl + F4) command enables you to select a default option of sentence, paragraph, or page to be cut or copied from your document. The desired entity to be cut or copied is determined by the cursor location. If you want to manipulate a unit of text other than a sentence, paragraph, or page, you can first mark the text as a block and then issue the Move command.

Most block commands, which are used to mark chunks of text for later manipulation, are of little use when you want to move only a column or rectangle of text. Before you can move a rectangle of text that is embedded in other text, you must paint the desired text by placing the cursor at the beginning of the text, issuing the Block (Alt + F4) command, and moving the cursor to the end of the desired text; then you issue the Move (Ctrl + F4) command. All of the text between the beginning and ending cursor locations is painted. After you tell WordPerfect that you want to execute the Rectangle or Column option, the rectangle or column of text is all that is painted—and cut or copied.

One of the real benefits of using block commands is that they allow you to store often-used pieces of text to disk for later use. This feature saves you a tremendous amount of time retyping the same text from one document to the next. Unless you use the **Append command**, data that you save to an existing file will destroy the data that is currently in that file and replace it with the marked block of text.

WordPerfect provides you with two ways to find text: The first merely locates text, which can then be manipulated or changed in any way you please; the second finds the text and replaces it with other text that you have previously chosen.

From time to time you will forget to check on the available amount of disk storage remaining on a diskette. When you try to save a file and receive a Disk Full error, you can use the List Files (F5) command to delete unwanted files to free enough disk space to save your file; or you can replace the full disk with a blank, formatted disk and save to the new disk, since the temporary file is usually completely contained in RAM.

Key Terms and Concepts

alignment character
Append command
backup files
block
Boldface command
case conversion
center block
Center command
codes
Copy option
Cut option
Date command
Delete option
Exit command
Flush Right command
hanging paragraph
Left Indent command
L/R Indent command
margin commands
Move command

Overstrike command
queue
Print Block command
rectangular block
Replace command
Reveal Codes command
Reverse Search command
Save Block command
Save command
saving files
Search command
Set-up Menu
subscript
superscript
Tab Align command
tab stops
temporary file
Underline command
wild-card technique

Chapter Quiz

Multiple Choice

1. The key sequence for the Print command is:
   a. F7
   b. SHIFT + F7
   c. F10
   d. SHIFT + F10

2. Which of the following commands is not a save command?
   a. Exit
   b. Save
   c. Terminate
   d. All of the above are Save commands.

3. Which of the following is *not* a Margin command?
   a. Line Format
   b. Left Indent
   c. Center
   d. L/R Indent
   e. All of the above are Margin commands.

4. Which of the following is an option provided in the Print Options Menu?
   a. Change the printer number.
   b. Print only this page.
   c. Print the entire document.
   d. Change the font.
   e. All of the above are print options.

5. Which of the following commands must be reissued for each paragraph from Line Format when resetting margins?
   a. Center
   b. Left Indent

   c. Tabs
   d. L/R Indent
   e. Margins

6. Which of the following commands is not used for a marked block of text?
   a. Save
   b. Delete
   c. Center
   d. Indent
   e. All of the above commands are for blocks.

7. Which of the following commands are used for rectangle block mode?
   a. Sentence
   b. Paragraph
   c. Page
   d. Retrieve
   e. None of the above

8. Which of the following statements is false?
   a. When a block is moved into the current document, it is placed at the current cursor location.
   b. When a block is written to disk, it is placed at the end of existing data in that file via the Append option.
   c. The cut option causes two copies of the blocked text to appear in a document.
   d. All of the above statements are true.
   e. Both a and c are false.

9. Which of the following commands is extremely important when you receive a disk full error message?
   a. Block delete
   b. List Files
   c. Copy
   d. Cut
   e. None of these are really important.

10. Which of the following is not an option in the Replace command of WordPerfect?
   a. Search backward.
   b. Ignore upper and lower case.
   c. Search only for whole words.
   d. Search for embedded codes.
   e. All of the above are options for the find and replace.

True/False

11. If you really mess up a file that you are editing, the safest thing to do is to issue the Exit command.

12. A major problem in using tabs is that the decimal points do *not* easily align in a straight column.

13. A .BK! file can be changed by using the Retrieve command.

14. A block must be marked before you are allowed to use the Append command.

15. The first files to delete after you receive a disk full error message are the files with a .BK! extension.

Answers

1. b 2. c 3. c 4. a 5. b and d 6. d 7. e 8. c 9. b 10. e 11. t 12. f 13. f 14. t 15. t

Exercises

1. Define or describe each of the following:
   a. temporary files
   b. backup files
   c. Tab Align command
   d. L/R Indent
   e. tab stops
   f. block
   g. superscript/subscript
   h. block write

2. The _____ command saves the file and exits WordPerfect.

3. The _____ command saves the file and returns you to your document.

4. The _____ command allows you to abandon a file being created or edited.

5. When you are working with large documents, it is a good idea to use the _____ command to avoid retyping them.

6. Special effects commands require you to issue _____ special effects commands.

7. You can interrupt any file that is printing by issuing the _____ command.

8. If you are editing an existing file, the file that you are actually making the changes to is the _____ file in RAM.

9. The _____ command as well as the Print command allows you to initiate the printing of a file.

10. The _____ or _____ command is used for setting the right-hand margin.

11. The _____, _____, or _____ command is used for temporarily resetting the left-hand margin.

12. The _____ command is used to underline text.

13. The _____ command is used to center text.

14. The _____ command is used to clear all tabs from the ruler line.

15. The _____ symbol is used to set a tab.

16. The _____ command is used to move the cursor to the next tab location.

17. The _____ command is used to indicate that numeric information is being entered and directs WordPerfect to align the numbers on the decimal point.

18. The _____ command is used to reset the left-hand margin of only one paragraph.

19. Backup files automatically created by WordPerfect have a _____ file extension.

20. Pressing the _____ key cancels any WordPerfect command.

21. The command to mark a block of text is _____.

22. A block of text is painted using _____ commands.

23. The command that creates a copy of a block of text is the _____ option of the Move command.

24. The command that moves a block of text to another location in a document and erases the original is the _____ option of the Move command.

25. The command that is used to place WordPerfect in column block mode is the _____ option of the Move command.

26. The block delete command is _____.

27. The command that is used to print text slightly above or below the current line is the _____ command.

28. The command that is used to record a marked block of text to disk is _____.

29. The command used to display the directory of your default disk is _____.

30. The command used to delete files while you are still entering or editing text in your document can be found as part of the _____ option.

31. Unless a block of text is first marked, only _____ character at a time is affected by the Super/Subscript command.

32. The Block command is accessed by pressing the _____ keys.

33. The Search forward command is accessed by the _____ keys, and the Search backward command is accessed via the _____ keys.

34. The _____ command is used to move back to the prior cursor location in a Search command.

Computer Exercises

Below is a summary of the WordPerfect commands covered in this chapter.

Save (F10)	Save a file to disk.
Exit (F7)	Save a file and either exit or start a new document.
Cancel (F1)	Undelete/Cancel command to restore deleted text or cancel a command.
Reveal Codes (Alt + F3)	Examine embedded codes that appear in a document.
Print (SHIFT + F7)	Print a document.
Center (SHIFT + F6)	Center text on a line.
Boldface (F6)	Boldface text.

Underline (F8)	Underline text.
Flush Right (Alt + F6)	Right-justify text on a line.
Date (SHIFT + F5)	Convert the system date to various formats.
Line Format (SHIFT + F8)	Set margins and tabs.
Indent (F4)	Indent the left-hand margin for a single paragraph.
L/R Indent (SHIFT + F4)	Indent both the left- and the right-hand margins for a single paragraph.
Margin Release (SHIFT + TAB)	Create a paragraph with a hanging indent.
Tab Align (Ctrl + F6)	Align numbers by a decimal point or text by any character.
Block (Alt + F4)	Mark a block of text in a document for use with another command.
Move (Ctrl + F4)	This command is used to cut or copy a unit or block of text to another position in a document.
Super/Subscript (SHIFT + F1)	This command prints superscripts and subscripts and spaces them properly.
Case Conversion (SHIFT + F3)	This command converts upper case to lower case and vice versa.
Search (F2)	Finds specified character strings in a document.
Replace (Alt + F2)	Finds and replaces character strings in a document.

1. Load the BOOKEXER file and then use the Exit command to clear the screen. Remain in WordPerfect.

2. Print out the entire BOOKEXER file, which is on the disk.

3. Print out only page 2 from the BOOKEXER file.

4. Using the BOOKEXER file, perform the following tasks:
   a. Position the cursor to the beginning of the file. Set the left-hand margin to 15. Set the right-hand margin to 65.
   b. Position the cursor to the second paragraph of page 2. Indent the left-hand margin two tab stops.
   c. Reset the left margin to 10 and the right margin to 74. Re-form the document.
   d. Position the cursor to the second paragraph of page 3. Issue a L/R Indent command and re-form the paragraph.
   e. Use the Reveal Codes command to examine the beginning of the second paragraph of page 2. Note the [Indent] codes that have been embedded by WordPerfect.

      Set the document for double spacing. Reset the margins to 25 for the left-hand and 60 for the right-hand.

      Use the Exit (F7) command to quit the document. Do not save the file.
   f. Reload the BOOKEXER file. Notice that the file is still in its original condition.

Position the cursor to the second paragraph. Issue two Indent commands. Notice how the document has changed. Use the Exit command to quit the file.

5. Clear the screen. Use the Center command to center the following text on separate lines.

WordPerfect

Using Centering Commands

Using Decimal Tabs

Delete all tab stops from the ruler line. Enter tab stops in columns 25 and 50. Enter the two columns of numbers below using only the Tab command; then, using the Tab Align command, reenter the columns of numeric data. The first column is placed with the decimal in position 25. The second column is placed with the decimal in position 50.

```
12.76          7.65
134.50         .531
1,965.75       10.50
12.65          9.6
```

Notice how the decimals are now lined up. Save the file under the name CH7EX5.

6. Type the following letter using the conventions that appear below:
   a. Use the Center command to center the text *Acme Computing*.
   b. Use the Flush Right command to enter today's date.
   c. Store the document to a file called CH7EX6.

```
                    Acme Computing


                                     January 15, 1989


Laura Miller
2117 Emerson
Bloomington, Il 61701


Dear Ms. Miller:

Thank you for submitting your application and
resume for the applications programmer/analyst
positions advertised for our data processing
department. After all of the resumes have been
screened we shall contact you about your status.
This process is expected to be completed by
March 25, 1989.

Sincerely yours,


Lucky Luciano
```

7. Enter the following table. Before starting, however, remove all tab stops and create new tab stops at positions 15, 40, 55, and 70. Use the Boldface and Center commands to center the title data, and use the Tab Align command for entering the numeric data. Note how the numbers move to the left until the decimal points are entered and afterward move to the right.

Ed's Microcomputer Shop
Projected Profit Margin

	1	2	3
Sales	325,000.00	347,588.00	371,745.00
Cost	195,000.00	208,553.00	223,047.00
Margin	130,000.00	139,035.00	148,698.00

Save the document to disk using the name CH7EX7.

8. Retrieve the following list of names and addresses from the disk file called CH7EX8. Using the block commands, arrange the names and addresses in alphabetical order by last name. Save the sorted names and addresses to a file called CH7EX8A.

Reza Ghorbani
4033 N. Wolcott
Chicago, Il. 60712

Debbie Acklin
408 E. Monroe
Bloomington, Il. 61701

Harvey Posio
1013 Hillcrest
San Diego, Ca. 94307

Juan Decesario
1214 Flores
Miami, Fl. 12562

Arthur Adams
115 Ginger Creek Ct.
Bloomington, Il. 61701

Russell Davis
707 Vale St.
Bloomington, Il. 61701

Fred Ficek
1215 Tamarack
Normal, Il. 61761

9. Using the same file of names and addresses, arrange them in order by ZIP Code. Save the sorted names and addresses to a file called CH7EX9.

10. Retrieve the file called BOOKEXER. Using the block commands, save the first paragraph to a file called CH7EX10A. Save the third paragraph to a file called CH7EX10B. Append the fifth paragraph to the CH7EX10A file. Quit the BOOKEXER file using the Exit command without saving the file. Open a file called EXER4C. Retrieve the PARAx files that you just created in order. Be sure to position the cursor to the end of a "chunk" of text, before retrieving the next file. Using the file delete commands, delete the PARAx intermediate files. Save the file.

11. Retrieve the BOOKEXER file. Locate each occurrence of the term *word processing*. Locate each occurrence of the word *program* and change it to *pogrom*. Experiment with other find commands using the BOOKEXER document. When you are finished, exit without saving the file.

12. Retrieve the CH7EX12 file. Using the Rectangle command, place the second column of names beneath the first. Save the finished product to a file called CH7EX12A.

```
Reza Ghorbani        Debbie Acklin
Harvey Posio         Juan Decesario
Arthur Adams         Russell Davis
Fred Ficek
```

13. Clear the screen and retrieve the CH7EX13 file. You will find text like that listed below. Using the Block command, perform each indicated task on the appropriate line. For example, the first line "Center this text" should be centered using the Block + Center commands. Save your work to the file CH7EX13A. Print out the entire file.

```
Center this text
Center and boldface this text
Center and underline this text
Center, boldface, and underline this text
Underline this text
Boldface and underline this text
Right justify this text
Underline and right justify this text
Delete this text
CONVERT THIS TEXT TO LOWER CASE
convert this text to upper case
```

Use the block command to print only the first five lines of the changed CH7EX13 file.

14. For this project, assume you are working for a newspaper that has received a guest column on purchasing microcomputers. Your editor feels that the work submitted by the writer is good, but is too long for a single column. Instead of presenting it as one column, it is to be broken into two parts.

The editor has made a number of changes to the article for you to incorporate to prepare it for publication. The various editorial changes have been indicated on the document. (The document follows these instructions.)

In indicating the changes to be made, your editor has used a number of common editing marks on the document. The marks along with their meanings are listed below:

       ⌗   Start a new paragraph at this location.

       ℓ   Delete this character(s).

       ∧   Insert a character(s) at this location.

       ⌣   Close up (get rid of unnecessary blank lines or blanks between characters).

       ]⌈   Place the enclosed text at this location in the document.

Because the author originally prepared the article using Word-Perfect, it was submitted on diskette. The name of the WordPerfect file is EDTARTCL. You are to open the EDTARTCL file and make changes indicated on the written document. Notice that the paragraphs are numbered on the written document but they are not numbered on the diskette file.

The paragraphs were numbered to make the instructions here easier for you to follow:

1. Change the original title to "Planning for a Computer Purchase." Center this title.

2. Delete the numbers in the first paragraph, and make certain that there is only one space between the remaining words.

3. Delete the various section headings within the document.

4. In paragraph 2, make the term *micro processor* one word.

5. In paragraph 3, move the marked sentence to the end of the paragraph.

6. In paragraph 4, move the marked sentence to the end of the paragraph.

7. In paragraph 5, insert the comma at the indicated location.

8. In paragraph 6, insert an apostrophe.

9. In paragraph 8, move the word *also.*

10. Block paragraphs 1 through 10 and save them to a file named `COLUMN1`. Issue a Block delete command to delete the first part of the file.

The file `COLUMN1` now contains the first microcomputer column for the newspaper. You are now ready to make changes to the remainder of the document, which will be used for the second guest column.

11. The title for the second column is "Computer Stores Need Close Study." Be sure to center the title.

12. Insert the following introductory paragraph:

    ```
    Although home computers are readily available
    at a number of different types of outlets, con-
    sumers should be careful where they shop.
    ```

13. Delete the numbers from paragraph 11. Make certain that there is only one space between the words.

14. In paragraph 14, change *they are* to *he is.*

15. In paragraph 15, create a new paragraph beginning with the phrase *Used computer stores.*

16. Delete the numbers from paragraph 16, and make certain that there is only one space between words. Change the indicated upper-case letters to lower-case.

17. In paragraph 17, change the capital *D* to a lower-case letter.

18. In paragraph 18, replace the % characters with the words *per cent.*

19. Move paragraph 19 to the indicated position following paragraph 20.

20. Before paragraph 21, insert the following paragraph:

    ```
    Generic software packages combine word pro-
    cessing, spreadsheets and data base on one
    diskette. These packages may not have the capa-
    bilities of larger, more expensive packages but
    are ideal for home use. This software, along
    with documentation, typically costs less
    than $30.
    ```

21. In paragraph 21, change the word *ten* to the numeral *10.* Then delete the word *also.*

22. Block off this document and store it to a file named COLUMN2. Once COLUMN2 has been created on diskette, the existing file is no longer needed. You may now issue an Exit command without saving the file. This leaves the original EDTARTCL file unchanged.

23. Print out the COLUMN1 and COLUMN2 files.

Purchasing a Home Computer

1.   This is the time of year when many consumers begin to ponder the idea of purchasing a microcomputer for home use. Over the past few years microcomputers have become fairly popular Christmas gifts either for children in the family or for the gift givers, themselves. A consumer must consider a number of important factors when purchasing a microcomputer for the home. The factors to consider are the 1. the typical computer system, 2. compatibility, 3. special requirements, 4. where to purchase the hardware, 5. software considerations, and 6. hidden costs.

~~Typical Computer System Components~~

2.   The typical microcomputer system is composed of four parts: 1. the microcomputer itself, 2. a storage device, 3. an input device, and 4. an output device. The microcomputer contains the internal memory (that portion available to the user), the actual micro processor, as well as all of the electronic components that are needed to make the device work.

3.   The storage device for the computer is used to store programs (pre-written instructions to the computer) and data. The common storage medium used today is the diskette. While some computers use cassette tape, this medium is extremely slow. There are a variety of sizes and types of diskettes on the market. Purchase only that type of disk for your system. All that you have to know is whether or not your computer is capable of recording on only one or both sides of the disk, and also whether or not the disk is single or double density (determines the quality of the surface).

4. The typical input device for giving instructions to the machine is the keyboard. No two manufacturers seem to make the same type of keyboard. Nothing can be more discouraging than getting a machine that has the keys arranged in a manner that is different from what you are accustomed to using. Before you buy a machine, make sure that you try out the keyboard.

5. The typical output devices are the monitor and the printer. The monitor is used to output any prompts to the user and for nonessential output that does not have to be saved. When you need information that has to be saved for historical purposes the printer is used. There are a number of different types of monitors and printers. The cost of these devices is typically directly related to the quality of output. The higher the quality of output the higher the cost of the device.

Issue of Compatibility

6. The most important issue to address when purchasing a microcomputer is compatibility. Different manufacturers' computers cannot always easily talk with other manufacturers computers. You must, therefore, decide exactly why you want the machine. At this in time, many consumers' purchasing decision becomes clouded by brand loyalty to some particular machine. This is the worst way to make a purchasing decision.

7. For example, do you want to be able to take work home from the office with you? In this case, your machine choice is limited to the types of microcomputer you use at the workplace. You do not want to purchase a computer that cannot read information generated by a machine at the office. If you are purchasing a machine for your children, will it be able to communicate with the childrens' computers at school? This allows a child to do work at home and then take it to school. Compatibility with school can be extremely important, since many schools have programs that also allow students to check out software for use at home.

~~Special Requirements~~[2]

8.   Today's microcomputers, unlike mini computers or mainframe computers, do not have

      many limitations on where they can be placed. They do not have any heat/cooling

      or humidity requirements that cannot be easily met within the typical household.

      Electrical requirements are minimal. You do not need a dedicated electrical circuit

      for the computer, but you do not (also) want to put it on the same circuit that

      already has the refrigerator, microwave oven, toaster, and coffee maker on it. A

      voltage/surge protector or lightning arrestor is also a good idea. Voltage/surge

      devices can cost upwards to $100, but a good lightning arrestor (all that is really

      needed) can be purchased for under $10 at your local hardware store.

9.   A combination of high heat along with high humidity might also cause the disk unit

      to develop problems in finding data or programs during the summer months.   This

      can many times be remedied simply by turning on the dehumidifier.

10.   The primary problem that many consumers encounter is that of static electricity.

      Static electricity, especially during the winter months, can be a real killer for the

      electronic circuits and chips inside the computer, printers, and disk drives. This

      problem can easily be resolved by purchasing an anti static mat, button, or other

      device you can touch to discharge any built up static electricity before you touch

      your computer.

] Computer Stores Need Close Study [

~~Where to Purchase the Machine~~ [2]

11.   There are basically four different sources of computers: 1. local computer specialty

      shops, 2. department/discount stores, 3. mail order, and 4. used computers.

12.   Local computer specialty shops have been the primary source of computers for

      consumers. These shops typically have trained technicians and sales staff who are able to handle most problems that arise. Service on the hardware is usually performed right on the premises. These shops also typically service only those machines that they sell.

13. Another source of computers is the department/discount store. Exceptional buys are possible at these locations. The sales staff, depending on the store, may or may not be able to answer questions about the capability of the hardware and/or software. Service on the machines is usually at a location other than where the machine was sold.

14. Mail order shops also offer tremendous buys on hardware. The consumer is expected to be fairly knowledgeable about the equipment that ~~they are~~ _he is_ purchasing. If something goes wrong with the equipment, it must be sent back for repair. Depending on the store, this can take anywhere from one to four weeks. Any questions that you have after the equipment arrives will usually cost a long-distance telephone call.

15. Used computers can be an exceptional buy. If the system is purchased from an individual, you may be able to purchase a complete system containing both hardware and software for a fraction of the original price. One disadvantage in purchasing such equipment is that the warranty has probably expired, and it might be hard to get the equipment repaired if anything goes wrong with it. Another disadvantage is that the owner of the equipment may have unreasonable expectations about the value of the old equipment. Used computer stores are also opening in large cities. These stores even provide a warranty for equipment purchased there.

Software Considerations

16. Once the machine has been purchased, the software (preprogrammed instructions) that allow you to make the machine useful must also be purchased. If you purchase name brand software, you can easily invest one half the cost of the hardware for programs. There are five basic sources for software: 1. Computer/Department

stores, 2. Mail order, 3. Public domain software, 4. Shareware, 5. Generic software.

17.   Computer and Department stores typically stock many types of software packages. It is not uncommon to see literally hundreds of different packages in a store. Unless you purchase a name brand or very popular software, the sales staff may not be able to answer questions that you have about its use. Also expect to pay close to full price for the programs.

18.   Mail-order vendors often have anywhere from a 20% to 60% discount on software prices. With such discounts, however, expect almost no support from the vendor. If you have any problems, you will probably have to call the manufacturer of the software.

19.   Shareware is software that is typically available free to you for evaluation purposes. If, after using the software, you decide that you want to keep it, instructions are included that direct you where to send in a nominal charge for complete documentation and rights to enhancements or updates. A number of good wordprocessing and spreadsheet packages are available in this manner.

20.   Public domain software is software that is available to you for about the cost of a disk. It is not pirated software, but software that has been designed and developed possibly for a user's group. While some of this software is excellent, much of it is a waste. Many times this type of software is available to you by joining a local users group for a specific type of computer.

Hidden Costs

21.   There are a number of costs that are not always considered in making the decision to purchase a home computer. These hidden costs include: software, disks, ribbon,

paper, and computer furniture. Software, as mentioned previously, can easily reach one half the cost of the hardware. Other costs include disks. It is not uncommon for a microcomputer owner to have a number of boxes of disks. This cost mounts up when the disks can cost anywhere from $10 to $50 a box (ten). If you purchase a printer, you will have to buy ribbon and paper for it also. You may also find that the table that you had originally planned to use with the computer is not the right height (typically typing or 27 inches from the floor), so you may need to purchase a computer table.

Summary

22. Examining the various options available for purchasing the computer as well as software for the home allows a consumer to make a more intelligent purchase decision. Facing the issues of compatibility and special needs of microcomputers allows you to be more comfortable about using the computer as well as allowing you to more completely enjoy the computer later on.

Chapter

8

Advanced Word
Processing with
WordPerfect

Chapter Objectives

After completing this chapter, you should be able to:

Discuss the Speller

Discuss WordPerfect's special Page Format commands

Discuss WordPerfect's special Print Format commands

This chapter introduces you to WordPerfect's Speller, as well as to format/print features that enable you to accent your document with page headings, footings, and a justified or ragged right-hand margin, among other things.

WordPerfect has productivity aids that make the user's life easier: Speller, which checks the spelling in WordPerfect documents; Thesaurus, which helps you find synonyms and antonyms for words; and Merge, which (among other things) enables you to generate personalized form letters. The examples presented use the README.WP file found in the training version of WordPerfect.

Speller

The Speller option helps you proofread a document that is on your screen by comparing every word in your document with the words contained in the Speller dictionary. Some of its features are the following:

1. A main dictionary that contains over 100,000 words
2. The ability to create and maintain a personal dictionary for words that are not in the main dictionary
3. The ability to tell WordPerfect to check spelling on a page, in a block, or in an entire document
4. The ability to find alternative spellings by a phonetic or pattern look-up
5. The detection of double occurrences of words (for example, the the) and to delete the second occurrence
6. The automatic detection of nonwords in the document
7. A count of the words that were checked for spelling in the text

WordPerfect contains a number of files that it uses in performing a spelling check:

Main Dictionary (LEX.WP). The LEX.WP file contains the main dictionary file, which holds over 100,000 words. The dictionary, because of its large size, is on a separate disk.

Supplemental Dictionary ({WP}LEX.SUP). The {WP}LEX.SUP file contains words that you add to WordPerfect's dictionary, such as words that are related to your specific discipline. It can be edited directly by WordPerfect. It is this file that is searched if WordPerfect cannot find a word in the main dictionary file.

Speller Utility (SPELL.EX). The SPELL.EX file contains the utility that allows you to modify and create dictionaries by adding, correcting, or deleting words.

The method of starting Speller depends on whether you are using a diskette-based or a hard disk–based computer.

Diskette-Based System. When you are using a diskette-based system, you first retrieve the document to RAM. Then remove the data disk from the disk drive (usually drive B) and replace it with the Speller (dictionary) diskette. Issue the Spell (Ctrl + F2) command to start the spelling check. You must leave the speller disk in drive B while the proofreading of your document is in process.

Hard Disk–Based System. When you are using a hard disk–based system, you must first retrieve the document to RAM. Issue the Spell (Ctrl + F2) command to start the spelling check.

This method assumes that both dictionaries are in the same directory as your WordPerfect files. If WordPerfect is unable to find the dictionary files, it displays a message in the status line similar to the following:

```
Main dictionary not found. Enter name: C:\WP\LEX.WP
```

If the dictionary files are in a subdirectory or another directory, you must change to that directory.

Once the Speller command has been given, the following menu appears at the bottom of your screen:

```
Check: 1 Word; 2 Page; 3 Document; 4 Change Dictionary; 5 Look Up; 6 Count
```

If you want to check only the word or page at the current cursor location, select option 1 or 2, respectively. Option 3 (the option most frequently selected) checks spelling of the entire document.

When you select option 4, a message similar to that below is displayed.

```
Enter new main dictionary name: LEX.WP
```

You can now enter the name of a separate main dictionary of your own creation for WordPerfect to use in its spelling check. For instance, if you were a medical student, you might want to use a dictionary of medical terms.

After you have chosen the new main dictionary, WordPerfect asks if you want to use a new supplementary dictionary:

```
Enter new supplementary dictionary name: {WP}LEX.SUP
```

Again, if you want WordPerfect to use a new supplementary dictionary, simply enter its name.

Option 5, the Look Up option, helps with words you don't know how to spell by looking for words in the main dictionary that include a particular pattern of letters. The words found are displayed at the bottom of the screen.

Option 6, the Count option, counts the words in your document without taking the time for a spelling check. When the Count is finished, the number is displayed at the end of the document.

Once the proofing process has started, the message `* Please Wait *` is displayed at the bottom of your screen and stays there until WordPerfect encounters a group of characters in your document that it cannot find in its dictionary. At that time, your screen splits into two parts, with text from your document at the top with the suspect word highlighted in reverse video, and Speller information at the bottom (see Figure 8.1). Let's examine the lines at the bottom of the screen:

```
Not Found! Select Word or Menu Option (0=Continue):0
1 Skip Once; 2 Skip; 3 Add Word; 4 Edit; 5 Look Up 6 Phonetic
```

The `Not Found!` message at the bottom of your screen is not relevant if suggestions for replacing the suspect word are displayed. Type the letter of the correct suggestion, and any occurrence of that word in your document

```
Instructions: While holding down the Ctrl key, push F2.  Next,
push 2 to check a page, and then follow the prompts and status
line as you like.

   We hold theese truths to be self-evedent, that all men are
   are created equal, that they are endoud by their Creator
   with certain unalienable Rights, that among these are Life,
   Liberty and the prusuit of Happiness.  That to secure these
   rights, Goverments are instituted among Men, deriving their
   just powers from the consent of the governed.This "readme" file is designe

===============================================================================

A. these




Not Found!  Select Word or Menu Option (0=Continue): 0
1 Skip Once; 2 Skip; 3 Add Word; 4 Edit; 5 Look Up; 6 Phonetic
```

is corrected. If the correct spelling is not displayed on the screen but options A through X appear, depress the ENTER key to display the next screen of
suggestions.

A suspect word is not always misspelled; WordPerfect may simply not
have your particular word in its dictionary. In this case, you can take the Skip
Once or Skip option. With the Skip option WordPerfect asks you no further
questions about that word during the current proofing session. The Add Word
option adds the word to the supplementary dictionary and the Speller then
resumes the proofing session.

If the suspect word is indeed incorrect and WordPerfect does not have a
correction in its dictionary, the Edit option must be selected to correct the
suspect word. Once the Edit option is selected, the message `Press Enter`
`when done` appears at the bottom of the screen, and the cursor appears
beneath the suspect word. You can now manually correct the spelling. When
you are finished, use the ENTER key to continue the proofing session.

You may have misspelled a word in such a way that WordPerfect cannot
make any suggestions. You may select the Look Up option to provide the
pattern of characters to be used in finding the correct spelling for the suspect
word once the message `Word Pattern: _` is displayed at the bottom of
the screen. If the correct word is not located, select the Edit option or go to
Webster's unabridged, and correct it manually.

WordPerfect provides wildcard characters for the Look Up operation.
You can represent a single letter, of which you are uncertain, by a question
mark (?) and more than one letter by an asterisk (*). For example, if you enter
the character string *p?ck*, the words *pack, peck, pick, pock,* and *puck* are displayed
on the screen. The Look Up character string *pack** generates *pack, package,
packaged,* and so on.

The Phonetic option tells WordPerfect to look up all words in the main
dictionary that sound like the suspect word. If the correct spelling now appears, the word can be corrected automatically; otherwise, it must be corrected
via the Edit option.

Figure 8.2
The Page Format screen contains various options that you can use to format text on a printed page.

```
Page Format

     1 - Page Number Position

     2 - New Page Number

     3 - Center Page Top to Bottom

     4 - Page Length

     5 - Top Margin

     6 - Headers or Footers

     7 - Page Number Column Positions

     8 - Suppress for Current page only

     9 - Conditional End of Page

     A - Widow/Orphan


Selection: 0
```

You may from time to time have to use a word that contains numeric characters. When WordPerfect encounters such a word, it displays the following message:

```
1 2 Skip; 3 Ignore words containing numbers; 4 Edit
```

When option 3 is selected, any words containing numbers will be ignored for the remaining portion of the proofing session.

One handy feature of the Speller is that it can locate double occurrences of a word (for example, the the). When a **double word** is found, the menu below is displayed.

```
Double Word! 1 2 Skip; 3 Delete 2nd; 4 Edit; 5 Disable double word checking_
```

Options 1 and 2 resume the proofing session. The Delete 2nd option automatically deletes the second occurrence of the double word in your document and resumes the proofing session.

Page Format

5.0

The **Page Format** (Alt + F8) **command** allows you to control the appearance of the text on the printed page. This command embeds codes into the document at the cursor location. After this command has been issued, the Page Format screen appears (Figure 8.2) on your monitor.

Page Number Position

The **Page Number Position option** provides nine alternatives for positioning page numbers on the output. When you select option 1, the menu depicted in Figure 8.3 appears on your monitor.

Figure 8.3
Page Number Position
screen.

```
Position of Page Number on Page

    0 - No page numbers

    1 - Top left of every page

    2 - Top center of every page

    3 - Top right of every page

    4 - Top alternating left & right

    5 - Bottom left of every page

    6 - Bottom center of every page

    7 - Bottom right of every page

    8 - Bottom alternating left & right



Selection: 0
```

5.0 Most of these menu selections are self-explanatory, but options 4 and 8 merit discussion. These options, used when you intend to bind the output in pamphlet or booklet form, cause even-numbered page numbers to occur on the left and odd-number page numbers on the right.

When the page number is at the top of the page, it prints on line 7. WordPerfect uses position 10 for the left corner page number, position 42 for the center, and position 74 for the right corner. After you have made your selection, you return to the Page Format Menu.

New Page Number

The **page numbering** of a document is automatically controlled by Word-Perfect. From time to time, however, you may want to alter this automatic numbering. For example, you may be working on a report that is composed of different files—part one residing in a file called REPORT1, say, and part two in REPORT2. Suppose that part one has ten pages, and you want the two parts to be numbered sequentially. The first page of REPORT2 should then be numbered page 11.

Entering a **new page number** is a two-step process: (1) enter the new page number and (2) specify its format. To accomplish this, place the cursor at the beginning of the REPORT2 file, enter the Page Format (Alt + F8) command, and select option 2. At that time the prompt New Page #: _ appears at the bottom of the screen. Enter the new page number, in this case 11. After you press the ENTER key, WordPerfect asks you to select **numbering style** with the prompt Numbering Style: 1 Arabic; 2 Roman; 0 (Arabic numbers are 1, 2, 3, and so forth; Roman numerals are i, ii, iii, iv, and so forth.) You can use Roman numerals for paginating the preface, foreword, table of contents, and so on. Select the Arabic option.

As soon as you change the page number, the new number appears on the status line. When you print out REPORT1, its pages will be numbered 1 to 10; then when you print REPORT2, WordPerfect will start the first page of this document with 11 instead of 1. Subsequent pages are numbered consecutively, based on the initial value that you entered.

Figure 8.4
Page Length screen.

```
Page Length

    1 - Letter Size Paper: Form Length = 66 lines (11 inches)
        Single Spaced Text lines = 54 (This includes lines
        used for Headers, Footers and/or page numbers.)

    2 - Legal Size Paper: Form Length = 84 lines (14 inches)
        Single Spaced Text Lines = 72 (This includes lines
        used for Headers, Footers and/or page numbers.)

    3 - Other (Maximum page length = 108 lines.)

Current Settings

    Form Length in Lines (6 per inch):  66

    Number of Single Spaced Text Lines: 54




Selection: 0
```

5.0   **NOTE**   When you use page numbers, WordPerfect subtracts two lines from the available 54 lines: one for the page number and one to keep a blank line between the text and the page number line. This leaves you with 52 printable lines (assuming single spacing). The soft page breaks shown on your screen accurately depict where the printed breaks will occur as long as you do not incorporate headers and footers.

Center Page Top to Bottom

The **Center Page option** centers information vertically on the printed page by inserting the same number of blank lines before and after the text. It is used to center short letters, figures, or tables. Make certain that you position the cursor at the beginning of the page before entering this command. Only the page on which the code is embedded is centered.

Page Length

WordPerfect assumes that a standard page (8½ by 11 inches) contains 66 lines, of which 54 contain text. This provides for one-inch (6-line) margins at the top and bottom. Upon selecting the **Page Length option**, you are shown the menu depicted in Figure 8.4.

If you want to have more printed lines on each page, select option 3. In the figure, the cursor is placed beneath the page length; but since you want to leave this as is, press the ENTER key. Now, change the 54 to whatever value you desire. The value that you enter is the number of lines of text that will appear on every page from this point on in your document.

In counting lines of text, WordPerfect includes headers, footnotes, one line of footer text, and page numbers in the total number of text lines.

NOTE   The top margin is not affected by this command. It will still continue to occupy the same amount of space (default of one inch).

Figure 8.5
Header/Footer screen.

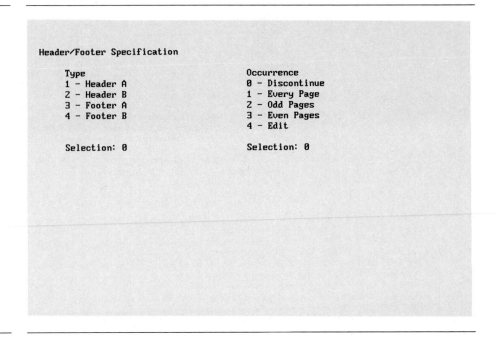

```
Header/Footer Specification

     Type                          Occurrence
     1 - Header A                  0 - Discontinue
     2 - Header B                  1 - Every Page
     3 - Footer A                  2 - Odd Pages
     4 - Footer B                  3 - Even Pages
                                   4 - Edit

     Selection: 0                  Selection: 0
```

Top Margin

5.0 The default size of the **top margin** is one inch or six lines (twelve half-lines). The Top Margin option of the Page Format command is used to change this setting beginning at the cursor location. Since the top margin is not shown on the screen, you must use Reveal Codes (Alt + F3) to see the top margin code.

Upon selecting Top Margin, the prompt Set half-lines (12/inch_ from 12 to _ is displayed at the bottom of the screen. If you want a margin of two-thirds of an inch instead of one inch, you enter 8 in response to the prompt. This now places the page number on line 5 instead of line 7.

If you are hand-feeding your paper to the printer, WordPerfect assumes that you have not already positioned the paper one inch down from the print head. When printing starts, it will move the paper up one inch.

Headers or Footers

Headers and **footers** are lines of text that are printed in the top and bottom margins, respectively. You need to enter these commands only once, at the beginning of the file; the headers and/or footers will be repeated as specified. The default is *no* header or footer. To create a header or footer, position the cursor at the top of the page on which you want the header or footer to start. Upon selecting the Headers or Footers option, the screen depicted in Figure 8.5 is displayed on your screen.

You first specify the header or footer you want (the first two options are headers and the second two are footers) and then tell WordPerfect how it is to position the text by selecting from the Occurrence menu. WordPerfect now clears the screen so you can enter the header or footer text. Any special features such as bold, center, underline, or flush right can be used. The status line of the header/footer text-entry screen contains the prompt Press EXIT when done along with the line and position data. When you are finished entering the header or footer, press the Exit (F7) key.

WordPerfect provides control over printing headers and footers. It prints headers beginning with the first text line of the page and automatically sub-

5.0   tracts the header lines plus a blank line from the total number of text lines. Therefore, if you have a one-line header, two lines are subtracted from the total lines (assuming the 54 line default); thus 52 text lines are actually printed from your document.

The first line of footer text is printed on the last text line of the page. A blank line is automatically inserted to separate the text from the footer. Any additional footer lines are printed in the bottom margin.

If you discover an error in a header or footer line, move the cursor to the line in the document that holds the [Hdr/Ftr] code. Use the Reveal Codes (Alt + F3) to locate the code, and position your cursor to the right of the code. You are now ready to correct the error. After you issue the Page Format (Alt + F8) command and select the Header/Footer option, the Header/Footer Specification menu is displayed on the screen. Select the appropriate header or footer and take option 4, the Edit command. The footer is now displayed on the header/footer entry screen. Make your changes and save them using the Exit (F7) command.

You may not want to have a header appear on the first page of your document, but you may want the footer to print there. In this case, you must place the header code anywhere after the end of the first line of the first page but before the first line of the second page. The footer must be specified before the last line of the first page. This results in the header line(s) printing at the top of the second page, rather than at the top of the first page.

The ^B (Ctrl + B) command sequence is used in the header or footer text line to include the page number in the header or footer. For example, the following sequence would cause WordPerfect to place the header and the appropriate page number at the top of every page of printed text in a file:

```
Four Software Tools Page ^B
```

Placing page numbers in a header or footer now presents a problem: If you previously told WordPerfect to print the page number, it will print every page number twice, once in the header and again at the bottom of each page. You must now tell WordPerfect, via the Format Print (Alt + F8), not to number the pages.

Page Number Column Position

This option allows you to tell WordPerfect the left corner, center, or right corner positions in which to place the page number. This is especially helpful if you are using 12 pitch rather than 10 pitch, because the right-hand margin changes to 89 using 12 pitch (elite) type. When you select this command, the screen depicted in Figure 8.6 is displayed on your screen.

To accept the current settings, press the ENTER key. To return the current settings to the WordPerfect defaults, select option 1. To enter your own settings, select option 2 and, using the conventions shown, enter your own.

Suppress for Current Page Only

This option allows you to turn off any page formatting for a page. First position the cursor to the very top of the page and then select this option. The screen depicted in Figure 8.7 is then displayed on your screen.

To suppress more than one of these options, concatenate (join) them with plus (+) signs.

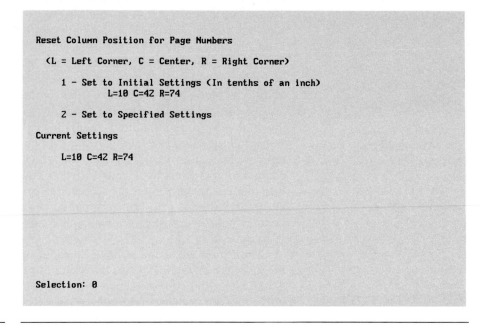

```
Reset Column Position for Page Numbers

    (L = Left Corner, C = Center, R = Right Corner)

        1 - Set to Initial Settings (In tenths of an inch)
                L=10 C=42 R=74

        2 - Set to Specified Settings

Current Settings

        L=10 C=42 R=74




Selection: 0
```

5.0 *Conditional End of Page*

The **Conditional End of Page command** specifies that if a page break occurs within a certain number of following lines, a hard page break will occur. After entering the command, you must tell WordPerfect how many lines from the cursor location are to be "page-break protected" with the prompt `Number of lines to keep together = _`. This command is useful for protecting text such as tables from being split by page breaks. For example:

```
                 Inflation During the 80s

                 1980          9.9%
                 1981          8.5%
                 1982          6.0%
                 1983          4.5%
```

In this example, the cursor is placed at the beginning of the text to be protected. The Page Format (Alt + F8) is issued and the conditional end of page command is selected. A 6 is now entered to tell WordPerfect to protect the next six lines from page breaks. This command gives you better control over how page breaks appear in a document; it can be used any number of times in a document.

Widow/Orphan

A *widow* occurs when only the first line of a paragraph appears at the bottom of a page. An *orphan* occurs when the last line of a paragraph appears at the top of a page. The Widow/Orphan option tells WordPerfect to avoid widow and orphan lines in a document if the cursor is at the beginning, or from the cursor location onward. After entering this command, the `Widow/Orphan Protect? (Y/N): N` prompt appears at the bottom of the screen. Enter Y to start the protection.

You typically use the conditional end of page feature of WordPerfect to protect tables, and you use this option to protect the first and last lines of

Figure 8.7
The Suppress Page Format for
Current Page Only screen.

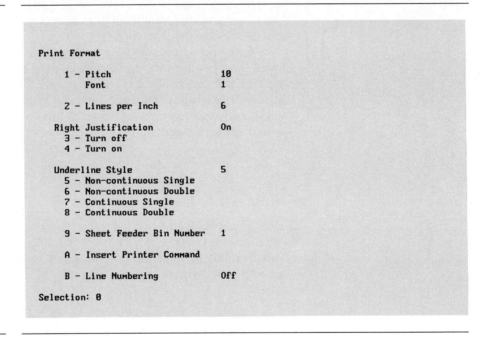

```
Suppress Page Format for Current Page Only

  To temporarily turn off multiple items, include a "+" between menu entries.
  For example 5+6+2 will turn off Header A, Header B, and Page Numbering
  for the current page.

     1 - Turn off all page numbering, headers and footers

     2 - Turn page numbering off

     3 - Print page number at bottom center (this page only)

     4 - Turn off all headers and footers

     5 - Turn off Header A

     6 - Turn off Header B

     7 - Turn off Footer A

     8 - Turn off Footer B

Selection(s): 0
```

Figure 8.8
Print Format Menu.

```
Print Format

     1 - Pitch                        10
         Font                         1

     2 - Lines per Inch               6

     Right Justification             On
     3 - Turn off
     4 - Turn on

     Underline Style                  5
         5 - Non-continuous Single
         6 - Non-continuous Double
         7 - Continuous Single
         8 - Continuous Double

     9 - Sheet Feeder Bin Number      1

     A - Insert Printer Command

     B - Line Numbering               Off

Selection: 0
```

5.0
ⷫ

paragraphs. This option can also be turned on and off within your document
any number of times.

*Print Format

The Print Format (Ctrl + F8) command embeds codes that give you control
over the appearance of the text on the printed page. After this command has
been issued, the screen depicted in Figure 8.8 appears on your monitor.

Pitch

This option enables you to change the **pitch** (the number of characters printed
per inch—ten is the default) and the **font** (the style of print used to generate
characters), beginning at the cursor location. The various fonts and pitches

5.0   that are available for your use are determined by the fonts provided by WordPerfect for the printer you are using.

Some sample pitches and fonts for a Star printer can be seen in Figure 8.9. When you select this option, you first change the pitch, and then you can change the font if you want to. If you are in doubt about which fonts are supported by WordPerfect for your printer, print the PRINTER.TST and PRINTER2.TST files.

When you change the pitch and/or the font, you may be employing larger or smaller characters; as a result, your line of text may no longer fit properly on the line. The solution to this problem is to change the margins at the same place in the document that you enter the pitch or font change.

Proportional Spacing. A popular font that usually requires a letter-quality printer is proportional spacing. **Proportional spacing** inserts increments of space equally between words in a line. This gives the text a finished, professional appearance similar to that of typesetting. To start proportional spacing, you enter a 13* for most printers.

Lines per Inch

You can change the number of lines printed per vertical inch: The default is six and can be changed to eight.

Care should be exercised in using this command because using both 6 and 8 lines per inch on the same page may cause your printer to think it has reached the end of the page prematurely. This causes problems with page breaks. If you select this option to set 8 lines per inch, you will also want to tell WordPerfect to print more than 54 lines of text per page; for example, you would probably want to set the page length to 84 and the number of text lines to 72.

Right Justification

This option spaces the printed text so that the right-hand margin is either even (right justified) or ragged. The command is embedded at the cursor location. The default is right justification on. Right justification should be on when you are using the proportional spacing font.

Underline Style

This option provides you with four alternatives for presenting underlined text. Continuous single is the default. Monochrome monitors show a true underline on the screen, whereas color monitors show underlined text in a different color.

The single and continuous single options use the single underscore (_), whereas the noncontinuous double and the continuous double options use the double underscore (=) (but single and double underscoring appear the same on the screen). The continuous options underscore blanks, and the noncontinuous methods do not. Samples of the underscore options appear below:

5. Noncontinuous Single

<u>ID</u>   <u>Name</u>   <u>Hours</u>   <u>Gross Pay</u>

WordPerfect Printer Test Document

| In this document each word associated with a feature is printed
| with that feature (e.g., bold, ~~super~~script, ~~sub~~script, and
| ~~strikeout~~). Over~~strike~~ is sometimes used to build new characters
| like ≠ å ⁿ. This paragraph is redlined. Redline will print a
| vertical bar or a plus symbol in the left margin.

Text can be centered   or flushed right.
If a feature described does not appear on your printout,
your printer may not have that capability.

Continuous_____	Double underlining	Continuous
Non-Continuous	Double underlining	style
Continuous	Single underlining	underlines
Non-Continuous	Single underlining	tabs.

WordPerfect has left, center, right, and decimal aligned tabs.
Centered tabs center on the tab stop, not between the margins.
Several types will be demonstrated with dot leaders included.

Left Aligned   Centered. . . . . Decimal.aligned
Left   Center $4.50

1   At this point, each line will   within columns. There are two
2   be numbered in the left margin.   types of columns, parallel and
3   The column feature allows text   newspaper. This is an example
4   to be right and left justified   of newspaper columns.
5
6   This document has been printed in 10 pitch with font 1. In the
7   next few lines, pitches and fonts will be changed as specified.
8   If your printer changes pitch when only a font change was
9   specified, your printer may be pitch/font specific, meaning the
10 pitch can only be changed with the font.

This is 12 pitch in font 1. You may notice that the margins are
a little different for this block of text. For one-inch margins
12 pitch, the margins should be set at 12 and 89.

This is 15 pitch in font 1. For one inch-margins 15 pitch, use
15 and 112. This paragraph is also printed in eight lines per
inch. Unless your printer prints 15 pitch in condensed print,
the lines may look too close with this character size.
This is 10 pitch in font 2.
This is 13* pitch in font 3. Font three is usually a proportionally
spaced font in WordPerfect. Notice the asterisk after the pitch
which specifies PS.
This is 10 pitch in font 4.
This is 10 pitch in font 5.
This is 10 pitch in font 6.
This is 10 pitch in font 7.
This is 10 pitch in font 8.

Advance up and down move text up or down 1/2 line.

Advance down   Text on a regular line   Advance up   Normal

For More Available Features, Refer To Printer2.tst

1

Auto page number is centered above.   This is a footer.

Figure 8.9
Sample fonts supported by WordPerfect.

5.0

6. Noncontinuous Double

ID	Name	Hours	Gross Pay

7. Continuous Single

ID	Name	Hours	Gross Pay

8. Continuous Double

ID	Name	Hours	Gross Pay

Sheet Feeder Bin Number

Some letter-quality printers have sheet feeders with multiple bins for feeding single sheets of paper to the printer automatically. This allows you to have different-sized paper in each bin. The default is 1. If you change the bin number, the printer begins using that bin at the cursor location; therefore, this code must be entered at the beginning of a page.

Insert Printer Command

This option embeds codes at the cursor location that control special functions of a printer or typesetter. As are other codes, they are invisible on the screen. These codes are the decimal equivalents of **escape codes**, sequences of characters that give a command to the printer and can be found in an appendix of your printer manual. Any code less than 32 decimal or greater than 126 must be entered in angle brackets <>.

When this command is invoked, the Cmnd: _ prompt appears at the bottom of the screen. You can now enter, for instance, the command <27>4. This command activates italic print on an Epson FX printer. The <27> represents the decimal value of the Escape command. Since most printer-oriented commands begin with an Escape, they are referred to as escape codes.

Line Numbering

This option prints line numbers at the beginning of each line of text in your document, starting at the cursor location. When the command is invoked, WordPerfect displays the menu depicted in Figure 8.10 on your screen.

The entries in the right-hand column are the defaults. You can decide whether or not you want to include the blank lines, and you can specify the location of the line number and whether or not to restart the numbering on each page.

Chapter Review

The Speller option allows you to check the spelling of any document file quickly. The two dictionaries used by this spelling checker are the main dictionary and the supplemental dictionary. The Speller option provides an easy-to-follow menu that gives alternative actions that can be performed on a suspect word. In addition, the appropriate part of the document is displayed (with the suspect word in reverse video) so that you can see the word in context.

Figure 8.10
Line Numbering Menu.

```
Line Numbering

    1 - Turn off                              Off
    2 - Turn on

    3 - Count blank lines?                    Y

    4 - Number every n lines, where n=        1

    5 - Position of number from left edge: 6
        (in tenths of an inch)

    6 - Restart numbering on each page?       Y




Selection: 0
```

WordPerfect enables you to control how information will appear on the page and provides flexibility in how the document will be printed. Some of the Page Format commands enable you to control page numbering, centering, length, and the top margin; insert headers and/or footers; insert Conditional End of Page commands; and control the occurrence of widow and orphan lines.

Other special printing features can be obtained by using the Print Format command. Options from this menu allow you to control the pitch and font, right justification, underlining style, and line numbering.

Key Terms and Concepts

Center Page option
Conditional End of Page command
double words
escape codes
font
footer
header
new page number

numbering style
Page Format command
Page Length option
page numbering
Page Number Position option
pitch
proportional spacing
top margin

Chapter Quiz

Multiple Choice

1. Which is the default for page numbering?
   a. Bottom center of every page
   b. No page numbers
   c. Top alternating left and right
   d. None of the above

2. The key sequence for invoking the Print Format command is
   a. Ctrl + F8
   b. Ctrl + F7
   c. SHIFT + F8
   d. Alt + F8
   e. None of the above

3. Which command is used to avoid widow and orphan lines?
   a. Print Format
   b. Print
   c. Page Format
   d. Conditional End of Page
   e. None of the above

4. Which of the following command(s) may not work properly on a dot-matrix printer?
   a. Headers or Footers
   b. Widows/orphans
   c. Proportional spacing
   d. Pitch
   e. All will work well.

5. Which command(s) are used to place one or more lines of text at the top and/or bottom of each page?
   a. Conditional End of Page
   b. Top Margin
   c. Headers/Footers
   d. Suppress for Current Page Only

True/False

6. The cursor does not play any role in issuing Print Format and Page Format commands.

7. The Speller can only check the entire document when the Spell (Ctrl + F2) command is issued.

8. WordPerfect does not allow you to change a header line; you must first delete the header and then reenter it.

9. WordPerfect allows you to center information both horizontally on a line and vertically on a page.

10. The ^B command is used to include the page number in a header or footer line.

Answers

1. b 2. a 3. c 4. c 5. c 6. f 7. f 8. f 9. t 10. t

Exercises

1. Define or describe each of the following:
   a. font   d. conditional end of page
   b. header line   e. underline style
   c. footer line

2. The _____ key sequence invokes the Page Format command.

3. The _____ key sequence invokes the Print Format command.

4. The default for the number of text lines on a page is _____ lines.

5. The features invoked using Print Format and Page Format commands are not visible until the document is _____ .

6. Many format commands must be entered at the _____ of a document.

7. The number of headers and footers that you can specify is _____ .

8. The top margin, unless otherwise specified, has _____ lines.

9. The default pitch in WordPerfect is _____ cpi.

10. The _____ style of numbering usually appears in a preface.

11. The _____ command allows you to initialize the page counter to a value other than 1 when printing a document.

12. When you specify a page number and print a document, _____ lines of text will print.

13. When you change the page length the _____ remains unchanged.

14. When printing letters or short memos, the _____ command makes the document appear more balanced.

15. When you are printing a large document, the _____ command is useful in starting the page numbering with a value other than 1.

16. Widow and orphan lines can be avoided by using the _____ command.

17. When _____ is used on a header or footer line, it results in page numbers appearing.

18. The column in which the page number is to be printed can be changed by using the _____ command.

19. The _____ command can result in erroneous page breaks.

20. The _____ command allows you to print a document with either a smooth or ragged right-hand margin.

Computer Exercises

Summary of Commands

Ctrl + F2	Speller
Page Format (Alt + F8)	This command allows you to determine how information will appear on each page.
Print Format (Ctrl + F8)	This command allows you to determine how information will appear on the printed page.

1. Retrieve the BOOKEXER file. If you move the cursor to examine the file, be sure to move it back to the beginning of the document before starting this exercise.

a. Tell WordPerfect to center the page number at the bottom of each page. Print the document. Compare this with the printout of this file from the previous chapter. Notice that there are two fewer lines of text per page.

b. Change the page length to 58. Decrease the top margin by two lines. Print the document and compare this to the previous printout.

c. Turn off page numbering. Create the following header:

BOOKEXER

Tell WordPerfect to print this header at the top of each page. Now create a footer that prints the word Page followed by the page number. Print the document and compare this printout with those from the two previous exercises.

d. At the beginning of the document, tell WordPerfect to turn on widow/orphan protect. Again, print the document.

e. Tell WordPerfect to use 5 as the beginning page number. Print the file. Is the new numbering in effect?

2. Use the Reveal Codes command to examine the codes now embedded at the beginning of your document. Identify which code was used for each task above.

* 3. Retrieve the BOOKEXER file. Turn off right-justification and print the document using 12 pitch. Change the left-hand margin to 12 and the right-hand margin to 84 and print the document again. Notice that 12 pitch "packs" more text per line.

* 4. Print the BOOKEXER file using the following font specifications. Exit without saving the file to disk, after you have printed the document.

a. For paragraph 1 of page 1 use font 1 and 12 pitch.
b. For paragraph 2 of page 1 use font 2 and 10 pitch.
c. For paragraph 3 of page 1 use font 2 and 12 pitch.
d. For paragraph 4 of page 1 use font 3 and 10 pitch.
e. For paragraph 5 of page 1 use font 3 and 12 pitch.
f. For paragraph 6 of page 1 use font 4 and 10 pitch.
g. For paragraph 1 of page 2 use font 4 and 12 pitch.
h. For paragraph 2 of page 2 use font 7 and 10 pitch.
i. For paragraph 3 of page 2 use font 7 and 12 pitch.
j. For paragraph 4 of page 2 use font 8 and 10 pitch.
k. For paragraph 5 of page 2 use font 8 and 12 pitch.

* 5. Print the BOOKEXER file using 15 pitch at 8 lines per inch. The page length must be set to 72, text lines to 66, left-hand margin to 15, and right-hand margin to 100. Print and then save the document.

6. Use the Reveal Codes command to display the codes from exercise CH7EX13a. Delete these codes. Your text should now appear as the original.

7. Print out the BOOKEXER document with each line numbered. Numbering should start over on each page.

8. Print the BOOKEXER to a file called CH8EX8. Exit WP and use the Pipe command to view the CH8EX8 file. It should have the text from the BOOKEXER file.

*These exercises cannot be done with the educational version of WordPerfect.

9. Enter the following financial statements for the Barrymore Corporation using the WordPerfect word processing software. Each financial statement should appear on a separate page within the file. To enter the financial statements, save as CH8EX9, and use the following conventions:
    1. Issue the Print Format (Ctrl + F8) command and tell WordPerfect to print the document in elite (12 cpi) pitch.
    2. Clear all of the existing tabs before you start entering the financial statements; set the right-hand margin to 90. (5.0 SHIFT + F8)
    3. Enter the financial statement titles and center them.
    4. For the Statement of Financial Position, set tabs at positions 14, 17, 20, 57, 71, and 85. When you enter the document, use regular Tab commands for the first three tab stops; use Tab Align commands for the remaining three tab stops.
    5. Before you enter new tab stops for the Income Statement, clear all existing tab stops. Enter new tab stops at positions 14, 55, and 74. Use a regular Tab command to position to the first tab stop; use Tab Align commands to position to the other tab stops.
    6. Use the Print Format (Ctrl + F8) (5.0 SHIFT + F8) command to set the underlining style to continuous double for grand totals. If your printer does not support the double underlining feature, use the equal sign (=) character. This is accomplished by positioning the cursor to the same position on the next line and entering the equal signs at the location of the double underscores. Of course, using this method results in some additional space between the number and the equal signs.
    7. Use the Print Format command to set the underlining style to continuous single for subtotal lines.

Barrymore Corporation
Comparative Statement of Financial Position
December 31, 1988 and 1987

	December 31 1988	December 31 1987	Increase (Decrease)
Assets			
Current assets:			
Cash	$ 110,000	$ 99,000	$ 11,000
Accounts receivable	231,000	154,000	77,000
Inventories	286,000	242,000	44,000
Total current assets	627,000	495,000	132,000
Land	357,500	220,000	137,500
Plant and equipment	638,000	696,300	(58,300)
Less: accumulated depreciation	(99,000)	(110,000)	11,000
Patents	33,000	36,300	(3,300)
Total Assets	$1,556,500	$1,337,600	$218,900

Liabilities and Shareholders' Equity			
Liabilities:			
Current liabilities:			
Accounts payable	$ 286,000	$ 220,000	$ 66,000
Accrued expenses	220,000	231,000	(11,000)
Total current liabilities	506,000	451,000	55,000
Deferred income taxes	154,000	110,000	44,000
Long-term bonds (due December 15, 1990)	143,000	198,000	(55,000)
Total Liabilities	803,000	759,000	44,000
Shareholders' Equity:			
Common stock, par value $5 authorized 100,000 shares, issued and outstanding 50,000 and 42,000 shares	275,000	231,000	44,000
Additional paid in capital	256,300	187,000	69,300
Retained earnings	222,200	160,600	61,600
Total Shareholders' Equity	735,500	578,600	174,900
Total Liabilities and Shareholders' Equity	$1,556,500	$1,337,600	$218,900

Barrymore Corporation
Income Statement
For the year ended December 31, 1988

Sales		$1,100,000
Expenses:		
Cost of sales	616,000	
Salary and wages	209,000	
Depreciation	22,000	
Amortization	3,300	
Loss on sale of equipment	4,400	
Interest	17,600	
Miscellaneous	8,800	881,100
Income before taxes and extraordinary items		218,900
Income taxes		
Current	55,00	
Deferred	44,000	99,000
Income before extraordinary item		119,900
Extraordinary item—gain on repurchase of long-term bonds (net of $10,000 income tax)		13,200
Net income		$ 133,100
Earnings per share (50,000):		
Income before extraordinary items		$ 2.40
Extraordinary item		.26
Net income		$ 2.66

Chapter
9

Beginning

Spreadsheet

with Lotus 1-2-3

Chapter Objectives

After completing this chapter, you should be able to:

Describe the concepts of spreadsheets and worksheets

Define and discuss common spreadsheet terminology

Discuss features that are common to many spreadsheet packages

Discuss the steps involved in using spreadsheet packages

Define and discuss the three parts of Lotus 1-2-3

Discuss the various aspects of the 1-2-3 screen

Discuss the various means of manipulating the 1-2-3 pointer (cursor)

Discuss the role of the various keys and their relationship to 1-2-3

Discuss various elementary features of the 1-2-3 packages

Enter a 1-2-3 worksheet

Introduction to Spreadsheets

The spreadsheet is the piece of software that has single-handedly caused American business to take the microcomputer seriously as a problem-solving tool. An electronic spreadsheet is simply the electronic equivalent of the accounting worksheet. Both the electronic worksheet and the accounting worksheet consist of a matrix composed of rows and columns. These rows and columns allow a person to organize information in an easy to understand format.

The terms *spreadsheet* and *worksheet* can be distinguished as follows: **spreadsheet** is the set of program instructions, such as VisiCalc or Lotus 1-2-3, that produces a worksheet; a **worksheet** is a model or representation of reality that is created using a spreadsheet software package. Spreadsheets can be used in completing any data manipulation involving numbers and text that is usually performed with pencil, paper, and calculator. Uses of spreadsheets in business include:

Budget preparation

Working trial balances

Business modeling

Sales forecasting

Investment analysis

Payroll

Real estate management

Taxes

Investment proposals

Electronic spreadsheet software greatly improves the user's accuracy, efficiency, and productivity. Once a worksheet has been prepared, other options ("what if" alternatives) can be easily considered simply by making the appropriate changes and instructing the spreadsheet to recalculate all entries to reflect these changes. This allows the user to spend more time on creative decision making.

Why Use Spreadsheet Software?

Suppose that you have a friend, Ed, who owns a grocery store with the following departments: Deli, Bakery, Liquor, Grocery, Produce, and Meat. It's the end of the year, and Ed would like to compare the sales of the various departments for last year and this year, keeping track of the overall change in sales (either positive or negative) and the percentage change in sales for each of the departments.

You have volunteered to help Ed develop this report manually. To ease the calculation process so that the correct numbers are included in each calculation, you have also decided to use some standard lined paper divided into a number of columns. This type of paper is many times referred to as worksheet paper.

In designing the report, you decide that the easiest way to present the data is to have the names of the departments along the vertical axis of the report and the column headings along the horizontal axis. You can now enter last year and this year sales figures for each department (Figure 9.1).

Once you have the data entered properly, you can use your calculator to compute the change in sales from last year to this year. This is accomplished by subtracting the sales for last year from the sales for this year and recording the change for each department in the Change column.

	Departments	Last Year	This Year	Change	% Change
1					
2	Deli	700	575		
3	Bakery	1000	1100		
4	Liquor	1200	1400		
5	Grocery	2500	2900		
6	Produce	950	1000		
7	Meat	1500	1410		
8					
9					
10					
11					

Figure 9.1 Manual worksheet containing labels and sales figures.

	Departments	Last Year	This Year	Change	% Change
1					
2	Deli	700	575	(125)	
3	Bakery	1000	1100	100	
4	Liquor	1200	1400	200	
5	Grocery	2500	2900	400	
6	Produce	950	1000	50	
7	Meat	1500	1410	(90)	
8					
9					
10					
11					

Figure 9.2 Manual worksheet with Change columns calculated.

In many business applications, negative numbers are represented as numbers between parentheses rather than with a minus sign. For example, to calculate the change for the Deli department, you are required to enter the equation 575 − 700 in your calculator and receive the answer of −125. Enter the −125 as (125) on your report. Once you have finished with all of the change calculations your report should now look like that in Figure 9.2.

You are now ready to compute the % Change entries. This is accomplished by dividing the Change figure by the Last Year sales entry for each

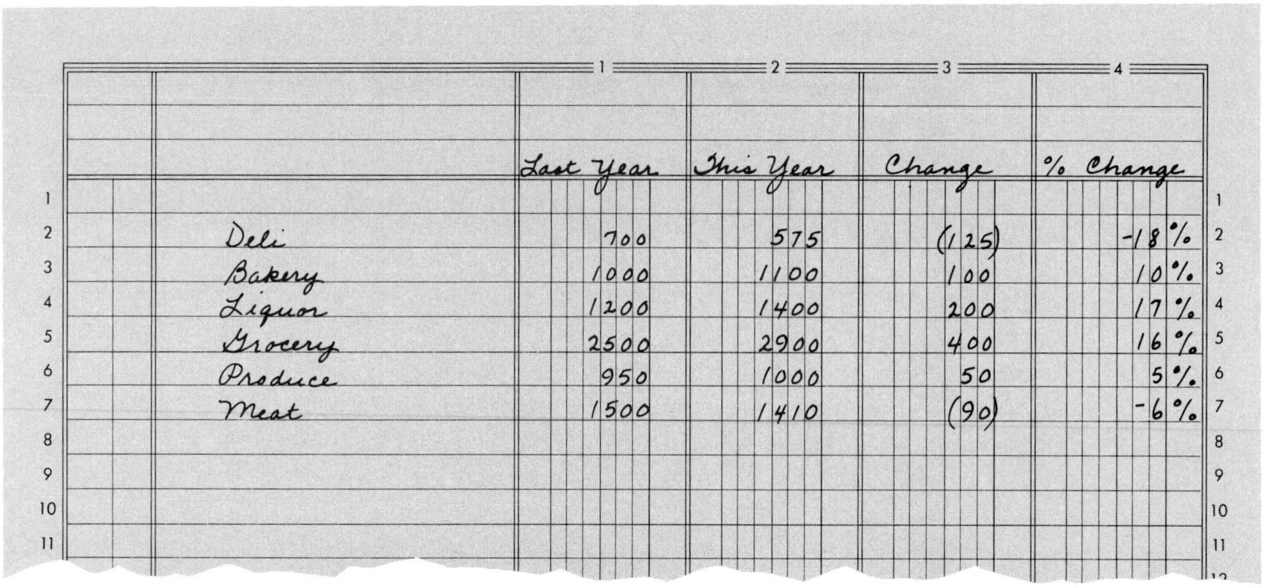

Figure 9.3   Manual worksheet with % Change calculation results shown.

department and converting the result to a percent. For example, to arrive at the % Change for the Deli department, you must divide -125 by 700. The result, $-.1786$, must now be converted to a whole percent. Since percentages are really just decimal fractions, the value to be placed in your report is -18%. Again you are required to perform the just-described steps for each department. Your report should now look like that in Figure 9.3.

You must now generate a total for each of the first three columns containing numbers—Last Year, This Year, and Change—and calculate the fourth column as before. This, of course, involves adding all of the numbers in a column together, recording the sum value, clearing the calculator, and starting over for the next column of numbers. Once you have generated the column totals, your report should appear like that in Figure 9.4.

Your report for Ed is now completed. You can present it to him to use in his decision making. What if, however, the sales for three departments change? Then, to use the report effectively, it would have to be entirely redone. Or what if Ed wants you to determine the impact of a 10% increase in This Year sales for each department? The ability to respond quickly to changes and reflect them in a report, as well as to respond to various "what if" questions, is what gives a spreadsheet package its tremendous power.

Suppose that instead of building this report manually you used a computerized spreadsheet package. The computer-generated report will appear to be amazingly similar to your manual report. All of the column headings, department names, and sales figures for each department would have to be entered. The calculation instructions (formulas) on how the spreadsheet package is to manipulate the figures are also entered. However, since the instructions are the same within a column, once a formula is entered, you can re-use it by copying it down the column. For example, you enter a formula for calculating the change data once and then copy that formula down the column. You do the same for the % Change formula. All that is left is to tell your spreadsheet package to calculate the total for the Last Year column of numbers. Since the other columns also have to be summed, you can copy this formula to them.

Departments	This Year	Lst Year	Change	% Change
Deli	700	575	(125)	-18 %
Bakery	1000	1100	100	10 %
Liquor	1200	1400	200	17 %
Grocery	2500	2900	400	16 %
Produce	950	1000	50	5 %
Meat	1500	1410	(90)	-6 %
Final Total	7850	8385	535	7 %

Figure 9.4   Manual worksheet with totals shown.

The real advantage of using a spreadsheet is that since it is formula driven, once a change is made to any of the sales figures, the spreadsheet automatically recalculates the report and generates the appropriate answers without any additional work on your part. Spreadsheet software thus makes answering "what-if" questions easy.

Spreadsheet Syntax

Each spreadsheet package allows the user to identify a unique address or **cell** at the intersection of a row and a column. A **row** is on a horizontal axis; a **column** is on a vertical axis. Worksheet cells are referred to by their COLUMN/ROW designation, and each may contain a label, a number, or a formula.

A **label** is alphanumeric text used to provide headings for the rows and columns, to make the worksheet easier to understand. Labels may be numeric (for example, quarters 1, 2, 3, or 4) or alphabetic (for example, the word *quarter*). A **number** is a numeric value entered in a cell; it may be either a constant or a variable—in which case it is the result of some type of mathematical calculation.

The **formula** contained in a cell creates relationships between values in other specified cells. For example, if the contents of cells E1, E2, E3, and E4 were to be added together, with the result to be placed in cell E7, the formula +E1+E2+E3+E4 would have to be placed in cell E7. Formulas used in cells can be more complex than just simple sums; they can contain financial calculations such as net present value or statistical expressions such as variance or standard deviation.

Understanding that formulas allow computations (based on the value in one cell) to determine values in other cells makes spreadsheets easy to use. It is imperative that anyone wishing to make effective use of spreadsheets be able to express relationships in terms of values—for example, gross margin = sales − cost of goods sold, or taxes = gross income × 35 percent. Once any such relationship has been defined and placed in a numeric format, any situation involving that relationship can be analyzed via an electronic worksheet.

One major strength of the electronic spreadsheet is that it presents and works with data in the familiar tabular format that is used to present or depict almost all data. A personal budget, for example, uses this tabular format: The budget categories are placed in a column, and the various time periods are placed as headings across the top row. Moreover, the spreadsheet is able to project and evaluate numerous alternatives to a single plan—the ubiquitous "what if" form of analysis—making it an important aid in decision making. The interrelationship of the cells enables the viewer to see immediately what effect changing the contents of one or more cells has on the rest of the worksheet.

Spreadsheets can be used in two basic ways: with your own worksheet, if you have a unique application or just have the time and want the practice (and if the application to be modeled is not very complex); or with a template. A **template** is much the same as an application program, except that someone has already done all the logical planning, designing, and implementing involved in building the template. Consequently, the individual using the template only has to enter some data and receive the results.

VisiCalc, an acronym for Visible Calculator, was the first spreadsheet introduced for microcomputers. It was designed by Dan Bricklin and Robert Frankston at a time when Bricklin was a student in the Harvard MBA program; he became interested in developing VisiCalc after growing tired of playing "what if" games in case studies that primarily required financial analysis. At the time, some software packages available for mainframe computers were capable of performing this type of manipulation, but they were difficult to use. One apocryphal story has Bricklin discussing the possible application of such a concept to the newly emerging microcomputers with one of his MBA professors, and being told that the idea would never be marketable.

Another person associated with VisiCalc is Dan Flystra, also a student in the MBA program at Harvard, who purchased the marketing rights to the product and founded Personal Software—later renamed VisiCorp (now defunct).

VisiCalc was originally designed to run on the Apple II computer and was responsible for many purchases of Apple computers by business. Since the introduction of the program, many different spreadsheet packages have been produced for microcomputers. Many of these reflect tremendous improvements in power and capability over the original VisiCalc. Probably the best known of these is the Lotus 1-2-3 spreadsheet program. Just as VisiCalc was responsible for business purchases of Apple microcomputers, Lotus 1-2-3 was responsible for business purchases of many IBM PC microcomputers.

Lotus 1-2-3 is the progeny of Mitch Kapor, a colorful character who taught himself programming after a number of other job endeavors. His first spreadsheet success was VisiTrend/Plot, a statistical and graphics package that he designed and programmed; it was purchased by VisiCorp and was capable of receiving data from VisiCalc.

With the money he earned from the sale of VisiTrend/Plot, plus some venture capital, Kapor set out to beat VisiCorp at its own game. He realized that the VisiCalc–VisiTrend/Plot hookup was cumbersome, since it required passing data, leaving one program, and then starting the other. He felt that this whole process could be made transparent to the end user.

Kapor and his staff designed Lotus 1-2-3 specifically for the IBM PC microcomputer; it was introduced early in 1983. A tremendous publicity campaign (and the superior quality of the software) helped Lotus 1-2-3 become an immediate success in the business community.

Problem-Solving Steps Using Spreadsheets

In approaching a problem, especially a complex problem, you should try to develop a plan for handling it as early in the process as possible. A lot of additional work can be avoided by prior planning; your end product will look better, and you will avoid redoing work. The planning process steps are: determining the purpose, planning, building and testing, and documenting.

Determining the Purpose. The first step is to determine exactly what the purpose or goal of the worksheet is. In other words, what do you want it to do for you? What inputs will be necessary to provide to the worksheet? What outputs do you want the spreadsheet to generate? Are printed reports needed to make the information the worksheet provides useful?

Planning. The second step is to plan a blueprint of your worksheet on paper. This blueprint should maintain the same rectangular format presented by the screen you are using and should include all screens that will have explanations to you or other users. Remember that you may only be using this spreadsheet once a year and may not remember all the nuances of your spreadsheet logic after such a long separation. You should also plan how you will manipulate your data.

Building and Testing. The third step is to build and test your worksheet. If you have planned everything properly, this should go smoothly. Testing the spreadsheet involves making sure that it manipulates the data correctly. A lot of things can go wrong—for instance, a formula might reference an incorrect cell, or it might be entered incorrectly—but a number of packages that you can process against a spreadsheet help in this process. Two of them, Spreadsheet Auditor and Docucalc, display the spreadsheet (as it appears on the screen), the cell values, and the corresponding formulas within cells used to manipulate data.

Documenting. The final step is to finish the documentation for using the worksheet. Some of this documentation is included within the worksheet itself, but a lot of other concepts may have to be covered to allow a user other than the worksheet's author to operate it effectively. In addition, limitations on inputs and outputs must be communicated, and if the worksheet is to be used as a template within an organization, its date of creation and its author's name and telephone number must be provided.

Introduction to Lotus 1-2-3

The Lotus 1-2-3 software package, as the name implies, has three logical and totally integrated parts: spreadsheet, data management, and graphing. **Integration** means that you do not have to leave the spreadsheet program, for instance, to get to the graphing or data management programs.

Parts of 1-2-3

Spreadsheet. The extremely powerful **spreadsheet** portion of Lotus manipulates the tabular accountinglike data. You can enter numbers, labels, or formulas into the worksheet. For example, you can list twelve numbers in a column and define one cell to hold the sum of those twelve numbers; thereafter, when any one of these numbers is changed, the sum is automatically updated to reflect the change.

Figure 9.5
(a) The Lotus Access System.
(b) The Lotus 1-2-3 copyright
screen.

```
1-2-3  PrintGraph  Translate  Install  View  Exit
Enter 1-2-3 -- Lotus Worksheet/Graphics/Database program


                    1-2-3 Access System
                      Copyright 1986
                 Lotus Development Corporation
                    All Rights Reserved
                       Release 2.01

     The Access System lets you choose 1-2-3, PrintGraph, the Translate utility,
     the Install program, and A View of 1-2-3 from the menu at the top of this
     screen.  If you're using a diskette system, the Access System may prompt
     you to change disks.  Follow the instructions below to start a program.

     o  Use [RIGHT] or [LEFT] to move the menu pointer (the highlight bar at
        the top of the screen) to the program you want to use.

     o  Press [RETURN] to start the program.

     You can also start a program by typing the first letter of the menu
     choice.  Press [HELP] for more information.
```

(a)

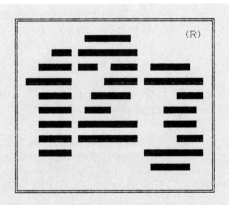

```
                      Copyright (C) 1986
                 Lotus Development Corporation
                     All Rights Reserved
                      1300656-4749219
                        Release 2.01
```

(b)

Data Management. The **data management feature** of Lotus 1-2-3 allows you to sort, summarize, and extract (make reports) portions of the individual records contained in a file. The major difference between this type of data management and other types is that here the entire file is contained in a worksheet.

Graphics. The **graphics feature** allows you to take information that you have entered in a worksheet and display it graphically to the screen (assuming you have graphics screen capability) or to the printer. You can display information

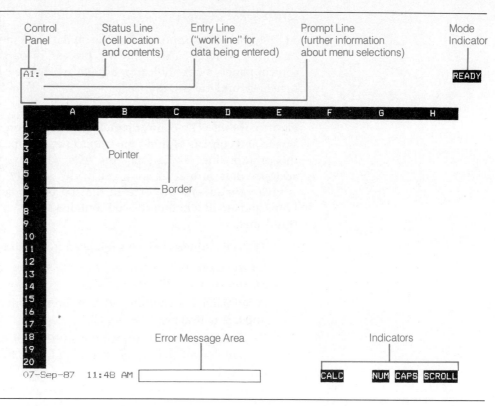

Figure 9.6
**The Lotus 1-2-3 worksheet
screen.**

in the form of a pie chart, bar chart, stacked bar chart, line, or *xy*. A regular monochrome monitor, however, will not display a graph; rather, the computer will simply beep.

Starting Lotus 1-2-3

Lotus 1-2-3 is a menu-driven software package, meaning that lists of options (*menus*) are displayed for you to choose from. Lotus 1-2-3 allows you to make a selection by either entering the first character of the option at the keyboard or positioning the pointer using a Right or Left arrow key and then depressing ENTER.

Starting Lotus 1-2-3 is a straightforward process. Simply place the Lotus System disk in disk drive A and your data disk in disk drive B. Turn on the computer (if the computer is already on, simply enter LOTUS). The computer will then display the **Lotus Access System** (see Figure 9.5a). This is the first example of a 1-2-3 menu structure. The first line with the 1-2-3, File-Manager, Disk-Manager, and so on, entries is the menu line containing the various options from which to choose. The second line contains a description of the highlighted menu option. Since the highlighted option is 1-2-3, the message `Enter 1-2-3 -- Lotus Spreadsheet/Graphics Database Program` is displayed. As you move the pointer from one entry to another via the Right and Left arrow keys, the message changes to reflect the new, highlighted menu option. At this time, either enter a 1 or depress the ENTER key. After some disk processing, a message will appear indicating that you are in Lotus 1-2-3 (see Figure 9.5b). After a short wait, the screen depicted in Figure 9.6 will then be displayed, and the directory of the default disk drive will be read by the system.

Lotus 1-2-3 Screen

At first, there may appear to be little on the worksheet screen, but looks in this case are deceiving. The following pieces are part of the worksheet screen: control panel, mode indicator, border, worksheet, pointer/cursor, error message area, and indicators.

Control Panel. The **control panel** is contained on the top three lines of your screen and consists of (first) the status line, (second) the entry line, and (third) the prompt line. The **status line** tells where you are, displaying the cell address, data format (if any), cell width and the cell contents; information is given about how the data in that particular cell are being processed by Lotus and about whether the cell contains a label, a value, or a formula. In the status line:

> The cell address is always followed by a colon—A1:.
>
> Information about a cell formatted using the / Range Format command appears in parentheses—(C2).
>
> A cell that has a column width different from the rest of the worksheet appears within brackets—[15].
>
> The protection status appears. If a PR appears in the cell, you cannot change this cell's contents. If a U appears, this cell's contents can be changed.
>
> The cell contents appear to the right of any of the above entries.

The **entry line** corresponds to a "scratch" area that contains any data you happen to enter. It also contains any "pre-entered" information destined for the cell location given in the status line. This information is not placed in either the cell or the status line until the ENTER key is pressed. The entry line may also contain a menu of options for performing various operations on your worksheet. The main menu can be invoked any time by entering the slash (/) command.

The **prompt line** contains further options or an explanation of a specific command when a 1-2-3 menu is displayed.

Mode Indicator. The **mode indicator**, in the upper right-hand corner of the screen, displays status information about what 1-2-3 is doing. Some mode indicators you will be seeing while you are working in this book are:

> READY—Lotus 1-2-3 is waiting for you to tell it to do something.
>
> VALUE—You are entering a number or formula to be contained in a cell.
>
> LABEL—You are entering text information to be contained in a cell.
>
> EDIT—You are changing the contents of a cell via the edit feature of 1-2-3.
>
> POINT—You are pointing to a cell or to a range of cells.
>
> MENU—You have a menu displayed before you and are selecting from it.
>
> HELP—You are using the 1-2-3 help feature.
>
> ERROR—Something went wrong, and 1-2-3 is waiting for you to depress the ENTER or Esc key to acknowledge the error.
>
> WAIT—1-2-3 is calculating the spreadsheet or performing a read/write operation and cannot accept more commands.

FIND—1-2-3 is using its data management feature to perform a find operation.

FILES—You are using a command that displays a listing of files.

Border. The **border** labels the rows and columns of your worksheet. The columns are labeled with letters of the alphabet (A, B, C, and so on), and the rows are labeled with numbers (1, 2, 3, and so on).

Worksheet. The **worksheet** contains whatever space is available to the user for problem solving. The worksheet has several key parts. They are cell, pointer, and window. As was noted earlier, a cell is the intersection point of a row and column and is referred to by its cell address COLUMN/ROW. For example, B5 refers to the cell located at the intersection of column B and row 5. A cell can contain either a label, a value, or a formula.

The **pointer**, also sometimes referred to as the cursor, is the reverse-video (light background with dark characters) bar. Its width depends on the width of the cell being referenced. The contents of the referenced cell are displayed in the status line of the control panel.

The 1-2-3 worksheet is large compared to many other spreadsheet packages. It contains 256 columns (A, B, C, D, . . . , IV) and 8,192 rows for a grand total of 2,097,152 cells. How large a piece of paper would you need to hold this size spreadsheet? If each cell were ¼ inch high and 1 inch wide, a piece of paper that could hold all of these rows and columns would have to be 170.6 feet high and 21.3 feet wide. The 1-2-3 worksheet is, indeed, large.

It goes without saying that all these cells cannot be displayed at one time on your small display screen. Instead, only small, rectangular sections of these 2,097,152 cells can be displayed at one time. The display, referred to as the **window**, always has twenty rows; the number of columns displayed depends on the column width.

Current Date and Time. The **current date** and **current time** are displayed here. Remember, for this time to be correct, you must respond to the Date and Time prompts when you boot the computer system.

Error Message Indicator. **Error messages** appear in the lower left-hand corner of the screen, giving a brief explanation of what has gone wrong. They are accompanied by a beep from the computer when a Lotus 1-2-3 rule has been broken. After you have read the message and wish to return control to the worksheet, simply depress the Esc or ENTER key.

Indicators. The old IBM keyboard does not tell you whether the Scroll Lock, Caps Lock, or Num Lock keys are on or off. The Lotus 1-2-3 **indicators** for each of these provide this information. If one of these keys is on, a message in reverse video will be displayed in the lower right-hand corner of the screen. A fourth indicator is CALC, which will be discussed in a later chapter.

Navigating Around the 1-2-3 Worksheet

Because Lotus 1-2-3 was designed specifically for the old IBM PC, it makes full use of all the keys on the keyboard—an especially important feature when it comes to moving the pointer quickly around the worksheet. Most pointer movement commands are accomplished by using the ten-key pad found on the right-hand side of the keyboard, and Lotus 1-2-3 automatically places these keys in cursor movement mode rather than in numeric mode. The movement keys work as follows:

> The **Down arrow** moves the pointer down one cell position (down one row).
>
> The **Up arrow** moves the pointer up one cell position (up one row).
>
> The **Right arrow** moves the pointer to the right one cell position (to the right one column).
>
> The **Left arrow** moves the pointer to the left one cell position (to the left one column).
>
> The **PgUp key** moves the pointer up twenty lines (one page) in its present column.
>
> The **PgDn key** moves the pointer down twenty lines (one page) in its present column.
>
> The **Home key** moves the pointer to cell position A1.
>
> The **End key**, when entered prior to an arrow key, positions the pointer in the same direction as the arrow key at the next nonblank boundary cell. For example, a worksheet will typically have blocks of cells with data, followed by blocks of blank, empty cells that are in turn followed by other cells with data. If the pointer is in a blank/empty region and the End key is depressed, followed by an arrow key, the pointer will be moved to the first nonblank cell. If the same command sequence is entered again, the pointer moves to the last nonblank cell in that block. Entering the same command sequence moves the pointer to the next nonblank area. When there are no longer any nonblank cells remaining in one direction of pointer movement, one of 1-2-3's boundaries will have been reached (for example, row 8,192 or column IV).
>
> The **TAB key**, located above the Ctrl key, moves the pointer to the right one screen (seventy-two characters) at a time. The **TAB** plus the **SHIFT key** moves the pointer to the left one screen (seventy-two characters) at a time.

The TAB key function can also be performed with two other sets of keystrokes:

> Moving to the right one screen at a time (also referred to as a *big right*): Ctrl + Right arrow.
>
> Moving to the left one screen at a time (also referred to as a *big left*): Ctrl + Left arrow.

The above keys move or skip the cursor across the worksheet. In contrast, the **Scroll Lock key** causes the worksheet to move under the cursor, rather than causing the cursor to move across the spreadsheet.

How Lotus 1-2-3 Uses Other Keys

Figure 9.7 shows where the various special purpose keys are located on the IBM PC keyboard and what they are used for. The remaining special purpose keys work as follows:

> The **/ key** is used to invoke the 1-2-3 Main Menu. The Main Menu (see Figure 9.8) is used to invoke other menus or commands. The various menus used in 1-2-3 account for over 115 different commands. The menus and the command prompts appear in the Control Panel of

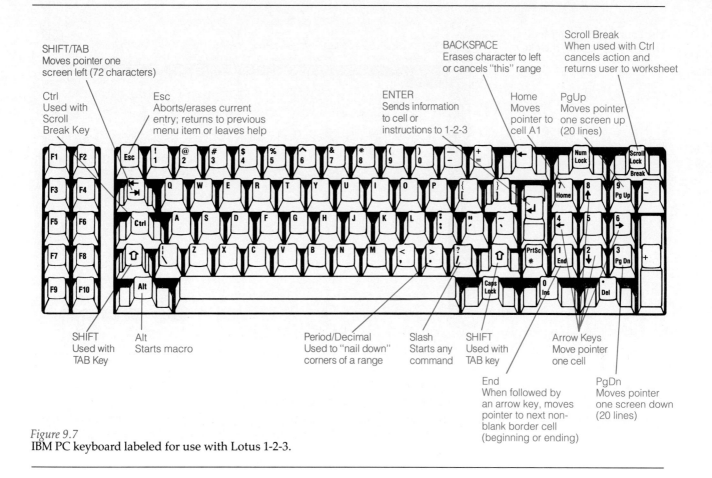

Figure 9.7
IBM PC keyboard labeled for use with Lotus 1-2-3.

the worksheet screen. A menu item can be selected by positioning the pointer to that item and pressing the ENTER key or by entering the first character of the command. When you are dealing with a menu item, the message in the prompt line describes the command or displays a submenu that will be executed if this option is selected. A menu item once selected may invoke another menu or it may execute a command. The various menus contained in 1-2-3 can be seen in Appendix B.

The **Esc key** is used to back out of a command sequence, if you are in a menu. If you are entering data in a cell, anything that appears on the entry line is simply erased when you depress Esc, and the original contents of the cell (if any) are left unchanged.

The **Ctrl key** plus the **Scroll Break key** is used to cancel any action taking place and return the user to the worksheet. This key sequence can be used to cancel printing, sorting, or any other 1-2-3 operation.

The **Macro (Alt) key** lets you give letter keys alternative meanings. If you find yourself repeating certain sequences of keystrokes, you can have 1-2-3 save these keystrokes in a **keyboard macro**; then you can direct 1-2-3 to execute them, by depressing the Macro key along with the coded one-letter name.

The **ENTER key** tells 1-2-3 that you have finished typing and want to send the information to the cell or give 1-2-3 an instruction.

Figure 9.8
The Lotus 1-2-3 Main Menu
invoked by pressing the / key.

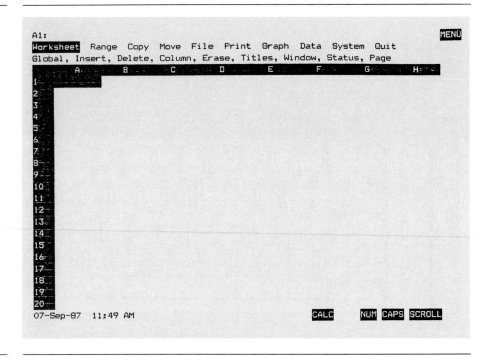

The **BACKSPACE key** deletes the character to the left of the pointer and can also cancel the current range.

The **function keys** are the ten keys lying together on the left-hand side or the twelve keys along the top of the keyboard. They are used to perform specially defined 1-2-3 functions with only one keystroke. The ten function keys perform the following tasks:

F1	HELP	Displays a help screen
F2	EDIT	Edits the contents of a cell
F3	NAME	Displays defined range names
F4	ABS	Defines a cell as an absolute value
F5	GOTO	Moves the pointer to a cell
F6	WINDOW	Jumps from one window to another
F7	QUERY	Performs the last query sequence
F8	TABLE	Performs the last table sequence
F9	CALC	Recalculates all the formulas in the worksheet
F10	GRAPH	Generates the graph last defined

Data Entry

Data entry is the process of placing values, labels, or formulas into the individual cells of a worksheet. A label cell can be printed or listed onto the screen, but it cannot be involved in a calculation. Therefore, you could say that the type of data stored in a cell dictates how that cell can be manipulated. The spreadsheet software must have some indication of the type of data you wish to store in a cell, and it is forced to make certain assumptions.

If you begin entering data of an alphabetic character within a cell, the spreadsheet will assume that you wish to enter **label data**. When 1-2-3 encounters alphabetic data, it automatically places a single quote (') at the beginning.

This presents a problem when you are entering formula-related information because the formula's reference to the cell location must start with an alphabetic character. The problem is solved by placing a + symbol before the cell location, so 1-2-3 recognizes the entry as a formula rather than as a label.

Numeric information is entered simply by typing the digits that they are composed of. (A negative number is represented by preceding the number with a minus sign ($-$); no such convention is needed if the number is positive.) This, however, presents a problem when you wish to have **numeric data** treated as a label. For example, how could the years *1988* and *1989* be presented to Lotus 1-2-3 as labels rather than numbers? Lotus 1-2-3 uses a very simple technique: in order to present *1988* as a label, all you need to do is place a single quote (') before the value to be treated as a label. For example, in this case you would enter the characters '1988 and Lotus would treat *1988* as a label.

Formulas explaining how numeric data are to be manipulated are entered as they would be processed algebraically. If the formula is entered properly, the spreadsheet will perform the operation; otherwise, an error message will be displayed in the lower left-hand corner of the screen, and the computer will beep. If this happens, the formula must be edited or reentered.

Entering Formulas

Operators. Formulas tell 1-2-3 what mathematical manipulations you wish it to perform on specific cell contents. The operations 1-2-3 can perform are invoked by using the following symbols in a formula:

    ^   Exponentiation

    *   Multiplication

    /   Division

    +   Addition

    $-$ Subtraction

Thus, to divide the contents of cell C3 by the contents of cell D3, you would enter the formula +C3/D3.

Precedence (Order of Operations). The order in which calculations are executed is called **precedence**. Operations are always performed in the following order, left to right within a formula:

    Exponentiation is performed first

    Then any multiplication and division, in the order that they occur

    Then any addition and subtraction, in the order that they occur

For example, the formula +A7/A1+B3*D4^3 would result in the following:

1. The contents of cell D4 are raised to the third power.
2. The contents of cell A7 are divided by the contents of cell A1.
3. The contents of cell B3 are multiplied by the result of step 1.
4. The result of step 2 is added to the result of step 3.

Parentheses and Precedence. Parentheses can be used to override the above order of operations. At the most general level, operations inside parentheses are performed before those outside; within the parentheses, however, the order of operations is the same. When multiple sets of parentheses are used, the operations within the innermost set are executed, followed by those within the next set.

For example, the formula `+C3-(A3+D3)` would result in the following:

1. The contents of cell A3 are added to the contents of cell D3.

2. The result of step 1 is subtracted from the contents of cell C3.

For a more complex example, the formula `+D3*D4+(C7+E4^3*F6 -(G6/F7+D3^2)+A1)` would result in:

1. The `(G6/F7+D3^2)` would be performed first because these operations reside in the innermost set of parentheses.
   a. The contents of cell D3 are raised to the second power.
   b. The contents of cell G6 are divided by the contents of cell F7.
   c. The result of step 1a is added to the result of step 1b.

2. The formula now logically appears as `+D3*D4+(C7+E4^3*F6 -Step1+A1)`, and the next part of the formula to be executed would be `(C7+E4^3*F6-Step1+A1)`.
   a. The contents of cell E4 are raised to the third power.
   b. The result of step 2a is multiplied by the contents of cell F6.
   c. The contents of cell C7 are added to the result of step 2b from which is subtracted the result of step 1 and to which is added the contents of A1.

3. The formula now logically appears as `+D3*D4+Step2`.
   a. The contents of cell D3 are multiplied by the contents of cell D4.
   b. The result of step 3a is now added to the result of step 2 to obtain the final result.

Circular References

One problem that almost all users of a spreadsheet like 1-2-3 encounter when entering formulas is the circular reference. A **circular reference** is a formula in a cell that, directly or indirectly, refers back to that same cell. A circular reference in a worksheet is indicated when a `CIRC` message appears at the bottom of the screen. When the circular reference is corrected, the `CIRC` message disappears. A circular reference would appear on the screen if the following formula appeared in cell B12:

`@SUM(B1.B12)`

The circular reference appears because the cell B12 is an operand in the operation as well as the cell designated to hold the answer. A cell cannot be both.

Built-in Functions

Built-in functions are processes or formulas that have already been programmed into the spreadsheet software package. These functions save the user a tremendous amount of effort and tedium in writing all the statements needed to perform some type of mathematical manipulation. In the Lotus spreadsheet package, a function is designated by the @ symbol. To sum the values contained in cells A3, B3, C3, D3, and E3 and place the result in cell G3, the following formula would be required in cell G3: `@SUM(A3.E3)`. While there are many others, some of the more common Lotus 1-2-3 functions are:

Mathematical
  Absolute value, arc cosine, arc sine, arc tangent, cosine, log, exponent, pi, random, round, integer, sine, square root, tangent

Logical
    True, false, if/then/else

Financial
    Internal rate of return, net present value, future value of an annuity, present value, payment

Statistical
    Average, minimum, maximum, standard deviation, variance

Correcting Errors on the Worksheet

There are basically five correction methods (plus one start-over method) for dealing with errors you've made while using the Lotus 1-2-3 package:

1. If you make an error while typing something in the "scratch" area of the control panel, use the BACKSPACE key to erase the mistake, and then retype any deleted data.

2. If you have entered something in the worksheet that you want to replace with other data, move the pointer back to that cell, type the new data, and hit ENTER. The new entry will take the place of the old.

3. If you have entered data in a cell of the worksheet that you want to blank out, position the pointer to that cell, and depress the key sequence /RE, and hit ENTER to erase the contents of that one cell.

4. If you start to enter data for a cell and then change your mind, simply depress the Esc key, and the data will not be entered in the cell. If you are inside a menu, you can depress the Esc key to get the previous level. If you want to return to the worksheet, depress Ctrl and Break simultaneously.

5. Suppose a cell that has an error in it contains a very long formula or label. You don't want to reenter all of the information because you will more than likely commit some other type of error in doing so. In this type of situation, you should depress the **Edit key (F2)**. The Edit key places the cell contents on the entry line, as well as on the status line. You can now use the following keys and perform "word processing" on the cell contents displayed on the entry line.

    Home   Places the cursor at the beginning of the line.

    End   Places the cursor at the end of the line.

    Del   Deletes the character under the cursor.

    BACKSPACE   Deletes the character to the left of the cursor.

    Esc   Returns the user to the worksheet without changes.

    Ctrl + Break   Stops what is being done and returns you to the worksheet in ready mode.

    [arrow key]   Moves the cursor in the direction of the arrow.

    To insert information on a line, position the cursor one position to the right of where you wish the new information to go, and start typing.

6. If everything is totally wrong and you have a complete mess on your hands, you may just wish to start over with a new worksheet, erasing what's already on the screen. To erase the current worksheet, enter the following commands: `/Worksheet Erase Yes`. This will erase the screen and RAM. You cannot recall anything, so use this command sequence carefully.

Getting Help

From time to time, you may forget where you are in a menu structure (see Appendix B for Lotus 1-2-3 command structure) or may not understand how a particular command operates. Since 1-2-3 has over 115 built-in commands, it's reasonable to assume that you will not be acquainted with all of them.

To aid you in remembering (or in becoming acquainted for the first time with) these commands, Lotus 1-2-3 provides a built-in tutor, known as the **help facility**, which you can activate by pressing the F1 key. The help facility displays information about the current menu options available to you or about the current command you are working on; it is made context-sensitive by the position of the pointer in a menu or a command sequence from a menu. To get out of help and back to the worksheet, simply press the Esc key.

For example, suppose that you needed help while you were at READY mode in your worksheet. If you pressed the Help (F1) key, the screen depicted in Figure 9.9 is displayed to your monitor. Notice that the control panel is displayed at the top of your screen and that the mode indicator says HELP. To leave, press the Esc key. Suppose now that you want more help about entries contained in the Main Menu. After you have invoked the Main Menu via the / key, press the Help (F1) key and a screen like that depicted in Figure 9.10 appears on your monitor. You can now obtain help about the Move command by highlighting that option. The help screen depicted in Figure 9.11 now appears on your screen with information about the Move command. When you have finished, press the Esc key to return to READY mode.

Entering a Sample Lotus 1-2-3 Worksheet

Let's assume that a friend of yours named Ed owns a grocery store with the following departments: Deli, Bakery, Liquor, Grocery, Produce, and Meat. It's the end of the year, and Ed would like to compare the sales of the various departments for last year and this year, keeping track of the overall change in sales (either positive or negative) and of the percentage change in sales for each of the departments.

Since Ed knows you are enrolled in a course that covers Lotus 1-2-3, you have been honored with a request to help him prepare a spreadsheet to perform the data manipulation. After carefully examining the problem, you decide that a worksheet like the following will present the information in an understandable format:

COMPSALS

Department	Last Year	This Year	Change	% Change
Deli	700.00	575.00	(125.00)	−18%
Bakery	1,000.00	1,100.00	100.00	10%
Liquor	1,200.00	1,400.00	200.00	17%
Grocery	2,500.00	2,900.00	400.00	16%
Produce	950.00	1,000.00	50.00	5%
Meat	1,500.00	1,410.00	(90.00)	−6%
Store Total	7,850.00	8,385.00	535.00	7%

In the course of this project, the following learning objectives in the use of Lotus 1-2-3 will be accomplished:

1. Introduction to pointer movement

2. Entering labels (text)

3. Use of the @SUM function

Figure 9.9
Help screen for READY mode.

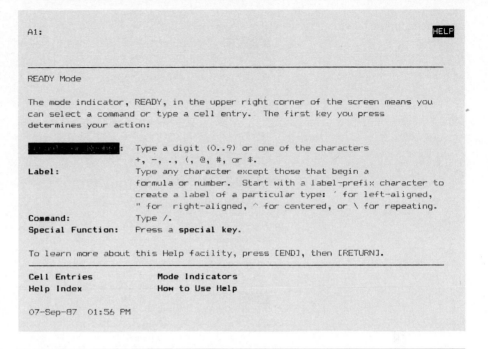

Figure 9.10
Help screen for Main Menu.

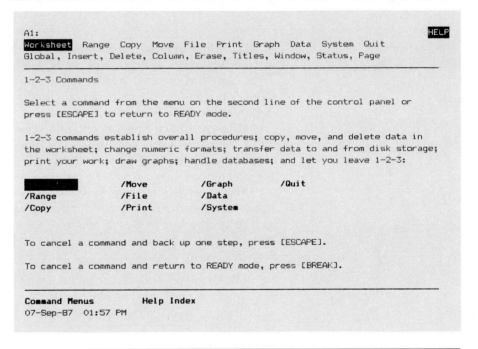

4. Entering 1-2-3 formulas

5. Changing column width for an entire worksheet

6. Global data format changes

7. Use of the Copy command

8. Use of the Range Format command

9. Use of the Range Erase command

10. Justification of text within a cell

11. Printing a worksheet

Figure 9.11
Help screen for the Move command.

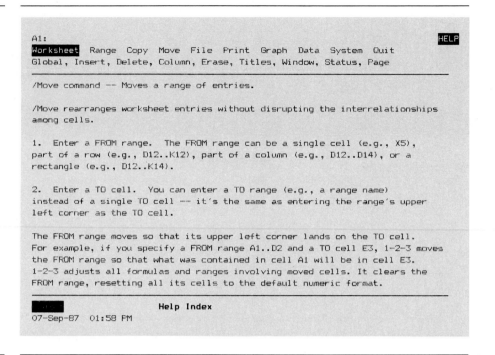

```
A1:                                                                    HELP
Worksheet  Range  Copy  Move  File  Print  Graph  Data  System  Quit
Global, Insert, Delete, Column, Erase, Titles, Window, Status, Page
────────────────────────────────────────────────────────────────────────
/Move command -- Moves a range of entries.

/Move rearranges worksheet entries without disrupting the interrelationships
among cells.

1.  Enter a FROM range.  The FROM range can be a single cell (e.g., X5),
part of a row (e.g., D12..K12), part of a column (e.g., D12..D14), or a
rectangle (e.g., D12..K14).

2.  Enter a TO cell.  You can enter a TO range (e.g., a range name)
instead of a single TO cell -- it's the same as entering the range's upper
left corner as the TO cell.

The FROM range moves so that its upper left corner lands on the TO cell.
For example, if you specify a FROM range A1..D2 and a TO cell E3, 1-2-3 moves
the FROM range so that what was contained in cell A1 will be in cell E3.
1-2-3 adjusts all formulas and ranges involving moved cells. It clears the
FROM range, resetting all its cells to the default numeric format.
────────────────────────────────────────────────────────────────────────
                            Help Index
07-Sep-87  01:58 PM
```

Format of Instructions. In accomplishing these objectives, you will have to perform a number of processing steps, which are detailed on the following pages. Any time you see a letter followed by a number (for example, B4), it signifies that you are to go to that cell location and enter the following data or execute the following instruction.

After you have finished entering the data or instruction, depress the ENTER key or an arrow key. Depressing the ENTER key takes the information from the entry line and places it in the cell, leaving the pointer on that cell. The pointer can then be moved to another cell via the appropriate arrow key.

To accomplish the same task with one less keystroke, simply depress an arrow key when you are finished entering data on the entry line. This action both enters the data in the cell and moves the pointer to the next cell location.

Step-by-Step Instructions for 1-2-3 Sample Worksheet–COMPSALS

1. Enter row and column labels. Don't worry if some of the labels won't fit in a cell. That will be taken care of later.

B1	COMPSALS
B3	Department
C3	Last Year
D3	This Year
E3	Change
F3	% Change
B5	Deli
B6	Bakery
B7	Liquor
B8	Grocery
B9	Produce

    B10   Meat

    B12   Store Total

2. Change the column width to 12 for the whole spreadsheet (global). Lotus 1-2-3 brings up a blank worksheet with a column width of 9.

    /—Brings up the Main Menu for Lotus 1-2-3.

    W—Selects the desired Worksheet selection from the Main Menu. You may select from a menu in either of two ways: (1) you can move the pointer with arrow keys to the selection and depress ENTER; or (2) you can enter the first letter of the option desired. You will notice that, as you move the pointer along the options, the prompt line changes from option to option. This gives the user additional information about each option.

    G—Tells 1-2-3 that the command to be entered will affect the entire worksheet.

    C—Signifies that the Column Width command has been selected from the menu.

    12—Changes the column width from 9 to 12 positions.

    ENTER—Tells 1-2-3 to execute the command.

3. Enter totals for the Last Year and This Year columns. Don't enter the commas or decimal points as presented above. You'll tell 1-2-3 what to do with these numbers later.

    C5   700

    C6   1000

    C7   1200

    C8   2500

    C9   950

    C10   1500

    D5   575

    D6   1100

    D7   1400

    D8   2900

    D9   1000

    D10   1410

4. At C12, demonstrate the use of the @SUM command.

    C12 [by manual pointer movement] @SUM(—Enters the beginning of the formula.

    C5 [by manual pointer movement]—Positions the pointer at cell C5.

    .—Marks the beginning of the range.

    C10 [by manual pointer movement]—Positions the pointer at cell C10—the last cell to be summed.

)—Stops the process with a).

    ENTER—Executes the sum function.

The above steps will produce the value 7850 in cell C12. The use of the @SUM function introduces the use of a function and illustrates 1-2-3's ability to point to data and then enter that pointed address into a formula. The @SUM function also introduces the concept of a **range**. As you no doubt noticed, the pointed range (adjacent cells included in the operation) appeared in reverse video. This convention allows a user to see exactly which cells will be included in an operation.

Note carefully what happens on the screen as you total the This Year column.

5. At D12, use the @SUM command to add the numbers in the This Year column.

> D12 [by manual pointer movement] @SUM(—Enters the first part of the formula.
>
> D5 [by manual pointer movement]—Positions the pointer at cell D5.
>
> .—Marks the beginning of the range.
>
> D10 [by manual pointer movement]—Positions the pointer at D10.
>
>)—Stops the process with a).
>
> ENTER—Executes the sum function.

The above steps will produce the value 8385 in cell D12.

6. Use a global change to put two positions to the right of the decimal point and to allow for commas between the hundreds and thousands digits.

> /—Brings up the Main Menu for Lotus 1-2-3.
>
> W—Selects the Worksheet option from the Main Menu (see task 2 above.)
>
> G—Tells 1-2-3 that the command to be entered will affect the entire worksheet.
>
> F—Tells 1-2-3 that the format (the manner in which data are presented on the worksheet) is to be selected.
>
> ,—Tells 1-2-3 that commas are to be placed where you would logically expect them. Negative numbers will be contained in parentheses. A fixed number of decimal places can also be specified.
>
> 2—Tells 1-2-3 that two decimal positions will be displayed.
>
> ENTER—Tells 1-2-3 to execute the instruction.

7. At E5, calculate the change between This Year and Last Year (using the pointer method).

> +—Indicates to 1-2-3 that a formula is to be entered.
>
> D5 [by manual pointer movement]—Positions the pointer at cell D5.
>
> −—indicates to 1-2-3 that the next cell is to be entered.
>
> C5 [by manual pointer movement]—Positions the pointer at cell C5.
>
> ENTER—Executes the command and places the result in cell E5.

You can use the pointer when entering a cell location in a formula. This works well when you don't remember the exact location.

8. Copy (replicate) this formula for the rest of the cells in the column.

Copying the formula into the other cells in the column can save a tremendous amount of time and can eliminate typing errors. Make sure that the pointer is at E5.

/—Brings up the Main Menu.

C—Selects the Copy option.

ENTER—Establishes the sending area. You only want to copy the contents of this cell (E5).

Down arrow to E6—Positions the pointer at the first cell in the range, to receive the formula contained in E5.

.—Indicates to 1-2-3 that this is the first cell to be referenced in a range—"nailing down" the beginning.

Down arrow to E12—Positions the pointer at the last cell in the range to receive the formula contained in E5.

ENTER—Tells 1-2-3 to execute the copy command.

Don't worry about the garbage in E11. You'll get rid of that later.

You will notice that the other cells now have answers in the change column that correspond to those at the beginning of this lesson. Move the pointer from one cell to another in the column. Notice that the cell addresses have been changed automatically by 1-2-3. This ability to change cell locations automatically during a copy or move is referred to as **relative addressing**.

9. Enter the formula to calculate the percentage change. You'll change the format of the column later. Position pointer to cell F5.

+E5/C5—Places this formula in cell F5.

ENTER—Executes the sum function.

You should have the value (0.18) in cell F5.

This method demonstrates that you are not required to point if you know the cell addresses. The pointing method, although impressive at first, can actually result in extra work for a worksheet user. This is especially true if the cell locations are far away on the worksheet.

10. Copy this formula for the rest of the column, after first positioning the pointer at cell F5.

/—Invokes the Main Menu.

C—Selects the Copy command.

ENTER—Establishes cell F5 as being the only cell holding data to be copied to other cells.

Down arrow to F6—Positions the pointer at the first cell that is to receive the formula to be copied.

.—Indicates to 1-2-3 that this is the first cell to be referenced in a range.

Down arrow to F12—Positions the pointer at the last cell in the range that is to receive the formula from cell F5.

ENTER—Tells 1-2-3 that the range has been established and that the command is to be executed.

11. To get rid of the two entries at E11 and F11, position the pointer at F11.

/—Invokes the Main Menu.

R—Selects the Range option from the Main Menu. The Range

option should be used whenever you wish to perform operations on only a part of the worksheet, rather than on all of it.

E—Tells 1-2-3 that you wish to erase the contents of a range of cells beginning with F11—not the entire worksheet.

Back arrow—Moves the pointer to the last cell in the range (E11).

ENTER—Tells 1-2-3 that the range has been established and that the command is to be executed.

Your spreadsheet should now look as follows:

```
COMPSALS
Department      Last Year  This Year   Change        % Change
Deli                700.00     575.00    (125.00)         (0.18)
Bakery            1,000.00   1,100.00     100.00           0.10
Liquor            1,200.00   1,400.00     200.00           0.17
Grocery           2,500.00   2,900.00     400.00           0.16
Produce             950.00   1,000.00      50.00           0.05
Meat              1,500.00   1,410.00     (90.00)         (0.06)

Store Total       7,850.00   8,385.00     535.00           0.07
```

12. Format column F for percentages, beginning with position F5.

/—Invokes the Main Menu.

R—Selects the Range option from the Main Menu.

F—Selects the Format to change a portion of the worksheet.

P—Tells 1-2-3 that you wish to use the Percent format to display data within a range.

O—Tells 1-2-3 that there are to be no positions to the right of the decimal.

ENTER—Marks cell F5 as the beginning of the range.

Down arrow to F12—Marks the rest of the cells in the range.

ENTER—Tells 1-2-3 that the range has been established and that the data format is now to be changed to percent.

13. Position the pointer at F3 to right-justify the column labels.

/—Invokes the Main Menu.

R—Selects the Range option from the Main Menu. You only want to right-justify one row of labels (a range).

L—Selects the Label Prefix command.

R—Tells 1-2-3 to right-justify the label within the cell and start the range with cell F3.

Back arrow to B3—Establishes the range of cells whose labels are to be right justified.

ENTER—Tells 1-2-3 to right-justify the labels within the marked range of cells.

14. Save the worksheet onto disk, using the name COMPSALS.

/—Brings up the Main Menu.

F—Selects the File option. This option is selected any time you wish to read or write data onto a disk.

S—Executes the Save command to save a worksheet to the disk in drive B.

COMPSALS—Responds to Lotus 1-2-3 prompt for the file name. If the file has already been saved before, 1-2-3 will ask if you want to cancel or replace: CANCEL would result in the command being canceled; REPLACE would overwrite the old file with the present worksheet in RAM.

15. Print the worksheet.

/—Brings up the Main Menu.

P—Selects the Print option.

P—Tells 1-2-3 that the output is to go to the printer.

R—Tells 1-2-3 that you wish to tell it what part of the worksheet is to be printed. (Remember there are 524,288 cells.)

A1 [by manual pointer movement]—Gives the first cell location (upper left-hand corner).

.—Tells 1-2-3 that a range is to be established.

F12 [by manual pointer movement]—Gives the last cell location (lower right-hand corner).

ENTER—Tells 1-2-3 that the range has been established.

G—Tells 1-2-3 to begin printing.

16. Go to next page of the printout, so the current page can be removed.

P—Tells 1-2-3 to go to the top of the next page.

A—Tells 1-2-3 that it is now at the top of the paper. If you forget to align the printer with this command, your worksheet may have a wide gap in the middle.

Saving and Retrieving Worksheet Files

The first time that you work on a worksheet, 1-2-3 prompts you to enter a name for the worksheet when you issue the command to save it to disk. Any worksheet file that you save to disk has the .WK1 file extension. The following commands are used to save a worksheet to disk:

/—Brings up the Main Menu for 1-2-3.

F—Selects the File option from the Main Menu. This option is selected any time that you wish to save or load a worksheet from disk.

S—Executes the Save command to save a worksheet to the disk in drive B.

The worksheet file can now be loaded at a later time and changes can be made to that worksheet. Use the following commands to load a worksheet:

/—Brings up the Main Menu for 1-2-3.

F—Selects the File option from the Main Menu.

R—Selects the Retrieve option to read a worksheet file from the disk in drive B. You can now either manually enter the name of the worksheet to be loaded or simply "point" to the appropriate worksheet file using the pointer and then depressing the ENTER key.

 Once you finish making any changes to the worksheet, you must again save it to disk. Since you indicated the name of the worksheet to 1-2-3 when you loaded it, when you issue the Save command, 1-2-3 displays that name as the default. By pressing the ENTER key, you accept that default. If you wish to enter another name, the current name disappears as soon as you press any other alphabetic or numeric key. If you press the ENTER key to accept the default name, 1-2-3 displays the following menu:

Cancel   Replace

The Cancel command tells 1-2-3 to stop this operation and returns you to READY mode.

The Replace command tells 1-2-3 to go ahead and save the contents of this worksheet to disk. This process destroys the original worksheet file and replaces it with the new worksheet.

Once you have saved a file to disk, you may want to verify that it actually was stored properly. You can verify that a worksheet was stored properly in two ways. First, you can simply reload the worksheet file from disk using the /File Retrieve commands. Second, you can use the List command from the File Menu. Issuing the /File List command results in a menu display from which you select the appropriate type of file that you wish to have displayed. In this case, you would enter the following commands:

/—Brings up the Main Menu of 1-2-3.

F—Selects the File option of the Main Menu.

L—Selects the List option of the File Menu.

W—Tells 1-2-3 to display all of the worksheet files (those files with a .WK? file extension) to the screen (Figure 9.12).

When you wish to return to 1-2-3, press the ENTER key.

Release 2.X of 1-2-3 stores worksheets with a file extension of .WK1. The older version of 1-2-3 (Release 1A) stored worksheets with an extension of .WKS. These older .WKS worksheet files can be read by Release 2.X of 1-2-3, but when a Save command is executed these files are saved using the .WK1 file extension. This means that when you retrieve a .WKS file and then subsequently save it, that file appears twice. One file contains the .WKS file extension and the other contains the .WK1 file extension. Once this occurs, you should use the /File Erase Worksheet command to erase the .WKS file. Otherwise you may make important changes, save the file, and later retrieve the unchanged .WKS file.

Your worksheet should now look exactly like the worksheet at the beginning of this lesson. If it doesn't you have done something wrong. Compare the contents of each cell with the contents listed below:

B1:	'COMPSALS
B3:	''Department
C3:	''Last Year
D3:	''This Year
E3:	''Change
F3:	''% Change
B5:	'Deli
C5:	700
D5:	575
E5:	+D5-C5
F5:	(P0) +E5/C5
B6:	'Bakery

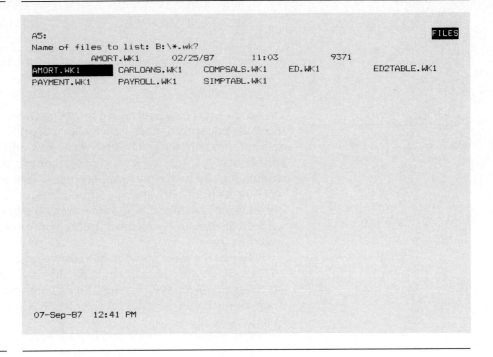

Figure 9.12
Type of screen displayed
when you enter the /Files List
Worksheet instruction.

C6:	1000	
D6:	1100	
E6:	+D6-C6	
F6:	(PO) +E6/C6	
B7:	'Liquor	
C7:	1200	
D7:	1400	
E7:	+D7-C7	
F7:	(PO) +E7/C7	
B8:	'Grocery	
C8:	2500	
D8:	2900	
E8:	+D8-C8	
F8:	(PO) +E8/C8	
B9:	'Produce	
C9:	950	
D9:	1000	
E9:	+D9-C9	
F9:	(PO) +E9/C9	
B10:	'Meat	
C10:	1500	
D10:	1410	
E10:	+D10-C10	
F10:	(PO) +E10/C10	
B12:	'Store Total	

C12:   @SUM(C5..C10)
D12:   @SUM(D5..D10)
E12:   +D12–C12
F12:   (PO) +E12/C12

Chapter Review

One of the most frequently used microcomputer applications in business is the electronic spreadsheet, which allows an individual to manipulate any data/information that can be placed in a row-and-column format. Most spreadsheet software packages have a number of features in common, including the ability to copy formulas or text, delete rows or columns, load worksheets from disk, insert rows or columns, change the format of data presentation, move text or formulas from one location to another, print the worksheet, save the worksheet, freeze portions (titles) of the worksheet, and split the screen.

Two of the most popular spreadsheet packages are VisiCalc and Lotus 1-2-3. VisiCalc was originally built for the Apple II microcomputer, and Lotus 1-2-3 was originally built for the IBM PC. Both software packages resulted in dramatically increased sales for their respective machines when they were first introduced.

When you are using a spreadsheet package you must follow a number of logical steps in planning, developing, and testing your worksheet, in order to ensure that the problem is properly modeled.

The Lotus 1-2-3 spreadsheet package is a menu-driven, integrated package composed of the functional parts of spreadsheet, graphics, and data management. Its screen consists of a control panel, border, mode indicator, special indicators, error message indicator, and worksheet area. Various keys of the keyboard are used to move the pointer around the worksheet area.

You can enter data and correct errors by making changes in the control panel area. After data are entered or changes made, they will be reflected in the appropriate cell if you press an arrow key or the ENTER key. Arithmetic manipulation of numeric data contained in cells can be accomplished by entering a formula or by telling 1-2-3 to use one of its built-in functions. A detailed example of worksheet formation involves the practical application of many of these functions.

Key Terms and Concepts

Alt key	entry line
BACKSPACE key	error messages
border	Esc key
built-in functions	formula
cell	function keys
circular reference	graphics feature
column	help facility
control panel	Home key
Ctrl + Scroll Break keys	indicators
current date	integration
current time	/ key
data entry	keyboard macro
data management feature	label
Down arrow	label data
Edit key (F2)	Left arrow
End key	Lotus Access System
ENTER key	Lotus spreadsheet

Lotus worksheet
Macro key
mode indicator
number
numeric data
PgDn key
PgUp key
pointer
precedence
prompt line
range
relative addressing

Right arrow
row
Scroll Lock key
spreadsheet
status line
TAB key
TAB + SHIFT keys
template
Up arrow
window
worksheet

Chapter Quiz

Multiple Choice

1. Which of the following terms is not related to a worksheet?
   a. Row
   b. Column
   c. DOS prompt
   d. Pointer
   e. Border
   f. All of the above terms are related to a spreadsheet.

2. Which of the following items is not allowed in a cell?
   a. Formula
   b. Label
   c. Function
   d. Number
   e. All of the above are allowed in a cell.
   f. None of the above are allowed in a cell.

3. Which of the following names is not related to spreadsheet software triumphs?
   a. Mitch Kapor
   b. Dan Bricklin
   c. VisiCalc
   d. Steve Jobs
   e. Lotus 1-2-3

4. Which of the following keystrokes does not result in cursor movement?
   a. Arrow key
   b. PgUp
   c. Alt
   d. TAB
   e. End + an arrow key
   f. All of the above result in cursor movement.

5. Which of the following items is not found in the control panel?
   a. Entry line
   b. Prompt line
   c. Error line
   d. Status line
   e. All of the above are part of the control panel.
   f. None of the above is part of the control panel.

True/False

6. Integrated packages allow you to pass information from one part to another without any real difficulty.

7. The mode indicator is used to show the current status of the worksheet.

8. A cell is referenced by using the ROW/COLUMN designation.

9. The built-in functions in 1-2-3 always start with a @ character.

10. When entering a formula, you need only enter the cell location and an operation symbol—for example, A2-B7.

Answers

1. c 2. e 3. d 4. c 5. c 6. t 7. t 8. f 9. t 10. f

Exercises

1. Define or describe each of the following:
   a. built-in function   f. mode indicator
   b. 1-2-3 data management   g. indicators
   c. 1-2-3 graphics   h. Edit key (F2)
   d. Lotus Access System   i. precedence
   e. control panel   j. on-line help

2. A spreadsheet is the software, while a(n) _____ is the work area.

3. Any cell can be referenced by referring to its corresponding _____ _____ and _____ .

4. List each of the types of contents a cell may have:
   a.

   b.

   c.

5. A(n) _____ is similar to a prepackaged program. You enter the data, and it computes the results.

6. List the steps involved in using a spreadsheet to solve a problem:
   a.

   b.

   c.

   d.

7. List the three integrated parts of Lotus 1-2-3:
   a.

   b.

   c.

8. List the three parts of the 1-2-3 control panel:

   a.

   b.

   c.

9. The _____ indicator is used to identify the current status of the Lotus 1-2-3 package.

10. The part of your worksheet that is visible on your screen is referred to as the _____ .

11. The second line of the control panel is the _____ line.

12. Explain the use of each of the following cursor movement keys:

    a. Arrow key

    b. PgUp

    c. PgDn

    d. End

    e. Home

    f. TAB

13. The _____ key is used to quit an instruction or back up a step in the menu.

14. The two keys _____ and _____ are used to stop any spreadsheet process or function.

15. A cell that contains text automatically has a(n) _____ placed in it.

16. Why is the concept of precedence important in entering formulas? Explain how 1-2-3 evaluates a formula and executes it using precedence. How can this order of precedence be changed?

17. Why are built-in functions so useful? List some functions that you might find useful, and beside each function list an application of it.

    a.

    b.

    c.

    d.

18. Explain how the use of each of the following keys changes when the Edit mode is entered by pressing the F2 key.

    a. Home

    b. Del

    c. BACKSPACE

    d. End

    e. Esc

    f. Arrow keys

19. The four keystrokes _____, _____, _____, and _____ are used to erase the entire worksheet.

20. Practice using the on-line help facility, which is activated by pressing the F1 key.

Computer Exercises

1. Use the / File Retrieve command to load the worksheet file called CALEN-DAR, which contains an appointment calendar for keeping track of various appointments. Practice moving the pointer around the worksheet using the following commands.

Part I

    a. Use the various arrow keys to move the pointer.
    b. Press the Home key.
    c. Press the PgDn key twice.
    d. Press the PgUp key three times; notice the beep.
    e. Position the pointer at 8:00.
    f. Press the End key, followed by the Down arrow key.
    g. Press the same two keys again; the pointer should be at row 2048.
    h. Press the End key, followed by the Right arrow key; the pointer should be at cell IV2048.
    i. Now enter any character at cell IV2048. You should receive a Memory Full error message. Even though 1-2-3 has a bountiful number of cell locations, the limited amount of RAM in your computer prevents you from using all of them. Press the Esc key to get rid of the error message.
    j. Press the End key, followed by the Up arrow key. You should now see "end of column" at cell IV1. Notice that there is a single quote mark in front of the text. This single quote tells 1-2-3 that the contents of this cell are text data. Although you can enter the single quote, 1-2-3 automatically places it in the cell for you.
    k. Press the Home key.
    l. Press the TAB key twice.
    m. Press the SHIFT and TAB keys together.
    n. Position the pointer at cell A5. This cell contains the 1-2-3 function @NOW. This function is used to get the date that you entered when you started Lotus 1-2-3. If you did not enter a date, this cell contains 01-Jan-80 (the DOS default).

Part II

    a. Press the Scroll Lock key.
    b. Use the various arrow keys to move the pointer.

    c. Press the PgDn key twice.
    d. Press the PgUp key once.
    e. Press the TAB key twice.
    f. Press the SHIFT and TAB keys together.

2. Use the / File Retrieve command to load the worksheet file called PAYMENT, which is a template that allows you to enter the amount of a loan, the interest rate, and the number of years for the loan. It then automatically calculates the amount of the payment and the total amount paid over the life of the loan.

    Before you do anything to the worksheet, let's explore some of its features. There are two areas in this worksheet: The first area will hold information about various loans, and the second contains the information about a loan that you are permitted to change. If you try to change any cells, the computer merely beeps and displays the error message Protected Cell. Press the Esc to continue. The high-intensity (bright) cells' contents can be changed, but the others can't. Note the PR entry on the status line for protected cells and the U entry of the high-intensity unprotected cells.

    You are therefore allowed to change the loan amount, the interest rate, and the life of the loan in years. Enter the loan amounts without using dollar signs or commas. For example, if a loan is for $10,000, enter it as 10000. The current interest rate is 12 percent, expressed as a decimal (.12). The final field that you are allowed to change is the length of the loan, which is currently set for 4 years. These two variables appear at the bottom of the screen.

    Notice that as soon as you change the contents of one field the worksheet automatically recalculates itself.

    Enter information about the following loans:

    a. $10,000 at 12 percent for 4 years
    b. $15,000 at 12 percent for 4 years
    c. $25,000 at 14 percent for 6 years
    d. $80,000 at 16 percent for 20 years
    e. $120,000 at 13 percent for 15 years

3. Use the / File Retrieve command to load the worksheet file called ERRORS, which contains a number of mistakes that you should correct.
    a. Reenter the following mistakes:
       twilve
       cumpany

    b. Use the F2 Edit command to remedy the following errors:
       The dog jumped ovr the lasy cat
       The childrun sat at hoam

    c. Use the / Range Erase command to delete each of the following:
       xxxxxxxxx
       ****

       \ \ \ \ \ \ \ \ \ \

4. You are to create a student's budget schedule that will subtract total expenses from total income for a 4½-month period (one semester) and set

net cash amounts for each month. In addition, the schedule should provide monthly totals for income and expense items, with grand totals as depicted in the example below.

The dollar figures, along with the budget categories in the example below, are only illustrative. You are to pick categories and supply amounts appropriate to your particular situation. You are to use formulas or the sum function to calculate column and row totals as well as the net cash amount.

```
                    SCHOOL YEAR BUDGET
TERM: FALL                                      YEAR: 198__
NAME:

INCOME      AUGUST   SEPTEMBER   OCTOBER   NOVEMBER   DECEMBER   TOTAL

WORK          150        300        300       300        150     1200
AWARDS         50        100        100       100         50      400
ALLOWANCE      25         50         50        50         50      225
OTHER           5         10         10        10         10       45

EXPENSES

TUITION       250        500        500       500        250     2000
BOOKS          75        150        150       150         25      550
HOME           25        100        100       100        100      425
CLOTHING       40         80         80        80         40      320
FOOD           40         90         90        90         40      350
TRANSPORT      20         35         35        35        100      225
OTHER          20         35         35        35         35      160

TOTALS

INCOME        230        460        460       460        260     1870
EXPENSES      470        990        990       990        590     4030
NET CASH     -240       -530       -530      -530       -330    -2160
```

Save the worksheet to a file called CH9EX4.

5. You are the manager of a car dealership. You have five salespeople working for you. Your boss has requested that you take the last two years of sales information for each sales rep and determine the difference between the two years in sales dollars. Your boss has requested the information in the following format:

Sales rep	Last Year	This Year	Change	% Change
Harry	125,000	178,000		
Sally	190,000	260,000		
Ben	76,000	68,000		
Marge	98,000	153,000		
Felix	230,000	198,000		
Carol	78,000	163,000		
Totals				

You are to enter the formulas that will calculate the Change and % Change column entries. Place a total at the bottom of any column containing numeric information.

Set the worksheet column width to 12.
Save the worksheet to a file called CH9EX5.

6. The band leader has asked you to help in the record-keeping for the high-school band members' fund-raising drive. The band members are selling candy (at $3.00 per can) to pay for a trip to Washington, D.C. The band leader has accounting information concerning the number of cans of candy checked out by each member and about the money turned in by each member. You have been asked to determine how much, if anything, each member owes and to provide any information you can on totals.

Band Member	Cans Taken	Money Received	Balance Due
Diane Collins	40	120.00	
Melvin Davis	30	66.00	
Jack Gibson	50	140.00	
Darlene Posio	25	60.00	
Chris Peterson	45	120.00	
Joan Rushing	30	90.00	
Totals			

Save this worksheet file to disk using the name CH9EX6.

7. The head of the accounting department is interested in a comparative income statement for the last two years and has asked you to prepare the financial statement using the information below. You have been asked to ascertain the dollar change between the various income statement entries, as well.

ACE Inc.
Income Statement (unaudited)

	Last Year	This Year	Change
INCOME			
Sales	150,000	175,000	
Cost	90,000	115,000	
Margin	60,000	60,000	
EXPENSES			
Materials	20,000	18,000	
Supplies	3,000	3,100	
Payroll	15,000	16,000	
Utilities	700	720	
Misc.	900	850	
Rent	6,000	6,000	
Totals			
NET INCOME			

Don't worry too much about getting the headings exactly centered.
Save this worksheet to a file called CH9EX7.

8. Prepare a worksheet that contains a quarterly summary report for the ABC Company by region. Each of the regions should have a column total. Set the global column width to 12, and right-justify the column headings using the Label Prefix command. Save as CH9EX8.

ABC Company
Quarterly Sales Report by Region

	Jan.	Feb.	Apr.
Region A	12,644.00	7,500.00	23,780.00
Region B	45,623.00	8,750.00	21,960.00
Region C	7,634.00	9,890.00	33,450.00
Region D	12,575.00	3,256.00	28,750.00
Region E	33,456.00	7,250.00	25,500.00
Totals	111,932.00	36,646.00	133,440.00

9. Prepare a worksheet containing the car sales report by sales representative for Nissan Motors. There are six sales representatives and five car models for which you wish to track sales. The global column width should be set to 10. The global column format should be comma with 0 decimal positions. A total should be calculated using the @SUM function for each sales representative as well as for the total sales for each model of car. Save as CH9EX9.

Nissan Motors
Car Sales Report
By Sales Representative and Auto Model

	Sentra	Maxim	Pulsar	Pulsar XE	Pathfinder	Sales Rep. Total
Fred	50,870	43,000	16,000	0	49,560	159,430
Harold	10,600	20,000	31,250	43,670	0	105,520
Jim	0	19,800	15,400	0	24,675	59,875
John	30,900	21,000	45,780	0	0	97,680
Madeline	43,000	62,500	30,790	47,760	0	184,050
Marie	22,000	19,450	0	18,900	72,450	132,800
Totals	157,370	185,750	139,220	110,330	146,685	739,355

10. Prepare a projected profit report for the XYZ Company for a five-year period. The sales for each year should increase 20%. The costs should always be assumed to be 60% of sales, while the profit is always equal to the sales minus the costs. After the worksheet has been finished, plug in a first-year sales figure of $60,000. Save as CH9EX10.

XYZ Company
Projected Profit Report

	Year 1	Year 2	Year 3	Year 4	Year 5
Sales	100,000	120,000	144,000	172,800	207,360
Costs	60,000	72,000	86,400	103,680	124,416
Profit	40,000	48,000	57,600	69,120	82,944

Chapter
10

Intermediate
Spreadsheet
with Lotus 1-2-3

Chapter Objectives

After completing this chapter, you should be able to:

Discuss in greater detail the concept of range

Discuss in detail 1-2-3's copy conventions

Discuss in detail 1-2-3's format conventions and the differences between a range format and a global format

Discuss adding and deleting rows and columns

Discuss the use of the Move command

Explain in detail the various options available under the Print Menu

Discuss other data entry topics

Discuss in greater detail 1-2-3's built-in functions

In Chapter 9, you were introduced to a number of different 1-2-3 commands, some of which had virtually self-explanatory names. The concept of a range and the Copy, Format, Move, and Print commands, however, must be covered in more detail. These commands give a 1-2-3 user additional power to simplify actions and to determine how output will appear.

Range

When you are using 1-2-3, a statement or a process you wish to perform may require your indicating a range of cells to 1-2-3. A *range* is any specially designated single cell or rectangular group of cells on a worksheet; it is defined by pointing to the cells with the pointer or by typing the addresses of cells at the opposite corners of the range. Remember that a cell is a rectangle and therefore has only four corners.

Figure 10.1a displays a valid range containing three cells:

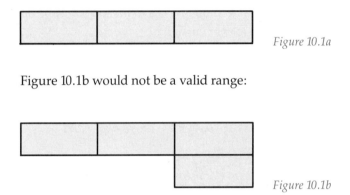

Figure 10.1a

Figure 10.1b would not be a valid range:

Figure 10.1b

You can give the cell locations of any pair of cells on opposite corners in defining a range of 1-2-3. For example, suppose you had a range containing a number of cells and having as its four corners the cells A, B, C, and D; to define the range, you would only have to give the cell addresses of two opposite corners, in whichever order you like—A and C, B and D, D and B, or C and A. Given any of these cell addresses, 1-2-3 will define the same range as is depicted in Figure 10.2:

Figure 10.2

From time to time a worksheet will contain range settings from a previous session with 1-2-3 that you no longer desire, such as print settings. You may wish to cancel a previous print range and specify another. Any range in any 1-2-3 command can be cancelled by depressing the BACKSPACE key. The new range can now be entered.

With the many spreadsheet commands that utilize ranges, one problem that many 1-2-3 novices face is when to "nail" the pointer down with a period

Figure 10.3
The cell to be copied is identified to 1-2-3.

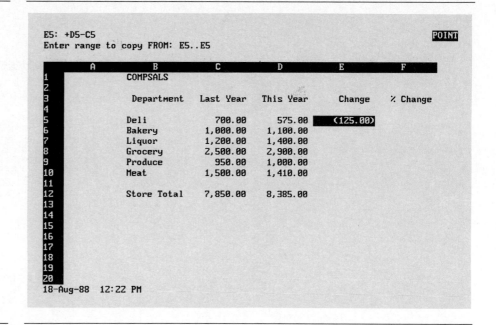

(.) and when to simply extend a range via pointer manipulation commands. This is easily solved for you via visual cues by 1-2-3. If you issue a command that does not have the pointer already nailed down, you receive a prompt that contains only one reference to a cell (A1, for example). On the other hand, if the pointer has already been "nailed" down by 1-2-3, you receive a prompt like A1..A1. This means that all you have to do is simply extend the range via pointer movement commands. If this range displayed by a command is incorrect, simply press the BACKSPACE key to cancel the range, move the pointer to the appropriate beginning cell, press the period key to "nail" the pointer, and extend the range via pointer manipulation commands.

The Copy Command

The **Copy command**, which takes information that has been entered in one or more cells and copies it to other cells on the worksheet, can save you many keystrokes and much time when building a worksheet. You will probably remember using the Copy command as part of your work on the sample COMPSALS worksheet in the last chapter, but you may not yet understand everything that it was doing. The Copy command involves setting up a **sending cell or cells** that contain the data to be copied, and then setting up a **receiving set of cells** to which the data will be copied. The following steps are required:

1. Select the Copy command from the Main Menu.
2. Indicate to 1-2-3 which cells are to be in the "From" range—that is, which cells hold data to be copied onto other cells. If only one cell is involved, simply hit the ENTER key; if a range of cells is involved, extend the range (the two periods [..] indicate that the beginning of the range is already fixed) and then move the pointer to the last cell in the range (or enter the cell address) and depress the ENTER key (see Figure 10.3).
3. Indicate to 1-2-3 which cells are to be in the "To" range—that is, which cells are to receive data currently held in the "From" cells. If only one cell is involved, simply hit the ENTER key. If a range of cells is involved, **nail down** the beginning of the range with a period (.), and

Figure 10.4
The cells to receive the contents of the cells to be copied are identified.

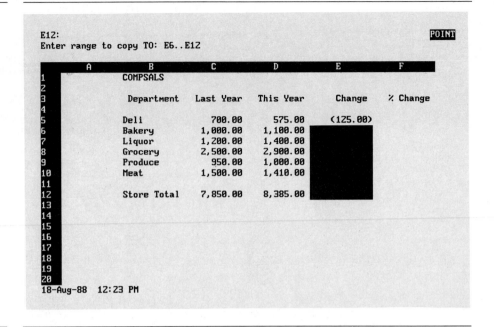

Figure 10.5
The worksheet after the Copy command has been executed.

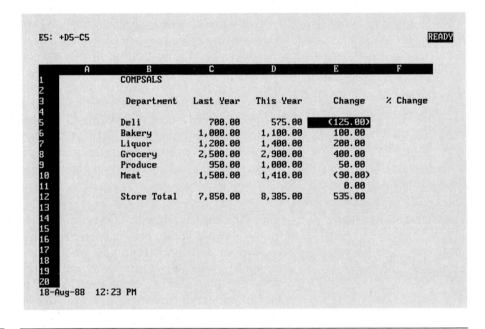

then move the pointer to the last cell in the range (or enter the cell address) and depress the ENTER key (see Figure 10.4).

Once the ENTER key is pressed, the indicated cells are copied (see Figure 10.5).

WARNING Make certain that your "From" cell range does not overlap your "To" cell range. If this happens, 1-2-3 simply overwrites the previous contents of cell(s), and the previous contents are irretrievably lost.

As was noted in Chapter 9, 1-2-3 automatically changes the cell references in a formula it is copying to reflect the new cell location of the formula. This is an example of the concept of relative addressing. Other text data are copied from one cell to another exactly as they appear. For example, if a cell having the label *Year* in it were copied to another cell, the receiving cell would also contain *Year*; and if the text in the sending cell is right justified, the text in the receiving cell will also be right justified.

The Copy command contains a time-saving feature you can use when copying a range of cells. Imagine that you wish to copy a range of cells two cells (columns) wide by twenty rows deep. You would establish the "From" range as before—by entering the cell addresses or by pointing—and 1-2-3 would then be informed that the sending range consists of two columns and twenty rows. When you tell 1-2-3 the "To" range, however, you can simply identify the address of the upper left-hand cell of the receiving range (or point to this cell) and hit the ENTER key. Because 1-2-3 retains in memory what the sending data looks like, it assumes that you want it to move the whole range and does so.

Formatting

The 1-2-3 spreadsheet package uses the FORMAT command to control the manner in which numeric information appears in a cell. As you have already seen, you can either *format* the entire worksheet via the **/ Worksheet Global Format option** or format a specific part of the worksheet via the **/ Range Format series of commands**. It is important to note that the Range Format takes precedence over the Worksheet Global Format, so any cell containing data not specifically formatted using the Range Format command can be changed using the Worksheet Global Format command.

Cell data can be formatted using the global or range options in various ways, including the following:

Fixed. This option displays a fixed number of decimal places (0–15), specified by the worksheet user. Examples; 10, 10.5, −120.00. When this command is used in a / Range Format command, the message (Fx) appears in the status line. The *x* denotes the number of decimal positions.

Scientific. This option displays data in the exponential scientific notation format. The worksheet user specifies the number of decimal places in the multiplier (0–15). The exponent is expressed as a power of 10 (E) from +99 to −99. Examples: 1.35E +11, −7.5E −19. When this command is used in a / Range Format command, the message (Sx) appears in the status line. The *x* denotes the number of decimal positions.

Currency. This option places a dollar sign ($) before each numeric cell entry, and commas after the thousand and million places in each entry large enough to have them. Negative numbers are placed in parentheses. The user indicates how many positions to the right of the decimal are desired. Examples: $13.50, ($6.75), $1.050. When this command is used in a / Range Format command, the message (Cx) appears in the status line. The *x* denotes the number of decimal positions.

, This option is identical to the Currency option, except that no dollar signs are used. When this command is used in a / Range Format command, the message (,x) appears in the status line. The *x* denotes the number of decimal positions.

General. This option, the default numeric display, suppresses trailing zeros after a decimal point. Extremely large or small numbers are displayed in exponential notation format. Examples: 17.66, −4.3, 2.4 + 10. When this command is used in a / Range Format command, the message (G) appears in the status line.

+/− This option displays a horizontal bar graph in which the number of symbols is the integer part of the value. + signs are used to represent positive integers, and − signs are used to represent negative integers; if the value is zero, a ⋅ is displayed. For example:

$$6 = + + + + + +$$
$$4 = + + + +$$
$$-3 = - - -$$
$$10 = + + + + + + + + + +$$
$$-5 = - - - - -$$
$$3.5 = + + +$$

When this command is used in a / Range Format command, the message (+) appears in the status line.

Percent. This option displays the numeric entry in a cell as a percentage (%). The user must specify how many decimal positions are desired. The value contained in the cell is the decimal equivalent multiplied by 100 and followed by a percent sign. Examples: 45%, 12.5%, −23%. When this command is used in a / Range Format command, the message (Px) appears in the status line. The x denotes the number of decimal positions.

Date. This option requests you to enter the format of date display desired from among the following possibilities:

1 DD-MMM-YY   (Example 09-Sep-89)
2 DD-MMM   (Example 09-Sep)
3 MMM-YY   (Example Sep-89)
4 (Long Intn'l) (Example 09/09/89)
5 (Short Intn'l) (Example 09/09)

The Time entries display a submenu for the following entries when you wish to format a cell containing a date function:

1 (HH:MM:SS AM/PM)   (Example 11:18:53 AM)
2 (HH:MM AM/PM)   (Example 11:18 AM)
3 (Long Intn'l)   (Example 11:18:53)
4 (Short Intn'l)   (Example 11:18)

When this command is used in a / Range Format command, the message (Dx) appears in the status line. The x denotes Date Format option selected. If the Time format was selected, a (Tx) appears in the status line.

Text. This option displays the formula—rather than the result of the formula—in a cell. Example: +D3/C3. When this command is used in a / Range Format command, the message (T) appears in the status line.

Hidden. This option allows you to inhibit the display of numbers, formulas, and text in a cell so that it does not appear on the screen. When the pointer resides on the cell that has been hidden, the contents of the cell appear in the Control Panel with the range indicator (H). This option is useful when you wish to embed comments/documentation concerning some aspect of your worksheet but you do not wish to have those comments appear when the worksheet is printed. When this command is used in a / Range Format command, the message (H) appears in the status line.

Reset. This option is used whenever you wish to change the format of a cell or a range of cells from the existing range format back to the global format.

Remember that the General Format option is the default format used by 1-2-3 to start a spreadsheet, and that the default column width used by 1-2-3 is nine positions wide. You can determine other default values used by 1-2-3 by entering the command / Worksheet Status.

Adding and Deleting Rows and Columns

From time to time, you may also wish to add or delete one or more rows or columns on the worksheet. This task simply involves pointing to where you wish to add or delete the row or column. The pointer plays a major role in this process. Columns are added to the *left* of the pointer position, and rows are added *above* the pointer position.

WARNING Make certain that there are not important areas of the worksheet off screen that may be affected by deleting a row or column. Remember, the entire column or row will be completely destroyed—not just what appears on the screen.

Let's add a column to the COMPSALS worksheet, which currently appears as follows:

Department	Last Year	This Year	Change	% Change
Deli	700.00	575.00	(125.00)	-18%
Bakery	1,000.00	1,100.00	100.00	10%
Liquor	1,200.00	1,400.00	200.00	17%
Grocery	2,500.00	2,900.00	400.00	16%
Produce	950.00	1,000.00	50.00	5%
Meat	1,500.00	1,410.00	(90.00)	-6%
Store Total	7,850.00	8,385.00	535.00	7%

 First, position the pointer where the addition or deletion is to take place. For example, if you want to add a column between present columns B and C, place the pointer anywhere in column C. Then issue the following commands:

/—Gets the Main Menu.

W—Takes the Worksheet option.

I—Takes the Insert option from the Worksheet Menu.

C—Tells 1-2-3 that you wish to insert a column.

ENTER—Executes the command.

The pointer in column C appears in reverse video. This means that the range is only one column wide. When you depress the ENTER key, the old column C will become the new column D. If you had wished to add two columns, you would have depressed the Right arrow key one time and then the ENTER key. The COMPSALS worksheet now looks as follows:

Department	Last Year	This Year	Change	% Change
Deli	700.00	575.00	(125.00)	-18%
Bakery	1,000.00	1,100.00	100.00	10%
Liquor	1,200.00	1,400.00	200.00	17%

Grocery	2,500.00	2,900.00	400.00	16%
Produce	950.00	1,000.00	50.00	5%
Meat	1,500.00	1,410.00	(90.00)	-6%
Store Total	7,850.00	8,385.00	535.00	7%

Now let's add two rows between the Deli and Bakery lines. First, position the pointer anywhere on the Bakery line; then issue the following commands:

/—Gets the Main Menu.

W—Takes the Worksheet option from the Main Menu.

I—Takes the Insert option from the Worksheet Menu.

R—Tells 1-2-3 to insert a row.

Down arrow—Extends the range to two rows.

ENTER—Tells 1-2-3 to add the rows.

The COMPSALS worksheet now appears as follows:

Department	Last Year	This Year	Change	% Change
Deli	700.00	575.00	(125.00)	-18%
Bakery	1,000.00	1,100.00	100.00	10%
Liquor	1,200.00	1,400.00	200.00	17%
Grocery	2,500.00	2,900.00	400.00	16%
Produce	950.00	1,000.00	50.00	5%
Meat	1,500.00	1,410.00	(90.00)	-6%
Store Total	7,850.00	8,385.00	535.00	7%

You are now free to use these new rows and columns to enter new departments and to enter summary information for sales from two years ago.

Deleting rows and columns involves essentially the same process, except that you mark the actual ranges (rows or columns) to be deleted instead of inserted.

Moving Cell Contents

You may want to add or delete a column or row from your worksheet, only to discover that another area of your worksheet would be disastrously affected by such an action. This is the time to use 1-2-3's **Move feature**, which allows you to relocate cell contents without disturbing other areas of your worksheet. The Move feature automatically retains all functional relationships of any formulas; it works by specifying sending and receiving areas on the worksheet (much like the copy statement—except that the sending contents are then destroyed).

WARNING Make certain that the receiving range does not overlap any valuable cells in your worksheet. All cells in the receiving range will be destroyed, and you will not be able to retrieve the data contained in them.

Suppose that you have a loan amortization worksheet that looks like the one at the top of the next page. Imagine that you want to center the information contained at the top of the worksheet in order to give it a more balanced look. To perform this task, which involves moving the information contained in eight cells one column to the right, you would have to execute the steps that follow the worksheet.

```
Interest                12.00%
Loan Amount             $1,200
Months                      20
Beginning Date          May-85
```

```
                                        TOTAL       BALANCE
        DATE    PRINCIPAL   INTEREST   PAYMENT   OUTSTANDING
        May-85     54.50      12.00      66.50       1145.50
        Jun-85     55.04      11.46      66.50       1090.46
        Jul-85     55.60      10.90      66.50       1034.86
        Aug-85     56.15      10.35      66.50        978.71
        Sep-85     56.71       9.79      66.50        922.00
```

/—Invokes the Main Menu.

M—Selects the Move option from the Main Menu.

A1 [by manual pointer movement]—Positions the pointer at A1 to establish the beginning of the "From" range.

.—Nails down the beginning of the "From" range.

C5 [by manual pointer movement]—Positions the pointer to the ending cell in the "From" range.

ENTER—Tells 1-2-3 that the "From" range has been defined.

B1 [by manual pointer movement]—Positions the pointer at the beginning of the "To" range.

ENTER—Tells 1-2-3 to move the cell contents.

The worksheet would now appear as follows:

```
        Interest                12.00%
        Loan Amount             $1,200
        Months                      20
        Beginning Date          May-85
```

```
                                        TOTAL       BALANCE
        DATE    PRINCIPAL   INTEREST   PAYMENT   OUTSTANDING
        May-85     54.50      12.00      66.50       1145.50
        Jun-85     55.04      11.46      66.50       1090.46
        Jul-85     55.60      10.90      66.50       1034.86
        Aug-85     56.15      10.35      66.50        978.71
        Sep-85     56.71       9.79      66.50        922.00
```

The Print Command

When you want to get something out of the computer or off disk so that you can examine it at your leisure, the **Print command** is an invaluable aid. On the other hand, if you don't understand how it generates output, the command can also be frustrating to use. The Print command allows you to print the whole worksheet or parts (ranges) of it. The output can be sent directly to a printer or placed in a disk file, from which it can later be used by a word processing program. The spreadsheets displayed in this book were originally created using 1-2-3, then saved to disk, and then accessed using WordPerfect's Retrieve command.

After you select the Print option from the Main Menu, 1-2-3 prompts you to tell it whether you want the output to go to a printer (the Printer option) or onto a disk file (the File option). If you select the File option, you will be asked to enter the file name to which 1-2-3 will add the extension .PRN. This is important to remember, because if you wish to access the file later, the file name you specify must include the .PRN extension.

Print Menu

At this point, the following **Print Menu** will be displayed in the control panel by 1-2-3:

```
Range Line Page Options Clear Align Go Quit
```

Let's examine in turn what each of these options does:

Range. The **Print Range option** is selected to tell 1-2-3 which part of the worksheet is to be printed. You can enter the cell addresses of two opposite corners of the range that is to be printed, or you can use the pointer to identify the range to 1-2-3.

Line. The **Line option** tells the printer attached to your computer to advance the paper one line. This command is useful when you wish to leave some blank space between ranges that are printing out.

Page. The **Page option** advances the paper in the printer to the top of the next page. It is useful if you wish to have printed output start on a new sheet of paper. After 1-2-3 is finished printing the range of cells that you indicated, it stops the printer at that location. To advance the page in the printer, simply take the Page option. This will also result in the printing of any footing lines (discussed later).

Options. The Options selection invokes the **Options Menu** (shown below), which allows you to place headings, footings, borders, and so forth, on the printout:

```
Header Footer Margins Borders Setup Pg-Length Other Quit
```

Options contained in this menu enable you temporarily to override defaults set by 1-2-3 for printing information. These overrides remain in effect until you change them or restart Lotus 1-2-3. If you save your spreadsheet and then call it back, Lotus 1-2-3 will remember the overrides because they will have become part of the worksheet file.

Header/Footer. These options allow you to enter one line of text to be used as a heading or footing for each page of printout generated. You will be prompted for the text and can place up to 240 characters on the line. In either a heading or footing line, the following special characters can be used to give printing instructions to 1-2-3:

> \#—Numbers the pages beginning with 1
>
> ¦ —Splits headings/footings into sections as follows:
>
>> The first is left justified
>>
>> The second is centered
>>
>> The third part is right justified
>
> @—Prints today's date

For example, in the footing of the sample worksheet `COMPSALS`, you could place the following text:

```
Page#¦COMPSALS¦@
```

This would develop a footing with the word *Page* and the page number in the first (left justified) section. The word `COMPSALS` would appear in the center part of the footing, its text centered. The date would appear in the third (right justified) section.

Lotus 1-2-3 always leaves two blank lines between the worksheet and any headings and footings. Headings and footings can be suppressed by selecting `Options Other Unformatted`, and they can be reinstated by selecting `Options Other Formatted`.

Margins. This option, which allows you to change the current margins (left, right, top, and bottom), is especially important if you have a dot-matrix printer and wish to print the worksheet using compressed print so that you get more characters per line. The maximum value allowed for resetting the right-hand margin is 240 characters.

Borders. This option allows you to specify horizontal or vertical borders that will be displayed on each page of a printed report. For example, you may have a worksheet that develops a loan amortization table and generates one line of output for each month of the loan; the borders option could be used in this case to print column headings on each page. All you have to do is select the row or column (depending on where you want the labels), and then specify the range of cells containing the desired text. To clear the borders, you would enter the commands `/PRINT PRINTER CLEAR BORDERS`. The Borders option, to work properly, must have the print range specified differently. When using borders, do not specify any border cells in the print range. Specify them separately in the border range. Otherwise the border cells print twice on the first page. See Figure 10.6.

Setup. This option tells your printer which escape code to use for printing the data. For example, for Epson FX or Epson-compatible printers, condensed printing (17.16 cpi) can be obtained by entering `\015` as the setup string. In order to get back to Pica (10 cpi) printing, you would have to enter `\PRINT PRINTER OPTIONS SETUP`, followed by `\018`. If you wished to print in elite (12 cpi), you would enter `\077` to turn elite on; to turn it off, you would enter `\080`. Depending on the setup string, you can print in 10, 12, or 17.1 character pitch.

Page-Length. This option, which allows you to tell 1-2-3 how many lines are on a page of paper, becomes important when you use something other than 11-inch paper.

Other. This option displays the following menu:

```
As-Displayed Cell-Formulas Formatted Unformatted
```

As Displayed. This option prints the output exactly as it appears on the screen.

Cell Formulas. This option prints one cell per line and displays the cell contents (text or formula).

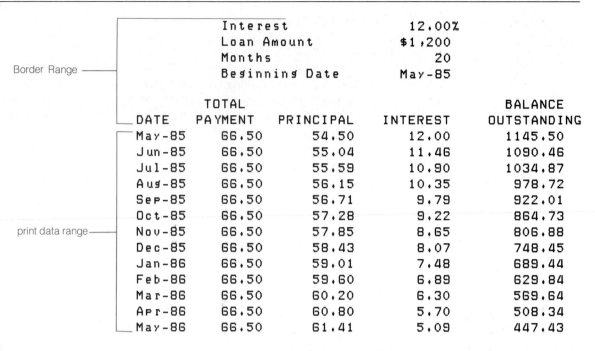

Figure 10.6

Unformatted. This option overrides any footings, headings, or page breaks, printing the output without any of these.

Formatted. This option restores any footings, headings, or page breaks that might have been suppressed.

Clear. As print specifications are entered, 1-2-3 stores them in RAM and uses them for any printing operations, and in addition stores them to your worksheet file when the file is saved onto disk. Occasionally, you may not want these various print settings to be stored in memory; by selecting the **Clear option**, you can return all print options to their default values. This option results in the following menu being displayed:

All Range Borders Format

All. Resets all print settings to the default values.

Range. Cancels the print range.

Borders. Cancels the border range.

Format. Cancels margins, page length and setup string and returns them to their default values.

Align. The **Align command** is used when 1-2-3 has lost track of where it is on a sheet of paper—for example, when a user turns the knob on the printer platen to roll the paper forward, rather than using the Line or Page options. When this happens, position the paper in the printer to the top of a new sheet and execute the Align command; 1-2-3 will immediately assume that it is at the top of a new page.

Go. The **Go option** tells 1-2-3 to send the designated range as output to the printer or to the named disk file, after which control is returned to the Print

Menu. This allows you to print other parts of the worksheet if you desire. If the printer is not on line, 1-2-3 will try to print and find that it can't; it will then beep and display an error message. You must depress the Esc key to continue. If you are storing data onto a disk file, the Go command tells 1-2-3 to put the information in the file.

What happens if you forget to enter the set-up string or print the wrong range? To stop printing, depress both the Ctrl and the Break keys; this will interrupt the printer and return control to the Print Menu. Use the page command to go to the top of the next page, or position the paper to the top of the next page manually and enter the Align command.

Quit. The **Quit option** tells 1-2-3 to terminate the print session and returns you to ready mode in the worksheet. When storing output data onto a disk file, you must use this command to close the file properly. If you do not, no data will be in the file when you try to access it later. When storing data onto a disk file, you must go through the following steps:

1. Name the file.
2. Establish the range and any options.
3. Enter the Go command to store data onto the disk file.
4. Enter the Quit command to close the disk file.

Print Default Settings

Lotus 1-2-3 has a number of defaults for printing. Depending on the type of printer you have, some may differ from those listed below. When a blank worksheet is started or when the Clear option is taken, 1-2-3 institutes or restores these default settings:

Left margin is 4

Right margin is 76

Top margin is 2 lines from the top of the page

Bottom margin is 2 lines from the bottom of the page

Page length is 66 lines per page

Auto-line feed is NO

Wait to insert a sheet of paper is NO

Interface is parallel

Set-up string is NO

1-2-3 and the Print Line Counter

The 1-2-3 software package has an internal line counter for keeping track of the current printer position on a page. As it prints each line of a worksheet, 1-2-3 automatically adjusts this line counter. Three of the Print Menu commands—Line, Page, and Align—also affect this counter. The Line command not only issues a line feed for the printer, but it also increments the internal 1-2-3 line counter by a value of 1. The Page command tells the printer to go to the top of the next page and sets the line counter back to a beginning value. The Align command just resets the line counter back to its beginning value.

You should be able to tell from the above discussion that you will not want to manually adjust the position of the paper within the printer; 1-2-3 has no way of knowing that you have moved the paper. It remembers only the current line counter value. When you manually position the paper at the top of the next page and try to print another worksheet, you will receive a ten-line gap wherever 1-2-3 "remembers" to issue a page break command to the printer. To solve this problem, issue a Ctrl + Break command and return to the Print Menu. Then, manually move the paper to the top of the next page and issue an Align command. The line counter will be reset, and you will be ready to start printing.

Forced Page Breaks

One problem that faced many 1-2-3 users of Release 1A was how to get the spreadsheet to force an end of page and start printing the next line at the top of the next page in a long worksheet. This has been remedied in the Release 2.X of 1-2-3 via the / Worksheet Page command. This command automatically forces a **page break** at the location in the worksheet in which it is entered. For example, if you wished to force a page break after the Grocery department line in the COMPSALS worksheet, you must first position the cursor to the Produce line and enter the / Worksheet Page command (see Figure 10.7). Once this command has been entered, a blank line appears within the worksheet with a :: entry. The :: entry tells 1-2-3 that when it reaches this line in the worksheet it should issue a page break and begin the next line at the top of a new sheet of paper.

WARNING When you issue a page break command with the / Worksheet Page command, 1-2-3 inserts a new row into your worksheet and then places the page break symbol :: in the cell at which the pointer resided when the command was issued. This means any portion of your worksheet off the screen also has this blank row added. You should, therefore, use this command carefully, since parts of your worksheet that are not currently viewed on your screen can also be affected. To get rid of an undesired page break, use the / Worksheet Delete Row command if you have just entered this command. If you have had this command embedded in your worksheet for some time, make certain that no worksheet entries are currently on this row. If there are text, numbers, or formulas, use the Move command or possibly the Range Erase command.

1-2-3 Functions

You have already used the 1-2-3 function @SUM to take the place of a number of other, longer instructions. Functions save time and increase accuracy because they reduce the number of keystrokes and the chance for error. A function contains a preprogrammed set of instructions that you issue by using what 1-2-3 refers to as a **function call** (this involves naming the function) and then telling 1-2-3 where to find the data to act on.

A typical 1-2-3 function consists of the following parts.

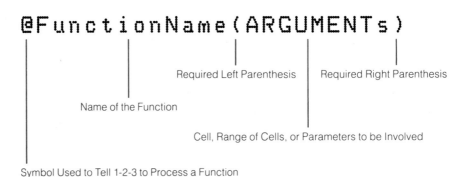

Figure 10.7
The COMPSALS worksheet
with a hard page break (::)
created with the pointer on
the Produce label.

```
COMPSALS
  Department      Last Year    This Year       Change    % Change
Deli                 700.00       575.00      (125.00)       -18%
Bakery             1,000.00     1,100.00       100.00         10%
Liquor             1,200.00     1,400.00       200.00         17%
Grocery            2,500.00     2,900.00       400.00         16%
::
Produce              950.00     1,000.00        50.00          5%
Meat               1,500.00     1,410.00       (90.00)        -6%
Store Total        7,850.00     8,385.00       535.00          7%
```

Some 1-2-3 functions that are used frequently in business and education are listed below. Other 1-2-3 functions can be found in Appendix B.

Date Functions:

@DATE (year,month,day)—Places the date for any day since 1/1/1900

@DAY (date)—Gets the day number from this date

@MONTH (date)—Gets the month number from this date

@YEAR (date)—Gets the year number from this date

@NOW—Gets the date from the DOS date register

Statistical Functions:

@COUNT (list)—Counts the number of entries in the specified list (range)

@SUM (list)—Sums the values of all cell contents in the list (range)

@AVG (list)—Averages the values of all cell contents in the list (range)

@MIN (list)—Finds the smallest value from the cells listed in the range

@MAX (list)—Finds the largest value from the cells listed in the range

@STD (list)—Finds the standard deviation from the values of the cells listed in the range

@VAR (list)—Finds the variance from the values of the cells listed in the range

Miscellaneous Functions:

@IF (cond,x,y)—Indicates that, if the condition is true, the value in x or the formula in x will be used; otherwise, the value in y or the formula in y will be used.

@ROUND (x,n)—Indicates that the number x will be rounded to n decimal positions: if the next position has a value of 5 or greater, the digit n will be rounded up; if that position has a value of 4 or less, the digit n will remain unchanged.

The value of functions is best appreciated if you view them as "black boxes" that accept input and produce the output (correct answer) in the designated cell (see Figure 10.8). The input to a function consists of the arguments (if any) contained between parentheses. The meaning of these arguments

Figure 10.8
The black box approach of
using functions.

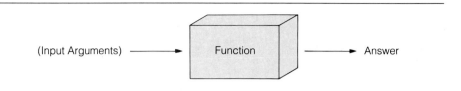

varies from function to function. If multiple arguments appear, they are separated by commas. Sometimes arguments may consist of a range of cells, and at other times they can have completely different roles. The point to keep in mind is that the function itself has all of the built-in routines required for producing the correct answer.

Functions can be **nested**—meaning that one function references another function. Suppose, for example, that you wish to get the number of the month from the system date (DOS). You could do this by using the nested function statement @MONTH (@NOW), which uses the output of the @NOW function as input to the @MONTH function.

Another example of nesting would be the statement @ROUND(@AVG‐(F3..F6),1), which averages the numbers in the range F3 to F6 and then rounds the results to one decimal place. When using nested functions, you must make certain that the number of left-hand parentheses equals the number of right-hand parentheses. If the numbers don't match, 1-2-3 will cause the computer to beep at you, indicating an error.

More on Data Entry

Changing the Column Width. When you are entering numeric data into a cell and receive asterisks (**********) in the cell, 1-2-3 is telling you that the column is not wide enough to display the number properly. You may also wish to expand a column to provide sufficient room to display row labels properly. A column can be expanded via the commands:

/—Gets the Main Menu

W—Selects the Worksheet option

C—Selects the **Column Width command**

S—Selects the Set command

＿＿—Enter the desired column width

ENTER—Executes the command

When you are entering the new column width, you can either enter a number or adjust the column width a character at a time by pressing your arrow keys. The right arrow increases the column width by one position each time it is pressed, and the left arrow decreases the column width by one position each time it is pressed. The new column width appears on the status line between brackets ([ ]). For example, a cell in a column set to a width of 15 would contain a [15] on the status line of the Control Panel.

NOTE For a numeric cell, 1-2-3 always reserves the rightmost character position to hold a right-hand parenthesis [)] or a percent sign (%).

Dates. The 1-2-3 package gives you tremendous flexibility when it comes to entering numeric or text data in a cell. One of the features of 1-2-3 is how it handles dates as a numeric value. Since a date is really a numeric entry for 1-2-3, there can be no overflow to the next cell like text data. The number generated by any date function represents the number of elapsed days since January 1, 1900. Since this number is meaningless, it must be converted to a useable form via the / Range Format Date commands. This means that the column width is extremely important no matter what date format has been selected. If the column width is not wide enough, 1-2-3 displays asterisks (******) in the affected cell. This means that the column is not wide enough to accept the text translation of the numeric date entry.

Text. When you enter text data within a worksheet cell, 1-2-3 automatically assumes that this text is to be left-justified within the cell and embeds a single quote (') to accomplish this task. If you wish to have text right-justified or centered within a cell, you must instruct 1-2-3 via a label prefix character how the data should be presented. The label prefix characters are:

'	left-justify text
"	right-justify text
ˆ	center text

While 1-2-3 automatically places the single quote in a cell for left-justifying text, you must manually enter a double quote (") or caret (ˆ) as the first character within a cell when you wish to right-justify or center text, respectively. Also keep in mind that the column has to be wide enough to properly display the text within the cell. For example, if you wish to right-justify the text Last Year within a cell; it would not appear properly justified if the column width were 9. To appear properly justified, the column width has to be greater than the text width.

WARNING You must never use a label prefix for a number that is to be involved in a calculation. When 1-2-3 sees a label prefix of ', ", or ˆ, it assumes that this is indeed text data exactly as you have indicated and as a result assigns a numeric value of zero to this cell. This means that if you sum a column of numbers that all have a label prefix, a value of zero will appear.

Repeating Text. When you want to enter a **repeating character** or string of characters within a cell, 1-2-3 requires you to use the backslash (\) as a shorthand notation to tell it to repeat the character. Any character or characters following the backslash will then be repeated until the cell is filled. The following examples assume that the column width of 9 has been used.

Cell Entry	Cell Display
\ –	– – – – – – – – –
\ABC	ABCABCABC
\DOG	DOGDOGDOG
\ =	= = = = = = = = =

This shorthand method is frequently used to create subtotal lines (––––––––––) and total lines (= = = = = = = = =) within business reports.

1-2-3 Sample

FUNCTION

Worksheet

Suppose you are taking an introductory class in statistics, and early in the semester the teacher asks that you examine the characteristics of four sets of numbers. For each set of numbers, you are to calculate the average, the standard deviation, and the variance; you are also to give the high, the low, the sum, and the number of entries for each set of numbers. You are aware that

1-2-3 would be an ideal aid in performing this homework assignment. The sets of numbers are:

1. 9, 12, 7, 5, 2, 1, 3, 4, and 8
2. 8, 36, 16, 9, 4, 0, and 12
3. 1, 16, 4, 9, 36, 25, 16, 23, and 17
4. 69, 60, 59, 65, 56, 77, 81, 91, and 85

After careful analysis, you conclude that the following worksheet will solve the problem.

```
FUNCTION

10-Jan-89

Homework assignment for Business Statistics:
Examine the statistical characteristics of four sets
of numbers.
```

	Set 1	Set 2	Set 3	Set 4
	9	8	1	69
	12	36	16	60
	7	16	4	59
	5	9	9	65
	2	4	36	56
	1	0	25	77
	3	12	16	81
	4		23	91
	8		17	85
==				
Sum:	51	85	147	643
Average:	5.67	12.14	16.33	71.44
Stand. Dev.:	3.4	10.86	10.26	11.83
Variance:	11.56	117.84	105.33	140.02
Maximum:	12	36	36	91
Minimum:	1	0	1	56
Count:	9	7	9	9

In doing this project, you will practice the following skills:

1. Using the @NOW and @DATE date functions
2. Changing the column width of one column
3. Using the F2 Edit function for correcting errors
4. Using statistical functions
5. Using the @ROUND function
6. Using nested functions
7. Copying a single-column range to multiple columns
8. Handling blank cells and cells with a blank on functions

Be sure that you enter the date before you start Lotus 1-2-3. It will become important later on. If you have already entered the date and there is material on the worksheet screen, you can erase it by typing:

```
/
W       Worksheet
E       Erase
Y       Yes
```

1-2-3 Sample

FUNCTION

Spreadsheet

1. Enter the name of the worksheet.

   ```
   A1   FUNCTION
   ```

2. "Stamp" the worksheet with today's date at cell A3, using the @NOW function.

   ```
   A3  @NOW
   ENTER
   ```

   In this sample worksheet, the @NOW function caused 32152 to be placed in the cell, signifying that 32,152 days have elapsed since December 31, 1899. That number must now be converted to a more useful format.

   You could also enter today's date manually, using the @DATE (yy,mm,dd) function. In this example, you would enter @DATE (88,1,10). You would receive the same result of 32152 in cell A3, however, and you would still need to format that cell in order for the information to become useful.

3. Change the number in cell A3 to a standard business format.

   /—Gets the Main Menu.

   R—Selects the Range option.

   F—Selects the Format option.

   D—Selects the Date command from Format.

   ENTER—Selects the first option of date (DD-MM-YY).

   ENTER—Executes the command.

4. You will notice that ********* (1-2-3's overflow indication) now appears in cell A3, indicating that the cell is not wide enough to display the data. This generally happens after some type of data manipulation; it does not happen with standard text data. In order to get rid of this error, you must change the width of column A to 15—a size large enough for labels that are to be entered later.

   /—Gets the Main Menu.

   W—Selects the Worksheet option.

   C—Selects the Column Width command.

   S—Selects the Set command.

   15—Enters the new desired column width for this column.

   ENTER—Executes the instruction.

5. Enter the text data exactly as it appears below (you'll correct any errors later).

```
A5    Homework assignment for Business Statistics:
A6    Examine the statistical characteristics of fours sets of numbers.
B8     ^Set 1
C8     ^Set 2
D8     ^Set 3
E8     ^Set 4
A19   "Sum:
A20   "Average:
A21   "Stand. Dev.:
A22   "Variance
A23   Maximum
A24   "Minimum:
A25   "Count:
```

The ^ character is found above the 6 key and is used to tell 1-2-3 to center the data within the cell. It is one of three commands that tell 1-2-3 how to position data within a cell. The three are:

'   Left-justify text within the cell

"   Right-justify text within the cell

^   Center text within the cell

Notice that text data and manipulated data are handled differently by 1-2-3. Text data is allowed to overflow its cell boundaries. For example, if you went to cell B6 and entered "new text," the words would appear in the middle of the text that was entered in A6.

6. You probably noticed that the text you entered above contains three errors: cell A6 says *fours* instead of *four*; cell A22 does not have a : mark after *Variance*; and cell A23 is not right justified and lacks a : mark. You could correct these errors by reentering all of the data, but to be more efficient you could also use the Edit function (invoked by the F2 key) as part of the following procedure:

A6 [by manual pointer movement]—Positions the pointer to cell A6.

F2—Displays the contents of cell A6 on both the status line and the entry line, and positions the pointer at the end of the line. The text is now available to the user for manipulation.

Back arrow to *s* of *fours*—Moves the pointer to the *s* of *fours*.

Del—Erases the *s*.

A22 [by manual pointer movement]—Positions the pointer at cell A22.

F2—Displays the contents of cell A22 for editing, with the pointer at the end of the line.

:—Enters the : at the end of the line.

ENTER—Tells 1-2-3 to change the data within the cell.

A23 [by manual pointer movement]—Positions the pointer at cell A23.

F2—Displays the contents of cell A23 for editing, with the pointer at the end of the line.

Home—Moves the pointer to the beginning of the line, under the ' mark.

Del—Deletes the single quote (').

"—Tells 1-2-3 to right-justify the contents of the cell.

End—Moves the pointer to the end of the text within the cell.

:—Enters the : mark at the end of the line.

ENTER—Tells 1-2-3 to change the data within the cell.

7. Enter the four sets of numbers.

B9 9	C9 8	D9 1	E9 69
B10 12	C10 36	D10 16	E10 60
B11 7	C11 16	D11 4	E11 59
B12 5	C12 9	D12 9	E12 65
B13 2	C13 4	D13 36	E13 56
B14 1	C14 0	D14 25	E14 77
B15 3	C15 12	D15 16	E15 81
B16 4		D16 23	E16 91
B17 8		D17 17	E17 85

8. Enter the total line for cell B18.

\ = —Repeats the equal sign throughout the cell.

ENTER—Tells 1-2-3 to enter the data in the cell.

The backslash (\) located above the Alt key is used by 1-2-3 as the repeat indicator. Any character(s) that appear after the backslash will be repeated throughout the cell. For example, \ABC would place ABCABCABC in the cell.

9. Copy the total line to the cell locations of C18, D18, and E18. Leave the pointer at cell B18.

/—Gets the Main Menu.

C—Selects the Copy command.

ENTER—Establishes cell B18 as the only cell in the "From" range.

C18 [by manual pointer movement]—Positions the pointer at cell C18 (the beginning of the "To" range).

.—Nails down the beginning of the range.

E18 [by manual pointer movement]—Positions the pointer at the last cell in the "To" range.

ENTER—Tells 1-2-3 to execute the copy instruction.

10. Enter the statistical functions for column B.
    a. Enter the @SUM function at B19 by pointing.

B19 @SUM(—Enters the first part of the @SUM function.

B9 [by manual pointer movement]—Positions the pointer at cell B9 (the beginning of the range).

.—Nails down the beginning of the range.

B17 [by manual pointer movement]—Positions the pointer at the end of the range.

)—Enters the right parenthesis.

ENTER—Tells 1-2-3 to execute the command, and places the result in cell B19.

This method demonstrates using the pointer to point addresses to a 1-2-3 function. In addition to entering the locations via pointing, you can also just give the locations directly to 1-2-3.

b. Enter the @AVG function at B20 by directly entering the cell addresses of the cells involved.

> B20 @AVG (B9.B17) ENTER

Since you already know the cell locations from having pointed out the @SUM locations, you now need enter only the cell location at the beginning of the range and the cell location at the end of the range. To execute the command, just depress the ENTER key.

c. Enter the remaining functions, either by pointing or by entering the cell addresses directly. Remember, only enter the formulas for column B; you'll be copying these to the other columns later.

> @STD—Standard Deviation
>
> @VAR—Variance
>
> @MAX—Maximum
>
> @MIN—Minimum
>
> @COUNT—Count

11. You can now see that the average, standard deviation, and variance entries all have six decimal positions; having this many positions to the right of the decimal point can be distracting to anyone wishing to use the information in report form. You could use the / Range Format command to change the output format of these three cells, but this is also an excellent opportunity to use nested functions. You will use the Edit feature of 1-2-3 and add the @ROUND function to the three cells containing average, standard deviation, and variance entries. First, position the pointer at cell B20.

F2—Invokes 1-2-3's Edit mode.

Home—Positions the pointer at the beginning of the line.

@ROUND(—Inserts @ROUND(at the beginning of the existing line.

End—Positions the pointer at the end of the line.

,2)—Tells 1-2-3 that you only want two positions to the right of the decimal.

ENTER—Tells 1-2-3 to enter the data in the cell.

Instead of seeing 5.6666666 in cell B22, you should now see 5.67.

12. Repeat the steps in task 11 to change the entries in cells B21 and B22.

13. Copy the formulas for the calculations from column B to columns C, D, and E. Position the pointer at B19.

/—Invokes the Main Menu.

C—Selects the Copy command.

B25 [by manual pointer movement]—Positions the pointer at the end of the "From" range.

ENTER—Tells 1-2-3 that the "From" range has been completely defined.

C19 [by manual pointer movement]—Positions the pointer at the first cell in the "To" range.

.—Marks the beginning of the "To" range.

E19 [by manual pointer movement]—Positions the pointer at the last cell in the "To" range.

ENTER—Tells 1-2-3 that the "To" range has been completely defined, and tells it to execute the command.

The reason you didn't have to give cell E25 as the last address has to do with how 1-2-3 remembers your definition of the "From" range. You defined the range as one column wide and going from cell B19 to cell B25. 1-2-3 is thus informed that the "From" range consists of seven rows of cells. Once you tell 1-2-3 in a Copy command where to put the first cell of the "From" range column, it will assume that you also wish to copy the rest of the cells in that column.

You gave three cells as the columns to receive the range. Each of these cells was in a different column, so 1-2-3 assumed that you wanted three copies of the "From" range—one for each column.

14. Examine the results of the calculations on the screen. Notice that column C has two blank entries and that the count is indeed equal to 7. 1-2-3 is capable of determining when to include a cell in a calculation, and when not to, based on its contents or lack of them. Now what will happen if you make a change in cell C16? Position your pointer at C16.

> Space—Adds a character space.
>
> ENTER—Tells 1-2-3 to enter the "data" in the cell.

Notice that, even though there isn't a value in C16, the results of the calculations on the screen have been altered dramatically. Notice also that a single quote (') appears in cell C16. Go back to cell C16 and enter the command / Range Erase. The results of the various statistical evaluations immediately return to their original values.

When using ranges that contain so-called blank cells, you should make certain that they really are blank. The single quote (') warns you that the contents of this cell will not work properly in any type of numeric calculation.

15. Save the worksheet using the file name FUNCTION.

> /—Gets the Main Menu.
>
> F—Takes the File option.
>
> S—Takes the Save command.
>
> FUNCTION—Enters the name FUNCTION as the file name.

16. Print the file, and put the date, page, and name of the file in a footing.

> /—Invokes the Main Menu.
>
> P—Selects the Print option.
>
> P—Directs the output to the printer.
>
> R—Selects the Range command.
>
> A1 [by manual pointer movement]—Positions the pointer at A1.
>
> .—Nails down the beginning of the print range.
>
> F25 [by manual pointer movement]—Positions the pointer at F25 (the end of the range), allowing all text to print.
>
> ENTER—Indicates to 1-2-3 that the range has been established.
>
> O—Selects the Options Menu entry from the Print Menu.
>
> F—Selects the Footer command from the Options Menu.
>
> Page# | FUNCTIONS | @—Tells 1-2-3 to divide the footing into three parts, as follows: the page number left justified in the left-hand part; the name of the file, FUNCTION, centered in

the middle part; today's date right justified in the right-hand part.

ENTER—Submits the footing to 1-2-3.

Q—Terminates the Options Menu, and returns to the Print Menu.

G—Prints the worksheet.

P—Prints the footing while going to the top of the next page.

Q—Quits and returns to the worksheet.

Your worksheet should now appear exactly like that at the beginning of this Sample Worksheet. If it doesn't, compare your cell contents to these:

FUNCTION Cell Contents

```
A1:  'FUNCTION
A3:  (D1) @NOW
A5:  'Homework assignment for Business Statistics:
A6:  'Examine the statistical characteristics of four
sets of numbers.
B8:  ^Set 1
C8:  ^Set 2
D8:  ^Set 3
E8:  ^Set 4
B9:  9
C9:  8
D9:  1
E9:  69
B10: 12
C10: 36
D10: 16
E10: 60
B11: 7
C11: 16
D11: 4
E11: 59
B12: 5
C12: 9
D12: 9
E12: 65
B13: 2
C13: 4
D13: 36
E13: 56
B14: 1
C14: 0
D14: 25
E14: 77
B15: 3
C15: 12
D15: 16
E15: 81
B16: 4
D16: 23
E16: 91
B17: 8
```

```
D17:  17
E17:  85
B18:  \=
C18:  \=
D18:  \=
E18:  \=
A19:  "Sum:
B19:  @SUM(B9..B17)
C19:  @SUM(C9..C17)
D19:  @SUM(D9..D17)
E19:  @SUM(E9..E17)
A20:  "Average:
B20:  @ROUND(@AVG(B9..B17),2)
C20:  @ROUND(@AVG(C9..C17),2)
D20:  @ROUND(@AVG(D9..D17),2)
E20:  @ROUND(@AVG(E9..E17),2)
A21:  "Stand. Dev.:
B21:  @ROUND(@STD(B9..B17),2)
C21:  @ROUND(@STD(C9..C17),2)
D21:  @ROUND(@STD(D9..D17),2)
E21:  @ROUND(@STD(E9..E17),2)
A22:  "Variance:
B22:  @ROUND(@VAR(B9..B17),2)
C22:  @ROUND(@VAR(C9..C17),2)
D22:  @ROUND(@VAR(D9..D17),2)
E22:  @ROUND(@VAR(E9..E17),2)
A23:  "Maximum:
B23:  @MAX(B9..B17)
C23:  @MAX(C9..C17)
D23:  @MAX(D9..D17)
E23:  @MAX(E9..E17)
A24:  "Minimum:
B24:  @MIN(B9..B17)
C24:  @MIN(C9..C17)
D24:  @MIN(D9..D17)
E24:  @MIN(E9..E17)
A25:  "Count:
B25:  @COUNT(B9..B17)
C25:  @COUNT(C9..C17)
D25:  @COUNT(D9..D17)
E25:  @COUNT(E9..E17)
```

Chapter Review

A range is any "box" of data cells that has four 90° angles. Various commands allow you either to point out a range of cells to be affected by a later command or to specify addresses of two opposite corners of the range, thereby identifying it.

The Copy command is used to copy the contents of one or more cells (the sending area) and place this in a receiving area of one or more other cells. There are two parts to the Copy command: specifying the sending area (the "From" range), and specifying the receiving area (the "To" range). Both areas are ranges that you can denote by giving the cell addresses or by using the pointer to point them out.

The Format command can be used in either a range or global manner. The Range option formats only a portion of the worksheet, whereas the

Global option formats the entire worksheet not currently under a Range command format. A number of format options are available, including fixed, currency, date, percent, or scientific.

The Print command allows you to specify exactly how you wish to print all or part of your worksheet—the range to be printed, and any options that you desire, such as margins, headings, or footings—and then lets you tell 1-2-3 to print.

The built-in functions of 1-2-3 may be simple or compound (the so-called nested functions, produced when one function is used as input to another function). A worksheet using a number of statistical functions can accommodate many of the spreadsheet concepts involved in these various commands.

1-2-3 allows you to perform a number of special purpose tasks to make certain that data are presented properly. It allows you to add and delete rows and columns, move text from one position in a worksheet to another, and issue page breaks within the worksheet for later printing.

1-2-3 also allows you to control how data appear within a cell. For example, it allows you to change the column width, right-justify, center text, and repeat text within a cell.

Key Terms and Concepts

Align command	Line option
Borders option	Margins option
Clear option	Move feature
Column Width command	nail down
Copy command	nested functions
Date	Options Menu
Footer option	Other option
Format Currency option	page break
Format Date option	Page-length option
Format Fixed option	Page option
Format General option	Print command
Format Hidden option	Print Menu
Format Percent option	Print Range option
Format Reset option	Quit option
Format Scientific option	/ Range Format commands
Format Text option	receiving cells ("To" range)
Format , option	repeating character
Format + / − option	sending cells ("From" range)
function call	Setup option
Go option	/ Worksheet Global Format option
Header option	

Chapter Quiz

Multiple Choice

1. Which of the following statements about ranges is false?
   a. A range must be either a rectangle or a square.
   b. A range can be defined by "pointing."
   c. A range can be defined by giving the cell addresses of two opposite corners.
   d. A range can be defined by pointing to the first cell and entering the address of the second cell.
   e. All of the above methods can be used to define a range to 1-2-3.

2. Which of the following statements about the Copy command is false?
   a. The first item to be defined is the sending cell/range.
   b. The second item to be defined is the receiving cell/range.
   c. The receiving range can overlap with the sending range without losing data.
   d. The receiving range can be larger than the sending range.
   e. All of the above statements are true.

3. Which of the following steps is not involved in printing a worksheet to a file?
   a. Name the file.
   b. Establish the range and any options.
   c. Issue the Go command.
   d. Take the Quit command to close the file.
   e. All of the above are necessary.

4. Which of the following is not available using the Print Menu?
   a. Specify the right margin.
   b. Specify the page length.
   c. Specify the subtotal point.
   d. Specify the heading and/or footing for each page.
   e. Specify the set-up string for printing.
   f. All of the above are print commands.

5. Which of the following statements is true for functions?
   a. It is difficult to nest functions.
   b. The character used to denote a function is *.
   c. The date functions are of relatively little use.
   d. The function @MONTH(@NOW) is used to get the month of the year when the date was entered after the boot process.

True/False

6. Functions can save you, the user, a tremendous amount of time.

7. Ranges are typically entered by using three cell addresses.

8. You can print a worksheet without specifying the print range.

9. The set-up string allows you to print in 10, 12, or 17.1 cpi.

10. Print footings allow you to print out the page number, today's date, and some text data.

Answers

1. d 2. c 3. e 4. c 5. d 6. t 7. f 8. f 9. t 10. t

Exercises

1. Define or describe each of the following:
   a. range   f. Align command
   b. Range Format   g. Line option
   c. Global Format   h. Page option
   d. set-up string   i. nested function
   e. footing

2. When using the Copy command, you must first define the _____ _____ range and then define the _____ _____ range.

3. When the receiving range overlaps the sending range, some data will be _____.

4. A(n) _____ format affects the entire worksheet, while a(n) _____ format affects only an area of the worksheet.

5. The _____ places a $ sign and any needed commas in a number.

6. Before the worksheet or a part of the worksheet can be printed out, the print _____ must be defined to 1-2-3.

7. In addition to dumping output to a printer, 1-2-3 can also place it in a(n) _____.

8. The _____ selection under the Options Menu allows you to change the print pitch.

9. The _____ command allows you to define *top of page* to 1-2-3.

10. The _____ command moves the paper a small increment, while the _____ command moves the paper to the top of the next page.

11. How does the role of the Quit command differ in creating printer output from its role in creating disk output?

12. What is the advantage of nesting functions?

13. List the functions you consider to be useful at this time.

14. When a number will not fit in a cell, 1-2-3 fills that cell with _____.

15. The _____ character tells 1-2-3 to repeat the text across the cell.

16. If you delete a row or a column, all of the _____ in that row or column will be deleted.

17. The _____ command is used to increase the width of a column.

18. The @NOW function results in _____ appearing in the cell in which it resides.

19. The label prefix _____ is used to center text.

20. The "repeat the following characters" command in 1-2-3 is the _____.

Computer Exercises

1. In this exercise, you are to prepare a payroll register. Enter the formulas that would be necessary to prepare the register shown on the next page. The Net Pay is calculated by subtracting the appropriate deductions and taxes from the Gross Pay figure that has been previously calculated. The deductions and taxes, for the sake of simplicity, are assumed to be 37%. The overtime rate = rate * 1.5. Set column A to a width of 20. Set the remaining columns to a width of 11. Your worksheet will not appear so crowded.

Employee	Total Hours	Rate	Overtime Hours	Overtime Rate	Gross Pay	Net Pay
Jones, Anthony	40.00	6.50	2.00	9.75	279.50	176.09
Adams, Sam	40.00	6.50		9.75	260.00	163.80
Smith, Luther	40.00	6.50		9.75	260.00	163.80
Hunt, Mary	40.00	6.50	3.00	9.75	289.25	182.23
Lora, Kathy	40.00	6.50		9.75	260.00	163.80
Kent, John	40.00	6.50		9.75	260.00	163.80
Lester, Ned	40.00	5.50		8.25	220.00	138.60
Sahara, Ohmar	40.00	5.50		8.25	220.00	138.60
Johns, Peter	40.00	4.25	10.00	6.38	233.75	147.26
Dix, Yvonne	40.00	7.50		11.25	300.00	189.00
TOTALS					$2,582.50	$1,626.98

Save your worksheet file using the name CH10EX1.

2. A teacher friend has asked your assistance in developing a worksheet for calculating grades. Your friend has developed the following criteria for the worksheet:

    a. It is important to have the worksheet stamped with today's date.

    b. The total possible points are to appear at the top of each column.

    c. The average, high grade, low grade, standard deviation, and variance statistics are to be calculated using 1-2-3 functions.

    d. The % of Total Points entry is to be calculated by dividing the total possible points by the average.

The following information contains the format for the worksheet:

    a. You must set column A to a width of 15.

    b. Set the rest of the columns to a width of 11.

    c. You must also use the @NOW function to "date-stamp" the worksheet in cell A1.

    d. The ¦ character is found above the Alt key.

```
10-Feb-89

                      Grading Template

                     ¦
         NAME        ¦ Exam I  Anot. Bib. Exam II
POSSIBLE POINTS      ¦  150       45        130
- - - - - - - - - - -¦- - - - - - - - - - - - - - - - -
                     ¦
Student 1            ¦  113       44        110
Student 2            ¦  116       42         90
Student 3            ¦  129       42         85
Student 4            ¦  133       44        125
Student 5            ¦  121       42         76
Student 6            ¦  139       41        115
Student 7            ¦  116       42         75
Student 8            ¦  130       39        120
Student 9            ¦  127       42         95
Student 10           ¦  120       42        115

- - - - - - - - - - -¦- - - - - - - - - - - - - - - - -
                     ¦
Average              ¦  124       42        101
% of Tot. Pnts.      ¦ 82.93%   93.33%    77.38%
High Grade           ¦  139       44        125
```

(Continued on page 288)

```
Low Grade      :     113        39         75
Std, Deviation :       8         1         18
Variance       :      65         2        312
```

Save this worksheet file using the name CH10EX2.

3. Print out your CH10EX2 worksheet file. Specify a heading that has "Intro-duction to Microcomputers" as the text to appear at the top of the page. Specify a footing that has the page number, name of the worksheet file, and the date at the bottom of the page. Refer to the print command structure chart in Appendix B, if you have questions about how to get to a command.

4. Print out your CH10EX1 worksheet file. Specify a condensed print setup so that the worksheet will print on one page of paper. Refer to the print command structure chart in Appendix B. You will also have to expand the right-hand column to a width of 120.

 5. Print out your CH10EX2 worksheet to a disk file called TEST. Leave 1-2-3 and access the TEST.PRN file with your word processing software, or use the DOS TYPE command to make sure that you created the file properly. Remember that 1-2-3 has placed the .PRN extension on the file.

6. Retrieve the worksheet CH10EX2. You just received word that your teacher friend forgot to include a student named Student5a in the list. This individual's scores are 100 for Exam 1, 41 for Anot. Bib., and 113 for Exam II. Add this individual to the existing grading worksheet, making any changes that are necessary. Store the changed worksheet to a file named CH10EX6.

7. You are now to add a column to replace the existing column A in the CH9EX5 file. This column should have a heading of Dept. The two different sales forces in the business are the new car sales staff and the preowned car sales staff. Sally, Marge, and Harry are in the Dept. 1 cells. Sort the file with Dept. as the primary key and Sales Rep as the secondary key. Place the results in a file called CH10EX7.

8. Prepare a worksheet that Gerry can use for his golf outing day. Gerry is interested in tracking scores for golfers over four rounds. He is interested in not only calculating the total strokes over the four rounds of golf but also in finding the average number of strokes for each golfer during the outing. Give the average score column a range format of fixed with one position to the right of the decimal. Save as CH10EX8.

```
              Gerry's Golf Outing Day
              Pebble Beach, California

                                                   Total      Outing
              Round 1   Round 2   Round 3   Round 4  Strokes    Average
Don Horsmann     75        73        70        80      298       74,5
Dak Zephyr       64        66        62        65      257       64,3
John Wells       68        64        66        70      268       67,0
Gerald McMillan  90        96       105        84      375       93,8
```

Chapter
11

Advanced
Spreadsheet with
Lotus 1-2-3

After completing this chapter, you should be able to:

Discuss commands that allow you more control over your environment

Explain the concept and use of range names

Discuss the use of dummy rows and columns in ranges

Discuss the use of the Sort command

Discuss the use of the Titles option

Discuss the differences in relative and absolute addressing

Discuss the merits of mixed cell addresses

Discuss the use of absolute range names

Discuss automatic versus manual worksheet recalculation

Discuss in greater detail the @PMT *and* @IF *functions*

Explain the use of the @DATE *function and its use in arithmetic manipulation*

Once you have initially built a worksheet, you are usually still not finished with it. There may be minor errors that you wish to correct, or enhancements that you wish to add to your worksheet to give it a more professional appearance.

This chapter will cover the following topics: controlling your worksheet environment, range names, adding and deleting rows and columns, moving, sorting, titles, absolute versus relative addressing, manual versus automatic recalculation, and more on the functions @IF, @PMT, and @DATE.

Controlling Your Worksheet Environment

The Lotus 1-2-3 package provides you with a number of options you can use to obtain more control over your worksheet environment. Many of these commands make it easier to generate reports with the exact columns desired, presentation of numeric information in the manner desired, changing directories on a fixed disk, and rearranging column and row data, as well as saving files with password protection.

Worksheet Zero Command

The Worksheet **Zero command** allows you to suppress any zeros that occur within numeric cells. These zeros can be either the answer generated by a formula or a zero that has been entered. The command / Worksheet Global Zero Yes tells 1-2-3 that no zeros are to be displayed in cells. The / Worksheet Zero Global Zero No tells 1-2-3 that zeros are again to be displayed in a cell.

GoTo Command

Up to this point, you have positioned the pointer to a location in your worksheet via pointer movement commands. 1-2-3 provides a faster way to go directly to the address of a cell via the **GoTo command** invoked by pressing the function key F5. Once the GoTo command has been issued, the prompt Enter address to go to : E14 is displayed. The cell address displayed once the command has been issued is the current pointer address. You can now enter the new location and press the ENTER key. The pointer then moves to that cell address. The GoTo command (F5) can save you many keystrokes when you are working on a large worksheet application.

System Command

1-2-3 allows you to temporarily exit 1-2-3 and enter DOS via the System command of the Main Menu. The **System command** allows you to run a program or execute a DOS command. For example, many people routinely forget to enter the date and time when they boot the system. Using the System command, you can drop to DOS and use the DOS DATE and TIME commands to enter this information (see Figure 11.1). Once you have finished with your tasks at the DOS level, enter the command EXIT and you return to your worksheet in READY mode.

Changing the Directory

When you use 1-2-3 on a fixed disk, 1-2-3 usually assumes that worksheet files are to be saved to the directory in which your 1-2-3 program files reside. You may wish to save worksheet files to another directory or even to a diskette in a disk drive (for example, drive B). To accomplish this, you must use the

Figure 11.1
Your screen after the 1-2-3 System command is executed.

```
          (Type EXIT and press [RETURN] to return to 1-2-3)


          The IBM Personal Computer DOS
          Version 2.10 (C)Copyright IBM Corp 1981, 1982, 1983

          A>date
          Current date is Tue  1-01-1980
          Enter new date: 9-11-87

          A>time
          Current time is  0:05:14.22
          Enter new time: 20:37


          A>
```

command / Worksheet Global Default Directory and then enter either the new directory path (for example, C:\wksfiles\school) or the disk drive followed by a backslash (for example, B:\).

Once you have entered the appropriate information, 1-2-3 returns you to the Default submenu. To make this change permanent so that 1-2-3 always uses the entity that you just described for storing any worksheet, issue the Update command. Most of the time, however, this is simply a temporary change. In that case, issue the Quit command and you are returned to READY mode.

You should note that when you issue the Quit command after changing the directory, the change has been made only for this worksheet session. If you use the Update command before you quit from the Default submenu, the change becomes permanent. This means that when you now leave 1-2-3 and start it at a different date, it will default to the directory/disk that it now finds in its default information file.

Column Hide

You may run into a situation where it is advantageous to print certain columns of a worksheet without printing certain embedded columns. This is accomplished via the / Worksheet **Column Hide command**. For example, suppose that you wished to print, as well as display, your COMPSALS (see Figure 11.2) worksheet without the Change column (column E). You must first position your pointer anywhere in column E and then issue the command.

/—Gets the Main Menu.

W—Selects the Worksheet option.

C—Selects the Column option.

H—Selects the Hide option.

ENTER—Tells 1-2-3 that this is the only column to be hidden. To hide multiple columns, expand the range.

The worksheet depicted in Figure 11.3 is now displayed on your screen. Even though column F's entries are dependent on the hidden column E, the data still are calculated properly. The only way that you can tell that column E has been hidden is to examine the row border labels. The hidden column has no detrimental impact on the rest of the worksheet. To make the hidden column reappear, issue the above command, but replace the Hide with the Display.

Figure 11.2
`COMPSALS` worksheet.

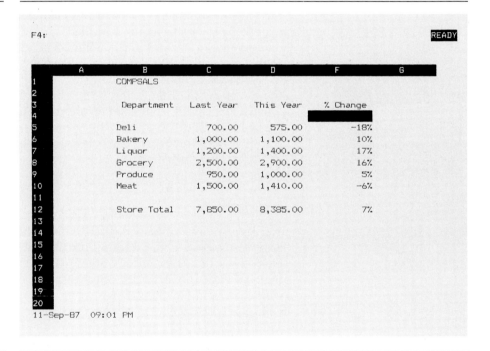

Figure 11.3
Worksheet with column E hidden.

Columns previously hidden reappear on the screen with an asterisk to the right of the column identifier in the column border (see Figure 11.4). To "unhide" the column, place the pointer in the column marked with the asterisk (column E) and press the ENTER key. The column has now been restored.

The real advantage of hiding columns is that you can hide columns containing intermediate results when it comes time to print a report. Only the columns that contain data meaningful for a specific report need be displayed on the screen and printed. This feature allows you to prepare reports that are more easily understood by their users.

Figure 11.4
Worksheet hidden column
marked with * using Display
command.

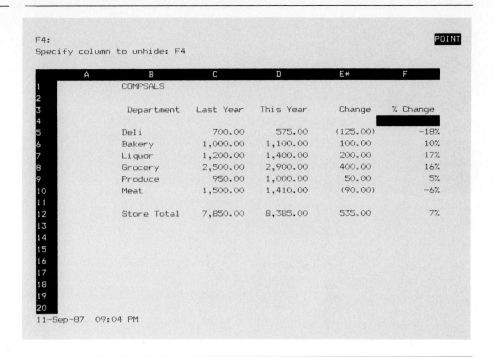

Figure 11.5
Worksheet with a circular
reference.

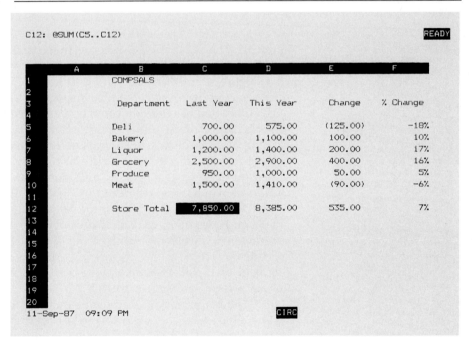

Finding Circular References and Status Commands

Suppose that you are working on an application like the COMPSALS work-sheet and suddenly a circular reference is indicated in your worksheet (see Figure 11.5). You have no idea what has caused this to occur. You don't even have any idea how long ago the CIRC reference indicator appeared on your screen, because you were not looking at the indicators area of the worksheet. Finding the location of the circular reference with the least amount of difficulty involves using the / Worksheet Status command.

Figure 11.6
Status screen for COMPSALS
worksheet.

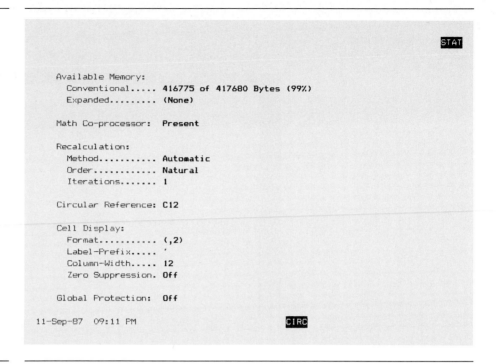

Once that command is issued to 1-2-3, a screen similar to Figure 11.6 appears. You see that 1-2-3 indicates that a circular reference exists in cell C12. You press the ENTER key to return to READY mode and find that the formula (see Figure 11.5) @SUM(C5..C12) is in cell C12. The problem is that cell C12 has been told to not only hold the answer but also to participate in the calculation. Once you use the Edit command and change the 12 in the formula to 10, the circular reference disappears from the screen.

If multiple circular references occur within a worksheet, 1-2-3 finds only one at a time. Since only one circular reference is indicated at one time, you must correct each as it is found and then issue another / Worksheet Status command to find the next.

Besides finding circular references, the / Worksheet Status command provides other valuable pieces of information. For example, it indicates the amount of memory available for a worksheet as well as the amount of memory used by your worksheet. It contains information about methods of recalculation, global format use, the current global column width, and whether or not zero suppression is in effect.

Another important status report can be invoked via the / Worksheet Global Default Status command. That report (see Figure 11.7) contains information about the defaults currently in effect in your worksheet. For example, it contains information about the printer interface used, margins, page characteristics, directory in use, and various formats that are in effect for punctuation, currency, and date and time presentation.

Password Protecting Your Worksheets

Release 2 provides you with the ability to **password**-protect your worksheet files.

WARNING If you have a bad memory, you should not use passwords. Once you save a file with a password, you will always be prompted for it before

Figure 11.7
The Default Status screen for
COMPSALS.

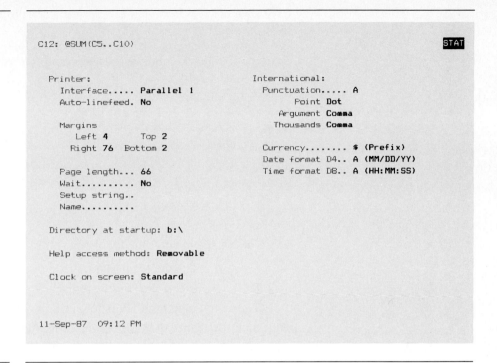

Figure 11.7
The Default Status screen for
COMPSALS.

1-2-3 will allow you to access the file. If you forget your password, 1-2-3 will deny you access to the worksheet.

The following example shows how to save the worksheet YEAREND with the password FINLCOPY.

/—Invoke the Main Menu.

F—Select the File option.

S—Tell 1-2-3 to save the worksheet file.

YEAREND P—Enter the name of the file, press the space bar, and enter a P. The P indicates to 1-2-3 that a password is to be assigned to this file.

FINLCOPY—Enter the password. (It does not appear on your screen, so be careful to enter it correctly.) The password may contain up to 15 characters.

FINLCOPY—1-2-3 now asks you to verify the password. To do so, you must reenter the original password and press the ENTER key. In this case, the FINLCOPY password is now operational.

To change or cancel a password, you must enter the / File Re-trieve command and enter the appropriate file name. 1-2-3 now prompts you for the password. You must enter the appropriate password before you can cancel it or enter a new one. To cancel a password, save the worksheet and press Esc or BACKSPACE when you are prompted for the password. The worksheet will now be saved to disk without a password.

Range Transpose

The / **Range Transpose command** allows you to rearrange the rows and columns within a range in your worksheet. Any alphanumeric or numeric label can be rearranged; however, you are not allowed to arrange any relative address formulas. Trying to do so will result in ERR messages in any cells that have formulas. If formulas are desired, rearrange the labels and then add the formulas.

Assume that you wish to rearrange the following worksheet's rows and columns so that the columns are rows (and vice versa):

```
COMPSALS

Department   Last Year   This Year
Deli             700.00      575.00
Bakery         1,000.00    1,100.00
Liquor         1,200.00    1,400.00
Grocery        2,500.00    2,900.00
Produce          950.00    1,000.00
Meat           1,500.00    1,410.00
```

You would need to enter the following commands:

/	Gets the Main Menu.
R	Selects the Range option.
T	Selects the Transpose option.
B3.D10 ENTER	Enter the Copy From Range (Transpose Range) either by entering the actual cell addresses or by manual pointer movement "painting" the affected area.
B16 ENTER	Tell 1-2-3 where to place the transposed range.

You will now see the following worksheet on your screen:

```
COMPSALS

Department   Last Year   This Year
Deli             700.00      575.00
Bakery         1,000.00    1,100.00
Liquor         1,200.00    1,400.00
Grocery        2,500.00    2,900.00
Produce          950.00    1,000.00
Meat           1,500.00    1,410.00

Department   Deli     Bakery     Liquor     Grocery    Produce    Meat
Last Year    700.00   1,000.00   1,200.00   2,500.00   950.00     1,500.00
This Year    575.00   1,100.00   1,400.00   2,900.00   1,000.00   1,410.00
```

Remember, only text can be moved using the Transpose command. Any formulas will move improperly, causing ERR messages to appear in the affected cells.

Range Names

By now, you have used ranges extensively in formatting, copying, and printing information from worksheets. One problem with using ranges is that you must always keep track of the cell addresses of two opposite corner cells in each range; to help avoid this problem, Lotus 1-2-3 has a feature that allows you to give a **range name** to a range of cells and thereafter refer to that range by the given name.

Let's reexamine the procedure involved in setting up function formulas for the FUNCTION worksheet you practiced on in Chapter 10. Every time you wanted to add a function in column B of the worksheet, you either had to point to the cell locations in the range or had to enter the previously recorded cell locations. Another alternative is to give the cell range a name like `COLB`; then every time 1-2-3 requests a range, you can simply use `COLB` (short for column B).

Another advantage of using range names is that they make a worksheet self-documenting and, therefore, more readable. This can be very helpful when you are setting up formulas to refer to a range name rather than merely a cell location. If you come back to a worksheet later, a formula using range names will make much more sense.

Name Menu

To give a range a name, you must invoke the Range option from the Main Menu, and select the Name option from the Range Menu. You then receive a menu that looks as follows:

```
Create   Delete   Labels   Reset   Table
```

Create. The **Create option** is used to give a name to a range of cells or to redefine the location of the named range. The range name can be one to fourteen characters in length (including special characters and spaces); Lotus recommends that you use only A–Z, 0–9 and the dash (–), without using spaces. After you select the Create option, you are prompted for the name you wish to give the range. You are then prompted to define the range to 1-2-3 (by pointing or by typing in the actual addresses).

At this point, you can use the F5 key (GoTo) to reference a range name or a cell address. You are not restricted in the number of times that you include a cell in different named ranges. When the worksheet is saved, the range names are also saved.

Delete. The **Delete option** is used to allow 1-2-3 to drop a named range from memory. The contents of the individual cells involved remain unchanged. After you select this option, you are prompted to enter the name of the range to be deleted or to point to the range to be deleted on the prompt line.

Labels. The **Labels option** is very similar to the Create option, except that the name for the range is taken directly from an adjacent label entry. You must make certain that the label to be used as the range name does not contain more than fourteen characters.

For example, assume that you have two adjacent entries like those shown below. Position your pointer at cell D3, and enter the command `/ Range Name Labels`. Press the ENTER key (or if there are multiple cells involved, indicate the end of the range). You must now tell 1-2-3 whether the named cells are right, down, left, or up with respect to the labels.

```
        D3              E3
      |Sales  |    $100.00|
```

Each entry is treated as a separate range name. You cannot delete them in one step, as you can create them; instead, you have to delete them individually or use the Reset option.

Reset. The **Reset option** makes 1-2-3 drop from its memory all range names that have been assigned.

Table. The **Table option** of the Name submenu allows you to construct a report containing all range names and their appropriate cell addresses in your worksheet. The pointer location is used as the upper left-hand corner of the report. Since the report actually takes up space within the worksheet, make certain that you are in an unused area; otherwise, a valuable portion of your worksheet model may be lost.

Naming Instructions

The steps needed to give the numbers in column B of the FUNCTION worksheet the range name COLB are as follows:

/—Gets the Main Menu.

R—Takes the Range option, and displays the Range Menu.

N—Takes the Name option of the Range Menu, and displays the Name Menu.

C—Takes the Create option of the Name Menu.

COLB—Specifies the range name to be used.

B9 [by manual pointer movement]—Points to the first cell in the COLB range.

.—Nail down the beginning of the range.

B17 [by manual pointer movement]—Points to the last cell in the COLB range.

ENTER—Tells 1-2-3 to execute the command.

You can now enter functions simply by referring to the range name, COLB. For example, you could enter the @SUM function as @SUM(COLB), without having to enter the cell addresses or pointing. You can also copy this formula to the other columns, in which case 1-2-3 keeps track of the range but not the range name.

More Range Name Examples

Load the COMPSALS worksheet and create the range names indicated in Figure 11.8. When you are finished, you should have the following range names: Header, Dept, Sales, and Print. Notice that as you are creating the range names, 1-2-3 displays them in alphabetical order on the prompt line (see Figure 11.9). Once you have created the named ranges, you can verify that, for instance, the Sales named range was created properly by going through the keystrokes required to create it.

Verifying Named Ranges. Once you have indicated (via highlighting the Sales range name and pressing the ENTER key), the cells contained in the Sales named range will be highlighted on your screen (see Figure 11.10). This method works well if you just wish to verify one named range, but if you wish to verify all of your named ranges, the best technique is to use the Table command of the Range name submenu. Position your pointer to cell B16 (this will become the upper left-hand corner of the report) and enter the following commands:

/—Gets the Main Menu.

R—Takes the Range option.

N—Takes the Name option.

Figure 11.8
Cells included in the specified named ranges.

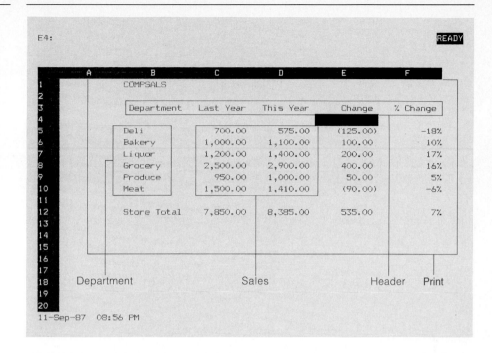

Figure 11.9
Named ranges in `COMPSALS` listed via the / Range Name Create command.

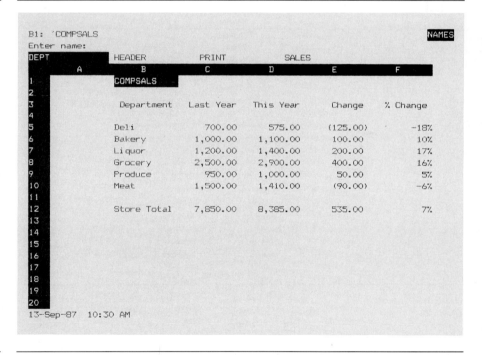

T—Takes the Table option.

ENTER—Tells 1-2-3 to create the report.

Your worksheet should now appear like that depicted in Figure 11.11. Notice that each range name appears on a separate line in the report. Also notice that the beginning and ending cell addresses are included in the report. The beginning cell is always viewed as the upper left-hand cell by 1-2-3, and the ending cell is always viewed as the lower right-hand cell. Therefore, for a named range composed of a single row, the first cell is really the upper left-hand

Figure 11.10
Verifying the named range
Sales via the Create
command.

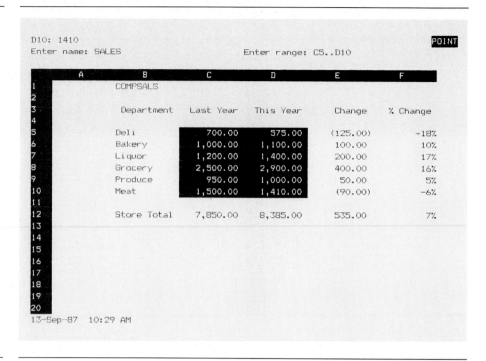

D10: 1410
Enter name: SALES   Enter range: C5..D10   `POINT`

	A	B	C	D	E	F
1		COMPSALS				
2						
3		Department	Last Year	This Year	Change	% Change
4						
5		Deli	700.00	575.00	(125.00)	-18%
6		Bakery	1,000.00	1,100.00	100.00	10%
7		Liquor	1,200.00	1,400.00	200.00	17%
8		Grocery	2,500.00	2,900.00	400.00	16%
9		Produce	950.00	1,000.00	50.00	5%
10		Meat	1,500.00	1,410.00	(90.00)	-6%
11						
12		Store Total	7,850.00	8,385.00	535.00	7%
13						
14						
15						
16						
17						
18						
19						
20						

13-Sep-87   10:29 AM

Figure 11.11
The output of the / Range
Name Table command.

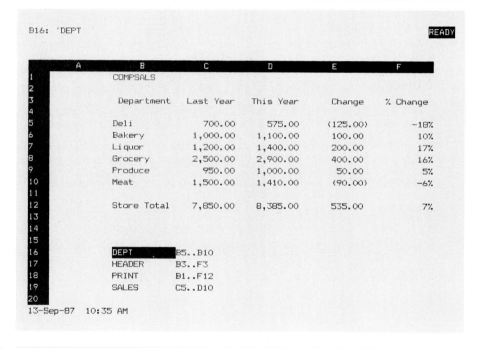

B16: 'DEPT   `READY`

	A	B	C	D	E	F
1		COMPSALS				
2						
3		Department	Last Year	This Year	Change	% Change
4						
5		Deli	700.00	575.00	(125.00)	-18%
6		Bakery	1,000.00	1,100.00	100.00	10%
7		Liquor	1,200.00	1,400.00	200.00	17%
8		Grocery	2,500.00	2,900.00	400.00	16%
9		Produce	950.00	1,000.00	50.00	5%
10		Meat	1,500.00	1,410.00	(90.00)	-6%
11						
12		Store Total	7,850.00	8,385.00	535.00	7%
13						
14						
15						
16		DEPT	B5..B10			
17		HEADER	B3..F3			
18		PRINT	B1..F12			
19		SALES	C5..D10			
20						

13-Sep-87   10:35 AM

corner of the range. Notice also that the entries generated by the Table command have actually become part of the worksheet and have been treated as
labels by 1-2-3 (notice the 'DEPT entry in Figure 11.11).

Using Named Ranges. Once you have created named ranges in your worksheet, you can use them in any command that requires a cell address or a
range of cells before it will work. For example, you can use named ranges with
the GoTo (F5) command. After pressing the F5 key, enter the named range
Dept, and your pointer moves to cell B5 (your pointer always positions to the
upper left-hand cell of a named range using the GoTo command).

Figure 11.12
Result of a Copy command
using the Names function
key.

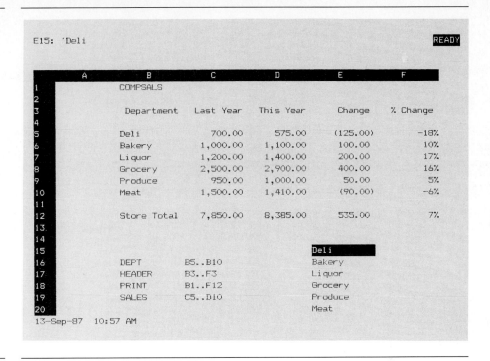

Instead of actually entering the characters contained in a named range, you can also use the Names (F3) function key. Once you are in a command that requires you to enter a cell address or a cell range and you want to use a named range, you can press the F3 key and highlight the named range to be included in this instruction. For example, the Names (F3) key can be used in conjunction with the Copy command. The following example will copy the Dept named range to cell E15 without extensive pointer movement. Position your pointer to cell E15.

/—Gets the Main Menu.

C—Takes the Copy command.

F3—Press the Names (F3) function key.

Dept—Highlight the Dept named range.

ENTER—Specify the Dept named range as the From cells.

ENTER—Specify cell E15 as the To range.

Notice that the cells contained in the Dept named range (see Figure 11.12) have been copied without positioning the cursor to cell B3, highlighting cells B3..F3, and then indicating that cell E15 is the destination cell. This technique is extremely useful when you have common text (such as lines of dashes used to indicate subtotals in a business report) required at multiple locations in a document.

Now use a named range to calculate the grand total for the This Year and Last Year columns. This grand total could be accomplished by the formula +C12+D12. This method would not, however, allow us to use a named range. Instead, enter the formula @SUM(SALES) in cell C13. Once this formula has been entered, the result of 16,235.00 is displayed in the cell. Notice that the entry in the status line shows C13: @SUM(SALES). Now delete the named range called Sales using the following commands:

/—Gets the Main Menu.

R—Takes the Range option.

Figure 11.13
Example of a formula after a
named range is deleted.

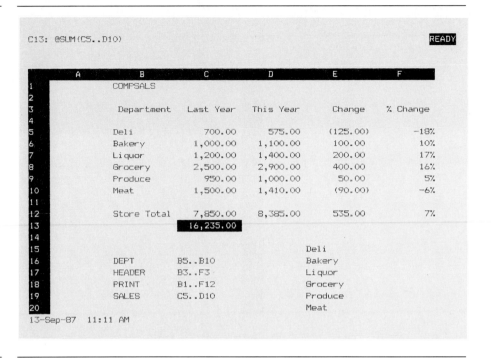

N—Takes the Name option.

D—Takes the Delete option.

Sales—Highlight the Sales named range using pointer movement commands.

ENTER—1-2-3 executes the command.

Notice that the @SUM function entry in the status line no longer contains the Sales named range but, instead, contains the cell address of C5..D10 (see Figure 11.13). Once you create a named range, 1-2-3 still keeps track of that range via the cell addresses that were entered when the named range was created. Instead of referring to a range via the addresses, 1-2-3 allows you to substitute a variable name. If you delete the variable name via the / Range Name Delete command, 1-2-3 simply substitutes the cell addresses that you initially used in creating the named range.

Use of Dummy Columns or Rows in Expanding Ranges

Dummy Columns. Load the file called COLSALES. Many times you will have an application in which you wish to create year-to-date sales totals for each department. You also want to set up the report so that it automatically expands as you insert a column to enter the sales for a new month. Such a report format requires a format similar to that in Figure 11.14. If you use the @SUM command like that depicted in Figure 11.14, you immediately have problems when you insert a new column for the figures for March. In order to generate the correct store totals, the @SUM function has to be changed each time a new month is added. Requiring this kind of change each month not only results in an inflexible worksheet, but also a worksheet that is sooner or later going to result in incorrect answers when someone forgets to change the @SUM function.

The solution to this problem is to use a **dummy column**. When you wish to add and delete rows and columns and have this reflected in any calculation

Figure 11.14
A typical worksheet tracking year-to-date totals.

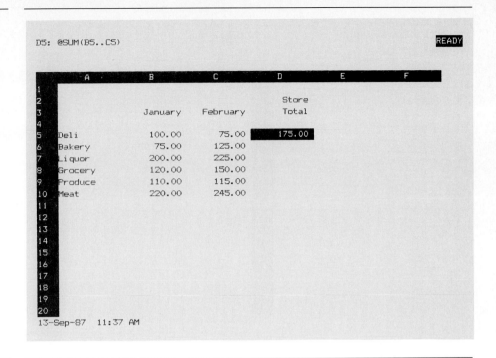

that references a range, like the @SUM function, your range must be set up so that any additions or deletions occur after the beginning cell in the range and before the ending cell in the range. To incorporate this into the worksheet depicted in Figure 11.14 requires a number of changes:

1. A blank column (the dummy column to be referenced later) must be inserted to the left of the grand total column (column D).
2. The new column D is set to a width of 1.
3. The @SUM function must be edited so that the ending cell in the range is D5 (the function should now be @SUM(B5..D5)).

Your worksheet should now look like that in Figure 11.15.

Now when you wish to add a new month and have the sales figures for that month automatically included in the Store Total, position the pointer to the dummy column, insert a new column, and enter the sales figures. Because the new column gets inserted to the left of the dummy column and, therefore, before the last cell in the @SUM function range, the new data are automatically included in the store total. You can now copy this new sum formula down column E.

 Dummy Rows. Load the file COMPSALS. If you wanted to incorporate the concepts just covered to allow you to add new departments so that they are automatically included in the yearly total, you have to change the @SUM functions to include the blank row entry after the Meat department. Your Last Year sum function in cell C12 now appears as @SUM(C5..C11). Of course, you must make the same change to the This Year column @SUM function. To add a new department (leaving the order of the others unchanged) so that it can be included in the total now requires you to position your pointer to row 11, insert a new row, and enter the new sales figures. The newly entered sales figures are now included within the total for that year.

Expanding the range of the @SUM function for the COMPSALS worksheet was a straightforward task, because a blank row existed that could be used

Figure 11.15
Worksheet with a dummy
column D.

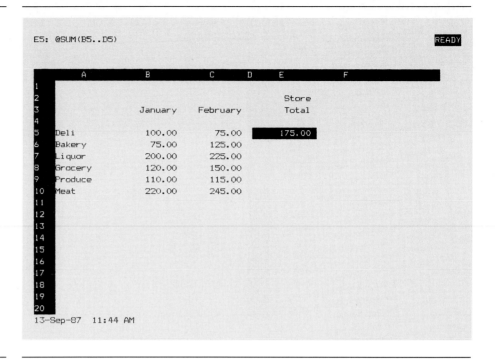

```
E5: @SUM(B5..D5)                                                      READY

            A            B            C        D    E           F
 1
 2                                                   Store
 3                     January     February          Total
 4
 5  Deli             100.00         75.00           175.00
 6  Bakery            75.00        125.00
 7  Liquor           200.00        225.00
 8  Grocery          120.00        150.00
 9  Produce          110.00        115.00
10  Meat             220.00        245.00
11
12
13
14
15
16
17
18
19
20
13-Sep-87   11:44 AM
```

as the **dummy row**. What happens, however, when you have an application like that depicted in Figure 11.16 that requires you to indicate subtotal lines with a cell of dashes (––––––) and a total line with a cell of equal signs (= = = = = = =)? If you remember back to the previous chapter, text entries are given the value of zero by 1-2-3. Since a value of zero does not affect the summation of a column of numbers, the dummy row can be the row containing the total or subtotal text indicators. You must, however, never use such a dummy row for statistical functions like @AVG, @MIN, @STD, and @VAR, since a cell with a zero value is included in these calculations. For example, a @AVG function that includes a text cell with a zero value has a deflated average.

Any time an application requires you to add several numbers together, you should use the @SUM function with a dummy ending cell. Later on, when you add numbers to that list, you don't have to change any formulas so that the new items are included in the list. Any range or named range including a dummy column or row will automatically expand and contract as columns are added to the left of a dummy column or above a dummy row. When you have the dummy row or column containing text data, make certain that you do not use functions that will be affected by a zero value.

Sorting

From time to time, you may want to rearrange data in a particular order. Some spreadsheets allow you to perform such a task via the Move statement; 1-2-3, however, contains a **Sort command**. This feature allows a worksheet to be constructed in a way that is logical for the individual building it, and then to be accessed by another user and rearranged in a manner that is logical for that person's application.

Sort Menu

The Sort command is found in the Data Menu, which is invoked from the Main Menu. When the Sort option is selected, the following menu is displayed:

Figure 11.16
Worksheet with a dummy
row containing equal signs
(=).

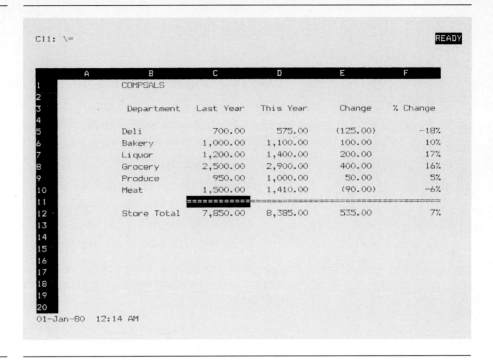

Data Range   Primary Key   Secondary Key   Reset   Go   Quit

Data Range. The **Data Range option** allows you to mark the area to be sorted—an operation that must occur before a sort can take place. Column headings and total lines are not included in the data range. It is wise to save a worksheet before you perform a sort; then if you really mess things up, you can just reload the worksheet from disk.

Primary Key. The **Primary Key option** allows you to select the column you want the data range to be sorted by. Since the entire range has been described to 1-2-3, all you have to do is point to a cell in the column; 1-2-3 will then prompt you to select the sort order, in either Ascending or Descending order.

Secondary Key. The **Secondary Key option** allows you to arrange date within the primary key when the sort is executed. For example, in a sort of name and address data, you could establish City as the primary key and Last Name as the secondary key; the data would then be sorted by city, and within each city would be sorted by last name.

Reset. The Reset option is selected to make 1-2-3 drop from its memory all the sort parameters you've given it.

Go. The **Go option** is the command that tells 1-2-3 to execute the sort.

Quit. The **Quit option** returns you to your worksheet and ready mode.

When you have a large worksheet, you may wish to set up a number of sorts for different data ranges. In this type of application, it is advisable to use the Reset before the next sort. This is especially important when you are going from an application that has both primary and secondary sort keys to an application that has only a primary sort. Unless you tell 1-2-3 to Reset the sort parameters, it still remembers the secondary key. In this type of situation, you would receive a Key column outside of sort range error message.

 ### Worksheet Practice with the Sort Command

Load in the CH10EX1 worksheet you created in Chapter 10, and try some experiments with the Sort command. The loading process is accomplished via the following commands:

/—Gets the Main Menu.

F—Selects the File option.

R—Selects the Retrieve option.

CH10EX1—Identifies the name of the worksheet.

ENTER—Tells 1-2-3 to get the worksheet.

You should now have the following worksheet loaded (since the entire worksheet will not normally fit on one page, spaces have been deleted to make it fit here):

Employee	Total Hours	Rate	Overtime Hours	Overtime Rate	Gross Pay	Net Pay
Jones, Anthony	40.00	6.50	2.00	9.75	279.50	176.09
Adams, Sam	40.00	6.50		9.75	260.00	163.80
Smith, Luther	40.00	6.50		9.75	260.00	163.80
Hunt, Mary	40.00	6.50	3.00	9.75	289.25	182.23
Lora, Kathy	40.00	6.50		9.75	260.00	163.80
Kent, John	40.00	6.50		9.75	260.00	163.80
Lester, Ned	40.00	5.50		8.25	220.00	138.60
Sahara, Ohmar	40.00	5.50		8.25	220.00	138.60
Johns, Peter	40.00	4.25	10.00	6.38	233.75	147.26
Dix, Yvonne	40.00	7.50		11.25	300.00	189.00
TOTALS			15.00		$2,582.50	$1,626.98

Once the worksheet has been loaded, you must tell 1-2-3 how to sort the information, by invoking the Main Menu and selecting the Data option from it. The following steps should now be taken:

S—Takes the Sort option from the Data Menu.

D—Selects the Data Range to define the area of the worksheet to be sorted.

A4 [by manual pointer movement]—Positions the pointer at A4 (the cell with the contents "Anthony Jones").

.—Nails down the beginning of the range.

G13 [by manual pointer movement]—Positions the pointer at cell G13 (the cell with the contents "189.00").

ENTER—Tells 1-2-3 that the data range is defined.

P—Selects the Primary Key option.

A4 [by manual pointer movement]—Positions the pointer at A4 (the cell with the contents "Anthony Jones"). Actually, the pointer could just as well be placed anywhere in column A inside the data range.

ENTER—Tells 1-2-3 to accept this information.

A—Tells 1-2-3 to perform the sort in ascending order.

ENTER—Indicates to 1-2-3 that the sort order has been completed.

G—Tells 1-2-3 to perform the sort.

Your worksheet should now look like the one shown below:

Employee	Total Hours	Rate	Overtime Hours	Overtime Rate	Gross Pay	Net Pay
Adams, Sam	40.00	6.50		9.75	260.00	163.80
Dix, Yvonne	40.00	7.50		11.25	300.00	189.00
Hunt, Mary	40.00	6.50	3.00	9.75	289.25	182.23
Johns, Peter	40.00	4.25	10.00	6.38	233.75	147.26
Jones, Anthony	40.00	6.50	2.00	9.75	279.50	176.09
Kent, John	40.00	6.50		9.75	260.00	163.80
Lester, Ned	40.00	5.50		8.25	220.00	138.60
Lora, Kathy	40.00	6.50		9.75	260.00	163.80
Sahara, Ohmar	40.00	5.50		8.25	220.00	138.60
Smith, Luther	40.00	6.50		9.75	260.00	163.80
TOTALS			15.00		$2,582.50	$1,626.98

This information is ideal if you're looking for a payroll listing of employees in the company. What happens, though, if you want to group individuals in alphabetic order by department? On this worksheet, doing so would involve adding a column to the left of the Employee column to contain the department number and setting the Dpt. column to a width of four positions and changing the format to zero decimal positions.

First, position the pointer anywhere in column A and add a column as follows:

/—Invokes the Main Menu.

W—Selects the Worksheet option.

I—Selects the Insert option.

C—Selects the Column option.

ENTER—Executes the Insert command.

Next, position the pointer in new column A and change it to a width of 4.

/—Invokes the Main Menu.

W—Selects the Worksheet option.

C—Selects the Column Width option.

S—Selects the Set option.

4—Specifies the new width.

ENTER—Executes the command.

Next, position the cursor to cell A4 (the one to the left of "Sam Adams"). Change the format to zero positions to the right of the decimal.

/—Invokes the Main Menu.

R—Selects the Range option.

F—Selects the Format option.

F—Selects the Fixed option.

0—Identifies the number of decimal positions.

ENTER—Executes the command.

A13 [by manual pointer movement]—Positions the pointer at the end of the range.

ENTER—Tells 1-2-3 to execute the command.

Enter the Dpt. heading and the following department numbers to your worksheet:

Dpt.	Employee	Total Hours	Rate	Overtime Hours	Overtime Rate	Gross	Net Pay
1	Adams, Sam	40.00	6.50		9.75	260.00	163.80
2	Dix, Yvonne	40.00	7.50		11.25	300.00	189.00
2	Hunt, Mary	40.00	6.50	3.00	9.75	289.25	182.23
1	Johns, Peter	40.00	4.25	10.00	6.38	233.75	147.26
2	Jones, Anthony	40.00	6.50	2.00	9.75	279.50	176.09
1	Kent, John	40.00	6.50		9.75	260.00	163.80
1	Lester, Ned	40.00	5.50		8.25	220.00	138.60
2	Lora, Kathy	40.00	6.50		9.75	260.00	163.80
2	Sahara, Ohmar	40.00	5.50		8.25	220.00	138.60
1	Smith, Luther	40.00	6.50		9.75	260.00	163.80
	TOTALS			15.00		$2,582.50	$1,626.98

More sort instructions must now be issued to tell 1-2-3 exactly how to sort information in the data range, including: giving a new sort range to 1-2-3 (remember, a field outside the old range has been added), specifying a new primary key, and specifying a secondary key. (Since the data range has not changed dramatically and both a primary and a secondary key sort will be executed, the Reset command does not have to be executed.) These tasks require the following steps:

/—Invokes the Main Menu.

D—Selects the Data option.

S—Selects the Sort option from the Data Menu.

D—Selects the Data Range option.

BACKSPACE—Cancels the existing range.

A4 [by manual pointer movement]—Positions the pointer at the left of the cell with "Sam Adams" in it.

.—Nails down the beginning of the range.

H13 [by manual pointer movement]—Positions the pointer at the end of the range.

ENTER—Tells 1-2-3 that the range has been established.

P—Selects the Primary Key option.

BACKSPACE—Cancels the existing range.

A4 [by manual pointer movement]—Positions the pointer at cell A4 (any other cell in column A inside the data range would do just as well).

ENTER—Tells 1-2-3 that the primary key range has been established.

ENTER—Tells 1-2-3 to sort in ascending order (default).

S—Selects the Secondary Key option.

B4 [by manual pointer movement]—Positions the pointer at cell B4 (any other cell in column B within the data range would do just as well).

ENTER—Tells 1-2-3 that the secondary key range has been established.

A—Tells 1-2-3 to sort in ascending order.

ENTER—Tells 1-2-3 that the order of the sort is specified.

G—Tells 1-2-3 to sort the worksheet.

Your worksheet should now look as follows:

Dpt.	Employee	Total Hours	Rate	Overtime Hours	Overtime Rate	Gross Pay	Net Pay
1	Adams, Sam	40.00	6.50		9.75	260.00	163.80
1	Johns, Peter	40.00	4.25	10.00	6.38	233.75	147.26
1	Kent, John	40.00	6.50		9.75	260.00	163.80
1	Lester, Ned	40.00	5.50		8.25	220.00	138.60
1	Smith, Luther	40.00	6.50		9.75	260.00	163.80
2	Dix, Yvonne	40.00	7.50		11.25	300.00	189.00
2	Hunt, Mary	40.00	6.50	3.00	9.75	289.25	182.23
2	Jones, Anthony	40.00	6.50	2.00	9.75	279.50	176.09
2	Lora, Kathy	40.00	6.50		9.75	260.00	163.80
2	Sahara, Ohmar	40.00	5.50		8.25	220.00	138.60
	TOTALS			15.00		$2,582.50	$1,626.98

Save this worksheet to a file called PAYSORT, as follows:

/—Invokes the Main Menu.

F—Selects the File option from the Main Menu.

S—Selects the Save option.

PAYSORT—Keys in the new worksheet name.

ENTER—Saves the file to disk.

Titles

By this time, you have surely noticed that it is inconvenient to work with large spreadsheets, like PAYROLL, whose width exceeds the display on the screen—especially when you are interested in gross pay and net pay information for an employee. You can see the net or gross pay numbers on the screen, but you can't see the employee names. You may have wished you could freeze a column of data or a row of text to act as labels for an off-screen row or column. Lotus, like many spreadsheet packages, has a feature that provides this capability (it is referred to as the **Titles option**).

When you are using the Titles option, the pointer again plays an important role. Any columns to the left of the pointer or any rows above the pointer that appear on the screen can be frozen to act as labels. You cannot move the pointer into a title area by using the arrow keys. In order to get the pointer into the titles area, you must press the F5 key and then enter the address of the cell. This causes two copies of the title cells to be displayed on the screen.

Titles Menu

The Titles command is invoked from the Worksheet Menu. It presents a menu consisting of the following options:

Both   Horizontal   Vertical   Clear

Both. The Both option freezes the rows above the pointer and the columns to the left of the pointer, creating a fixed border of headings for vertical and horizontal scrolling through the worksheet.

Horizontal. The Horizontal option freezes the rows above the pointer, creating fixed headings for vertical scrolling through the worksheet.

Vertical. The Vertical option freezes the columns to the left of the pointer, creating fixed line labels for horizontal scrolling through the worksheet.

Clear. The Clear option causes any rows or columns that have been frozen to return to unfrozen status. (Note that in order for a cell to be frozen on the screen it must appear on the screen at the time that the Titles option of the Worksheet Menu is selected. If a cell does not physically appear on the screen, it cannot be frozen on the screen.)

Titles Instructions

Using the Titles command to freeze the employee names would require the following steps:

Home—Positions the pointer at cell A1.

C1 [by manual pointer movement]—Positions the pointer at cell C1.

/—Gets the Main Menu.

W—Selects the Worksheet option.

T—Selects the Titles option.

V—Selects the Vertical Titles option.

When you move the pointer to the Net Pay column, the Employee column will remain on the screen and your display will look as follows:

	Employee	Overtime Hours	Overtime Rate	Gross Pay	Net Pay
1	Adams, Sam		9.75	260.00	163.80
1	Johns, Peter	10.00	6.38	233.75	147.26
1	Kent, John		9.75	260.00	163.80
1	Lester, Ned		8.25	220.00	138.60
1	Smith, Luther		9.75	260.00	163.80
2	Dix, Yvonne		11.25	300.00	189.00
2	Hunt, Mary	3.00	9.75	289.25	182.23
2	Jones, Anthony	2.00	9.75	279.50	176.09
2	Lora, Kathy		9.75	260.00	163.80
2	Sahara, Ohmar		8.25	220.00	138.60
	TOTALS	15.00		$2,582.50	$1,626.98

Relative and Absolute Addressing

As you have already seen, a formula can be copied across a row or down a column, and 1-2-3 will automatically adjust the formula placed in each cell to reflect its new location and the location of any participating cells. This is the concept behind relative addressing. But what happens if you don't want 1-2-3 to change a formula automatically to reflect a new cell location? How do you tell 1-2-3, without directly entering a different formula in each cell, to refer to only one cell in a series of calculations?

Let's examine a concrete application of this question. How would you find out what percentage each individual's gross pay was of the total gross pay in the CH10EX1 worksheet? You could insert a column between the Gross Pay and Net Pay columns, but how could you enter a formula and copy it to the other cells in the column in such a way that it would always refer to the contents of the total gross pay cell in calculating the percentage?

The first possibility, manually entering the required formula for each row in the column, is feasible with the few employees that are currently in the worksheet, but it would be a tremendous amount of work if you were dealing with 100 employees. The easiest way to solve the problem is to use a technique referred to as **absolute addressing**.

An absolute cell reference is easy to distinguish from a relative cell reference because it appears with one or more dollar signs ($) in the cell reference—for example, A1, $A1, or A$1.

Let's begin by examining why the relative addressing feature of 1-2-3 is inappropriate for this application.

Load the worksheet file PAYSORT, if it is not already on your screen.

1. Position the pointer anywhere in column H (Net Pay), and insert the new column, using the following instructions:

    /—Gets the Main Menu.

    W—Selects the Worksheet option.

    I—Selects the Insert option from the Worksheet Menu.

    ENTER—Executes the Insert command.

2. Enter the column headings.

    ```
    H1 % of Total
    H2 ^Gross
    ```

    Center (^) the second line of the heading.

3. At cell H4, enter the formula for calculating the percentage of total gross pay, using the relative addressing convention.

    ```
    H4 +G4/G15
    ```

    When you depress ENTER, you should see 0.10 as the cell contents.

4. Set the column to a percentage format with one decimal position.

    /—Invokes the Main Menu.

    R—Selects the Range option.

    F—Selects the Format option from the Range Menu.

    P—Selects the Percent format.

    1—Sets the number of decimal positions to one.

    ENTER—Tells 1-2-3 that this part of the command is finished.

    H13 [by manual pointer movement]—Positions the pointer at the last cell in the range.

    ENTER—Tells 1-2-3 that the range has been defined and that the command is to be executed.

5. Copy this formula to the rest of the cells in the column.

    H4 [by manual pointer movement]—Positions the pointer at cell H4.

    /—Invokes the Main Menu.

    C—Selects the Copy command option.

    ENTER—Indicates to 1-2-3 that cell H4 is the only "From" cell.

    H5 [by manual pointer movement]—Positions the pointer at cell H5, the beginning of the "To" range.

    .—Nails down the beginning of the "To" range.

    H13 [by manual pointer movement]—Positions the pointer at the last cell in the "To" range.

ENTER—Tells 1-2-3 to execute the Copy command.

You should now see the following worksheet (with more spaces) on your screen:

Dpt.	Employee	Total Hours	Rate	Overtime Hours	Overtime Rate	Gross Pay	% of Total Gross	Net Pay
1	Adams, Sam	40.00	6.50		9.75	260.00	10.1%	163.80
1	Johns, Peter	40.00	4.25	10.00	6.38	233.75	ERR	147.26
1	Kent, John	40.00	6.50		9.75	260.00	ERR	163.80
1	Lester, Ned	40.00	5.50		8.25	220.00	ERR	138.60
1	Smith, Luther	40.00	6.50		9.75	260.00	ERR	163.80
2	Dix, Yvonne	40.00	7.50		11.25	300.00	ERR	189.00
2	Hunt, Mary	40.00	6.50	3.00	9.75	289.25	ERR	182.23
2	Jones, Anthony	40.00	6.50	2.00	9.75	279.50	ERR	176.09
2	Lora, Kathy	40.00	6.50		9.75	260.00	ERR	163.80
2	Sahara, Ohmar	40.00	5.50		8.25	220.00	ERR	138.60
	TOTALS			15.00		$2,582.50		$1,626.98

Obviously something is drastically wrong with this worksheet. What happened? When 1-2-3 copied the formula +G4/G15 to the other cells in the column, it automatically changed the formula for each cell as it proceeded down the column; as a result, cell H5 contains the formula +G5/G16, and cell H6 has the formula +G6/G17. But cells G16 and G17 do not contain any numeric values—hence the error message ERR.

1-2-3 did not want to use the contents of the total gross pay cell for each of the calculations after the Copy command was used because no absolute cell references are contained in the original formula entered in H4.

Go to cell H4, and enter the formula +G4/G15. Then use the instructions contained in step 5 above to copy the formula to the other cells in the column. Afterward, your screen should have a display like the following:

Dpt.	Employee	Total Hours	Rate	Overtime Hours	Overtime Rate	Gross Pay	% of Total Gross	Net Pay
1	Adams, Sam	40.00	6.50		9.75	260.00	10.1%	163.80
1	Johns, Peter	40.00	4.25	10.00	6.38	233.75	9.1%	147.26
1	Kent, John	40.00	6.50		9.75	260.00	10.1%	163.80
1	Lester, Ned	40.00	5.50		8.25	220.00	8.5%	138.60
1	Smith, Luther	40.00	6.50		9.75	260.00	10.1%	163.80
2	Dix, Yvonne	40.00	7.50		11.25	300.00	11.6%	189.00
2	Hunt, Mary	40.00	6.50	3.00	9.75	289.25	11.2%	182.23
2	Jones, Anthony	40.00	6.50	2.00	9.75	279.50	10.8%	176.09
2	Lora, Kathy	40.00	6.50		9.75	260.00	10.1%	163.80
2	Sahara, Ohmar	40.00	5.50		8.25	220.00	8.5%	138.60
	TOTALS			15.00		$2,582.50		$1,626.98

The dollar signs in the amended formula tell 1-2-3 that it is to leave this part of the formula exactly the same as it copies it from one cell to another. Relative addressing will not affect any part of the formula containing dollar signs.

In the above example, the formula containing the absolute cell reference had a cell address of G15. As was noted earlier, you can also use addresses like $A1 or A$1. Since this type of cell reference has elements of absolute addressing and relative addressing, it is referred to as a **mixed cell address**.

The relative part of a mixed cell address will change; the absolute part will remain the same. For example:

$A1 (**$ column row**). The absolute address portion of this reference is the column portion of the reference, so the row can change within the address, but the column must remain as A. This formula could be read as "any row in column A."

A$1 (**column $ row**). The absolute address portion of this reference is the row portion of the reference, so the column can change within the address, but the row must remain as 1. This formula could be read as "any column in row 1."

It is important to be aware that mixed cell addresses cannot be used with range names. If absolute addresses are desired for range names (for example, $COLB), the range name will be treated as though both the column and the row portions of the address are absolute—that is, it will be wholly an **absolute range name**.

Automatic Versus Manual Worksheet Recalculation

Each time you press the ENTER key, 1-2-3 automatically recalculates the entire worksheet. This is not a problem when the worksheet is small, but when the worksheet is large and involves many calculations it can become very time-consuming.

To avoid this problem, 1-2-3 has the ability to turn off its **Automatic Recalculation feature**, allowing the user to tell it when to recalculate. This is accomplished by entering the following command sequence:

/—Invokes the Main Menu.

W—Selects the Worksheet option.

G—Selects the Global option from the Worksheet Menu.

R—Selects the Recalculation option from the Global Menu.

M—Executes the Manual command.

If you make changes to any cell after this **Manual Recalculation option** has been selected, 1-2-3 tells you by displaying a CALC message at the bottom of your screen next to the indicators area. To get 1-2-3 to recalculate the worksheet, you must depress the F9 function key.

If you save the worksheet file onto disk, the Manual Recalculation setting is saved in the worksheet file. If you wish to reset the spreadsheet to automatic, all you need do is enter the above commands replacing the M with an A (for Automatic).

More on Functions

@PMT

Lotus has incorporated a financial function that is a true time-saver. The @PMT (principal,interest, periods)—payment per period—**function** calculates the payment of a loan or mortgage based on the three pieces of information: principal, interest, and number of periods. Using this function allows you to avoid entering the following formula:

```
Prin*Inter/12/(1-1/(1+Inter/12)^Periods)
```

@IF *and Logical Operators*

The @IF **function** allows Lotus 1-2-3 to check for certain conditions and then take actions based on the results of the check. The format of the @IF function is `@IF(condition,true,false)`. The "condition" portion of the function allows you to set up an equation to check for specific results or cell contents; the "true" portion contains instructions that will be executed if the condition is true; the "false" portion contains instructions that will be executed if the condition is false.

The operators allowed in a 1-2-3 `@IF` function are:

Relational:

=   equal to

‹   less than

‹=   less than or equal to

›   greater than

›=   greater than or equal to

‹›   not equal to

Logical:

`#NOT#`   not (the opposite of any equation or relation must be the case before the true option is executed)

`#AND#`   and (both conditions must be true before the true option is executed)

`#OR#`   Or (either action can be true for the true option to be executed)

These operators can be used to set up a number of different conditions:

`+B13=60#OR#D17<20`   The value contained in cell B13 is equal to 60, or the value contained in cell D17 is less than 20.

`+H14>0#AND#D19>1985`   The value contained in cell H14 is greater than zero, and the value in cell D19 is greater than 1985.

`#NOT#(YEAR=1985)`   The value stored in the cell named `YEAR` is not 1985.

`(B15-C10)=D3#AND#C5>D7`   The value of cell B15 minus the value of cell C10 is equal to the value contained in cell D3, *and* the value contained in cell C5 is larger than the value contained in cell D7.

These new conditions also have places in the order of precedence discussed earlier. The complete listing of this order is as follows:

The Operator Order of Precedence

Operator	Meaning	Level
^	exponentiation	7
−	negative	6
+	positive	6
*	multiplication	5
/	division	5
+	addition	4
−	subtraction	4
=	equal	3
<	less than	3
<=	less than or equal	3
>	greater than	3
>=	greater than or equal	3
<>	not equal	3
#NOT#	logical not	2
#AND#	logical and	1
#OR#	logical or	1

@DATE *and Arithmetic*

You were introduced to some aspects of the @DATE **function** when you entered the FUNCTION worksheet. The information returned by the @NOW and @DATE functions is numeric and represents the number of elapsed days since December 31, 1899. Thus, when 1-2-3 displays a date via one of the three formats listed below, it is merely formatting numeric information for display. If you loaded the FUNCTION worksheet and looked in cell A3, you would see a number that corresponds to today's date. 1-2-3 displays date information in one of the following formats:

(D1) 1(dd-mmm-yy) 29-Jan-88

(D2) 2(dd-mmm)   29-Jan

(D3) 3(mmm-yy)   Jan-88

Displaying a date is a two-step process: first, you get the data via the @DATE or @NOW function, causing a number to appear on the screen and in the cell; second, you use the Range Format commands on the cell to hold one of the above formats, causing a date display to appear on the screen.

The numeric method that 1-2-3 uses to display dates can be very beneficial in manipulating dates. Since the date is really numeric, any arithmetic operations can be performed on it. To get the date for a week from today, for example, you simply add 7 to the existing numeric date. Or if you want to find out how many weeks there are between two dates, you can subtract the ending date from the beginning date, divide by 7, and round the result using the @ROUND or @INT functions, and find out how many intervening weeks there are.

With date arithmetic involving months, you must be careful. You can't simply convert a month to thirty days and expect it to work. Adding a number like 30.5 doesn't work well either, unless the period covered is small. The following method assumes that payment will occur on or before the twenty-eighth day of the month:

1. Add 31 to the previous date.

2. Subtract the current @DAY from the present number to bring you back to the present day of the prior month.

3. Add @DAY to the original number to move you forward to the proper day in the next month.

This allows you to advance from one month to the next, if the day of the month is 1 through 28.

You can also compare the value of the @NOW function with another date already entered on the worksheet or with a date in a formula. To do this requires using the command @IF(@NOW>@DATE(88,2,1),x,y). The x represents the action to be taken if the condition is true, while the y represents the action to be taken if the condition is false. More information on 1-2-3 functions appears in Appendix B.

Worksheet Practice

A number of the topics discussed in this chapter are used in the next few pages to prepare two worksheets: the first worksheet involves generating a loan amortization table; the second serves as the basis for evaluating various automobile loan alternatives.

Loan Amortization Worksheet

The following loan amortization table requires you to enter the loan amount, the interest on the loan, the length of the loan in months, and the starting date of the loan. It will then generate a table that includes the amount of the payment, the month of the payment, the portion applied toward the principal, the portion applied to the interest, and the outstanding balance.

In doing this project, you will practice the following skills:

1. Using the @PMT function
2. Using the @IF function
3. Using date arithmetic
4. Using absolute addressing

The worksheet is as follows:

```
Interest                        12.00%
Loan Amount                     $1,200
Months                              20
Beginning Date                  May 88
                TOTAL                                      BALANCE
DATE          PAYMENT        PRINCIPAL        INTEREST     OUTSTANDING
May-88          66.50           54.50           12.00        1145.50
Jun-88          66.50           55.04           11.46        1090.46
Jul-88          66.50           55.59           10.90        1034.87
Aug-88          66.50           56.15           10.35         978.72
Sep-88          66.50           56.71            9.79         922.01
```

To present the information in the above format, you'll obviously have to use absolute addressing to allow each line of formulas to refer to the data at the top of the worksheet. In addition, you'll have to use date arithmetic to advance the date month by month from one line to the next; you'll have to use the @PMT function for easy calculation of the payment (you could place this piece of information at the top also); and later you'll have to use the @IF function to generate the worksheet properly.

The various column amounts are calculated as follows:

The payment is calculated via the @PMT function.

The interest is calculated by multiplying the outstanding balance by the interest rate, and dividing that result by 12 (interest for one month).

The principal is calculated by subtracting the interest amount from the payment amount.

The new outstanding balance is calculated by subtracting the amount of the payment applied toward the principal from the old outstanding balance.

Now let's go through the individual tasks involved in creating this worksheet.

1. Set the global column width to 10.

/—Invokes the Main Menu.

W—Selects the Worksheet option of the Main Menu.

G—Selects the Global option of the Worksheet Menu.

C—Selects the Column Width option.

10—Specifies the new column width.

ENTER—Tells 1-2-3 to execute the command.

2. Enter label information in the appropriate cells.

A2 Interest
A3 Loan Amount

```
A4  Months
A5  Beginning Date
A8  ^DATE
B7  ^TOTAL
B8  ^PAYMENT
C8  ^PRINCIPAL
D8  ^INTEREST
E7  ^BALANCE
E8  ^OUTSTANDING
```

3. Enter the loan information.

```
C2  .12
C3  1200
C4  20
C5  @DATE(88,5,1)
```

4. Format cell C2 for percentage, with two decimal positions.

> C2 [by manual pointer movement]—Positions the pointer at cell C2.
>
> /—Invokes the Main Menu.
>
> R—Selects the Range option.
>
> F—Selects the Format option from the Range Menu.
>
> P—Selects the Percent option.
>
> ENTER—Takes the default of two decimal positions.
>
> ENTER—Tells 1-2-3 to format only this cell.

5. Format cell C3 for currency, with zero decimal positions.

> C3 [by manual pointer movement]—Positions the pointer at cell C3.
>
> /—Invokes the Main Menu.
>
> R—Selects the Range option.
>
> F—Selects the Format option from the Range Menu.
>
> C—Selects the Currency option.
>
> 0—Tells 1-2-3 the number of decimal positions.
>
> ENTER—Tells 1-2-3 to accept the decimal position information.
>
> ENTER—Tells 1-2-3 to format only this cell.

6. Format cell C4 for whole months.

> C4 [by manual pointer movement]—Positions the pointer at cell C4.
>
> /—Invokes the Main Menu.
>
> R—Selects the Range option.
>
> F—Selects the Format option from the Range Menu.
>
> F—Selects the Fixed Format option.
>
> 0—Specifies the number of decimal positions.
>
> ENTER—Tells 1-2-3 to accept the decimal position information.
>
> ENTER—Tells 1-2-3 to format only this cell.

7. Format cell C5 for the date.

> C5 [by manual pointer movement]—Positions the pointer at cell C5.

/—Invokes the Main Menu.

R—Selects the Range option.

F—Selects the Format option from the Range Menu.

D—Selects the Date option.

3—Selects the (MMM-YY) option.

ENTER—Tells 1-2-3 to format only this cell.

The information on the first line of the schedule also represents the first payment. As a result, the formulas in this row will be a little bit different from those in subsequent rows.

8. Copy the beginning date onto the schedule.

A9 [by manual pointer movement]—Positions the pointer at cell A9.

+C5—Tells 1-2-3 to refer to the contents of cell C5 and place them here also. (If the contents of cell C5 change, the contents of this cell will also change.)

ENTER—Tells 1-2-3 to execute the command.

9. Format cells A9 and A10 for the date.

A9 [by manual pointer movement]—Positions the pointer at cell A9.

/—Invokes the Main Menu.

R—Selects the Range option.

F—Selects the Format option from the Range Menu.

D—Selects the Date option.

3—Selects the (MMM-YY) option.

Down arrow—Includes cell A10.

ENTER—Tells 1-2-3 to execute the command.

10. Enter the formula to calculate the monthly payment in cell B9.

```
@PMT(C$3,C$2/12,C$4)
```

The first parameter above provides the address of the cell containing the principal; the second parameter provides the address of the cell containing the interest; the third parameter provides the address of the cell containing the number of periods. Since each of these pieces of information must be referenced in each row, absolute addressing is required; the absolute portion of each parameter freezes the location to a particular row. The formula can now be copied correctly.

11. Enter the formula to calculate the interest portion of this payment in cell D9.

```
+C$3*C$2/12
```

The amount must be divided by 12 to provide the amount of interest for this particular month rather than for the whole year.

12. Enter the formula to calculate the amount of the payment applied toward the principal in cell C9.

```
+B9-D9
```

13. Enter the formula to calculate the outstanding balance in cell E9.

    ```
    +C3-C9
    ```

14. Format the entire worksheet for two decimal positions.

    /—Invokes the Main Menu.

    W—Selects the Worksheet option.

    G—Selects the Global option from the Worksheet Menu.

    F—Selects the Format option from the Global Menu.

    F—Selects the Fixed command.

    ENTER—Takes the default and re-formats the worksheet.

15. Copy the payment and principal formulas (which will stay the same) to the next line. (The cells will contain the correct results after the next steps are finished.)

    B9 [by manual pointer movement]—Positions the pointer at cell B9.

    /—Invokes the Main Menu.

    C—Selects the Copy command.

    C9 [by manual pointer movement]—Positions the pointer at the last cell in the "From" range.

    ENTER—Tells 1-2-3 that the "From" range has been established.

    B10 [by manual pointer movement]—Positions the pointer at the beginning of the "To" range.

    ENTER—Tells 1-2-3 to copy the formulas.

16. Enter the formula to advance the date incrementally in cell A10.

    ```
    +A9+31-@DAY(A9+31)+@DAY(A9)
    ```

    This command provides you with the ability to advance the date by the proper increment from one month to the next, as long as the loan begins on day 1 through 28. This formula can now be copied to the rest of the rows.

17. Enter the new formula for calculating the interest in cell D10.

    ```
    +E9*C$2/12
    ```

    You now have a formula that can be easily copied to other rows.

18. Enter the new formula for calculating the outstanding balance in cell E10.

    ```
    +E9-C10
    ```

    You now have a formula that can be easily copied to other rows.

19. Copy the formulas contained in row 10 down enough rows. (Enough rows depends on the maximum number of periods that you wish to allow in a loan; you'll copy this one down forty rows. Remember, the more rows you have, the longer your worksheet will take to recalculate.)

    A10 [by manual pointer movement]—Positions the pointer at cell A10.

/—Invokes the Main Menu.

C—Selects the Copy option command.

E10 [by manual pointer movement]—Positions the pointer at the last cell in the "From" range.

ENTER—Tells 1-2-3 that the "From" range has been defined.

A11 [by manual pointer movement]—Positions the pointer to cell A11, the first cell in the "To" range.

.—Nails down the beginning of the "To" range.

PgDn [twice]—Moves the pointer down the worksheet forty rows.

ENTER—Tells 1-2-3 to copy the formulas and recalculate the worksheet.

Now sit back and watch 1-2-3 do all the work! When you look at your worksheet, everything seems to have worked until about row 29—when negative numbers suddenly begin popping up in the worksheet. What happened? The loan was completely paid, but 1-2-3 wasn't aware of it, so the balance went from positive to negative.

Somehow, you have to indicate to 1-2-3 to take appropriate action when the balance is completely paid to get rid of the negative numbers. Let's review the logic and determine which are the critical formulas.

On examination, the two most important calculations seem to be the outstanding balance and the payment. When the oustanding balance equals a few cents or less, that means that the loan is paid off. (The outstanding balance never comes out to exactly zero because of rounding errors.) All other calculations are based on the contents of either the outstanding balance or payment entry; so if you can get these fields to zero out, the other fields will also contain zeros.

To examine the contents of a cell and check for a value, you must use the @IF function.

20. Change the method of recalculation from automatic to manual to save waiting time.

/—Invokes the Main Menu.

W—Selects the Worksheet option.

G—Selects the Global option from the Worksheet Menu.

R—Selects the Recalculation option from the Global Menu.

M—Selects the Manual command.

21. Position your pointer at cell E10, and either reenter the formula or use the Edit feature to enter changes. Your new formula should now look like the following:

```
@IF(E9<=1,0,@ROUND(+E9-C10,2))
```

This formula can be translated as: if the result of the old balance is just a few cents, put a zero in this cell; otherwise, calculate the new rounded outstanding balance.

22. You also have to do something to make the payment column stop printing. Position your pointer at cell B10, and either enter the new formula or use the Edit feature to enter changes.

```
@IF(E9<=1,0,@PMT(C$3,C$2/12,C$4))
```

This formula can be translated as: if the contents of the outstanding balance cell are just a few cents, place a zero in the payment cell; otherwise, execute the payment function.

23. Copy these new formulas onto the rest of the worksheet, using the commands from step 19 above.

24. Tell 1-2-3 to recalculate the worksheet, by pressing the [F9] Calc function key.

25. Center the information at the top of the spreadsheet to give it a more balanced appearance.

> A2 [by manual pointer movement]—Positions the pointer at cell A2.
>
> /—Invokes the Main Menu.
>
> M—Selects the Move command.
>
> C5 [by manual pointer movement]—Positions the pointer at cell C5, to establish the "From" range.
>
> ENTER—Tells 1-2-3 that the "From" range is defined.
>
> B2 [by manual pointer movement]—Positions the pointer at the beginning of the "To" range.
>
> ENTER—Executes the Move instruction.

26. Save the worksheet under the name LOANAMOR. You should now have a worksheet that looks like the following:

```
     Interest                12.00%
     Loan Amount             $1,200
     Months                      20
     Beginning Date          May-89

              TOTAL                          BALANCE
DATE        PAYMENT    PRINCIPAL   INTEREST   OUTSTANDING
May-88       66.50       54.50      12.00      1145.50
Jun-88       66.50       55.04      11.46      1090.46
Jul-88       66.50       55.59      10.90      1034.87
Aug-88       66.50       56.15      10.35       978.72
Sep-88       66.50       56.71       9.79       922.01
Oct-88       66.50       57.28       9.22       864.73
Nov-88       66.50       57.85       8.65       806.88
Dec-88       66.50       58.43       8.07       748.45
Jan-89       66.50       59.01       7.48       689.44
Feb-89       66.50       59.60       6.89       629.84
Mar-89       66.50       60.20       6.30       569.64
Apr-89       66.50       60.80       5.70       508.84
May-89       66.50       61.41       5.09       447.43
Jun-89       66.50       62.02       4.47       385.41
Jul-89       66.50       62.64       3.85       322.77
Aug-89       66.50       63.27       3.23       259.50
Sep-89       66.50       63.90       2.60       195.60
Oct-89       66.50       64.54       1.96       131.06
Nov-89       66.50       65.19       1.31        65.87
Dec-89       66.50       65.84       0.66         0.03
Jan-90        0.00         .00        .00         0.00
Feb-90        0.00        0.00       0.00         0.00
Mar-90        0.00        0.00       0.00         0.00
Apr-90        0.00        0.00       0.00         0.00
```

Car Loan Evaluation Worksheet

In doing this project, you will practice the following skills:

1. Using mixed cell addressing
2. Observing the effects of copying mixed cell addresses

A friend of yours, Sandy, is trying to decide which vehicle to purchase, and a major part of the decision-making process involves the size of the monthly payment. Sandy wishes to finance the purchase over four years, but she also wants to easily change the loan length. The vehicles being considered, along with the amount to be financed, are as follows:

Conversion van	$18,000
Toyota pickup	8,000
Chrysler LeBaron	10,000
Ford Thunderbird	11,000

Sandy has also visited a number of financial institutions to find the interest rate offered. They are:

Credit Union	11%
Car Manufacturer	15.5%
Bank 1	12.5%
Bank 2	13%

The following spreadsheet allows you to present the above information in a tabular format to assist your friend's decision-making process.

```
                          Sandy's Loan Evaluation
                     Amount      Credit        Car
                     Financed     Union       Manuf.      Bank 1      Bank 2
                                  11.0%        15.5%       12.5%       13.0%
Conversion van       $18,000     465.22       505.53      478.44      482.89
Toyota pickup        $8,000      206.76       224.68      212.64      214.62
Chrysler LeBaron     $10,000     258.46       280.85      265.80      268.27
Ford Thunderbird     $11,000     284.30       308.93      292.38      295.10


Number of Years             4
```

The @PMT function is perfect for this application. Mixed cell addressing, combining absolute and relative addressing, will also be useful.

Entering the spreadsheet involves a number of steps.

1. Position the pointer in column A, and change the width of column A to 20.

   /—Invokes the Main Menu.

   W—Selects the Worksheet option.

   C—Selects the Column Width command from the Worksheet Menu.

   S—Sets the column width.

   20—Specifies the new width.

   ENTER—Executes the command.

2. Enter the label data.

   C1 Sandy's Loan Evaluation

```
B2   Amount
C2   "Credit
D2   "Car
B3   Financed
C3   "Union
D3   "Manuf,
E3   "Bank 1
F3   "Bank 2
C4   ,11
D4   ,155
E4   ,125
F4   ,13
A5   Conversion van
A6   Toyota pickup
A7   Chrysler LeBaron
A8   Ford Thunderbird
B5   18000
B6   8000
B7   10000
B8   11000
A12  Number of Years
B12  4
```

3. Format the percentages. Begin by positioning the pointer at cell C4.

   /—Invokes the Main Menu.

   R—Selects the Range option.

   F—Selects the Format option from the Range Menu.

   P—Selects the Percent format.

   1—Specifies the number of desired decimal positions.

   ENTER—Submits the decimal positions to 1-2-3.

   F4 [by manual pointer movement]—Extends the range to cell F4.

   ENTER—Executes the format change.

4. Format the amount financed to currency. Begin by positioning the pointer at cell B5.

   /—Invokes the Main Menu.

   R—Selects the Range option.

   F—Selects the Format option from the Range Menu.

   C—Selects the Currency format.

   0—Specifies the number of desired decimal positions.

   ENTER—Submits the decimal positions to 1-2-3.

   B8 [by manual pointer movement]—Extends the range to cell B8.

   ENTER—Executes the format change.

5. Set the worksheet format to two decimal positions.

   /—Invokes the Main Menu.

   W—Selects the Worksheet option.

   G—Selects the Global option.

   F—Selects the Format option from the Global Menu.

   F—Selects the Fixed option.

   ENTER—Changes the worksheet format.

6. Format the length of loan cell to fixed with 0 decimal positions. Begin by positioning the pointer to cell B12.

   /—Invokes the Main Menu.

   R—Selects the Range option.

   F—Selects the Format option of the Range Menu.

   F—Selects the Fixed option.

   0—Specifies the number of desired decimal positions.

   ENTER—Submits the decimal positions to 1-2-3.

   ENTER—Executes the format change.

7. Enter the @PMT function for cell C5.

   ```
   @PMT($B5,C$4/12,$B$12*12)
   ```

   The principal entry, $B5, keeps 1-2-3 returning to column B of "this" row. The interest entry, C$4, keeps 1-2-3 returning to "this" column of row 4. It is divided by the twelve months of the year.

   The periods entry, B12, keeps 1-2-3 returning to cell B12. It is multiplied by the 12 monthly payments.

8. Copy this formula to the rest of the spreadsheet. Begin by positioning the pointer to cell C5.

   /—Invokes the Main Menu.

   C—Selects the Copy command.

   ENTER—Establishes the "From" range.

   .—Nails down the beginning of the "To" range.

   F8 [by manual pointer movement]—Moves the pointer to the end of the "To" range.

   ENTER—Executes the Copy command.

9. Save this worksheet to the file CARLOANS.

Cell Contents Listing for Amortization Worksheet

```
B2:  'Interest
D2:  (P2) 0.12
B3:  'Loan Amount
D3:  (C0) 1200
B4:  'Months
D4:  (F0) 20
B5:  'Beginning Date
D5:  (D3) @DATE(84,5,1)
B7:  ^TOTAL
E7:  ^BALANCE
A8:  ^DATE
B8:  ^PAYMENT
C8:  ^PRINCIPAL
D8:  ^INTEREST
E8:  ^OUTSTANDING
A9:  (D3) +D5
B9:  (F2) @PMT(D$3,D$2/12,D$4)
C9:  (F2) +B9-D9
D9:  (F2) @ROUND(+D$3*D$2/12,2)
```

```
E9:   (F2) @ROUND(+D3-C9,2)
A10:  (D3) +A9+31@DAY(A9+31)+@DAY(A9)
B10:  (F2) @IF(E9<=1,0,@PMT(D$3,D$2/12,D$4))
C10:  (F2) +B10-D10
D10:  (F2) +E9*D$2/12
E10:  (F2) @IF(E9<=1,0,@ROUND(+E9-C10,2))
A11:  (D3) +A9+31@DAY(A9+31)+@DAY(A9)
B11:  (F2) @IF(E10<=1,0,@PMT(D$3,D$2/12,D$4))
C11:  (F2) +B11-D11
D11:  (F2) +E10*D$2/12
E11:  (F2) @IF(E10<=1,0,@ROUND(+E10-C11,2))
A12:  (D3) +A9+31@DAY(A9+31)+@DAY(A9)
B12:  (F2) @IF(E11<=1,0,@PMT(D$3,D$2/12,D$4))
C12:  (F2) +B12-D12
D12:  (F2) +E11*D$2/12
E12:  (F2) @IF(E11<=1,0,@ROUND(+E11-C12,2))
```

Cell Contents Listing for Car Loan Worksheet

```
C1:   'Sandy's Loan Evaluation
B2:   'Amount
C2:   "Credit
D2:   "Car
B3:   'Financed
C3:   "Union
D3:   "Manuf.
E3:   "Bank 1
F3:   "Bank 2
C4:   (P1) 0.11
D4:   (P1) 0.155
E4:   (P1) 0.125
F4:   (P1) 0.13
A5:   'Conversion van
B5:   (C0) 18000
C5:   @PMT($B5,C$4/12,4$B$12*12)
D5:   @PMT($B5,D$4/12,4$B$12*12)
E5:   @PMT($B5,E$4/12,4$B$12*12)
F5:   @PMT($B5,F$4/12,4$B$12*12)
A6:   'Toyota pickup
B6:   (C0) 8000
C6:   @PMT($B6,C$4/12,4$B$12*12)
D6:   @PMT($B6,D$4/12,4$B$12*12)
E6:   @PMT($B6,E$4/12,4$B$12*12)
F6:   @PMT($B6,F$4/12,4$B$12*12)
A7:   'Chrysler LeBaron
B7:   (C0) 10000
C7:   @PMT($B7,C$4/12,4$B$12*12
D7:   @PMT($B7,D$4/12,4$B$12*12)
E7:   @PMT($B7,E$4/12,4$B$12*12)
F7:   @PMT($B7,F$4/12,4$B$12*12)
A8:   'Ford Thunderbird
B8:   (C0) 11000
C8:   @PMT($B8,C$4/12,4$B$12*12)
D8:   @PMT($B8,D$4/12,4$B$12*12)
```

```
E8: @PMT($B8,E$4/12,4$B$12*12)
F8: @PMT($B8,F$4/12,4$B$12*12)
A12: Number of Years
B12: 4
```

Chapter Review

1-2-3 provides several commands that allow you to control your worksheet environment. The Worksheet Zero command allows you to suppress any cell that has a zero. The GoTo (F5) command allows you to quickly position the pointer to a specific cell. The System command allows you to temporarily leave 1-2-3 and issue commands at the system (DOS) level. You are allowed to hide columns so that they appear neither on the screen nor in print. You can use the Worksheet Status command to find circular references. You can password protect your worksheet. And you can use the Range Transpose command to rearrange text within a worksheet.

After a worksheet has been created, you will probably want to make a number of improvements to it. One of these, making cell formulas self-documenting and easier to read, can be accomplished easily by the use of range names. A single cell or a range of cells can be given a name and accessed under that name in such applications as calculations, uses of the Copy command, and printing a portion of your worksheet.

The Sort feature included with 1-2-3 enables you to arrange data in an order that is logical for any given application. Another handy (and more common) feature is the Titles feature, which allows you to freeze column or row headings on the screen so that they are visible no matter where you are in the worksheet. This makes it much easier to track information in large spreadsheets.

The ability to reference a single cell over and over, even when the formula is copied down a column, is often useful. In 1-2-3, this is called absolute addressing. An entire address can be absolute, or only the row or column can be; the latter is referred to as a mixed cell address.

Because the worksheet automatically recalculates itself when any cell's contents are changed, long delays can often result in a large worksheet after a simple change has been made. In such a case, you can direct 1-2-3 to recalculate the worksheet only when the F9 key has been pressed. This option is known as manual recalculation.

The @IF function allows you to embed logic within the worksheet that enables the function to perform one action if the logic is satisfied and perform another if it is not.

Key Terms and Concepts

absolute addressing
absolute range name
#AND#
Automatic Recalculation feature
Column Hide command
$ column row
column $ row
Create option
Data Range option
@DATE function
Delete option
dummy column, row

Go option
GoTo command
@IF function
Labels option
Manual Recalculation option
mixed cell address
#NOT#
#OR#
password
@PMT function
Primary Key option
Quit option

range name
/ Range Transpose command
Reset option
Secondary Key option
Sort command

System command
Table option
Titles option
Zero command

Chapter Quiz

Multiple Choice

1. Which of the following statements about range names is (are) true?
   a. Range names can be used to enhance readability.
   b. Range names make cell formulas self-documenting.
   c. Using range names in formulas is better than using cell addresses.
   d. A range name created via the label option takes its name from the contents of an adjacent cell.
   e. All of the above statements are true.
   f. All of the above statements are true except d.

2. Which of the following statements is false about the Sort command?
   a. It is safest to save your worksheet before you do any sorting.
   b. Three levels of sorts or keys can be specified.
   c. All or part of a worksheet can be sorted.
   d. The Sort command allows you to rearrange data quickly within the worksheet.
   e. None of the above statements is false.

3. Which of the following statements is false about an absolute address?
   a. It can have both the column and row absolute—CR.
   b. It can have only the column portion absolute—$CR.
   c. It can have only the row portion absolute—C$R.
   d. It can actually be a range name—$EXPENSES.
   e. All of the above responses are correct.

4. Which of the commands below allows you to freeze portions of the worksheet so that they can be used as column or row headings on the screen?
   a. Titles
   b. Labels
   c. Borders
   d. Legend
   e. None of the above responses is correct.

5. Which command allows you to detect circular references within your worksheet?
   a. Worksheet Hide
   b. Directory Status
   c. Worksheet Status
   d. Worksheet Reference Hide
   e. None of the above

True/False

6. Using manual recalculation slows down the operation of the spreadsheet.

7. The Titles command allows only horizontal text to be frozen on the screen.

8. Relative addressing is used whenever you wish a formula that is to be copied down a column or across a row to refer to the identical cell.

9. It is impossible to create a mixed range name by using a mixed cell address.

10. The function @IF allows you to embed sophisticated logic within your worksheet quickly.

Answers

1. e 2. b 3. e 4. a 5. c 6. f 7. f 8. f 9. t 10. t

Exercises

1. Define or describe each of the following:
   a. range name   d. absolute address
   b. titles   e. mixed cell address
   c. manual recalculation   f. date arithmetic

2. One of the greatest benefits of range names is that they allow a cell formula to be self-_____.

3. Positioning the pointer at a word (cell) and then making that word the range name is accomplished via the _____ option of the Range Menu.

4. The Create and Delete commands reside in the _____ Menu.

5. A hidden column is so indicated by a(n) _____ when the / Worksheet Column Display command is issued.

6. The option of the Range Name submenu that is used to create a report of the various named ranges created within the worksheet is _____.

7. The _____ command can be used to reset the date or time without leaving 1-2-3.

8. A(n) _____ key will have information sorted in order inside a(n) _____ key.

9. The Sort option is found in the _____ Menu.

10. Before you use the Sort command, it is probably wise to _____ _____ your worksheet file.

11. The _____ command allows you to freeze rows and/or columns on the screen for use as headings.

12. _____ addressing allows cell references to change as they are copied. _____ addressing maintains all or part of the cell address from one cell to the next.

13. _____ cell addressing allows one part of the cell address to change while keeping the other part intact.

14. _____ recalculation enables you to avoid waiting for long spreadsheets to recalculate each time a cell is changed or a new cell is entered.

15. The function key _____ is pressed when you wish 1-2-3 to recalculate a worksheet while you are in manual recalculation mode.

16. The message _____ appears at the bottom of the screen when a change has been made to the contents of some cell during manual recalculation mode.

17. The _____ function allows you to embed logic in your worksheet.

18. The logical operators _____, _____, and _____ allow you to specify how comparisons are to interact.

19. The operators $<$, $>$, and $<=$ are referred to as _____ operators.

20. The `@DATE` function is extremely useful because it allows you to perform _____ to advance the date from one month to the next.

Computer Exercises

1. Ed has been approached to invest in a microcomputer store that will specialize in selling relatively low-cost microcomputers. Ed has done an excellent job of collecting information about this proposed business venture. He is interested in modeling the next four years of business activity. He wants a worksheet built to present information in two basic areas—an input area and an income statement area—as appears at the top of next page.*

   The following criteria must be applied to the worksheet:
   1. The input area will start in column A. Column A should be set to a width of 25.
   2. The income statement will start in column F.
   3. Sales are expected to be 300 units the first year.
   4. Rent for each year is $7,500 per year.
   5. Salaries are equal to 10% of sales (commission sales).
   6. Supplies are 1.5% of sales.
   7. Clerical costs are $4,000 the first year, and 6% more each additional year.
   8. Advertising costs are $50,000 plus 7% of sales the first year; $25,000 plus 7% of sales the second year; and 5% of sales in subsequent years.

```
INPUT AREA
UNITS SOLD (YEAR 1)         300
COST PER UNIT             $650
ANNUAL SALES GROWTH      15.00%
ANNUAL PRICE REDUCTION    7.00%
PRODUCT MARGIN           40.00%
```

---

*Adapted from Arthur Andersen & Co. materials.

```
                              ED'S MICROCOMPUTER SHOP
                           Projected Financial Statements

                            1          2          3          4
                         --------   --------   --------   --------
       Sales             325,000    347,588    371,745    397,581
       Cost              195,000    208,553    223,047    238,549
                         --------   --------   --------   --------
       Margin            130,000    139,035    148,698    159,032

       Expenses:
        Advertising       72,750     49,331     18,587     19,879
        Salaries          32,500     34,759     37,174     39,758
        Rent               7,500      7,500      7,500      7,500
        Supplies           4,875      5,214      5,576      5,964
        Clerical           4,000      4,240      4,494      4,764
        Other Costs       10,000     10,500     11,025     11,576
                         --------   --------   --------   --------
       Total Expenses    131,625    111,544     84,357     89,441
                         --------   --------   --------   --------
       Income b/f Taxes   (1,625)    27,491     64,341     69,591
        Income Taxes           0     13,746     32,170     34,796
                         --------   --------   --------   --------
       Net Income         (1,625)    13,746     32,170     34,796
                         --------   --------   --------   --------
```

9. There is a 50% tax rate.

10. Other costs are $10,000 the first year, and 5% more each additional year.

11. An @IF statement must be set up to check for a positive income b/f taxes.

12. The following range names will be used:

Units Sold	Units
Costs per Unit	Cost
Annual Growth	Growth
Annual Price Reduction	Ann.red
Profit Margin	Margin
First Year Sales	Sales
Year 1 Net Income	Year 1
Year 2 Net Income	Year 2
Year 3 Net Income	Year 3
Year 4 Net Income	Year 4

13. Column F will be set to a width of 16.

14. The global column will be set to a width of 11.

15. For year 1, the following sales formula will be used:

    `$UNITS*($COST/(1-$MARGIN))`

16. For years 2–4, the following sales formula will be used:

    `+SALES*(1+$GROWTH)*(1-$ANN.RED)`

17. The following cost formula for year 1:

    `$SALES*(1-$MARGIN)`

18. Generate a report of named ranges and print it out. Save this worksheet to a file called CH11EX1.

2. Retrieve the worksheet CH11EX2. Locate and correct all circular references contained in the worksheet. Be sure to use the GoTo command to position the pointer directly to each circular reference, once you have located it.

3. Retrieve the CH9EX5 file. Use the 1-2-3 Sort command to place the rows of the worksheet in order by the last name of the sales representatives. Don't include any total or heading lines in the sort. Save the sorted worksheet to a file called CH11EX3.

4. Load the worksheet CH11EX4. Set the worksheet up so that any additional monthly sales data are automatically included in the total for each salesperson. Also set the vertical totals such that a new person can be added at the bottom of the column. Enter sales for April and May. (You supply them.) A new person, George, is added in March. His sales figures are 4,500 for March and 3,700 for April.

5. Retrieve the CH10EX2 worksheet. To the right of the worksheet enter a Final Percentage column as depicted below. Take the students' total earned points and divide them by the total possible points to calculate the current percentage grade.

```
10-Feb-89

                        Grading Template

            NAME        ¦  Exam I  Anot.Bib.  Exam II   FINAL %
    POSSIBLE POINTS      ¦    150       45        130        325
    ------------------   ¦------------------------------------------
    Student 1            ¦    113       44        110     82.15%
    Student 2            ¦    116       42         90     76.31%
    Student 3            ¦    129       42         85     78.77%
    Student 4            ¦    133       44        125     92.92%
    Student 5            ¦    121       42         76     73.54%
    Student 6            ¦    139       41        115     90.77%
    Student 7            ¦    116       42         75     71.69%
    Student 8            ¦    130       39        120     88.92%
    Student 9            ¦    127       42         95     81.23%
    Student 10           ¦    120       42        115     85.23%
    ------------------   ¦------------------------------------------
    Average              ¦    124       42        101     82.15%

    % of Tot. Pnts.      ¦  82.93%   93.33%    77.38%
    High Grade           ¦    139       44        125
    Low Grade            ¦    113       39         75
    Std. Deviation       ¦      8        1         18
    Variance             ¦     65        2        312
```

Save this worksheet using the name CH11EX5.

6. Develop a loan amortization schedule for a 15-year mortgage. The principal is $20,000. The interest rate is 13.5%. You select the beginning date. Each line in the amortization schedule should have the month, payment amount, principal reduction amount, amount applied toward interest, and the remaining outstanding balance. (Remember that you must multiply the periods (years) by 12 when dealing with months.)

In solving this problem and looking at the worksheet, you must use the Horizontal Titles option to keep the column headings on the screen. You must also design the worksheet so that it quits calculating and outputting negative numbers when the principal is completely paid.

Print this worksheet using the Borders option. This will print the column headings at the top of each page of the printout, making the output more readable. Save this worksheet under the name CH11EX6.

7. Develop a worksheet that allows users to investigate a number of different principal amounts plotted against a number of different interest rates for home mortgages. Start with the principal amounts of $20,000, $40,000, $60,000, $80,000, $100,000 and $120,000. Use interest rates of 11.5%, 12.5%, 13%, 14%, 14.5%, 15%, and 15.5%. Refer to the Car Loan Evaluation Worksheet for ideas. The loans are all for 25 years. Save this file using the name CH11EX7.

8. Load the CH10EX1 worksheet containing the payroll information. Sort it alphabetically by rate of pay—that is, so that rate of pay is the primary key and last name is the secondary key. Save this file using the name CH11EX8.

9. Load the CH11EX6 worksheet. Move the input labels to column A. Hide the Total Payment column. Print the first three years of payments.

10. You are to prepare a straight-line depreciation schedule that allows a firm to depreciate an asset over a period up to twenty years. The formula for calculating straight-line depreciation is as follows: 1 / Number of periods of estimated useful life * (Cost − Salvage Value). The example below shows a depreciation schedule for an asset valued at $100,000 with a salvage value of 12,000 at the end of 10 years. The depreciation base is calculated by subtracting the estimated salvage value from the asset cost. Generate a total figure for the Depreciation Expense column to serve as a check figure to make certain that the depreciation total equals the depreciation base. Save as CH11EX10.

```
                      ABC Company
              Straight-Line Depreciation Schedule

        Asset Cost                          $100,000
        Estimated salvage value             $12,000
        Estimated useful life (yrs)              10
        Depreciation base                   $88,000
        --------------------------------------------------------

                    Year    Dep. Exp.      Book Value
                                          $100,000.00
                     1      $8,800.00       $91,200.00
                     2      $8,800.00       $82,400.00
                     3      $8,800.00       $73,600.00
                     4      $8,800.00       $64,800.00
                     5      $8,800.00       $56,000.00
                     6      $8,800.00       $47,200.00
                     7      $8,800.00       $38,400.00
                     8      $8,800.00       $29,600.00
                     9      $8,800.00       $20,800.00
                    10      $8,800.00       $12,000.00
```

```
                    11              $.00              $.00
                    12              $.00              $.00
                    13              $.00              $.00
                    14              $.00              $.00
                    15              $.00              $.00
                    16              $.00              $.00
                    17              $.00              $.00
                    18              $.00              $.00
                    19              $.00              $.00
                    20              $.00              $.00
          -------------------------------------------------------

                           $88,000.00
```

11. One of the most difficult areas for both school boards and teachers unions to deal with is contract negotiation. The union and the school board must sit down and try to negotiate a new contract for teachers. Depending on the school district, this process must be performed every one to five years.

   This process becomes complex because it is extremely difficult for both the school board and the union to determine quickly the economic impact of a proposal or counterproposal. Because of the different types of job steps and educational categories often found in education, this is an ideal application for Lotus 1-2-3. After a proposal or counterproposal has been presented, it can be quickly modeled using 1-2-3.

   This particular exercise attempts, as much as possible, to keep the negotiation model simple and easy to use. The model itself has five different parts: Input/Impact areas, Salary schedule, Individuals in each category, Salary subtotals for each category, and a financial statement.

   The Input/Impact areas of the worksheet can be seen following this discussion. The Input area allows you to change three pieces of data. The beginning salary is the salary received by anyone hired directly from college with a bachelor's degree. The job step increment is the amount that is added to an individual's salary for each year worked. The educational increment is the amount that is added to a teacher's salary for obtaining additional education.

   The Impact area shows the current total amount paid for salaries, as well as other information. The results of any changes made to the Input area are reflected in these entries. For instance, once a change has been entered in the base salary, job step increment, or educational increment entries, the change is reflected in the Impact area.

   The Impact area is also affected by changes in projections for next year's revenues and expenditures in the financial statement. You are allowed to change the Est. %Increase column of the financial statement. The projected expenditures are subtracted from the expected revenues to arrive at the Present Available Monies entry. The Total Differential Cost is now subtracted from the Present Available Monies to arrive at the Difference with Proposal.

   Let's now examine each of the other different areas of the negotiation model. First, let's take a look at the information contained in Table 1, which shows the salary for each job category. The job step (vertical) entries represent the salary based on longevity, or length of service with the school district. The educational increment (horizontal) entries represent the salary increments that accrue to teachers based on additional education that a teacher receives.

Table 2, the teachers by education and job steps, shows how many people are in each separate category. A check figure indicating the total number of teachers in the table is used to guard against data entry errors.

Table 3, salary totals of each job category, is calculated by multiplying each entry in the salary schedule by the corresponding number of individuals in that entry. A grand total of all subtotals in this table is generated and used in the Impact area of the worksheet.

Table 4, the financial statement, contains this year's revenue and expenditures. It also contains a projected percent increase column used for generating each category of next year's projected revenue and expenditures. The projected expenditures subtracted from projected revenues generates the available monies entry in the Impact area.

Most of the entries in the financial statement are self-explanatory, but a few merit some explanation. Let's examine the Revenue portion of the financial statement first.

1. The Governmental Divisions entry is composed of revenue received from a number of state and federal programs such as general state aid, driver education, special education, vocational education, gifted education, and federal subsidies.

2. The Student and Community Services is composed of revenue received from tuition from regular or adult education programs, as well as revenue from textbooks, lunch programs, and snack bars.

3. The Anticipation Warrants Receivable entry represents a source of short-term financing. These warrants are securities issued in anticipation of the receipt of the tax levy and are repaid when the tax levy is distributed.

Now let's look more closely at the Expenditures portion of the financial statement.

1. The Administration category includes monies expended for administrators and their support personnel, as well as contractual entries for legal services.

2. The Fixed Charges category includes monies expended for the employer's share of retirement systems payments, various insurance policies provided for employees, and interest on anticipation warrants.

3. The Capital Outlay category includes new equipment for educational programs, as well as for replacement equipment.

4. The Debt Service category includes the total for anticipation warrants payable.

Hints for Building the 1-2-3 Model (CH11EX11)

1. Design the Input and Impact areas so that they appear on different screens. Reach them by pressing the PgDn and PgUp keys.

2. Arrange each of the schedules so that they can be reached by pressing the TAB key.

3. Set column A to a width of 22 and the first column of your financial statement to a width of 32.

4. Enter the current Salary Base total as a numeric constant so changes can be tracked. This figure is the only figure, besides the financial statement figures, that has to be manually changed.

5. The beginning salary figure in Table 1 (15,700) must appear via a cell reference to the Input area. If that figure subsequently changes, the change will automatically be reflected in the table. The same holds true for the vertical and horizontal increments. They must also be accessed via cell references. Some form of absolute addressing is required.

6. Make certain that you sum the teachers in the various categories in Table 2. This provides you with a check figure that indicates whether or not you have all of the teachers entered. It does not, however, indicate whether the teachers have been entered in the appropriate categories.

7. The grand total of Table 3 provides you with the total cost of any changes that are made in the Input area. Use the @SUM function to sum each category subtotal.

8. The impact area entries are calculated as follows:
   a. The Current Salary Base Total is derived via a cell reference to the Instruction cost entry in the Financial Statement of Table 4. This figure does not change.
   b. Total Cost of Change is derived by summing the entries contained in Table 3.
   c. Total Differential Cost is derived by subtracting Current Salary Base Total from the Total Cost of the Change.
   d. The Percentage Change is derived by dividing the Total Differential Cost by the Total Cost of Change.
   e. Average Salary Increase is derived by dividing the Total Differential Cost by the number of teachers.
   f. Present Available Monies is derived by subtracting the total expenses from the total revenues of Table 4.
   g. The Difference with Proposal is derived by subtracting the Present Available Monies from the Total Differential Cost.

Input Area

Beginning Salary	15,700
Job Step Increment (Vert)	500
Educational Increment (Horiz)	375

Impact Area

Current Salary Base	1,545,250	Before Change
Total Cost of Change	1,545,250	
Total Differential Cost	0	
Percentage Change	0.0%	
Average Salary Increase	0	
Present Available Monies	31,804	
Difference with Proposal	31,804	

Table 1
Salary schedule

Your School District For the Year 19xx
Education and Job Steps

Step	B.S.	B.S. +8	B.S. +16	B.S. +24	M.A.	M.A. +8	M.A. +16
1	15,700	16,075	16,450	16,825	17,200	17,575	17,950
2	16,200	16,575	16,950	17,325	17,700	18,075	18,450
3	16,700	17,075	17,450	17,825	18,200	18,575	18,950
4	17,200	17,575	17,950	18,325	18,700	19,075	19,450
5	17,700	18,075	18,450	18,825	19,200	19,575	19,950
6	18,200	18,575	18,950	19,325	19,700	20,075	20,450
7	18,700	19,075	19,450	19,825	20,200	20,575	20,950
8	19,200	19,575	19,950	20,325	20,700	21,075	21,450
9	19,700	20,075	20,450	20,825	21,200	21,575	21,950
10	20,200	20,575	20,950	21,325	21,700	22,075	22,450
11	20,700	21,075	21,450	21,825	22,200	22,575	22,950
12	21,200	21,575	21,950	22,325	22,700	23,075	23,450
13	21,700	22,075	22,450	22,825	23,200	23,575	23,950
14	22,200	22,575	22,950	23,325	23,700	24,075	24,450
15	22,700	23,075	23,450	23,825	24,200	24,575	24,950
16		23,575	23,950	24,325	24,700	25,075	25,450
17		24,075	24,450	24,825	25,200	25,575	25,950
18		24,575	24,950	25,325	25,700	26,075	26,450
19		25,075	25,450	25,825	26,200	26,575	26,950
20			25,950	26,325	26,700	27,075	27,450
21				26,825	27,200	27,575	27,950
22				27,325	27,700	28,075	28,450
23					28,200	28,575	28,950
24							29,450

Table 2
Teachers by job step and education

Your School District For the Year 19xx
Individuals in Education and Job Steps

Step	B.S.	B.S. +8	B.S. +16	B.S. +24	M.A.	M.A. +8	M.A. +16
1	1		1	1	1	1	0
2	1						
3		1					
4		1					
5			4			1	3
6	1	2			1		
7	1			1			
8	1		2				
9					3		1
10	2					1	
11		3	1	2			
12	1						
13			3	1	2		2
14	1						
15						4	
16		1		1			
17							
18							
19		1		2		2	1
20			1			3	
21				0			
22					2	1	
23							3
24							
Total Teachers	70						

Table 3
Salaries by job step and
education

Your School District For the Year 19xx
Salary Totals of Individuals in Education and Job Steps

Step	B.S.	B.S. +8	B.S. +16	B.S. +24	M.A.	M.A. +8	M.A. +16
1	15,700	0	16,450	16,825	17,200	17,575	0
2	16,200	0	0	0	0	0	0
3	0	17,075	0	0	0	0	0
4	0	17,575	0	0	0	0	0
5	0	0	73,800	0	0	19,575	59,850
6	18,200	37,150	0	0	19,700	0	0
7	18,700	0	0	19,825	0	0	0
8	19,200	0	39,900	0	0	0	0
9	0	0	0	0	63,600	0	21,950
10	40,400	0	0	0	0	22,075	0
11	0	63,225	21,450	43,650	0	0	0
12	21,200	0	0	0	0	0	0
13	0	0	67,350	22,825	46,400	0	47,900
14	22,200	0	0	0	0	0	0
15	0	0	0	0	0	98,300	0
16	0	23,575	0	24,325	0	0	0
17	0	0	0	0	0	0	0
18	0	0	0	0	0	0	0
19	0	25,075	0	51,650	0	53,150	26,950
20	0	0	25,950	0	0	81,225	0
21	0	0	0	0	0	0	0
22	0	0	0	0	55,400	28,075	0
23	0	0	0	0	0	0	86,850
24	0	0	0	0	0	0	0

Table 4
School income statement
with next year's projections

Your School District Financial Statement for the Year 19xx
EDUCATIONAL FUND

REVENUE	This Year	Est. %Inc.	
Beginning Balance	$ 6,704.63		$ 6,704.63
Local Taxes	1,156,300.00	2.00%	1,179,426.00
Governmental Divisions	592,870.00	1.50%	601,763.05
Student and Community Services	237,640.00	2.50%	243,581.00
Other Revenue	1,300.00	2.00%	1,326.00
Anticipation Warrants Rec.	435,170.37	2.50%	446,049.63
TOTAL ESTIMATED REVENUE	$2,429,985.00		$2,478,850.31
EXPENDITURES			
Administration	$ 174,825.00	3.00%	$ 180,069.75
Instruction	1,545,250.00		1,545,250.00
Health	7,650.00	1.50%	7,764.75
Maintenance	7,200.00	1.50%	7,308.00
Fixed Charges	65,150.00	1.50%	66,127.25
Student & Community Services	319,810.00	2.00%	326,206.20
Capital Outlay	50,000.00		50,000.00
Debt Service	240,000.00	1.80%	244,320.00
Contingency	20,000.00		20,000.00
TOTAL PROPOSED EXPENDITURES	$2,429,885.00		$2,447,045.95

12. ***Part A—General Instructions (CH11EX12)***

1. Enter the following financial statements using Lotus 1-2-3.

2. Prepare a financial analysis of the Treadstone 21 Company based on information contained in the various financial schedules as they currently appear. If there is sufficient information available, explain how the various increases/decreases within the statements occurred.

3. In addition to examining the various financial statements, you are also to prepare the other financial analysis measures contained on the last page of this assignment and include these in your paper.

4. You are responsible for gathering information concerning the formulas for the required ratios.

5. What information not included would allow you to prepare a better analysis?

6. Would you recommend investing in this company? Be sure to carefully state your rationale.

7. Determine the impact on the Treadstone 21 Company and your decision on whether or not to purchase stock if the following changes occurred for 1988:
   a. Sales returns and allowances increased 10 percent.
   b. Accounts receivable increased by 15 percent.

c. Long-term liabilities are $200,000.

d. Sales increase 5 percent (gross profit percentage constant).

Just enter the above changes and examine their impact on the worksheet. Do not try to make the debits balance the credits.

8. You do not currently have any information about what type of business the Treadstone 21 Company is engaged in. Assume that the company could be in any one of the following five businesses. You are also given information about three of the ratios to be calculated. Based on the information from the ratios for each of the proposed businesses, would you invest in Treadstone 21? Give a rationale for each type of possible business.

	Retail	Electric	Machinery	Grocery	Clothing
Quick ratio	1.3	0.9	1.8	0.8	1.1
Liability to Equity	60.2	210.0	57.4	34.2	43.7
Asset to Sales	74.0	173.0	65.0	16.3	39.2

Part B—Format Instructions

1. Set the Global Column Width to 12.

2. Use the Copy feature of 1-2-3 as much as possible.

3. Use WordPerfect or some other word processing package to write your paper.

4. Save each of the schedules to disk as a print file (you may want to review this process from Chapter 10 and the discussion on the Quit command from the Print submenu), and use the WordPerfect Retrieve command to include them in your report. 1-2-3 may embed some strange-looking end of file indicators at the bottom of your .PRN file. You can get rid of them by issuing a delete to end of line (Ctrl + End) command. Also, make certain that if you have double spacing in effect, you change it to single spacing when you load in the schedules. You may also have to reset your pitch and/or margins to get the schedules to print properly.

5. Design your 1-2-3 worksheets so that data need be changed in only one location to affect the other financial statements and ratios. This means that one income statement's figures will refer to the other's and change as the other changes. You accomplish this cross-reference by first deciding which income statement is to be changed and which is to reflect the changes entered on the other. For example, assume you decide that the horizontal analysis income statement is to be the part of the worksheet that will receive any changes and that the vertical analysis income statement will reflect the changes made to the horizontal worksheet. To accomplish this you must first build the horizontal analysis income statement. After you have done this, copy the various row and column headings from that area of the worksheet to the area that will hold the vertical analysis income statement. All that now remains to be done is to direct 1-2-3 to load the information into the vertical analysis cells. You do this by referencing the first cell in the other worksheet (for example, +V11). You can now copy this reference down this column. You will have to replace any zero entries with the appropriate rows of dashes.

6. Within the body of your spreadsheet, you are to give the various reports the following range names:
   a. Comparative Balance Sheet — Balance1
   b. Comparative Schedule of Current Assets — Balance2
   c. Horizontal Analysis Income Statement — Income1
   d. Vertical Analysis Income Statement — Income2
   e. Retained Earnings Statement — Retained
   f. Ratio Analysis Data and Ratios — Ratio

   You can now give the range name to 1-2-3, instead of pointing out the range when printing.

7. Turn in your report along with the diskette containing your Word-Perfect and 1-2-3 files. The worksheet should reflect the changes from item 7 of Part A. The worksheets of the financial statements in the body of your report should have the same format as those on the following pages.

Treadstone 21 Company
Comparative Balance Sheet
December 31, 1988 and 1987
Horizontal Analysis

	1988	1987	Increase (Decrease) Amount	Percent
Assets				
Current assets	$635,713	$591,883	$43,830	7.4%
Long-term investments	106,000	183,000	(77,000)	−42.1%
Plant assets (net)	485,000	510,000	(25,000)	−4.9%
Intangible assets	35,000	35,000	0	0.0%
Total assets	$1,261,713	$1,319,883	($58,170)	−4.4%
Liabilities				
Current liabilities	$200,000	$247,000	($47,000)	−19.0%
Long-term liabilities	150,000	225,000	(75,000)	−33.3%
Total liabilities	$350,000	$472,000	($122,000)	−25.8%
Stockholders' Equity				
Preferred 6% stock, $100 par	$160,000	$155,000	$5,000	3.2%
Common stock, $10 par	550,000	550,000	0	0.0%
Retained Earnings	201,713	142,883	58,830	41.2%
Total stockholders' equity	$911,713	$847,883	$63,830	7.5%
Total liab. & stckhos.' equity	$1,261,713	$1,319,883	($58,170)	−4.4%

Treadstone 21 Company
Comparative Schedule of Current Assets
December 31, 1988 and 1987

	1988	1987	Increase (Decrease)	
			Amount	Percent
Cash	$116,780	$89,683	$27,097	30.2%
Marketable securities	105,000	85,000	20,000	23.5%
Accounts receivable (net)	132,233	125,000	7,233	5.8%
Merchandise inventory	275,000	287,000	(12,000)	−4.2%
Prepaid expenses	6,700	5,200	1,500	28.8%
Total Current Assets	$635,713	$591,883	$43,830	7.4%

Treadstone 21 Company
Income Statement
For Years Ended December 31, 1988 and 1987
Horizontal Analysis

	1988	1987	Increase (Decrease)	
			Amount	Percent
Sales	$1,607,025	$1,234,000	$373,025	30.2%
Sales returns and allowances	35,750	34,000	1,750	5.1%
Net sales	$1,571,275	$1,200,000	$371,275	30.9%
Cost of merchandise sold	1,095,150	820,000	275,150	33.6%
Gross profit	$476,125	$380,000	$96,125	25.3%
Selling expenses	$185,000	$141,000	$44,000	31.2%
General expenses	100,000	93,400	6,600	7.1%
Total operating expenses	$285,000	$234,400	$50,600	21.6%
Operating income	$191,125	$145,600	$45,525	31.3%
Other income	8,500	11,000	(2,500)	−22.7%
	$199,625	$156,600	$43,025	27.5%
Other expenses	6,000	13,000	(7,000)	−53.8%
Income before income tax	$193,625	$143,600	$50,025	34.8%
Income tax	85,195	61,985	23,210	37.4%
Net income	$108,430	$81,615	$26,815	32.9%

Treadstone 21 Company
Comparative Income Statement
For Years Ended December 31, 1988 and 1987
Vertical Analysis

	1988		1987	
	Amount	*Percent*	*Amount*	*Percent*
Sales	$1,607,025	102.3%	$1,234,000	102.8%
Sales returns and allowances	$35,750	2.3%	$34,000	2.8%
Net sales	$1,571,275	100.0%	$1,200,000	100.0%
Cost of merchandise sold	$1,095,150	69.7%	$820,000	68.3%
Gross profit	$476,125	30.3%	$380,000	31.7%
Selling expenses	$185,000	11.8%	$141,000	11.8%
General expenses	$100,000	6.4%	$93,400	7.8%
Total operating expenses	$285,000	18.1%	$234,400	19.5%
Operating income	$191,125	12.2%	$145,600	12.1%
Other income	$8,500	0.5%	$11,000	0.9%
	$199,625	12.7%	$156,600	13.1%
Other expense	$6,000	0.4%	$13,000	1.1%
Income before income tax	$193,625	12.3%	$143,600	12.0%
Income tax	$85,195	5.4%	$61,985	5.2%
Net income	$108,430	6.9%	$81,615	6.8%

Treadstone 21 Company
Comparative Retained Earnings Statement
For Years Ended December 31, 1988 and 1987

	1988	1987	Increase (Decrease)	
			Amount	*Percent*
Retained earnings, January 1	$142,883	$100,568	$42,315	42.1%
Net income for year	108,430	81,615	26,815	32.9%
Total	$251,313	$182,183	$69,130	37.9%
Dividends:				
On preferred stock	$9,600	$9,300	$300	3.2%
On common stock	40,000	30,000	10,000	33.3%
Total	$49,600	$39,300	$10,300	26.2%
Retained earnings, December 31	$201,713	$142,883	$58,830	41.2%

Additional Data Needed For Ratio Analysis

	1988	1987
A/R Beginning of Year Balance	125,000	140,000
Total Assets Beg. of Year	1,314,400	1,187,500
Tot. Ass.—Long-Term Invest.	1,131,400	1,010,000
Shares Outstanding Common	50,000	50,000
Price per Share of Common	$20.50	$13.50
Dividend/Share of Common	$ 0.80	$0.60

Financial Ratio Analysis

	1988	1987
Current Ratio		
Acid Test		
Accounts Receivable Turnover		
No. of Days' Sales in Recbles.		
Plant Assets to Long-Term Liab.		
Stockholders' Equity to Liab.		

PROFITABILITY ANALYSIS
Net Sales to Assets
EPS on Common Stock
Price Earnings Ratio
Dividend Yield

Chapter
12

Introduction to Data
Base Management

After completing this chapter, you should be able to:

Discuss the differences between the traditional approach to information processing and the data base approach

Discuss the role of the DBMS

Discuss the advantages of a DBMS

Describe the parts of a DBMS

Describe the role of the data base administrator

Discuss some data base organization methods

Discuss in detail how indexes are created

Discuss the steps involved in planning a data base file

One challenge that faces a user of information most frequently is how to store data in a file so that information can be easily retrieved. Historically, one problem was that once the fields had been defined and data stored, it was a highly complicated task to add or delete fields in a record. Also, to access information from a file required the user to consult with a systems analyst/programmer who could design and write programs to access the needed information. The programs themselves might take several months to design, write, test, and debug. If conditions and information needs changed, it took a fair amount of time to get information to meet the new requirements. Data base management systems have totally revolutionized the ability to supply a user with timely information.

In this chapter, we first examine the traditional manner of supplying information to a user via files and then the data base approach. We discuss the parts of a data base management system, the data base itself, and the role played by the data base administrator.

Traditional Approach to Information Processing

The **traditional approach** to providing information to a user is file-oriented. Each application area has its own set of master and transaction files, which are used for storing, processing, and retrieving data (Figure 12.1). The files for each application are specifically designed for that application at the time of system design. No provisions are made for sharing data between departments or divisions of an organization. Each functional area of an organization has its own set of files and programs for manipulating that data. If a change must be made in the way that data are physically stored in the personnel file (for example, expanding the zip code field to handle ten characters instead of five), any program that accesses this file must also be changed to reflect the change in the zip code field of the "new" personnel file.

The traditional approach centers around the master file for that application. Any time changes are made, the impact of the change is recorded to the master file by subtracting a value from one field or by adding a value to another field. The information from this master file is then used as the basic source for providing information to the user.

Problems of the Traditional Approach

The traditional approach, while still frequently used, also has some built-in problems. These problems are data redundancy, program and data dependency, and lack of flexibility.

Data Redundancy. The problem of having identical information stored in multiple files is **data redundancy**. This means that the same data have to be recorded by more than one application. The record structures in Figure 12.2 show that a number of fields are identical between payroll and personnel files. Having to store the same data in more than one file means that it is more costly to maintain and edit because the same work is being done more than once.

Keeping data of these common fields identical between applications is naturally a problem. The data should be identical, but most of the time there will be many discrepancies from one file to the next. This problem of errors occurring in a file relates to **data integrity** and means that the fields of a specific entity's record will be inconsistent from one file to another. A lack of data integrity results in reports being generated that have errors.

Let's examine this problem of data integrity with an example. Joe, an employee of the company, moves. It's around the end of the year, and Joe wants to make certain that he receives his W-2 form (summary of earnings for the

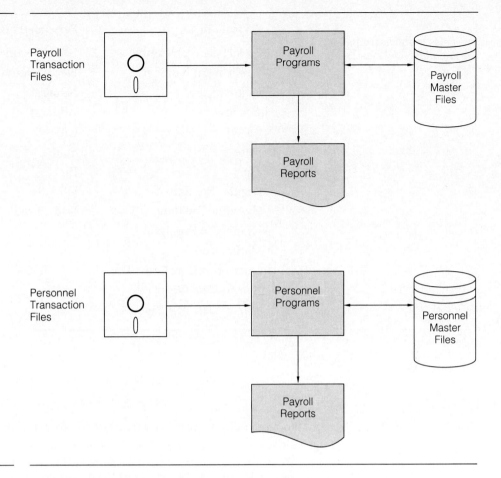

Figure 12.1
With the traditional approach to information processing, each application has its own set of master and transaction files.

year that is sent to the IRS for tax purposes) at his new address. Joe is also a very busy person and has time only to make certain that the change is made with the payroll department. Because he neglects to inform the personnel department, his address data are no longer correct. Any reports that are generated in personnel now have incorrect data (Joe's address) in them.

Program and Data Dependency. One problem with the traditional approach to information processing is that a change to a field cannot be made directly to the file. If a field is to be added, deleted, or changed, a new file must first be created that reflects the desired change. A program must be written that reads a record from the old file and then saves this record in the new format to the new file. If a new field has been added to the record, this information must be entered manually for each record.

Another problem with the traditional approach to information processing is that each field contained in a file must be defined perfectly so that the program can properly access the file. This means that any time a field is added, deleted, or changed in a file any program that accesses the changed file must be changed so that the description of the file actually matches the changed file.

Lack of Flexibility. When a change is needed that results in a change to a file in a traditional information system, it is extremely difficult to implement because the file and any programs that access that file also must be changed. The ability to quickly make a change, or the **flexibility** of a system, is greatly diminished in a traditional information-processing environment. Because every report generated by a system requires a special program to be written, the ability

Figure 12.2
The fields found in the payroll and personnel master
files.

Payroll File	Personnel File
Social Security Number	Social Security Number
Department Number	Department
Name	Name
Address	Address
City	City
State	State
Zip	Zip
Regular Pay Rate	Job Title
Overtime Pay Rate	Date Hired
Number of Exemptions	
Marital Code	
Quarter-to-Date Gross Pay	
Year-to-Date Gross Pay	
Year-to-Date Net Pay	

to respond quickly to user requests for special reports is made extremely difficult. This is especially compounded if the data for the request are in several
files. The complexity of the program and its logic design will probably make
the cost of obtaining the data exceed the benefit of that data.

Role of the Data Base Management System

A **data base management system (DBMS)** is a complete set of programs that
serve as the interface between a user or application program and allows data
to be created, deleted, or changed in an integrated data base. These data can
then be used to create reports that are useful to the user. The term **integrated**
refers to DBMS's ability to logically relate one record with another such that
any data related to a specific topic can easily be retrieved via simple requests to
the DBMS. DBMS software represents the interface between the user and the
data that are needed for that user's application (Figure 12.3). Data base processing in a large organizational context using mainframe computers would provide access to data via an application program. When microcomputer-based
DBMSs are used, however, the user typically has direct access to the DBMS by
entering instructions at the keyboard.

Data Base Management System Example

Let's examine a typical application that could use a DBMS. Suppose that you
are the personnel manager for a manufacturing company that employs around
1,000 employees. The president of the company has just received an information request from a federal government agency that is concerned with the
number of male and female employees over the age of fifty-five. The agency
wants the names and addresses of males and females listed separately. The
president of the company has delegated this task to you; you have three weeks
to provide these reports to the agency.

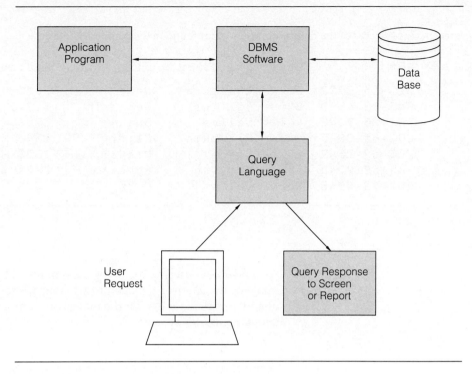

Figure 12.3
The DBMS acts as the interface between a user (or application program) and the data base.

The personnel information for these employees is located in three five-drawer filing cabinets. The personnel records are stored in manila folders and are in alphabetical order. All you must do is go through each folder and see if any employee is over the age of fifty-five. If any are, you check the gender and write the name and address of males on one list and females on the other list. Imagine the number of hours that you would spend in accomplishing this task.

Let's examine what would be required if the personnel information is in a computer-based DBMS. Instead of searching manila folders contained in a filing cabinet, you now sit at your computer keyboard to access the personnel data base pictured in Figure 12.4. Each row depicted in Figure 12.4 represents a record, and each column represents a field of data.

The steps involved in actually accessing the personnel file from the computer are

Turn on the computer and the printer.

Place the disk with the DBMS software and personnel data base file in their appropriate drives or change to the appropriate directory on the fixed disk and start the DBMS (enter the command DBASE).

Give the command to open the personnel data base file.

Give the command to search all records in the data base file and print those names and addresses of females over the age of fifty-five. When this is finished, do the same for males over fifty-five.

If you were using the dBASE III Plus DBMS, the following statements would accomplish this task:

```
.USE EMPLOYEE
.LIST FIRST,LAST,ADDRESS,CITY,STATE,ZIP FOR SEX='F' .AND. AGE>55 TO PRINT
.LIST FIRST,LAST,ADDRESS,CITY,STATE,ZIP FOR SEX='M' .AND. AGE>55 TO PRINT
```

Figure 12.4
A few fields of several of the thousand or so records found in the personnel data base file.

```
SS#            Dept   Last Name    First Name   Address
323-45-6732    232    Anderson     Jane         1536 N. Delmore Lane
345-23-4959    345    Billingham   George       113 Delane Dr.
567-36-7948    441    Boling       Susan        6789 W. University
283-85-3905    445    Clayburn     Cliff        2345 N. Adelaide
203-59-2848    232    Crane        Fraser       1676 W. Freud
345-56-2342    556    Croxton      Roberta      234 N. Main St.
202-76-4848    656    Doring       Fran         1674 W. Gregory
```

As a result of entering the above commands, all records that meet the criteria (male or female over the age of fifty-five) are sent to the printer. Two reports, one for females and one for the males, are generated. This entire process might take ten minutes at most.

Advantages of Data Base Management Systems

The data base approach to information processing solves many of the problems that have been associated with the traditional approach to information processing. The solutions include data independence, eliminated data redundancy and increased data integrity, integrated data from other files, enhanced security, and standardized reports.

Data Independence. With the traditional approach to information processing, the data needed for an application was stored in a separate set of transaction–master files. With data base information processing, all data relative to a general application can be stored in a data base. If any changes must be made, they can be incorporated in the data base without changing each program that might access the data base. This is possible because a DBMS provides for two views of the data stored in it.

The **physical view** of the data base is related to how data actually appear in the data base. It deals with the actual location of the data on a storage device. The **logical view** represents data that are needed by the user or programmer (Figure 12.5). The emphasis here is on making fields of data easily available to a user; the user does not have to know exactly how data are stored in the data base and does not have to provide the data base with this description. This greatly facilitates access to data in a data base. All that the user must know is the name of the file to be accessed and the field names of the necessary data fields. The advantage of viewing the data logically is that the user is totally insulated from where and how the data are stored. DBMS software takes care of accessing the data and makes it available to the user.

Eliminated Data Redundancy and Increased Data Integrity. Because all data related to a single general application are stored in one place, if a change occurs it only has to be made in one location.

Integrated Data from Other Files. A user can obtain all the important data related to an application by creating relationships among records in other files.

Figure 12.5
A user of an application program needs only a logical view of data stored in the data base.

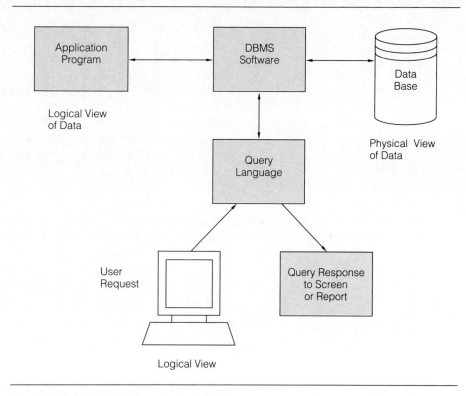

This greatly enhances the flexibility of generating reports that require information to be integrated from several files.

Enhanced Security Through Management of Data Access. Advanced DBMS packages can be instructed to examine a user's request for data and verify that the particular user is allowed to "see" the data found in a requested field. This ability to deny unauthorized users access to restricted data greatly enhances data security and further ensures data integrity.

Standardized Reports. A DBMS allows a user to request a program be run to produce a standardized report. It can be used to fulfill queries (requests for data in a specified format) to the data base. The data base can be used by a personnel program that was written to generate a report of employees' birthdays so that a small gift can be sent to them. As indicated in the previous personnel example, it can be used to generate a query to produce records that meet certain criteria such as age or gender.

Parts of a Data Base Management System

A DBMS is a complicated set of programs that have been created to provide the flexibility, ease of use, and easy access to the data found in a data base. As mentioned previously, the DBMS acts as the interface between the user and the data base. A DBMS has four parts: a query language, a report generator, a data-definition language, and a data-manipulation language.

Query Language

Most individuals who use a DBMS find the query language to be the easiest vehicle to use in obtaining information from the data base. The query language is especially useful when reports that are generated periodically do not have

Figure 12.6
The structure of the dBASE
INVENTRY inventory file.

```
Structure for database: B:Inventry.dbf
Number of data records:  25
Date of last update : 01-01-89
Field  Field Name  Type         Width  Dec
    1  INVID       Character     10
    2  NAME        Character     36
    3  ONHAND      Numeric        4
    4  REORDER     Numeric        4
    5  OPTIMUM     Numeric        7     2
**Total**                       62
```

the exact, needed information. In this type of situation, it is the **query language** that allows you to interrogate the DBMS about the specific data for which you are searching from the data base. Let's examine an inventory application and see how you can use the query language of dBASE III Plus to obtain information about your inventory file. The following are some queries that could be asked against the inventory file and the answers received through the dBASE query language.

List all inventory items that have an on-hand value less than the reorder value. This allows us to see which items are in danger of being out of stock.

List all inventory items that have a total inventory value greater than $7,500. The inventory value is calculated by multiplying the unit cost by the number on hand. This allows us to keep an eye on the "big ticket" items to make certain that major pilferage is not occurring.

To answer these requests requires just a few hours of introduction to the query language of the DBMS package that your firm is using. The DBMS package that you will be receiving hands-on instruction with is, of course, dBASE III Plus. By the end of Chapter 15, you will know enough to answer the above requests by using the query language of dBASE to form queries against the inventory file. Figure 12.6 shows the structure for the inventory file, IN-VENTRY, used in this example. The dBASE queries used are as follows:

```
USE INVENTRY
LIST FOR ONHAND<REORDER
LIST FOR PRICE*ONHAND>7500
```

Figure 12.7 lists the result of the requests.

Report Generator

The report generator for a DBMS is a feature that is most frequently found in microcomputer-based DBMS packages. The **report generator** greatly simplifies the task of generating a professional-looking report with appropriate report headings, page numbers, report date, column headings, grand totals, and so on. Figure 12.8 shows an example of a report generated using the dBASE III Plus REPORT command and the INVENTRY file. This dBASE REPORT command will be covered in detail in a later chapter.

Data-Definition Language

The **data-definition language (DDL)** designs the logical structure of the data base. This logical structure contains information about all fields—their names,

Record#	INVID	NAME	ONHAND	REORDER	OPTIMUM	PRICE
1	3625a1	crt lamp	13	50	100	149.00
6	3970-8a1	multi-purpose back shelf	25	30	50	110.00
7	4400a1	workstations	9	12	20	699.00
8	4430a1	workstations	5	8	15	650.00
9	4440	triangle extension	15	18	20	185.00
10	4442	rectangle extension	100	120	150	175.00
12	4446	wristrest	35	45	50	39.00
13	4838	footrest	120	130	150	35.00
14	4858a1	manager's chair	8	10	12	549.00
15	4857	associate's chair	12	15	18	359.00
16	4856	clerical chair	33	40	54	299.00
17	4765	associate's chair	55	60	75	340.00
18	4447a1	copyholder	88	92	99	120.00
19	4270	42" customizer	30	40	45	190.00

(a)

Record#	INVID	NAME	ONHAND	REORDER	OPTIMUM	PRICE
3	8093a1	serial microbuffer	45	30	100	379.00
5	6582a1	computer vacuum	85	75	120	139.00
10	4442	rectangle extension	100	120	150	175.00
16	4856	clerical chair	33	40	54	299.00
17	4765	associate's chair	55	60	75	340.00
18	4447a1	copyholder	88	92	99	120.00
30	4288a1	suspension bar	4853	21	34	33.00
42	7177a1	tape i.d. system	1000	900	1000	115.00
44	2955	applesaver	89	92	95	99.00
66	7180	data strike data eraser	110	120	160	69.00
69	6580	portable computer vacuum	99	120	135	112.00
100	4003	84" high data storage	18	36	84	575.00

(b)

Figure 12.7
The output from the queries to the dBASE inventory file. (a) ONHAND<REORDER.
(b) PRICE*ONHAND>7500.

Figure 12.8
An example of a finished report using the dBASE REPORT command and the INVENTRY file.

```
Page no.      1
01/01/89
```

Inventory Sales Report

Item	Description	Price	Units Sold	Extension
3625a1	crt lamp	149.00	9	1341.00
3970-8a1	multi-purpose back shelf	110.00	5	550.00
4270	42" customizer	190.00	88	16720.00
4271	72" customizer	250.00	2	500.00
4272a1	42" side extension	115.00	50	5750.00
4273	72" side extension	135.00	1	135.00
4276	flat shelf	68.00	85	5780.00
4278a1	suspension bar	39.00	45	1755.00
4279	back extension foot	40.00	9	360.00
4400a1	workstations	699.00	9	6291.00
4430a1	workstations	650.00	5	3250.00
4440	triangle extension	185.00	2	370.00
4442	rectangle extension	175.00	7	1225.00
4444	copyholder	99.00	55	5445.00
4446	wristrest	39.00	0	0.00
4447a1	copyholder	120.00	18	2160.00
4545a1	ready files set	39.50	20	790.00
4765	associate's chair	340.00	55	18700.00
4838	footrest	35.00	12	420.00
4856	clerical chair	299.00	28	8372.00
4857	associate's chair	359.00	35	12565.00
4858a1	manager's chair	549.00	5	2745.00
6137a1	IBM nylon cartridge ribbon	5.95	10	59.50
6582 a1	computer vacuum	139.00	85	11815.00
8093a1	serial microbuffer	379.00	45	17055.00
Total		5208.45	685	14153.50

the type of data (character, numeric, and date, for example) that are contained in the field, and the field length. This logical structure is also called the **schema**. A **subschema** is the way in which a specific application program or user is allowed to access the data found in this particular file. The subschema allows limited access to the fields of the file to specific users or applications and specifies that type of allowed access. For instance, in a payroll application, a payroll clerk should be able to field questions from employees who have bona-fide questions about their paychecks. The clerk can view fields such as pay rate, hours worked, gross pay, net pay, and year-to-date totals to answer questions. This clerk, however, would not be able to change any values found in the data base. A subschema can be prepared for any program or user who will be accessing the data base.

The DDL defines the characteristics of each record: the fields to be contained in it, their names, the data type, and the field length. It also limits access to fields and defines what access rights (read-only or read-with-write privileges) individuals have once they have gained access to a particular field of data.

Data-Manipulation Language

The **data-manipulation language (DML)** has all the stored routines that allow a user to store, retrieve, change, delete, or sort data or records within the data base. Each of these routines takes the form of a single command that the user can use; the following are some common dBASE III Plus commands:

```
BROWSE
CREATE
DISPLAY
LIST
SORT
```

Each command can be customized further by providing additional information about the fields to be included or a value to be used in executing the command. The DML evaluates all requests for data that have been issued through the query language of the DBMS.

In many microcomputer-based DBMS systems, the DDL and DML are combined into one language, which is usually referred to as the DML. The DDL is most commonly found in mainframe-based DBMS systems where the need for many different users to access a single data base and the subsequent need for security is far greater than that found in a microcomputer environment.

Role of the Data Base Administrator

In large organizations that make use of a DBMS, many different users want access to the data base and have very differing information needs. The data contained in a data base are extremely important to both small and large organizations. In large organizations, however, there are many more people who can have access to the data base, make changes to the data base, and take actions that can directly or indirectly harm the data contained in the data base. In large organizations, there is usually a **data base administrator (DBA)** who has been appointed by management and who works with users to create, maintain, and safeguard the data found in the data base. Whereas a DBA in a large organization will have several staff members, individuals using a microcomputer-based DBMS perform this task by themselves.

A DBA in any environment has several important roles. These include maintaining a data dictionary, a transaction log, configuration control, security, and proper backup of the data base. Let's examine each of these areas.

Data Dictionary

The **data dictionary** contains the meaning of each piece of datum found in the data base; it includes data names, type of data, and field size, and describes any interrelationships between this piece of datum with other data items. Because a data base can be used by multiple users, it is important to keep data names unique within an application. Many DBMS systems now combine the DDL with an active data dictionary. In this type of DBMS, the DBMS uses the dictionary as a reference tool. When a data item is requested, the DBMS automatically refers to the data dictionary to determine the location of the requested data.

Transaction Log

A **transaction log** contains a complete audit trail of all activity of a data base for a given period of time. This log aids in the backup process if any data are destroyed; the log has a record of all changes that can be used to re-create or restore the data base to its original condition before it was damaged or erased. The transaction log also provides the means to track any illegal accesses to the data base by unauthorized individuals. The transaction log keeps track of not only what was done to the data base but also who performed the action. Not all DBMS packages for microcomputers have transaction-logging abilities. dBASE III Plus does have a HISTORY command, however, which allows you to record instructions that are entered from the keyboard. Mainframe- or minicomputer-based DBMSs automatically dump information from the transaction log to a tape or disk file.

Configuration Control

Configuration control allows only the DBA to make changes to the schema of a data base. Because many different users can access a data base, it is important that fields cannot be summarily added or deleted by one user without agreement on the part of other users who must also access this particular data base.

In this context of configuration control, the DBA also works with users to determine what types of edit controls should be placed on any new field. This means that the DBMS can be told what type of data is expected in a particular field and can perform some elementary validity checks to ensure that the appropriate data type or values have been entered into the field.

Security

The **security** aspect of a data base relates to which individuals should have access to which fields of data and the type of access rights that each user should have. Thus, individuals might be classified as having no access to a field/file, read-only access privileges, or read-and-write privileges.

This security concern also relates to measures that are taken to provide for the most efficient recovery if a disaster strikes the organization and the information in the data base is lost. Many of these concerns are discussed in a later chapter dealing with internal control.

Backup and Recovery

One very important concern of a DBA is to ensure that proper backup of the data base is performed. **Backup** refers to the copies made of the data base and to all changes that have been made to it. Then if something happens to the data base that seriously damages or destroys the data in it, the data base can be reconstructed (**recovered**) using the backup. The transaction log, of course, plays an important role in recording any changes and transactions that have occurred to the data base. The backup copy of a data base can be saved to a removable disk device, tape, or, when the file is small, a diskette medium.

Data Base Organization Methods

The way a data base is organized determines how fast data can be retrieved and how complex your interaction with the data base can be. It is important for you to know how the organization method affects the amount of time the system needs to process data. Some methods are much slower than others because they require large portions of a file to be read before a record is located. Some of the more common data base organization methods are discussed below.

Figure 12.9
List structure keeping track
of unpaid invoices for a single
customer.

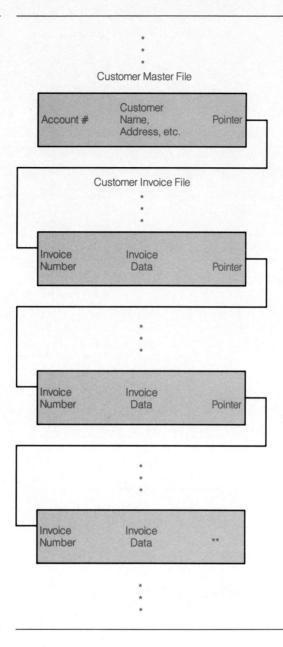

List Structures

One organization method, called a **list structure**, links records together
through the use of pointers. A **pointer** is a data item in a record that identifies
the storage location of another record that is logically related. Records in a
customer master file, for example, contain the names and addresses of every
customer, and every record in this file has an identifying account number.
During an accounting period, a customer may buy a number of items on credit
on different days, and the company wants to maintain an invoice file of such
transactions. A list structure can be used to show unpaid invoices at any given
time. Every record in the customer file contains a field that points to the record
location of the first invoice for that customer in the invoice file (Figure 12.9).
The first invoice record is linked to all later invoices for the customer. The last
invoice in the chain is identified by a special character.

Figure 12.10
Hierarchical (tree) structure.

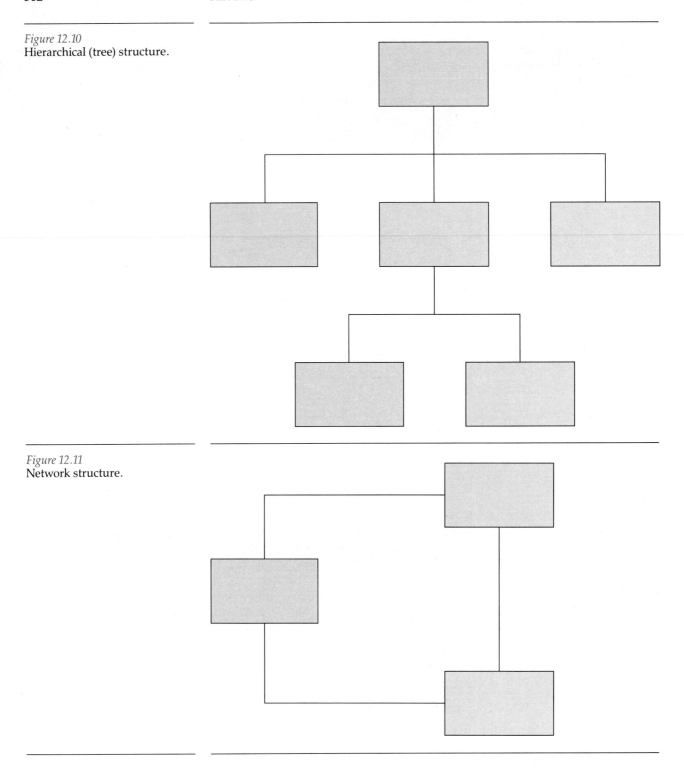

Figure 12.11
Network structure.

Hierarchical (Tree) Structures

Another organization method, called a **hierarchical (tree) structure**, arranges units of data in levels that graphically resemble an upside-down tree, with the root at the top and branches below. A hierarchical (tree) structure reflects a superior–subordinate (owner–owned) relationship. Below the single-root data component are subordinate elements called **nodes**, each of which in turn owns one or more other elements, or none. Each element (or branch) in this

Figure 12.12
Relational structure linking college courses with professors, locations, and other data categories.

Course/Instructor Relation	
Course	Instructor
English 110	Meyer
Math 107	Garner
Spanish 115	Fiero
*	*
*	*
*	*

Course/Location Relation	
Course	Location
English 110	Stevenson 101
Math 107	Schroeder 223
Spanish 115	Stevenson 323
*	*
*	*
*	*

Other Relations
For example, course related to time of meeting, days of meeting, or hours of credit.

structure has a single superior (Figure 12.10): The equal branches in a tree structure are not connected to each other.

Network Structures

A third data base organization method, called a **network structure**, differs from the tree in permitting the connection of the nodes multidirectionally (see Figure 12.11). In this system, each node may have several owners and may own any number of other data units. This data management software enables the extraction of information to begin at any record in a file.

Relational Structures

Another data base organization method, a **relational structure**, consists of one or more tables on which data are stored in the form of relations. For example, relation tables can be used to link a college course with its instructor and the location of the class (see Figure 12.12). To find the name of the instructor and the location of an English class, you order a search of the course/instructor relation (which produces the name *Meyer*) and the course/location relation (which produces the class location, Stevenson 101). Many other relations are, of course, possible. Relational structures are a relatively new and very popular data base structure for microcomputer packages.

Indexing

An index enables you to keep track of the various relations in a relational data base environment and to access any record in a file quickly and easily; without it, the relational form of data base organization would not be possible. Thus

Figure 12.13
Customer address file,
indexed in state order.

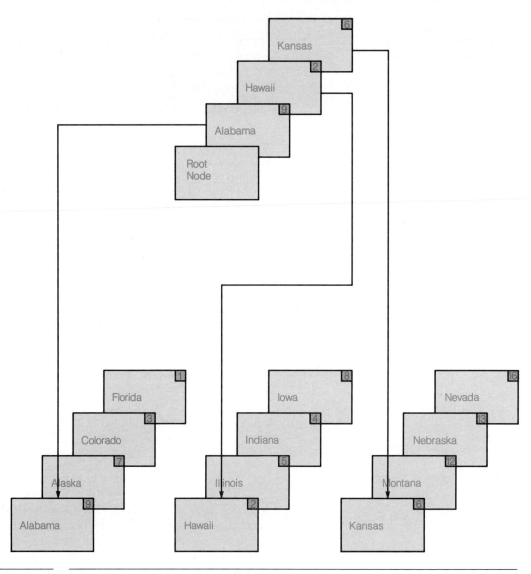

Figure 12.13
Customer address file, indexed in state order.

any relational data base package must use an index for direct access to records.

The **index** contains one or more key fields for ordering a file. When you use an index, the physical record remains in the same physical position in the file, but the key of each record (along with its record number) is placed in the index, producing a file that has been logically reordered by one or more key fields.

The index has a treelike structure. Once a branch in the tree is chosen, you never have to go backward: Only the subbranches of the chosen branch need to be considered.

In an index, information is held sequentially and in multiple data levels. Figure 12.13, for example, illustrates two levels, each of which divides its portion of the data into smaller parts at junctions or branching points called **nodes**. The top level is the **root node**, at which every search for a particular record key starts. The root node in Figure 12.13 has three keys: Alabama, Hawaii, and Kansas. All alphabetic entries from Alabama to Hawaii are pointed to by the lower-left node; all those from Hawaii to Kansas are in the middle node; and all those from Kansas on are in the lower-right node.

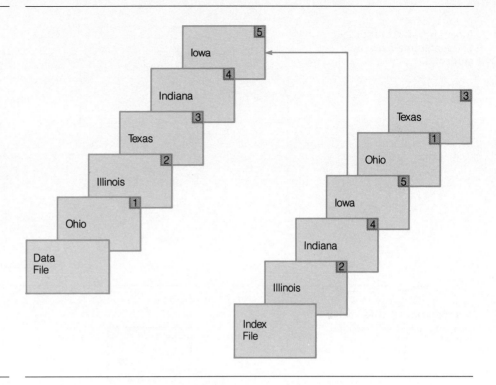

Figure 12.14
Process dBASE follows in accessing an address found by indexing from a hard disk.

Suppose the indexing program is required to find the record for Indiana. The program first looks at the root node; and since Indiana is between Hawaii and Kansas alphabetically, the program examines only the middle node. Because the tree in this case has two levels, Indiana is found in the next node examined.

The index merely contains the location of the desired record(s) in the data base file. After finding the address of the appropriate record, the data base management software can access it from a hard disk in about two to three seconds. Figure 12.14 illustrates this point.

Accessing a relational data base record requires two steps. First, the index must be searched to find the location of the desired record in the file. Second, the desired record must be accessed in the file.

It is the subdivision of indexes that produces the ability to run through a file rapidly. Fast access to every key depends on the index tree's being in balance. As keys are added, the index grows and the nodes fill. When a node gets full, the data base management software splits it, creating two half-full nodes that can now accommodate additional records.

Indexing has the distinct advantage of being able to maintain data in several orders at the same time. Information about clients or customers can also be ordered simultaneously by last name, Social Security number, city, and state. Indexes can be used, therefore, to cross-reference a data file, giving a relational data base tremendous accessing power.

Suppose, for example, that you have to find out the classes in which Sam Thomas was enrolled at a college. Student information is in one file and class information is in another; each of these files has an index file. The program first looks at the student file, checking through the student index by name (see Figure 12.15). This leads (through several index levels not shown) to the index entry containing Sam Thomas's name and student ID (4417). The data base

Figure 12.15
Index entries of the student
file, containing name and
student ID.

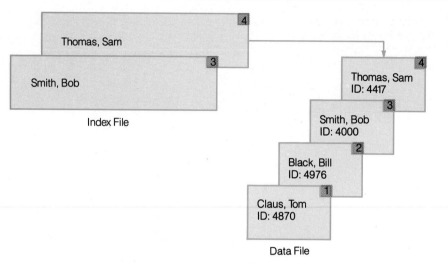

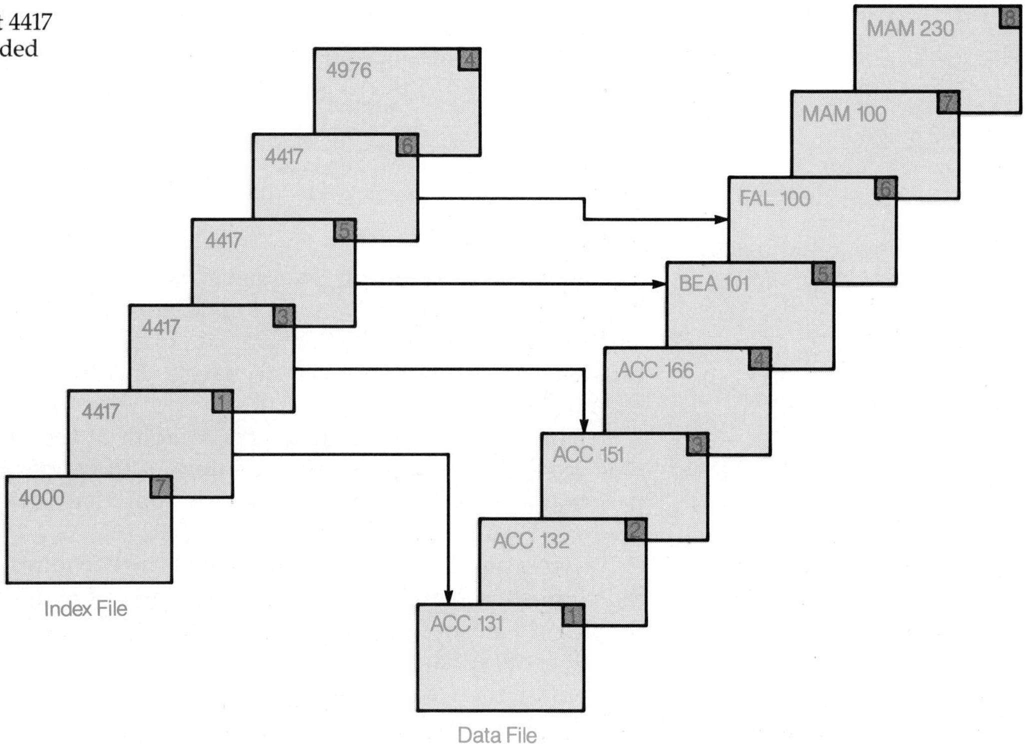

Figure 12.16
Index entries for student 4417
pointing to classes attended
records.

program now switches to the class file indexed by student ID (see Figure 12.16), searching for the first occurrence of 4417. This process points to record 1. The program is satisfied that no other classes for this individual exist, since the class index file is ordered in such a way that all 4417 class entries occur together in the class index file.

Because of its ability to index, the microcomputer is adequate for many data base needs. The advantage of indexing is that altering or retrieving information in the data base no longer entails sitting through a lengthy sort program; queries to the data base are answered quickly.

Sequential (Traditional) File Data
Processing Versus Relational Data Base

Relational file organization is much more efficient than sequential (traditional) file organization and greatly improves computer performance. Users do not have to wait repeatedly for time-consuming file sorts to be performed, access to data is much quicker, and adding records to existing files is also quicker.

The following table illustrates some of the differences between sequential (traditional) file organization and relational data base techniques.

	Sequential File Processing	Data Base (one index)
Building a file	Append newer record(s) after older records and sort when finished.	Append newer records after older records and update index.
Preparing for processing	Place records physically in ascending or descending order according to the contents of one or more fields.	Leave records in original order but generate an index of required key fields that point to the corresponding record on disk.
Accessing a record	Perform a sequential or binary search.	Use index to find location of record and go to that location on disk.
Adding a record	Append record and re-sort entire file	Append record and update index.
Obtaining a different file order	Re-sort the file.	Use another index or generate a new index.

Building a Data Base

The **data base** holds information that is related to a specific application. In this context, the term is considered to be synonymous with *file*. This is especially true when dealing with dBASE.

A **record** relates to the entity that contains information about a specific business transaction in the data base. There are usually records in a data base.

A **field** holds information about one part of a transaction. For example, the LASTNAME field holds information about the last name of the individual who created the transaction. A record contains one or more fields.

Information from one or more fields is used to form a *key*, which is used to identify the records in a file. The record key makes the process of retrieving records from a file easier, and it plays an important part in the ordering of a file. Often the records in a file are placed in key order.

Commonly, several keys are used in a file. The primary key is the unique identifier for a particular record. The primary key in a dBASE data base is the physical record number. If a record occupies the fifth record location, it has the record number 5, which is the primary key for that record.

Data in a file are usually arranged in some order that is based on the contents of one or more fields; this order is known as the **secondary key**. For example, a file might be arranged in order by Social Security field or by name. You are not usually limited in the number of keys that you can develop for an application.

The following entries of a customer address data base file further illustrate these definitions:

Alfred A. Conant
2645 W. Hartford
Moosejaw, IL 61703
(309)367-8934

The preceding four lines constitute one record of the customer address data base file: Each line contains one or more fields of information about a customer in the data base. One important difference between human data base managers and computer data base management systems is that humans can easily differentiate the various fields of information, almost intuitively, whereas a computer has to have the information described in minute detail. For example, when arranging a series of records by customers' last names, a human being easily detects where the first-name and middle-initial parts of a name end and the last-name part of a name begins, but a computer must have detailed instructions.

Nor is a computer capable of telling the address line from the telephone line without help from the human being who sets up the data base. The fundamental difference between a human data manager and a computer is that the computer can't detect differences in data that are based on context. It is therefore necessary to structure a data base in a rigid enough way that the computer does not err when it tries to access and process a data base record.

What is this process of describing the data base to the computer? First, you must decide exactly what data should be stored; and to do this, you have to break the data down into meaningful units of information. For example, in the customer address data base, the following fields (schema) are needed for each record:

```
FIRST NAME
MIDDLE INITIAL
LAST NAME
ADDRESS
CITY
STATE
ZIP
PHONE
```

Thus it is desirable that every data base record be capable of holding all of these fields. Notice that there are eight fields of data for each record; the fact that there are only four lines of information does not mean that there are only four fields of data per record. If only one field is assigned per line, problems can surface later. For example, if you want the records to be ordered by last name, it would be extremely difficult for a computer to arrange records in last name order if you were working with whole-line fields. With the above arrangement, however, it is easy because every logical piece of data is also a complete and unique field of data on the record.

Learning to define the various meaningful items of information in a record is an important aspect of data base management. Given the proper data base structure, the information can be arranged or sorted by last name; and the data base can be searched for individuals in a given last-name range because the last-name field is isolated from the first-name and middle-initial fields. It therefore becomes a meaningful piece of data with which the computer can work.

In the example above, the computer is instructed that there are eight fields. The first field is FIRSTNAME, the second is MIDDLE INITIAL, the third is LASTNAME, and so on. If Chicago, Il 60603 is stored in the FIRSTNAME field, the computer will not object; it will store Chicago, Il 60603 as the first name and proceed from there. The user, therefore, must put the correct data in the appropriate field if the data are to be accessible.

The **structure** of the data base determines the manner in which the various pieces of information are arranged for each record, the type of characters (numeric or alphanumeric) that are used to store each field, and the number of characters that are required by each field.

Once the data base has been structured, it can be managed. This involves issuing instructions directing the computer to perform actions that include adding new records, changing existing records, sorting and arranging records into a new order for the user's convenience, searching the data base for specific types of records, printing data, and deleting data.

Certain operations are obviously desirable: From time to time, customers are added to the data base, it may occasionally be necessary to sort the records into some higher order (for example, alphabetically by last name within a city), or it may sometimes be advantageous to find all those records that meet certain criteria (for example, all records of customers who live in Peoria and have a 61603 zip code). Thus a provision must be included for updating old records when a customer moves or for deleting records of customers who die or move out of state.

The choice of field(s) to use as a key for a record depends on what type of processing you want to accomplish. If you want a report based on customers' names, you will probably want a key that combines the last and first names. If you want a report based on the customer's location, you will want a key that contains the last and first names and the city.

The concept of the computerized data base assigns to the computer the work of finding, replacing, and printing reports about specific types of records. It remains the responsibility of the user, however, to make certain that the information in the computer has been stored accurately.

Chapter Review

The traditional approach to information processing requires that each application have its own set of master and transaction files. This arrangement leads to such problems as data redundancy, lack of data integrity, program and data dependency, and lack of flexibility. A data base management system (DBMS) is a set of software that resides between a user and the data stored in a data base. The view of the data stored in the data base (logical view) is translated by the DBMS software so that it can easily retrieve the data from the data base (the physical view). A DBMS has four basic parts: the query language, a report generator, a data-definition language, and a data-manipulation language.

A data base administrator (DBA) is the individual within an organization who is responsible for the day-to-day planning and control of the data base. It is the DBA who is responsible for maintaining a data dictionary and transaction log. It is also the DBA, along with members of the staff, who ensure that the integrity of data stored in the data base is maintained. Data integrity is maintained by keeping out unauthorized users. This person is also responsible for allowing for proper backup and control of the data base.

A number of organizational methods are used to arrange data in a data base, including list structures, hierarchical (tree) structures, network structures, and relational structures. The relational structure has been favored by computer scientists because it is fairly easy to use. The indexing used by relational structures, however, proved difficult to implement properly until the microcomputer (with its independent power) was introduced.

The heart of the relational organization method is the index, which uses a treelike structure for holding record keys. The index allows you to access a record directly; it contains the field from each record indexed, along with the record's location on disk. The index is split into branches, and data are kept in sequence within a node of each branch. As a result, only a small portion of the index has to be searched to find the location of any record.

One of the greatest benefits of a relational data base is that a general understanding of how indexes work is all you need to know before using the index feature.

The index also enables you to use pieces of data to link one or more files together for processing. For instance, you may have to look up a record to get a piece of information that in turn enables you to access a record directly from a second file.

The term *data base* is usually taken to be synonymous with *file* when microcomputers are involved in processing data. A data base consists of records that hold information about some type of business entity or transaction. Each record is composed of pieces of data, called fields, that relate to the transaction.

When you are designing the format of the file to hold data, you must design it to handle future processing needs. This may mean separating name fields into `lastname`, `firstname`, and `middle initial` fields so that the computer can arrange the information in alphabetical order by last name.

Key Terms and Concepts

backup and recovery
configuration control
data base
data base administrator (DBA)
data base management system
  (DBMS)
data-definition language (DDL)
data dictionary
data independence
data integrity
data-manipulation language (DML)
data redundancy
data security
field
flexibility
hierarchical (tree) structure
index
integrated (DBMS)

list structure
logical view
network structure
nodes
physical view
pointer
program and data dependency
query language
record
relational structure
report generator
root node
schema
secondary key
structure
subschema
traditional approach
transaction log

Chapter Quiz

Multiple Choice

1. In which of the following data base organizations is a node owned by several higher nodes?
   a. Relational
   b. Hierarchical

   c. Network
   d. List structures
   e. None of the above

2. Which data storage entity is used to store information about a transaction?
   a. File
   b. Record
   c. Element
   d. Field
   e. None of the above

3. Which of the data base organizations makes use of tables to arrange data for access logically?
   a. Relational
   b. Hierarchical
   c. Network
   d. List structure
   e. None of the above

4. Which of the following statements about index structures is false?
   a. An index contains a number of branches.
   b. The field being indexed and the address on disk are stored for each record.
   c. Once a search is started for a record in an index, it will probably require going through several branches to find the desired record.
   d. Branches must be in balance (contain about the same number of entries) for searches to be efficient.
   e. All of the above statements are true.

5. In which data base organizations can ordered data be viewed as a table?
   a. Relational
   b. Hierarchical
   c. Network
   d. List structure
   e. None of the above

True/False

6. In discussions about managing data bases on microcomputers, *data base* and *file* usually mean the same thing.

7. A properly designed record layout allows you easily to order the file in a number of different ways.

8. Managing a data base includes such tasks as creating reports, adding, deleting, and changing records.

9. The librarian controls access to the data base.

10. Even though data are not in the proper order in a relational data base, the index holds information that allows you to order the file logically.

Answers

1. c 2. b 3. a 4. c 5. a 6. t 7. t 8. t 9. f 10. t

Exercises

1. Define or describe each of the following:
   a. data base management system
   b. data base
   c. data base administrator
   d. data-definition language
   e. relational structure
   f. root node
   g. index

2. The _____ approach has a set of files for each information processing activity.

3. Two problems with the traditional approach are
   a.

   b.

4. The problem with the traditional approach that does not allow changes to be easily made to a file is called _____ dependence.

5. List the four parts of a DBMS.
   a.

   b.

   c.

   d.

6. How a user accesses data from the data base is called the _____ view, and how the data are stored in the data base is called the _____ view.

7. A _____ of a data base holds data about any accesses or changes that have been made to a data base.

8. _____ means that only a DBA can make changes to the schema of a data base.

9. The part of a data base called the _____ allows you to add fields or to create new files within the data base.

10. The _____ for a data base holds information about each piece of datum, such as data name, type of data, and field size, found in the data base and any interrelationships for this piece of datum.

11. In the _____ structure a node can be owned by a number of different nodes.

12. In the _____ structure a node can be owned by only one superior node.

13. The _____ structure uses tables to organize the records in the file logically.

14. Creating a new relation involves simply creating a new _____.

15. The top node of an index is called the _____.

16. The index contains which two pieces of information about each record in an indexed file?
   a.

   b.

17. Data in an index are stored _____.

18. The field that identifies a record is called a(n) _____.

19. The maximum number of records allowed in a dBASE III Plus file is _____.

20. The terms *file* and _____ are really the same when used in the context of microcomputers.

21. The _____ is used to record information about a transaction.

22. A(n) _____ holds one piece of information contained in a record.

23. In designing a record, it is important that the _____ organize the fields properly for later processing.

24. The process of creating reports, adding records, deleting records, and changing records is called _____ the data base.

25. The _____ has a superior–subordinate relationship with data.

Chapter
13

Beginning Data Base
Management with
dBASE III Plus

Chapter Objectives

After completing this chapter, you should be able to:

Discuss the parts of a dBASE III Plus screen

Discuss how to issue commands to dBASE III Plus

Discuss how to create dBASE III Plus files

Discuss how to add and edit data

Discuss some elementary dBASE III Plus commands

Discuss the limitations of dBASE III Plus

Discuss the dBASE III Plus Assist feature

Discuss dBASE III Plus menu options

This chapter introduces you to **dBASE III Plus**. It also introduces you to the **menu-driven** (default) and **command-driven modes** of dBASE III Plus and to the `CREATE`, `USE`, `APPEND`, `HELP`, and `EDIT` commands. A disadvantage of the menu-driven mode for an experienced user is the amount of time that it takes to display menus and receive or execute instructions: Several menus may be displayed before one action can be accomplished, and control may have to be returned to previous menus before the next. However, menu-driven programs are useful for users without programming experience and when internal control is an important aspect of an application. Thus the Assistant menu mode is emphasized in this and the following chapters, although after you know the commands, you may prefer the command mode.

Introduction to dBASE III Plus

The dBASE package is the best-selling relational data base package on the market. The current version of dBASE (dBASE III Plus) evolved from dBASE II. Ashton-Tate originally developed dBASE II for 8-bit microcomputers that used the CP/M operating system. When IBM introduced the IBM PC, Ashton-Tate revised dBASE to run on the PC/MS DOS operating systems.

When Ashton-Tate first thought of developing dBASE II, it was envisioned as being a software package for the rather narrow market of systems developers rather than for the general public. The dBASE II developers, therefore, assumed that users would have certain programming and systems development skills not usually found in the general public. This resulted in a package that was not user friendly.

This lack of a user friendly interface was a problem when the package became tremendously popular and began to sell to users who were unskilled in programming. To overcome this total lack of user friendliness and to take advantage of the power of the IBM's 16-bit microprocessor, Ashton-Tate introduced the dBASE III package in 1984. This new dBASE III package had an ASSIST feature that provided a low-level user interface and the capacity for many more fields per record.

However, users demanded an even friendlier program with even more power. Ashton-Tate responded by introducing dBASE III Plus in the latter part of 1985. This version has the ability to network and a full-featured user interface. The new interface operates by menu selections and thereby avoids making the user enter instructions from a **dot prompt**. This means that a user can concentrate on solving a problem rather than spending time learning dBASE language rules.

Limitations of dBASE III Plus

Anyone who wants to use the full version of dBASE III Plus should be aware of the following limitations that the package places on an application: (1) The package requires an IBM PC or compatible 16-bit computer with a minimum of 256K of memory (more memory is faster); (2) the system should have either two 360K diskette drives or a hard disk and one diskette drive; (3) a limit of one billion records is placed on any file; (4) the maximum record size is 4,000 characters and 128 fields; (5) a character field can have a maximum length of 254 positions; (6) a numeric field is limited to 15 positions; (7) a memo field is limited to 4,096 positions; (8) no more than ten data base files can be open at one time; and (9) only seven indexes can be specified as active for a file at one time. Most applications are not affected by these limitations.

The version of dBASE III Plus covered in this and the following chapters is the student demonstration version. The only difference between the full version and the student version is that the student version limits file size to 31 records.

Modes of dBASE III Plus

The dBASE III Plus package provides you with three different modes. The first, Assistant mode, provides an easy to use menu-driven interface that enables you to issue commands without an in-depth understanding of dBASE. The second, Command mode, requires some understanding of dBASE because instructions are entered at the dot prompt (.) and does not display help menus for most commands. The third, Program mode (also referred to as batch mode), enables you to store instructions in a program file and execute all of them by issuing one command.

Starting dBASE III Plus

The manner in which you start dBASE III Plus depends on whether you are using a diskette or hard disk microcomputer.

Diskette Systems. To start dBASE III Plus on a diskette system requires you to boot the computer with the DOS system disk and then enter the date and time if you want to have this information in the directory of any files that you create.

   You no doubt realize that when you use a diskette system, you usually place your program diskette in drive A and the diskette that is to hold your data files in drive B. To get dBASE III Plus to execute requires entering the command DBASE at the A> DOS prompt.

   Once the necessary files contained in the first diskette are loaded, you are prompted to insert the second disk in the drive and press the ENTER key.

Hard Disk Systems. To start dBASE III Plus on a hard disk system requires that after turning on the system you tell DOS to activate the directory in which your dBASE III Plus program files reside. This is accomplished by using the Change Directory (CD) DOS command. If, for instance, your dBASE III Plus directory is named DB3PLUS, enter the command CD \DB3PLUS. After you have activated the directory, you can start dBASE by entering the command DBASE at the DOS prompt.

The Assistant Menu Screen

Once you issue the DBASE command to start dBASE III Plus, the copyright screen (see Figure 13.1) is displayed on your monitor. The copyright screen contains such information as the individual who purchased the package, the company at which this person works, the serial number of the package, and conditions of the copyright agreement. This screen disappears after a few seconds or when you press the ENTER key. At that time the Assistant menu is displayed (see Figure 13.2).

   Whether you start dBASE from a hard disk or a diskette, the Assistant menu screen will be virtually identical. The Assistant menu provides, across the top of the screen, a number of options from which you can select. You select an option by either positioning the pointer (via the arrow keys) or entering the first character of the command. As you make selections, the pull-down menus change. For instance, the menu displayed when the Position option is

Figure 13.1
Copyright screen of dBASE
III Plus.

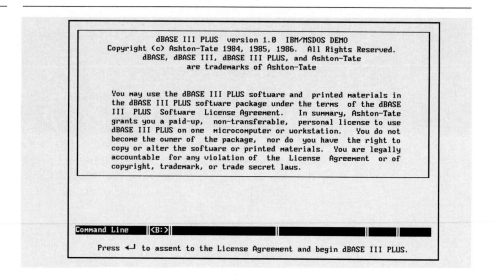

Figure 13.2
The dBASE III Plus screen
with the Assistant menu
activated.

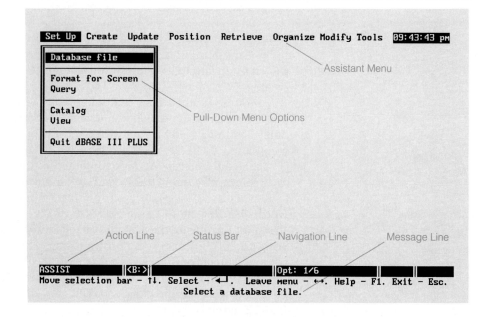

selected (see Figure 13.3) is different from the Set Up menu that is automatically displayed by the Assistant (see Figure 13.2). Every option in the menu bar has its own pull-down menu with its own set of options (see Figure 13.4). And a pull-down menu may have a submenu with options.

Other components of the Assistant menu—the action line, status bar, navigation line, and message line—are discussed below.

Action Line. The **action line** is the line above the bar near the bottom of the screen. It displays the command being generated by your menu or submenu selection.

Status Bar. The **status bar** is in reverse video near the bottom of your screen. The status bar displays information about the current status of dBASE III Plus; for instance, the current drive, the file (if any) in use, the current record number or the option from the menu or submenu in use, whether the Ins or

Figure 13.3

Assistant screen after the Position option has been selected.

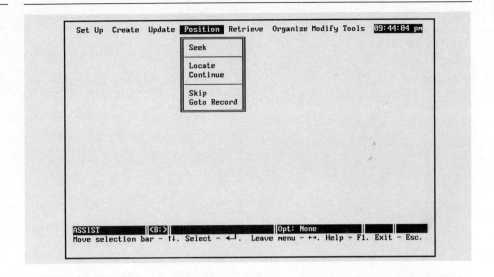

Figure 13.4

Various menus available from the Assistant menu.

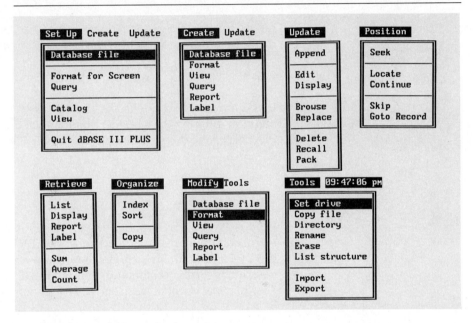

Del option is in use (during the edit process), and the status of the Caps Lock key (CAPS if the Caps Lock key is on).

Navigation Line. The **navigation line** appears just beneath the status bar and provides instructions for moving from one menu option to another or for moving from one submenu to another.

Message Line. The **message line** is beneath the navigation line and displays an explanation of the current menu option along with any action you are to take.

Leaving the Assistant Menu. If you make a mistake on a menu selection, you can back up one level by pressing the Esc key. If you are at the menu line, however, upon pressing the Esc key you leave the Assistant menu and drop to the so-called dot prompt mode. In dot prompt mode, no menus are displayed;

Figure 13.5
The Help screen for the
CREATE command.

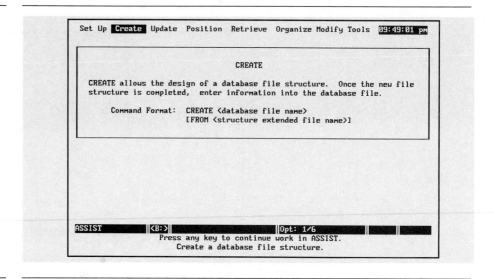

rather, the dot prompt (.) appears on the action line. The status bar and the message line are also visible. The message line contains the prompt:

`Enter a dBASE III PLUS command.`

If you have pressed the Esc key by mistake, you can get back to the Assistant menu by entering the ASSIST **command** at the dot prompt and then pressing the ENTER key. The Assistant menu (see Figure 13.2) is redisplayed on the screen.

The Help Facility

Help is available by highlighting any item in the Assistant menu or any submenu and then pressing the F1 function key. For instance, if you want help on the CREATE command, press the F1 key while that option is highlighted; a description of that command (see Figure 13.5) is displayed on your screen. Another way to obtain assistance is by responding Y to the prompt:

`Do you want some help? (Y/N)`

This prompt appears when you commit an error in entering a command at the dot prompt. Once you respond Y the Help Main menu (see Figure 13.6) is displayed on your screen.

If you want information about a dBASE command, all you have to do is enter the HELP **command** at the dot prompt and press the ENTER key. The Help Main Menu appears on your screen. Select option 1, Getting Started, and enter the command about which you want additional information. For example, if you want information about the REPORT command, enter REPORT in the message line, and after you press the ENTER key, information about that command is displayed on your screen (see Figure 13.7).

Note that when you are in Help mode, the navigation line contains prompts about how to move from one screen to the next by pressing the PgUp or PgDn keys. It also instructs you to move to the previous menu by depressing the F10 key or to exit to the dot prompt by pressing the Esc key. If you want information about any other dBASE command, simply enter that command in the message line.

Figure 13.6
The Help Main Menu for the
REPORT command.

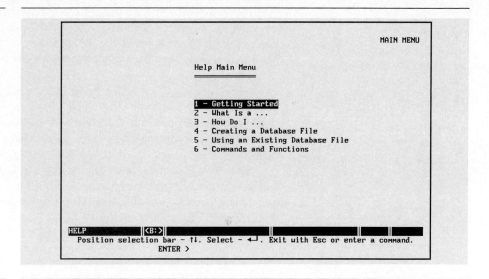

Figure 13.7
The Help screen generated
for the REPORT command.

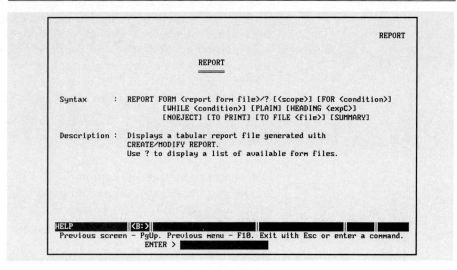

You can save yourself one step by entering the HELP command and then the command about which you want the information. To get the immediate information about the REPORT command, enter the following command at the dot prompt:

.HELP REPORT

Once the command is entered, the appropriate screen of information (see Figure 13.7) is displayed on your monitor.

Leaving dBASE III Plus

When you have finished a dBASE III Plus session, you must remember to use the QUIT **command**, which closes any files that might still be open. If a file has had records added to it and is not closed properly, the end of the file marker will be misplaced and records may be lost. To execute QUIT, you must move the Assistant pointer to the SET UP command and, once the Set Up menu is displayed, move the pointer bar to the Quit dBASE III PLUS selection and press the ENTER key.

If you wish to enter the QUIT command from the dot prompt, simply press the Esc key once or twice to receive the dot prompt on the action line and then type QUIT and press the ENTER key. No matter which method you choose, a message and the DOS prompt appear on your screen.

Communicating with dBASE III Plus

At the computer, start the dBASE III Plus program by the methods detailed earlier in this chapter. You will then see the Assistant menu, which provides you with a list of alternatives and is an excellent tool for learning how to use dBASE.

The dBASE package also enables you to enter the command mode once you have mastered how commands are built by observing them on the action line. This is accomplished by pressing the Esc key once or twice, which gives the dot prompt on the action line:

.

The period (.) is the dBASE III Plus command mode prompt. This means that dBASE is now waiting for you to enter a command. Remember to press the ENTER key after each command to tell dBASE to execute your instruction.

In its command-driven mode, dBASE III Plus requires that you state the task you want to perform in a language that dBASE can understand. For example, suppose that you want to use the CUSTOMER file to list those who live in the state of Hawaii. This would require the following commands:

```
USE CUSTOMER
LIST FOR STATE = "Hawaii"
```

Before you can effectively communicate with dBASE III Plus in the command mode, you must learn some grammatical rules for constructing sentences in accordance with the syntax of dBASE's language. The parts of a dBASE sentence are

```
COMMAND   SCOPE   NOUN   CONDITION
```

The command portion of the sentence tells dBASE III Plus exactly what action to perform. Common commands include LIST, USE, DISPLAY, and REPORT. The *scope* portion of the sentence limits the range of the command, determining whether all or only a small part of the file is to be processed by the command. The noun is the object—a file, a field, or a variable—on which the command acts. The condition portion specifies the fields or files to be acted upon. A dBASE III Plus command need not have all four parts; it may consist of the command part alone.

The advantage of using the Assistant menu is that you do not have to concern yourself with the parts of a command. This menu-driven mode automatically constructs the commands on the action line and then executes them for you. This ability of dBASE to build instructions and then execute them frees novices from the tedium of learning the dBASE language syntax and enables them to concentrate on solving problems.

 ### Setting the Default Drive

Unless told otherwise the dBASE program automatically assumes that data files are on the same disk as the dBASE III Plus program files. If you are using a diskette-based system, however, you will not want to record your data files

Figure 13.8
The Tools option used to set the default drive to B and the dBASE command on the action line that has been generated by the menu selections.

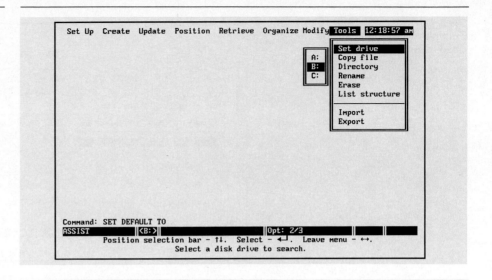

on the limited disk space of the dBASE system disk. To record data files on a different disk, you select the Tools option from the Assistant menu and then press the ENTER key to obtain the Set-drive entry of this submenu (note that the action line contains the entry (SET DEFAULT TO). Next, move the bar that indicates the next submenu to B: (see Figure 13.8) and press the ENTER key. Henceforth, commands entered without a drive specifier will operate on the assumption that the file resides in drive B.

Full-Screen Cursor Menus

The full-screen feature of dBASE enables you to move the cursor to various formatted locations on the screen. The dBASE III Plus package also offers full-screen menus (see Figure 13.9) that contain directions on how to use the cursor. This facility can be turned off by using the SET MENU ON/OFF command at the dot prompt. The ON displays the menus when dBASE goes into full-screen mode. The OFF results in no menus being displayed.

Creating a dBASE III Plus File

Before a file can be used by dBASE III Plus, you must provide some specific information about the file (its name) and the data fields (name, data type, and length), using the following rules:

1. A file name can contain a maximum of eight characters. Do not give the file an extension because the dBASE III Plus package automatically places a .DBF extension on all data base files.

2. A field name consists of a maximum of ten characters. Acceptable characters are the letters A through Z, the digits 0 through 9, and the underscore mark (_). The data to be stored in a field determine the type of the field: character string (C), numeric (N), logical (L), Memo (M), and Date (D).
   a. A *character string field* can hold any alphanumeric character (number, letter, or special character).
   b. A *numeric field* is restricted to numerals and the decimal point (.); the decimal point must be counted as part of the field length.
   c. A *logical field* will be marked Y (yes) or N (no) and is always only one position in length.

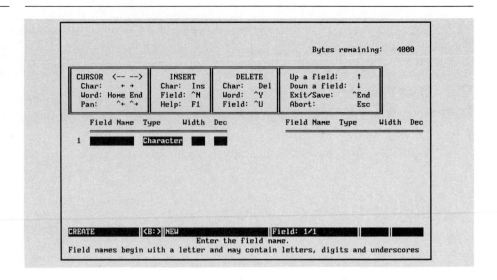

d. A *Memo field* can hold a maximum of 4096 characters and is therefore ideal for containing large amounts of text data.

e. A *Date field* contains eight positions and automatically has the slashes (/) in their correct locations; an empty Date field appears as __/__/__.

Once again, let's review the CUSTOMER data base application. The following ten data items will be used to compose a data record for each customer:

First Name
Middle Initial
Last Name
Address
City
State
Zip
Phone
Amount Owed
Payment Date

After deciding which pieces of information to store, you must decide the type of data to be stored in each field and how long each field should be. Character data will be used for all fields except for the amount owed and payment date fields. Why would you want to use character data for the zip field when a zip code is comprised of numeric digits? Zip codes are easier to store as character data for two reasons. First, a common rule of thumb is that data should be stored as character data unless they are to be used in calculations. Second, character data are easier to include in indexing.

The phone field is also character data because the area code appears between parentheses ( ) and a hyphen appears between the exchange and the number in that exchange. The only field that is numeric is the Amount Owed field. It will have two positions to the right of the decimal point. The Payment date will use the Date field data type. The breakdown of field names, data types, and field lengths is as follows:

Figure 13.10
Select the disk drive on which the file is to be created.

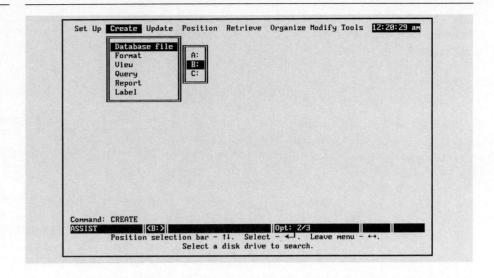

Field	Data Type	Field Length
FIRST	C	10
INIT	C	1
LAST	C	12
ADDRESS	C	25
CITY	C	15
STATE	C	2
ZIP	C	5
PHONE	C	13
AMOUNT	N	8,2
DATE	D	8

It is important not to use too many fields in a record or to define fields that are too large to hold the data. The size of the fields determines how much space they will take on disk. All fields are stored as described, and any unused field positions are filled with blanks. Thus, reserving too much room for a field wastes the disk storage space.

The `CREATE` **command** from the Assistant menu is used to build the template for a dBASE III Plus file. The Database File option from the `CREATE` command is then selected by pressing the ENTER key. dBASE now prompts you for the disk drive on which the file is to be created (see Figure 13.10) and then for the file name to be created (see Figure 13.11).

At this point, the cursor control menu is displayed at the top of the screen (see Figure 13.12). The status line contains important pieces of information: the name of the instruction being executed (`CREATE`), the name of the file (`CUS-TOMER`) and the disk on which it is to be recorded (`B:`), and the fact that the pointer is on field 1 of 1 (no others have been created). In the upper right-hand corner of the screen is the number of bytes that remain for this record.

You can now define each field to dBASE. A field name can be up to ten characters and must start with an alphabetic character. After you have entered the field name, press the ENTER key. (Field names always appear in uppercase characters regardless of the status of the Caps Lock key.) The data type is the next information to be entered, and the default is character. Thus, for any character field, simply press the ENTER key. Next, enter the width and press ENTER. The only time you are prompted for decimal positions is when the field has been defined as numeric.

Figure 13.11
Enter the file name of the file to be created.

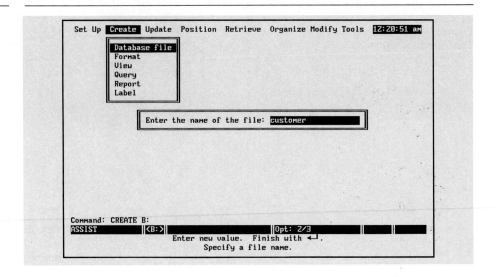

Figure 13.12
The Create screen that appears for a file to be created.

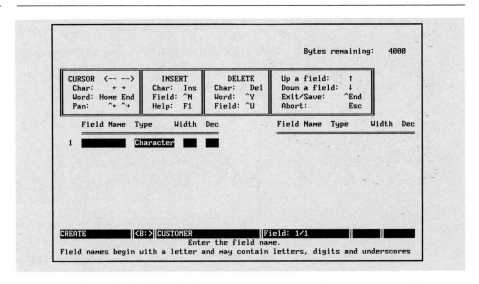

You are now ready to define the next field. When you enter the last payment date data type, the width is automatically assumed to be eight positions (Figure 13.13).

Correcting errors that you spot is a straightforward process: Use the cursor positioning keys on the key pad to move the cursor to the desired field and reenter the data.

When you have finished defining the fields in the record, press ENTER in response to the prompt for a field name, without entering any information. You then receive a prompt to review the file (see below). When you press the ENTER key again, the file definition is finished. Pressing any other key enables you to go back and make any needed changes.

```
Press ENTER to confirm. Any other key to resume. _
```

You now see the message `Please Wait....` as dBASE records this information to the disk. It then asks

```
Input data records now? (Y/N) _
```

Figure 13.13
The completed Create screen for the CUSTOMER.DBF file.

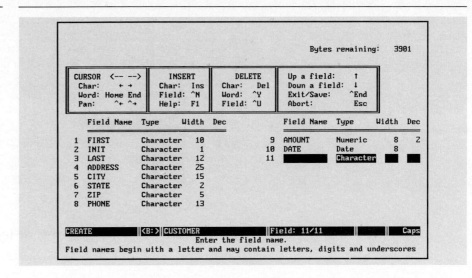

Type Y to enter the five records below:

```
                        Name and Address Data Base
--------------------------------------------------------------------------------

      Last        First    Init     Address               City          St  Zip
  Ghorbani      Reza       R.  4033 N. Wolcott          Chicago         Il  60712
                               (312)245-0324      125.00    01/17/88

  Ghorbani      Ann        B.  4033 N. Wolcott          Chicago         Il  60712
                               (312)245-0324      250.00    03/23/88

  Acklin        Douglas    C.  408 E. Monroe            Bloomington     Il  61701
                               (309)663-8976       55.00    04/01/88

  Walters       Barbara    A.  1981 Crestlawn           Arlington       Va  13411
                               (703)237-3727       75.00    12/23/88

  Adams         Arthur     V.  115 Ginger Creek Ct.     Bloomington     Il  61701
                               (309)828-7290       35.00    03/15/88
```

The dBASE III Plus package clears the screen and places a blank record form on the screen (see Figure 13.14). The full-screen cursor menu appears at the top of the screen, the status line with the name of the file and the current record number at the bottom of the screen, and each field name in the left-hand column. Fill in the appropriate blanks. Each field appears in reverse video to indicate the field length. When you have reached the end of a field, the computer's bell rings, and the cursor automatically advances to the next field. If you finish entering data before the end of the field is reached, simply press the ENTER key. When the last field is filled or the ENTER key is pressed, a new blank form for the next record is displayed (see Figure 13.15).

When you enter numeric information, dBASE III Plus automatically right-justifies the number in the field when you press ENTER. If the number does not have decimal positions, you do not have to enter a decimal point; dBASE will automatically place it appropriately.

When the form has been filled with the data for the first record, it should look like Figure 13.15.

As each record is entered, dBASE raises the record number in the status

Figure 13.14
Blank record form for the
CUSTOMER file.

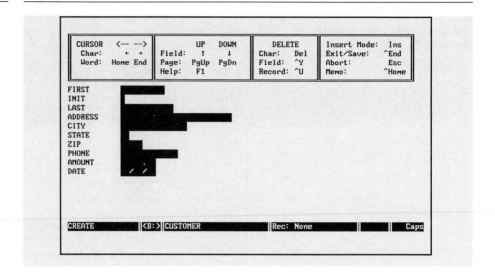

Figure 13.15
Filled-in form for the first
data record of the
CUSTOMER.DBF file.

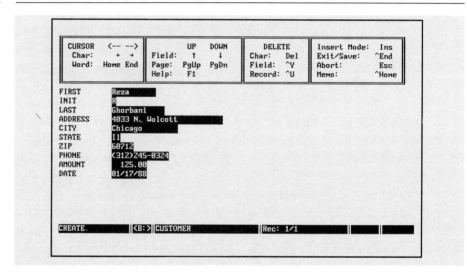

bar of the screen. When you have finished entering all five of the records, press ENTER when you are shown the first field of the next blank form. dBASE then assumes that you have finished entering data and returns you to the Assistant menu. You can now enter your next command. If you mistakenly press the ENTER key, select the Update command from the Assistant menu and press ENTER when the pointer is on the Append option. A new, blank form is now displayed on the screen.

Activating
the Data Base

You have now created the CUSTOMER data base file and recorded five records in it. If you are still in dBASE and have not activated any other files, all you have to do to add records to the CUSTOMER file is select the Update option from the Assistant menu and press ENTER when the Append option has been highlighted with the pointer.

If you quit dBASE and then later want to add records to the CUSTOMER file, you must reenter dBASE and perform the following steps:

1. Select the Tools option of the Assistant menu, select the Set Drive option, and set the default drive to B: (assuming you are using a data disk in disk drive B).

Figure 13.16
Specifying a data base file to be opened.

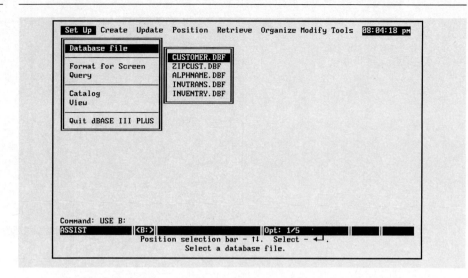

Figure 13.17
Specifying the data base file to open.

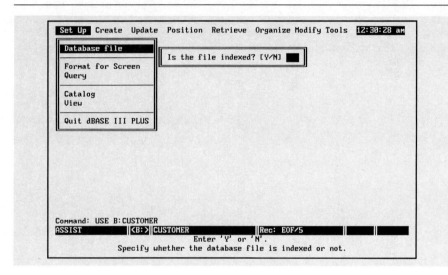

2. Select the Set Up option of the Assistant menu, specify the drive (press ENTER if step one has been performed), point to the file and press the ENTER key (see Figure 13.16), and respond N (in this case) to the prompt asking you whether or not the file is indexed (see Figure 13.17).

3. Select the Update option of the Assistant menu and press the ENTER key when the pointer has highlighted the Append option. A screen similar to that depicted in Figure 13.14 is displayed on your monitor. The only difference is that the status bar contains the command APPEND rather than CREATE.

Once the file has been activated, you can look at the organization of the file by invoking the Tools option of the Assistant menu and then selecting the List Structure option and entering N to the prompt Direct the output to the printer? (see Figure 13.18).

Once the LIST STRUCTURE command has executed, dBASE displays the message Press any key to continue work in ASSIST._ Press any key, and the Assistant menu appears on your monitor.

The dBASE package keeps track of the current number of records in the file and includes the .DBF extension in the file name. If you remembered to

Figure 13.18
Output of the LIST
STRUCTURE command for
the CUSTOMER.DBF data
base file.

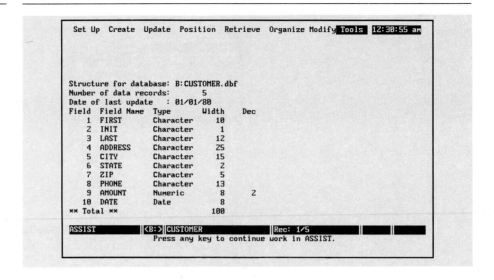

Figure 13.19
Assistant screen to implement the LIST command.

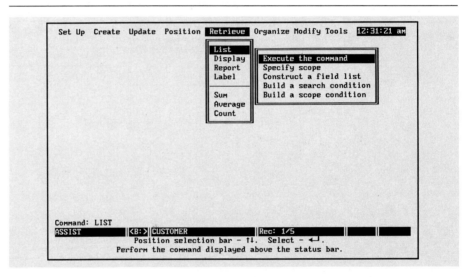

enter the date when you booted DOS, dBASE also keeps track of the date of
the last update; if you forgot to do so, the date will be 01/01/80. You can also
see the name, character type, and length of each field. The total bytes of
storage used by each record is at the bottom of the display.

The total number of bytes is one more than the sum of the individual
field sizes, to reserve a position for the delete indicator (*).

Now that you've looked at the structure of the data base, you should list
the contents of the file to guarantee that you haven't done anything wrong.
Select the Retrieve option of the Assistant menu, position the pointer to the
List option, and press ENTER; then position the pointer to the Execute the
command line (see Figure 13.19) and press ENTER.

Once the command has been executed, the prompt Direct the output to the printer? is displayed on the monitor. Simply press the EN-
TER key to have the records displayed (see Figure 13.20). The prompt Press
any key to continue work in ASSIST._ is now at the bottom of
the screen. Once a key is pressed, you are returned to the Assistant menu.

The LIST command starts at the beginning of your data file and lists
all records to the screen. For readability, dBASE lists the names of the fields

Figure 13.20
Output of the LIST
command.

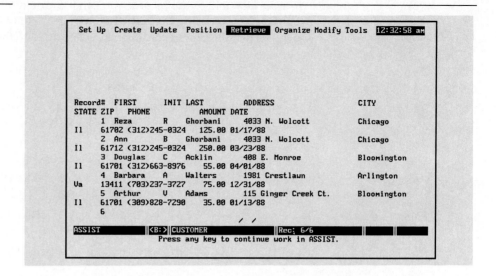

Figure 13.21
The Append screen.

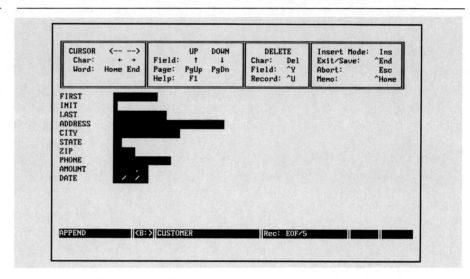

above the data, and it continues displaying records on the screen until the end of the file is reached. dBASE keeps track of where it is in a file by the use of a pointer, or record number, which is simply the file location of the current record being worked on by dBASE. The first record in a file is 1, the second is 2, and so forth.

Adding Records to the File

To add records to the data base file, select the UPDATE command from the Assistant menu, position the pointer to the APPEND **command**, press the ENTER key. Any records added to a file via the APPEND command are placed at the end of the existing file. When the APPEND command is executed, a number of actions are performed by dBASE: The screen is cleared and a blank record form is displayed, the record number in the status bar is updated for the new record, and a blank entry screen (see Figure 13.21) is displayed on your monitor.

You can now enter more records, as you did after the file was initially created. The next blank record screen is automatically displayed when the last field of this record is filled, or when the ENTER key is pressed with the cursor in the last field of the record. You can indicate to dBASE III Plus that you have finished by pressing ENTER when the first field of a blank form appears.

The following records can now be added to the existing CUSTOMER file:

Last	First	Init	Address	City	St Zip
Davis	Russell	B. 707 Vale St.		Bloomington	Il 61701
		(309)662-1759	35.00		02/27/88
Acklin	Debbie	C. 408 E. Monroe		Bloomington	Il 61701
		(309)827-1395	35.00		03/21/88
Posio	Harvey	B. 1013 Hillcrest		San Diego	Ca 94307
		(619)271-9871	1250.00		04/03/88
Pietrowiak	Ben	A. 3334 N. Foster		Normal	Il 61761
		(309)452-9126	20.00		03/23/88
Acklin	Sandy	C. 408 E. Monroe		Bloomington	Il 61701
		(309)829-9901	35.00		02/25/88
Ficek	Fred	R. 1215 Tamarack		Normal	Il 61761
		(309)454-7123	0.00		04/05/88
Decesario	Juan	C. 1214 Flores		Miami	Fl 12562
		(305)719-1363	10.00		04/01/88

When these records have been entered, you can list the file via the RE-TRIEVE and LIST commands to ensure that you did not forget to enter a record. Your file should look something like the following:

Record#	FIRST	INIT	LAST	ADDRESS	CITY
	STATE ZIP PHONE		AMOUNT DATE		
1	Reza	R	Ghorbani	4033 N. Wolcott	Chicago
	Il 60712 (312)245-0324		125.00 01/17/88		
2	Ann	B	Ghorbani	4033 N. Wolcott	Chicago
	Il 60712 (312)245-0324		250.00 03/23/88		
3	Douglas	C	Acklin	408 E. Monroe	Bloomington
	Il 61701 (309)663-8976		55.00 04/01/88		
4	Barbara	A	Walters	1981 Crestlawn	Arlington
	Va 13411 (703)237-3727		75.00 12/31/88		
5	Arthur	V	Adams	115 Ginger Creek Ct.	Bloomington
	Il 61701 (309)828-7290		35.00 03/13/88		
6	Russell	B	Davis	707 Vale St.	Bloomington
	Il 61701 (309)662-1759		35.00 02/27/88		
7	Debbie	C	Acklin	408 E. Monroe	Bloomington
	Il 61701 (309)827-1395		35.00 03/21/88		
8	Harvey	B	Posio	1013 Hillcrest	San Diego
	Ca 94307 (619)271-9871		1250.00 04/03/88		
9	Ben	A	Pietrowiak	3334 Foster	Normal
	Il 61761 (309)452-9126		20.00 03/23/88		
10	Sandy	C	Akclin	408 E. Monroe	Bloomington
	Il 61701 (309)829-9901		35.00 02/25/88		
11	Fred	R	Ficek	1215 Tamarack	Normal
	Il 61761 (309)454-7123		0.00 04/05/88		
12	Juan	C	Decesario	1214 Flores	Miami
	Fl 12562 (305)719-1363		10.00 04/01/88		

Figure 13.22
An edit screen for record 10 of
the CUSTOMER file.

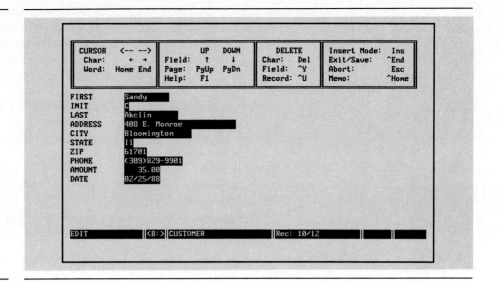

 Editing Records in the File

There should be twelve records in the file. Examine each record to make certain that there are no errors. Notice that in record 10 the last name is spelled incorrectly. This can be corrected via the EDIT **command**, which can be invoked from the Update option of the Assistant menu. Once the EDIT command has been invoked, a blank screen appears and the contents of the last record are displayed. You can now use the PgUp and PgDn keys to move backward and forward, respectively, in the file.

Once record 10 is located (see Figure 13.22) you can now use any of a number of commands to change the record.

You can advance the cursor to the next field by pressing the ENTER key. In addition to using the full-screen cursor movement commands, you can also exercise cursor control with the following commands:

Cursor Control Key	dBASE Command	
	CTRL + A	Moves cursor one word to the left.
	CTRL + F	Moves cursor one word to the right.
←	CTRL + S	Moves cursor one position to the left.
→	CTRL + D	Moves cursor one position to the right.
↑	CTRL + E	Moves cursor up one line. At the top line it displays the prior record.
↓	CTRL + X	Moves cursor down one line. At the bottom line it displays the next record.
Del	CTRL + G	Deletes the character at the cursor position and moves the text one position to the left.
	CTRL + Y	Deletes the contents of an entire field.
	CTRL + W	Writes the changes back to the file. It then returns you to the Assistant menu.
PgUp	CTRL + R	Writes the current record to disk and displays the previous record.
PgDn	CTRL + C	Writes the current record to disk and displays the next record.

Ins   `CTRL + V`   Toggles between overwrite and insert mode.
                            When you are in insert mode, the `INS` message
                            is displayed in the status bar.

             `CTRL + U`   Deletes or undeletes a record. When a record is
                            deleted a `Del` is displayed in the status bar.

To correct the error in record 10, press the ENTER or the Down arrow key twice to move the cursor to the `LAST` field. You can then position the cursor to the *k* by entering `CTRL + D` twice or by pressing the Right arrow key twice; type over the error by entering `cK`. Press the Ctrl + End or Ctrl + W keys to exit the `EDIT` process and return to the Assistant menu.

Use these commands to correct errors in your data base file. As those of you acquainted with WordStar have no doubt noticed, the full-screen `EDIT` cursor movement commands use either the cursor movement keys or WordStar commands, making the `EDIT` feature easy to use for **full-screen editing**.

dBASE III Plus
File Types

As was mentioned earlier, dBASE automatically places a .DBF file extension on any file that is generated via the `CREATE` command. In addition to .DBF files, dBASE also generates other files. Each of these files is discussed briefly below and will be introduced in more detail later.

Data Base Files

Date base files have a .DBF file extension and contain records that contain information about a business happening or transaction and are comprised of fields of data.

Memo Files. Memo files have a .DBT file extension and are capable of storing the large blocks of information found in the memo fields of a data base file. The information in a memo field is actually stored in a separate file.

Index Files. Index files have a .NDX file extension and provide dBASE with the ability to appear to arrange information in a file without actually sorting it.

Format Files. Format files have a .FMT file extension and store custom screen forms or custom report forms.

Label Files. Label files have a .LBL file extension and are used for printing labels with the `LABEL` command.

Memory Files. Memory files have a .MEM file extension and are used to store the active memory variables to disk. A memory variable represents a temporary memory location that can hold the result of one or more computations.

Report Form Files. Report form files have a .FRM file extension and hold the parameters used to create a stored report form.

Text Files. Text files have a .TXT file extension and can hold data that have been copied from a data base file to this temporary file. This allows other applications packages (such as word processing packages) to access this data.

Catalog Files. Catalog files have a .CAT file extension and contain all of the names of a set of related data base files and their related files.

Query Files. Query files have a .QRY file extension and contain information about the conditions for displaying records from an existing data base file.

Screen Files. Screen files have a .SCR file extension and contain information about the screen layout of a custom data entry form.

View Files. View files have a .VUE file extension and are used for relating data base files with their related indexes, format fields, and other information defining the relationships among all these files.

Chapter Review

Before creating a dBASE file, you must plan the field name, the field length, and the type of data that is to be used for each field. The CREATE command from the Assistant menu is used to build a template for a data base file. Once the template is created, you can enter records immediately; the APPEND command is used to add records to the file later.

Accessing a file requires using the SET UP command from the Assistant menu (this issues a USE command). The Tools option of the Assistant menu is used to invoke the LIST STRUCTURE command to display the structure of the file to show the field names, data types, and field size.

Listing the records to the screen requires selecting the Retrieve option from the Assistant menu and then selecting the Execute the Command option. The field name along with each field's contents of all records are displayed to the monitor.

To change a record requires selecting the Update option of the Assistant menu and then positioning the pointer to the Edit option. The last record accessed is displayed to the screen. Full-screen cursor movement commands as well as WordStar cursor movement commands can now be used to position the cursor and to move from one record to the next within the file.

The QUIT command is used to leave dBASE III Plus. The QUIT command is required any time that you have added records to an indexed file. If QUIT is not used, the records may not be added and the index will have to be rebuilt.

Key Terms and Concepts

action line
APPEND command
ASSIST command
command-driven mode
CREATE command
dBASE III Plus
dot prompt
EDIT command

full-screen editing
HELP command
menu-driven mode
message line
navigation line
QUIT command
status bar

Chapter Quiz

Multiple Choice

1. Which is not a true statement about dBASE III Plus?
   a. The package can be used only in menu mode.
   b. No statements can be saved to a file and executed later.

  c. Once the dot prompt is reached, the Assistant menu cannot be
     reactivated.
  d. All of the above statements are false.

2. Which of the following commands enable(s) you to place records in a data
   base file?
   a. USE
   b. CREATE
   c. LIST
   d. APPEND
   e. ADD

3. The LIST command is used for the following:
   a. Looking at records contained in a file
   b. Invoking a data base file
   c. Displaying the structure of a data base file
   d. Exiting the dBASE III program
   e. Making changes to a file

4. Which of the following commands enables you to make a change to an
   existing data base file?
   a. EDIT
   b. LIST
   c. USE
   d. CREATE
   e. QUIT

5. Which of the following are valid data types for use with dBASE III Plus?
   a. Character
   b. Numeric
   c. Memo
   d. Date
   e. Logical
   f. All of the above

True/False

6. The dBASE III Plus package in Assistant mode is menu driven.

7. The dBASE III Plus package uses the period (.) as the default user
   prompt.

8. It is advisable to use the QUIT command from the dot prompt or the
   QUIT dBASE III PLUS from the Set Up option of the Assistant
   menu to avoid data loss.

9. The dBASE III package EDIT command makes use of the cursor pad as
   well as WordStar-like commands for cursor manipulation.

10. The EDIT and APPEND commands use the full-screen feature of
    dBASE III Plus.

Answers

1. d 2. b and d 3. a and c 4. a 5. f 6. t 7. f 8. t 9. t 10. t

Exercises

1. Define or describe each of the following:
   a. command-driven   c. full-screen editing
   b. menu-driven   d. record number

2. The maximum number of records allowed in a dBASE III Plus file is _____.

3. The line of the Assist menu that indicates the current disk drive and the name of the file in use is the _____ line.

4. The HELP command can be invoked by pressing the _____ function key.

5. Before you turn off the computer you must issue the _____ command to avoid data loss.

6. Exiting the Assistant menu is achieved by pressing the _____ key.

7. The default mode for dBASE is the _____ menu.

8. A dBASE record can have up to _____ characters.

9. The _____ command is used to describe a record to dBASE.

10. A file is made available to dBASE by entering the _____ command.

11. The _____ gives the physical location of a record in a file.

12. The _____ should be used to exit dBASE.

13. The _____ command is used to look at the structure of a dBASE file.

14. The _____ command is used to add data to an existing data base file.

15. The APPEND and EDIT commands make use of the _____ screen editing feature of dBASE.

16. The EDIT command uses _____-like cursor movement commands.

17. The _____ edit command is used to save the changes to the current record and return control back to dBASE.

18. The _____ edit command deletes the contents of an entire field.

19. When you use the LIST STRUCTURE command, what pieces of information are provided before the field list?
    a.

    b.

    c.

20. List and describe three types of files used by dBASE III Plus.

Computer Exercises

1. Create a file called PAYMAST. It should have the following structure:

```
STRUCTURE FOR FILE:   A:PAYMAST .DBF
NUMBER OF RECORDS:    00012
DATE OF LAST UPDATE:  01/01/80
PRIMARY USE DATABASE
FLD       NAME       TYPE WIDTH      DEC
001    EMPLOYID     N    004
002    FIRSTNAM     C    010
003    LASTNAM      C    012
004    PAYRATE      N    006       002
005    YTDGROSS     N    009       002
**TOTAL**                00042
```

2. Enter the following records:

ID	NAME	RATE	GROSS
4908	Richard Payne	4.45	556.00
5789	Connie Reiners	3.35	450.00
5323	Pamela Rich	6.00	780.00
6324	Mark Tell	5.50	980.00
2870	Frank Terlep	3.80	670.00
4679	Kenneth Klass	4.90	780.00
8345	Thomas Momery	4.70	580.00

3. List the contents of the file by using the LIST command.

4. Add the records below:

5649	Toni McCarthy	5.20	667.00
5432	Alan Monroe	5.20	1340.00
5998	Paul Mish	4.90	887.00
4463	Edward Mockford	4.90	775.00
456		0.00	0.00

5. Use the EDIT command to correct any errors. Also use the EDIT command to place your name in the name area for record #12.

Chapter 14

Intermediate Data Base Management with dBASE III Plus

Chapter Objectives   After completing this chapter, you should be able to:

Discuss various dBASE III Plus file manipulation commands that can be issued from the Assistant menu and from the dot (.) prompt

Discuss pointer movement commands

Discuss the `CREATE REPORT` *command*

This chapter describes a number of dBASE III Plus commands used for file manipulation.

Access and Display Commands

The USE, LIST, and LIST STRUCTURE commands have already been introduced; the DISPLAY command, the ? character, and the RECNO( ) function have not.

Command Execution from the Assist Menu

Example 1   USE

The USE **command** makes a file available to the user. You can execute a USE command as follows:

1. Select the Tools option of the Assistant menu.
2. Select the Set Drive entry to set the default drive to B.
3. Select the Set Up option from the Assistant.
4. Select the Data base file entry (note that the command USE now appears on the action line).
5. Select drive B (the default specified in the previous step; note that B: also appears on the action line).
6. Point to the customer file (note that USE B:CUSTOMER now appears on the action line).
7. Respond N to the prompt Is the file indexed? [Y/N].

The customer file is now activated and ready for use by dBASE.

Example 2   LIST STRUCTURE

If you want to examine the structure of the CUSTOMER file, you must select the Tools option of the Assistant menu and then select the LIST STRUC-TURE **command** (DISPLAY STRUCTURE now appears on the action line). Upon receiving the prompt Direct the output to the printer? [Y/N], enter an N. A list of the record structure is displayed (see Figure 14.1), allowing you to examine the structure of a record and providing information such as name of the file, number of records currently in the file, date of last update, names of the fields, data types of the fields, and field lengths. At the end of the structure report, the total number of bytes of storage occupied by each record is given.

Example 3   LIST

The LIST **command** enables you to display the contents of the CUSTOMER file on the screen. To execute a LIST command, select the Retrieve option of the Assistant menu (you will then see LIST on the action line); a submenu (see Figure 14.2) now appears. After you select the first option, Execute the command, and respond N to the prompt Direct the output to the printer? [Y/N], the contents of the file CUSTOMER are displayed on your screen (see Figure 14.3).

Once the LIST command has finished executing, press any key to continue working in Assist mode.

The unmodified LIST command starts at the beginning of the file and lists all fields of each record. When a regular LIST command is executed,

Figure 14.1
Output of the LIST STRUCTURE command accessed through the Tools option of the Assistant menu.

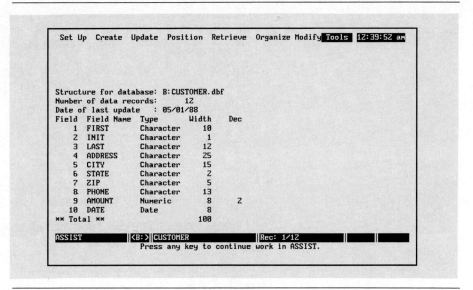

Figure 14.2
The List screen prompts.

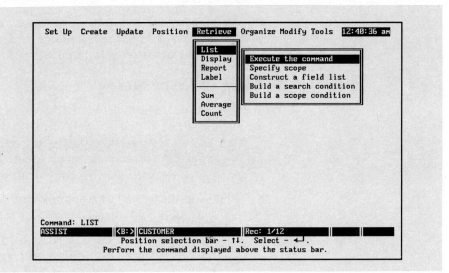

Figure 14.3
Output of the LIST command executed against the CUSTOMER file.

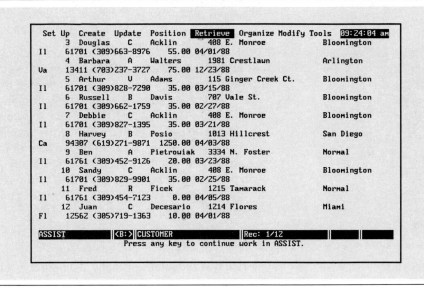

Figure 14.4
Construct a field list screen.

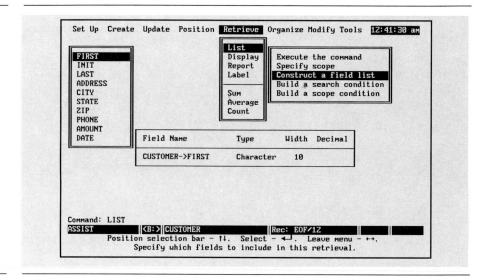

dBASE searches the entire file for records. The L I S T command moves the pointer automatically to the beginning of the file, and when the search ends, the pointer is located at the last record.

Example 4   LIST field list

You can control which fields of records are listed by executing the C o n - s t r u c t   a   f i e l d   l i s t option of the List submenu. The C o n s t r u c t   a f i e l d   l i s t option enables you to determine which fields from records to list on the screen. For example, to list the first names, initials, and last names in the file, you use the following commands from the Assistant menu.

1. Select the R e t r i e v e option of the Assistant menu.
2. Take the L i s t option (L I S T now appears on the action line).
3. Select the C o n s t r u c t   a   f i e l d   l i s t option of the List submenu; the fields in the C U S T O M E R record are now displayed (see Figure 14.4).
4. Move the pointer with the Up and Down arrow keys to display the characteristics of each field in the middle of the screen.
5. Press the ENTER key to select field (the pointer automatically moves down to the next entry).

As each field is selected, dBASE adds that field name to the L I S T command in the action line (see Figure 14.4). After all of the desired fields (F I R S T , I N I T, and L A S T) have been selected, the action line should have the following content: L I S T   F I R S T , I N I T , L A S T. Upon pressing a Right or Left arrow key, you are returned to the List submenu, and the C o n s t r u c t   a   f i e l d   l i s t entry is now in low-intensity video and unavailable for further selection. To execute the new L I S T command, select the E x e c u t e   t h e   c o m m a n d entry with the pointer, press the ENTER key, and respond N to the prompt D i r e c t o u t p u t   t o   t h e   p r i n t e r ?   [Y / N]. The records are now listed on the screen (see Figure 14.5).

Example 5   LIST field list

To list the first names, initials, last names, and amounts for all the records, you use the same steps as described above but add the A M O U N T field. The com-

Figure 14.5
Output of the L I S T command using selected fields.

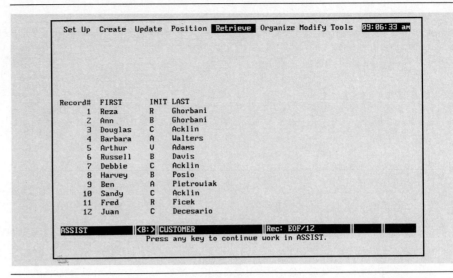

Figure 14.6
The L I S T command with an additional field.

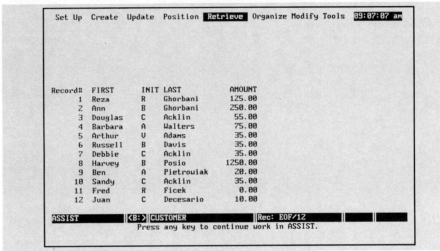

mand that now appears on the action line is LIST FIRST, INIT, LAST, AMOUNT. The new output (see Figure 14.6) now includes the AMOUNT field.

Example 6   *LIST NEXT*

You can use the L I S T command to display the next *x* number of records in a file by adding the NEXT **option** to the basic L I S T command. First, however, since you are not including all records from the file in this command, you must reposition the pointer at the beginning of the file by means of the Assistant menu Position command. Once the Position command has been executed, select the Goto Record option and then the TOP command (see Figure 14.7). The pointer is now positioned at the beginning of the file.

You can now select the Retrieve option from the Assistant menu. Once the List option has been selected from this menu, select the Specify scope option of that submenu. A Scope submenu now appears on the screen, from which you select the NEXT option. An entry then appears that asks you to enter the number of records that you want to have listed on the screen (see Figure 14.8). Enter the number 5 and press the ENTER key. Now specify the FIRST, INIT, LAST, and AMOUNT fields to be included in the LIST

Figure 14.7
The Assistant screen for positioning the pointer at the beginning of the file.

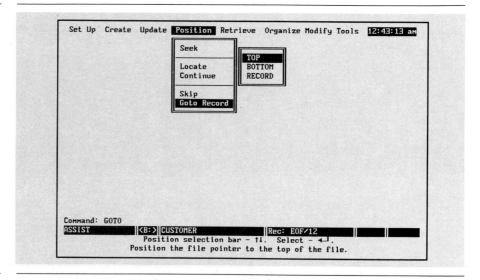

Figure 14.8
The Assistant screen for specifying the scope.

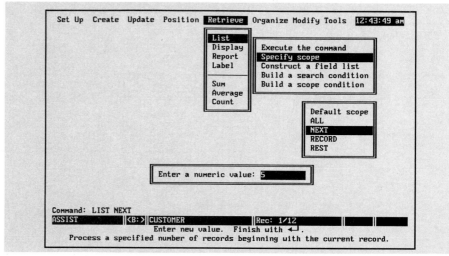

command by selecting the Construct a field list option. Once you have finished this task, you are now returned to the List submenu and must now select the Execute the command option. Do not route the output to the printer. The first five records are displayed on your screen (see Figure 14.9).

 ### Example 7   *LIST FOR*

You can also use the LIST command to display records that meet a certain criterion by entering the FOR **parameter** and the selection criterion after the LIST command. For example, you might want to list all records that have an amount greater than $100. This is accomplished by selecting the Retrieve option from the Assistant menu and then executing the LIST command. Once the List submenu is displayed, select the Build a search condition option. This displays the record fields to the screen. Select the Amount field by positioning the pointer to that field (see Figure 14.10).

Once the field has been selected, a condition menu appears on the screen, and you must select (in this example) the > Greater Than option (see Figure 14.11). The enter the value of 100 at the prompt Enter a numeric

Figure 14.9
Output of the LIST NEXT
5 RECORDS command.

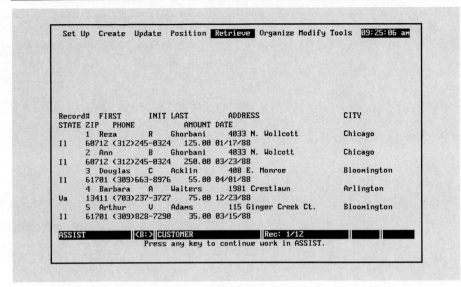

Figure 14.10
A field marked for a search
condition.

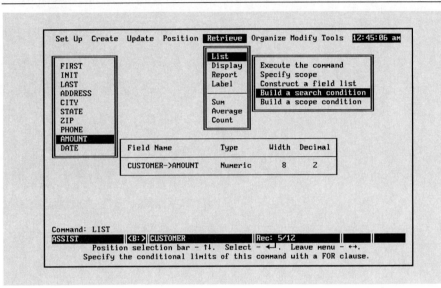

Figure 14.11
The Condition screen.

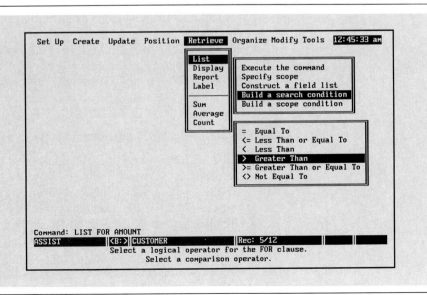

Figure 14.12
The More Conditions prompt.

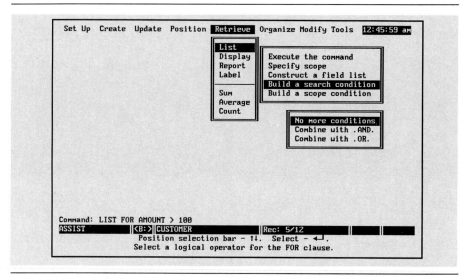

```
   Set Up  Create  Update  Position  █Retrieve█ Organize Modify Tools  █12:45:59 am█
                  ┌─────────┐┌──────────────────────────────┐
                  │█List   █││ Execute the command          │
                  │ Display ││ Specify scope                │
                  │ Report  ││ Construct a field list       │
                  │ Label   ││█Build a search condition     █│
                  │         ││ Build a scope condition      │
                  │ Sum     │└──────────────────────────────┘
                  │ Average │   ┌──────────────────────┐
                  │ Count   │   │█No more conditions    █│
                  └─────────┘   │ Combine with .AND.    │
                                │ Combine with .OR.     │
                                └──────────────────────┘




   Command: LIST FOR AMOUNT > 100
  █ASSIST       █║<B:>║CUSTOMER            ║Rec: 5/12   ║   ║   █
                    Position selection bar - ↑↓.  Select - ◄┘.
                    Select a logical operator for the FOR clause.
```

Figure 14.13
The records listed for the command LIST FOR AMOUNT > 100.

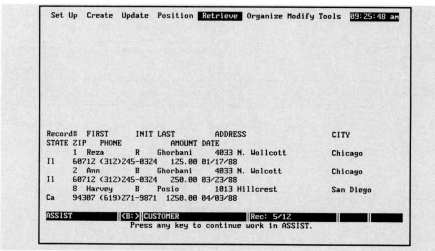

```
   Set Up  Create  Update  Position  █Retrieve█ Organize Modify Tools  █09:25:48 am█




  Record#  FIRST     INIT LAST        ADDRESS              CITY
  STATE ZIP   PHONE          AMOUNT DATE
       1  Reza      R    Ghorbani     4033 N. Wollcott     Chicago
  Il   60712 (312)245-0324   125.00 01/17/88
       2  Ann       B    Ghorbani     4033 N. Wolcott      Chicago
  Il   60712 (312)245-0324   250.00 03/23/88
       8  Harvey    B    Posio        1013 Hillcrest       San Diego
  Ca   94307 (619)271-9871  1250.00 04/03/88
  █ASSIST       █║<B:>║CUSTOMER            ║Rec: 5/12   ║   ║   █
                    Press any key to continue work in ASSIST.
```

value:_. You now receive a prompt inquiring whether or not there are more conditions (see Figure 14.12) and should select the No more conditions entry (the command LIST WHILE AMOUNT > 100 is in the action line). Then select the Execute the command entry of the List submenu. Three records (see Figure 14.13) are now on the screen.

Example 8   LIST, with selection criteria and specified fields

The LIST command probably generated more output than you need or want. To list only selected fields (in this case, the first and last names and the amount) of records that meet a criterion, you must position the pointer to the beginning of the file and select the Construct a field list option of the List submenu to specify the field list containing these fields; then take the Build a search condition option to enter your criterion. Once this has been done, you should see the command LIST FIRST, LAST, AMOUNT WHILE AMOUNT > 100 in the action line. List the records to the screen (see Figure 14.14).

Figure 14.14
List of specific fields for a
condition.

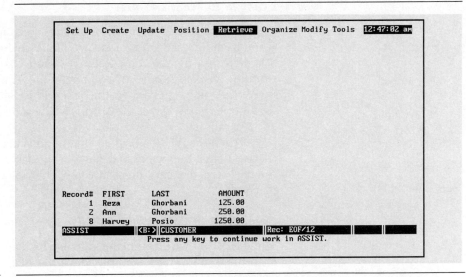

Figure 14.15
The result of a DISPLAY
command when the pointer
is located at the end of the
file.

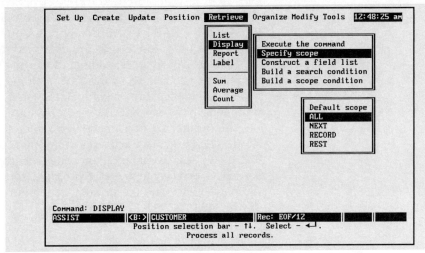

DISPLAY

The DISPLAY **command** works similarly to the LIST command except that
only the record at the pointer location is displayed. The DISPLAY ALL command causes sixteen lines to appear on the screen. dBASE then gives a WAIT-
ING prompt, signifying that you may press any key to have the screen display
the next sixteen lines.

Unlike the LIST command, the DISPLAY command does not go immediately to the beginning of the data file; rather, it causes the display to begin
at the record at which the pointer is currently positioned. The DISPLAY
command is found in the Retrieve submenu.

Example 9 DISPLAY

If a DISPLAY command is issued after the pointer has moved to the bottom
of the file (for example, after a LIST command has been executed), no record
is displayed. In this example, the pointer is at the end of a file after execution
of the above list statement. Since it has reached end of file, no record is
displayed; only the field headings appear on the screen (see Figure 14.15).

Example 10   DISPLAY ALL

To list all the records in the file onto the screen in the same fashion that would result from the LIST command, you must include the ALL **parameter**. This is accomplished by selecting Retrieve, then Display, then Specify scope from the Display submenu, and finally the ALL option. The command DIS-PLAY ALL now appears on the action line. Select the Execute the command option and direct the output to the screen (see Figure 14.16); press any key to continue.

When the DISPLAY ALL command is used, dBASE automatically stops (pauses) after 16 lines of text have been displayed on the screen. To display the next screen of text, press any key. This will continue until the end of file is reached.

Example 11   DISPLAY ALL field list

The DISPLAY ALL command can also be used to list specific files or records onto the monitor. For example, once the ALL scope has been specified, the fields first, last, and amount can be specified in the same manner as for the LIST command. Once the process is completed, the command DISPLAY ALL FIRST, LAST, AMOUNT appears on the action line. Once the command is executed, the records are displayed to the monitor (see Figure 14.17).

The DISPLAY ALL command can use any of the field list, scope, or conditions options used by the LIST command.

Crude reports can be generated by using the LIST and DISPLAY ALL commands in two ways. First, you can issue a printer command by responding Y to the prompt Direct output to the printer? [Y/N]. This command, when executed, activates the printer, prints the output of the LIST or DISPLAY ALL command, and then deactivates the printer. The second method is used from the dot prompt. You must issue a SET PRINT ON command to activate the printer, issue your command, and turn the printer off with a SET PRINT OFF command.

DIR

Example 12   DIR

The DIR **command** also can be used to list data base files onto the screen. The directory (DIR) command can be accessed from the Tools entry of the Assistant menu by selecting the Directory option. Once the Directory option is selected, you are prompted for the drive to be used (the pointer automatically moves to the default drive); enter the appropriate drive. If you have selected drive B:, the prompt on the action line is now DIR B:. You must now point to the type of file that you want displayed (in this case, .dbf) and press the ENTER key (see Figure 14.18). The files are now displayed on your screen.

Access and Display Commands Entered from the Dot Prompt

The Assistant menu of dBASE III Plus enables you to create dBASE commands without knowing much about the dBASE language syntax. As you have seen in the preceding examples, dBASE shows the commands it is following in the action line; these commands are the same as those you would enter at the dot prompt. The commands for each of the above examples are given in this

Figure 14.16
Output of the DISPLAY
ALL command.

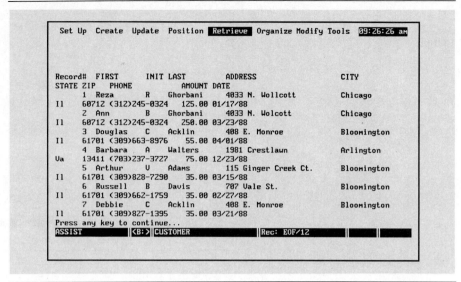

Figure 14.17
Output of the DISPLAY
ALL FIRST, LAST,
AMOUNT command.

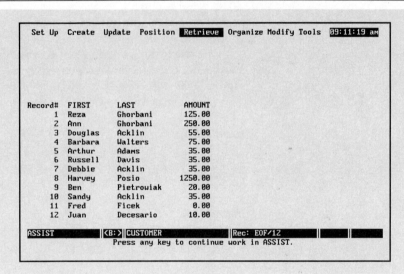

Figure 14.18
Screen for the DIR
command.

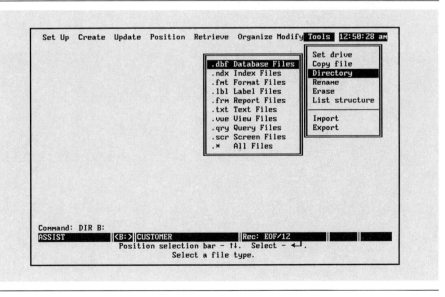

Figure 14.19
The dBASE screen with dot
prompt.

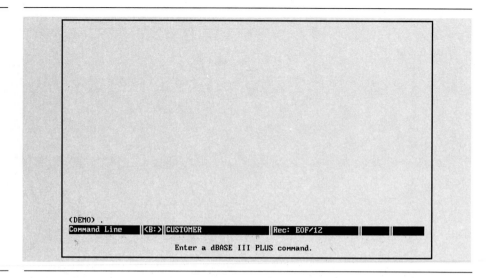

section. Since the output is very similar, only the commands issued at the dot prompt are given.

To reach the dot prompt (.) press the Esc key one or more times. You should now see a blank screen with the dot prompt on the action line (see Figure 14.19).

The instructions required for each example are as follows:

Example 1

```
. set default to b:
. use customer
```

Example 2

```
. list structure
```

Example 3

```
. list
```

Example 4

```
. list first, init, last
```

Example 5

```
. list first, init, last, amount
```

Example 6

```
. goto top
. list next 5 first, init, last, amount
```

Example 7

```
. list for amount > 100
```

Example 8

```
. list first, last, amount for amount > 100
```

Example 9

```
. display
```

Example 10

```
. display all
```

Example 11

```
. display all first, last, amount
```

Example 12

```
. dir *.dbf
```

As you can see, the Assistant menu enables you to gradually construct your dBASE commands without much knowledge of the syntax, and the command mode (.) requires that you have a good understanding of how to form a dBASE command. As you get more and more acquainted with dBASE, you will probably spend more time at the dot prompt.

Some forms of the preceding commands just cannot be entered through the Assistant menu. For example, a version of the LIST/DISPLAY command(s) can be used to search for rather loose criteria. For instance, you might not know how to spell someone's name exactly, but you do know how the name starts. In this situation, it is best to use the **substring function ($)**. The following command could be translated as "list the first name and last name fields of any record that has the characters *Gho* in the last-name field."

```
. list first, last for 'Gho' $last
Record# first     last
      1 Reza      Ghorbani
      2 Ann       Ghorbani
```

The following command generates a list of every record that has a capital *A* in the first-name field.

```
. list first, last for 'A' $first
Record# first     last
      2 Ann       Ghorbani
      5 Arthur    Adams
```

The following command generates a list of every record that has the characters *ar* anywhere in the first-name field.

```
. list first, last for 'ar' $first
Record# first     last
      4 Barbara   Walters
      8 Harvey    Posio
```

? and RECNO( ) Commands

The **? character** is used any time that you want some piece of information displayed on the screen. The RECNO ( ) **function** is used to obtain the pointer location from dBASE. Using ? and RECNO ( ) together produces a command to identify the location of the pointer and display that number on the screen, as follows:

```
. ? recno()
        5
```

Pointer Position Commands

Pointer positioning commands can be entered easily from the dot prompt. Entering them from the Assistant menu takes too many keystrokes for many users. A number of pointer position commands are included in dBASE. These commands activate (make available) records for dBASE processing; they include the GOTO, GO, GOTO TOP, GOTO BOTTOM, and SKIP commands. (Of course, such commands as LIST and DISPLAY also result in a change of the pointer position.)

GO and GOTO

The GO and GOTO commands can be used interchangeably. The following examples illustrate the joint use of the GOTO and DISPLAY commands to enable you to examine the content of a record. In each case, the DISPLAY command generates a display of the record pointed to by the GOTO command, as follows:

```
. goto 5
. display

Record#  FIRST       INIT    LAST        ADDRESS              CITY
    STATE ZIP     PHONE             AMOUNT DATE
      5  Arthur       V      Adams       115 Ginger Creek Ct.Bloomington
    Il      61701  (309)828-7290     35.00 03/13/88

. goto 10
. display

Record#  FIRST       INIT    LAST        ADDRESS              CITY
    STATE ZIP     PHONE             AMOUNT DATE
     10  Sandy        C      Acklin      408 E. Monroe        Bloomington
    Il      61701  (309)829-9901     35.00 02/25/88
```

The GOTO portion of a pointer position command (except in the cases of GOTO TOP and GOTO BOTTOM) can be implied simply by entering the desired record number after the dot prompt. For example, the following command sequence suffices.

```
. 2
. display first, last, amount
Record#  FIRST       LAST        AMOUNT
      2  Ann         Ghorbani    250.00

. list next 4 first,last
Record#  FIRST       LAST
      2  Ann         Ghorbani
      3  Douglas     Acklin
      4  Barbara     Walters
      5  Arthur      Adams
```

SKIP

The SKIP **command** advances the pointer one record forward in the file. It can be followed by a number (positive or negative): A positive number moves the pointer forward that number of records, and a negative number moves the pointer backward that number of record positions. When the SKIP command is issued, the new pointer position is displayed on the screen. For example, with the pointer currently situated at record 5 (as the result of the preceding file manipulation), the unmodified SKIP command advances the pointer as follows:

```
. SKIP
Record no.        6
. display first,last,amount
Record# first     last     amount
      6 Russell   Davis    35.00
```

With the pointer currently located at record 6, the following SKIP command moves the pointer backward three records in the file:

```
. skip -3
  Record no.        3
. display

Record#  FIRST       INIT    LAST          ADDRESS              CITY
   STATE ZIP    PHONE              AMOUNT DATE
      3  Douglas     C       Acklin        408 E. Monroe        Bloomington
   Il      61701 (309)663-8976      55.00 04/01/88
```

With the pointer located at record 3, the following SKIP command moves the pointer forward six records in the file:

```
. SKIP 6
  Record no.        9
. display

Record#  FIRST       INIT    LAST          ADDRESS              CITY
   STATE ZIP    PHONE              AMOUNT DATE
      9  Ben         A       Pietrowiak    3334 Foster          Normal
   Il      61761 (309)452-9126      20.00 03/23/88
```

GOTO TOP

The GOTO TOP **command** positions the pointer at the first record in the file, as follows:

```
. GOTO TOP
. ?RENCO()
          1
```

The GOTO TOP command can also be used with the DISPLAY command to position the pointer at the beginning (top) of the file and display that record, as follows:

```
. goto top
. display first, last, amount
RECORD#    FIRST   LAST      AMOUNT
        1  Reza    Ghorbani  125.00
```

GOTO BOTTOM

The GOTO BOTTOM **command** positions the pointer at the last record in the file, as follows:

```
, GOTO BOTTOM
, ?RECNO()
            12
```

Other Commands and Functions

DATE

If you want to access the system date while you are in dBASE, use the DATE function. The date that you entered during the boot process is now displayed; or if you did not enter a date, 01/01/80 is displayed. The command and display are as follows:

```
, ? DATE()
03/13/87
```

End of File (EOF)

The **end of file (EOF) function** senses the end of the file—the location beyond the "last" record in the file. A sample EOF command follows:

```
, GOTO BOTTOM
, ? EOF ()
,F,
```

Notice that the value returned is F (false), meaning that the end of the file was not detected. This is because the pointer is now at the beginning of the last record. To activate the EOF function, a SKIP command must be issued to move the pointer past the last record.

```
, SKIP
Record no,          13
, ? EOF ()
,T,
```

Beginning of File (BOF)

The same technique applies to the **beginning of file (BOF) function**; as appears below, dBASE doesn't realize that it is actually at the top of the file until you try to access a record that isn't there.

```
, GO TOP
, ?bof()
,F,
, SKIP -1
    Record no,          1
, ?bof()
,T,
```

SUM

dBASE can be directed to perform arithmetic via the SUM **command**. For instance, if you want to know the grand total owed, you can find out by using

Figure 14.20
The Sum screen for summing
the AMOUNT field.

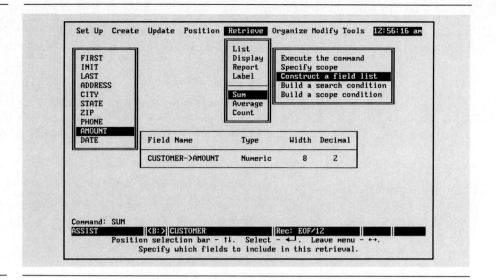

the Retrieve option of the Assistant menu. You now select the Sum option and then the Construct a field list option and point to any numeric fields that you want to sum (in this example, you can sum only the AMOUNT field). Once these commands have been given (see Figure 14.20), you are ready to execute the command.

Once control is returned to the Sum submenu, the command SUM AMOUNT appears on the action line. After the command is executed, the following message appears on your screen:

```
12 records summed
amount
1925.00
```

You might also be interested in knowing the grand total for customers that have a $100 or greater balance. To determine this, enter the search condition FOR AMOUNT > 100, after the AMOUNT field has been selected. After executing this command, you should see the following on your screen:

```
3 records summed
amount
1625.00
```

dBASE also enables you to generate the numeric average of a field within a data base file. For instance, you might want to know the average amount owed in the CUSTOMER file. This information can also be obtained via the Retrieve option of the Assistant menu. Now select the Construct a field list option and then select the appropriate numeric fields (in this example, only the AMOUNT field is numeric) and execute the command (see Figure 14.21).

Before the command is executed, the action line contains AVERAGE AMOUNT. Once the command is executed, the following data should be displayed on your screen:

```
12 records averaged
average
160.42
```

Figure 14.21
The Average screen of the
Assistant menu.

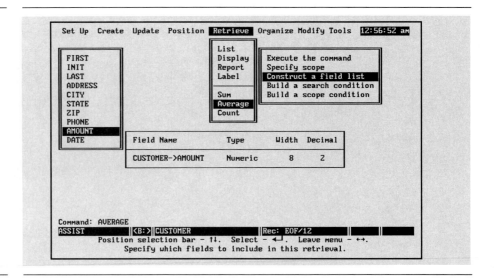

Record Alteration Commands

You have already seen how to make changes in a record by using the EDIT command. Other alterations can be made by using the REPLACE, DELETE, PACK, and RESTORE commands. The command-level dot prompt mode is used in the following examples. Although this mode provides maximum flexibility, the Assistant menu could be used in some of these examples.

REPLACE

Instead of accessing each record and displaying it for full-screen editing, you can use the REPLACE **command** to institute the change. For example, assume that Reza Ghorbani paid his bill in full. To change the amount in his record to zero, enter the REPLACE command shown below. A message telling you how many records were replaced will then be displayed. To verify that the RE-PLACE command has accomplished its task, enter the LIST command that follows it.

```
. replace amount with 0 for first = 'Reza'
        1 record replaced
. list first, last, amount
```

Record#	first	last	amount
1	Reza	Ghorbani	0.00
2	Ann	Ghorbani	250.00
3	Douglas	Acklin	55.00
4	Barbara	Walters	75.00
5	Arthur	Adams	35.00
6	Russell	Davis	35.00
7	Debbie	Acklin	35.00
8	Harvey	Posio	1250.00
9	Ben	Pietrowiak	20.00
10	Sandy	Acklin	35.00
11	Fred	Ficek	0.00
12	Juan	Decesario	10.00

This example limits the criteria for the replacement. If you want to change every record by the same amount, you can add the scope parameter ALL. For example, you could add five cents to each record's amount by issuing the

REPLACE command shown below. Clearly, if you need to make a change that will affect all the records in a file, or a large number of records, the REPLACE ALL command will do the job in significantly less time than the EDIT command requires. The following example illustrates how it works:

```
. replace all amount with amount + .05
    12 records replaced
. list first, last, amount

Record#  first     last           amount
      1  Reza      Ghorbani         0.05
      2  Ann       Ghorbani       250.05
      3  Douglas   Acklin          55.05
      4  Barbara   Walters         75.05
      5  Arthur    Adams           35.05
      6  Russell   Davis           35.05
      7  Debbie    Acklin          35.05
      8  Harvey    Posio         1250.05
      9  Ben       Pietrowiak      20.05
     10  Sandy     Acklin          35.05
     11  Fred      Ficek            0.05
     12  Juan      Decesario       10.05
```

You can easily return the file to its former status by issuing another REPLACE command.

```
. replace all amount with amount - .05
    12 records replaced
. list first, last, amount

Record#  first     last           amount
      1  Reza      Ghorbani         0.00
      2  Ann       Ghorbani       250.00
      3  Douglas   Acklin          55.00
      4  Barbara   Walters         75.00
      5  Arthur    Adams           35.00
      6  Russell   Davis           35.00
      7  Debbie    Acklin          35.00
      8  Harvey    Posio         1250.00
      9  Ben       Pietrowiak      20.00
     10  Sandy     Acklin          35.00
     11  Fred      Ficek            0.00
     12  Juan      Decesario       10.00
```

Now put 125.00 back in the Ghorbani record.

DELETE, PACK, and RECALL

From time to time, you will want to delete records from a data base file. This is a two-step process: (1) the record is marked for deletion via the DELETE **command**; and (2) the file is recopied, with all records that were marked for deletion left out and with all records packed together via the PACK **command**. The first step is sometimes referred to as *logical deletion*; although the record is marked, it is not removed from the file. Consequently, it can still be read and processed. The example that follows illustrates marking a record (record 7) for deletion. First the pointer is positioned at record 7; then part of the record is displayed to make certain that the desired record has been located; then the DELETE command is issued. The message displayed on the screen indicates that the record has been marked; the **delete indicator (*)** appears between the record number and the first field of the record. The command (with dBASE response) is as follows:

```
. 7
. display first, last
Record# first        last
       7 Debbie      Acklin
. delete
       1 record deleted
. display
Record# FIRST        INITIAL LAST         ADDRESS         CITY
       STATE ZIP     PHONE           AMOUNT DATE
       7 *Debbie     C       Acklin        408 E. Monroe   Bloomington
       Il     61701 (309)827-1395     35.00 03/21/88
```

The asterisk (*) shows that the record has been marked for deletion, takes up one byte of storage on a dBASE record, and accounts for the extra position reserved for the fields in a record. In a listing of all the file records, the record marked for deletion is recognizable at once:

```
. list first, last, amount

Record#  first       last          amount
      1  Reza        Ghorbani       125.00
      2  Ann         Ghorbani       250.00
      3  Douglas     Acklin          55.00
      4  Barbara     Walters         75.00
      5  Arthur      Adams           35.00
      6  Russell     Davis           35.00
      7 *Debbie      Acklin          35.00
      8  Harvey      Posio         1250.00
      9  Ben         Pietrowiak      20.00
     10  Sandy       Acklin          35.00
     11  Fred        Ficek            0.00
     12  Juan        Decesario       10.00
```

Once a record has been marked for deletion, it can be undeleted (as long as a PACK command has not been issued) by using a RECALL **command**. If you want to undelete a record, you must first position the pointer at that record and then issue the RECALL command. To undelete all of the records in a file, enter a RECALL ALL command. Since the pointer is still on record 7 in the present case, a pointer positioning command does not have to be entered. After a RECALL command is entered, the number of records undeleted is displayed on the screen.

```
. 7
. recall
       1 record recalled
. display first ,last
Record# first       last
       7 Debbie      Acklin
```

Assume that record 13 is to be deleted from the file (you will first have to add it to the file using the APPEND command). The following steps have to be taken to delete record 13:

1. The pointer is positioned at record 13.
2. The record is displayed to ensure that the pointer is properly positioned.
3. The DELETE command is entered.
4. Part of the file is listed to ensure that the record has been marked.
5. The file is packed via the PACK command, physically removing the record.
6. Portions of each record are then listed to ensure that the record is gone.

On your screen, these steps appear as follows:

```
. 13
. display
Record#  FIRST      INITIAL LAST      ADDRESS              CITY
    STATE ZIP    PHONE        AMOUNT DATE
    13  Eric       C       Wild      207 S. Broadmore      Felix
    Ks    34762              0.00   /  /

  . delete
    1 record deleted
  . list first,last,amount

    Record#  first      last        amount
        1  Reza       Ghorbani    125.00
        2  Ann        Ghorbani    250.00
        3  Douglas    Acklin       55.00
        4  Barbara    Walters      75.00
        5  Arthur     Adams        35.00
        6  Russell    Davis        35.00
        7  Debbie     Acklin       35.00
        8  Harvey     Posio      1250.00
        9  Ben        Pietrowiak   20.00
       10  Sandy      Acklin       35.00
       11  Fred       Ficek         0.00
       12  Juan       Decesario    10.00
       13 *Eric       Wild          0.00
  . pack
    12 records copied
  . list first,last,amount

    Record#  first      last        amount
        1  Reza       Ghorbani    125.00
        2  Ann        Ghorbani    250.00
        3  Douglas    Acklin       55.00
        4  Barbara    Walters      75.00
        5  Arthur     Adams        35.00
        6  Russell    Davis        35.00
        7  Debbie     Acklin       35.00
        8  Harvey     Posio      1250.00
        9  Ben        Pietrowiak   20.00
       10  Sandy      Acklin       35.00
       11  Fred       Ficek         0.00
       12  Juan       Decesario    10.00
```

Figure 14.22
Options screen of the
CREATE REPORT
command.

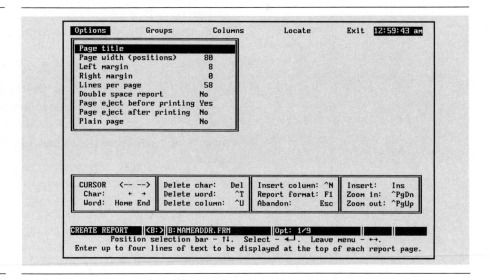

Report Template and the CREATE REPORT Command

Having data stored in a computerized file is not worth much by itself; for it to be useful in practical terms it must be placed in report form on paper. This is accomplished by using the CREATE REPORT command in dBASE. The CRE-ATE REPORT command builds a **report template** on disk containing the report format, headings, and fields to be included in the report (see p. 428).

The template is created by filling in fields presented in dBASE screens that prompt you through the process. All you have to do is to respond to the prompts on each screen.

From the Assistant menu, enter the command CREATE and select the REPORT option from the submenu. dBASE now prompts you for the drive on which the report is to reside as well as the name of the report to be created. You must also have a data base file open; if you don't, dBASE will also prompt you for the name of the file to be used. Enter a report name of NAMEADDR.

The first screen displayed is the Options screen, which enables you to change a number of print options and enter the report heading (see Figure 14.22). When you select the Page Title option, a square box (see Figure 14.23) opens on the screen for the title. Enter the following title:

ABC COMPANY

CUSTOMER NAME AND ADDRESS REPORT

Don't worry about trying to center the information in the line; dBASE does this automatically when the report prints.

The next set of entries enables you to specify the width of the report, the number of positions in the right and left margins, the number of lines per page, whether or not you want the report double-spaced, printer eject options, and paper options.

When you have finished entering the title (see Figure 14.23), issue the End (Ctrl + End) command to return to the Options menu. Now position the bar to the Left Margin option and press the ENTER key. Pressing the ENTER key unlocks this entry: change the left margin to 2. Press the Right arrow key to move to the next menu option (Groups).

Some of the maximum values for the Options screen entries are as follows:

1. Up to four lines of titles can be entered.

2. Up to 500 characters per line can be specified.

Figure 14.23
Report title box of the
Options screen.

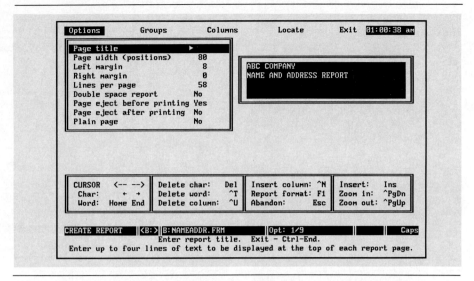

Figure 14.24
Groups screen of the
CREATE REPORT
command.

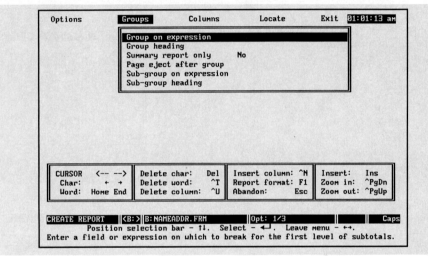

3. Default left margin is 8 characters.

4. Default right margin is 0 characters.

5. Default is single spacing for lines per page.

6. The default for Page Eject before Printing is Yes.

7. The default for Page Eject after Printing is No.

8. The default for Plain Page is No. If Yes, the page numbers and the system date are not printed. In such a situation the report heading is printed only on the first page of the printout.

The Groups screen (see Figure 14.24) enables you to establish subtotals for a report. Subtotals can be used only on a sorted or indexed file; and since NAMEADDR is not accessing a sorted or indexed CUSTOMER file, you do not want to enter any information about subtotals. Press the Right arrow key to advance to the Columns screen.

The Columns screen enables you to specify each field that you want to have printed on a line (see Figure 14.25). Use the top box to enter the names of the fields (unlock a field by pressing the ENTER key). If you have forgotten the field name, simply press the ENTER key to get into the Contents entry and

Figure 14.25
The Columns screen.

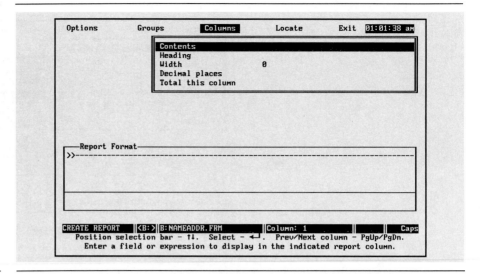

Figure 14.26
The dBASE F10 help facility
for fields. Both the field name
and information about the
data are displayed.

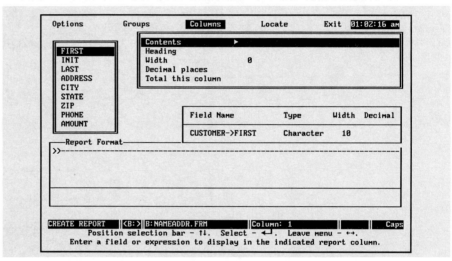

press the F10 key. This results in a screen display of the fields for this file in a box in the left margin along with a description of the fields in a middle box (see Figure 14.26).

When the heading for that field is to be entered, a box appears in the middle of the screen and allows you to enter up to five lines of text (see Figure 14.27). Hit the PgDn key when you are finished. The width of the field (if you want it set to a size other than that specified in the record structure) can also be entered. If you are entering information about a numeric field, you will also be prompted to state the number of decimal positions and whether or not dBASE should total that column in the report. The box at the bottom of the screen depicts the report format.

Enter the following information for the indicated fields:

```
Field      Heading    Total
FIRST
LAST       NAME
ADDRESS    ADDRESS
CITY       CITY
STATE      ST
AMOUNT     AMOUNT     Y
```

Figure 14.27
Columns screen field-
heading box for a report
column heading.

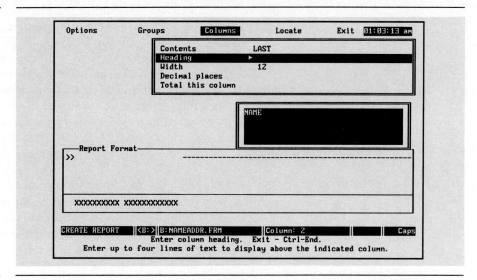

Figure 14.28
Completed Report Format
box of the Columns screen.

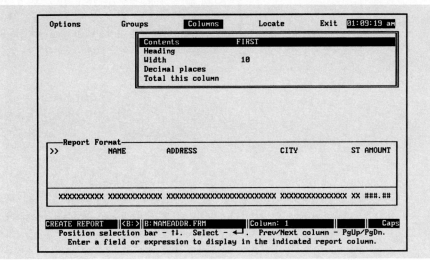

Should you make an error in entering a valid field name, dBASE will beep, display an error message at the bottom of the screen, and direct you to press any key to continue. If you can't remember the name of the field, press the F10 key (see Figure 14.26) for a listing of the valid field names for the file in use.

After you have entered a field and proceeded to the next field-definition box by depressing the PgDn key, dBASE shows you how the report will appear in the Report Format box (see Figure 14.28). dBASE takes the previously specified column headings and places them at the top of the box. The width of a character field is indicated by XXXXs and the width of a numeric field by ####.## (see Figure 14.28).

dBASE automatically takes the field length from the record and places that number in the Width entry for each field. If you want to trim a column, simply decrease the number. This results in rightmost truncation for character fields. For example, if a field width that was 25 is changed to 18, characters to the right of position 18 will not print on this line but will wrap to the next line. The only time that information does not wrap to the next line is when there are rightmost unused positions for this field in all records.

dBASE also automatically places one space between each column.

The Locate option of the REPORT command menu generates a screen containing all of the fields that are used by this report form. You can examine one of these fields by positioning the pointer to that field and pressing the ENTER key. The report window for that field is now displayed to the screen.

To save the report, simply issue the EXIT command from the REPORT command menu. You now receive a two-prompt menu: Save and Abandon. To save this report form to disk, select the Save option. To exit the REPORT CREATE command without saving the template to disk, select the Abandon option. You then receive the prompt Are you sure you want to abandon operation? [Y/N]. Press the Y key to return to the Assistant menu.

Printing a Report

You are now ready to use the report template and the REPORT FORM command to generate a report. First select the Retrieve option from the Assistant menu and then the Report option from this submenu. Indicate that the report template resides on the default drive (B: in this case). Select the NAMEADDR.FRM report form. At this time, you should see the following command on the action line: REPORT FORM B:NAMEADDR. Select the Execute the command option. If you respond Y to the prompt Direct the output to the printer? [Y/N], dBASE appends TO PRINT to the command on the action line; otherwise, the output is sent to the screen.

```
Page No,    1
04/15/89
                              ABC COMPANY
                    CUSTOMER NAME AND ADDRESS REPORT
            NAME          ADDRESS             CITY          ST    AMOUNT
Reza     Ghorbani     4033 N, Wolcott      Chicago        Il    125,00
Ann      Ghorbani     4033 No, Wolcott     Chicago        Il    250,00
Douglas  Acklin       408 E, Monroe        Bloomington    Il     55,00
Barbara  Walters      1981 Crestlawn       Arlington      Va     75,00
Arthur   Adams        115 Ginger Creek Ct, Bloomington    Il     35,00
Russell  Davis        707 Vale St,         Bloomington    Il     35,00
Debbie   Acklin       408 E, Monroe        Bloomington    Il     35,00
Harvey   Posio        1013 Hillcrest       San Diego      Ca   1250,00
Ben      Pietrowiak   3334 Foster          Normal         Il     20,00
Sandy    Acklin       408 E, Monroe        Bloomington    Il     35,00
Fred     Ficek        1215 Tamarack        Normal         Il      0,00
Juan     Decesario    1214 Flores          Miami          Fl     10,00
*** Total ***
                                                              1925,00
```

When dBASE executed the above command, it accessed the disk for the NAMEADDR.FRM file and loaded it. It then accessed the customer file.

Once you build a report template, you can use it over and over. You can also limit the records that are included in a report by use of the FOR parameter via the Build a search condition. For example, you may want to print an exception report containing only those customers whose balance is over $100. The following example illustrates such a report.

You enter the same commands as in the previous example. But instead of immediately telling dBASE to execute the command, select the Build a search condition option, select the AMOUNT field, select the > Greater Than option, enter 100, and press the ENTER key. Tell dBASE there are no more conditions. At this time you should see the following command on the action line: REPORT FORM B:NAMEADDR FOR AMOUNT > 100. Tell dBASE to execute the command, and the following report is generated.

```
Page No,     1
04/15/89
                            ABC COMPANY
                  CUSTOMER NAME AND ADDRESS REPORT
            NAME        ADDRESS           CITY        ST  AMOUNT
Reza     Ghorbani    4033 N, Wolcott    Chicago      Il   125,00
Ann      Ghorbani    4033 N, Wolcott    Chicago      Il   250,00
Harvey   Posio       1013 Hillcrest     San Diego    Ca  1250,00
*** Total ***

                                                         1625,00
```

You might also want to print a report of amounts owed by customers in a specific region. The following command entered at the dot prompt (.) produces a list of all customers who live in Bloomington and generates a grand total of the amount owed:

```
,  report form nameaddr for city = 'Bloominston'
```

```
Page No,     1
04/15/89
                            ABC COMPANY
                  CUSTOMER NAME AND ADDRESS REPORT
            NAME        ADDRESS             CITY          ST  AMOUNT
Douglas  Acklin     408 E, Monroe       Bloominston     Il   55,00
Arthur   Adams      115 Ginger Creek Ct, Bloominston    Il   35,00
Russell  Davis      707 Vale St,        Bloominston     Il   35,00
Debbie   Acklin     408 E, Monroe       Bloominston     Il   35,00
Sandy    Acklin     408 E, Monroe       Bloominston     Il   35,00
*** Total ***

                                                             195,00
```

You could also specify the Build a search condition and specify the CITY field as the field to use in this operation. When prompted with Enter a character string (without quotes):, respond with Bloominston, press the ENTER key, tell dBASE there are no more conditions, and then tell it to execute the command.

To make changes to a report template requires selecting either the Create or Modify options of the Assistant menu and then the Report option. Once the drive and the template name have been specified, you can change any of the screen information.

Chapter Review

The dBASE III Plus package provides commands for manipulating data. The LIST command can be used to display (a) the contents of an entire file, (b) selected records that meet selection criteria, or (c) selected fields of records. The DISPLAY ALL command works like the LIST command except that it stops when it has displayed sixteen lines on the screen.

A number of pointer movement commands are provided, including the explicit and implied GO and GOTO commands and the SKIP command, which enable you to move forward or backward in the file, a record at a time or a number of records at a time.

The REPLACE command enables you to change one record, selected groups of records, or all records in the file at one time, in accordance with stated selection criteria. This provides you with another method, besides the EDIT command, for changing the field contents of records.

The substring command ($) is a powerful command that enables you to search for characters in a field of data. It can be used in conjunction with such commands as REPLACE and LIST using DBASE.

The dBASE III Plus package does not automatically delete a record from a file when you issue the DELETE command. Instead, it only "logically" deletes the record, which means it marks it with dBASE's delete indicator, the asterisk (*), for future deletion. After a record has been marked for deletion, it can be undeleted by using the RECALL command. Physically removing a record from a file requires using the PACK statement following the DELETE. The PACK statement copies the entire file to a new location on disk, dropping any records marked for deletion.

The CREATE REPORT command enables you to generate a formatted report via a report template from information contained in a file. The CREATE REPORT feature provides a number of full-screen editing windows for you to use in describing the report, including screens for specifying report and column headings and any fields you want to print. The feature also generates totals for any numeric fields.

Key Terms and Concepts

ALL parameter
beginning of file (BOF) function
CREATE REPORT command
DELETE command
delete indicator (*)
DIR command
DISPLAY command
end of file (EOF) function
FOR parameter
GO command
GOTO command
GOTO BOTTOM command
GOTO TOP command
LIST command
LIST STRUCTURE command

NEXT option
PACK command
RECALL command
RECNO() function
REPLACE command
REPORT FORM command
report template
SKIP command
substring function ($)
SUM command
TO PRINT option
USE command
WHILE parameter
? character

Chapter Quiz

Multiple Choice

1. Which of the following dBASE command(s) can be used to change records in a file?
   a. LIST
   b. EDIT
   c. REPORT
   d. REPLACE
   e. CHANGE

2. If you use the SET PRINT ON command, reports could be generated using which of the following statements?
   a. LIST
   b. REPORT
   c. DISPLAY
   d. All of the above
   e. Only the REPORT

3. The report feature of dBASE III Plus enables you to do which of the following?
   a. Establish a report title
   b. Print column headings
   c. Number each page
   d. Print totals
   e. All of the above
   f. Only a, b, and c

4. Which of the following commands does not move the record pointer?
   a. SKIP
   b. GOTO BOTTOM
   c. GOTO TOP
   d. .5
   e. SKIP −5
   f. All of the commands move the record pointer.

5. Which of the following statements is true about the LIST and DISPLAY commands?
   a. The DISPLAY does not allow you to display selected fields.
   b. Both the LIST and DISPLAY prohibit arithmetic selection criteria.
   c. The DISPLAY shows the next 16 lines of record text and then pauses.
   d. The DISPLAY automatically lists all of the records in the file.
   e. None of the above statements is false.

True/False

6. The DISPLAY ALL command gives you more control than the simple LIST command.

7. The DELETE command physically removes a record from a file.

8. The RECALL command automatically unerases all deleted records within a file.

9. The DISPLAY command shows the record at the current pointer location.

10. The SUM command can be used to total numeric fields from selected records in a file.

Answers

1. b and d 2. d 3. e 4. f 5. c 6. t 7. f 8. f 9. t 10. t

Exercises

1. The command DISPLAY _____ will display all records in the file on the screen and pause after each sixteen lines.

2. The _____ command displays the record at the current pointer location.

3. List the pointer positioning commands:
   a.

   b.

   c.

   d.

4. The GOTO _____ places the pointer at the end of the file.

5. The _____ command can be used to move forward or backward in the file.

6. The _____ command is used to display the current record number.

7. The GOTO _____ command is used to position the pointer at the beginning of the file.

8. The _____ command can be used to change records in the file.

9. The function _____ is used to find a character string in a field.

10. The _____ command is used to mark a record for deletion.

11. The _____ command is used to undelete a record.

12. The _____ command is used to remove records from a file that have been marked for deletion.

13. The _____ command is used to generate a total of a field from the records in a file.

14. The _____ command sends any output on the screen to the printer.

15. The _____ command is used to build a report template that can be used later.

Computer Exercises

The following exercises require using the PAYMAST file, created previously.

1. Look at the format of the data base records.

2. Look at the employee and pay rate of each record.

3. Look at only those employees with a gross of more than $850.

4. Total the gross pay field.

5. Total the gross pay field for those with a gross of more than $900.

6. Give Mark Tell a raise of .50.

7. Give everyone a raise of .25.

8. Go to record 5 and display it to the screen.

9. Delete and recall record 9.

10. Delete record 5.

11. Pack the file.

12. Use the $ function to find any record with a P in the first or last name.

13. Create the following report and print it out.

```
PAGE NO. 00001
04/13/89

                                    PAYROLL SUMMARY
       ID          EMPLOYEE              PAY RATE         GROSS
     4908  Richard     Payne               4.45          556.00
     5789  Connie      Reiners             3.35          450.00
     5523  Pamela      Rich                6.00          780.00
     6324  Mark        Tell                5.50          980.00
     2870  Frank       Terlep              6.80          670.00
     4679  Kenneth     Klass               4.90          780.00
     8345  Thomas      Momery              4.70          580.00
     5649  Toni        McCarthy            5.20          667.00
     5432  Alan        Monroe              5.20         1340.00
     5998  Paul        Mish                4.90          887.00
     4463  Edward      Mockford            4.90          775.00
      456                                  0.00            0.00
    ** TOTAL **
                                                        8465.00
```

14. Use the report template you developed to generate a report for employees with a gross pay of more than $800.

Chapter 15

Advanced Data Base Management with dBASE III Plus

Chapter Objectives   After completing this chapter, you should be able to:

Discuss the dBASE III Plus SORT _command_

Discuss the dBASE III Plus INDEX _command_

Discuss locating records in sequential and random files

Discuss ordered reports

Discuss some miscellaneous file commands

Discuss the BROWSE _command_

This chapter introduces you to dBASE techniques that allow you to arrange, rearrange, and locate data in the manner most suitable to your application. The commands covered in this chapter include SORT, INDEX, LOCATE, FIND, DELETE, and BROWSE.

Arrangement Commands

SORT

The SORT command is used to physically rearrange records in a file according to values contained in a specific field of each record. To do this, the sort does not rearrange the content of the file itself but specifies the order in which an output file will hold the original file's content. The SORT command has the following syntax:

```
SORT <field list> TO [<output file>]
```

The following are defaults for the SORT command. The TO file, which holds the output of the sort, has a .DBF file extension unless you specify another extension in the file name. Sorts are in ascending order (/A) unless you specify otherwise.

The SORT command has some general rules for its use. When you sort on multiple fields, the most important field is placed first. Up to ten fields can be specified. Place a comma between fields. You may not sort logical or memo fields.

Ascending order (the default setting) sorts the information in alphabetical order A to Z and in numeric order 0 to 9. If you specify descending order, alphabetic sorts are placed in order Z to A and numeric information in order 9 to 0.

Sorting the CUSTOMER file in zip code order requires setting the default drive to B: (if you have not already done so), activating the CUSTOMER file, selecting the ORGANIZE option of the Assistant menu, and then selecting the SORT option of this submenu (the action line now contains SORT ON). A listing of the fields contained in the CUSTOMER file, with information about each highlighted field, is now displayed on your screen (see Figure 15.1). Highlight the ZIP field, press the ENTER key, and then press the Right arrow key to return to the Organize submenu. Select the default drive (B:) to hold the sorted output file by pressing the ENTER key. You are now prompted for the name of the output file (see Figure 15.2). Enter the name ZIPCUST and press the ENTER key. The command SORT ON ZIP TO ZIPCUST has now been executed by dBASE, and the file ZIPCUST now holds the sorted information from the CUSTOMER file.

Once the sort starts the following lines appear at the bottom of your screen:

```
00%
100%           12 Records Sorted
```

The SORT command keeps you informed as to how much of the file has been sorted. When the sort is completed, the 100% xx Records Sorted message is displayed on the screen. You now have two files: the original CUSTOMER file on disk, which remains unchanged, and the newly created ZIPCUST file, which contains the data from the CUSTOMER file arranged by the contents of the ZIP field. Because you have not changed the file specified via a USE statement, the CUSTOMER file remains active. You can confirm that its order has not changed by using the RETRIEVE com-

Figure 15.1
Field list for specifying key
fields in a sort.

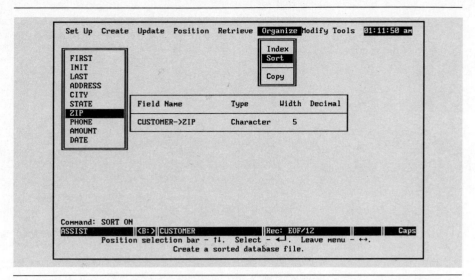

Figure 15.2
Screen for specifying the output file in a sort operation.

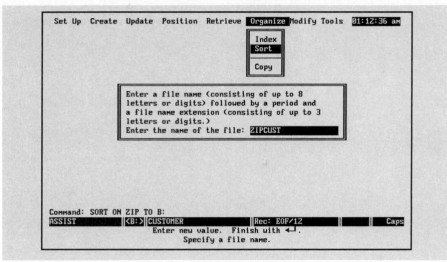

mand of the Assistant menu and listing the file by the fields FIRST, LAST,
CITY, STATE, and ZIP (see Figure 15.3).

To verify that you have created the ZIPCUST file properly, issue the SET
UP command from the Assistant menu, activate the ZIPCUST file, select the
RETRIEVE command from the Assistant menu, specify the same fields, issue
the LIST command, and execute (see Figure 15.4). Notice that the records are
not in the same order as in the CUSTOMER file but are arranged by the contents
of the ZIP field. This means that the record numbers are also different, having
been changed to reflect their new locations in the ZIPCUST file.

The process of sorting information by two fields is just as straightforward. Suppose you want to sort the CUSTOMER file by name. When two
customers have the same last name, you will want the first names to be in
alphabetical order. In this case, the primary sort key (first field specified) is the
last name, and the secondary sort key (second field specified) is the first name.
Specify your sort fields in the manner previously indicated and place the
output in the file ALPHNAME. Once the SORT command is executed, the
information is placed in first-name within last name order. Activate the

Figure 15.3
Output of the unchanged
CUSTOMER file via the LIST
command.

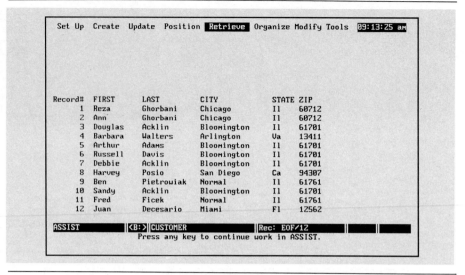

Figure 15.4
The sorted ZIPCUST file.

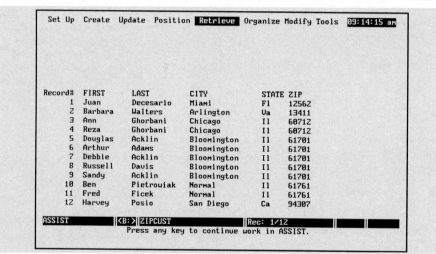

ALPHNAME file and list it in LAST, FIRST, CITY, STATE, and ZIP order (see Figure 15.5).

The dBASE command that created the ALPHNAME file is SORT ON LAST,FIRST TO B:ALPHNAME.

The SORT command is not usually the best way to arrange data within a file. Several restrictions apply to it:

1. It usually takes a lot of computer time. Although this is not evident with a small file such as CUSTOMER, an attempt to use SORT on a file containing 3,000 records would make it obvious.

2. The SORT command generates a new file every time it is executed. This takes up a large amount of disk storage when you are dealing with large files.

3. The record numbers change from one file to another. The record number of a record in the unsorted file will be useless to you in the sorted file.

Figure 15.5
Result of a L I S T command against the sorted ALPHNAME file.

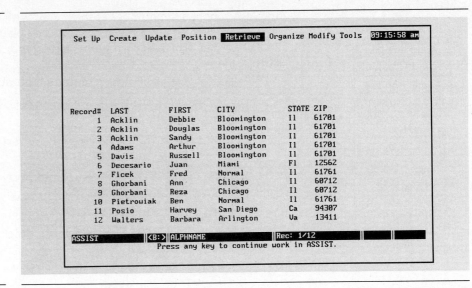

INDEX

The easiest way to overcome these shortcomings of the SORT command is by using the <u>INDEX</u> **command**. This command can generate two types of indexes: single field and multiple field.

Single-Field Indexes. A **single-field index** file is ordered by one field only. The ordering of an indexed file is fundamentally different from that of a sorted file: Instead of reordering the original data physically, as the SORT command does, the INDEX command reorders it logically without moving records. This is accomplished by using an Index Construct to create an index file in which each specified field points to the appropriate record in the specified file. The contents of the original file remain unchanged, with the same physical file order and the same record numbers, whereas the index file created by the INDEX command holds the logical order of the file.

To prepare for the following examples, activate the CUSTOMER file via the SET UP command in the Assistant menu.

Logically arranging the CUSTOMER file in zip code order requires selecting the ORGANIZE option of the Assistant menu, selecting the INDEX option from the submenu, and responding with the field ZIP to the prompt for entering an index expression. Now indicate that you want this index placed on the default drive (in this example, B:) by pressing the ENTER key. Name the index file to be created (ZIP). The CUSTOMER file is now logically arranged in ZIP field order, and the ZIP.NDX file is created on the default drive.

Once the indexing process starts, the following information is displayed on your screen:

```
00%
100% Indexed    12 Records Indexed
```

These steps generate the command INDEX ON ZIP TO ZIP in the action line. The result is an index file called ZIP.NDX; each record in the ZIP.NDX file contains the ZIP field for a record in the CUSTOMER file

Zip Code	*Record Number*
12562	00012
13411	00004
60712	00001
60712	00002
61701	00003
61701	00005
61701	00006
61701	00007
61701	00010
61761	00009
61761	00011
94307	00008

Figure 15.6
Information contained in the ZIP.NDX file: the zip code and the location of each record.

and also contains the number of the record with that particular zip code value (see Figure 15.6). When the records are displayed, dBASE first accesses the ZIP.NDX file, which in turn points to the appropriate record from the CUSTOMER file.

To activate the ZIP index requires a number of steps:

1. Use the SET UP option of the Assistant menu to select the CUSTOMER file.

2. Indicate that the file is indexed by responding Y to the prompt Is the file indexed? [Y/N].

3. Point to the ZIP.NDX entry and press the ENTER key.

4. Press a Right or Left arrow key to activate the index (the command USE CUSTOMER INDEX ZIP appears on the action line).

5. Select the RETRIEVE option of the Assistant menu and take the LIST option.

6. Specify that the fields LAST, FIRST, CITY, STATE, ZIP, and AMOUNT be displayed.

7. Execute the command.

The information from the CUSTOMER file (see Figure 15.7) is now displayed.

When dBASE lists the records from an indexed file, it performs a number of tasks automatically. First, it goes to the ZIP.NDX file (see Figure 15.6) and finds zip 12562. It also finds that record 12 of the CUSTOMER file holds the data for this index entry. dBASE now accesses record 12 of the CUSTOMER file. It then moves to the second index entry and repeats the process until all index entries have been processed.

As you can see from this example, using the Assistant menu to create indexes and then invoke the file using that index requires a number of steps and even more keystrokes. Creating indexes and then verifying that you have created them correctly using the LIST command requires less time in command mode at the dot prompt (.). The remaining indexes will therefore be created using the command mode of dBASE III Plus.

Another bonus from using command mode is that after an index is created, it is automatically invoked by dBASE. This means that you do not have to issue a USE FILENAME INDEX command to list the records from the file for the created index.

To verify that the contents of the CUSTOMER file remain physically unchanged, you could issue the following commands:

```
. use customer
. list first,last,city,state,zip
```

Record#	FIRST	LAST	CITY	STATE	ZIP
1	Reza	Ghorbani	Chicago	Il	60712
2	Ann	Ghorbani	Chicago	Il	60712
3	Douglas	Acklin	Bloomington	Il	61701
4	Barbara	Walters	Arlington	Va	13411
5	Arthur	Adams	Bloomington	Il	61701
6	Russell	Davis	Bloomington	Il	61701
7	Debbie	Acklin	Bloomington	Il	61701
8	Harvey	Posio	San Diego	Ca	94307
9	Ben	Pietrowiak	Normal	Il	61761
10	Sandy	Acklin	Bloomington	Il	61701
11	Fred	Ficek	Normal	Il	61761
12	Juan	Decesario	Miami	Fl	12562

Figure 15.7
The CUSTOMER file listed via the ZIP.NDX index.

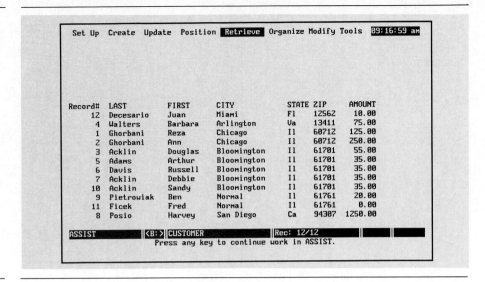

```
     Set Up  Create  Update  Position  Retrieve  Organize Modify Tools  09:16:59 am




    Record#  LAST        FIRST     CITY         STATE ZIP     AMOUNT
         12  Decesario   Juan      Miami        Fl    12562     10.00
          4  Walters     Barbara   Arlington    Va    13411     75.00
          1  Ghorbani    Reza      Chicago      Il    60712    125.00
          2  Ghorbani    Ann       Chicago      Il    60712    250.00
          3  Acklin      Douglas   Bloomington  Il    61701     55.00
          5  Adams       Arthur    Bloomington  Il    61701     35.00
          6  Davis       Russell   Bloomington  Il    61701     35.00
          7  Acklin      Debbie    Bloomington  Il    61701     35.00
         10  Acklin      Sandy     Bloomington  Il    61701     35.00
          9  Pietrowiak  Ben       Normal       Il    61761     20.00
         11  Ficek       Fred      Normal       Il    61761      0.00
          8  Posio       Harvey    San Diego    Ca    94307   1250.00

    ASSIST          <B:> CUSTOMER              Rec: 12/12
                    Press any key to continue work in ASSIST.
```

If you want to see the file arranged in logical order of last name, issue the INDEX and LIST commands:

```
. index on last to last
  12 records indexed
. list last, first, city, state, zip, amount
```

Record#	LAST	FIRST	CITY	STATE	ZIP	AMOUNT
3	Acklin	Douglas	Bloomington	Il	61701	55.00
7	Acklin	Debbie	Bloomington	Il	61701	35.00
10	Acklin	Sandy	Bloomington	Il	61701	35.00
5	Adams	Arthur	Bloomington	Il	61701	35.00
6	Davis	Russell	Bloomington	Il	61701	35.00
12	Decesario	Juan	Miami	Fl	12562	10.00
11	Ficek	Fred	Normal	Il	61761	0.00
1	Ghorbani	Reza	Chicago	Il	60712	0.00
2	Ghorbani	Ann	Chicago	Il	60712	250.00
9	Pietrowiak	Ben	Normal	Il	61761	20.00
8	Posio	Harvey	San Diego	Ca	94307	1250.00
4	Walters	Barbara	Arlington	Va	13411	75.00

Multiple-Field Indexes. A single-field index is inappropriate for many applications. For instance, what do you do if you want the file to appear in order by the first-name and last-name field contents? The INDEX command manages this task easily by enabling you to **concatenate** (join) fields in creating the index. The result is a **multiple-field index**. The first multiple-field index here will be created using the Assistant feature of dBASE, but others will be created at the dot prompt.

Reenter the Assistant mode by entering ASSIST at the dot prompt, and then press the ENTER key.

Once the file has been properly activated (it already is unless you have just started dBASE), perform the following steps:

1. Select the Organize option of the Assistant menu.

2. Enter the fields to be indexed (see Figure 15.8). The statement on the action line is now INDEX ON LAST + FIRST TO.

3. Press the ENTER key.

Figure 15.8
Screen used to concatenate fields for creating the LFNAME index file.

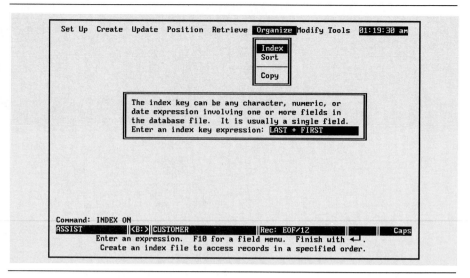

Figure 15.9
The listing of selected fields from the CUSTOMER file in alphabetical order via the LFNAME index.

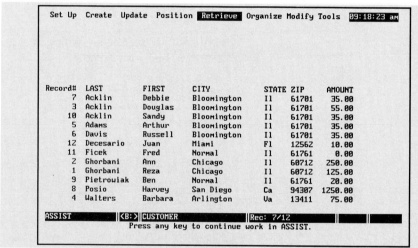

4. Indicate that the index file is to be placed on the default drive (in this case B:); the dBASE command on the action line is now INDEX ON LAST + FIRST TO B:.

5. Enter the index file name LFNAME and press ENTER. dBASE appends the file name to the command so that it becomes INDEX ON FIRST + LAST TO B:LFNAME. The file is now indexed by dBASE, and the message 100% Indexed   12 Records indexed appears at the bottom of your screen.

6. Use the Set Up option of the Assistant menu to activate the Customer file using the LFNAME index.

7. Press the Left or Right arrow key.

8. Use the Retrieve option of the Assistant menu, and then select the List option.

9. Construct a field list containing the LAST, FIRST, CITY, STATE, ZIP, and AMOUNT fields.

10. Execute the command.

A listing of the file in alphabetical order by last name (see Figure 15.9) is now displayed. You can see that within the last-name order the Acklin and the

Ghorbani records are now listed in alphabetical order by the first-name field contents.

The remaining examples of multiple-field index fields will be entered via command mode at the dot prompt. Notice that you do not have to enter the drive identifier in front of the index file name since dBASE automatically creates it on the default drive (in these examples drive B).

Extending the index order to three fields is done with the following INDEX command, which logically arranges the file in order by zip code, last name, and first name:

```
. index on zip + last + first to ziplfnam
  12 records indexed
. list last, first, city, state, zip, amount
```

Record#	LAST	FIRST	CITY	STATE	ZIP	AMOUNT
12	Decesario	Juan	Miami	Fl	12562	10.00
4	Walters	Barbara	Arlington	Va	13411	75.00
2	Ghorbani	Ann	Chicago	Il	60712	250.00
1	Ghorbani	Reza	Chicago	Il	60712	125.00
7	Acklin	Debbie	Bloomington	Il	61701	35.00
3	Acklin	Douglas	Bloomington	Il	61701	55.00
10	Acklin	Sandy	Bloomington	Il	61701	35.00
5	Adams	Arthur	Bloomington	Il	61701	35.00
6	Davis	Russell	Bloomington	Il	61701	35.00
11	Ficek	Fred	Normal	Il	61761	0.00
9	Pietrowiak	Ben	Normal	Il	61761	20.00
8	Posio	Harvey	San Diego	Ca	94307	1250.00

Assume that you now want to access the CUSTOMER file by last-name first-name order. You do not have to re-create the LFNAME index because it is still on the disk under the name LFNAME.NDX. All you have to do is type the name of the file and the name of the corresponding index to use in accessing the data. The commands are as follows:

```
. use customer index lfname
. list last, first, city, state, zip, amount
```

Record#	LAST	FIRST	CITY	STATE	ZIP	AMOUNT
7	Acklin	Debbie	Bloomington	Il	61701	35.00
3	Acklin	Douglas	Bloomington	Il	61701	55.00
10	Acklin	Sandy	Bloomington	Il	61701	35.00
5	Adams	Arthur	Bloomington	Il	61701	35.00
6	Davis	Russell	Bloomington	Il	61701	35.00
12	Decesario	Juan	Miami	Fl	12562	10.00
11	Ficek	Fred	Normal	Il	61761	0.00
2	Ghorbani	Ann	Chicago	Il	60712	250.00
1	Ghorbani	Reza	Chicago	Il	60712	125.00
9	Pietrowiak	Ben	Normal	Il	61761	20.00
8	Posio	Harvey	San Diego	Ca	94307	1250.00
4	Walters	Barbara	Arlington	Va	13411	75.00

You can also have the data sorted in some numerical order. The INDEX command operates only on character data, unless the created index refers exclusively to a numeric field of the original file. The data in an index are always stored as character data, not as numeric data; therefore, to create a

mixed data multiple-field index (an index that uses both numeric fields and character fields), the numeric fields in the original file must first be changed to character data using the STR **function.**

The following example illustrates the creation of an index ordered by the AMOUNT field only. The file can then be listed in ascending order by the amount owed. Keep in mind that the index entry is now character data, whereas the data in the original file remain numeric. The commands used and the list produced are as follows:

```
. use customer
. index on amount to amount
     12 records indexed
. list last, first, city, state, zip, amount
```

Record#	last	first	city	state	zip	amount
11	Ficek	Fred	Normal	Il	61761	0.00
12	Decesario	Juan	Miami	Fl	12562	10.00
9	Pietrowiak	Ben	Normal	Il	61761	20.00
5	Adams	Arthur	Bloomington	Il	61701	35.00
6	Davis	Russell	Bloomington	Il	61701	35.00
7	Acklin	Debbie	Bloomington	Il	61701	35.00
10	Acklin	Sandy	Bloomington	Il	61701	35.00
3	Acklin	Douglas	Bloomington	Il	61701	55.00
4	Walters	Barbara	Arlington	Va	13411	75.00
1	Ghorbani	Reza	Chicago	Il	60712	125.00
2	Ghorbani	Ann	Chicago	Il	60712	250.00
8	Posio	Harvey	San Diego	Ca	94307	1250.00

Creating a mixed data multiple-field index that refers to one or more numeric field(s) requires the use of the STR (string) function: otherwise, an error message is displayed. The STR function works only if you provide the name of the field to be converted, the field length, and the number of positions to the right of the decimal point that are involved. To create an index using the zip code and amount fields, you would issue the following commands:

```
. index on zip + str(amount,8,2) to zipamoun
     12 records indexed
. list last, first, city, state, zip, amount
```

Record#	last	first	city	state	zip	amount
12	Decesario	Juan	Miami	Fl	12562	10.00
4	Walters	Barbara	Arlington	Va	13411	75.00
1	Ghorbani	Reza	Chicago	Il	60712	125.00
2	Ghorbani	Ann	Chicago	Il	60712	250.00
5	Adams	Arthur	Bloomington	Il	61701	35.00
6	Davis	Russell	Bloomington	Il	61701	35.00
7	Acklin	Debbie	Bloomington	Il	61701	35.00
10	Acklin	Sandy	Bloomington	Il	61701	35.00
3	Acklin	Douglas	Bloomington	Il	61701	55.00
11	Ficek	Fred	Normal	Il	61761	0.00
9	Pietrowiak	Ben	Normal	Il	61761	20.00
8	Posio	Harvey	San Diego	Ca	94307	1250.00

Ancillary Commands. There are two versions of the DELETE and LIST commands related to files. To delete files (such as the no longer needed CUSTZIP file), you can use the <u>DELETE FILE</u> **command**.

```
. delete file zipcust.dbf
FILE HAS BEEN DELETED
```

You may sometimes want to list various families of files on the screen, which you can accomplish by using the <u>LIST FILES LIKE</u> **command**. You do not have to use an extension for data base files because when no extension is given, dBASE automatically inserts a .DBF extension. To list index files, however, you must use the **.NDX extension**. Wildcards can be used in LIST FILES LIKE commands such as the following:

```
. list files like *.ndx
ZIP      .NDX       LAST     .NDX       LFNAME   .NDX
ZIPLFMAN.NDX       ZIPAMOUN.NDX       AMOUNT   .NDX
   5120 bytes in       6 files.
330752 bytes remaining on drive.


. list files like *.dbf
CUSTOMER.DBF       PAYMAST.DBF        ALPHNAME.DBF
   3286 bytes in       3 files.
334848 bytes remaining on drive.
```

Managing Index Files. One of the major benefits of using index files is that they do not have to be constantly re-created as you add records to or delete records from them. You can specify as many as seven indexes in a USE statement. Any indexes that are specified following the INDEX portion of the USE statement are automatically **updated** when an APPEND, DELETE, or PACK command is executed against the file. For example, to make certain that all of the indexes created in this chapter are updated to reflect all future changes in the CUSTOMER file, you would issue the following command:

```
. use customer index ziplfnam,last,lfname,zipamoun,amount,zip
```

Any time a new record is appended or an indexed field is changed (via the EDIT or BROWSE commands), the appropriate indexes are automatically updated. Only the first index you specify, however, is **active**. In this example, the result is that the CUSTOMER file can be accessed only via the ZIPLFNAM index.

It is important to specify appropriate indexes after the file name when you are about to pack a file. The PACK command automatically re-creates each of the specified indexes once the PACK statement has compressed the file; but if you do not specify the indexes before you pack the file, you will have to re-create each index separately. Should you forget to re-create any of the indexes and later try to use the old index to list the revised file contents, you will receive a RECORD OUT OF RANGE error message.

Reports Using Indexes. When you are generating a report, an index can be used to determine the order in which the data file will be used. For instance, to generate a report in zip code, last name, and first name order, you would use the following commands:

```
• use customer index ziplfnam
• report form nameaddr to print
```

Page No.   1
05/10/89

ABC COMPANY
NAME AND ADDRESS REPORT

NAME		ADDRESS	CITY	ST	AMOUNT
Juan	Decesario	1214 Flores	Miami	Fl	10.00
Barbara	Walters	1981 Crestlawn	Arlington	Va	75.00
Ann	Ghorbani	4033 N. Wolcott	Chicago	Il	250.00
Reza	Ghorbani	4033 N. Wollcott	Chicago	Il	125.00
Debbie	Acklin	408 E. Monroe	Bloomington	Il	35.00
Douglas	Acklin	408 E. Monroe	Bloomington	Il	55.00
Sandy	Acklin	408 E. Monroe	Bloomington	Il	35.00
Arthur	Adams	115 Ginger Creek Ct.	Bloomington	Il	35.00
Russell	Davis	707 Vale St.	Bloomington	Il	35.00
Fred	Ficek	1215 Tamarack	Normal	Il	0.00
Ben	Pietrowiak	3334 N. Foster	Normal	Il	20.00
Harvey	Posio	1013 Hillcrest	San Diego	Ca	1250.00

*** Total ***

                                                                 1925.00

A report can also be easily generated using the "numeric" (actually, character) AMOUNT.NDX index file by entering the following commands:

```
• use customer index amount
• report form nameaddr to print
```

Page No. 1
04/15/89

ABC COMPANY
NAME AND ADDRESS REPORT

NAME		ADDRESS	CITY	STATE	AMOUNT
Fred	Ficek	1215 Tamarack	Normal	Il	0.00
Decesario	Juan	1214 Flores	Miami	Fl	10.00
Ben	Pietrowiak	3334 N. Foster	Normal	Il	20.00
Davis	Russell	707 Vale St.	Bloomington	Il	35.00
Arthur	Adams	115 Ginger Creek Ct.	Bloomington	Il	35.00
Debbie	Acklin	408 E. Monroe	Bloomington	Il	35.00
Sandy	Acklin	408 E. Monroe	Bloomington	Il	35.00
Douglas	Acklin	408 E. Monroe	Bloomington	Il	55.00
Barbara	Walters	1981 Crestlawn	Arlington	Va	75.00
Reza	Ghorbani	4033 N. Wolcott	Chicago	Il	125.00
Ann	Ghorbani	4033 N. Wolcott	Chicago	Il	250.00
Harvey	Posio	1013 Hillcrest	San Diego	Ca	1250.00

*** Total ***

                                                                 1925.00

Location Commands

Up to this point, you have used either the LIST or DISPLAY commands to locate a record. Both commands start at the beginning of a file and display all of the records that meet the specified search criteria. If you want to display only one relevant record at a time—rather than all of the relevant records at once—you can use either the `LOCATE` or `SEEK` command.

LOCATE

The `LOCATE` **command** is used to perform a sequential file search, starting at the beginning of the file and progressing through it until a "hit" occurs. (A hit occurs when a record's content meets the specified search criteria.) For example, assume that you want to find all the records of clients who live in the town of Normal. When you are setting up the criteria for a character field, make certain that you enter the characters exactly as they appear in the field. Accomplishing this would require the following statements:

```
. use customer
. locate for city = 'Normal'
Record =        9
. continue
Record =       11
. continue
End of LOCATE scope
```

The dBASE program displays the record number of the first record in the file that meets the search criteria. Any number of simple or complex search criteria can be used to find records via the `LOCATE` command. The `CONTINUE` **command** sends dBASE looking for the next record that meets the search criteria. This process continues until the last record in the file is processed, at which point the message `End of LOCATE scope` is displayed. You can now use the `EDIT` command to examine any or all of the displayed record numbers.

The preceding example can also be executed from the Assistant menu, but then the information is not displayed together. The following discussion takes place from the Assistant.

SEEK

The `SEEK` **command** can be used only for accessing a **random file** (any dBASE file that has an index). Both the file and the index must be referenced in a `USE` statement before the `SEEK` command is issued.

The `SEEK` command operates differently from the `LOCATE` command. The `LOCATE` command results in a sequential search of the data file itself, whereas the `SEEK` command uses the index to find any record(s) that match the search criteria, and the entry in the index then points to the record location in the data file. Since the information in the index is all character data, the search criteria must be contained inside single quotes.

Again, the number of keystrokes in using the Assistant menu in conjunction with a `SEEK` command are many more than those required by the dot prompt. The following examples are executed at the dot prompt.

The `SET HEADINGS OFF` **command** turns off the field headings for a displayed record.

Assume that you are going to use the `CUSTOMER` file via the `ZIP` index. To find those records that have a 61761 zip code, you would use the following commands:

```
. use customer index zip
. set headings off
. seek '61761'
. display
     9  Ben        A Pietrowiak   3334 N. Foster          Normal
IL 61761 (309)452-9126      20.00
. skip
Record no.     11
    11  Fred       R Ficek        1215 Tamarack           Normal
Il 61761 (309)454-7123      0.00
. skip
Record No.      8
     8  Harvey     B Posio        1013 Hillcrest          San Diego
Ca 94307 (619)271-9871    1250.00
```

Notice that dBASE does not give the END OF FILE ENCOUNTERED message. When the SEEK command is executed, the first occurrence of zip code 61761 is found in the index file (see Figure 15.6), and dBASE positions the pointer to that record (in this case, record 9). After accessing this 61761 record, the only way to find out if there are any more 61761 records is to advance via the index to the next zip record. This is also a 61761 record. The second SKIP command advances you (via the index) to a 94307 zip code. Since the zip code found is no longer 61761, you know that there are no more 61761 records.

The SEEK 61761 command directs dBASE to find the first occurrence of the 61761 zip in the ZIP index. Unless the NO FIND **message** is displayed, dBASE positions the pointer at that record location. The record is displayed via the DISPLAY command. The next occurrence of the 61761 zip is located via the SKIP command, which positions the pointer at the next record that is pointed to in the ZIP index. This process is repeated until all of the 61761 zip codes have been located.

To use the AMOUNT index to find all customers in the CUSTOMER file who owe $35.00, you would need to issue the following commands:

```
. use customer index amount
. seek 35.00
. display
     5  Arthur     V  Adams            115 Ginger Creek Ct.    Bloomington
Il     61701 (309)828-7290      35.00 03/15/90
. skip
Record No.     6
. disp
     6  Russell    B  Davis            707  Vale  St.          Bloomington
Il 61701 (309)662-1759      35.00 02/27/90
. skip
Record No.      7
. disp
     7  Debbie     C  Acklin           408  E.  Monroe         Bloomington
Il 61701 (309)827-1395      35.00 03/21/90
. skip
Record No.     10
. disp
    10  Sandy      C  Acklin           408  E.  Monroe         Bloomington
Il 61701 (309)829-9901      35.00 02/25/90
. skip
Record No.      3
. disp
     3  Douglas    C  Acklin           408  E.  Monroe         Bloomington
Il 61701 (309)663-8976      55.00 04/01/90
```

The following commands will also work:

```
. seek '    35.00'
. display
```
```
   G  Russell    B Davis           707 Vale St.          Bloomington
Il 61701 (309)662-1759        35.00 02/27/88
```

These examples illustrate that when you are using a single-field numeric index you do not have to be extremely careful in specifying search criteria. The same is not true, however, of specifications for a multiple-field relationship. An example of this type of application is to access the CUSTOMER file using the ZIPAMOUN index, as follows:

```
. use customer index zipamoun
. seek '6170135.00'
NO FIND
.? RECNO()
                    13
```

Why was the NO FIND message displayed despite your having typed 61701 for the zip code and 35.00 for the amount? Remember, the amount field comprises eight positions, and the zip code field comprises five positions; each of these thirteen positions must be included in the search criteria if the search is to be successful. Notice also that the value returned by the RECORD function was 13 because no such records could be found. The following commands find any record with a zip code of 61701 and an amount-owed field of $35.00:

```
. seek '61701   35.00'
. display
   5  Arthur      V Adams          115 Ginger Creek Ct.   Bloomington
IL 61701 (309)828-7290        35.00 01/13/88
. skip
Record no.        7
. display
   7  Debbie      C Acklin         408 E. Monroe          Bloomington
Il 61701 (309)827-3195        35.00 03/21/88
. skip
Record no.        3
. display
   3  Douglas     C Acklin         408 E. Monroe          Bloomington
Il 61701 (309)663-8976        55.00 04/01/88
. skip
Record no.        1
. display
   1  Reza        R Ghorbani       4033 N. Wolcott        Chicago
Il 61702 (312)245-0324       125.00 01/17/88
```

As before, this process is continued until a record is displayed that does not meet the established criteria. The first SEEK command causes dBASE to find the first record that meets the criteria; the subsequent SKIP commands are used to determine whether any more records in the file exist that also meet the search criteria.

Aspects of random and sequential access can be combined to generate a listing of records that meet a certain criterion. Suppose that you want to list only those records in the file that have a zip code of 61701. If you use the LIST command, dBASE will start at the beginning of the file and read through it sequentially to the end—a procedure that can consume a tremendous amount of time if you are dealing with a large file.

You can avoid this problem by using an index that incorporates the desired information in a continuous group. You tell dBASE to go to the beginning of the desired group of records via a SEEK command, and then you issue a LIST command to list all records that meet the criterion. The statements that follow use the CUSTOMER file and the ZIP index. The beginning of the 61701 records is encountered, and all records are then listed as long as they match the 61701 zip code criteria. As soon as the characteristics of the records in the index no longer match the search criterion, the search is stopped. You would use the following commands:

```
. use customer index zip
. seek '61701'
. list first, last, address, zip while zip = '61701'
   3  Douglas    Acklin    408 E. Monroe         61701
   5  Arthur     Adams     115 Ginger Creek Ct.  61701
   6  Russell    Davis     707 Vale St.          61701
   7  Debbie     Acklin    408 E. Monroe         61701
  10  Sandy      Acklin    408 E. Monroe         61701
```

This very useful process of going randomly to a point in a file and then processing sequentially from that point is called **skip sequential processing**.

BROWSE

The BROWSE **command** enables you to change fields of records in a file rapidly. It is especially useful for a file that contains an index. Whereas the EDIT command displays complete records on one or more screens, the BROWSE command enables you to determine which field of each record you want displayed.

In posting payments from customers to the CUSTOMER file, you can have the payment information sorted in alphabetical order by last name. For this type of application, you need only the fields FIRST, LAST, and AMOUNT, because the FIRST and LAST fields enable you to determine whether you have the correct record, and the AMOUNT field enables you to enter the new balance after the payment is made.

Activate the Assistant menu and then do the following tasks: (1) invoke the CUSTOMER file with the LFNAME index; (2) select the Update option of the Assistant menu, point to Browse, and press the ENTER key. The entire record is now available to you (see Figure 15.10). Use the menu at the top of the screen for cursor movement.

The disadvantage of using the Assistant is that you are overwhelmed with data from the file. It would be much better if you were able to limit the number of fields that are displayed. This can be accomplished at the dot prompt using the BROWSE command, which has the following format (field names must be separated by a comma):

BROWSE FIELDS [list of fields]

The two necessary words are BROWSE and FIELDS; the list of fields to be displayed on the screen follows. To access the CUSTOMER file in alphabetical order, you would issue the following commands (see Figure 15.11):

Figure 15.10

The BROWSE command as it is executed from the Assistant menu.

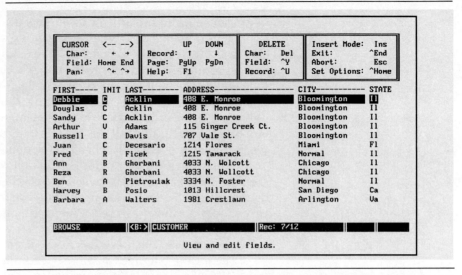

Figure 15.11

The BROWSE command used against selected fields.

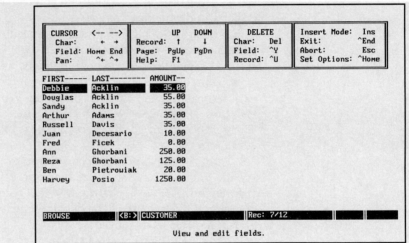

♦ use customer index lfname
♦ browse fields first,last,amount

    The record number currently being changed is displayed at the top of the screen. The field names are displayed at the top of each display column. The first record displayed (in this case, record 3) is in reverse video. The cursor movement keys can be used to make changes. In this case, you want to move to the amount field, a task that requires entering two CTRL + F commands (you could also just hold down the Right arrow key). Each subsequent CTRL + F (or Down arrow) command moves you to the AMOUNT field of the next record. Clearly, this method is much faster than the EDIT command in making scattered changes in a file.

Chapter Review

The dBASE package provides two ways to order records within a file: via the SORT command and via the INDEX command. The SORT command enables you to create a file in which the records are sorted by one or more specified fields. For large files it is a time-consuming command.

The INDEX command creates an index whose contents consist of the key field of each record and the location of each record on disk. The data file is left in its original order, whereas the index is arranged in the desired order. To access a record, dBASE first goes to the index file to find the location of the desired record and then goes to the identified location in the data file. An index file can be built using a number of fields and will produce the information in only one pass. For example, the file could be logically arranged in last-name first-name order with only one statement. The term *logically* is used to emphasize that the original file remains in its original order; only the index file is arranged to reflect the changed relationship.

When you are using multiple-field indexes, you often want changes in the data file to be reflected in every index. This is done by placing the names of any indexes that you want to be updated after the USE statement. Up to seven indexes can be specified. When a change is made that affects any of the specified indexes, the indexes will automatically be changed, too. Remember, however, that only the first index can be used with a SEEK command.

The dBASE package contains several commands that enable you to perform DOS-like actions. With them you can list files that meet certain criteria, or you can delete files from disk.

The REPORT command can be used with sorted or indexed files to generate reports that contain ordered data. With ordered files, the subtotal feature of the REPORT generator can be used.

Sequential files (sorted files without indexes) can be searched for relevant records via the LOCATE command. When the end of the file is reached, the END OF FILE ENCOUNTERED message is displayed on the screen. The next occurrence of that record type is located by issuing the CONTINUE command.

Indexed files can be searched for relevant records via the SEEK command. You must have specified the appropriate index on the USE statement beforehand. The next occurrence of that record type is located via the Skip command. If no record of the desired type is found in the entire file, the NO FIND message is displayed.

The BROWSE command enables you to change records by making use of the full-screen editing feature of dBASE. BROWSE differs from EDIT in enabling you to specify which fields to display on the screen. By using this command, you can quickly move through the file in an index file order and manually make changes to selected records.

Key Terms and Concepts

active index
BROWSE command
concatenation
CONTINUE command
DELETE FILE command
INDEX command
LIST FILES LIKE command
LOCATE command
mixed data multiple-field index
multiple-field index

.NDX extension
NO FIND message
random file
SEEK command
SET HEADINGS OFF command
single-field index
skip sequential processing
SORT command
STR function
updating multiple indexes

Chapter Quiz

Multiple Choice

1. Which of the following statements about sorting is false?
   a. It takes more computer time than indexing.
   b. It takes up more disk space than indexing since an output file has to be created.
   c. A multiple key sort is simply impossible.
   d. You are allowed to sort on only one field at a time.
   e. All of the above statements are true.

2. Which of the following statements is false about indexing?
   a. The original file is left the same.
   b. The index file that "logically" orders the file is created.
   c. First the index must be accessed and then the data file, if the records are desired in indexed order.
   d. The index holds the contents of each data record.
   e. All of the above statements are true.

3. A version of the _____ command is used to list the files on disk.
   a. DISPLAY
   b. BROWSE
   c. LIST
   d. INDEX
   e. USE

4. Which of the following commands enable(s) you to make changes in a record?
   a. BROWSE
   b. REPLACE
   c. EDIT
   d. All of the above
   e. None of the above

5. Which command is used to locate records in an indexed file?
   a. SEEK
   b. LOCATE
   c. SKIP
   d. CONTINUE
   e. None of the above

True/False

6. A file must be indexed before the LOCATE command can be used.

7. The SKIP command is used to find the next record that meets the search criteria for a sequential search.

8. An indexed file can be processed in sequential order by the indexed field.

9. When multiple indexes are specified, only the first index name can be used to find records.

10. Sorting files is usually faster than indexing them.

Answers

1. c 2. d 3. c 4. d 5. a 6. f 7. f 8. t 9. t 10. f

Exercises

1. Define or describe each of the following:
   - a. index
   - b. multiple-field index
   - c. active index
   - d. sequential file
   - e. indexed file
   - f. concatenation

2. Physically reordering the records within a file and creating a new file is done by using the _____ command.

3. The records in a file can be sorted in either _____ or _____ order.

4. The SORT command enables you to sort files using single or _____.

5. The _____ file contains both the key field contents and the record location.

6. Listing records from an indexed file requires going to the _____ file, which then points to the record _____ in the file.

7. Indexing a file usually takes _____ time than sorting a file.

8. Joining two or more fields to form one index is the process known as _____.

9. Numeric fields can be included in an index, but they must first be converted to _____ characters.

10. The command _____ file CUSTZIP can be issued to erase the CUSTZIP file.

11. When several indexes follow the USE statement, only the _____ index can be used to find records.

12. When several indexes follow the USE statement, the PACK command will result in _____ index(es) being rebuilt.

13. An ordered report can be generated by using either a _____ or an indexed file.

14. Totals can be incorporated in a report only when a field is _____.

15. The _____ is used to locate records via an index.

16. The _____ is used to locate records in a sequential file.

17. When you are using the SEEK command, the character string must appear inside _____.

18. The _____ is used to find the next record in a sequential file search.

19. The _____ command enables you to display only desired fields when changing or updating records.

20. The BROWSE command makes use of the dBASE _____ screen editing feature.

Computer Exercises

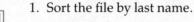

The following exercises require the PAYMAST file, created previously:

1. Sort the file by last name.

2. Sort the file by gross pay.

3. Index the file by employee id. List the file.

4. Index the file by last name. List the file.

5. Index the file by gross pay. List the file.

6. Index the file by last name and first name. List the file.

7. Use the last-name index to list the file.

8. Find all the employees who have a gross pay of $780.00. Use the SEEK command.

9. Use the LOCATE command to find all the employees who have a pay rate of $4.90.

10. Create a report using the last-name index.

11. Create a report using the gross-pay index.

12. Use the BROWSE command to examine selected fields of your records.

PART THREE

APPLIED CONCEPTS

After completing this chapter, you should be able to:

Discuss presentation graphics, graphics editors, and design graphics

Discuss the steps used in creating a graph

Discuss the four common types of graphs

Discuss some of the capabilities of paint programs

Discuss the drawing tools of the Paintbrush toolbox

Discuss the abilities of computer aided–design software

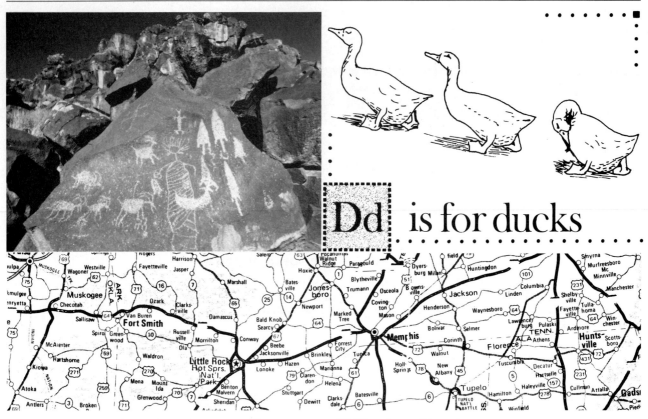

Figure 16.1   Commonly used graphic images. (Photo courtesy of William James Warren)

In our lives, as they were in our ancestors' lives, graphics are ever present. Cave dwellers recorded important events in petroglyphs. Pictures teach children to connect words with objects. Maps guide us to our destinations. Graphic images help us to universalize, simplify, and communicate information (Figure 16.1).

Most people conceive computers as being data processors, word processors, and number crunchers. But computers are as well suited to displaying information as they are to processing it. Given the vital roles both graphics and computers play in communication, it's not surprising that software designers have turned the computer into an image maker. **Computer-generated graphics** are particularly helpful in business settings, where charts and graphs are indispensable for conveying information (Figure 16.2).

This chapter examines the hardware needed to support graphics applications packages, the types of packages on the market, and the types of charts and graphs microcomputers can create with these packages. We'll examine the graphics capabilities of Lotus 1-2-3 and Ashton Tate's Presentation Pack. And we'll introduce the graphics editor/paint program Paintbrush.

Graphics Hardware

To support graphics software, a computer system must have a screen to display graphics, a printer or plotter to draw the graphics, and, for those computers without built-in graphics circuitry, a special adapter graphics card.

A computer creates graphic images by converting data into numbers that correspond to its screen's X/Y (width/height) coordinates. The numbers dictate which of the screen's pixels are to be used to create the image. Graphic images can be displayed to a screen as bits (dots) or vectors (lines).

Figure 16.2
Numeric data can be summarized in a graph to allow us to spot trends.

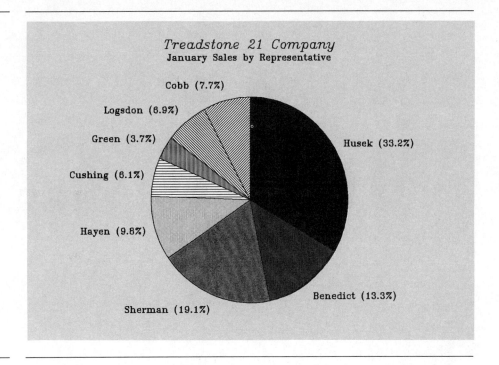

Bit-mapped graphics treat film, paper, and video screens as fields or grids, creating dot-pattern graphics out of various colored inks (on the printed page) or pixels (on the screen). The higher the pattern's dot density is, the more detailed are the graphics. Most printers and monitors use bit mapping to create graphics.

Vector graphics use a special type of screen that draws with straight or curved lines instead of pixels. Vector screens are more expensive than those used in bit mapping, but they generate more detailed graphics and are frequently used in applications such as engineering, where accuracy is critically important.

Graphics Output

Early in the evolution of computer graphics, screen technology quickly surpassed the capabilities of available software. The software drivers of packages like Lotus 1-2-3 did not interface well enough with high-quality color monitors to produce multicolored charts. The situation changed with the introduction of faster computers, EGA/VGA graphics boards, and EGA/VGA monitors (see Chapter 2). Today's graphics software and sophisticated screens can produce graphics containing up to 256,000 colors.

Computer users are now waiting for color-print technology to catch up with screen output. Plotters and dot-matrix printers, the standard printing devices, have limited capabilities for combining text and graphics. Plotters are quite good at drawing color graphics, but generate choppy text. Some dot-matrix printers can't produce graphics, and, of those that can, only the most advanced produce high-quality color output.

Desktop publishing systems may blaze the trail to better color printing. The corporate world has responded enthusiastically to desktop publishing and yearns for more advanced systems. In response, computer manufacturers have produced laser printers that generate high-quality text and graphics and are quieter and faster than are their plotter and dot-matrix predecessors. Although they do not yet match the capabilities of the most sophisticated screens, laser printers likely will figure prominently in the future of color graphics.

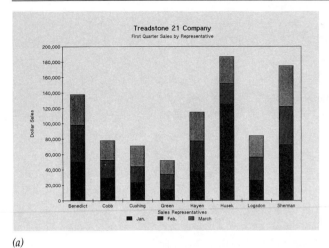

(a)

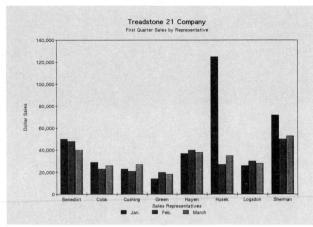

(b)

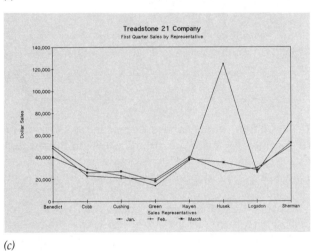

(c)

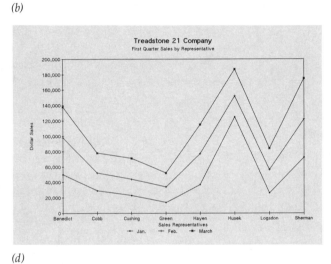

(d)

Figure 16.3
(a) A stacked-bar chart. (b) A side-by-side bar chart. (c) A regular line chart. (d) An area line chart.

Types of Computer Graphics Applications

Let's look at three types of computer graphics applications: presentation graphics, graphics editors, and design graphics.

Presentation Graphics

Graphics offer great advantages in presenting complex information in readily understandable form. For example, one of the most daunting forms of printed information is the statistics-filled spreadsheet. However, a user can interpret hundreds of statistics at a glance if the numbers are rendered into a well-designed graph.

Presentation-graphics software enables computer users to turn numeric information and data relationships into graphics. People use **presentation graphics** in business to highlight key information, direct thinking, show relationships, make comparisons—in short, to simplify complex processes. According to studies, people perceive presentations that include graphics to be better organized, more interesting, more comprehendible, and more persuasive than presentations that do not. The chart shown in Figure 16.2 depicts the January sales of Treadstone 21 sales representatives in presentation-graphics form.

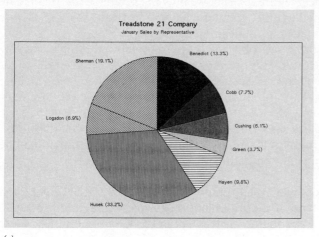

(e)

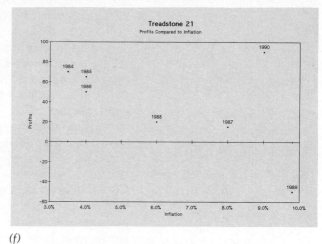

(f)

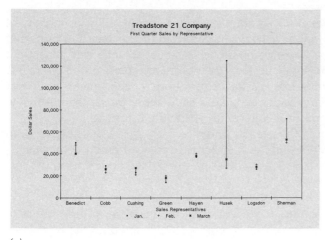

(g)

(h)

Figure 16.3 (continued)
(e) A pie chart. (f) A scatter plot, or XY graph. (g) A hi-lo graph. (h) A combination bar and line graph.

Types of Charts and Graphs. Presentation-graphics software allows users with little artistic skill to create attractive and informative graphs and charts, including the following.

A **bar chart** consists of horizontal or vertical bars that are stacked, floating, or clustered side by side. A stacked-bar chart layers bars to form a larger bar representing a category's combined total. In the example in Figure 16.3a, the monthly sales of each employee are combined into one bar. A side-by-side bar chart compares data in distinct categories, such as monthly sales (Figure 16.3b).

A **line graph** illustrates lows, highs, and trends with a line or series of lines. Line graphs are ideal for showing trends over time or the distribution of one variable over another (Figure 16.3c). An area line graph can represent combined entries much like a stacked-bar chart (Figure 16.3d).

A **pie chart** compares the proportional parts of a whole. Pie charts are useful for comparing component shares with one another and with the combined total. Figure 16.3e shows each sales representative's January sales as a percentage of total January sales.

A **scatter plot**, or **XY graph**, is a two-dimensional graph consisting of points whose coordinates represent values on the **X (horizontal)** and **Y (vertical) axes**. Scatter graphs illustrate in easy-to-read form the relationship of one variable to other variables. Figure 16.3f shows how the profits of the Treadstone 21 company are compared to inflation rates over several years. Year labels have been placed above the plots to give meaning to the graph.

A **hi-lo graph** is often used by newspapers to show the high and low selling points of stocks. Hi-lo graphs emphasize the range between the highest and lowest values within a category by connecting them with a line. Figure 16.3g shows a hi-lo graph of Treadstone 21 sales representatives' first-quarter sales.

Graph characteristics also can be combined. For instance, the graph shown in Figure 16.3h highlights January sales by representing them in a line graph while depicting the other monthly sales as bars.

Creating Graphs. Users can create graphics with either special integrated software packages or stand-alone presentation packages. Integrated software packages with graphics capabilities, such as Lotus 1-2-3, Symphony, Microsoft Works, and Excel, enable the user to generate graphics from the package's spreadsheets or data bases.

Stand-alone presentation-graphics packages permit the user to convert into graphic form data that have been entered from the keyboard or imported from an applications package. Stand-alone packages usually can generate a greater variety and more sophisticated graphics than can integrated packages. For example, some stand-alone packages can store screen images and later display them in a specific sequence (like a slide-show presentation) on the computer screen, in a printout, or in camera-generated pictures.

A major benefit of both types of graphics packages is that the user can repeatedly change a graph until it is just right. To create a graph, a user needs data to be graphed, labels to identify these graphed data, and explanatory text where necessary.

Creating Graphs with Lotus 1-2-3. Assume, for instance, a user wants to graph first-quarter sales for each sales representative noted on the worksheet in Figure 16.4. First, the user must select from the package's menu or submenu the graph type that would best represent the data. If the user were using Lotus 1-2-3, he or she would go to the Type Menu to select a Line, Bar, XY, Stacked-Bar, or Pie chart.

After selecting a graph type, the user enters the set or sets of data points to be graphed. Lotus 1-2-3 permits up to six data-point sets to be described. The user assigns the sets successive letters from the Graph Menu's A–F options. In the example shown for Figure 16.4, three data-point sets (one for each month) will be graphed, so only options A, B, and C are used. The user attaches identifying labels to the sets with the Graph Menu's X option. Afterward, the graph depicted in Figure 16.5 is ready for viewing or printing.

Data Labels and Documentation. As effective as they are at conveying information, graphs and charts need some sort of text or identifying labels to indicate what they are depicting. Someone unacquainted with the worksheet in Figure 16.4 could deduce little from the graph in Figure 16.5. However, the graph would be readily comprehendible if it were supplied with a legend stating what each bar represents and title lines identifying the company, what is being graphed, and the X and Y axes.

Figure 16.6 shows what the graph looks like with these additions, which were executed on a Lotus 1-2-3 integrated graphics package using the Graph Menu's Option entry. To make the graphed data points easily distinguishable, the user can use the Legends option to indicate variables by symbol, color, or hatching (shading lines).

Figure 16.4
A sales worksheet that can be
used to generate a graph.
Various data ranges have
been marked for later reference in this chapter.

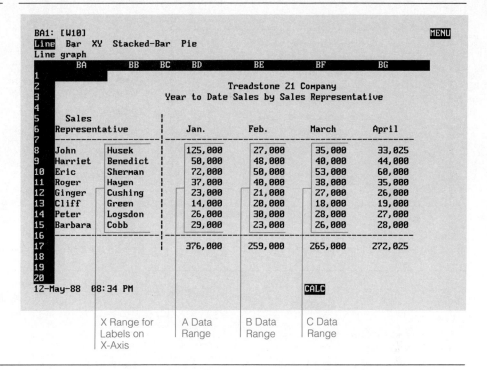

Figure 16.5
A graph without identifying label information except for the
X data option.

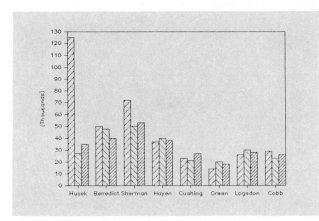

Figure 16.6
A finished Lotus 1-2-3 graph with various lines of
documentation.

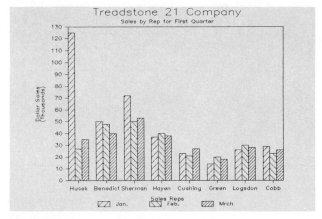

Creating Graphs with Stand-Alone Packages. Stand-alone packages permit users to enter and graph data from application programs that lack graphing capability, such as dBASE III Plus. Some stand-alone packages such as Ashton Tate's Presentation Pack—which includes Chart-Master, Sign-Master, and Diagram-Master software—allow users to generate much more than graphs of numeric data. Let's examine some of the Presentation Pack's capabilities.

Chart-Master. The menu-driven Chart-Master package generates graphs from data that are either read from a file or entered at the keyboard. Worksheet data depicted in Figure 16.4 were rendered into charts with the Chart-Master program. The user starts building a graph by selecting the Create-a-Chart option from the program's Main Menu (Figure 16.7).

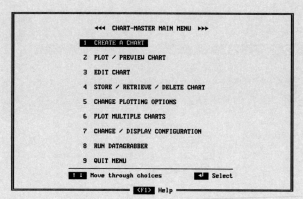

Figure 16.7
The Chart-Master Main Menu.

Figure 16.8
The titles for the graph are entered.

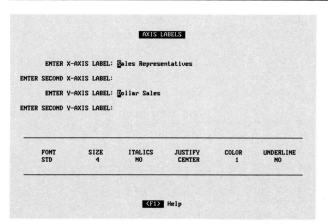

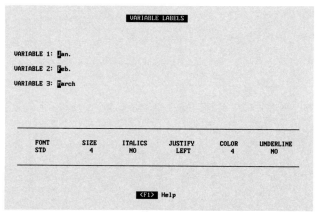

Figure 16.9
The X- and Y-axis labels for the graph are entered.

Figure 16.10
The variable labels for the graph are entered.

After the user selects the Create-a-Chart option, Chart-Master prompts for a title entry to be displayed at the top of the graph. Three title lines were used for the graph in Figure 16.8. At the bottom of the screen, the computer displays a description of how this data will appear on the printed graph. In the example, this display indicates the titles will be centered, tinted the first color selection, and size 7 (fairly large). Chart-Master now prompts for the X- and Y-axis labels. Each axis bears a single-line label, but the software provides for two-line axis labels (Figure 16.9).

Next, Chart-Master prompts for data on how to build the graph, asking first for the number of variables the graph will use. Figure 16.10 shows three variables—January, February, and March. Chart-Master then prompts for the number of observations and asks that each variable be labeled. In the example, the eight sales representatives are the observations, and their names serve as the labels. Next, Chart-Master prompts for all of variable 1's observations, then all of variable 2's observations, and so on until data for all variables have been entered (Figure 16.11).

Upon receipt of all observation data, the software returns the user to the Main Menu. The user then can instruct the computer to complete the graph and display it to the screen by selecting a chart type (clustered-bar chart, for example) from the Plot/Preview Chart option (Figure 16.12). If the displayed

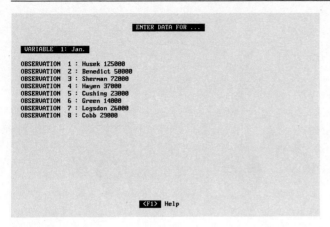

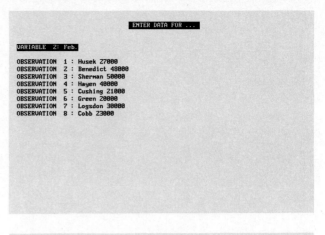

Figure 16.11
The data are entered for the graph.

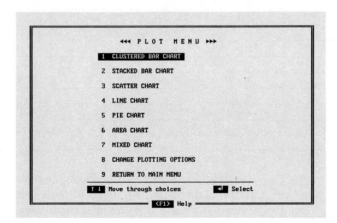

Figure 16.12
The Plot/Preview menu.

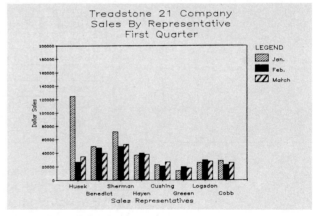

Figure 16.13
A plotted clustered-bar chart.

graph is satisfactory, the user can print it. A plotter generated the clustered-bar chart shown in Figure 16.13). The user can return to the Plot Menu and select other graph types for the software to compose from the inputted data, printing each type (Figure 16.14).

Sign-Master. Sign-Master enables users to generate graphics that can be used as signs, inserted into reports, or displayed on overhead projectors. Figure 16.15 shows a sign that was included in the Sign-Master package's sample file.

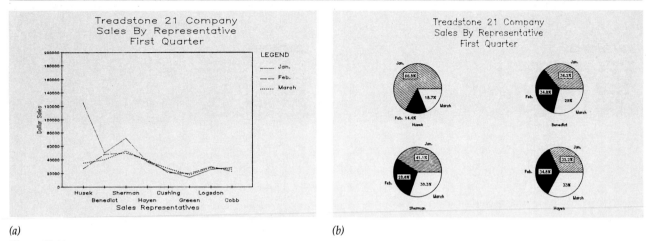

(a)   *(b)*

Figure 16.14
(a) A line graph and (b) multiple pie charts generated by Chart-Master.

Figure 16.15
Printout of a sample Sign-Master graphic.

Job Performance and Job Satisfaction

What is their bottom-line value to an organization?

DESIGN CONCERN	HAS AN EFFECT ON		
	Job satisfaction	Job performance	Ease of communication
Degree of enclosure			✔
Layout			✔
Temperature/air quality	✔		
Lighting	✔	✔	
Windows	✔	✔	
Access control		✔	
Noise	✔		
Speech privacy			✔
Comfort	✔		
Participation	✔	✔	
Flexibility	✔		

Diagram-Master. Diagram-Master allows users to create Gantt charts, organization charts, and other types of graphics. Gantt charts are used to plan and track projects by showing what tasks have to be done and which of these have been completed or are underway. Figure 16.16 shows graphics generated from Diagram-Master's sample files.

Graphics Editors/Paint Programs

Graphics editors/paint programs turn the computer screen into a luminous canvas or drawing pad on which the user can generate or modify graphics using computerized art tools. PC Paintbrush+, Publisher's Paintbrush, Hot Shot Graphics, and Microsoft Paintbrush are some popular graphics editors on the market today. With these programs, a user can create business graphics such as company logos and visual devices for reports, newsletters, and finan-

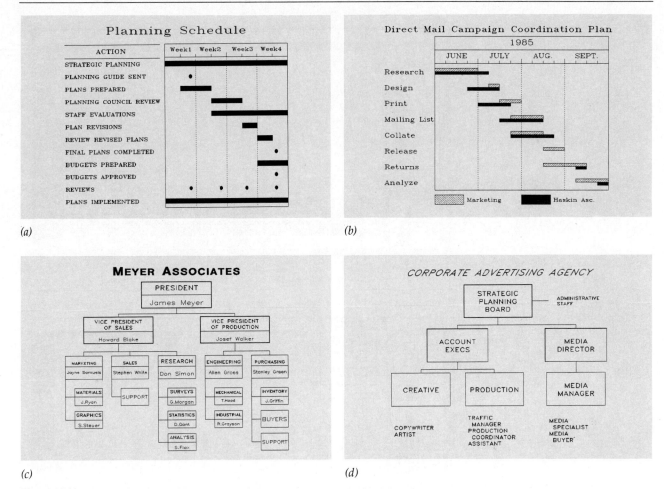

(a)

(b)

(c)

(d)

Figure 16.16
Organization charts and Gantt charts generated by Diagram-Master's sample files.

cial statements. After the desired image has been created, the user can save it to a disk file, recalling it later to incorporate in a document or poster created with other software programs.

Most of these packages present the user with a toolbox, a menu, a palette of colors or patterns, a variety of shapes (boxes and circles), some method of controlling line width, and the capability to zoom in (enlarge) parts of the drawing (Figure 16.17). Let's look at PC Paintbrush, by Z-Soft, to see how paint programs work.

PC Paintbrush supports a two-button mouse for drawing, command issuance, and tool and menu-option selection. The mouse's movements are represented on the screen by either a dot (while on the drawing area) or an arrow (when off the drawing area). Using the mouse as a pointer, the operator selects a pull-down menu and highlights the desired option (Figure 16.18). In the screen's lower left-hand corner is the drawing-width scale, from which the user selects a drawing-line thickness by positioning the pointer on the proper setting and pressing the left-hand mouse button. In Figure 16.19, the bottom line was drawn with the default line-width setting, and the top line was drawn in the thinnest line width.

The user colors and shades line drawings with the palette at the bottom of the screen, selecting the active pattern by positioning the pointer on the

Figure 16.17
The Microsoft Paintbrush
screen.

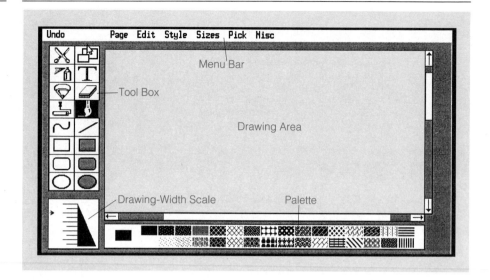

Figure 16.18
Mouse pointer indicating a
pull-down menu selection.

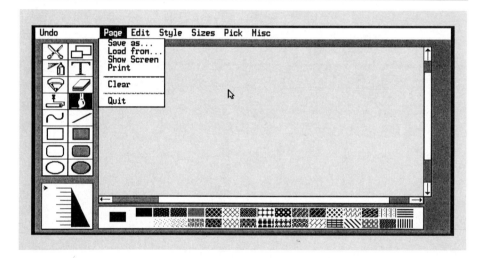

appropriate box and clicking the mouse. The box immediately to the right of the drawing-width scale indicates the active color or shading pattern (Figure 16.20).

The toolbox, located on the screen's left-hand side, contains various drawing tools, which are represented by icons. The various tools draw, erase, airbrush, set type, and fill in areas with colors or patterns, as described next (Figure 16.21).

> Scissors cut out nonrectangular objects, which the user can move or copy to another part of the drawing area. To move an object, the user clicks the left mouse button and draws a line around the object with the mouse pointer. Next, the user positions the pointer inside the circle, clicks the right mouse button, then holds down either mouse button and moves the object to the desired position. An object created with the scissors also can be copied by encircling it with a line and simultaneously pressing a mouse button and the SHIFT key.

> The Spray Can sprays the active drawing color, in the active width, on selected drawing parts. The user paints by holding down either mouse button and moving the pointer across the screen.

Figure 16.19
Examples of line widths offered by the drawing-width
scale.

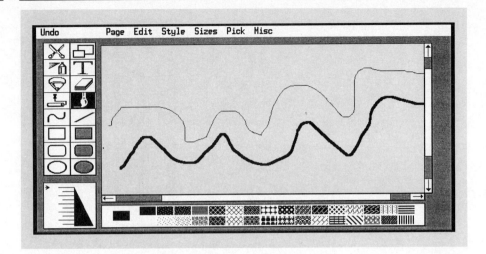

Figure 16.20
Examples of the selected
colors and patterns.

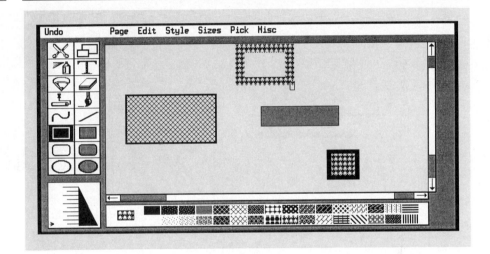

The Color Eraser erases the active drawing color from selected parts of
the picture. The user holds down either mouse button and moves the
pointer over the area to be erased.

The Paint Roller fills an enclosed area with the active color. The user
clicks either mouse button to paint over solid colored areas and clicks
only the right mouse button to completely paint over a pattern.

The Curve draws a curved line in the active drawing color and width.
The user clicks the left mouse button to mark the starting point of the
curve and clicks the right mouse button to mark the ending point. Each
curve's end can be bent with the pointer until the curve is of the desired
arc. After each end has been formed correctly, the user clicks the right
mouse button to set the arc.

The Hollow and Filled Boxes outline and color rectangles. The user clicks
the left mouse button to set one corner, shapes the box with the pointer,
and clicks the right mouse button to set the opposite corner.

Hollow or Filled Circles draw outlines of filled circles and ellipses. The
user clicks the left mouse button to mark the center of the circle or
ellipse, moves the mouse to shape the figure, then clicks the right mouse
button to set the size.

Figure 16.21
The toolbox's various tools.

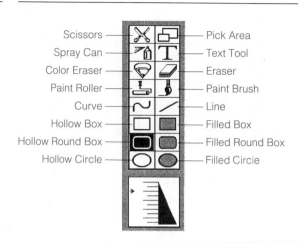

Scissors — Pick Area
Spray Can — Text Tool
Color Eraser — Eraser
Paint Roller — Paint Brush
Curve — Line
Hollow Box — Filled Box
Hollow Round Box — Filled Round Box
Hollow Circle — Filled Circle

Figure 16.22
A drawing of a microcomputer using PC Paintbrush.

Figure 16.23
The monitor outline as drawn with the rounded-rectangle tool.

The Pick Area works like the scissors, except it marks and cuts out a rectangular chunk of the picture. The user alters the picked area's size and orientation by clicking the left mouse button to set (establish the position of) one corner of the rectangle and clicking the right mouse button to set the other.

The Text Tool enables users to add text to a picture. The user selects typeface (character style), point size (character size), and other text options from the Style and Sizes menus, then places the pointer where the text is to be inserted and begins typing.

The Eraser erases anything drawn in the drawing area. The user holds down either mouse button and uses the pointer like an eraser.

The Paintbrush paints an image in the active drawing color and width. The user holds down either mouse button and moves the pointer across the screen as if it were a paintbrush.

The Line draws a line between two points in the active drawing color and width. The user clicks the left mouse button to mark the line's starting point, extends the line the desired length, then clicks the right mouse button to mark the line's ending point.

By combining the above operations, a user could draw the microcomputer depicted in Figure 16.22. The process would proceed as follows.

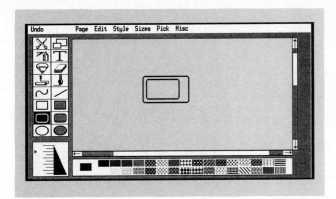

Figure 16.24
The monitor screen is added.

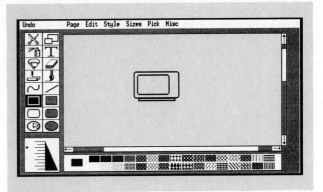

Figure 16.25
The monitor stand is added.

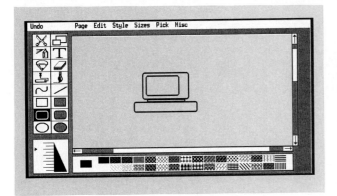

Figure 16.26
The computer shell is drawn with the rounded-rectangle tool.

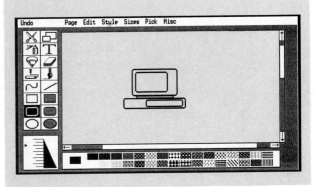

Figure 16.27
The disk drive bays are drawn by the rounded-rectangle tool.

First the user selects the rounded box icon from the toolbox by positioning the pointer on that box and clicking the left mouse button. With this tool the user outlines the microcomputer monitor by positioning the pointer at an appropriate spot on the screen and pressing the left mouse button to draw the monitor's left-hand corner. The user repeats the procedure, pressing the right mouse button, to create the outline's lower right-hand corner. The resultant outline would look like Figure 16.23. If a mistake is made, the user moves the pointer to the eraser icon and presses the left mouse button. The pointer changes to a square to indicate it is in eraser mode; the user then erases with it while holding down either mouse button.

Using the rounded-rectangle icon again, the operator repeats the above outline procedure to draw the monitor screen, monitor support, computer shell, and disk drive bays, as depicted in Figures 16.24–16.27.

Next, the user adds the logo with the rectangle outline again, first resetting the line width by positioning the pointer to the drawing-width scale's second hash mark (Figure 16.28). The user indicates that the computer's drive bay contains two disk drives by selecting the line icon from the toolbox and drawing appropriate-length lines to represent the drives (Figure 16.29). The user next draws in the monitor knobs using the circle icon (Figure 16.30).

The screen is ready to be colored (Figure 16.31). The user selects the gray icon from the palette and activates it by clicking the left mouse button. (The

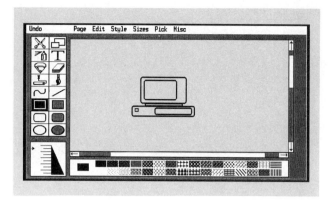

Figure 16.28
The computer with logo added.

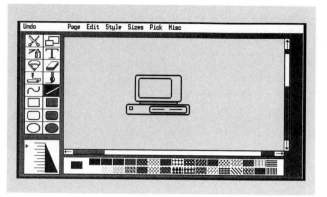

Figure 16.29
The two disk drives represented by lines.

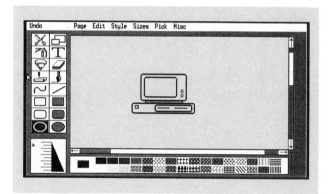

Figure 16.30
The monitor knobs drawn by the circle tool.

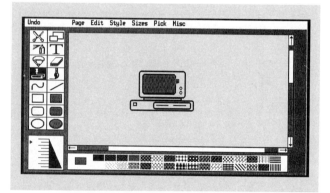

Figure 16.31
The monitor screen "painted" by the paint roller.

user can verify that gray is the active color by checking the square immediately to the right of the line-drawing scale.) The user activates the paint roller in the toolbox, positions the paint can on the screen graphic, presses the left mouse button, and paints in the screen.

Design Graphics

Design graphics help designers draw everything from automobile styles to skyscrapers. They are best exemplified by the application programs called Computer Aided Design (CAD), Computer Aided Manufacturing (CAM), and Computer Aided Engineering (CAE), all of which have greatly reduced the cost of designing and manufacturing products in several fields.

Examples of design-graphics software include Generic CAD, Auto CAD, and Microsoft's EasyCAD. Using CAD/CAM programs, manufacturers can create in a day drawings that used to take days or weeks to complete. CAD/CAM programs can rotate a drawing, layer it to show detail, and display it in various scales or three dimensions (Figure 16.32).

The industrial sector's enthusiastic use of CAD sparked the interest of architects, electrical engineers, theatrical designers, landscape designers, illustrators and artists, film animators, and others who have since made CAD part of their professional tools (Figure 16.33).

Figure 16.32
A sample file from the
EasyCAD program.

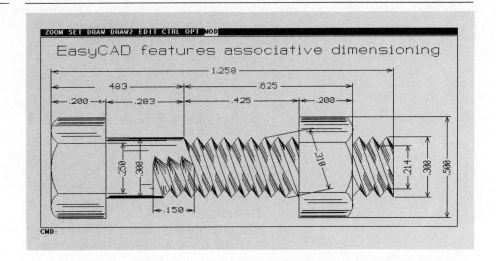

Figure 16.33
A floor plan generated using
a sample EasyCAD file.

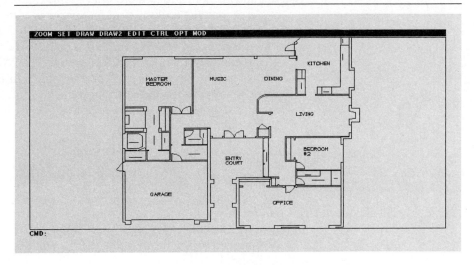

Using computers shortens almost any product's design time, not only because drawing and revising by CAD are far faster than doing so by hand, but also because designs can be tested on computer-aided engineering systems for integrity before they are manufactured. Before the advent of CAE systems, new product ideas were tested by first being turned into prototypes, expensive early-version models. Engineers subjected the prototypes to various tests to determine the product's durability and suitability. Now, a designer can create a product with CAD and test it on a CAE system more rigorously than is possible using real-world prototypes.

Computer-aided manufacturing systems help produce the finished products by creating artwork masters (such as blueprints), compiling lists of required components, and controlling machine operations. For example, a CAM may be used to precisely control assembly-line robots that weld together car body panels.

Manufacturers can also use CAM systems to estimate the cost of making a product. An architect could use a CAD package to design a floor plan, then employ a CAM program to estimate the cost of its construction. If the floor plan is changed, the CAM system will automatically refigure the cost estimate.

Chapter Review

Graphics enhance communication by connecting pictures with ideas and words. Businesses rely on graphics to summarize numeric information in readily understandable pictorial form.

Before a user can create graphics on a computer system, the system must have a built-in or an added-on graphics circuitry, a monitor (a color screen is needed for some applications), and a hard-copy output device such as a pen plotter, laser printer, or dot-matrix printer.

The business world uses three types of graphics packages: presentation graphics, graphics editors/paint programs, and design graphics. Presentation graphics render numeric data into charts and graphs. Four common types of graphs are the bar chart, line graph, pie chart, and scatter plot. Presentation graphics also may be used to create signs, Gantt charts, and organization charts.

Graphics editors or paint software is used to generate drawings or to edit existing graphic images that are stored on disk. Once a picture has been correctly drawn, it can be printed separately, inserted in a desktop-published document, or included in another graphic. Most paint programs have a drawing area, palette, toolbox, and menus for issuing commands.

CAD software exemplifies design-graphics packages. This software allows the user to perform in minutes tasks that once required hours or days. Originally used by manufacturing concerns, CAD packages are now popular with a variety of businesses. Designers often link CAD packages to CAE software, in order to test new product designs, and to CAM software, in order to facilitate the manufacturing process by generating parts lists and managing industrial robotics.

Key Terms and Concepts

bar chart
bit-mapped graphics
computer-generated graphics
design graphics
graphics editor/paint program
hi-lo graph
line graph

pie chart
presentation graphics
scatter plot (XY graph)
vector graphics
X (horizontal) axis
Y (vertical) axis

Chapter Quiz

Multiple Choice

1. Which of the following is a use for computer graphics?
   a. Computer games
   b. Drawing presentation charts
   c. Organization charts
   d. None of the above
   e. All of the above

2. Which of the following is or might be required for computer graphics applications?
   a. A graphics board
   b. A color monitor
   c. A pen plotter
   d. A laser printer
   e. All of the above

3. Which of the following is not a tool found in the toolbox of Paintbrush?
   a. Spray Can
   b. Drawing-width scale
   c. Scissors
   d. Paintbrush
   e. All of the above

4. Which of the following is not a part of defining a graph?
   a. Specifying the data to plot
   b. Specifying the titles
   c. Specifying the width of the bars
   d. Specifying the axes labels
   e. All of the above

5. CAD packages can be used for which of the following applications?
   a. Landscaping design
   b. House design
   c. Theatrical design
   d. All of the above
   e. None of the above

True/False

6. Monitors that use bit-mapped graphics are the most common graphics display devices.

7. Pen plotters are usually preferred over laser printers as output devices for graphic displays.

8. One of the benefits of presentation-graphics software packages is that they allow you to change a graph until it exactly suits your purpose.

9. Graphics editors/paint software cannot usually be used by a novice.

10. Computer-aided design packages are used only in manufacturing.

Answers

1. e 2. e 3. b 4. c 5. d 6. t 7. f 8. t 9. f 10. f

Exercises

1. One of the most commonly used graphic tools used when traveling is the _____.

2. Two types of presentation-graphics packages are
   a.

   b.

3. When building a graph, you have to provide a number of different pieces of information to the software package. Three of these pieces of information include
   a.

   b.

   c.

4. An example of a software package with an integrated graphics module is _____.

5. An example of a stand-alone presentation graphics package is _____.

6. The four basic types of graphs that can be generated are
   a.

   b.

   c.

   d.

7. The output device for graphics that is preferred most is the _____.

8. A _____ generates excellent graphics, but text quality is limited.

9. A graphics-display device that represents lines as continuous lines between two points rather than as dots uses _____.

10. The software package covered in this chapter that is capable of producing organization charts is _____.

11. Software packages that allow you to create a drawing are called _____.

12. Paint programs usually use a device called a _____ for issuing instructions and drawing.

13. The area of the screen called the _____ has a number of devices used in creating a drawing.

14. The _____ contains the different colors or patterns used in a drawing.

15. The _____ assumes different shapes depending on whether you are inside or outside the drawing area.

16. The size of a line is determined by the _____.

17. Selecting a menu option from the menu lines results in a _____ menu appearing on the screen.

18. The software application that was first used extensively in the engineering field is _____.

19. Three features that can be included in the CAD package are
    a.

    b.

    c.

20. The _____ can be used to develop parts lists, pricing, and instructions that will later be used by robots in assembling a product.

Questions for
Thought

1. Compare and contrast two presentation graphics packages. What are the relative strengths and weaknesses of the packages? Which package do you prefer? Be sure to state your rationale.

2. Find out what the best-selling paint programs are. What particular market is each package appealing to?

3. List applications that you could use a paint program for. Which paint program would best meet your needs?

4. Conduct a market survey of CAD packages that cost less than $200. Would you consider purchasing one of these packages yourself?

5. Prepare a report on business use of CAD/CAM packages.

Chapter
17

Graphing with 1-2-3

Chapter Objectives   *After completing this chapter, you should be able to:*

Discuss in detail the various options contained in the Graph Menu

Discuss the steps involved in building a graph

Discuss the various types of graphs that can be constructed by 1-2-3

Discuss the method of saving graph settings for later use

Discuss additional items for graphs, such as Titles and Legends

Discuss the steps involved in saving a graph onto disk for later printing

Discuss the steps involved in using the PrintGraph utility

This chapter is divided into three parts: the first deals with the various options provided in the Graph Menu; the second deals with building graphs; and the third deals with printing graphs.

The information presented in Chapters 9–11 demonstrates how 1-2-3 can be used to manipulate information arithmetically through the use of formulas for processing data that have been entered on the worksheet. The worksheet is automatically updated and completely recalculated whenever information is entered in a cell, allowing you to play a number of "what if" games to see how a change will affect the rest of the worksheet.

These characteristics alone may satisfy your needs when a worksheet containing small amounts of data is being used, but what happens when you have large amounts of data or when you cannot make sense of the small amount of data that is in the worksheet? The answer lies in the old maxim "a picture is worth a thousand words": 1-2-3 allows you, with only a small amount of effort, to depict the data that have been entered in a worksheet on the screen, in the form of a graph.

If you wish to use this feature, your computer must have either an EGA, VGA, or color graphics board and a color (or regular) monitor or a board that makes it possible to display graphics on a monochrome monitor. If you don't have this hardware (see Figure 17.1), your computer will only beep when you try to display the graph; in this case, you must save the graph onto a file and then print the graph via the PrintGraph feature of the Lotus Access System.

If your computer has both a monochrome monitor and a color monitor attached to it, 1-2-3 will use the monochrome monitor to display the worksheet and the color monitor to display the graph.

Steps in Building a Graph and Printing the Graph

The process of building a graph using 1-2-3 involves the following simple, easy-to-follow steps:

1. Selecting and loading in a worksheet file from disk, or using the current worksheet
2. Selecting the graphing menu via the command sequence / Graph
3. Selecting the type of graph to be used (line, bar, XY, stacked-bar, or pie)
4. Telling 1-2-3 which data ranges are involved in the graph (up to six ranges of data can be depicted in a graph)
5. Telling 1-2-3 to include any labels or extra information
6. Displaying the graph on the screen
7. Making any changes in the graph
8. Saving the graph onto disk for later printing, if desired (in which case 1-2-3 will place a .PIC extension on the graph file)
9. Printing the graph with PrintGraph

After you become accustomed to using the Graph option, you can go through this process easily in three to five minutes.

You can also enter "what if" changes in your data and automatically regraph the new information via the **F10 Graph key**, without going back through the Graph Menu.

Graph Menu

The **Graph Menu** is invoked by entering a / Graph command sequence. Unless you wish to add information to a "naked" graph, you can build the entire graph from this menu, without entering any submenus; the submenus

(a)   *(b)*

Figure 17.1
(a) Hercules graphics board. (b) Monochrome screen with Hercules graphics board. (Courtesy of Hercules)

allow you to dress up a graph with meaningful, descriptive data. Appendix B includes a chart of the graph command structure.

The Graph Menu that appears on your screen when you depress the command sequence / Graph is as follows:

```
Type X  A B C D E F  Reset  View  Save  Options  Name  Quit
```

Type

The **Type option** of the Graph Menu allows you to select the type of graph you wish to display from the following menu:

```
Line  Bar  XY  Stacked Bar  Pie
```

Line. The standard one-dimensional line graph presents the data on the Y (vertical) axis and the label of the data on the X (horizontal) axis. Up to six lines (sets of data) can be depicted. When graphing multiple sets of data, 1-2-3 automatically uses different data-point symbols for each set of data.

Bar. The standard one-dimensional bar graph (when multiple data ranges are used) places the bars for each data point from the data ranges side by side. Different shadings are used for each data range.

XY. An XY graph (scatter plot) is a two-dimensional graph with a set of data points referenced on both the X axis and the Y axis. For example, if you want to graph a company's profits compared to inflation over a period of years, you would select this option.

Stacked Bar. A stacked-bar graph stacks multiple ranges of data on top of each other instead of next to one another. Different shadings are given to each range of data to differentiate among them.

Pie. The pie chart, as the name implies, is a circle divided into wedges; it is used to depict a single data range. Because of its nature, the pie chart cannot depict multiple data ranges.

X. The **X command** defines a range of the worksheet to be used for a horizontal label of the graph. When you take the X option, you must give the addresses of or point to the cell(s) containing the label information. Often, these are row or column labels from the worksheet.

ABCDEF

The **ABCDEF commands** are used to specify up to six data ranges to be depicted on your graph. The first data range must be labeled A, the second B, and so on. You can enter the cell addresses or point to the cells to be included in each data range; then depress the ENTER key when you have finished.

1-2-3 remembers each data range you specify; to respecify an existing range, reselect it and specify a new data range to be graphed. If you wish to cancel a data range, you must use the Reset option. 1-2-3 requires you to define at least one data range, regardless of the type of graph that has been selected.

Reset

The **Reset option** selects the Reset Menu for the graphing function. The options of the Reset Menu allow you to cancel either the entire graph or portions of it. The Reset Menu options are as follows:

```
Graph X   A B C D E F   Quit
```

Graph. The **Graph command** allows you to cancel the entire graph. If this option is taken, the entire graph will have to be respecified to 1-2-3.

X. The X command allows you to cancel the labeling of the graph's horizontal axis.

ABCDEF. The ABCDEF commands allow you to cancel one or more data ranges of a graph. If you cancel all of them, 1-2-3 acts as though you do not have a graph specified.

Quit. The **Quit command** returns you to the Graph Menu.

View

The **View command** allows you to display the currently specified graph on the monitor, after which you can depress any key on the keyboard to return to the Graph Menu.

You can also obtain a display of a graph, showing the specified settings, while you are in the worksheet in ready mode. To do so, simply depress the F10 graph function key. You can return to the worksheet by depressing any key.

Save

The **Save command** is used to store the currently specified graph onto a disk file. Such a file is referred to by 1-2-3 as a "graph" or "picture" file and contains a .PIC extension.

Anyone with a regular monochrome monitor must use the Save command to save a graph file, since this type of monitor is not able to display a graph. The file must then be printed using the PrintGraph option from the Lotus Access System Menu.

Options

The **Options** selection allows you to dress up a graph with various options. When this option is selected the following menu is displayed:

```
Legend  Format  Titles  Grid  Scale  Color  B&W  Data Labels  Quit
```

Legend. The **Legend option** displays a menu that allows you to specify characters for the legend to be used to represent the various ranges of data. Up to nineteen characters can be shown, but as few as possible should be selected. The following menu is displayed:

```
A B C D E F
```

You now select the appropriate data range, and 1-2-3 displays the current legend for it. If you wish to change the legend, enter the new characters; if you wish to leave it unchanged, depress the ENTER key. The legend is displayed beneath the X-axis title entry.

Format. The **Format option** is used to change how the specified graph is displayed—that is, what characters are used to represent the displayed data points and how those data points are connected on the graph. The following menu is displayed when this option is selected:

```
Graph  A B C D E F  Quit
```

Graph. By selecting this option, you can determine how the data are to be presented on the graph. The following menu is displayed:

```
Lines  Symbols  Both  Neither
```

> *Lines.* This command will connect each data point within a range with a line.
>
> *Symbols.* This command will display each data point in a data range with the same character or symbol.
>
> *Both.* This command uses both lines and symbols in representing data points in a data range.
>
> *Neither.* This command uses neither lines nor symbols, requiring the legends for data points to be specified in legend option commands.

ABCDEF. This command option allows you to select a data range. When you have done so, 1-2-3 prompts you in exactly the same way it does when you select the Graph option in this menu.

Quit. This command returns you to the Options Menu.

Titles. The **Titles option** enables you to label the graph with up to two lines of text; these will appear at the top of the graph. The Titles option can also be used to enter a one-line text label for each axis. When you select the Titles option, you will be presented with the following menu:

```
First   Second   X Axis   Y Axis
```

First. This command allows you to enter the first line of text that is to be placed at the top of the page.

Second. This command allows you to enter the second line of text that is to be placed (below the first line) at the top of the page.

X Axis. This command allows you to enter one line of text to be displayed along the X (horizontal) axis.

Y Axis. This command allows you to enter one line of text to be displayed along the Y (vertical) axis.

Grid. The **Grid option** allows you to choose grid lines for display on a graph. When selected, it displays the following menu:

```
Horizontal   Vertical   Both   Clear
```

Horizontal. This command places horizontal grid lines on the graph when it is displayed. Grid lines can be used to make the relative size of plotted points clearer.

Vertical. This command places vertical grid lines on the graph when it is displayed.

Both. This command places both horizontal and vertical grid lines on a graph when it is displayed.

Clear. This command clears any grid lines from the display.

Scale. The **Scale option** allows you to set the scaling and format of a graph for either the X or Y axis. When you have selected the axis, the following menu of options will be displayed:

```
Automatic   Manual   Lower   Upper   Format   Indication   Quit
```

Automatic. With this option, the scaling on the graphs is automatically calculated by 1-2-3 to keep the entire graph visible on the display.

Manual. With this option, you select the scaling.

Lower/Upper. These options must be used if the Manual command was selected. They allow you to select the upper and lower scale limits, giving you more control over how data are presented. Small differences can be made to seem much greater.

Format. This option allows you to decide how numeric data will be used with scaling. When the graph is displayed, the numbers will appear in the selected format.

Indicator. Allows you to turn the scale indicators on a graph on or off when the graph is displayed to the screen via the View command.

Quit. This option returns you to the Options Menu.

Color/B&W. The **Color option** displays the information in colors that have been preselected by 1-2-3. The **B&W option** displays the data in standard black-and-white, with cross-hatching on the bars.

Data/Labels. The **Data option** allows you to specify a range of cells whose contents will be used to label the data points of a data range (A–F). First choose the range (A–F); then specify the cells to be included in the range; then, for line and XY graphs, select the alignment of the labels in relation to the data points (Centered, Left, Above, Right, Below), using the **Labels option**. Select the Quit option when you are finished, and you will return to the Graph Menu. The next time the graph is displayed, the cell contents of the specified range(s) will be displayed as data points.

Name

The **Name option** allows you to load in graph settings that were previously saved using the Create option of the Name Menu, reset the graph options to those for this graph, and then draw the graph using the specified features. When selected, the name option displays the following menu:

```
Use    Create    Delete    Reset
```

Use. The **Use command** allows you to make graph file settings that are contained in RAM memory current by entering the name or by pointing to the file with the pointer. The selected graph will then be displayed.

Create. The **Create command** allows you to save graph settings of the current graph. It can later be accessed via the Use command.

Delete. The **Delete command** is used to delete any graph settings contained in memory. To do this, enter the graph name and depress ENTER or point to the graph and depress ENTER.

Reset. The Reset command erases all named graphs from the computer's memory.

Quit

The Quit option returns you to the Main Menu of 1-2-3.

Generating Graphs

Simple Bar Graphs

The first exercise below is to generate a simple bar graph using the "This Year" information contained in the COMPSALS worksheet. The graph you produce should look like those in Figure 17.2.

    1. Load in the COMPSALS worksheet.

        /—Gets the Main Menu.

        F—Selects the File Menu.

        R—Selects the Retrieve command.

COMPSALS—Identifies the worksheet (or you can point to the worksheet name).

ENTER—Executes the command.

2. Select the Graph Menu and tell 1-2-3 to generate a bar graph.

/—Gets the Main Menu.

G—Selects the Graph Menu.

T—Selects the Type option from the Graph Menu.

B—Tells 1-2-3 to generate a bar chart.

3. Establish the X-axis label range (department names).

X—Indicates that the X-axis label range is to be specified.

B5 [by manual pointer movement or address entry]—Positions the pointer at cell B5.

.—Nails down the beginning of the range.

B10 [by manual pointer movement or address entry]— Positions the pointer at the last cell in the label range.

ENTER—Tells 1-2-3 that the range is established.

4. Establish the "This Year" column as the A data range.

A—Tells 1-2-3 that you wish to specify the A data range.

D5 [by manual pointer movement]—Positions the cursor at the beginning of the "This Year" data.

.—Nails down the beginning of the range.

D10 [by manual pointer movement]—Positions the pointer at the last cell to be included in the A data range.

ENTER—Tells 1-2-3 that the A data range is established.

5. Execute the View command (V) to display the graph on the screen (see Figure 17.2a). You may notice that the labels on the X axis are run together if you have a color screen. They will print correctly (see Figure 17.2b), but it is distracting to see this mess on the screen. Right now you're going to deal with the problem by entering abbreviated labels in column A and telling 1-2-3 to use those for the X-axis labels. The method of entering abbreviated labels you use will depend on the type of monitor and graphics adapter that you are using.

6. Go back to the Graph Menu, by depressing any key on the keyboard.

7. Leave the Graph Menu, by taking the Quit option (Q), to make changes to the COMPSALS worksheet.

8. Enter the abbreviated department labels in column A.

```
A5      Deli
A6      Bkry
A7      Liqr
A8      Groc
A9      Prod
A10     Meat
```

9. Return to the Graph Menu.

/—Gets the Main Menu.

G—Selects the Graph Menu.

10. Reset the X-axis labels.

X—Takes the X option from the Graph Menu.

Figure 17.2
Simple bar graph of the "This Year" information from the COMPSALS worksheet (a) as it appears on the display of a color screen, and (b) as it appears when printed out.

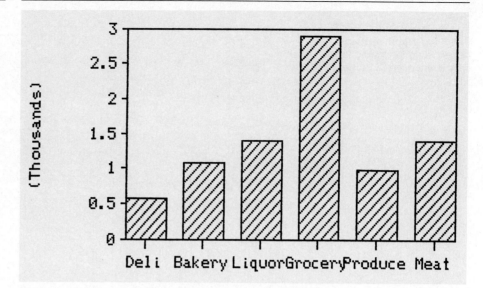

(a)

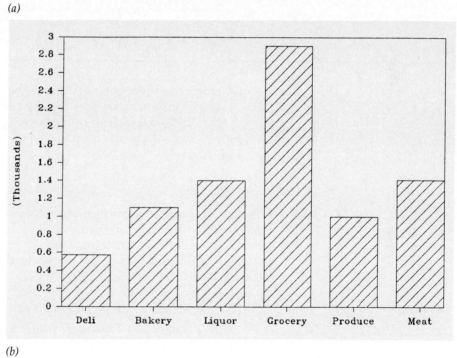

(b)

BACKSPACE—Cancels the current range. (This step is necessary because 1-2-3 remembers the range you previously established for the X option.)

A5 [by manual pointer movement or address entry]— Positions the pointer at cell A5, the beginning of the range. (Remember, you can pick any two opposite corners.)

.—Nails down the beginning of the range.

A10 [by manual pointer movement or address entry]—Marks the end of the range.

ENTER—Tells 1-2-3 to accept the range for the X axis.

Figure 17.3
Screen display of the COMP-
SALS bar graph, as it ap-
pears after abbreviated labels
have been inserted in the
worksheet.

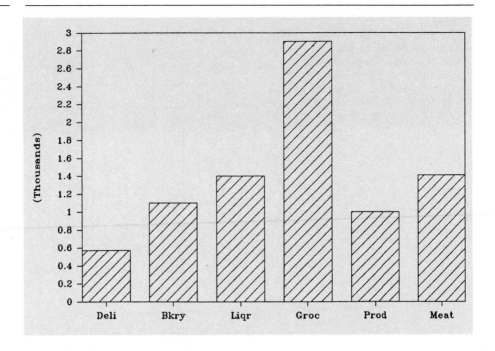

11. Select the View option (V) from the Graph Menu, and look at the graph. It should now look like the one pictured in Figure 17.3. Notice that the X-axis labels no longer overlap.

12. Depress any key to return to the Graph Menu.

Entering Titles

Although the graph in the just-completed exercise looks okay, if you want it to mean anything at a later date, you should probably put some descriptive labels on it. Lotus 1-2-3 allows you to put a two-line title at the top of the graph and a one-line title on each axis of the graph. In this exercise, you will place the following labels on the bar chart (Figure 17.4):

Line 1	Ed's Supermarket
Line 2	This Year's Sales
X axis	Departments
Y axis	Dollar Sales

Placing these labels on the graph involves the following steps:

1. The Options selection from the Graph Menu will allow us to place the labels on the bar chart.

O—Selects the Options Menu from the Graph Menu.

T—Selects the Titles option from the Options Menu.

F—Selects the First line option.

Ed's Supermarket—Specifies the title.

ENTER—Tells 1-2-3 to accept the title.

T—Selects the Titles option.

S—Selects the Second line option.

Figure 17.4
Bar graph of This Year's
COMPSALS sales, with
graph and axis titles in place.

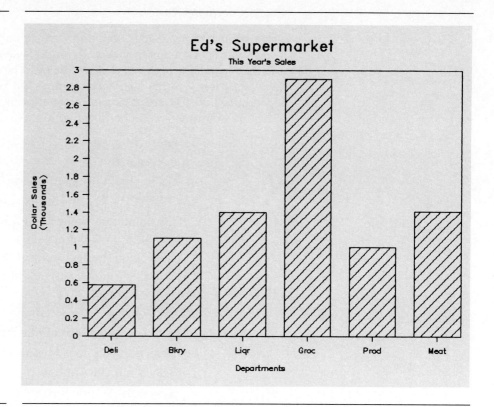

This Year's Sales—Specifies the title.

ENTER—Tells 1-2-3 to accept the title.

T—Selects the Titles option.

X—Selects the X-axis title option.

Departments—Specifies the title.

ENTER—Tells 1-2-3 to accept the title.

T—Selects the Titles option.

Y—Selects the Y-axis title option.

Dollar Sales—Specifies the title.

ENTER—Tells 1-2-3 to accept the title.

Q—Quits the Options Menu and returns to the Graph Menu.

2. View the graph by depressing the V option. Your graph should now look like the one in Figure 17.4.

3. Depress any key to return to the Graph Menu.

4. Save the graph's settings onto the worksheet, so it can easily be retrieved later.

N—Selects the Name option of the Graph Menu.

C—Selects the Create option.

TYSALE—Names the group of graph settings.

ENTER—Tells 1-2-3 to accept these graph settings.

If you want to take a look at this graph again, you don't have to reenter all the keystrokes; you just tell 1-2-3 to load TYSALE as the settings to generate a graph. These graph settings are also saved to a worksheet file when a save operation is performed.

Changing Data Ranges

The current graph settings contain instructions for creating a graph of This Year's sales for Ed's Supermarket. To graph Last Year's sales, the A data range and the second line of the worksheet title must be changed. You have to change the A data range to the Last Year column, and put "Last Year's Sales" in the second title line. The remaining graph specifications can be left unchanged.

    The steps involved in performing this task are as follows:

1. Get to the Graph Menu.
2. Change the A data range.

> A—Selects the A option from the Graph Menu.
>
> BACKSPACE—Cancels the existing range.
>
> C10 [by pointer movement or address entry]—Establishes the first cell in the A range.
>
> .—Nails down the beginning of the range.
>
> C5 [by pointer movement or address entry]—Establishes the end of the A range.
>
> ENTER—Tells 1-2-3 to accept the A data range.

3. Change *This* to *Last* in the second title line.

> O—Selects the Options Menu from the Graph Menu.
>
> T—Selects the Titles option.
>
> S—Selects the Second line option, causing "This Year's Sales" to be displayed.
>
> Home—Moves the pointer under the *T* in *This*.
>
> Del Del Del Del—Deletes the word *This*.
>
> Last—Enters the word *Last*.
>
> ENTER—Tells 1-2-3 to accept the changed title.
>
> Q—Quits the Options Menu and returns to the Graph Menu.

4. View the changed graph, using the View command (V) from the Graph Menu. The graph should now look like the one shown in Figure 17.5.
5. Depress any key to return to the Graph Menu.
6. Save these worksheet settings for later use.

> N—Selects the Name option from the Graph Menu.
>
> C—Selects the Create option.
>
> L Y S A L E—Names the group of graph settings.
>
> ENTER—Tells 1-2-3 to execute this command.

Side-by-Side Bar Graphs

You now have two bar graphs showing sales for this year and last year. Ed, however, wants to be able to make a direct comparison between the two years via one bar graph. Because you saved the settings of the T Y S A L E bar graph, all you have to do is load in those graph settings and change them in accordance with Ed's request. The following steps are required:

1. Get to the Graph Menu.
2. Replace the current graph settings with those contained in T Y S A L E (and stored in the spreadsheet).

> N—Selects the Name option from the Graph Menu.

Figure 17.5
Bar graph of Last Year's
COMPSALS sales, with graph
and axis titles in place.

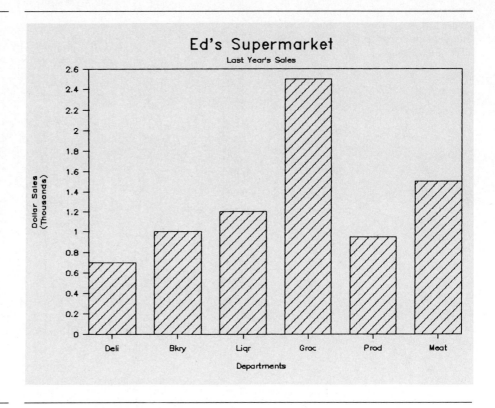

U—Selects the Use option from the Name Menu, enabling you to replace current graph settings with previously stored settings.

TYSALE—Specifies the graph settings to be stored.

ENTER—Tells 1-2-3 to execute the command.

3. The graph TYSALE is now displayed on the screen. Depress any key to return to the Graph Menu.

4. Establish the B range as the numbers in the Last Year column.

B—Tells 1-2-3 to expect the B data range.

C5 [by pointer movement or address entry]—Establishes the beginning of the B data range.

.—Nails down the beginning of the range.

C10 [by pointer movement or address entry]—Establishes the end of the B data range.

ENTER—Tells 1-2-3 to accept the B data range.

5. Change the second title line of the graph.

O—Selects the Options Menu.

T—Selects the Titles option.

S—Selects the Second line option.

Left arrow—Positions the pointer to the right of the *S* in *Sales*.

vs. Last Year's—Identifies new characters to be inserted.

ENTER—Accepts the new second title line.

Q—Quits the Options Menu and returns to the Graph Menu.

Figure 17.6
Side-by-side bar graphs of
COMPSALS sales.

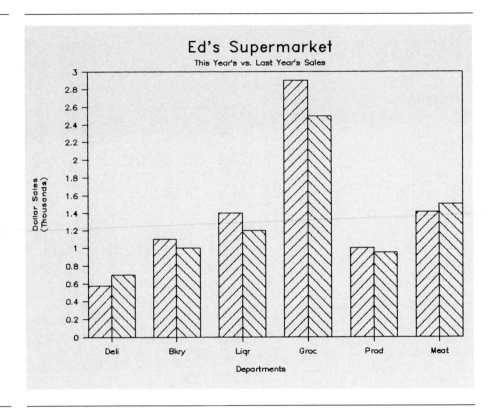

6. View the graph, using the V command. It should now look like the graph shown in Figure 17.6.
7. Depress any key to return to the Graph Menu.
8. Save the graph onto disk, so it can be printed later.

> S—Takes the Save option.
>
> LYTYSALE—Names the graph.
>
> ENTER—Tells 1-2-3 to execute the Save command.

9. Save these graph settings for later use.

> N—Selects the Name option from the Graph Menu.
>
> C—Selects the Create option from the Name Menu.
>
> LYTYSALE—Specifies the name of the graph settings to be saved.
>
> ENTER—Records these settings to the worksheet.

Converting to Line Graphs

Ed would also like to see the bar graph information depicted as a line graph. The following steps are involved:

1. From the Graph Menu, change the graph type.

> T—Selects the Type option from the Graph Menu.
>
> L—Tells 1-2-3 to generate a line graph.

2. View the graph, using the V command. It should now look like the graph shown in Figure 17.7.

Figure 17.7
Line graph of this year's and
last year's COMPSALS sales.

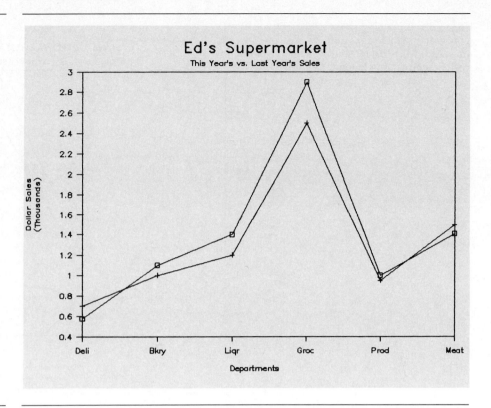

Entering Legends

Now Ed's confused because he can't tell the difference between this year's sales and last year's sales on the line graph. You will solve this problem by providing a legend that tells what symbols represent what data ranges.

The following steps are involved when you begin from the Graph Menu.

1. Add the legends.

   O—Selects the Options Menu.

   L—Selects the Legend option.

   A—Selects the A data range to hold the first legend text.

   TYSales—Identifies the text of the legend.

   ENTER—Tells 1-2-3 to accept the legend.

   L—Selects the Legend option.

   B—Selects the B data range to hold the second legend text.

   LYSales—Identifies the text of the legend.

   ENTER—Tells 1-2-3 to accept the legend.

   Q—Leaves the Options Menu and returns to the Graph Menu.

2. View the graph, using the V command. It should now look like the graph shown in Figure 17.8.

3. Depress any key to return to the Graph Menu.

4. Save these graph settings.

   N—Selects the Name option from the Graph Menu.

   C—Selects the Create option from the Name Menu.

Figure 17.8
Line graph of last year's and this year's COMPSALS sales, with accompanying legend.

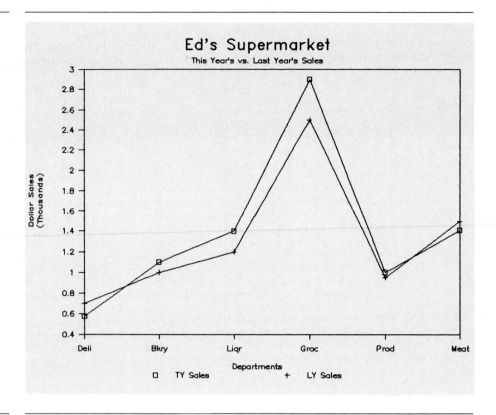

LYTYLINE—Names the graph settings.

ENTER—Tells 1-2-3 to save the graph settings.

5. Save the graph to a file for later printing.

S—Selects the Save option from the Graph Menu.

LYTYLINE—Identifies the graph to be saved.

ENTER—Tells 1-2-3 to execute the Save command.

Reconverting to Bar Graphs

Ed is very impressed with 1-2-3 and now wants the double-bar graph to include a legend for its bars. You need to take the following steps:

1. Get to the Graph Menu.
2. Select a new graph type.

T—Selects the Type option from the Graph Menu.

B—Tells 1-2-3 to create a bar graph.

3. View the graph, using the V command. It should now look like the graph shown in Figure 17.9.

Pie Charts

Ed wants more. You will try to satisfy him by putting the original bar chart information about this year's sales into the form of a pie chart. This involves the following:

1. Get to the Graph Menu.

Figure 17.9
Bar graph of last year's and
this year's COMPSALS sales,
with accompanying legend.

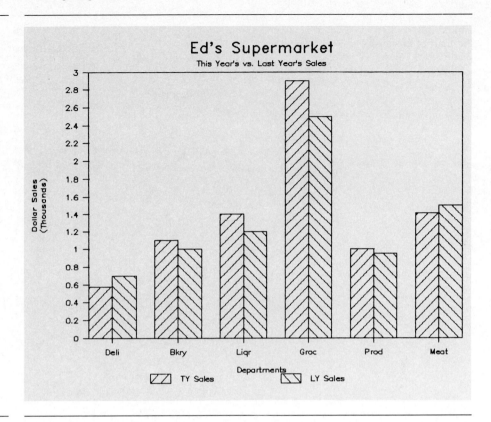

2. Reset the graph settings to TYSALE.

N—Selects the Name option from the Graph Menu.

U—Selects the Reset command, telling 1-2-3 which graph settings to use.

TYSALE—Specifies the settings to use.

ENTER—Tells 1-2-3 to change the settings of the current graph.

3. Get to Graph Menu and change the graph type.

T—Selects the Type option from the Graph Menu.

P—Tells 1-2-3 to draw a pie chart.

4. View the graph, using the V command. It should now look like the graph shown in Figure 17.10. 1-2-3 remembers all of the titles from the TYSALE graph settings.

5. Save the graph to a file.

S—Selects the Save option from the Graph Menu.

TYPIE—Names the graph.

ENTER—Tells 1-2-3 to save the graph.

Exploded Pie Chart

1-2-3 provides you with the ability to create an exploded pie chart showing one or more slices separated from the rest of the chart. To create this effect, you must set up a separate B data range. The A range contains the values to be plotted. The B range tells 1-2-3 the colors (or patterns, if viewed on a noncolor screen) to be used and which wedges (if any) are to be exploded.

Figure 17.10
Pie chart of this year's
COMPSALS sales.

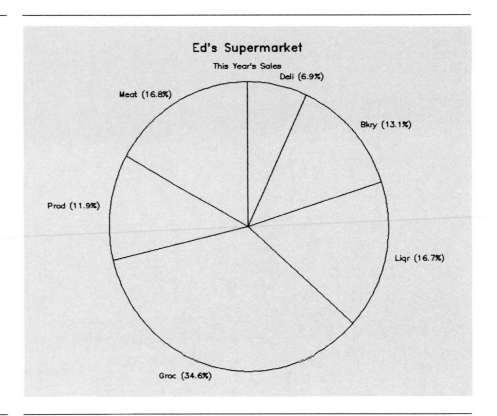

Plotting an exploded pie chart requires you to set up a new B data range in column G with values for the colors of each wedge to be plotted. These are given as single digits 0 through 8. The digits 0 and 8 are used for nonshaded wedges, the digits 1 through 7 for a shade or pattern. Add 100 to the appropriate shading value of exploded wedges. For example, if the shaded value of a wedge is 4 and you wish to have that wedge appear exploded from the pie, enter 104.

The worksheet displayed in Figure 17.11 generates the exploded pie chart in Figure 17.12. Don't worry if the graph appears a little "squashed"; it will appear fine when printed.

Stacked-Bar Charts

Ed would now like a stacked-bar graph showing the combined sales of each department for last year and this year. Once you have reached the Graph Menu, the steps are as follows:

1. Get the settings from the LYTYSALE graph that you stored previously.

    N—Selects the Name option from the Graph Menu.

    U—Selects the Use option from the Name Menu.

    LYTYSALE—Specifies the graph settings to use.

    ENTER—Puts the graph on the screen.

2. Depress any key to get to the Graph Menu.

3. Select a new graph type.

    T—Selects the Type option from the Graph Menu.

Figure 17.11
Worksheet for generating the
graph in Figure 17.12.

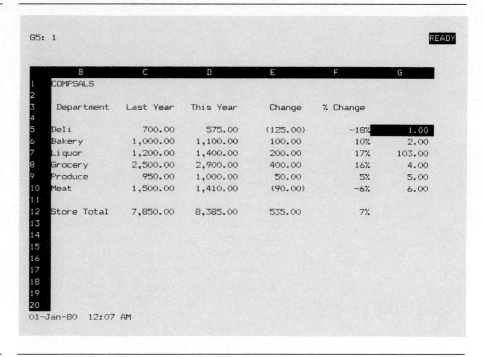

Figure 17.12
Exploded pie chart of data
depicted in Figure 17.11.

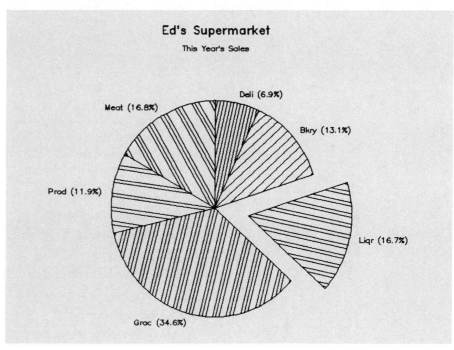

S—Tells 1-2-3 to generate a stacked-bar graph.

4. Enter a new second title line for the graph.

O—Selects the Options Menu from the Graph Menu.

T—Selects the Titles option from the Options Menu.

S—Selects the Second title line.

Left arrow—Moves the pointer under the *v* of *vs*.

Del [three times]—Deletes the word *vs*.

          +—Identifies the character to be added.

          ENTER—Tells 1-2-3 to accept the changed second line.

          Q—Quits the Options Menu and returns to the Graph Menu.

5. View the graph, using the V command. It should look like the graph shown in Figure 17.13.

6. Depress any key to return to the Graph Menu.

7. Resave the worksheet file so that 1-2-3 remembers the various named graph settings.

XY Graphs

Up until now, Ed has been requesting only one-dimensional graphs—graphs in which only Y data points are plotted. Now Ed has come up with an application that requires you to plot a set of Y data points against a set of X data points. Ed has accumulated seven years of profit figures that he would like to compare to each year's rate of inflation. To build such a graph, you must use the XY option from the Type Menu. Ed's figures are listed below.

| | PROFIT | |
| | | Inflation |
Year	Profit	Rate
1985	70	3.5%
1984	65	4.0%
1983	50	4.0%
1982	15	8.0%
1981	20	6.0%
1980	− 50	9.8%
1979	90	9.0%

    This information has been entered in a worksheet called PROFITS. The cell that contains "1985" is cell A6. Either load or create this worksheet. At this point, the following steps must be performed to get the XY graph.

1. Get the Graph Menu.

          /—Gets the Main Menu.

          G—Takes the Graph option.

2. Select the graph type.

          T—Selects the type option of the Graph Menu.

          X—Tells 1-2-3 to generate an XY graph.

3. Tell 1-2-3 the A data range.

          A—Selects the A data range option from the Graph Menu.

          B6 [by manual pointer movement]—Positions the pointer at the first A range cell.

          .—Nails down the beginning of the range.

          B12 [by manual pointer movement]—Positions the pointer at the end of the range.

          ENTER—Submits the A data range to 1-2-3.

4. Tell 1-2-3 the X data range.

          X—Selects the X data range option from the Graph Menu.

          C6 [by manual pointer movement]—Positions the pointer at the first X range cell.

Figure 17.13
Stacked-bar graph of last
year's and this year's
COMPSALS sales.

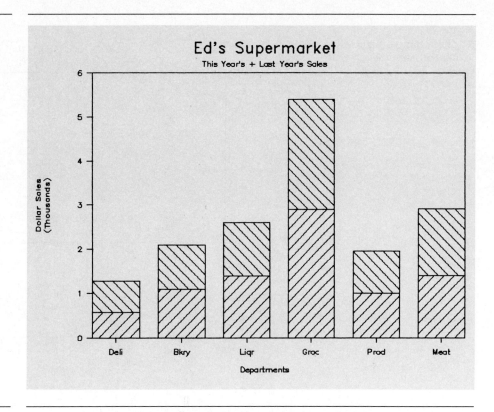

.—Nails down the beginning of the range.

C12 [by manual pointer movement]—Positions the pointer at
the end of the range.

ENTER—Submits the X data range to 1-2-3.

5. Enter the titles for the graph.

O—Selects the Options Menu.

T—Selects the Titles option.

F—Selects the First line.

Ed's Supermarket—Identifies the first line title.

ENTER—Submits the title to 1-2-3.

T—Selects the Titles option.

S—Selects the Second line.

Profits Compared to Inflation '79-'85—
Identifies the second title line.

ENTER—Submits the title to 1-2-3.

T—Selects the Titles option.

X—Selects the X-axis title.

Inflation—Identifies the X-axis title.

ENTER—Submits the title to 1-2-3.

T—Selects the Titles option.

Y—Selects the Y-axis title.

Profits—Identifies the Y-axis title.

ENTER—Submits the title to 1-2-3.

Q—Quits the Options Menu and returns to Graph Menu.

Figure 17.14
XY graph comparing profits
to inflation over a seven-year
period.

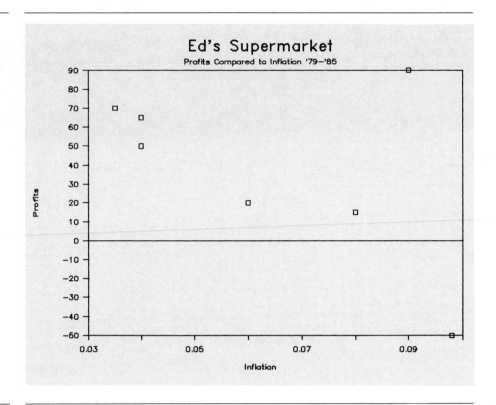

6. Tell 1-2-3 not to connect the data points with lines.

   O—Selects the Options Menu.

   F—Selects the Format option.

   G—Selects the Graph option.

   S—Selects the Symbols Only option.

   Q—Quits the Format Menu and returns to the Options Menu.

   Q—Quits the Options Menu and returns to the Graph Menu.

7. View the graph, using the V command. It should now look like the graph shown in Figure 17.14.

8. Depress any key to return to the Graph Menu, then save to XY1GRAPH picture file.

Formatting the X and Y Numeric Scaling

9. Change the format of the X and Y numeric scaling—the manner in which the scale numbers are displayed.

   O—Selects the Options Menu.

   S—Selects the Scale option.

   Y—Specifies the Y scale as the scale to be changed.

   F—Selects the Format option from the Scale Menu.

   F—Selects the Fixed option of the Format Menu.

   ENTER—Changes the format to two decimal positions.

   Q—Quits the Scale Menu and returns to the Options Menu.

Figure 17.15
Reformatted XY graph comparing profits to inflation over a seven-year period.

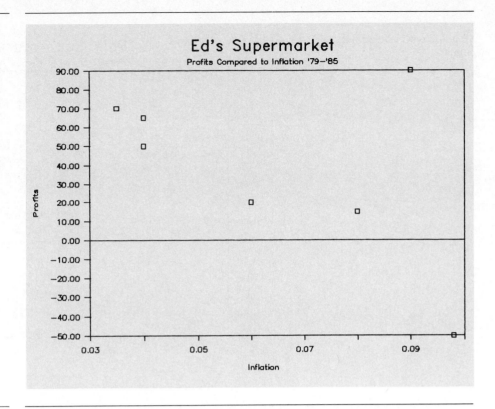

S—Selects the Scale option.

X—Specifies the X scale as the scale to be changed.

F—Selects the Format option from the Scale Menu.

F—Selects the Fixed option of the Format Menu.

ENTER—Changes the format to two decimal positions.

Q—Quits the Scale Menu and returns to the Options Menu.

Q—Quits the Options Menu and returns to the Graph Menu.

10. View the graph, using the V command. It should now look like the graph shown in Figure 17.15.

11. Save to a .PIC file called XY2GRAPH.

Labeling Graph Data Points

XY graphs can sometimes be rather hard to read. The data points represented are not properly labeled because the X option (atypically used for labeling the X axis) is used for plotting a set of data points. This can be eliminated through the use of the Data Labels feature of 1-2-3. Using the Data Labels feature involves the following steps:

1. Establish the Data Labels.

O—Selects the Options Menu.

D—Selects the Data Labels option of the Options Menu.

A—Selects the A data range option.

A6 [by manual pointer movement]—Positions the pointer at the first A range cell.

Figure 17.16
XY graph with labeled data
points.

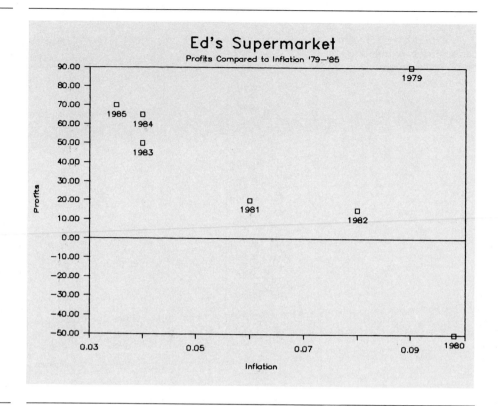

.—Nails down the beginning of the range.

A12 [by manual pointer movement]—Positions the pointer at
the end of the range.

ENTER—Submits the A Data Labels range to 1-2-3.

B—Tells 1-2-3 to place the labels below the data point
representation (square).

Q—Quits the Data Labels Menu.

Q—Quits the Options Menu.

2. Tell 1-2-3 to display the graph shown in Figure 17.16.

Graph Printing

Lotus 1-2-3 does not provide you with facilities for directly printing your graphs
from the 1-2-3 spreadsheet program. This is one of the few areas in which
Lotus's integration breaks down; but if this feature had been implemented,
1-2-3 would require much more RAM memory than it does now.

To print a graph, you must leave the 1-2-3 spreadsheet software and
return to the Lotus Access System Menu, where you take the **PrintGraph
option.** If you have been using 1-2-3, you will be instructed to insert the
PrintGraph disk in drive A. If you have previously saved your graph files and
wish to print them out, you can boot directly from the PrintGraph disk, which
also contains a copy of the Lotus Access System.

Make certain that the disk containing the graphs you have saved is inserted in drive B, and get your PrintGraph disk ready. If you have 1-2-3 running
on your computer, follow the instructions below. If the computer is off, boot
the system, then insert the PrintGraph disk in drive A; with that disk start
PrintGraph, skipping the instructions below. The steps involved in accessing
PrintGraph from 1-2-3 are as follows:

Figure 17.17
(a) The PrintGraph disk
prompt. (b) The PrintGraph
copyright screen.

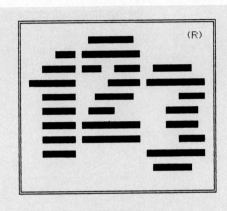

```
Insert PrintGraph Disk into your diskette drive

Press [RETURN] to continue or [ESCAPE] to quit
```

(a)

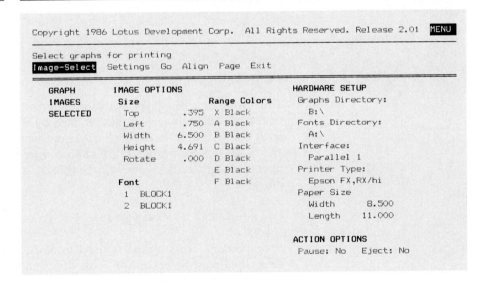

```
                              (R)

          P R I N T G R A P H
          Copyright (C)  1986
      Lotus Development Corporation
            All Rights Reserved
              Release  2.01
```

(b)

Figure 17.18
The PrintGraph Menu.

```
Copyright 1986 Lotus Development Corp.  All Rights Reserved. Release 2.01  MENU

Select graphs for printing
Image-Select  Settings  Go  Align  Page  Exit

  GRAPH        IMAGE OPTIONS                    HARDWARE SETUP
  IMAGES       Size              Range Colors   Graphs Directory:
  SELECTED     Top       .395    X Black          B:\
               Left      .750    A Black        Fonts Directory:
               Width    6.500    B Black          A:\
               Height   4.691    C Black        Interface:
               Rotate    .000    D Black          Parallel 1
                                 E Black        Printer Type:
               Font               F Black         Epson FX,RX/hi
               1  BLOCK1                        Paper Size
               2  BLOCK1                          Width     8.500
                                                  Length   11.000

                                               ACTION OPTIONS
                                               Pause: No   Eject: No
```

/—Gets the Main Menu.

Q—Selects the Quit option.

Y—Affirms leaving 1-2-3, and in a few seconds, elicits a display of the Lotus Access System Menu.

P—Selects the PrintGraph option.

At this point you will be directed to insert the PrintGraph disk in drive A (see Figure 17.17a), unless you have a fixed disk. Once you insert the PrintGraph disk, the screen depicted in Figure 17.17b is displayed on your monitor. Once PrintGraph is loaded, the PrintGraph screen in Figure 17.18 appears.

Figure 17.19
Menu of graph (.PIC) files.

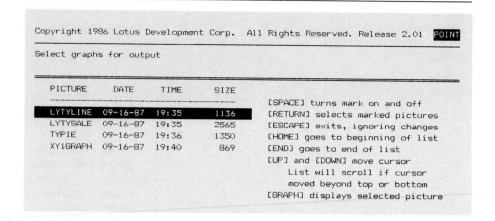

Figure 17.20
Graphs marked for printing.

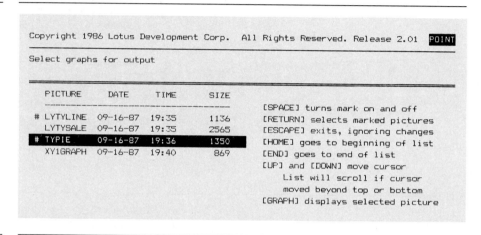

PrintGraph Menu

The information displayed beneath the PrintGraph menu details status information about the various options used by the utility, including what paper sizes are expected; what fonts have been selected; where files are to be found; and what type of printer PrintGraph is currently configured for. When you have properly started the PrintGraph utility, the following menu will be displayed:

```
Image-Select   Settings   Go   Align   Page   Exit
```

Image-Select. This option is used to mark graphs for printing. When you select the **Image-Select option**, a display of all graph files contained on the disk in drive B appears on the screen. Across the top file is a wide pointer, which is moved up and down by means of the up and down arrow keys. To tag or mark a file for printing, simply depress the Space Bar; a **pound sign (#)** will then appear to the left of that graph file entry (Figures 17.19 and 17.20).

Up to sixteen graph files can be selected for printing. If more than one file is selected, they are printed in the order in which they appear, from top to bottom. The computer then prints each graph in turn and automatically takes care of advancing the paper for the next graph. When you have selected all the files you wish to print, simply depress the ENTER key to return to the PrintGraph Menu. Depressing the space bar a second time will "unmark" the file.

Figure 17.21
Settings Menu.

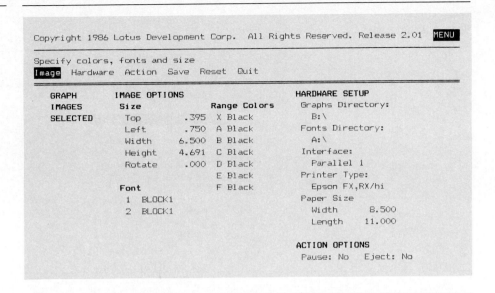

Figure 17.22
Image Menu.

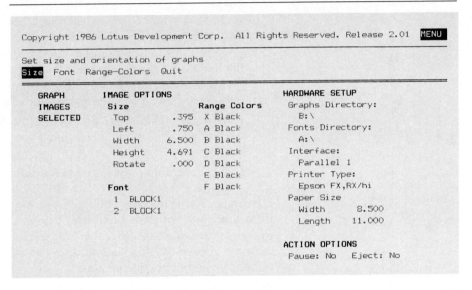

This convenient feature, known as **batch printing**, allows you to do something else (like catch up on your reading) while your graphs are being printed.

Settings. Upon selecting the **Settings option**, the following menu is displayed (Figure 17.21):

```
Image    Hardware    Action    Save    Reset    Quit
```

Image. The Image option (Figure 17.22) displays the following submenu when it is selected:

```
Size    Font    Range-Colors    Quit
```

Size. The **Size option** allows you to specify the height and width of the graph to be printed.

Figure 17.23
Font marked for use.

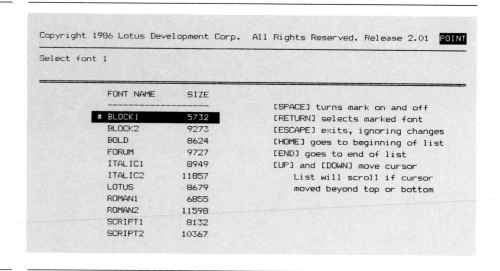

Copyright 1986 Lotus Development Corp. All Rights Reserved. Release 2.01 POINT

Select font 1

```
         FONT NAME      SIZE
         -----------    ----          [SPACE] turns mark on and off
      #  BLOCK1         5732          [RETURN] selects marked font
         BLOCK2         9273          [ESCAPE] exits, ignoring changes
         BOLD           8624          [HOME] goes to beginning of list
         FORUM          9727          [END] goes to end of list
         ITALIC1        8949          [UP] and [DOWN] move cursor
         ITALIC2        11857              List will scroll if cursor
         LOTUS          8679              moved beyond top or bottom
         ROMAN1         6855
         ROMAN2         11598
         SCRIPT1        8132
         SCRIPT2        10367
```

Font. The **Font option** allows you to select up to two fonts from eleven possible fonts in generating dot matrix output. Font 1 is used only for the first line of the graph title, font 2 for any other text. Fonts are selected in the same way that files are: Use a pointer to highlight the desired option, and then press the space bar to choose the font (Figure 17.23).

Range-Colors. This option allows you to assign a different color to each data range. This option is selected if you have the ability to generate color graphs.

Quit. This option returns you to the Settings Menu.

Hardware. The **Hardware option** allows you to configure 1-2-3 to the type of print that your printer is capable of printing, as well as to tell 1-2-3 where to find the graph files and font files. Most likely these tasks have already been done for readers of this textbook, so this option—as well as the remaining options—will not be covered here.

Quit. Returns you to the PrintGraph Menu.

Go. The **Go option** results in the graph being printed.

Align. The **Align option** resets the top-of-page. If the graph did not print properly (for example, if there is a blank area in the middle), simply move the paper manually to a perforation and press the Align command. PrintGraph now knows where the top of the page is.

Page. The **Page option** moves the paper in the printer forward to the top of the next page.

Step-by-Step PrintGraph Instructions

To print the graph files TYPIE and LYTYLINE that were created earlier, start from the PrintGraph Menu. Then:

1. Move the pointer to the Image-Select option (see Figure 17.19) and press ENTER.

2. Move the pointer (via the up and down arrows) to positions at the two desired graph names. Mark them by pressing the space bar so that a # symbol appears to the left of each. Hit ENTER when both have been marked (see Figure 17.20).

3. Take the Settings selection.

4. Take the Image option.

5. Take the Font entry of the Image Menu. Select font 1 and choose block2 by pointing, pressing the space bar, and hitting the ENTER key (see Figure 17.23).

6. Take the Font entry of the Image Menu again. Select font 2, and choose block1 by pointing, pressing the space bar, and hitting the ENTER key.

7. You've finished with the Image, so take the Quit option.

8. Quit from Settings Menu.

9. Make sure the printer is at the top of a new page; then select the Align option.

10. You're going to accept all the defaults for printing. The next step is to take the Go option to start printing.

The following options are now executed by PrintGraph:

1. The font files are loaded.

2. The graph file is loaded, and the picture is generated.

3. The graph file is printed.

PrintGraph displays various pieces of status information while it prints. In the menu area it identifies the graph file currently printing, and below the current printing file it displays a list of the files that were selected for printing.

PrintGraph's printing process is very slow in comparison to regular printing because the printer has shifted to graphics mode, which is generally slower than text mode.

The files selected for printing can be seen in Figure 17.24.

Chapter Review

To build a graph using 1-2-3, you must do the following: (1) select a worksheet file that contains information you wish to graph; (2) obtain the Graph Menu; (3) select the type of graph you want, and identify the pieces of data to be included; (4) enter any additional titles, labels, and legends; (5) view the graph on the screen; (6) make any further changes or enhancements.

The 1-2-3 package allows you to develop the following graphs: line, bar, XY, stacked-bar, and pie. Each of these graphs, except the XY graph, is one-dimensional—meaning that only one set of data points interacts across an unchanging X axis. If you wish to graph two sets of data points against each other, you must use an XY graph.

Each of the graph selections, except the pie chart, can use more than one set of Y data points. Each subsequent set of data points produces an additional line or bar, depending on the type of graph selected. The pie chart, by its very nature, is only able to plot one set of data points at a time.

After a graph has been finished, the settings for that graph can be saved onto an area of the worksheet by using the Name option of the Graph Menu. At this point, another graph, termed the "current" graph, can be built. You can make the graph settings you previously saved become the current graph by entering the Name option and specifying which group of graph settings is to be used. The graph itself can be saved, too, but it (unlike the graph setting)

Figure 17.24

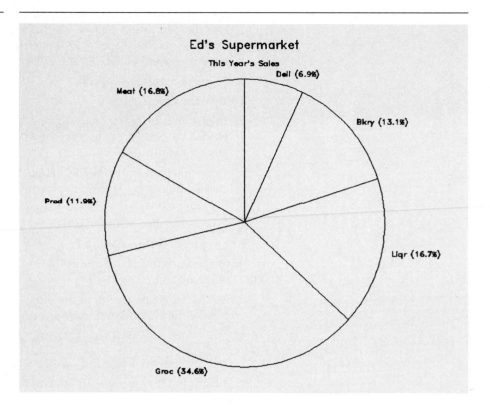

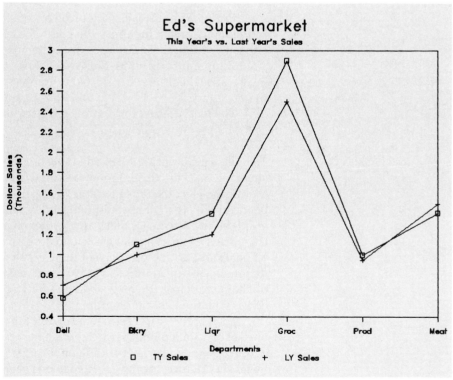

is saved to disk as a separate file. After a graph has been saved onto disk, it can be printed out via the PrintGraph utility supplied by Lotus.

   The PrintGraph utility, the program used to print any 1-2-3 graph that has been saved onto disk, allows you (depending on the printer that you are using) to determine the density of the graph to be printed and the fonts to be used for any text data on the graph. Font 1 is used for titles; font 2 is used for any other text data.

Printing graphs is a time-consuming process. PrintGraph's batch printing feature allows you to specify a number of graphs to be printed automatically, without your having to oversee any remaining steps in the printing process.

Key Terms and Concepts

ABCDEF commands	Legend option
Align option	Name option
batch printing	Options
B&W option	Page option
Color option	pound sign (#)
Create command	PrintGraph option
Data option	Quit command
Delete command	Reset option
Font option	Save command
Format option	Scale option
F10 Graph key	Settings option
Go option	Size option
Graph command	Titles option
Graph Menu	Type option
Grid option	Use command
Hardware option	View command
Image-Select option	X command
Labels option	

Chapter Quiz

Multiple Choice

1. Which of the following graph types can only have one set of Y data points?
   a. Line
   b. Bar
   c. Pie
   d. Stacked-bar
   e. XY
   f. All of the above can have more than one set of Y data points.

2. Which of the following is not considered to be a title?
   a. The two lines at the top of the graph
   b. X-axis title
   c. Y-axis title
   d. Legends
   e. All of the above are titles.

3. A B C D E F are
   a. Grades assigned for this exercise.
   b. X-axis data points.
   c. Y-axis data points.
   d. Data point labels.
   e. None of the above responses is correct.

4. Which of the following is not a feature of PrintGraph?
   a. Exists as a separate program available under the Lotus Access System
   b. Allows you to specify up to four fonts in a graph
   c. Allows you to batch-print graphs
   d. All of the above are features of PrintGraph.

5. Which of the following statements is not true about the Name feature of the Graph Menu?
   a. The stored graph settings are all active.
   b. The "current" graph settings can be saved onto the worksheet using this option.
   c. When the worksheet is saved onto disk, any graph settings are also saved.
   d. You can delete selected graph settings individually or all at once.
   e. All of the above statements are true.

True/False

6. The PrintGraph utility is one of the nonintegrated features of 1-2-3.

7. Once a set of graph settings is selected via the Use option of the Name Menu, the graph built with these settings is automatically displayed on the screen.

8. It is possible to reset selected parts of a graph or the complete graph.

9. Using legends allows you to distinguish among the various sets of Y data points.

10. The XY graph is the only 1-2-3 graph type that allows you to create a two-dimension graph.

Answers

1. c and e 2. d 3. c 4. b 5. a 6. t 7. t 8. t 9. t 10. t

Exercises

1. Define or describe each of the following terms.
   a. X axis
   b. Y axis
   c. legend
   d. scaling
   e. batch printing

2. List the steps involved in building and then printing a graph.
   a.

   b.

   c.

   d.

   e.

   f.

   g.

h.

i.

3. 1-2-3 automatically places the extension _____ on the file of any graph that is saved onto disk.

4. The _____ option allows you to label each set of Y data points, in order to make a graph more readable.

5. Graph settings can be saved onto the worksheet using the _____ _____ option of the Graph Menu.

6. The _____ command of the Graph Menu enables you to see the graph.

7. The _____ command is used when you wish to delete a portion of all of the current graph settings.

8. The _____ command is used to store a graph onto disk.

9. Any range can be canceled by pressing the _____ _____ key.

10. The format in which numeric data appear on a graph can be controlled by using the _____ option.

11. The _____ command is usually enlisted to produce labels across the bottom of the graph.

12. Explain the difference between a one-dimension graph and a two-dimension graph.

13. _____ bar charts combine entries into one set of Y data points, whereas _____ bar charts allow you to see differences immediately by comparing bars.

14. The _____ option of Print Graph allows you to specify a number of graphs to be printed and then leave to do whatever you want.

15. When you are using two fonts, _____ is used for the heading, while _____ is used for the rest of the graph.

16. Basically, _____ sizes of graphs can be printed.

17. PrintGraph is separate from 1-2-3 because it takes up too much _____ _____.

18. Explain how graphs are selected for printing.

19. You can mark graphs for printing by pressing the _____ key.

20. List the actions PrintGraph performs in printing a graph.
    a.

    b.

    c.

Computer Exercises

In building the following graphs, feel free to refer to the graph command structure in Appendix B. This will help you greatly in locating the various graph commands.

1. Retrieve the CH9EX5 worksheet file.
   a. Generate a pie chart, using the This Year column data.
   b. Generate a bar graph, using the same data. Save these graph settings to a named area called TYEAR.
   c. Compare the two years of sales, using a line graph. Save these graph settings to a named area called TYLYSALE.
   d. Generate a bar graph of the named graph TYEAR, using all the stored graph settings, but change the column to be graphed to Last Year.
   e. Generate a line graph of the named graph TYLYSALE, and enter legends at the bottom of the graph. Save these settings to a named area called LEGENDS.
   f. Using the TYLYSALE settings, change the graph type to a bar graph. Save this file to a picture file using the name BAR2SALE.
   g. Enter the following headings:

1st	FRED'S AUTO SALES
2nd	YEARLY SALES COMPARISON
X Axis	Sales Reps
Y Axis	Dollar Sales

   h. Save the graph to a picture file called BARTITLE.
   i. Save the graph settings to a named area BARTITLE.
   j. Exit from the Graph Menu. Change the contents of cells in the sales range. View the graph by depressing the F10 key.
   k. Resave the worksheet file. This will also save the named graphs.

2. Retrieve the CH9EX7 worksheet file.
   a. Graph the expenses for each year, using a line graph. Enter appropriate headings, labels, and legends. Save the file to a graph picture called EXPENSES.
   b. Generate a pie chart for each year's expenses. Save them to files called PIE1 and PIE2. You will have to reset the B data range to accomplish this.

3. Use the PrintGraph utility to print the above graphs. Refer to the Print-Graph portion of the chapter for instructions on using this utility.

Telecommunications

After completing this chapter, you should be able to:

Define the term telecommunications

Describe the role played by a modem in data communications

Differentiate between serial and parallel modes of data transmission

Differentiate between simplex, half-duplex, and full-duplex transmission

Differentiate between the asynchronous and synchronous protocols

Discuss the various types of networks that can be used to link computers

Discuss the roles of distributed data processing and local area networks

Discuss some of the media that are used for transmitting messages

Describe some of the desirable features available in communications software

Differentiate between multiplexors, concentrators, and front-end processors

Discuss the role of a local area network

Before the advent of electronic computers, businesses relied on the postal system to send and receive printed information. It is easy to imagine how long such a process took. The president of a shoe manufacturer asked for sales data in a letter to one of the company's outlets. A few days later, the outlet received the letter, compiled the requisite information and mailed off a reply. Two weeks after the president wrote the letter of request, the sales data arrived.

With computers to process and output information, today's corporate world produces far more information than it did just a few decades ago. This has produced a new need—the ability to transfer quickly vast amounts of computer-generated data from business to business.

Accordingly, the past decade has witnessed a boom in computer communications. Communications technology enables computers and computer operators to "talk" together in highly efficient networks. The computer communications explosion is fueled in part by plummeting hardware costs and the development of software that makes communications ever faster and easier.

The ability of computers to communicate with one another has profoundly affected our control of information. Using information-systems personnel, organizations can distribute information-processing resources throughout its structure and cut labor, paperwork, and turnaround time in the process. This chapter examines how computers are linked in two types of communication networks: distributed data processing (DDP), which entails the distribution and management of computer resources over a wide area, and the local area network (LAN), which links several computers and peripherals on the same premises.

Computer Communications

Telecommunications can be defined as the transfer of information from one computer to another computer or terminal by phone lines, satellite transmission, microwave links, coaxial cable, or radio transmission. Telecommunications enable the microcomputer user to

Employ the "electronic cottage concept"—performing work at home and transmitting it electronically to a distant office

Retrieve financial information from and sell or purchase stock on the Dow Jones Network

Send and receive electronic mail

Search electronically a computerized bibliography and receive a listing of articles, books, and papers that meet specific criteria

Data Transmission

Communication between computers is called data transmission. Data transmission requires both computers to recognize the transmission format in which the data is being transmitted, to transmit and receive at an established rate, to "know" the direction the data is being sent, and to operate according to common rules (protocols) governing data transfer. Let's take a detailed look at these requirements.

Data Conversion

Data are transmitted in either analog (continuous waves) or digital (binary) form. As noted in Chapter 2, computers generate and process data in binary code (typically ASCII). Binary code is transmitted in choppy jumps called **digital signals**, which usually are represented by two distinct states—the pres-

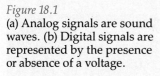

Figure 18.1
(a) Analog signals are sound waves. (b) Digital signals are represented by the presence or absence of a voltage.

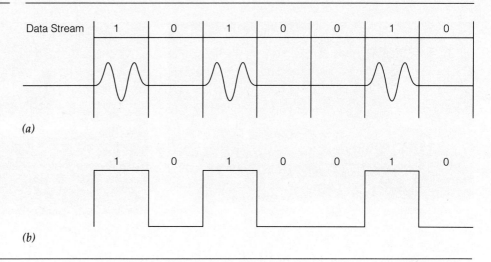

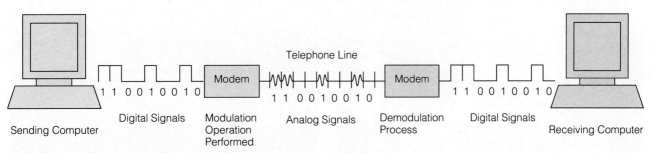

Figure 18.2
Sending and receiving computer data across telephone lines requires converting digital signals to analog (sound) signals and back again.

ence of a voltage (1) or the absence of voltage (0) (Figure 18.1b). In contrast, telephones handle and transmit sound waves (Figure 18.1a). To be transmitted over standard telephone lines, computer-stored data must first be converted from digital to analog, or sound, form.

Computer users usually transmit data long distance over telephone lines in analog form. However, in recent years telephone companies have begun to construct communication lines out of fiber optics instead of copper cables. Unlike copper, fiber-optics cables readily carry digital transmission signals. Nevertheless, computer users will likely depend on analog data transmission for some years to come.

For computers to communicate over a telephone line, the transmitting computer's digital signals must be converted into **analog signals** and sent to the receiving location, where they must be reconverted into digital signals for the receiving computer. The process of converting a digital signal to an analog signal is called **modulation**; converting analog signals into digital signals is called **demodulation** (Figure 18.2). The device that performs this task is called a *modem* (short for *mo*dulation–*dem*odulation).

Modems can be either external, residing outside the computer, or internal, residing inside the computer (Figure 18.3). An **internal modem** is a circuit board that fits into an expansion slot of an open-bus computer. An **external modem** connects to a microcomputer's serial interface. The most common serial interface is the RS-232. External modems, unlike internal modems,

(a)   *(b)*

Figure 18.3
Examples of (a) internal and (b) external modems. (Courtesy of Hayes)

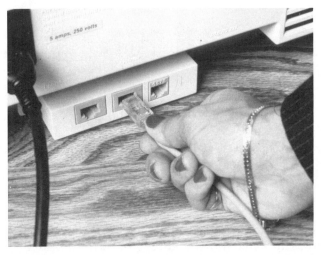

Figure 18.4
Most modems plug directly into the telephone-jack receptacle. (Courtesy of AT&T)

Figure 18.5
Some modems allow users to connect a telephone. (Courtesy of Digital Equipment Corporation)

work with a wide variety of microcomputers. However, they require an independent power source and usually cost more than internal modems. Many lap-top (portable) computers have built-in modems to facilitate intercomputer communication.

To facilitate data transmission, most modems use a standardized plug that connects directly to a telephone-jack receptacle (Figure 18.4). Many modems also allow users to plug a telephone into the modem, so the telephone functions normally when the modem is not in use (Figure 18.5).

Transmission Speed

Users can send data by either serial transmission, a bit (1 or 0) at a time, or parallel transmission, a character at a time. Data transmission speed is measured in bits per second (bps). The term *baud* is often erroneously used as a synonym for bits per second, but *baud* actually refers to the number of signal-

Figure 18.6
Parallel transmission sends all bits of a byte of storage at one time.

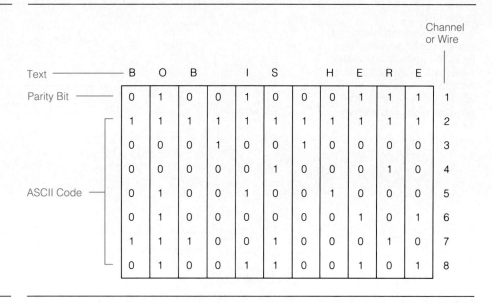

ling events per second. Bps and baud rates can be equivalent in transmissions of 300 baud, but not at transmissions of 1,200 baud or faster, in which several bits are sent in every signal event.

Serial transmission sends information 1 bit at a time over a single communication link. Computers always transmit over telephone lines in serial form. **Parallel transmission** sends all 8 bits needed to represent 1 character (1 byte) at once and requires at least eight connecting wires, one for each bit.

Parallel transmission is measured in characters per second and is usually faster than serial transmission. However, parallel transmission is limited to around fifteen feet, so it is most suitable for transmissions between a computer and nearby connecting peripherals, such as disks and printers (Figure 18.6).

Modems vary in transmission speed from 300 to 19,200 baud, or from about 30 to 1,920 characters per second. The upper rate for microcomputer modems is 9,600 baud, and the price of the hardware tends to rise with transmission speed. Businesses want faster modems not only to save time but also to save money on long-distance telephone calls. However, there is a practical limit on a modem's baud rate because the grade, or **bandwidth**, of a communications line dictates maximum transmission speed. For example, high-speed modems (over 9,600 baud) may not be able to transmit at full rate over regular telephone cables because such lines are of insufficient bandwidth.

Direction of Data Transmission

Data transmission over a communications line can be directed in three ways— simplex, half-duplex, and full-duplex (Figure 18.7). **Simplex transmission** occurs in one direction; data can be sent but not received, or received but not sent. Radio and television broadcasts are everyday examples of simplex transmission. Broadcasting towers are simplex transmitters that send data but cannot receive it. Conversely, the radios and televisions tuned in to these broadcasts are simplex receivers and cannot transmit a response.

Half-duplex transmission sends or receives data, but not both simultaneously. CB radios and home intercoms are examples of half-duplex transmitters. To send a message on either of these devices, a person must press a button while speaking; to receive a response, the person must release the button.

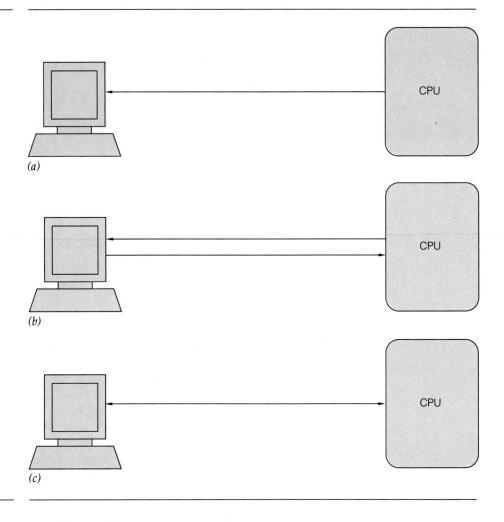

Figure 18.7
(a) Simplex transmission only sends or only receives data. (b) Half-duplex transmission sends and receives data but not simultaneously. (c) Full-duplex transmission simultaneously sends and receives data.

(a)

(b)

(c)

CPU

CPU

CPU

Full-duplex transmission sends and receives information simultaneously. A telephone is a common full-duplex device; two people engaged in a telephone conversation can talk simultaneously.

Simplex transmission is rarely used in computer communication because information processing usually requires that data be both sent and received.

Communications Protocol Modes

In sending or receiving data, computers follow a set of rules called a **protocol**. There are two protocol modes, asynchronous and synchronous (Figure 18.8). **Asynchronous protocol** transmits data a character at a time and uses several control features, including inserting a start bit before each character and one or more stop bits after each character. This control process is called **handshaking**.

Synchronous protocol sends and receives groups of characters, called packets, at fixed quantities and intervals. The transmitting terminal or computer must be able to store these blocks of characters. The synchronous mode is much faster and more complex than is the asynchronous mode. It is rarely used in microcomputer-based communication links but is a standard protocol for IBM mainframe computers.

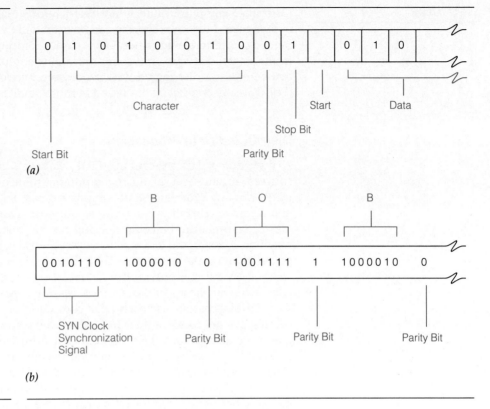

Figure 18.8
The difference between (a) asynchronous and (b) synchronous transmission protocols.

Communications Software

Computer communications require special software to perform such functions as terminal emulation, file transfers, accessing a specific computer, and logon procedures. Most modems are sold with supporting communications software.

Terminal emulation enables a microcomputer to serve as a computer terminal for another system. Common terminals that computer systems can link up with include ASCII terminals, dumb terminals, and teletypes. A **dumb terminal** is an ASCII terminal that contains no built-in processing powers; it simply sends and receives data.

Among the communication software's most important duties are the uploading and downloading of files. **Uploading** a file entails sending a file from a computer to another computer; **downloading** involves accessing another computer system's information and storing it in the downloaded computer. Uploading and downloading permit computer users to send and receive electronic mail, obtain free public-domain programs from bulletin-board services, or issue stock puts and calls using the Dow Jones Net.

Other types of features that communications software can support, with the requisite circuitry, include auto-dial or auto-answer. A modem with auto-dial automatically dials computer telephone numbers entered by the user on a keyboard. The auto-answer feature allows the user to call his or her computer from another location and access information (the receiving modem and computer must be connected and running). Dialing directories enable users to store and auto-dial frequently used computer numbers. At the user's command, the computer dials a directory number and "logs on" with the dialed system by providing information such as user number and access password.

Computer communication is not restricted to two machines at a time. Data exchange and resource sharing can be extended to several, geographically dispersed computers. Such a network includes computers (micro-, mini-, or mainframe), data, software, and communications equipment. A computer network can be either a distributed data processing network or a local area network. (Local area networks are discussed in more detail later in this chapter.)

Distributed Data Processing

A **distributed data processing (DDP)** network distributes and manages resources among several microcomputers, minicomputers, mainframe computers, or any combination of computer types. DDP systems can save money and improve reliability. For example, suppose a business employs a DDP system of one mainframe computer and several microcomputers. The business may find it easier and less expensive to perform certain tasks on its microcomputers than on the mainframe computer. And, because the DDP system consists of several computers, the failure of one computer in the system won't cripple the business's information processing capabilities.

Employees can use each DDP computer, or node, as a stand-alone processing system to solve their individual application needs. This is one of the major advantages of a DDP system. For example, suppose a large brewery switched from using a single mainframe computer to a DDP system that included microcomputers and the mainframe. Using their own microcomputer node, employees at the brewery's distribution centers now can record their monthly beer sales to the DDP's data records. Such on-site use helps reduce error because it puts data processing resources into the hands of those who are most familiar with their application needs instead of a few central-computer operators. However, DDPs make all users responsible for maintaining accurate, updated files.

DDP systems can be tailored to an organization's needs. An organization may supply its autonomous branches with applications nodes so the branches can process their own data. Conversely, a branch that relies on the organization's central computer for all its processing needs may require only a simple terminal. For example, the brewery hypothesized above installs a microcomputer at each of its distribution warehouses so each can track inventory. Suppose, however, that the brewery is small and has only a single, nearby distribution warehouse. With minimal processing needs, the warehouse might require just a simple terminal with which to send data to the brewery's computer for processing.

Constructing a DDP can present several difficulties: Communication costs may be too high; the system may have to use the business's existing hardware, which may be ill suited for distributed data linkage; and widely varying user needs may necessitate a complex system design. Also, storage of multiple copies of key files must be kept to a minimum on a DDP because every change in a file's data must be recorded on all copies. Security, too, can be problematic on a DDP. The more nodes a system has, the easier it is for unauthorized users to gain access to sensitive data unless special safeguards are built into the system.

Data Transmission Considerations

Most firms want their communication systems to send as much data as possible and as fast as possible to keep the per-byte transmission costs to a minimum. A business can increase its communication system's cost efficiency by carefully selecting an appropriate transmission medium and by using special hardware to boost transmission speed.

Communication Media

Computer networks require some form of transmission medium, a channel or route that will carry the data much like a highway carries automobiles. Communication media vary widely in efficiency and cost. And because businesses want to communicate the most data for the least cost, the choice of a transmission medium often involves a number of trade-offs. Typically, a business selects a communication medium for its computer network based on speed, cost, and message-range considerations.

Twisted-pair wiring is the most common and inexpensive communication medium for small local area networks with an operating speed of 1 megabit per second or slower. This medium uses two twisted, insulated copper wires and is frequently found in telephone systems. Twisted-pair wires have a low bandwidth and transmit relatively few characters per second.

Coaxial cable, which is used to hook television sets to cable service, consists of copper wire surrounded by insulation, which itself is surrounded by a signal shield of metal mesh. Coaxial cable will carry up to 10 megabits per second and is used to connect higher-speed local area networks where its higher transmission ability offsets the added wiring cost (Figure 18.9).

Fiber optics is a relatively new technology that is replacing copper wires as the dominant message-transmission medium for both telephone and computer-network systems. Fiber-optic cables consist of hair-thin glass strands that carry light pulses (Figure 18.10). Fiber-optic cables are less expensive and far more efficient than comparable coaxial cables. A standard coaxial cable can carry around 5,000 voice channels, whereas a much thinner fiber-optic cable can carry ten times that amount. As telephone companies convert to fiber optics, computer-network users will experience a dramatic increase in their data-communications capabilities.

Modems and telephone lines suffice for connecting widely separated computers that communicate in low-volume data. However, regular phone lines are often inadequate for high-baud transmission. Businesses that must daily transmit high volumes of data often rent or lease a dedicated line, which is specially prepared to reduce background noise and handle higher transmission speeds.

Data transmission doesn't always require wires or cables every step of the way. Microwave signals, short radio waves that are transmitted between relay towers, are frequently used in telephone communication systems. Businesses can employ microwave transmission to quickly and inexpensively relay data throughout a computer-communication system. Using such a transmission can be more affordable than leasing a dedicated telephone line.

Satellite communication enables users to send microwave computer data vast distances. Today, mainframe computers easily send data from one country to another via satellite transmission.

Multiplexors and Concentrators

When multiple users are connected to a computer by separate lines, the computer continually polls or checks each station to see if there are data to be sent. This **polling** process occurs many times each second (Figure 18.11). Often, a computer polls a terminal many times between a user's data entries. To increase the speed and efficiency of this system, especially when long-distance telephone lines are used, many businesses install special hardware called multiplexors and concentrators. These devices increase a communication system's efficiency by allowing more peripherals to be connected to a computer at a lower cost per connection and by relieving the receiving computer's CPU of many housekeeping and control functions.

A **multiplexor** routes the output from several terminals or computers into a single channel (Figure 18.12). This allows one telephone link to carry a transmission that normally would require several such links. It also allows for faster baud transmission. For example, a multiplexor can route four 300-baud terminal lines into a 1200-baud link to a distant computer. The multiplexor allocates to each terminal line one-fourth of the fast line's capacity. The device polls the terminals in succession for transmission bytes, which are sent one at a time down the fast line. If a terminal line has no byte to transmit, the multiplexor will insert a "blank" character instead.

The receiving computer demultiplexes, or breaks down, the transmission into its component messages and routes them to the proper application pro-

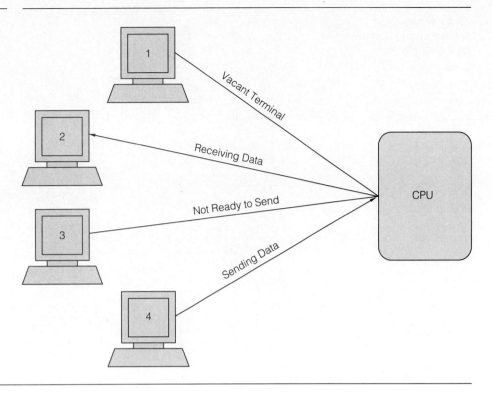

Figure 18.11
Multiple-line terminal communication with a computer.

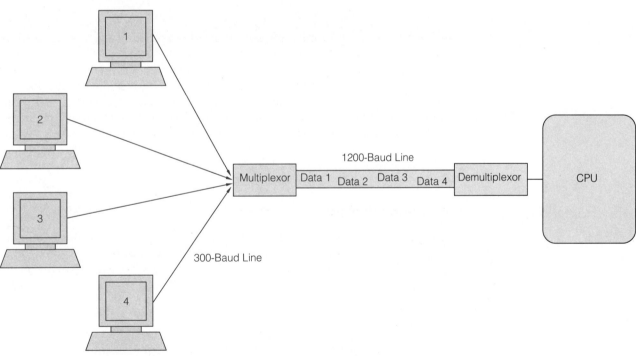

Figure 18.12
A multiplexor accepts input from several terminals, combines it, and sends it to the receiving computer, where it is demultiplexed.

grams. The multiplexor then sends the resultant output back to the appropriate terminal or computer.

A **concentrator** is a multiplexor with built-in computer circuitry (Figure 18.13). It, too, combines several slow lines into one fast line, but it is more

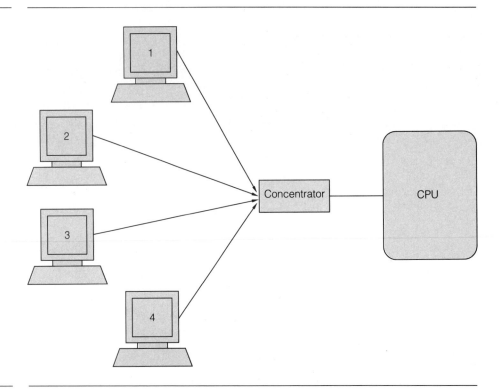

Figure 18.13
A concentrator is an intelligent multiplexor.

efficient in how it performs this task. Instead of reserving a character location, concentrators allocate time on the fast line as it is needed. This allows busy terminals to have more time than slow or unoccupied terminals.

Concentrators also can be programmed to compress data, send the data over the telephone line, and then uncompress the data at the other end. And, unlike multiplexors, concentrators can perform error-detection and error-correction procedures. Finally, concentrators can convert messages from one binary code to another (from ASCII or EBCDIC, for example), allowing otherwise incompatible terminals to link to the same network.

Front-End Processor

A **front-end processor** is a minicomputer that, besides performing general-purpose processing, frees a DDP's mainframe computer from such time-consuming housekeeping tasks as polling terminals for data, synchronizing the message packet, and error checking (Figure 18.14).

Network Topologies

The arrangement pattern of computers in a DDP is called the system's network topology. A network topology can assume many configurations.

In a **star network**, computer nodes radiate like spokes from a central, or hub, computer (Figure 18.15). A node on the network may be a computer of any size. Communication between spoke computers must pass through the hub computer. A bank with computers at several branches could utilize a star topology. A branch could process its transactions with an on-site node, then store the day's data on the master data files at the hub, or main branch, computer.

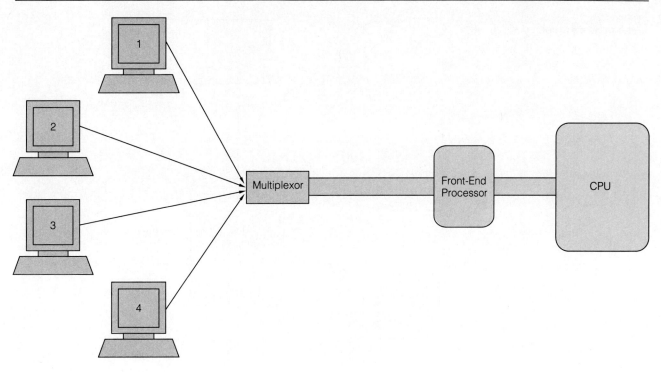

Figure 18.14
A front-end processor relieves the mainframe of many housekeeping tasks involved with data communications.

A **ring network** joins each computer in the system to two other computers, in opposing directions, forming a circle (Figure 18.16). A message destined for a specific node must travel around the ring from node to node until it reaches the designated computer. The major disadvantage of the ring network is that if one node becomes inoperative the entire network fails. Many ring networks control data exchange with a token-passing protocol. A **token** is a control signal that is passed from one node to the next, indicating which node is allowed to transmit. Only one token is passed around, so just one computer at a time can transmit data.

A **bus network** connects several nodes or computers with a single cable along which computers can send messages in either direction (Figure 18.17). To send a message, a computer seizes control of the cable or bus, transmits, then releases control of the bus. Bus networks are prone to message congestion (called contention), which can delay transmissions, thus tending to use the communication channel less efficiently than do the other topologies.

Bus networks often direct transmission traffic and avoid contention with a special protocol called carrier-sensed multiple access (CSMA). This protocol system is similar to a telephone party line, which any system member can use as long as someone else is not already calling on it. Special circuitry in the bus network ensures only one node transmits data at a time.

In a **fully distributed network**, all nodes can communicate directly with each other (Figure 18.18). This network topology speeds communication between computers, but the additional hardware and software costs may make it prohibitively expensive for many companies.

Figure 18.15
A star network topology.

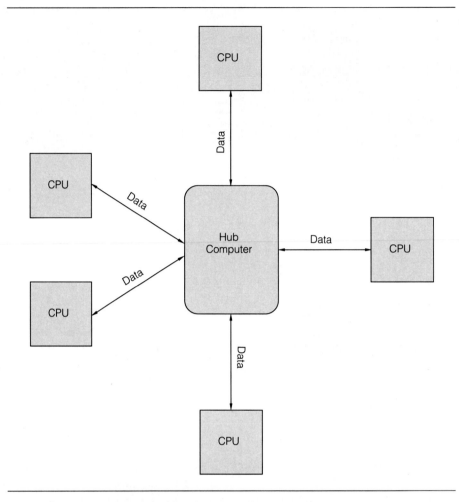

Figure 18.16
A ring network topology.

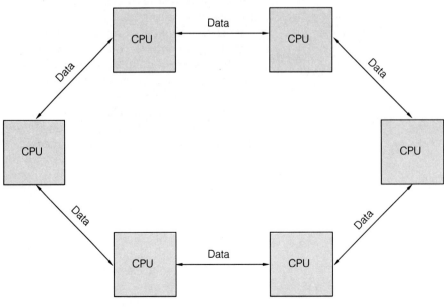

Figure 18.17
A bus network topology.

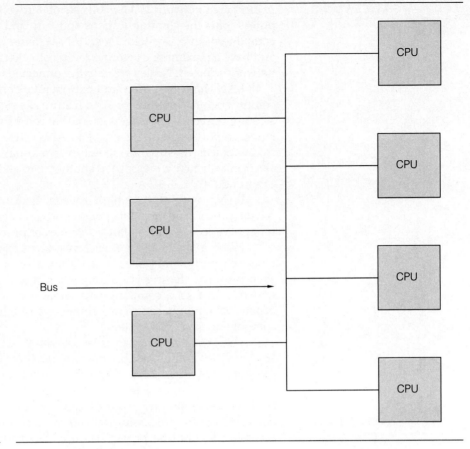

Figure 18.18
A fully distributed network, in which all computers can talk directly to any other node.

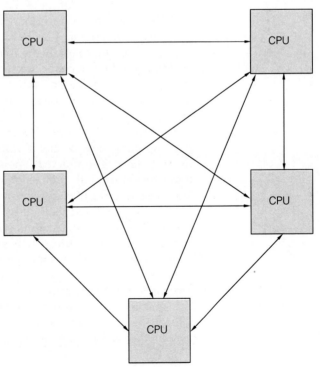

Local Area Networks

A **local area network (LAN)** consists of software, peripherals, and microcomputers, plus the communications software and hardware required to link the components into a system. Most LAN systems are confined to a single building and have a maximum operating radius of 1,000 to 7,000 feet, depending on the network selected. Nodes are usually connected to the network by coaxial cable.

LANs link computers and peripherals, permit data transmission between computers, and provide for such features as electronic mail. Electronic mail is a computer-based message system that routes word processed text—memos, letters, reports—among users of a LAN system. The prime advantage of electronic mail is its superior speed over manual message routing. A user can electronically mail a message to another user and receive a response in a matter of seconds.

LANs work at very high speeds; data often are transmitted over the coaxial cables at 50 megabits per second or faster. Accordingly, LANS are ideal for applications requiring large data files or processing high quantities of data.

LANs allow sharing of such resources as laser printers and fixed disks. However, peripheral prices have declined so dramatically in recent years that such resource sharing is no longer a primary rationale for installing a local network. In fact, a company with modest processing needs may find it less expensive to purchase several printers or fixed disks than to connect a few such components in a LAN system.

The greatest advantage users derive from a LAN is the ability to share key data files and data bases, thereby reducing data redundancy and increasing data integrity. LANs make vital stored information—such as customer, payroll, or patient master files—available to several users at once. To avoid confusion, file sharing requires software that can "lock" records that have been selected for processing. A user can lock a record, preventing others from accessing it, until he or she has updated and released the record. Locking ensures accurate updating of records.

To understand how important the locking capability is, imagine how data sharing would operate for a nonlocking accounts-receivable master file.

Suppose that a retailer employs several accounts-receivable clerks to track customer credit purchases. Each clerk has his or her own copy of the accounts-receivable master file and must post on it all applicable changes, payments, and credit purchases. Tracking these master-file changes would require a separate program to compare each customer's beginning balance with the current balance in each clerk's file. If a customer's current balance is greater than his or her beginning balance, the difference is added to a temporary record; if lower, the difference is subtracted. The software continues this subtraction and addition process until all the customer's transactions are processed and the final tally posted to the master file.

This convoluted method would not only require complex programming, it would provide the accounts-receivable clerks with inaccurate information. For instance, one clerk's file may show a customer overdrawn by $10,000, while another clerk's file shows the same customer as having a $1,000 balance.

By contrast, a lock-equipped LAN system would keep the accounts-receivable file neatly and constantly updated. Although all clerks could read the same file record simultaneously, only one could write to it. After updating a record, a clerk would release it, enabling another clerk to update it. In this way, all the clerks would be accessing a single version of the file.

File security is another important LAN advantage. An organization installing a LAN can add a variety of security controls if it wants to limit user access to the system's files. Logon/Password controls allow only those individuals who know a designated password and logon procedures to access the network. Trustee security limits user access to specific network directories.

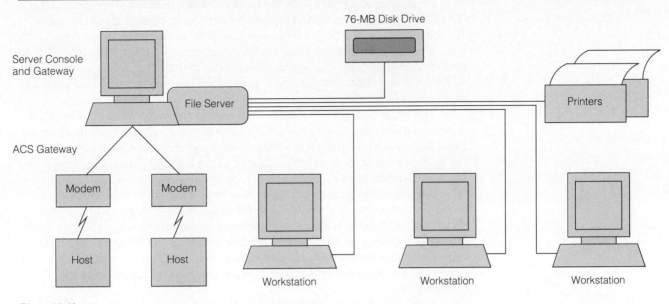

Figure 18.19
A Novell single-server network topology with an ACS gateway permitting remote access via modems.

Directory security dictates the type of actions users can take within a network directory. File-attributes security establishes whether a particular user can write to or merely read from a file.

The Novell Corporation produces a popular LAN with at least three parts (Figure 18.19). Microcomputers serve as workstations. A file server is a computer designated to store common-use software, including the one that monitors the network operation. Printers and fixed-disk storage hook directly to the file server. Cabling and connection hardware include the cables and connecting hardware used to link a node to the file server and the interface cards (circuit cards that go in the file server and workstations). A bridge is an optional component that allows a network to communicate with other, both like and unlike, network topologies. A gateway provides for communication with other computers by modems. The asynchronous communications server (ACS) gateway enables the network to communicate by modem with other computers.

Chapter Review

In the past decade, intercomputer communication has assumed vital importance in the corporate world. The ability to transmit data is called telecommunications. Telecommunications between computers usually occurs over some type of telephone network. To be transmitted, computer signals must be converted into analog form by a device called a modem. A modem at the receiving end reverses this process.

Data must be communicated over telephone lines in serial mode, or 1 bit at a time. Information can be transmitted between a computer and peripherals in parallel mode, or 1 character at a time. The transmission of data over a telephone line can be in simplex, half-duplex, or full-duplex form. Users need to both send and receive data and so usually transmit in either half-duplex or full-duplex mode.

A protocol is a set of transmitting rules. Two protocols, asynchronous and synchronous, are used to send messages. Asynchronous protocol transmits 1 character at a time and is the most common method of transmitting data. The synchronous method sends packets, or groups of characters, at a time. This protocol is most often used with IBM mainframe computers.

Communications software is a set of programs that handles the sending and receiving of data. Communications software usually includes such things as terminal emulation, the ability to upload and download files, and auto-dial and auto-answer abilities.

The process of distributing and managing computer resources is called distributed data processing (DDP). A number of advantages and disadvantages are associated with DDP systems. Computer networks are connected by twisted-pair wires, coaxial cable, fiber-optic cables, dedicated telephone lines, microwave-communication links, or satellite-communication links.

A major concern network users face is the efficiency with which the communication process occurs. Multiplexors, concentrators, and front-end processors all help to speed up the communication process.

The topology of a computer network describes the system's configuration. Computer network topologies include star, ring, bus, and fully distributed systems. Ring networks use a token to indicate which computer can transmit data.

Local area networks (LANs) permit users to share data files and high-cost peripherals, as well as employ special capabilities such as electronic mail. LANs are usually contained in one building. A LAN should provide for several levels of security.

Key Terms and Concepts

analog signals	handshaking
asynchronous protocol	internal modem
bandwidth	local area network (LAN)
bus network	modulation
coaxial cable	multiplexor
concentrator	parallel transmission
demodulation	polling
digital signals	protocol
distributed data processing (DDP)	ring network
downloading	serial transmission
dumb terminal	simplex transmission
external modem	star network
fiber optics	synchronous protocol
front-end processor	telecommunications
full-duplex transmission	terminal emulation
fully distributed network	token
half-duplex transmission	uploading

Chapter Quiz

Multiple Choice

1. Which network topology is sometimes referred to as a hub network?
   a. Ring
   b. Star
   c. Bus network
   d. Fully distributed
   e. None of the above

2. Which network topology makes use of a token to control which computer has access to the network?
   a. Ring
   b. Star
   c. Bus network
   d. Fully distributed
   e. None of the above

3. Which of the following statements is false?
   a. Digital communication commonly takes place using telephone lines.
   b. A modem is only used with fiber-optic cables.
   c. A digital signal still requires the use of at least one modem.
   d. All of the above are false.
   e. None of the above are false.

4. Which of the following is not a concern for security on a LAN?
   a. Who is actually using a terminal?
   b. Does the person have read/write privileges to this file?
   c. Does this password have access rights to this directory?
   d. None of the above is a security concern for a LAN.

5. Which of the following is usually false with respect to telephone-transmitted computer links?
   a. Data is usually transmitted digitally.
   b. Simplex transmission is frequently used.
   c. Synchronous transmission is infrequently used.
   d. All of the above are false.

True/False

6. Fiber-optic cables can be used for transmitting digital data.

7. Only an external modem can be used on an open bus computer.

8. The grade or bandwidth of a telephone line dictates the speed of a data transmission.

9. The "handshake" is simply the set of rules that are followed when transmitting data.

10. Downloading refers to copying a file from a computer and transferring it to your computer via a communication link.

Answers

1. b 2. a 3. d 4. a 5. d 6. t 7. f 8. t 9. t 10. t

Exercises

1. Define the following terms:
   a. telecommunications
   b. distributed data processing
   c. protocol
   d. handshaking
   e. network topology
   f. LAN

2. The transmission of any data over a communications link is called _____.

3. The process of translating a digital signal to an analog signal is called _____.

4. The device that performs the modulation–demodulation process is called a(n) _____.

5. The measurement in units of _____ is used to measure the number of bits per second (bps) for data transmission.

6. Data transmitted 1 byte at a time refers to _____ transmission of data, whereas data transmitted 1 bit at a time refers to _____ transmission.

7. The grade or _____ of a communications line determines the speed at which data can be sent.

8. The _____ data transmission only sends or receives data.

9. The _____ data transmission both sends and receives data at the same time.

10. The _____ data transmission sends and receives data but not at the same time.

11. The _____ transmission protocol sends information 1 character at a time.

12. The process of preceding and following a character with stop and start bits is a process called _____.

13. The process of sending a file from your computer to another computer via a communications link is called _____.

14. The process of distributing computer power and then managing a network is called _____.

15. A computer in a network is sometimes referred to as a(n) _____.

16. The medium usually used to connect telephones is referred to as _____.

17. A cousin of this communications medium _____ is also used to connect televisions.

18. The process called _____ is used to check to see if a terminal has data to send.

19. A _____ is a device that uses a high-speed communications line to combine low-speed messages.

20. A _____ is a device that can allocate line time based on terminal activity.

21. A _____ network topology has each computer connected to one in front and one in back.

22. A _____ is a control signal passed from one computer to the next to determine which computer on the network can send data.

23. A _____ network topology connects several computers with one cable.

24. The biggest advantage of a local area network is the ability to share _____ between users.

25. The four areas of security that should be addressed for a LAN are

a.

b.

c.

d.

Questions for
Thought

1. Prepare a report on the benefits that the new fiber-optic cable technology offers to both voice and data communications.

2. Examine the modem market. What features are offered? What features do you believe are desirable? What are the relative costs of modems that transmit at various speeds?

3. Prepare a report on the different types of LANs that are currently available on the market. Which type of LAN appears to be the best?

4. Prepare a report that describes how modems are able to send data at such high speeds over telephone lines without losing characters.

5. Create a list of the communications applications that our complex society relies on for proper functioning.

Chapter

19

Integrated Software

Systems

After completing this chapter, you should be able to:

Explain the parts of the integrated software package PC Works

Explain how information is passed from one part of the package to another

Explain how to build a data base using PC Works

Explain how to build charts using PC Works

Explain how word processing, spreadsheet, and chart data can be combined in one document

This chapter introduces integrated software by focusing on the software package PC Works, developed by Microsoft. It is marketed as an easy-to-learn microcomputer package for small businesses or home use. Microsoft also offers Apple Works for owners of Apple computers. Both packages are intended for small- or medium-sized applications. **PC Works** is capable of spreadsheet processing, graphing, word processing, data base applications, and intercomputer communications. It can also pass information easily from one application to another. For instance, a word processing document produced by Works can also contain a graph created by Works.

Works is a menu-driven package much like Lotus 1-2-3. However, there is a major difference. Software instructions for previously covered packages have been entered from the keyboard. Works instructions can be entered from the keyboard or with a mouse (covered in Chapter 2). If a mouse is not present on the machine, instructions can still be entered from the keyboard by pressing the Alt key and invoking the Menu Bar (like the Lotus 1-2-3 Main Menu). Once the Menu Bar appears on the screen, instructions can be entered as with Lotus 1-2-3. The appropriate command is highlighted by pressing a Right or Left arrow key and then pressing ENTER or by entering the boldfaced character that appears in the command.

A great advantage of integrated packages like Works is that the menus for each package have common elements. For example, all Works tools have a File menu and a Window menu. All tools that have a Print command contain similar commands (some may have additional special feature commands). Most of the application tools also have Edit, Select, Format, and Options menus with commands tailored to that specific tool. The following is a list of the common menu commands found in each tool, along with the function performed by that menu option:

File	Creates new files, opens existing files, saves and closes files, and exits Works
Edit	Copies, moves, inserts, and deletes data
Print	Selects the printer, prepares and prints a file
Select	Goes to and searches for specified data
Format	Changes the appearance of selected data on the screen and determines the way they print
Options	Changes the appearance of data and the way they calculate
Window	Gets Help, gets the tutorial, switches between open files, and changes Works settings

The application we use to illustrate Works involves a small-business owner who wishes to computerize his record keeping. Jim owns the Basket Tree, a crafts business in Normal, Illinois, that markets handmade baskets, brooms, wreaths, and other crafts. Some items are imported from the Philippines or Thailand, whereas other items are ordered from domestic wholesalers. Jim uses three different methods to sell his products. The first is direct-response advertisements placed in craft magazines for two items: decorated baskets, which Jim offers in four different colors, and decorated cinnamon-root brooms, which he offers in three sizes. Customer orders are taken over the telephone. Customers living in Illinois must have state sales tax added to their invoice, whereas individuals living outside the state do not pay sales tax. Jim wants to create invoices for all telephone orders easily.

The second sales method is participation in craft shows held in malls, in exposition halls, and at special events. Jim also participates in spring garden shows staged throughout the Midwest. Jim offers a greater variety of merchandise at these shows than he does for telephone orders. The craft magazines require advertisers to supply items in high volume for as long as six months after an ad appears. The people who frequent the shows, however, want a variety of merchandise, and many want to purchase one-of-a-kind wreaths or centerpieces for their homes.

Jim's third method of sales is wholesaling items to other Midwest retailers, using sales representatives who work for a 10–15 percent commission. A 10 percent commission is paid on imported items; a 15 percent commission is paid on domestically manufactured items. Jim has twelve sales representatives in five different states, and he wants to calculate their commissions easily.

Jim is expanding his business in Normal and recently leased a facility in a new commercial development called Normandy Village. This facility will allow him to add a retail outlet to his production area. Because he is frequently out of town, this retail outlet is primarily for special sales or exhibits. To properly advertise these special exhibits, Jim must develop a mailing list of individuals living within a fifty-mile radius of Normal. Jim wants to send a personalized exhibit announcement to each potential customer two weeks before an exhibit.

Jim wants his inventory on the computer to help with end-of-the-year tax preparation. He also wants to compare sales results from each type of marketing. After reading a favorable article on PC Works in a small-business magazine, Jim decides the Works package can accommodate his various needs and purchases it. He also buys a used Compaq computer with a fixed disk to run the system and a Hewlett-Packard laser printer.

Introduction to PC Works

The MS DOS version of Works requires an IBM or IBM-compatible computer with a minimum of 384K of internal memory. It also requires a computer with two 360K floppy disk drives, one 720K disk drive, or a fixed disk and a floppy disk of some type. To use the communications module of Works, the consumer also must purchase a modem.

Starting Works

Diskette-Based System. Starting Works using a diskette-based system requires booting the computer, placing the disk with Works in drive A, entering the command WORKS, and then pressing the ENTER key.

Fixed-Disk System. Starting Works using a fixed-disk system requires booting the computer, entering the command to switch to the subdirectory with Works (CD WORKS), entering the command WORKS, and pressing the ENTER key.

When the Works program is put into action, a copyright screen appears, followed by the Works Main Menu (Figure 19.1). The Main Menu allows access to Word Processor, Spreadsheet, Database, or Communications. Like Lotus 1-2-3, Works incorporates the graphics module inside the spreadsheet. An option is selected by using the mouse to point to the appropriate option between parentheses and pressing the left-hand button or by entering the first character of the option at the keyboard. Once the appropriate option is selected, Works asks if an existing file will be used or if a new file will be created. To open a new file, click the mouse to New. To access an existing file, select the **Open option**. If a mistake has been made, select the **Cancel option**.

To select a file that was created earlier with the Open command, a screen like that depicted in Figure 19.2 is displayed on the monitor. The top of this screen contains the active disk/directory. The first box contains the files, the second box contains the drives on this machine, and the third box contains the

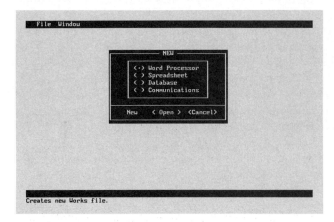

Figure 19.1
The Works Main Menu allows you to select the type of
application you want.

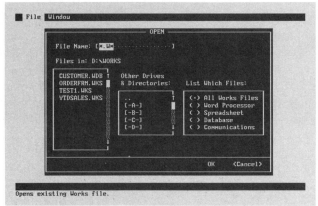

Figure 19.2
The screen used for loading existing files into Works.

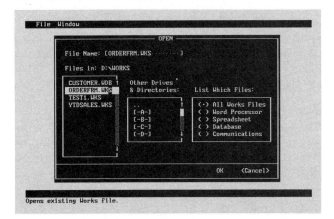

Figure 19.3
The file ORDERFRM.WKS is selected for loading into
Works.

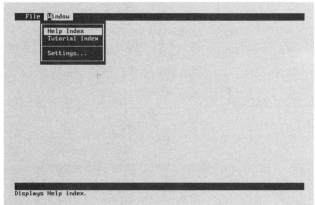

Figure 19.4
The subdirectory is displayed once the Window option is
selected.

different file types that can be displayed. All files created by Works contain an
extension that starts with a *W*. The various types of files are

Word processor files	.WPS
Spreadsheet files	.WKS
Data base files	.WDB
Communications files	.WCM

Figure 19.2 shows that all files in the subdirectory WORKS on drive D are
to be displayed (the default). Click the mouse to the appropriate type of file,
and only that file type will be listed. For example, if Works word processor files
are clicked, only files with a .WPS file extension are displayed in the left-hand
column. Use the mouse to click the file to be loaded. Once the file has been
selected, it appears in a bar as well as in the file name at the top of the screen.
Figure 19.3 shows that the file ORDERFRM.WKS has been selected for loading
into Works. Once a file has been selected, the **OK option** is clicked and that file
is loaded.

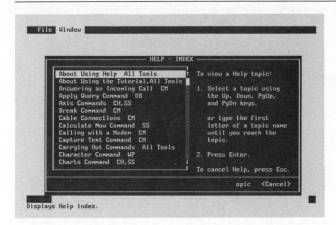

Figure 19.5
The Help screen is displayed once the Help feature is selected.

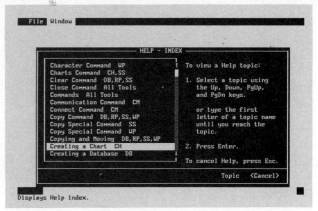

Figure 19.6
The Help screen for selecting the Creating a Chart CH option from the Help feature of Works.

Help Feature

Once any Works application is entered, help with a command is readily accessible via the Windows option of any Works menu. When the **Window option** is selected, a three-option submenu appears on the screen (Figure 19.4). The Help feature of Works is always accessed via the **Help Index option**, which is displayed on the screen (Figure 19.5). Use the mouse to highlight the desired command. If the command is not displayed on the screen, use the mouse to click the arrow in the lower right-hand corner of the command box or use the Up or Down arrow keys to position to the desired command. For instance, if information about the Chart command is desired, the screen depicted in Figure 19.6 is used to select that command, and the Help screen depicted in Figure 19.7 appears on the monitor.

When the desired information has been received, you can return to the Index by clicking the mouse on that option. An interactive lesson is started by selecting the Lesson option. To return to the Works application, select the Cancel option.

Exiting Works

To temporarily leave Works to perform a task in DOS and then later return, take the **File option** of a Works menu (this option is to leave Works for any reason). The DOS option drops to DOS and permits any commands (Figure 19.8). To return to Works, enter the command EXIT at the DOS prompt.

To return to DOS permanently after using Works, select the Exit option of the File command. To return to the Works Main Menu, select the Close command (Figure 19.9). To start another application, select the File command and then take the New or Open option.

Word Processing

Jim wants to send a letter to the landlord of Normandy Village finalizing his lease agreement. He first enters Works, taking the Word Processing option, and opens a new file. A blank word processing screen like that depicted in Figure 19.10 appears on the monitor. The first line is the Menu Bar with various

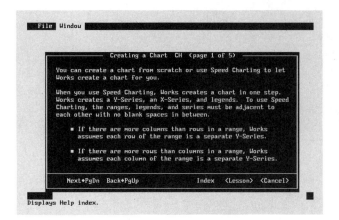

Figure 19.7
The Help screen (first of five) for creating a chart using Works.

Figure 19.8
After temporarily leaving Works by using the DOS option of the File command, issue the EXIT command to return to Works.

Figure 19.9
You are returned to the beginning Works Menu after the Close command has been issued.

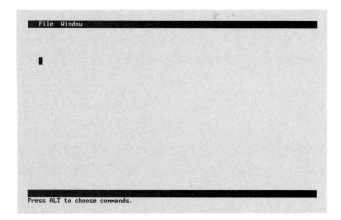

command options. The next line is the page ruler. The bracket ([) on the left-hand side marks the left margin, whereas the right bracket (]) marks the right-hand margin. The numbers indicate the inches per line. The default for a new page of text is a line length of six inches. The > > marks the beginning of your document; the diamond character marks the end of the file. The status line is the bar that appears toward the bottom of the screen. It indicates the page shown on the screen and the total number of pages contained in the document. The other entry (WORD1.WPS, in this case) contains the name of the file. A WORDn entry is used to indicate that this is a new file that has not yet been named and stored using the **Save** or **Save As options** of the File command. The last line of the screen is the message line, which shows messages related to the command currently being executed.

Jim wants to confirm his decision to lease the property at 12 Normandy Village in Normal, Illinois, and he decides to write a letter like that in Figure 19.11.

After Jim has entered the letter using Works, he notices that the word *Basket* has been misspelled (Figure 19.12). Because he is not a good typist or proofreader, Jim uses the Works built-in spelling checker by taking the Options command of the Menu Bar and then selecting the **Check Spelling option**.

Figure 19.10
A blank word processing
screen with the parts labeled.

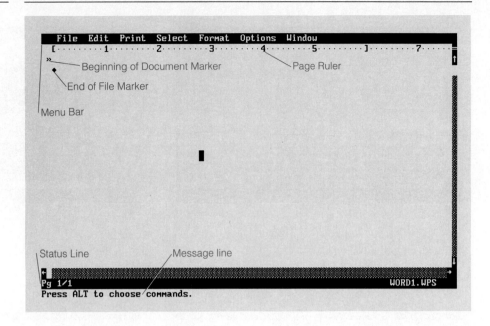

Figure 19.11
Jim's lease confirmation letter
(CONFIRM.WPS).

```
The Basket Tree
Box 1049
Bloomington, IL  61701

August 23, 198x

Hal Jamieson
Heritage Enterprises
1059 S. Main Street
Normal, IL  61761

Dear Mr. Jamieson;

The purpose of this letter is to confirm our agreement for
me to lease the property at 12 Normandy Village in Normal,
Illinois beginning October 1st.  The price that we agreed
upon Tuesday appears to be appropriate.  It should be noted
that per our agreement if a year's rent is paid by February
15th a 10 percent deduction against the total rent can be
taken by the lesee.

I also look forward to being able to take possession of the
property beginning on September 1st to prepare it for
occupancy without incurring any additional rental
obligation.

It is also my understanding that any changes in the color
scheme or carpeting are my responsibility financially.
It is also my understanding that I will be responsible for
heating, cooling, and water costs, but that insulation rated
at R40 will be placed in the ceiling no later than November
1st of this year.

I look forward to being at Normandy Village for several
years.

Sincerely Yours,



Jim
The Basket Tree
```

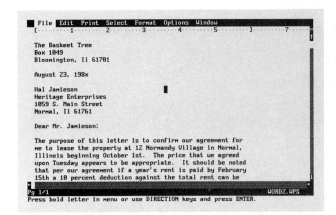

Figure 19.12
Letter with a word misspelled.

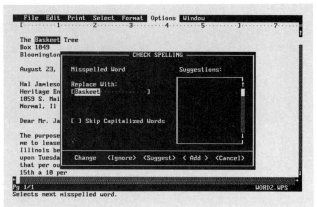

Figure 19.13
The spelling checker of Works has located a misspelled word.

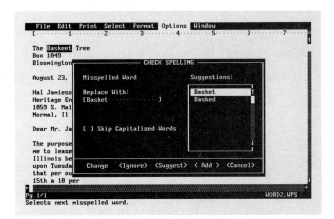

Figure 19.14
Works offers some suggestions for the misspelled word.

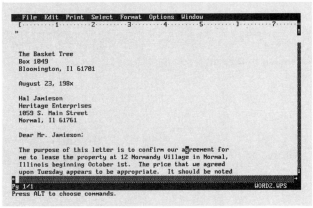

Figure 19.15
The corrected document on the monitor.

This starts the spelling check of the document. Once the spelling check starts, each word is compared to words held in the Works dictionary. The speller stops when it locates the word *Baskeet* (Figure 19.13) and highlights the suspect word. When the Suggest option is taken, the speller indicates alternate spellings for *Baskeet* (Figure 19.14). The appropriate word can be selected via the mouse or by using the Up and Down arrow keys. When the Change option is selected, the suspect word is replaced with the selected word (Figure 19.15).

The Works word processing commands are similar to the commands used in WordPerfect. Many of these commands, like those in WordPerfect, are used in combination with a Block command. The equivalent of the Block command in Works is the **Extend command (F8)**. The Extend command requires (a) positioning the cursor at the beginning of the text block, (b) entering the Extend command (press F8), (c) using the arrow keys to highlight the text, (d) issuing the Works command to be used against the block, and (e) canceling the block using any cursor movement command. To cancel a block without issuing a command against the marked block of text, shrink the text using the Shrink Extend (SHIFT + F8) command and cancel the Extend using the Esc key.

Word Processing Command Summary

Function Key Names	*Key/Combination*
Help	F1
Tutorial	SHIFT + F1
Move	F3
Copy	SHIFT + F3
GoTo	F5
Next Window	F6
Previous Window	SHIFT + F6
Repeat Search	F7
Repeat Copy or Format command	SHIFT + F7
Extend Selection	F8
Shrink Selection	SHIFT + F8
Paginate Now	F9

Cursor Movement/Selection Commands

Left a Character	Left arrow
Right a Character	Right arrow
Up a Line	Up arrow
Down a Line	Down arrow
Left a Word	Ctrl + Left arrow
Right a Word	Ctrl + Right arrow
Up a Paragraph	Ctrl + Up arrow
Down a Paragraph	Ctrl + Down arrow
To Beginning of Line	Home
To End of Line	End
To Beginning of File	Ctrl + Home
To End of File	Ctrl + End
Up a Screen	PgUp
Down a Screen	PgDn
To Beginning of Screen	Ctrl + PgUp
To End of Screen	Ctrl + PgDn
Start Extend	F8
Quit Extend	Esc
Extend Selection	F8
Shrink Selection	SHIFT + F8
Cancel Selection	Any cursor movement key

Text Formatting Commands

Old	Ctrl + B
Underline	Ctrl + U
Italic	Ctrl + I
Strikethrough	Ctrl + S
Superscript	Ctrl + SHIFT + =
Subscript	Ctrl + =
Plain Text	Ctrl + Space Bar
Center Text	Ctrl + C
Right Alignment	Ctrl + R
Left Alignment	Ctrl + L
Single Spacing	Ctrl + 1
Double Spacing	Ctrl + 2
1 Line Before Paragraph	Ctrl + 0
0 Lines Before Paragraph	Ctrl + E
Normal Paragraph	Ctrl + X

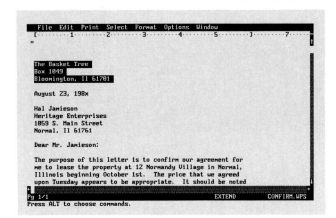

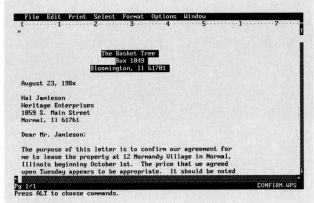

Figure 19.16
Text marked via the Extend command.

Figure 19.17
Marked text has been centered on the screen.

Editing

Delete Character Left	BACKSPACE
Delete Character	Del
Move	F3
Copy	SHIFT + F3
Undo	Alt + BACKSPACE

Special Commands

Tab	TAB
End of Paragraph	ENTER
Manual Page Break	Ctrl + ENTER
Print Page Number	Ctrl + P
Print Date	Ctrl + D
Print Time	Ctrl + T
Print File Name	Ctrl + F
Current Date	Ctrl + ;
Current Time	Ctrl + SHIFT + ;

Commands Using Extend

When Jim has finished his letter he decides to center and boldface his address. Rather than erasing and then reentering the text, he uses the Extend command to first mark the text and then issue the center and boldface instructions. He positions the cursor to the first character of his address, issues the Extend (F8) command, and then highlights all three lines of his address (Figure 19.16). He then issues the Center command (Ctrl + C) to center the text as depicted in Figure 19.17. To boldface the text, he issues the Bold command (Ctrl + B), and the text is boldfaced (Figure 19.18). Once a command of any kind has been issued against a marked block of text, any cursor movement command cancels the Extend command and unmarks the block of text (Figure 19.19).

Spreadsheet

Because the Works spreadsheet is similar to that of Lotus 1-2-3, only the differences between the two packages are noted. Figure 19.20 shows the worksheet parts. The spreadsheet name, as well as other pieces of information, is con-

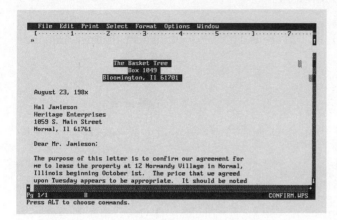

Figure 19.18
Marked text has now been boldfaced.

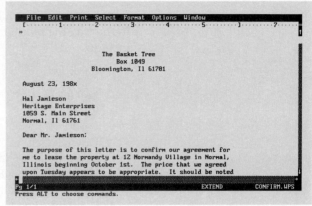

Figure 19.19
Any cursor movement command cancels the block.

Figure 19.20
The parts of a Works worksheet screen.

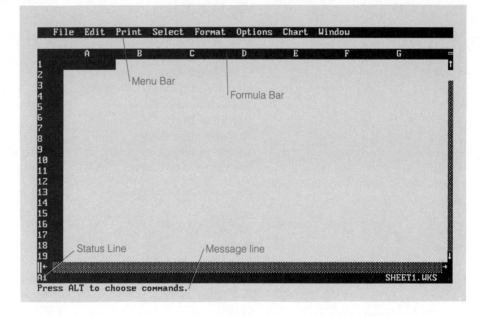

tained in the status line. The location of the pointer is given in the left-hand portion of the status line; the cell contents are at the top of the screen in the formula bar. This spreadsheet package allows for 4,096 rows and 256 columns. Worksheets prepared by Lotus 1-2-3 or VP-Planner can be loaded directly into the Works spreadsheet. Some of the advanced features, such as string handling and macros, will not directly convert, but the majority of worksheets can be loaded without difficulty.

One difference between Works and Lotus 1-2-3 is that formulas begin with a plus sign (+) in 1-2-3 and with an equal sign (=) in Works. As a 1-2-3 worksheet is read into memory, formulas are automatically converted to begin with a plus sign. However, 1-2-3 conventions can be started with formulas using an equals sign. The Works spreadsheet simply places an equal sign in front of the formula when the ENTER key is pressed to store the formula.

Works' built-in functions work similarly to those of Lotus 1-2-3. The only difference is that Works functions do not start with the at (@) sign. You must always start a Works function with either an equal sign (=) or a plus sign (+).

Pointer Movement Commands

While some pointer manipulation commands are similar, there are differences in the way the pointer is moved around a Works worksheet. These commands include:

Direction	Key/Combination
Left a Cell	Left arrow
Right a Cell	Right arrow
Up a Cell	Up arrow
Down a Cell	Down arrow
Left a Cell in a Range	SHIFT + TAB
Right a Cell in a Range	TAB
Up a Cell in a Range	ENTER
Left Unlocked Cell	TAB
One Block Left	Ctrl + Left arrow
One Block Right	Ctrl + Right arrow
One Block Up	Ctrl + Up arrow
One Block Down	Ctrl + Down arrow
One Screen Left	Ctrl + PgUp
One Screen Right	Ctrl + PgDn
One Screen Up	PgUp
One Screen Down	PgDn
To Beginning of Row	Home
To End of Row	End
To Beginning of File	Ctrl + Home
To End of File	Ctrl + End
Quit Extend or Collapse Selection	Esc

Function Key Commands

Help	F1
Tutorial	SHIFT + F1
Edit	F2
Move	F3
Copy	SHIFT + F3
Reference	F4
GoTo	F5
Next Window	F6
Previous Window	SHIFT + F6
Repeat Search	F7
Repeat Copy or Format command	SHIFT + F7
Extend Selection	F8
Select Row	Ctrl + F8
Select Column	SHIFT + F8
Select Spreadsheet	SHIFT + Ctrl + F8
Manual Calculate	F9
Exit Charting	F10
View Chart	SHIFT + F10

Works and Ranges

Works handles ranges differently than does Lotus 1-2-3. Lotus 1-2-3 typically requires (a) the pointer to be positioned at the beginning cell of a range, (b) the issuing of a command to be used against a range of cells, and (c) an indication of which cells are to be included in a range, either by entering the beginning and ending cell address or by pointing and executing the command. Works, however, requires highlighting the affected cells by including them in an Extend command and then issuing the desired command. After a command has been issued, any pointer movement command cancels the extended range. To cancel an Extend operation before a command has been issued, press the Esc key twice.

To manually indicate a range of cells to Works, use the same conventions as Lotus 1-2-3, but use a colon instead of a period. For example, to include cell B2 through cell C6 within a range, do the following:

Lotus 1-2-3	B2.C6
Works	B2:C6

If a period is used in a Sum function that tries to add all entries in those cells, a screen like that in Figure 19.21 is displayed. The cell range references are also highlighted to indicate where Works thinks the problem occurs.

All cells in a row, column, or the entire worksheet are often included in a command. With Works the cell addresses can be given manually or by highlighting the cells using keyboard commands. The commands are

Define a Column	SHIFT + F8
Define a Row	Ctrl + F8
Entire Worksheet	SHIFT + Ctrl + F8

Remember, an entire row or column is defined (extended) and will be affected by any Works command. To avoid having all cells affected (for example, all cells within a row), use the Extend command to define the cells to be included.

The **Define a Column** and **Define a Row commands** are also used in adding or deleting columns and rows. To add a column to the left of an existing column, first mark that column using Define a Column (SHIFT + F8), select the Edit option of the Menu Bar, and then select the Insert command. A column to the left of the marked column is now added to the worksheet. The same tasks are performed for adding a row. The only difference is that rows are added above the defined row.

Clear/Erase Command

The Works **Clear command** functions in the same fashion as the Range Erase of Lotus 1-2-3. The only difference is that the range of cells must be highlighted via the Extend command before Clear can be executed. The Clear command is found under the Edit option of the Menu Bar (Figure 19.22).

Copy Command

Another important command found in the Edit menu is the Copy command. Works executes a copy command in three ways: a standard copy, where a block of cells is copied from one area of the worksheet to another; a Fill Right command, which copies the first column of selected cells into the selected cells to the right; and a Fill Down command, which copies the first row of selected cells into the selected cells below.

Copy. The **Copy command** copies a block of cells from one area of the worksheet to another. Once the cells to be copied have been defined using an Extend (F8) command (Figure 19.23), the Menu Bar is activated, the Edit menu is

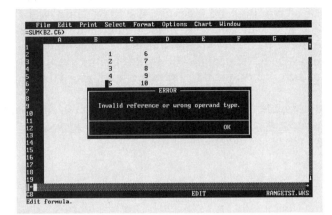

Figure 19.21
An error message appears if a range of cells has been incorrectly defined.

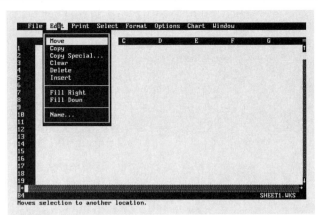

Figure 19.22
The Edit menu.

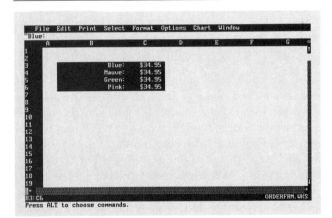

Figure 19.23
The cells to be copied are highlighted.

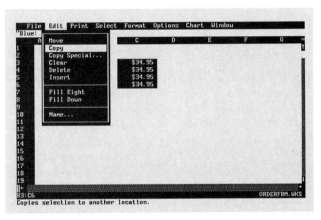

Figure 19.24
The Copy command from the Edit menu is selected.

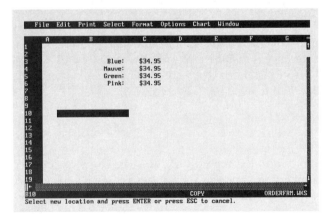

Figure 19.25
The pointer is moved to the receiving location.

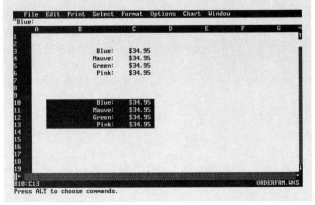

Figure 19.26
When the ENTER key is pressed, the information is copied.

selected, and the Copy command is selected (Figure 19.24). The pointer is then positioned to the worksheet cell where the copy is to be placed (Figure 19.25), and the ENTER key is pressed to make the copy (Figure 19.26).

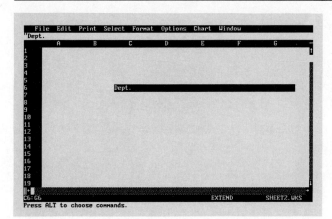

Figure 19.27
The cell to be copied and the cells to receive the copy must be included within the range.

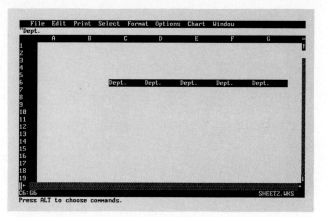

Figure 19.28
The copied cells using the Fill Right command.

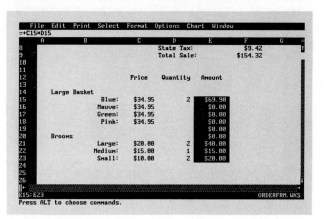

Figure 19.29
The cells to be included in a Fill Down command must be selected.

Figure 19.30
A completed Fill Down command used to copy formulas down a column.

Fill Right. The **Fill Right command** is used to copy a cell, a column of text, or formulas to the right. The cell containing the data to be copied, as well as the cells to receive the data, must be included in the extend range (Figure 19.27). Once the Fill Right command from the Edit menu has been selected, the data are copied to the remaining cells in the range (Figure 19.28).

Fill Down. The **Fill Down command** is used to copy a cell, a row of text, or formulas down a column. The cell containing the data to be copied, as well as the cells receiving the data, must be included in the extend range (Figure 19.29). Once the Fill Down command from the Edit menu has been selected, the data are copied to the remaining cells in the range (Figure 19.30).

Format Command

Changing the appearance of numeric cell screen displays is accomplished via the **Format command**. To format the cells, include the pertinent cells within an Extend command (Figure 19.31) and select the Format option of the Menu Bar (Figure 19.32). Then select the proper format for this group of cells and specify

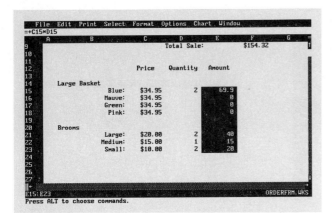

Figure 19.31
The cells to be formatted are included in an Extend range.

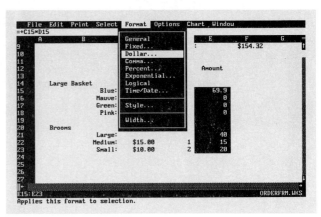

Figure 19.32
The Dollar option of the Format menu is selected.

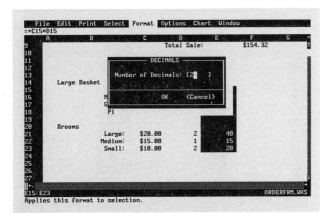

Figure 19.33
The number of decimal positions is specified.

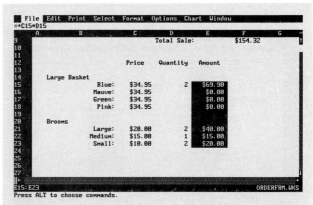

Figure 19.34
The newly formatted cells in the worksheet.

the number of positions to the right of the decimal (Figure 19.33). Figure 19.34 shows the selected cells after they have been formatted using the **Dollar option**.

The Format option is also used to reset the width of a specific worksheet column via the **Width command**. The pointer must reside on a cell within the column to be changed.

Printing the Worksheet

In Works the entire worksheet is printed unless a range of cells has been selected using the Extend command. The "entire worksheet" is a rectangle composed of any cells that have entries. The upper left-hand corner is always cell A1; the lower right-hand corner is defined as the cell that is as far right as the right-most used cell of the worksheet and as far down as the lowest used cell in the worksheet.

Once the **Print command** has been issued (Figure 19.35), you can change the layout by activating a dialogue box via the **Layout command** (Figure 19.36). The defaults can be changed to fit print needs. Items that can be changed include margins, paper size, and headers and footers.

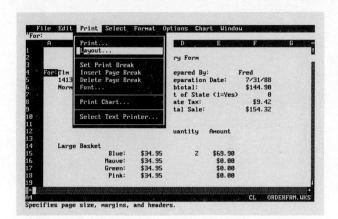

Figure 19.35
The Print menu.

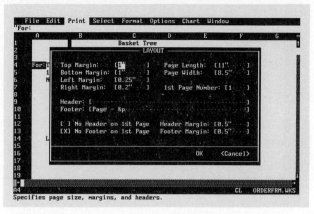

Figure 19.36
The Layout dialogue box that allows tailoring of the print operation.

Figure 19.37
Jim's telephone order/invoice worksheet.

```
                        Basket Tree
                  Telephone Order Entry Form

      For:Tim Duffy                Prepared By:         Fred
           1413 S. Cottage Ave.    Preparation Date:    8/31/88
           Normal, Il 61761        Subtotal:            $144.90
      Visa                         Out of State (1=Yes)        0
      /MC                          State Tax:             $9.42
        #: _____        Total Sale:          $154.32


                           Price    Quantity    Amount

           Large Basket
                    Blue:   $34.95       2      $69.90
                   Mauve:   $34.95               $0.00
                   Green:   $34.95               $0.00
                    Pink:   $34.95               $0.00

           Brooms
                   Large:   $20.00       2      $40.00
                  Medium:   $15.00       1      $15.00
                   Small:   $10.00       2      $20.00
```

Jim has built a worksheet that allows him to take orders over the telephone, record those orders, and automatically calculate the amount owed. Figure 19.37 shows this worksheet, which also acts as an invoice. Because sales tax is not collected for out-of-state sales, the worksheet checks the cell containing the out-of-state reference. If the reference is 0, sales tax is calculated. You can load the file called ORDERFRM.WKS to view this worksheet.

Charting

Jim wants to track his year-to-date revenues for each type of sale—telephone orders, shows, wholesale, and his new retail outlet. He also wants to graph this information to depict the contributions made by each area. To accomplish this, he has created a worksheet that allows him to enter monthly sales totals for each type of sale (Figure 19.38). This worksheet is easy to use and can be expanded by adding a row above the totals line. Jim examines this worksheet by loading the file YTDWORKS.WKS.

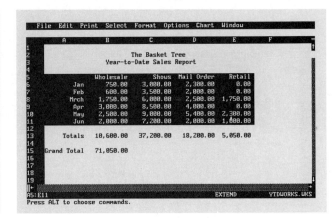

Figure 19.38
Jim's year-to-date sales-tracking worksheet.

Figure 19.39
To use the Speed Charting feature, first indicate which cells are to be graphed using the Extend command.

Figure 19.40
The finished graph using Speed Charting.

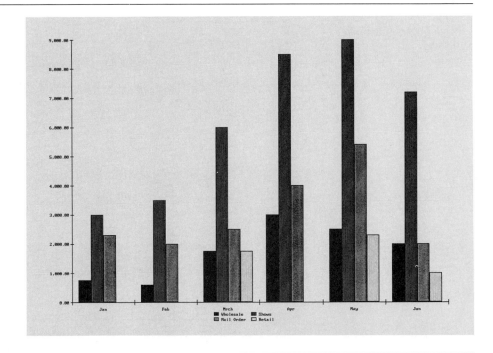

To quickly create a chart representing his worksheet data, Jim uses the Works Speed Charting feature to generate his first graph. This requires use of the Extend command to make rows and columns for the graph. It assumes that each column is a separate Y series of data points. The text left of the numbers is used as the X series label text. The text (column headings) above the Y series becomes the legend. After the text has been highlighted via the Extend command (Figure 19.39), the Chart option of the Main Menu Bar is invoked, and New is selected. From the Chart menu, the View option is selected to see the graph depicted in Figure 19.40.

Jim adds labels to the chart by selecting the Data option of the Chart menu (Figure 19.41) and taking the Titles command. After the Titles option is selected, a dialogue box appears on the screen. Jim provides the information he wants to appear on the graph (Figure 19.42). He notices that the print on the graph from Figure 19.40 is too small. To make it more readable, he takes the

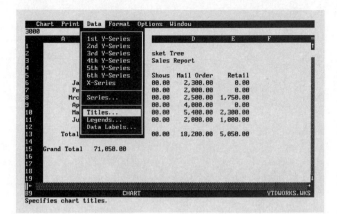

Figure 19.41
The Data menu for charting.

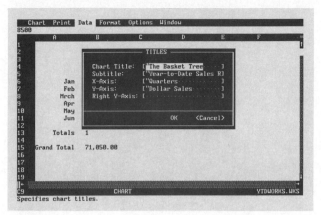

Figure 19.42
The dialogue box used for entering the various labels for the graph shown in Figure 19.40.

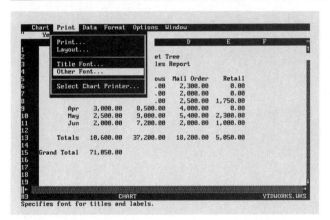

Figure 19.43
The Print submenu from the Chart menu showing the two font selection options.

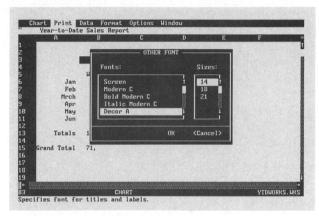

Figure 19.44
The dialogue box for selecting charting fonts.

Print option of the Chart menu. This allows him to change fonts via two options (Figure 19.43). He selects the Other Font option to change the size and style of text for the majority of the graph. A dialogue box like that depicted in Figure 19.44 is displayed, and Jim decides to select font Decor A and place the bulk of the text into size 14. He also sets the Title font to size 21. Figure 19.45 shows the finished graph. Notice that the text on the screen differs dramatically from the final output.

Jim now wants to create a pie chart depicting his total sales. His first Y series contains the cells B13:E13. The X series is composed of cells B5:E5. The two title lines from the previous graph should be used. The Title Font is Modern C 17, while the rest of the graph is printed in Modern C 14. Figure 19.46 shows this graph.

Data Base

To retain information about individuals who make purchases at the various shows, Jim stores data in a file called CUSTWORK.WDB. He wants the ability to access such data as first name, middle initial, last name, street address, city, state, zip code, and telephone number. To do this, he selects the **Data Base**

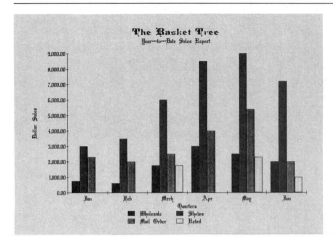

Figure 19.45
The chart with the new fonts.

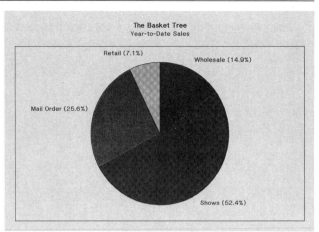

Figure 19.46
A pie chart of the year-to-date totals.

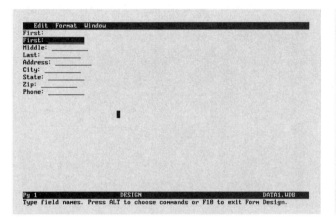

Figure 19.47
The constructed data-entry screen for the CUSTWORK.WDB file.

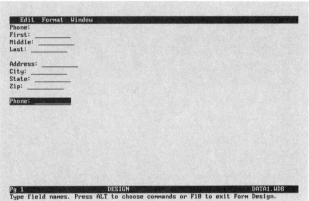

Figure 19.48
The data-entry screen with blank lines inserted.

option and then tells Works he wants to create a new file. Works now displays a monitor screen that allows him to specify the field names. Each field name entered must be followed by a colon to tell Works that this is the end of the name. A field name can contain a maximum of fifteen characters. The next field is positioned via the Down arrow or by positioning the cursor via the mouse. After Jim has finished building his data-entry screen, it looks like that depicted in Figure 19.47.

Jim decides to have blank lines between the name and address and between the address and phone entries. This requires positioning to the Address field, selecting the Edit option of the Menu Bar, and then selecting the Insert command. A blank line now appears on the entry form. He now positions to the Phone field and does the same thing. The data-entry form now appears like that in Figure 19.48.

Jim now wants the field lengths the same length as the data that will be recorded in them. The field name must be accommodated when determining the field length. To provide 12 spaces for the first name, the field length must be 19. Resetting the field length is accomplished via the Format command. Once the Format menu is displayed to the screen, select the Width option, and

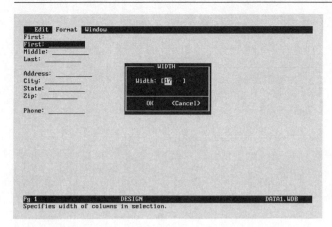

Figure 19.49
The dialogue box for changing the field length.

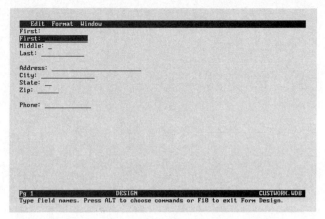

Figure 19.50
The completed data-entry screen.

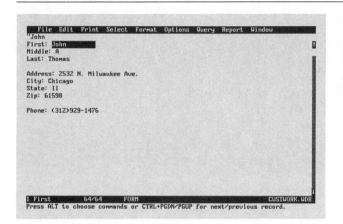

Figure 19.51
Once the data-entry form has been created, it can be used
to store data to the file.

Figure 19.52
The file is displayed as lines of text using the View List
command.

a length dialogue box appears on the screen (Figure 19.49). Change the 17 to 19
and press ENTER.

Jim must now change the settings for the rest of the fields by selecting a
field and taking the Format and Width commands. The field settings for the
remaining fields follow:

Middle	9
Last	18
Address	34
City	21
State	9
Zip	11
Phone	20

Figure 19.50 shows the finished data-entry screen.

After the screen has been created, it is saved under the name CUSTWORK.
After exiting from the design via the Edit command, data can be entered by
filling the blanks of the entry form (Figure 19.51). To see all the file data with
each record appearing on a line, select the Options entry of the Menu Bar and

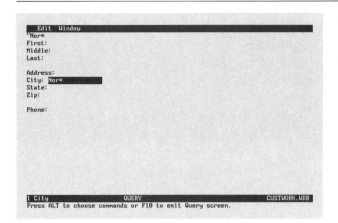

Figure 19.53
A completed query definition screen.

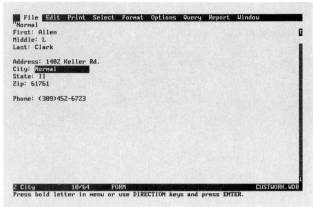

Figure 19.54
A record that meets the query criteria is displayed to the screen.

execute the View List command. Each record is displayed as a line on the screen (Figure 19.52).

To move through the file in View List mode, the pointer manipulation commands are the same as those used for the spreadsheet, and data can be copied by using similar spreadsheet copy commands.

Querying the Data Base

Jim wants to quickly locate in his data base a customer who lives in Normal. To do this, he constructs a query form via the **Query option** of the Menu Bar. When the Query menu is displayed, he takes the Define option, and a screen similar to a data-entry screen appears on his monitor (Figure 19.53). He places the Nor* in the City field to tell Works he wishes to locate a record with this characteristic. He then exits via the Exit Query of the Edit command.

When the Data Base Menu Bar is displayed, the Query option is again selected, and the Apply Query command is executed. The first record containing a "Nor" is now displayed on the screen (Figure 19.54). Other records can be located by using the Ctrl + PgUp or Ctrl + PgDn commands. When performing queries, Works does a sequential search of the file.

Sorting

As Jim adds to the data base, new records are placed at the end of the file. Because access to the file is sequential, these records usually must be sorted before a record can be generated. This is especially true if Jim wishes to create a level-break report. Jim wants his information to be sorted in alphabetical order by zip code. His primary key is the zip code, his secondary key is last name, and his tertiary key is the first name. A sort is accomplished by the Sort command under the Query option of the Menu Bar. Once this has been executed, a dialogue box appears on the screen. Jim now enters his sort keys (Figure 19.55) and presses ENTER, and the file is sorted (Figure 19.56). He is careful to use the Show All Records option of the Query menu if a Query is still active.

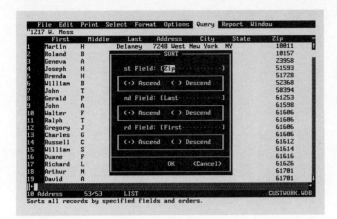

Figure 19.55
Specifying the sort keys.

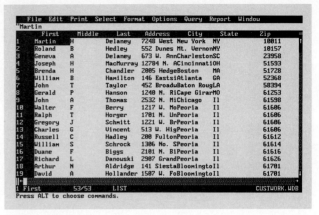

Figure 19.56
The sorted file.

Reporting

Jim now wants to generate a customer name and address report. This report lists his customers alphabetically by zip code. This is accomplished by taking the **Report option** of the Menu Bar and choosing the New command. The Report Menu, along with the Report definition screen, appears on his monitor (Figure 19.57).

Works keeps track of several types of lines when generating a report. These include

Intr Report	What follows this is printed at the beginning of the report.
Intr Page	What follows this is printed at the beginning of each page.
Intr 1st Break Field	This is printed at the beginning of the first break field.
Intr 2nd Break Field	This is printed at the beginning of the second break field.
Intr 3rd Break Field	This is printed at the beginning of the third break field.
Record	These are the fields from each record that print.
Summ 1st Break Field	This will print as the subtotal for the first break field.
Summ 2nd Break Field	This will print as the subtotal for the second break field.
Summ 3rd Break Field	This will print as the subtotal for the third break field.
Summ Page	This will print as the subtotal for the entire page.
Summ Report	This will print as the subtotal for the entire report.

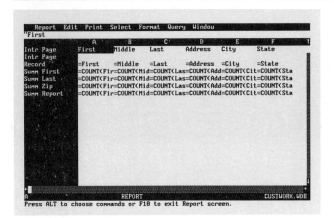

Figure 19.57
The Report definition screen.

Figure 19.58
The break indicators are turned off in the Sort dialogue box.

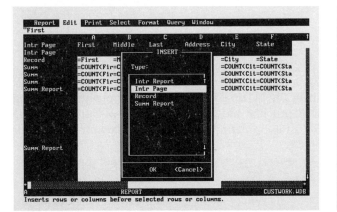

Figure 19.59
When the Insert command is given, Works must be supplied with the line type to be added to the report.

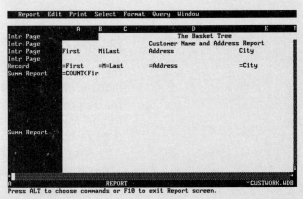

Figure 19.60
The changed report Works template.

Once the report definition is displayed, Works must be told that a level-break report is not desired. This is accomplished by selecting the Query option and executing the Sort command. A dialogue box now appears, and you must click the break boxes to turn off the level break (no *x*'s should appear). Figure 19.58 shows this box.

Jim marks the first two lines of the Report definition and uses the Edit command to insert lines. Upon receiving the Insert command, Works asks what type of lines are to be inserted. He selects the Intr Report option (Figure 19.59) and presses ENTER. He now marks the three subtotal lines using an Extend command and deletes them. Beginning with column B of the Summ Report line, he extends through column H and issues a Clear command (Figure 19.60). The Count command in column A gives a count of the records when the report is printed.

Jim sets the field widths so that the information appears properly within a cell. To print all report information on one sheet, he selects a font of Prestige and a size of 7. When he runs his report it appears like that in Figure 19.61. After making minor changes to his report, Jim saves his data base back to disk.

Figure 19.61
The finished report.

```
Martin     H   Delaney    7248 West New York  NY    10011 (212)635-8925
Roland     B   Hedley     552 Dunes Mt. VernonNY    10157 (914)329-5483
Geneva     A   Delaney    673 W. AnnCharlestonSC    23958 (803)689-4958
Joseph     H   MacMurray  12784 N. ACincinnatiOH    51593 (513)263-9485
Brenda     H   Chandler   2005 HedgeBoston    MA    51728 (617)748-9883
William    B   Hamilton   146 EastsiAtlanta   GA    52368 (404)263-8347
John       T   Taylor     452 BroadwBaton RougLA    58394 (504)784-9345
Gerald     P   Hanson     1240 N. RiCape GirarMO    61253 (314)928-3584
John       A   Thomas     2532 N. MiChicago   Il    61598 (312)929-1476
Walter     F   Berry      1217 W. MoPeoria    Il    61606 (309)673-9483
Ralph      T   Horger     1701 N. UnPeoria    Il    61606 (309)674-7834
Gregory    J   Schmitt    1221 W. BrPeoria    Il    61606 (309)676-9742
Charles    G   Vincent    513 W. HigPeoria    Il    61606 (309)676-8971
Russell    C   Hadley     200 FultonPeoria    Il    61612 (309)673-8475
William    S   Schrock    1306 No. SPeoria    Il    61614 (309)672-8936
Duane      F   Biggs      2101 N. BiPeoria    Il    61616 (309)673-8450
Richard    L   Danowski   2907 GrandPeoria    Il    61626 (309)673-8959
Arthur     N   Aldridge   141 SiestaBloomingtoIl    61701 (309)663-9210
David      A   Hollander  1507 W. FoBloomingtoIl    61701 (309)828-4361
Robert     L   Holtz      1225 HilltBloomingtoIl    61701 (309)452-1189
Donald     F   Manahan    215 OrleanBloomingtoIl    61701 (309)663-7843
James      L   Bender     328 Riley Bloomingtoil    61702 (309)662-8493
Alan       C   Darby      709 W. LocBloomingtoIl    61702 (309)828-7463
Gladys     R   Easton     1509 N. CaBloomingtoIl    61702 (309)828-3748
Thomas     P   Lane       434 PrisciBloomingtoIl    61702 (309)662-9065
Ronald     H   Hamilton   1202 HastiGalesburg Il    61723 (309)845-8923
Glenn      H   Lawrence   728 W. WalSpringfielIl    61729 (217)766-8933
Paul       W   Bowen      1490 GodfrNormal    Il    61761 (309)452-8935
Donald     C   Charlett   911 E IrviNormal    Il    61761 (309)452-8394
Allen      L   Clark      1402 KelleNormal    Il    61761 (309)452-6723
Arnold     D   Hall       1202 N. ScNormal    Il    61761 (309)452-7385
Richard    D   Jensen     619 S. KinNormal    Il    61761 (309)452-1935
Brian      J   Johnson    202 S. RooNormal    Il    61761 (309)452-3894
Raymond    B   Mitchell   22 HillcreNormal    Il    61761 (309)452-3584
Raymond    R   Preston    1905 WidemNormal    Il    61761 (309)452-7836
Keith      R   Shanks     1602 E. JaBloomingtoIl    61761 (309)829-4328
Andrew     T   Fisher     405 E. OliSouth BendIN    61783 (219)385-9476
Charles    E   Dunn       1304 AirpoCharlestonIl    61820 (217)343-6958
Walter     J   Bowyer     2145 VermoParis     Il    61920 (217)463-6899
Steven     J   Mckinzie   890 S. WebDanville  Il    61938 (217)444-6174
Craig      W   Thomas     6174 N ColDenver    CO    71677 (303)214-8943
Mark       P   Wagner     2111 Todd JacksonvilFL    71825 (904)749-3294
Evelio     H   Alvarez    390 GlouceSan Diego CA    71872 (619)783-9586
Harold     O   Ashton     1255 AlexaKnoxville TN    73846 (615)828-4395
Ronald     W   Brewer     1204 HighlChicago   Il    76114 (312)777-6138
Mark       R   Latham     1303 W. WeBurlingtonIA    76173 (319)263-4593
Samuel     J   Benjamin   214 S. WauAnn Arbor MI    76828 (313)828-3688
William    P   Miller     17023 ParkDallas    TX    82546 (214)642-8946
William    P   Miller     17023 ParkDallas    TX    82546 (214)642-8946
Michael    R   Graning    202 West HFt. Worth TX    82946 (817)428-3894
Murray     V   Jacobs     2404 ArcadSanta RosaCA    83591 (707)825-1352
Stanley    A   Larue      1011 WashiKenosha   WI    83720 (414)288-3481
```

Integration

Jim secured a loan from a local bank to finance his business. As part of the loan agreement, he submits quarterly income reports to the bank in the form of a letter. This quarter Jim wants to integrate word processing, spreadsheets, and graphs into his letter. This requires opening a word processing document, loading his YTDWORKS spreadsheet, and activating his pie chart. Jim then returns to his word processing document by using the Window command.

To include the worksheet data into his letter, Jim activates the worksheet using the Window command, marks the text to be copied using the Extend command, issues the Copy command, returns to his word processing document via the Window command, positions to where he wants to receive the text, and presses ENTER. The worksheet is now copied to his letter.

To include the graph, Jim selects the **Insert Chart command** from the Edit option. He is asked to indicate which worksheet chart is desired, and he marks the appropriate chart. The following tag is then placed within the document: *chart YTDWORKS.WKS:Chart1*.

Once the chart has been placed as a tag within the document, it must be sized to fit the available space. This is accomplished by placing the cursor at the tag and selecting the Paragraph command from the Format option. The size of the graph is now entered (Figure 19.62). Jim finishes his letter and prints it (Figure 19.63).

Figure 19.62
The dialogue box used to set
the size of the graph.

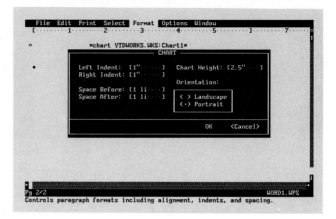

Figure 19.63
The finished letter integrating
word processing, spread-
sheet, and chart data.

```
The Basket Tree
12 Normandy Village
Normal, Il 61761

July 5, 198x

Hal Rogers
Loan Department
Twin City Bank
Bloomington, Il 61701

Dear Mr. Rogers:

As per our agreement, here is a quarterly report detailing
my year-to-date income.  I have provided a worksheet with my
total sales by business classification by month.  I have
also included a pie chart depicting the percentage
contribution of each.
```

The Basket Tree
Year-to-Date Sales Report

	Wholesale	Shows	Mail Order	Retail
Jan	750.00	3,000.00	2,300.00	0.00
Feb	600.00	3,500.00	2,000.00	0.00
Mrch	1,750.00	6,000.00	2,500.00	1,750.00
Apr	3,000.00	8,500.00	4,000.00	0.00
May	2,500.00	9,000.00	5,400.00	2,300.00
Jun	2,000.00	7,200.00	2,000.00	1,000.00
Totals	10,600.00	37,200.00	18,200.00	5,050.00

The Basket Tree
Year-to-Date Sales

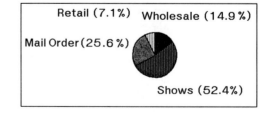

Retail (7.1%)   Wholesale (14.9%)

Mail Order (25.6%)

Shows (52.4%)

```
If you have any questions, please feel free to call me.

Sincerely,
```

Figure 19.64
The word processing letter
template.

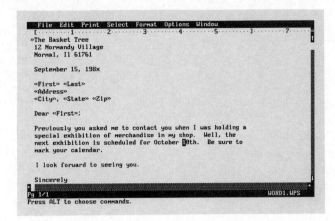

In preparation for an exhibit at 12 Normandy Village, Jim is sending invitations to all persons with a 309 or 217 area code, which includes everyone within a fifty-mile radius. He loads his CUSTWORK.WDB data base file and defines a query criteria of ==" (309*"|=" (217*" for the telephone field to limit the number of records selected. He then opens a new word processing document and enters the letter depicted in Figure 19.64. The data base field names are entered using the Insert Field command of the Edit option. Each of these must correspond to a field in the data base to be merged. A dialogue box opens and allows Jim to select one field that will be placed at the cursor location in the document. Desired spaces and punctuation must be inserted between fields.

Ready to print his letters, Jim takes the Print Merge command of the Print option, specifies the open data to be merged, specifies the number of copies and the print quality, and starts the job by pressing ENTER. The letters are printed (Figure 19.65).

Jim saves this file to the file named CUSTMERG.WPS. After saving his Merge document file, Jim changes his template letter so that it can be used to generate mailing labels for his Merge application. He deletes everything from the letter except the field name references and executes the Print Labels command of the Print Option. Works now requests information about the labels in a dialogue box (Figure 19.66). When the ENTER key is pressed, the labels are printed (Figure 19.67). Jim saves this to the file LABELMRG.WPS.

Chapter Review

PC Works by Microsoft combines word processing, spreadsheets, data base, charting, and communications software into one package. Works was designed for small- and medium-sized applications. It allows more than one file to be open at a time so that data can be traded between files. Each software application has a similar menu in the Menu Bar. The submenus are also similar, but there are some differences. The similarity in the software interface between applications makes learning the next application easier. Only the menu differences have to be explained.

Many of the WordPerfect word processing concepts can be used in operating Works, but there are differences with specific instructions. For instance, the Block command of WordPerfect becomes the Extend command in Works. The spreadsheet application allows you to directly import worksheets created by Lotus 1-2-3 or VP-Planner. Works automatically changes formulas to match

```
        The Basket Tree
        12 Normandy Village
        Normal, Il 61761

        September 15, 198x

        Roland Hedley
        552 Dunes Apt. 4
        Mt. Vernon, NY 10157

        Dear Roland;

        Previously you asked me to contact you when I was holding a
        special exhibition of merchandise in my shop.  Well, the
        next exhibition is scheduled for October 10th.  Be sure to
        mark your calendar.

        I look forward to seeing you.

        Sincerely


        Jim
```

```
        The Basket Tree
        12 Normandy Village
        Normal, Il 61761

        September 15, 198x

        Martin Delaney
        7248 West End Ave.
        New York, NY 10011

        Dear Martin;

        Previously you asked me to contact you when I was holding a
        special exhibition of merchandise in my shop.  Well, the
        next exhibition is scheduled for October 10th.  Be sure to
        mark your calendar.

        I look forward to seeing you.

        Sincerely


        Jim
```

Figure 19.65
Sample letters generated
from this Merge operation.

```
        The Basket Tree
        12 Normandy Village
        Normal, Il 61761

        September 15, 198x

        Geneva Delaney
        673 W. Annabelle
        Charleston, SC 23958

        Dear Geneva;

        Previously you asked me to contact you when I was holding a
        special exhibition of merchandise in my shop.  Well, the
        next exhibition is scheduled for October 10th.  Be sure to
        mark your calendar.

        I look forward to seeing you.

        Sincerely


        Jim
```

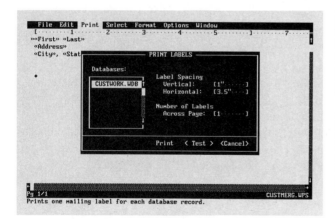

Figure 19.66
The Print Labels dialogue box requests information about
the print job to be performed.

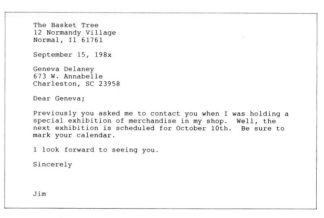

```
Martin Delaney
7248 West End Ave.
New York, NY 10011
```

```
Roland Hedley
552 Dunes Apt. 4
Mt. Vernon, NY 10157
```

```
Geneva Delaney
673 W. Annabelle
Charleston, SC 23958
```

Figure 19.67
Labels that were generated using the Print Labels
command.

the format it requires. For instance, all formulas must begin with an equal sign (=); functions start with a plus sign (+) or equal sign instead of an at sign (@); and ranges include a colon (:) instead of a period (.).

Charting in Works is easy. The speed charting facility quickly builds a bar chart without labels, and the labels can be added after the initial graph is built. It also can produce a wide variety of graphs using various fonts. This is especially easy with a laser printer.

The Works data base feature uses sequential access for storing and accessing records. It does not have any of the indexing capabilities found in dBASE III Plus. All records in a file must be loaded into RAM before any queries to the file can be made. Works does have a report feature that generates regular reports or reports requiring level breaks.

Key Terms and Concepts

Cancel option	Help Index option
Check Spelling option	Insert Chart command
Clear command	Layout command
Copy command	OK option
Data Base option	Open option
Define a Column command	PC Works
Define a Row command	Print command
Dollar option	Query option
Extend command (F8)	Report option
File option	Save As option
Fill Down command	Save option
Fill Right command	Width command
Format command	Window option

Chapter Quiz

Multiple Choice

1. Works does not include which of the following software applications?
   a. Spreadsheet
   b. Outliner
   c. Data base
   d. Graphing facility
   e. All of the above are part of Works.

2. Which command is used to include a spreadsheet in a word processing document?
   a. Attach
   b. Attach From
   c. Fill Left
   d. Copy
   e. Fill Down

3. The line of a Works screen that contains information about the highlighted command is the
   a. Menu Bar
   b. Status bar
   c. Message line
   d. Pull-down menu
   e. None of the above

4. Which of the statements about a Works data base are false?
   a. A data-entry form containing the field name and space for entering the data can be built for entering and accessing records from the file.
   b. The data base can be viewed either using the data-entry form or a line at a time.
   c. A screen similar to the data-entry screen is accessed via the Define Query command.
   d. Records not matching the query criteria can be accessed via the Show All Records command.
   e. All of the above statements are true.

5. The Works spreadsheet command that is similar to the Lotus 1-2-3 Range Erase command is
   a. Erase
   b. Delete
   c. Clear
   d. None of the above

True/False

6. Only the Charting feature of Works cannot be directly entered from the Works Main Menu.

7. The easiest way to save multiple files that you have opened is via the Save All command found under the File option of the Menu Bar.

8. The Window command of the Menu Bar allows you to move from one open application file to another.

9. During a Query operation, Works can start at the end of the file and move backward.

10. The Works spreadsheet has many incompatibilities with Lotus 1-2-3.

Answers

1. b 2. d 3. c 4. e 5. c 6. t 7. t 8. t 9. f 10. f

Exercises

1. The _____ at the top of the screen stays the same from one Works application to another.

2. The _____ displays screens with explanations about how a specific command operates in Works.

3. Commands can be entered in Works either by using the keyboard or by using a _____.

4. Until a new word processing file has been saved, it is called _____ in the status line.

5. The _____ command is used to mark blocks of text in the word processor.

6. In all Works applications, the Extend command is invoked by pressing the _____ function key.

7. The Works spreadsheet has a high compatibility rating with _____.

8. All formulas in the Works spreadsheet must begin with a(n) _____.

9. Ranges are marked _____ when a command is executed in Works.

10. If you wish to copy a formula down a column, the _____ Works command must be used.

11. If you wish to copy a formula across a row, the _____ Works command must be used.

12. Instead of using a period to specify a range of cells, Works requires that you use a _____.

13. The _____ command of the Print option of Works applications allows you to specify margins, headers and footers, and paper size.

14. When you first define a data base, Works requires that you enter the field name of each record and specify the field _____.

15. The _____ command is used to specify the characteristics of records to be located within a file.

16. The _____ data base command is used to display records that do not match the query criteria.

17. When you define a data base report, Works wants to know what type of heading and _____ lines to include.

18. The _____ command is used to transfer a worksheet to a word processing document.

19. When a chart is to be included within a document, Works places a _____ in the document at the location the chart is to be placed.

20. Data base fields are included in a document to be merged via the _____ command found in the Edit option.

Questions for Thought

1. Prepare a market study of the top five integrated software packages that are currently on the market.

2. What are the strengths and weaknesses of each package you studied in question 1?

3. List applications that can be made easier through the use of integrated software.

4. Which integrated package do you believe would best support your current and projected needs? Be certain to justify your choice.

5. How many of the packages identified in question 1 use the mouse as a pointing device? What is your opinion of the mouse as an input device?

Chapter 20

Management Information Systems and System Analysis

Chapter Objectives

After completing this chapter, you should be able to:

Describe a management information system

List the four levels of decision making

List the four types of reports

Describe a decision support system

Describe a system

List the characteristics common to systems

Define system analysis

List the phases in the system development life cycle

List various sources of information

Describe the function of a data-flow diagram

Describe the role of decision tables

Describe the role of pseudocode

Discuss the importance of structured walkthroughs

Discuss the need for testing

Discuss the three methods of system conversion

Imagine the following scenario. Shortly after expanding into walking shoes, a small company named Treadwell Shoes begins enjoying record profits. Walking shoes became the company's single largest revenue maker. But success also brings the company problems. A flood of orders for walking shoes has put the company's production line two months behind schedule and knocked the shipping department into disarray. Moreover, the company's managers lack enough information to decide whether the company should devote more capital to developing its new product. Treadwell's managers decide they can resolve these problems and handle more growth only if the company's antiquated manual information system is revamped and computerized.

Throughout this book, we've identified the computer as an information processor. This chapter examines the roles computers and information play in the decision-making process. We look at decisions—what types there are, who makes them, and what information is needed to make them. Next, we examine management information systems, which provide managers with the information they require to make decisions. Finally, we cover system analysis, which provides a formula for analyzing and solving problems.

Management Information Systems

Information is vital to business operations; consider the following:

Organizations incur half their operational costs handling information.

Most managerial problems are solvable with better information.

Organizations rely on information to meet their primary goals: decreasing costs and increasing productivity.

Managers often don't know what information they require to improve their decision making.

A **management information system (MIS)** is a formal process using both manual and computerized tools to control information. The goal of an MIS is to provide managers with vital information when they need it.

Decision-Making Levels

Management can be divided into low, middle, and top levels. Every manager requires data to make decisions. However, the kinds of decisions and the data the manager needs to make them vary with the manager's level. Top-level managers generally make strategic decisions; middle-level managers, tactical decisions; and low-level managers, operational decisions (Figure 20.1).

Strategic decision makers set objectives for an organization and devise long-range plans. **Strategic decision making** might include deciding what new products to manufacture, which new markets to target, where to build new plants, and how to raise capital. Because their decision making is directed toward the future and on a wide, sometimes global, scale, top-level managers have a great need for external information, such as economic forecasts, employment trends, and resource availability.

Tactical decision makers implement strategic decisions by allocating an organization's resources. Typically, **tactical decision making** requires making decisions about personnel, budgeting, production scheduling, and allocation of working capital.

Operational decision makers ensure that employees perform tasks efficiently by measuring their output against preset standards. **Operational decision making** involves such questions as who is assigned what job, whether to accept credit, how much inventory to reorder, and what raw materials are needed.

Figure 20.1
To be effective, an MIS needs
to provide information for
three types of decision making: strategic, tactical, and
operational.

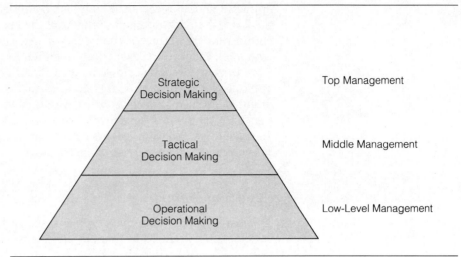

The decision-making process varies from level to level, as Table 20.1 describes. Low-level managers usually have highly structured roles that are standardized in written operational procedures. Because they deal with day-to-day operations, these managers have a high need for instant access to internal information (from within the organization) and fairly limited need for external information. Low-level managers work in real-time systems and tend to make fewer independent judgments than do tactical and strategic decision makers.

High-level managers perform almost opposite roles. They have no written procedures to guide them in solving the problems they face, so they frequently exercise independent judgment. They have a high need for external information because they decide what direction their organization should take in the future to operate effectively against competing companies.

Between these two extremes are middle-level managers, whose roles are moderately structured. They need moderate amounts of both internal and external information to perform their duties: external information in order to understand the strategies formulated by high-level managers and internal information in order to direct low-level managers on how to implement those strategies in the workplace.

Types of Decisions

Within these three decision-making levels, the MIS must address two types of decisions, structured and unstructured.

Structured decisions occur most frequently at the operational level and can be addressed by established procedures. For example, a loan officer engages in structured decision making when granting or denying a car loan to a person based on the applicant's age, income, years employed, credit standing, and so on. In a manual environment, written procedures dictate whether the

Table 20.1 Characteristics of the Three Levels of Decision Making

Characteristic	Operational	Tactical	Strategic
Degree of structure	High	Moderate	Low
Need for external information	Low	Moderate	High
Need for internal information	High	Moderate	Low
Need for real-time information	High	Moderate	Low
Degree of judgment	Low	Moderate	High

applicant should receive the loan. For example, the procedures may state that the loan should be denied if the applicant is unemployed or younger than eighteen years of age. Although structured decisions can be executed on a computer, they are routinely performed without computer assistance.

Unstructured decisions resolve ill-defined or unstructured problems. Typically, these decisions are made at the strategic level and entail future-oriented problems, such as what products to produce or which markets to penetrate. These problems involve many variables that are difficult to quantify. To solve them, decision makers often turn to computer tools that enable them to project the outcome of several alternatives.

Reporting Methods

To satisfy their decision-making needs, the various management levels require information presented to them in specific forms. Lower-level managers need information structured in detailed, real-time form. This form of information serves managers well for everyday decisions involving payroll, inventory, accounts receivable, and manufacturing. Middle- and top-level managers need their data organized so they can summarize it across functional lines (for example, the total payroll for a particular period). Accordingly, management information systems are designed to provide upper-level decision makers with the following special reports.

Scheduled Reports. **Scheduled reports** usually contain large amounts of detailed information, much of which is often irrelevant to high-level managers. Organizations produce these reports on a regular basis, such as daily or weekly. Although currently most are circulated on paper, scheduled reports increasingly are being displayed on monitor screens as real-time processing replaces batch processing.

Exception Reports. **Exception reports** alert management that an activity or process needs corrective action. An exception report could, for example, list customers with bills outstanding ninety or more days.

Demand Reports. A manager will request a **demand report** to obtain specific information. For example, a vice-president of sales may request a demand report detailing which sales representatives earned more than $100,000 in commissions for the year. Operators can produce a demand report in minutes by using a software package that handles a query language. For example, a user could obtain a demand report from a dBASE SALESREP file by issuing the following commands:

```
USE SALESREP
LIST FIRST, LAST, GTCOMMISN FOR GTCOMMISN>100000 TO PRINT
```

The first statement instructs dBASE to invoke SALESREP, the file containing data on the business's sales representatives. The second statement directs dBASE to list to the printer the first name, last name, and commission total of any sales representative whose annual commissions exceeded $100,000.

Predictive Reports. Managers use **predictive reports** in their planning process. Users create these reports by commanding the appropriate software to construct "what-if" scenarios, which may involve statistical and modeling techniques such as simulation or regression. For example, a manager who wants to project how the penetration of a new market would affect the company's revenues could command Lotus 1-2-3 to compute several "what if" alternatives. The alternatives could include how different unit-sales levels and fixed- and variable-product costs would affect net income. The manager could alter any item in the model, and the software will project a result.

MIS Versus Transaction Processing Systems

A **transaction processing system** (often simply referred to as data processing) processes transactions and outputs the results. A long-used system, it still represents the bulk of computerized processing.

Transaction processing systems enable users to process on computers such business tasks as inventory control, payroll, and accounts receivable. The user processes a transaction on the appropriate file, examines the impact, and records any subsequent change. For example, when an inventory manager records item purchases on the inventory file, the transaction processing system reduces the item's amount-on-hand value in the file by the appropriate amount. Later, the manager can examine the amount-on-hand value to determine whether it must be reordered. If it must, the user can employ the system to generate a purchase order.

Transaction processing systems are well suited to providing internal, real-time information. Thus, their primary users have been operational managers. Tactical and strategic managers rarely employ transaction processing because it does not provide the type of information they need to make decisions.

However, users can upgrade a transaction processing system so that it can be queried to produce decision models. In such cases, the system becomes an MIS, for it provides the decision support tools upper-level managers require. A major distinction between the two systems is that an MIS always has a transaction processing component, but a transaction processing system does not necessarily constitute an MIS.

Accordingly, users can view a computer system's ability to manage information as a matter of degree. The more an organization depends on strategic decision making for growth or survival, the more likely it utilizes powerful MIS capabilities. For example, a ten-employee company may be able to formulate strategy with a transaction processing system that has only weak MIS capabilities. Conversely, a multinational corporation would rely on a powerful MIS to remain competitive or gain advantage in the marketplace.

Decision Support Systems and MIS

Management information systems excel at providing information for routine, predictable decisions, and they permit easy acquisition to large data stores. However, they have been less successful in providing support for unstructured decisions, such as where the company should locate its next factory.

An optional extension of an MIS called a **decision support system (DSS)** provides user-friendly languages or programs that a decision maker can employ to retrieve or store data and perform modeling to solve unstructured problems. A **model** is a mathematical representation of the problem or system being examined. Many decision makers use microcomputers with spreadsheet software for decision support purposes. Many of these packages, such as Lotus 1-2-3, enable the user to combine spreadsheet, graphics, and data base management to model a problem. The user can alter the model easily when the environment produces unanticipated changes in the problem's structure.

Figure 20.2
(a) The subsystems (the parts) of an automobile. (b) An integrated system.
(Courtesy of Ford)

In large organizations, the MIS staff is assigned the duty of providing decision makers with appropriate information. Systems analysts are responsible for ascertaining managers' information needs and developing a program or system of programs to meet those needs.

What Is a System?

A **system** is a set of interrelated parts that work together to achieve a common goal. Each of us interacts daily with a variety of systems: traffic systems, sanitary systems, education systems, the human body's circulatory system. A system's parts can themselves be viewed as smaller systems or subsystems. For example, a water system is composed of pipes, valves, pumps, water retention devices, and the people who make the system work. In turn, the water system's pumps are subsystems comprising motors, springs, valves, gaskets, and other parts.

Systems often possess capabilities not inherent in any component part. This quality of a system being greater than the sum of its parts is called **synergism**. The automobile provides a good example of the synergistic principle. An automobile is a collection of such subsystems as brakes, drive train, electrical, and cooling components, each of which is made of wires, stamped sheet metal, glass, bearings, and so on. Each subsystem has a limited function: None by itself can transport a driver safely and comfortably on the highway. However, when assembled, these components form an integrated, functional system of considerable use and value (Figure 20.2).

An information system comprises smaller subsystems that perform specified tasks to aid the organization as a whole in achieving its goals. For example, a cash receipts subsystem serves an organization's more encompassing financial reporting system. Users send data from the cash receipts subsystem to the accounts receivable subsystem, which in turn provides information to the general ledger system. The organization then uses the general ledger system's information as raw material for the financial reporting system, which managers rely on to determine the financial health of the company.

A typical information system contains four generic parts: a data gathering subsystem, a processing subsystem, an output subsystem, and a data storage subsystem (Figure 20.3).

Figure 20.3
The four general parts of any information system.

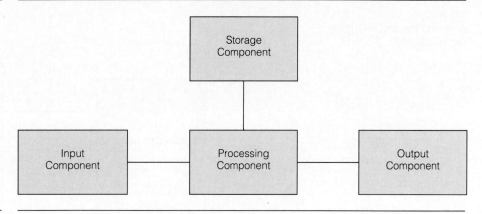

Figure 20.3
The four general parts of any information system.

Figure 20.4
The U.S. Postal Service acts as the interface between a credit card holder and the credit card company.

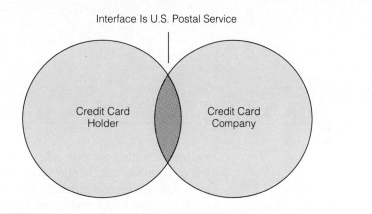

Figure 20.4
The U.S. Postal Service acts as the interface between a credit card holder and the credit card company.

System Characteristics

Systems share these characteristics: boundaries, interaction with the environment, purpose, and feedback.

Boundaries. A **boundary** defines the limits of a component, the collection of components, or the entire system. For example, a department in a company is one boundary; several departments that work together constitute another. Anything outside a system is the environment, and the system cannot control it. An automobile manufacturer cannot dictate events outside the factory, such as inflation rate, changes in tax laws, or the price of gasoline.

Subsystems, too, have boundaries, but none as well defined as the boundary between a system and its environment. This is because subsystems are interdependent: They cannot be completely separate from one another if the system is to function. The point where subsystems overlap is called the **interface**. It is also where the subsystems connect; one subsystem's output becomes another's input. No change occurs at the interface. For example, the U.S. Postal Service acts as the interface when a cardholder sends a check to pay a VISA bill (Figure 20.4).

Interaction with the Environment. Although distinct from their environment, systems must interact with it. Systems accept and process environmental inputs, generate outputs, and then send the outputs back into the environment (Figure 20.5). For example, a payroll system accepts time-card information from the environment (in this case, other departments residing outside the payroll

Figure 20.5
A system interacts with its
environment.

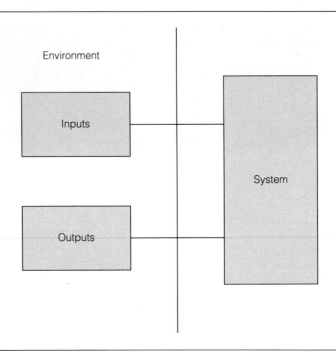

system's boundary), processes those inputs, and generates outputs back into the environment in the form of paychecks.

Environmental inputs to an automobile plant would include raw materials such as sheet metal and assembly parts. The plant would process these parts through stamping, assembling, and painting. The output would be the finished automobile.

A system cannot function properly without interacting with its environment. No system that involves humans is closed—that is, not interacting with and depending on its environment. If a factory produces cars that consumers in the environment don't want, it will go out of business. The factory will just as surely be forced to close its doors if it cannot procure from the environment those raw materials it needs to make cars.

Purpose. Systems must have a specific **purpose**. The goal of most companies is to make a profit for its shareholders. The objective of a payroll system is to fulfill contractual obligations related to remuneration of employees. The purpose of the circulatory system is to maintain life.

Feedback. Finally, all systems need some means to regulate and correct themselves so they can maintain a steady state. A system regulates itself through the feedback process. **Feedback** is accomplished by sampling output from one part of the system and sending it back into the system as input (Figure 20.6). Through feedback, the system can check the functioning of its component parts. If a sample output is not within established tolerances, the system takes corrective action.

The most common feedback example is the thermostat that heating and cooling systems use to maintain a set temperature. A house thermostat set to 70 degrees turns on the furnace when the temperature drops below 69 degrees. The furnace heats the home until the temperature climbs to 71 degrees, at which point the furnace shuts off. Environmental temperature provides the input to the thermostat.

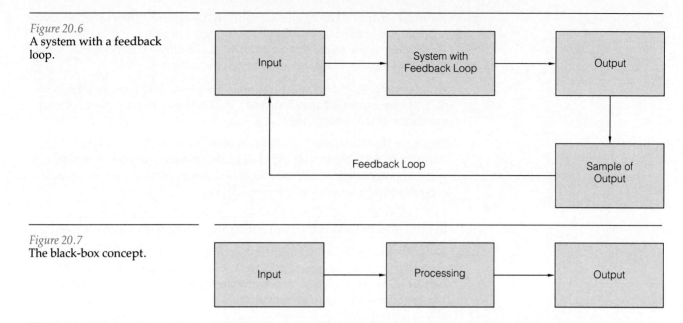

Figure 20.6
A system with a feedback loop.

Figure 20.7
The black-box concept.

Feedback also can take the form of quality control. For example, a feedback device may check parts to ensure that they are milled to within set tolerances. Parts that exceed the tolerances can be remilled or removed from the assembly line.

Black-Box Concept. Because the transformation of inputs into outputs can be extremely complex, the process is often represented in simplified, graphic form by the **black-box concept**. Rather than describing the process in detail, the black box defines it as simply input, process, and output (Figure 20.7). To construct a black box, the user only needs to know the input and output components. The transformation step, in which input is processed to generate output, is represented as a black box. The black box enables managers to easily conceptualize a complex task or series of tasks.

System Analysis

Few people in a complex system are aware of how their actions impact the system as a whole. For example, a vice-president of manufacturing may decide to increase production 20 percent, yet he or she may not realize how much more personnel, raw materials, and inventory space such an increase would necessitate. Likewise, it is difficult to ascertain what effects our daily, personal decisions will have. For example, when we go out to dinner or buy a new car, we rarely stop to consider what impact our spending has on the local economy.

System analysis is the procedure of developing management information systems that provide the information managers need to make decisions. System analysis is the process of helping management improve an organization's work methods by studying and modeling the organization's systems. This task is performed by a systems analyst, who serves as an adviser to the organization. A systems analyst usually provides management with several alternative ways to solve a particular problem. Although the analyst may recommend a particular solution, management makes the final decision.

A systems analyst may recommend changes in a company's manual procedures, or he or she may suggest the organization install a new, computerized information system. An analyst helps an organization decide what actions will yield the most return on the money invested in the system. The system analysis will succeed or fail based on economic or strategic terms.

An organization might investigate the feasibility of developing a new information system for a number of reasons, including:

Rapid Growth. Rapid growth strains existing systems. Transactions may increase so much that the company's staff cannot process them without putting in extensive overtime.

Data Considerations. Managers may require more accurate data to improve their decision making. The primary benefit of computerized systems is accuracy; a correctly designed computerized system always correctly processes properly inputted data.

Changes in Technology. Companies can adopt technologically advanced hardware to process data more efficiently, saving both time and money.

Reducing Human Effort. Computerizing applications usually enables an organization's employees to process transactions much faster and to handle more work. This is especially important in geographic areas where it is difficult to find clerical staff.

System Development Life Cycle

System analysis is performed in a series of formal steps called the **system development life cycle (SDLC)**. During the active life of a system, analysts often will repeat many of the following SDLC steps:

Feasibility Study. A **feasibility study** defines the problem and determines whether a solution can be implemented within budget constraints. The team usually limits its data gathering to interviews.

System Analysis. In this step, the system analysis team gathers data on all aspects of the organization's existing information system in order to decide how to correct or replace the system. The analysis team identifies how the system works as a whole, describes the subsystems' roles, and documents any problems. The team then formulates possible solutions and describes what needs to be done to realize these solutions. Finally, the team sends a system analysis report, containing a recommended solution, to management.

System Design. The analysis team designs the solution selected by management, constructing the new system according to the requirements identified in the system analysis phase. The team then decides what the system's parts should be and how those parts should function. It also develops a test plan with which they can later evaluate the system's accuracy and soundness.

Hardware Evaluation and Selection. The team members decide what hardware will best fulfill their system design needs and procure it.

System Development. The team determines what software the new system requires, procures or designs the software, and tests it.

System Implementation. The organization implements the new system and trains its personnel in its use.

System Audit and Maintenance. The analysis team evaluates the new system on how well it solves the problems identified in the system analysis (or feasibility study) phase. Required changes or improvements are made and the system is reevaluated.

Let's examine the system analysis steps in a hypothetical situation. Mary owns a drugstore in a Midwestern metropolitan area of 200,000 people. She has discovered that her ability to compete in the pharmacy business is hampered because her store cannot offer all the services provided by the big chain drugstores. Her strategic goals are to improve her store's service in order to compete more effectively. She also wants to track her inventory better for economic reasons. Mary hopes that computerizing her operations will enable her to meet these goals. She hires ABC Consultants to perform a system analysis on her business.

The first task ABC Consultants performs is a feasibility study on the computerizing of Mary's business. A feasibility study addresses whether a company should pursue a project from a cost–benefit perspective—that is, whether the benefits of solving the problem outweigh the costs of implementing the solution. The consultants gather documents and interview managers.

In discussing her needs, Mary informs the ABC analysts that she wants the system to generate a year-to-date summary for any patient within one minute and generic equivalents for prescriptions within three to five seconds. She also wants the system's costs to be manageable.

The consultants use their gathered data to do the following:

1. Identify the problem

2. Describe the project

3. List possible solutions

4. List performance requirements of the new system

5. Describe the data that must be gathered and the sources for that data

6. Draft a preliminary schedule for conducting the analysis

After interviewing Mary and her drugstore managers, pharmacists, and clerks, the consultants conclude that Mary has three basic problems:

1. She is losing her ability to compete from both price and service perspectives. Competitors have computerized systems that enable them to quickly provide customers with generic alternatives for prescription drugs. These competitors also prepare end-of-year summaries for each client's income taxes.

2. Her inventory costs are too high. She should reduce these costs by 20–25 percent.

3. She is spending too much time preparing regulatory government reports.

ABC states that computerization will not only help Mary resolve her three basic problems but also help her and her employees:

Keep accurate records on each client's pharmacologic needs

Provide customers with year-end, itemized prescription purchases for tax purposes

Eliminate the possibility of running out of stock and reduce the amount of on-hand inventory

Identify potentially dangerous prescription combinations and possible allergic reactions to certain drugs

Generate more effective and timely reports for management

Reduce the time spent on preparing regulatory government reports

Now Mary must decide whether the benefits of computerizing her operations described by the consultants are worth the cost.

Figure 20.8
Organization chart of Mary's
Pharmacy.

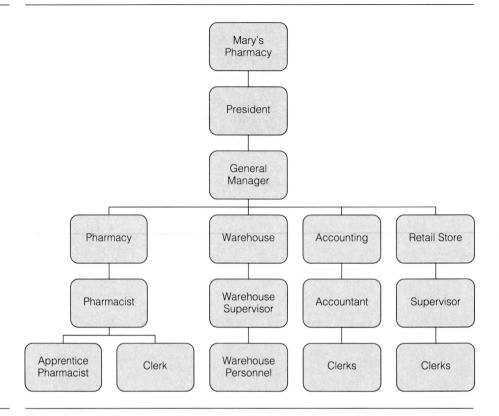

Data Gathering

Once a project is approved by management, the analysis team must gather data about the system and document its various operations. The project dictates what type and how much data are to be collected. Data can be classified into internal and external categories.

Internal Sources of Data. The analysis team can collect a variety of data from within an organization, including organization charts, interviews, documents, observation, and questionnaires.

Organization Charts. Organization charts (Figure 20.8) help analysts to determine quickly which areas of a firm may be affected by problems. Analysts also use their charts to decide whom they should interview for information about the current system and suggestions on how to improve it.

Interviews. The interview is one of the analyst's most important data gathering tools. Effective interviewing requires good communication skills, especially the ability to listen well. Analysts normally conduct at least two interviews. The preliminary interview provides data on the status of the current system, its operations and procedures, and the user's views of what the system lacks. Analysts conduct follow-up interviews to verify they have accurately and completely described the operations of the existing system. Thorough interviews always will ask interviewees if they have any suggestions on what aspects of the system should be examined.

Documents. Analysts also gather data from the documents an organization uses in its day-to-day operations. Invoices, receipts, reports, order forms, and policies and procedures manuals provide valuable information about the or-

Figure 20.9
The various symbols used in
a data-flow diagram.

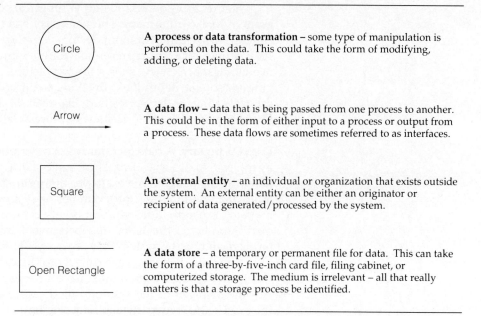

Figure 20.9
The various symbols used in
a data-flow diagram.

Circle — **A process or data transformation** – some type of manipulation is performed on the data. This could take the form of modifying, adding, or deleting data.

Arrow — **A data flow** – data that is being passed from one process to another. This could be in the form of either input to a process or output from a process. These data flows are sometimes referred to as interfaces.

Square — **An external entity** – an individual or organization that exists outside the system. An external entity can be either an originator or recipient of data generated/processed by the system.

Open Rectangle — **A data store** – a temporary or permanent file for data. This can take the form of a three-by-five-inch card file, filing cabinet, or computerized storage. The medium is irrelevant – all that really matters is that a storage process be identified.

ganization's operations. They also provide insight on how information is used by the various parts of the organization.

Observation. Analysts learn valuable information by observing how people perform tasks and comparing the performances with the way the tasks are supposed to be done. Through observation, the analysis team often discovers problems that probably would go undetected using other data gathering techniques.

Questionnaires. Properly constructed questionnaires can quickly and inexpensively gather data about a system from a large number of users. A questionnaire should require only a minimum amount of the respondents' time and effort. Multiple-choice, true-false, and fill-in-the-blank questions receive the best response. Open-ended essay questions should be avoided.

External Sources of Data. External sources of data include trade journals, books, conversations with customers and suppliers, and contacts with other companies that have developed information systems. It is especially important to talk to customers and suppliers if changes in the information system will affect them. By talking with firms that have already adopted systems it is considering, the analysis team can determine the strengths and weaknesses of their various solutions.

Documentation and Data Analysis Tools. One of the analysis team's most important tasks is documenting the existing system to discover how it processes data. Some of the tools discussed below are first used during the early data gathering stage. These tools are designed to help analysts, users, and management understand exactly why an operation or procedure is used.

Data-Flow Diagrams. Analysts use **data-flow diagrams** as their principal graphic tool to show how a system works. Data-flow diagrams are easy to understand because they use only four symbols to show how data flows through a system (Figure 20.9). Any system can be depicted with these four symbols.

Figure 20.10 depicts a simple, **physical (current system) data-flow diagram** of Mary's Pharmacy. The pharmacy has to interact with customers, the Federal Drug Administration, doctors, suppliers, and the accounting function. A data-flow diagram represents a complex process in two perspectives: An overall, or macro, view shows the big picture; a detailed, or micro, view provides a more in-depth look. Breaking the process into smaller components is called leveling, or decomposition. Figure 20.10 shows the macro view of Mary's Pharmacy, and Figure 20.11 shows a more detailed, or leveled, view.

Data Dictionary. A **data dictionary** is a description of each piece of datum used by the system. It serves a vital function because words carry different meanings for different people. For example, the term *data set* means a data file to an individual working as a programmer or systems analyst, but it also means a modem to an individual who works with communications equipment. The data dictionary helps the team members avoid misunderstandings when using terms related to the system they are examining.

The data dictionary ties directly to the data-flow diagram. Any data element listed in the diagram must have a corresponding entry in the dictionary. Anyone involved in the system project can refer to the dictionary to discover the exact role of any particular data element.

The team might write the following entries into the data dictionary to define the various data elements used to record an individual's name and address in a customer history form.

```
CUSTOMER NAME
          CUSTOMER ADDRESS, which consists of the
          following:
                One or both of the following:
                    STREET ADDRESS
                    POST OFFICE BOX NUMBER
                CITY
                STATE
                ZIP
```

Process Descriptions. To computerize a task, analysts must first document the data manipulation steps required to perform that task. This is especially true if the analysts are trying to computerize a complex, manually performed application. Such documentation not only helps analysts revamp the old system but also provides a record that can be referred to when it is time to update the new system.

Two tools used in this documentation process are structured English and decision tables.

Structured English. **Structured English** is plain English with certain restrictions, which derive from its structural similarity to program code. Structured English is limited to four basic structures, with which any set of processing steps can be depicted (Figure 20.12).

Decision Tables. Analysts use **decision tables** in conjunction with structured English to document processes that entail a large number of data manipulation steps. A decision table documents—in an easily comprehendible, tabular format—numerous conditions and corresponding actions. Figure 20.13 illustrates a decision table that documents our pharmacy example.

Figure 20.10
A physical data-flow diagram
showing the overall view of
the Mary's Pharmacy system.

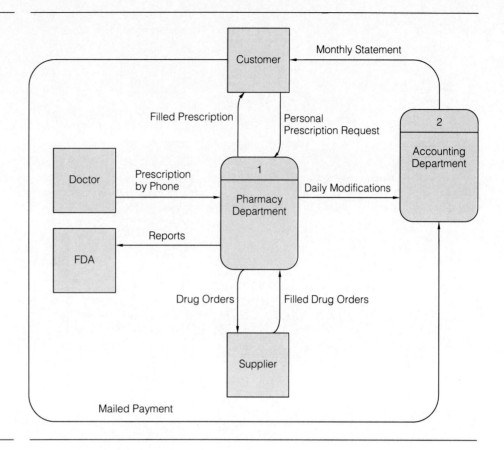

Decision tables are read from right to left and top to bottom. Each table consists of four parts (Figure 20.14). The upper left-hand quadrant represents the condition stub; the user checks here for various conditions or rules. The upper right-hand quadrant is the condition entry; the user can read here whether a condition applies. The lower left-hand quadrant represents the action stub; the user looks here for all possible actions that could be taken. The lower right-hand quadrant is the action entry; the user checks here to determine what actions should be taken if the entries in the condition stub apply.

The System Analysis Report

The system analysis phase concludes when the analysis team presents management with a report describing the present system and their recommendations for its improvement. Management must approve this report before the project can proceed to the design state—remember, the systems analysts only serve as advisers. Management either approves the team's recommendations, possibly with changes, or cancels the project.

The **system analysis report** contains the following sections:

1. An opening statement describing the problem, the scope of the project, and the objectives of the system analysis.

2. A description of the present system, the procedures it uses, and any problems or bottlenecks it manifests in processing data. System constraints are also noted.

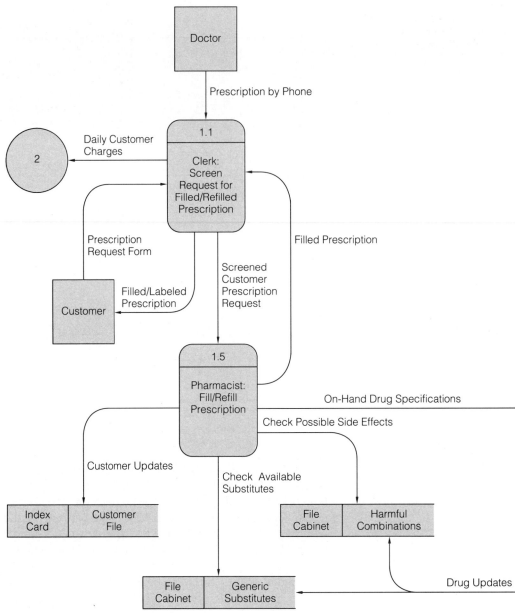

Figure 20.11(a)
Leveled physical data-flow diagram of the pharmacy.

3. Various alternatives for solving the problem. At least three alternatives are usually presented to management. One alternative may be to improve the processing methods of the system so that it can handle more transactions. A second solution might be to purchase new software (often, software that works with microcomputers is recommended). A third suggestion might be that the information systems staff design a system to solve the problem. This solution would be selected only if there isn't existing software that addresses the system's problems. One of these alternative solutions will be recommended to management.

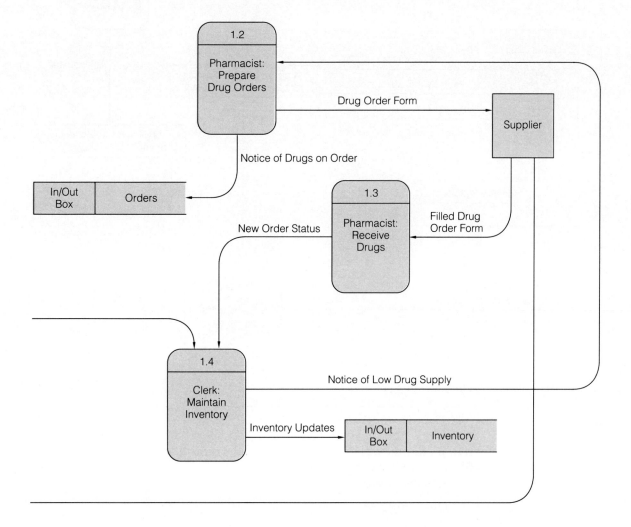

Figure 20.11(a)   (*continued*)

The analysis team usually presents these solutions in terms of their financial impact on the firm. To determine this, the team estimates the hardware and software costs for each alternative and describes what economic benefits the firm can expect to realize from each solution.

Costs and benefits can be classified as tangible or intangible. Tangible costs and benefits are quantified in financial terms and estimated according to the firm's internal data. For example, if a new system will reduce the current system's $60,000 labor costs by 30 percent, then implementation of the new system will save the firm $18,000. Intangible costs and benefits are not so easy

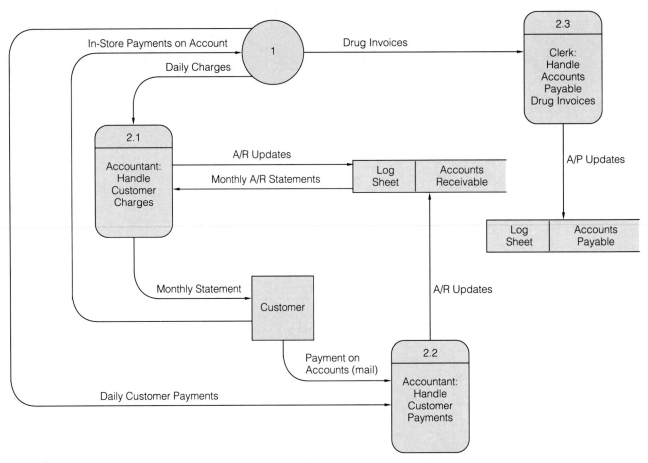

Figure 20.11(b)
Leveled physical data-flow diagram of the accounting process.

to quantify. The team evaluates intangible items with a "best guess" or an arbitrary formula. Consider, for example, the difficulty of quantifying the benefits of improving customer service.

Tangible costs include:

Operating costs

Maintenance costs

Purchase of software or hardware

Site preparation

Training

Intangible costs include:

Negative impact on employee morale

Negative impact on customer relations that might reduce business

Negative impact of employee errors

Tangible benefits include:

Reduced personnel costs

Reduced inventory costs—space as well as turnover

Reduced accounts receivable

Reduced operating costs

Sequence Structure	Selection Structure	Loop Structure	Case Structure

```
Sequence Structure        Selection Structure       Loop Structure            Case Structure
(DO)                      (IF-THEN-ELSE)            (DO-WHILE)                (SELECT-CASE)
   Do operation X          If condition X is true     Do X while Y is true      Select the rule that
   Do operation Y          THEN                                                 applies:
                              Do operation Y                                    Case 1   A<1
                           ELSE                                                    Do operation X
                              Do operation Z                                    Case 2   A≥1 and A≤10
                           ENDIF                                                   Do operation Y
                                                                                Case 3   A>10
                                                                                   Do operation Z
```

(a)

```
If the amount of the prescription exceeds $75
      IF the customer has a bill more than 90 days old
      THEN
                Do not extend credit
      ELSE (customer's credit is good)
                Extend credit
      ENDIF
ELSE (prescription amount is $75 or less)
      IF the customer has a bill more than 90 days old
      THEN
                Get pharmacist's approval
      ELSE (the customer's credit is good)
                Extend credit
      ENDIF
ENDIF
```

(b)

Figure 20.12

(a) The four structured-English primitives (structures) and (b) their implementation.

Figure 20.13
A decision table for the
pharmacy application.

		Rules		
Credit Approval Policy	1	2	3	4
1. Prescriptions > $75	Y	N	Y	N
2. Bill overdue by 90+ days	Y	Y	N	N
1. Extend credit			Y	Y
2. Deny credit	Y			
3. Get pharmacist's approval		Y		

Figure 20.14
The four parts of a decision
table.

Condition Stub	Condition Entry
Action Stub	Action Entry

Intangible benefits include:

Automation of day-to-day decisions

More accurate data used in the decision-making process

Improved employee morale

More accurate data for the planning process

System Design

Once management has accepted the system analysis report and decided on a solution, the analysis team begins designing the system. The first task is to break the system into easily understandable parts.

In writing a new system's program, the team divides the program into distinct, logical components called modules. Each module contains a set of program instructions that perform one task. A program will enter only at the beginning of a module and leave only at its end.

Structure Chart. The primary tool used in system design is the **structure chart**. It depicts in graphic form the system's various modules and their hierarchical relationships. Figure 20.15 shows a structure chart of Mary's Pharmacy.

A structure chart starts with a general process and breaks it into component tasks. Each rectangle of the hierarchy represents a module for which logic (processing steps) will have to be provided. A module might represent a subsystem, a program, or a subroutine (a set of programming language statements), depending on its relation to the rest of the hierarchy chart.

Data-Flow Diagrams for Design. The next step is to document the design of the new system in the structure chart. The analysis team creates a **logical data-flow diagram** for each major task, leveling those comprising additional steps. Figure 20.16 depicts the data-flow diagram for the accounting module. Notice that the data storage medium is not mentioned; only the storage process itself must be identified.

Hardware Evaluation and Selection

After describing the new system's processing steps, the analysis team can determine the system's hardware requirements. For example, if the agreed-on solution calls for several microcomputers sharing one data storage, then the firm will have to procure hardware to build a computer network.

The team establishes criteria for selecting vendors and estimates how much data the system must be able to process and how quickly. The firm puts all the hardware requirements in a request-for-proposal document and sends copies to potential hardware vendors. Each vendor returns a proposal, which the organization may evaluate using a sample program called a benchmark. A **benchmark** approximates the processing demands of the new system's program. By running a benchmark through each vendor's equipment, the analysis team can estimate the hardware's speed and processing capability and measure throughput.

System Development (Module Design)

With the various modules identified, the analysis team now can determine what logical operations will transform the input into the desired output. This step should be fairly easy if the structured English and supporting decision tables were developed properly. Programmers add input, output, and control statements to the structured English, converting it to a programlike code called pseudocode. Unlike true computer code, **pseudocode** does not follow the syntax rules of the computer-programming language being used (Figure 20.17). The pseudocode and decision tables also become essential parts of the documentation of the modules' internal design.

Structured Walkthroughs. The entire analysis team reviews the pseudocode logic and supporting decision tables. This process of peer review by other team members is known as a **structured walkthrough**. During the review, the designer of the module or program logic presents his or her design to the other group members. These members now ask questions or request clarification for any part they don't understand. It is far less expensive to locate and correct problems in the logic at this stage than later in the project development.

The logic of a module must be easy to understand because changes in the firm's environment may necessitate altering the system after its implementation. It is especially important to be able to make changes easily after a system has been implemented. Most information systems staffs spend 80 percent of their programming budgets on maintaining existing information systems.

Programming. Next programmers code the modules, using a programming language such as COBOL. The top module of the hierarchy chart is coded first, and subordinate modules are coded sequentially in a process known as **top-down coding** or programming.

Testing. Programmers test each module as they code it, thereby ensuring the integrity of higher-order modules. Modules residing on the same level of a hierarchy chart can be coded concurrently. As they code, programmers also review the modules in a process known as desk checking. **Desk checking** manually traces any data that could possibly be processed through the module (this includes both valid and invalid data). Sometimes walkthroughs are also conducted on the module code.

After a module's logic accuracy has been established, the code is compiled but not executed by the computer. This allows programmers to examine the output of the compilation process and locate any compiler diagnostics (error messages) that might be present. These diagnostic messages appear whenever the program code does not exactly follow the computer language syntax. This process often must be performed several times.

Top-down programming also enables programmers to code and test each module as it is being designed without having to code all the subordinate modules by stub testing. **Stub testing** involves coding dummy modules that are called by the module above. They are modules with minimal code and may simply display a message to the screen or to the printer that the appropriate module was reached and that control was returned to the calling module.

Programmers use extensive amounts of test data when determining whether all modules within a program are working properly. Test data consist of all possible types of valid or invalid data that could ever be processed by the module. Proper **testing** demands that every line of code in a program be executed so the programmer can verify that the program works as planned.

The program also must be tested with other programs that might exist in the same subsystem. **String testing** verifies that a program functions properly with other programs in the same subsystem. It verifies that the program logic is correct and that the program passes data to other program files properly. The major objective of string testing is to ensure that files are passed correctly from one program to the next.

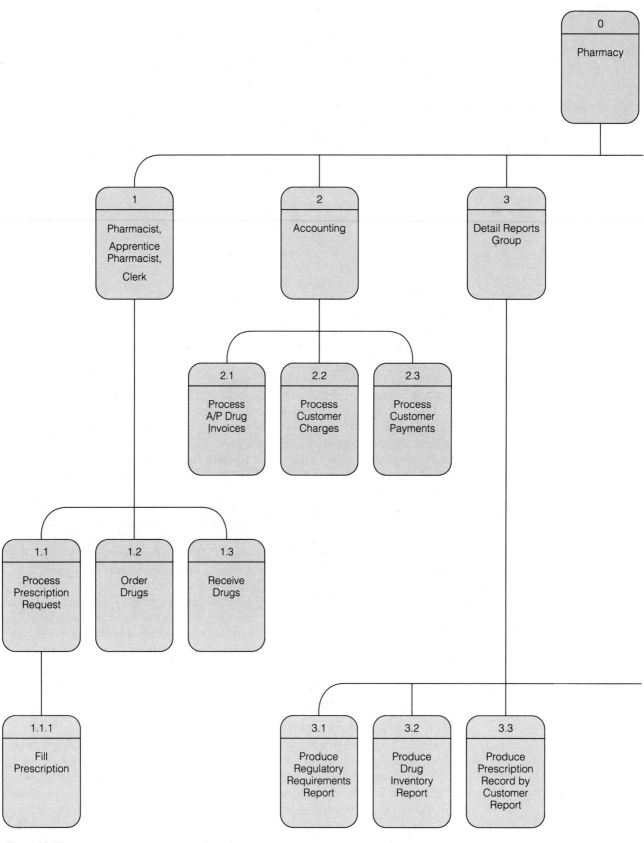

Figure 20.15
A hierarchy chart for the pharmacy application.

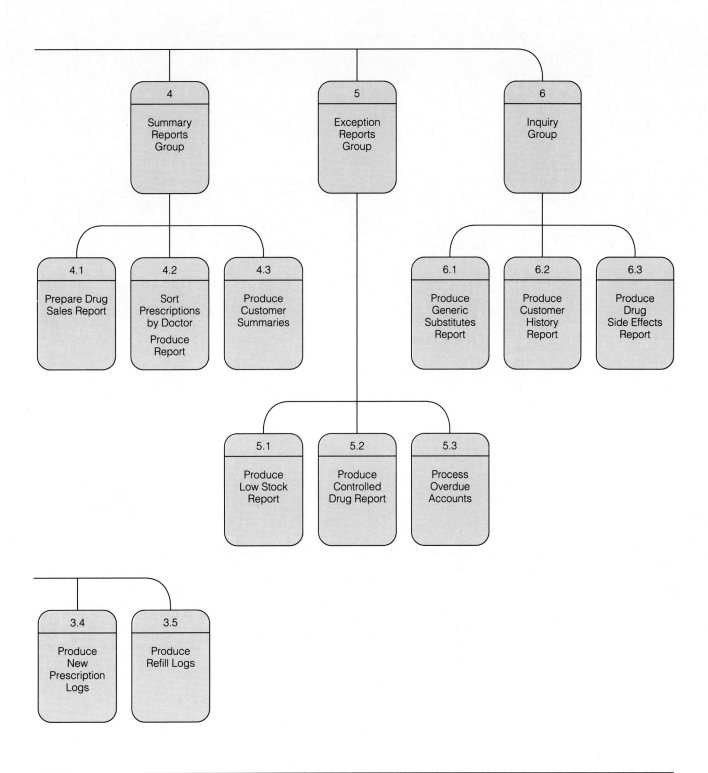

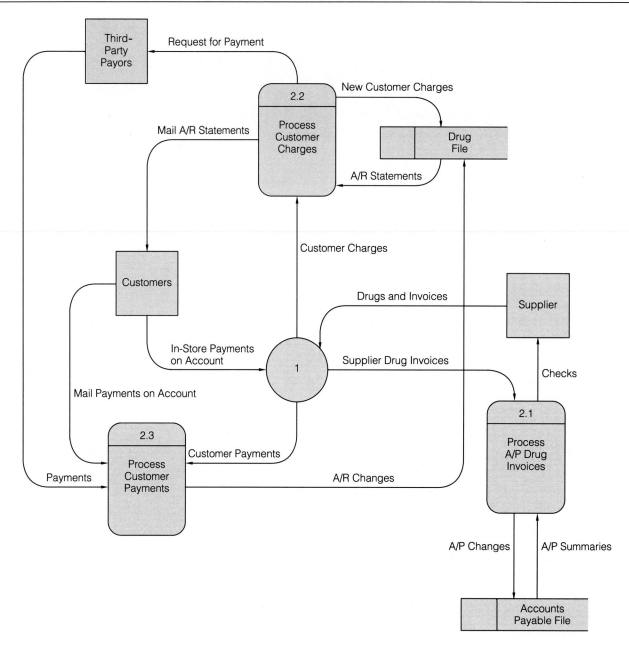

Figure 20.16
The logical data-flow diagram for the accounting module of the hierarchy chart depicted
in Figure 20.15.

The final test is the system test. A **system test** verifies that all parts of the
system work properly: Programs work, data is passed properly from one file
to another and from one subsystem to the other, and both manual and automated portions of the system function well.

System Implementation

During the system conversion stage, the system analysis team must address
several concerns prior to implementing the system.

Figure 20.17
A portion of pseudocode
used for designing a module.

```
DOWHILE not end of file (there are still more records)

    Read a record
    IF today's date is greater than 90 days from the
    date of last payment
        Compute the total owed
        Compute penalties
        Compute grand total
        Place overdue notice on bill
    ELSE
        Compute the total owed
    ENDIF
    Print the bill
ENDDO
```

Site Remodeling and Data Conversion. If the new system requires that the firm acquire considerable hardware, the existing hardware system site may have to be enlarged. The addition of a mainframe computer may require the firm to build a separate room with special electrical hookups and a temperature control system. Wiring for a networked system may have to be installed within existing walls.

File conversion, converting files from the old system to the new, usually takes more time and effort than any other system conversion task. If a manual system is being computerized, the firm may need to hire temporary help to assist in the conversion of paper files into computer files. Before converting an already automated system into another automated system, the firm may have to code and test file conversion programs to ensure that they function properly. Even though the firm uses a file conversion file to perform the data conversion, some fields may still have to be entered manually.

Personnel. The analysis team must train the firm's employees in how to use the new system. Many employees may be adverse to this training: Some may be intimidated by computers, others may see the system as a threat to their job security, and still others may be unsure of their ability to learn something new. The team's approach to this training influences greatly how well the employees accept the system. The team should hold an orientation session to tell employees what the training entails. Training sessions should not be used as an evaluation tool because some people learn faster than others.

Occasionally, employees lose their jobs when a new system is implemented. The personnel department often finds these employees other positions with the firm. If employees must be laid off, the firm should help them locate jobs with other employers.

System Conversion. Computer system implementation involves switching from the old system to the new. There are three basic methods of performing the switch:

Parallel Conversion. In a **parallel conversion**, both the new and the old systems operate side-by-side for a period of time. Such a conversion method provides built-in backup and recovery. If the new system fails, the firm can fall back on the old system.

Direct Conversion. In a **direct conversion**, the firm switches from the old system to the new all at once. Direct conversion is used only if the two systems' hardware or software are completely different. The old system is eliminated and replaced by the new system, which has no backup should something go wrong. Because its risk factor is extremely high, this type of conversion should be used with extreme caution.

Pilot Conversion. In a **pilot conversion**, only a small portion of the organization (for example, a single department) is converted to the new system. If the new system should fail, only part of the organization will be adversely affected. After all of its bugs have been worked out and it functions satisfactorily for the pilot department, the new system can be implemented for the remainder of the organization.

System Audit and Maintenance. After the organization has used the system for a while, management should obtain feedback from employees on the system's performance. To ensure that the system audit is objective, it is usually performed by someone other than those who designed and implemented the system.

The audit should address the following points:

1. Does the system meet the objectives identified in the feasibility study and system analysis stages? Specifically, does the system perform as promised and produce the anticipated benefits? Was the project completed on time and within budget?

2. Are the system controls being followed? Are these controls sufficient, or are additional controls needed?

3. Do the users accept, understand, and have confidence in the system?

System auditors also deal with the system's maintainability. For example, they may need to correct problems in the system or alter it to accommodate changes in the environment. Or they may need to upgrade the system so that it can handle new information needs identified by management. The system's documentation must be revised to reflect any maintenance work.

Chapter Review

A management information system (MIS) is a formal process that relies on manual and computerized tools to provide management with the information it needs to make decisions. The goal of an MIS is to get needed information to a decision maker on time. This goal is complicated by the three levels of decision making: strategic, tactical, and operational. Decisions also can be structured or unstructured. Information is provided in the form of reports—scheduled, exception, demand, and predictive—that are used by decision makers to obtain information.

An MIS provides decision makers with the information they need to make structured decisions. Unstructured decisions require decision support systems (DSS) to provide information for unstructured decisions. A DSS represents problems in mathematical terms. Spreadsheets are common DSS support tools for microcomputers.

It is the information system department's responsibility to provide the information management needs. To supply this data, information system personnel build information systems, using the processes of system analysis and system development life cycle (SDLC). The SDLC provides a methodology for computerizing manual information systems or for improving computerized systems.

All information systems are open systems—that is, they interact with their environment. Open systems accept input from the environment, process that input, and send output into the environment. Systems employ feedback to ensure that intermediate processes generate output that is consistent with established standards. Any complex system can be depicted graphically with the black-box concept.

The feasibility study relies on interviews to define the problem, establish its scope, and determine whether the project is cost justifiable. A report with a recommendation to management is prepared. If management decides to pursue the project, the system analysis phase begins.

The analysis team collects both internal and external data. It also documents the current system with physical data-flow diagrams, which can depict an overall (macro) view of the system or be leveled (decomposed) to provide a detailed (micro) examination. Structured English and decision tables document the processes identified in the data-flow diagram. The analysis phase culminates in the system analysis report, which is sent to management. The report describes several possible solutions, recommends a particular solution, and provides initial cost estimates. If management decides to continue with the project, the design phase begins.

In the design phase, the systems analysis team uses information from the system analysis phase to generate logical data-flow diagrams of the new system. After management approves the system's design, the analysis team evaluates hardware, sends requests-for-proposals to vendors, runs benchmarks on proposed hardware, and finally selects the most appropriate hardware.

In the system development phase, the team develops modules using logical data-flow diagrams, structured English, and decision tables. A hierarchy chart shows the top-down relationship of the system's modules; the actual modules are developed accordingly. As programmers develop logic for each module, they test it by conducting a walkthrough with the team's other members. Next, programmers code the modules and test them with desk checks, program tests, string tests, and system tests.

Developed systems are converted by preparing the site for new equipment, training personnel, and converting data files. The team can install the new system by parallel conversion, direct conversion, or pilot conversion.

After the system has been working for a while, an audit of the system is performed to ensure that it is working within the parameters established during the feasibility and system analysis phases. The firm must maintain the system by correcting errors in it or upgrading it in response to changes in the environment.

Key Terms and Concepts

benchmark	feedback
black-box concept	interface
boundary	logical data-flow diagram
data dictionary	management information system
data-flow diagram	(MIS)
decision support system (DSS)	model
decision table	operational decision making
demand report	parallel conversion
desk checking	physical data-flow diagram
direct conversion	pilot conversion
environmental interaction	predictive report
exception report	pseudocode
feasibility study	purpose

scheduled report	system analysis
strategic decision making	system analysis report
string testing	system development life cycle (SDLC)
structure chart	system test
structured decisions	tactical decision making
structured English	testing
structured walkthrough	top-down coding
stub testing	transaction processing system
synergism	unstructured decisions
system	

Chapter Quiz

Multiple Choice

1. Which of the following is a type of decision that is supported by a management information system?
   a. Tactical decision
   b. Operational decision
   c. Strategic decision
   d. Both a and b
   e. All of the above

2. Which of the following statements is false?
   a. Management information systems work best for unstructured types of decisions found in the strategic decision-making process.
   b. The heart of decision support systems is the model of the problem being investigated.
   c. A decision support system allows you to ask "what-if" questions about a problem.
   d. A common microcomputer-based tool in a decision support system is an integrated spreadsheet package.

3. Which of the following is *not* a characteristic common to systems?
   a. A feedback loop is established to check the output to ensure that it follows preset standards.
   b. Systems have little, if any, interaction with their environment.
   c. The area outside the boundaries of the system is called the environment.
   d. The area of overlap between two systems is called an interface.

4. Which of the following is *not* a phase found in the system development life cycle?
   a. System development
   b. System analysis
   c. Programming
   d. System implementation
   e. None of the above

5. Which of the following data gathering or documentation tools is (are) used by an analyst during the system analysis phase of a project?
   a. Data-flow diagrams
   b. Structured English
   c. Interviews
   d. Questionnaires
   e. All of the above

True/False

6. A decision support system is not part of a management information system.

7. Strategic planning makes use of masses of internal information.

8. Structured decisions can be most easily supported by a management information system.

9. Systems analysts require little involvement by management concerning selection of what systems to computerize.

10. A walkthrough allows other analysts to examine the logic of a module to ensure that it will perform a task properly.

Answers

1. e 2. a 3. b 4. c 5. e 6. f 7. f 8. t 9. f 10. t

Exercises

1. Define or describe each of the following:
   a. management information system
   b. decision support system
   c. system
   d. system analysis
   e. system development life cycle

2. The _____ level of decision making deals with the allocation of resources that are required to meet the objectives of an organization.

3. The _____ level of decision making deals with the day-to-day operations of the organization to ensure that processes stay within the parameters of preset standards.

4. The _____ level of decision making deals with the future.

5. The _____ decisions are those decisions for which preset standards have already been established.

6. A _____ is a device used to present information to a user and can be on either paper or a CRT.

7. A _____ report is one that is generated at regular intervals.

8. A _____ report is generated at the request of the user using some type of query language.

9. A decision support system is most frequently used to help with _____ decisions.

10. The key part of a decision support system involves building a _____ or mathematical representation of the problem.

11. A _____ is a set of interrelated parts that work toward a common goal.

12. _____ is the concept where the whole is greater than the sum of its parts.

13. The overlap of two systems or subsystems where no processing occurs is called the _____.

14. A(n) _____ system interacts with its environment.

15. The process of sampling output and sending it back into the system as input to verify that it is within established parameters is referred to as _____.

16. The _____ concept allows any system to be depicted as input, process, and output.

17. _____ is the process of studying and modeling systems.

18. The phases that are used in the system analysis process represent a methodology that is called the _____.

19. The _____ phase defines the problem and determines whether a system can be cost justified.

20. Three internal sources of data that can be used during the feasibility study and system analysis phases are
    a.

    b.

    c.

21. A data-flow diagram uses four symbols to document any system. List and state the purpose of each symbol.
    a.

    b.

    c.

    d.

22. A _____ data-flow diagram is used to depict the flows of data within an existing system.

23. A _____ is used during the system analysis phase to document each data item.

24. If many decision-making factors are involved in processing data, these factors can be depicted in a tabular format called a(n) _____.

25. The output of the system analysis phase that is received by management is called the _____.

26. When the system design phase begins, the various modules are depicted in a document referred to as a _____ chart.

27. The data flows of the new system are depicted in the _____ data-flow diagram.

28. A _____ is sent to potential hardware vendors.

29. A _____ is a sample program that is used to test a potential vendor's equipment to see if it performs as required.

30. _____ resembles structured English with input, output, and control statements and is used to design the logic for a module.

31. A _____ is conducted by other analysts to verify that the logic of a module functions as it is supposed to function.

32. The process of coding higher modules before lower modules are coded is called _____ coding.

33. _____ testing verifies that information is passed correctly from one file to the next.

34. _____ conversion makes certain that the files have been properly created for the new system.

35. Before employees can use the new system, they have to be _____ or educated as to how the new system operates.

36. The _____ conversion method runs both the old system and the new system side by side.

37. The _____ conversion method makes all changes at one time.

38. The _____ conversion method implements the system for only a small portion of the organization at one time.

39. The _____ conversion method provides the best backup if something goes wrong with the new system.

40. The process of examining the new system to ensure that it operates as it is supposed to is called the _____.

Questions for Thought

1. Examine the impact of data base technology on the ability of management information systems to respond to management's request for information to support the decision-making process.

2. Prepare a paper that differentiates between an organization that has only a transaction processing system and an organization that has a management information system.

3. Prepare a paper that examines how organizations can use information systems as strategic weapons in their business. In other words, how can organizations use information systems to gain an advantage over their competitors?

4. Prepare a paper that examines some of the tools used in system analysis that are not covered in this chapter. What are the strengths and weaknesses of these system analysis tools?

5. Examine the impact of a decision support system on an organization. What types of information processing resources are required to support a DSS?

Chapter
21

Ethics, Social Issues, and Computer Security

Chapter Objectives

After completing this chapter, you should be able to:

Define the term ethics

Analyze how computer education should be provided

Discuss computers in relation to employee monitoring and job security

Discuss the role of ergonomics and the use of computers

Identify computer crime

Discuss the role of a virus as an example of computer crime

Discuss how software piracy represents an ethical violation

Discuss the characteristics of a computer criminal

Discuss the impact computers have on individual privacy

Discuss two federal laws that apply to privacy

Define security as it relates to computers

Discuss the various applications of internal control to computers

Imagine the social chaos that would ensue if computers were to suddenly cease to operate. Patients in hospitals would die, trains and airplanes would become unsafe, roads would become snarled with cars as traffic lights failed, communications would break down, and production and manufacturing would come to a standstill. Given our dependence on computers, it is inevitable that we ask ourselves whether the machines, on the whole, benefit society and whether we use them ethically.

Ethics is the study of conduct and moral judgment. This chapter addresses the ethical use of the computer by government, businesses, and individuals. We examine what obligation schools have to teach computer use. We also raise issues about computers in the workplace. We discuss the individual's right to privacy and whether the gathering of computer data on people violates that right. Finally, we look at ways users can safeguard their computer systems.

Education and Computer Literacy

In the near future, say some business and education professionals, an individual who wants a good job will find it is as important to possess computer skills as to know the three *R*s. If this is so, we are ethically bound to incorporate computer instruction in school curriculums and ensure that students are "computer literate" by the time they are ready to enter the work force.

However, there is no consensus on what constitutes computer literacy. Some define the term as the ability to write a program that enables a computer to perform some task. Using such a standard, our educational system could fulfill its obligation to teach computer skills by introducing elementary grade students to simple languages such as BASIC or LOGO. Others maintain that computer literacy entails more practical skills, such as the ability to use and solve problems with various applications software packages. Still others insist that schools should be more concerned with teaching students about the impact computers have on society than training them in technical skills.

At any rate, the corporate world wants schools and colleges to teach students how to solve business-oriented problems using spreadsheet, word processing, and data base management software packages. Accomplishing this will require more than adding new classes to school curriculums: It will necessitate a wholesale retraining of teachers themselves, at all educational levels, in computer use and technology.

Computers in the Workplace

While it is common knowledge that computers have made blue- and white-collar workers more productive, little is known about how employees view the machines. Few studies have been done on what effects the computer has on job security, but many workers are understandably worried that their skills will be rendered obsolete by computer technology. Already, computers have eliminated several employment positions, changed how workers perform their duties, and created a variety of new jobs.

Job Security

While computer advocates note that computer technology has created millions of new jobs, detractors say it will put millions out of work. Conscientious companies retrain those employees who lose jobs to computerization. Generally, those jobs that require the least technical skills are computerized. For example, many manufacturing jobs that require routine welding, sorting, or assembly tasks are now performed by robots. In the office, manual filing and typing chores are being replaced by computerized counterparts (Figure 21.1).

Figure 21.1
Example of an automated assembly line in a manufacturing plant. (Courtesy of Chrysler Corporation)

Privacy and Job Monitoring

A potentially explosive subject is the computerized monitoring of employee work performance. Managers can program computers to track how many mistakes a typist or a data-entry clerk makes, how much time a worker spends away from his or her terminal, or how many transactions an accountant handles in a day. Computer monitoring could substantially increase the amount of stress workers feel on the job.

Health Considerations

Millions of employees spend their workday in front of a computer monitor and receive eye, back, and muscle strain for their efforts. Unions and employee groups have asked what health risks long-term monitor use poses to workers. Unfortunately, that question has not been answered conclusively by the several studies conducted on the subject. A few studies suggest that monitor use is hazardous; some studies show otherwise.

Looking at a monitor all day may or may not be dangerous, but there is little doubt it can cause red eyes and sore muscles. Users can minimize eyestrain by taking a break after every hour of viewing. They can also ergonomically design their workplaces to reduce muscle strain and increase efficiency.

Ergonomics is the science of adapting work and working conditions to suit the individual worker. Ergonomics can be applied in many ways. For example, hardware manufacturers now build sloping keyboards for a more comfortable typing position and put monitors on swivel bases so that screens can be adjusted to suit the user's viewing angle. Manufacturers now also offer consumers a variety of screen colors—including white, green, and amber—which reduce eyestrain. Ergonomically designed furniture helps office workers reduce backache and muscle strain (Figure 21.2). Ergonomically designed work

Figure 21.2
Examples of ergonomic fur-
niture. (Courtesy of Digital
Equipment Corporation)

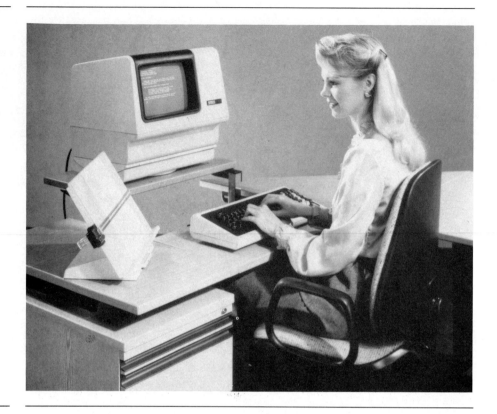

Figure 21.2
Examples of ergonomic fur-
niture. (Courtesy of Digital
Equipment Corporation)

environments are more costly to construct than are traditional offices, but increased worker productivity more than compensates for the added expense.

Computer Crime

Computer crime is the commission of unlawful acts by using computer technology. Some experts claim that only one-tenth of the computer crimes committed in the United States are actually reported. One reason for this lopsided ratio is that many firms are reluctant to report computer crime for fear it will cause stockholders to lose confidence in them.

Examples of Computer Crime

Following are several widely reported cases of computer crime.

Equity Funding. A former favorite of Wall Street investors, Equity Funding Corporation comprised a group of investment and insurance companies. Several top-level managers from some of these companies colluded to attract additional investors by lying about company profits. They also created 50,000 bogus insurance policies on the computer and sold them, packaged with bona fide policies, to other insurance companies. The group coded the fake policies in such a way that the company's auditors could not distinguish them from bona fide policies. Eventually, after the manager's actions caused losses as high as $20 million, the fraud was uncovered, and more than twenty people were convicted on federal charges.

Pacific Telephone. Jerry Schneider is a computer wizard who built his own computer system at the age of ten. Years later Schneider began raiding the garbage dumpsters of Pacific Telephone to retrieve the company's discarded computer printouts and other documents providing account numbers, passwords, and computer procedures. Using this information, Schneider would dial into the Pacific Telephone inventory-control system, order equipment to be delivered to himself, and then erase all traces of the transaction.

Schneider became so successful that he had to hire assistants. One of those assistants, who had asked his boss for a raise and been turned down, reported Schneider to the police.

414 Gang. The 414 gang was a group of teenage Wisconsin computer hackers who used microcomputers to gain access to computer systems across the country. Gang members would obtain or guess passwords to a system, examine files, run programs, and discover as much about the system as possible. During their electronic forays, they damaged key files of several companies. They also penetrated a hospital system used to monitor critically ill patients. A doctor stated several people could have died if the gang had damaged the system. The members of the 414 gang wound up having their computers confiscated, and some had to pay fines.

Enough Is Enough! A young man stole 50,000 pounds from the English firm that employed him, then manipulated computer data to cover the theft. The fraud was discovered, but management declined to prosecute for fear the publicity would worry the company's stockholders. The young man then demanded management provide him with a letter of recommendation, which it did. He used this recommendation to obtain a job at another firm. Four years later, the firm traced a 150,000-pound fraud to him. Again, management refused to prosecute, and again the thief demanded a letter of recommendation. But the thief pushed too hard when he demanded 3,500 pounds in severance pay. The firm filed charges.

Viruses. A new form of computer crime is the spreading of **software viruses**. Like their biological counterpart, these viruses can infect many parts of the host system—application programs, data files, and disk operating systems—and are self-replicating. Systems can be infected by on-line services, electronic bulletin boards, and users swapping disks. Once in a computer's RAM, the virus can infect other programs loaded for execution.

Software viruses wreak havoc by destroying data, modifying data, or sabotaging printing. The bug may command the computer to display the message "GOTCHA" and reboot the system, causing everything in RAM to be lost; it may destroy the file allocation table so that files cannot be found by DOS; or it might format a disk containing crucial information—a particularly harmful event for a fixed-disk user.

Software viruses are created and released by programmers, sometimes as a prank but often for malicious purposes. "Scores," the most widespread virus to infect Apple Macintosh microcomputers, was originally designed to attack custom applications used by a Texas company. The virus creates difficulty in running certain Apple programs and printing from applications and causes systems to crash when certain applications are started.

Software Piracy. **Software piracy** is the illicit duplication of software, a continual problem for the software industry. Software manufacturers estimate that for every popular microcomputer application package sold, pirates make four unauthorized duplications. Piracy costs software developers millions of dollars a year and increases the cost of original copies.

Illegal copying may be done by an individual who wants an inexpensive means of obtaining a particular software package or it might be committed by a company or individual who wants to sell pirated software to others. Selling pirated software copies is particularly prevalent in foreign countries, especially Brazil, Taiwan, and Saudi Arabia. Businesses have been caught making up to 100 copies of a single software program.

To battle piracy, software manufacturers have started two organizations. The Software Publishers Association (SPA) offers a $100 bounty to the first person who provides information about a person or company disseminating illegal software copies. Another group, ADAPSO, fights software piracy in corporations, schools, and foreign countries.

The primary legal protection software manufacturers have is **copyright** protection. This is the easiest and least expensive form of protection a software manufacturer can obtain, but it does not provide as much protection as a patent would—federal laws are unclear about what rights a copyright provides a software developer.

Many firms have tried placing copy-protection schemes on their software disks to prevent piracy. However, copy-protection schemes make it difficult for a user to create backup copies of legally purchased software. Software-protection schemes also may produce changes to the disk operating system, adversely affecting its functioning. Many people strongly object to software-protection schemes, which they feel wrongfully penalize honest software users. As a result, most software producers no longer install copy protection on their popular applications packages.

Many software developers do not sell software to consumers but sell rather the license to use a particular package on one computer (Figure 21.3). These so-called shrink-wrap licenses provide neither warranty on the software nor compensation provisions if the software malfunctions. The rationale for such sales policies is that users can buy a software program, copy it, and then return the purchased copy, claiming it is defective.

Eventually, the courts will determine whether shrink-wrap licenses are valid. In the meantime, there is much confusion over how software can be used. For instance, no one is sure whether a user who purchases a word processing software disk licensed for one computer can use the disk both at the office and at home if it is for the same work.

Shrink-wrap licenses are particularly problematic for schools. With software groups offering bounties for information about illegal copies, many schools have initiated policies stating that anyone caught copying school-owned software can be flunked and expelled from school. An easy way for a user to avoid trouble is to not copy software he or she has not purchased.

Characteristics of a Computer Criminal

Donn B. Parker, an expert on computer crime, lists the following profile of the typical computer criminal:

The person is a male.

The person is a white-collar employee.

The person is eighteen to thirty years of age.

The person is in a trusted position within the firm.

The person has never been in trouble before.

The behavior of this person does not deviate markedly from that of his peers.

Figure 21.3
Example of a Lotus Corporation License Agreement.

VP-Planner Plus

PAPERBACK SOFTWARE INTERNATIONAL
Software License Agreement

Before opening this package, read the following terms and conditions carefully.

OPENING THIS PACKAGE, OR USING THE SOFTWARE OR ANY COPY OF THE SOFTWARE ENCLOSED IN THIS PACKAGE, MEANS THAT YOU ACCEPT THESE TERMS AND CONDITIONS. IF YOU DO NOT AGREE TO THESE TERMS AND CONDITIONS, RETURN THE UNOPENED PACKAGE TO YOUR DEALER FOR A REFUND OF THE PURCHASE PRICE.

The Software in this package is offered only on the condition that you agree to the following terms and conditions:

1. You agree that this Software remains the property of Paperback Software International (PSI), but that PSI grants you a nonexclusive license to use this Software subject to this Agreement. This Software and this Manual are copyrighted.

2. You agree that this Software and this Manual are licensed to you for your use, and that this license is not a sale of this original Software or any copy.

3. You agree that you may make backup or archival copies of this Software to protect your investment from loss and/or to run this Software from a fixed disk or other disk media.

4. You agree that neither this Software disk nor any of the copies made may be given, distributed, transferred, loaned, leased, or sold to any other person, company, or entity unless you also transfer this Manual and transfer or erase any and all copies of this Software which you have made, and that the person, company, or entity to whom or which this Software is transferred consents to the terms of this Agreement.

5. You agree that you may not make any copies of this Software and/or this Manual other than those which are specifically authorized above or without the separate express written approval of PSI.

6. You agree that you may not disassemble, change, or modify this Software or any copy, and/or this Manual or any copy, in whole or in part, for any purpose, without express written authorization from PSI.

7. You agree that this Software will only be used on one computer by one person at one time.

8. You agree that PSI designed this Software for use with the computer system(s) listed in this Manual, and that with proper application this Software will perform substantially as described in this Manual. You also agree that PSI does not warrant that the functions contained in this Software will meet your particular requirements or that the operation of this Software will be uninterrupted or error-free. The diskette(s) delivered to you on which this Software is recorded are free from defects in materials and faulty workmanship under normal use. The representations above do not cover items damaged, modified, or misused after delivery to you.

   If a diskette should prove defective or if this Software does not perform as described in this Manual, you shall immediately return any defective diskette or non-conforming Software to PSI and, as your sole remedy, PSI shall either replace the diskette or Software or refund the purchase price at PSI's election.

   THE FOREGOING WARRANTIES ARE LIMITED IN DURATION TO THE PERIOD OF 90 DAYS FROM THE DATE OF ORIGINAL DELIVERY TO YOU. THE FOREGOING WARRANTIES ARE IN LIEU OF ALL OTHER WARRANTIES, EXPRESS OR IMPLIED, INCLUDING, BUT NOT LIMITED TO, THE IMPLIED WARRANTIES OF MERCHANTABILITY AND FITNESS FOR A PARTICULAR PURPOSE ON THE DISKETTES AND THE SOFTWARE. PSI SHALL IN NO EVENT BE LIABLE FOR ANY INDIRECT, INCIDENTAL, OR CONSEQUENTIAL DAMAGES, WHETHER RESULTING FROM DEFECTS IN THE DISKETTE(S) OR FROM ANY DEFECT IN THE SOFTWARE ITSELF OR DOCUMENTATION THEREOF. IN NO EVENT SHALL THE LIABILITY OF PSI FOR DAMAGES ARISING OUT OF OR IN CONNECTION WITH USE OR PERFORMANCE OF THE SOFTWARE OR DISKETTE(S) EXCEED THE LICENSE FEE ACTUALLY PAID BY YOU.

   Any implied warranties which are found to exist are hereby limited in duration to the 90-day life of the express warranties on the diskettes given above. Some states do not allow the exclusion or limitation on how long implied warranties last, so these exclusions or limitations may not apply to you. Warranties give you specific legal rights and you may also have other rights which vary from state to state.

9. You agree that if you violate any of the terms and conditions in this Agreement, PSI may terminate this Agreement and the license granted and shall be entitled to all rights and remedies available in law or equity, including, without limitation, specific performance. Upon termination of this Agreement, you agree to return your copy of this Software and this Manual to PSI at your expense and to erase any and all copies of this Software which you have made.

10. This Agreement is construed in accordance with, and governed by, the laws of the State of California and the United States of America. Should any part of this Agreement be declared invalid or unenforceable, the validity and enforceability of the remainder of this Agreement shall not be affected thereby. This Agreement can only be modified by a written agreement signed by you and PSI.

The person is typically trying to overcome some type of personal problem, typically financial in nature.

The person considers his or her acts justifiable because they are against a corporation rather than a person.

The gender attribute is changing as more women enter the work force. It is not surprising that most computer criminals are young because financial burdens are likely to be heaviest early in a professional's career. Often, the computer criminal is trying to support a family on limited resources. It is also reasonable that the person have a white-collar job and not have been in trouble before—the typical computer criminal is not the kind of person to rob someone at gunpoint. Stealing from a faceless entity like a corporation is another matter. The white-collar characteristic will also change as the computer becomes a tool for people in all sorts of occupations.

Part Three

Federal Law Dealing with Computer Crime

In 1984 President Reagan signed into law the **Comprehensive Crime Control Act of 1984**. This law prohibits an unauthorized individual from accessing computer records to obtain information protected by the Right to Financial Privacy Act of 1978 or data contained in the files of a consumer-reporting agency. It also prohibits unauthorized individuals from using, modifying, destroying, or disclosing information stored on government-owned computers or sabotaging government computers or software.

Software Development

Ethical software developers thoroughly test their software before selling it to users. This can literally be a life or death matter when the software drives systems that monitor hospital patients, control air traffic, regulate traffic lights, provide switching for rail-based transportation, and automate nuclear power plant operations (Figure 21.4).

Consider the following case. A programmer made a minor change in the program used to update the New York City Welfare Department's master file. The programmer considered the revision "trivial" and did not test the program after making the change. In the following months, welfare recipients contained in the master file died, moved away, or lost their eligibility to receive payments.

Normally, these recipients would be deleted from the welfare rolls when the master file was updated. However, the change caused the updated program to ignore batch-entered deletions to the master file and kept open files that should have been closed. During the next three months, the system's printers spewed out thousands of checks to people who were dead, had left the city, or were no longer entitled to receive payments. Field workers began to report that welfare payments were still being paid to closed cases. By the time the error was discovered, $7.5 million had been paid to people who should have been deleted from the files.

Welfare workers were able to find out who received the checks, but getting the money back was another matter. Most of the checks were for less than $300; just filing a suit to recover funds from one recipient would cost New York City $150, prosecuting would incur additional costs. The city could easily have spent more than $7.5 million trying to retrieve the money. In the end, New York City taxpayers wound up paying millions of dollars for the programmer's mistake.

Individual Privacy and Computers

Computers have a nearly incredible capacity to store and retrieve information. This capacity, some people feel, makes it easy for government or businesses to infringe on our right to privacy. **Privacy** has been defined as the claim of individuals, groups, or institutions to determine for themselves when, how, and to what extent personal information about them is communicated to others.

An individual who seeks an auto loan will be asked by the bank to provide information on his or her place of employment, outstanding loans, names and current balances of any credit cards, and other personal financial information. The applicant will then be asked to sign a statement that permits the bank to check the applicant's credit status.

Institutions that store data on individuals include schools, banks, credit offices, drivers license bureaus, state internal revenue offices, federal internal revenue offices, law enforcement offices, libraries, insurance companies, and many more. The federal government alone has thousands of data-collection and storage systems. Usually, these data are used to our benefit. However, it is possible for this information to be used maliciously to cause harm.

Figure 21.4
Proper control is essential for such sensitive systems as those that control nuclear power plants. (Courtesy of ERC)

Data stored in one computerized information system can be matched against data in other systems. For example, by matching a computer record of federal government employees and a computer listing of student loan defaulters, the government identified more than 47,000 of their own workers who failed to pay back their student loans.

In another example of record matching, the employees of a federal agency charged with the recovery of arrears child-support payments were themselves computer checked for compliance to child-support laws. The government discovered 540 employees who were behind in child-support payments.

Such matching can be performed with any number of computerized information systems. Opponents of computer matching decry the process as a danger to privacy and want it controlled. Proponents claim record matching is an effective method to discover fraud and enforce the law.

Electronic funds transfer (EFT) systems also pose a threat to privacy. An EFT system electronically transfers an individual's paycheck to a bank account. The person then uses a debit card to make purchases of groceries, gasoline, books, and so on. The amount of each purchase is automatically debited from the individual's account, recorded, and transferred to the appropriate vendor's account. Not surprisingly, this system is very popular among vendors because it makes bad check writing a thing of the past. Banks benefit from the system because it cuts the paperwork required to process checks.

At the end of the month, the bank sends its EFT–account holders a detailed listing of all the places they made purchases. However, such systems paint a detailed financial portrait of account holders: The question is, Who is allowed access to this information? Some people believe that these systems pose an unprecedented threat to privacy and freedom, arguing that governmental access to EFT information smacks of "Big Brother" control.

The U.S. Supreme Court has yet to review a case that has demanded a direct ruling on exactly what rights to privacy a citizen has under the Constitution. However, in a number of landmark cases, the Supreme Court has ruled that a right to privacy is implied by the First, Third, Fourth, Fifth, and Ninth Amendments.

The U.S. Congress and several state legislatures have passed legislation to safeguard an individual's privacy. Some important federal legislation on privacy includes the following.

Fair Credit Reporting Act of 1970. Congress passed this act to mitigate problems associated with the collection and use of credit, insurance, and employment information. Under the law, credit bureaus and investigatory reporting agencies must permit individuals on whom they maintain records the opportunity to inspect their files. If an individual challenges the accuracy of his or her file, the organization holding the records must review the data and correct any errors.

Privacy Act of 1974. This act regulates how the federal government manages information collected on citizens. The act stipulates that the government must annually report all of its data banks in the Federal Register. Federal agencies must report how they intend to use the data they maintain on individuals; if an agency plans to use its information for any but the stated purpose, it must first acquire the permission of the affected individual. Individuals have the right to review information stored about them, except when the files contain classified information or are part of a law enforcement data base. If the individual feels that his or her file information is inaccurate, the act provides a set of procedures for correcting the data.

It seems inevitable that computers will be used to store information on individuals. But, in a democracy, how that information is used and who uses it are not inevitable. Ultimately, the citizenry must decide how to reconcile the right to privacy and the need for information.

Computer Security and Controls

Organizations can help safeguard the privacy of data and reduce their chances of becoming computer crime victims by instituting a **security** system. A security system must include an **internal control** program: organizational procedures designed to protect computer facilities, hardware, software, and data bases.

Information is one of the most precious resources an organization possesses. The goal of computer security and internal control is to protect that resource. However, a company must strike an appropriate balance between security costs and the replacement costs of the assets being protected. Before implementing extensive security measures, many firms undertake a risk-analysis study to determine their security needs and how much meeting those needs will cost.

The cost of security may involve more than the price of installing a system. Unnecessarily strict internal controls can interfere with an organization's work flow. Employees may try to circumvent such controls so they can work faster and may create havoc with the security system in the process.

Controls can be broken into three basic categories: general controls, program controls, and documentation.

General Controls

General controls regulate access to a computer system. They consist of access controls, hardware controls, organization controls, system controls, data and procedural controls, and emergency or hazard controls.

Access Controls. **Access controls** protect the computer equipment and facilities. Typical access controls for a mainframe environment include locating the computer equipment in a windowless room separate from the organization's offices. Access control may require nothing more than locating computer equipment behind a locked door. Or it may involve elaborate hardware or procedures: combination door locks, ID card checks at entry points, or closed-circuit camera surveillance of computer rooms.

Access controls for a microcomputer may be as simple as bolting the machine to a desk to discourage theft and locking the power switch so only authorized personnel can use the computer.

Passwords often serve as an access control in computer systems comprising a network of remote-terminal users. To access the system, users must type in the right password when logging on. Some password systems notify security personnel if the user doesn't provide the right password within three tries. This prevents unauthorized users from guessing their way onto the system. On-line systems require special security protection. Some on-line systems are designed to automatically log off a user who has not entered data for a specific period of time—say, twenty minutes. This security measure prevents unauthorized individuals from accessing or altering sensitive data bases on an unattended computer or terminal.

Organizations can restrict data access in a number of ways. Companies that use mainframe computers often employ a data librarian to control who gains access to data files. A locked drawer may provide sufficient access control for microcomputer disks or other removable storage media.

Hardware Controls. **Hardware controls** are incorporated into computers to regulate who can use the machines. For example, a person may have to type a password into a mainframe computer before the machine permits the user to process data. Mainframe computers and minicomputers may also be equipped with **console logs**, devices that record what actions users perform on the machines. These devices even log what tapes were mounted on which drives by the operators, which files the operator altered, and what responses the operator gave to the computer's prompts or instructions.

Organization Controls. **Organization controls** divide data processing operations among several users. For example, one person's duty may be to collect accounts-receivable data, and another person's job may be to record the data. Such control measures make it necessary for two or more culprits to commit fraud or other computer crimes. A company's organization controls may direct that programming and operating of the computers be done by different individuals, that a librarian control the data files, or that operators rotate when running sensitive programs.

Organizational controls can also be used to ensure the smooth functioning of the company. For example, companies often separate their information-system department from other departments. This allows the computer department to function with the best interests of the organization in mind. For example, it could be detrimental for a company to have computer-department personnel report to a manager in the comptroller's office—the computer department could wind up devoting more attention to the comptroller's office than to other departments.

System Controls. **System controls** ensure the proper development of information systems. The most important of these controls entails the participation of users and management in a system's development (see Chapter 20). Implementation of a new system requires conversion controls such as record counts and file comparisons to ensure that all the old system's records are safely converted. The company must then test the new system. Finally, to keep system errors to a minimum, a company must control what changes can be made to a system and who can make them.

Data and Procedural Controls.

Data controls safeguard data or ensure their proper entry. In batch processing, workers often send a batch-control slip along with the documents the computer operators will be transcribing into machine-readable form. These control slips state how many documents are in the batch and provide control totals, field sums that can be used to check the accuracy of the transcription. For example, a control total for an accounts-receivable application might be the grand total of all charges made by the customers listed in a file.

Hash, or "nonsense," totals can also be used to check the accuracy of transcription. These totals are nonsense in that they don't truly represent a sum in the way control totals do. An example of a hash total would be the summed value of the Social Security numbers in all records processed.

Control and hash totals serve to indicate that records have been excluded from processing. These totals can be compared from one processing step to the next. If the totals match, then all of the records have been processed. If the totals do not match, it means that the operator purposely or mistakenly did not include a record or records for processing.

Perhaps the most important data control involves the creation and safeguarding of backup files. Backup files are copies of original files; they can serve as replacements if the original files are destroyed. Backup files are sometimes stored away from a company's computer center so they are safe even if the computer center catches on fire. Data controls also help ensure that records that have been suspended from processing due to errors are corrected and appropriately processed.

Procedural controls are sets of written instructions provided to those who operate and maintain a computer system. These instructions serve as source material, which operators can consult when there is a problem. If the problem is not adequately covered in the procedures, the instructions should provide the name and number of someone who can give more detailed assistance.

Hazard Controls.

Hazard, or emergency, **controls** provide provisions in case fire, flood, earthquake, or other disasters threaten a company's computer system. For example, fire-protection measures might include installing smoke detectors and fire-extinguishing systems.

More comprehensive emergency plans provide contingency actions if a company loses its entire computer operation. For example, two firms could agree to share computer equipment and processing with the other if one of them should lose its computer system. However, unless the firms are very small, this is rarely a viable alternative. Larger firms sometimes establish contingency contracts with vendors who will provide computer hardware in the event of a disaster. In such cases, the firms can continue to process data if they have safeguarded their backup software and data bases.

Program Controls

Program controls verify that data are entered and processed properly and that the resultant information is correctly outputted. These controls are commonly referred to as input, processing, and output controls.

Input Controls.

Input controls represent some of the most vital controls, for they help ensure that the data that users enter into a system are correct. Input controls can include batch-control slips (in batch systems) and limit tests, which determine if the value entered in a field exceeds an established maximum. For example, a limit test for a payroll application could check weekly time card totals to ensure that no employee has more than, say, sixty work hours. Tests can also be performed to check whether the field data is numeric (as it is supposed to be), a field contains blanks, a field contains a positive or negative value, and an employee or entity on whom data are being recorded exists in the master file.

The program or module that contains the various program-control checks is usually called the "edit program" in a batch system and the "edit module" in a real-time system. Batch records found to contain errors are suspended from processing and recorded to a list of such records. In real-time processing, the computer usually displays the erroneous field with an error message so that the user can immediately make the requisite corrections.

Processing Controls. **Processing controls** provide evidence that data are being processed properly. A common processing control is the control total. A program generates a control total that the user can compare with the output of the previous step. The user can note and correct any discrepancies in the totals.

Other processing controls include external labeling on disks or tape. Proper labeling ensures that the user loads the right storage medium for a job.

Logic controls within a program make certain that key values in an application are reasonable. For example, it would be unreasonable for the inventory-on-hand value to be negative. If this occurred, the program would display an error message.

Output Controls. **Output controls** involve reconciling the control totals from one job step to another and scanning the output to make certain that the data were processed correctly. They can also involve delivering output to the authorized individual.

Documentation

Most people tend to think of documentation as a necessary evil, not as a control device. However, a system's documentation is one of the most important assets an organization has. It provides information on the analysis, design, and implementation of a system and serves as a reference source for the system's users. New employees can use system documentation as a training tool. Large organizations often maintain system documentation libraries.

Chapter Review

Ethical use of computers entails a wide variety of considerations. Educators are concerned with how to construct curriculums that will help students become computer literate. In the workplace, ethics make it incumbent on employers to provide safe and efficient computer environments for their employees. Ergonomically designed furniture and computer equipment can help companies realize this goal.

Computer crime is the commission of unlawful acts with computer hardware, software, or data. The most pervasive computer crime is software piracy—the illicit duplication of software.

Ethical software development calls for proper testing of new software; software that fails to perform as the developers promise can wreak harm on companies and society.

Privacy is the claim of individuals, groups, and institutions to determine for themselves when, how, and to what extent personal information about them is communicated to others. Computerization is making it increasingly difficult to ensure privacy. Innovations such as EFT systems and computer-record matching threaten to provide institutions with intimate details of our daily lives. The Fair Credit Reporting Act of 1970 and the Privacy Act of 1974 have played important roles in protecting the privacy of individuals.

Security and internal control systems protect a company's computer assets from theft or unauthorized use. These controls are divided into general controls, program controls, and documentation controls. The general controls are divided into access controls, hardware controls, organization controls, system controls, data and procedural controls, and hazard, or emergency, controls.

Key Terms and Concepts

access controls
Comprehensive Crime Control Act of 1984
computer crime
console log
copyright
data controls
electronic funds transfer (EFT)
ergonomics
ethics
Fair Credit Reporting Act of 1970
general controls
hardware controls
hazard controls

input controls
internal control
organization controls
output controls
privacy
Privacy Act of 1974
procedural controls
processing controls
program controls
security
software piracy
software virus
system controls

Chapter Quiz

Multiple Choice

1. Which of the following would not be considered to be an ethical concern related to computers?
   a. Coverage of computers in schools
   b. Coverage of computers in Sunday school
   c. The proper testing of software systems that deal with life-threatening applications
   d. The proper testing of a trial balance worksheet
   e. All of the above are of ethical concern.

2. Which of the following statements is false?
   a. Illegal copying of software is fine as long as it is only used at home.
   b. Software developers are protected by copyright and patent laws.
   c. Some software developers have banded together to find and prosecute people who illegally copy their software.
   d. All of the above statements are false.
   e. Only a and b are false.

3. Which of the following is *not* a characteristic of a typical computer criminal?
   a. The person is young.
   b. The person is suffering financial difficulty.
   c. The person's actions differ dramatically from their peers due to financial stress.
   d. The person has never been in trouble before.
   e. All of the above are characteristics of a computer criminal.

4. Which of the following presents a possible source of violation of privacy?
    a. Improper review of school records
    b. Improper use of credit information
    c. Access to EFT information
    d. None of the above
    e. All of the above

5. Maintaining and reviewing a console log is an example of which control?
    a. Access control
    b. Hardware control
    c. Organization control
    d. Systems control
    e. None of the above

True/False

6. Ethics applied to computers also involves concern with employees' welfare in the workplace.

7. The Privacy Act of 1974 applies to businesses as well as to the federal government.

8. A password is an example of the application of an access control.

9. Hazard controls involve contingency plans for making certain that an organization can still provide for information needs in the event of a natural disaster.

10. Documentation is not a form of internal control.

Answers

1. b 2. e 3. c 4. e 5. b 6. t 7. f 8. t 9. t 10. f

Exercises

1. Define the following terms:
    a. ethics   d. security
    b. ergonomics   e. internal control
    c. privacy

2. The term _____ refers to the computer keeping track of an employee's performance.

3. Furniture that is _____ helps to ease backache and muscle strain.

4. The term _____ refers to the illegal duplication of applications software.

5. The theft, attack, misappropriation, or misuse of computer hardware, software, or data is called _____.

6. Four characteristics common to computer criminals are
    a.

    b.

    c.

    d.

7. The claim of individuals to determine for themselves when, how, and to what extent information about them is communicated to others is known as _____.

8. The _____ is federal legislation that only applies to data banks maintained by the federal government.

9. *Griswold v. Connecticut* held that the right to privacy was implied in the _____ amendments of the Constitution.

10. _____ is the set of policies, procedures, and safeguards that are taken by an organization to protect its assets.

11. The three families of controls are
    a.

    b.

    c.

12. A locked door to the computer room is an example of a(n) _____ control.

13. A batch-control slip is an example of a(n) _____ control.

14. _____ controls provide for contingencies in the case of a natural disaster.

15. Making certain that testing is properly carried out is an example of a(n) _____ control.

16. A console log is an example of a(n) _____ control.

17. _____ controls verify that information is being entered, processed, and output properly in an application.

18. A(n) _____ control examines a document to ensure that calculations were properly performed.

19. A(n) _____ control ensures that the printouts are delivered to the appropriate person within an organization.

20. Besides describing a system, _____ is used as a training aid and a control.

Questions for Thought

1. Do you believe that it is ethical for companies to use a computer to make "cold" sales calls to prospective customers? Be certain to justify your response.

2. Prepare a paper on the impact of viruses on the computer and business sectors of our society. Find out which laws, if any, are being used to prosecute individuals who introduce viruses into a computer system.

3. Examine the regulations regarding software piracy at your institution. Should these rules be changed?

4. Conduct some research about what exactly constitutes "intellectual property." Based on this research, does your answer to question 3 change?

5. Should law enforcement agencies have ready access to data files from financial institutions, schools, or social agencies for use in attempting to locate lawbreakers or potential lawbreakers?

Chapter

22

Desktop Publishing

After completing this chapter, you should be able to:

Define desktop publishing

Describe the characteristics of desktop publishing

Describe the hardware needs of desktop publishing

Differentiate between the two types of laser printers

Differentiate between bit-mapped and formula-generated characters

Discuss the role of a scanner in a desktop-publishing system

Discuss the role of desktop-publishing software

The vice-president for the Western division of a nationwide real estate firm notifies a Seattle branch office she will be stopping by in two days to see how local sales are going. She asks the branch office broker to prepare a report on the office's sales. The broker compiles such information as area sales volumes, transaction prices, and local residential and commercial developments. He wants the report to include text, several charts, and a photograph of all the office agents who received awards at the annual Board of Realtors' banquet. There isn't the time or money to have the report prepared by a print shop, but the broker doesn't need one—his office has a desktop-publishing system. Within a day, the broker produces his report, which contains all the elements he wanted to include. The visiting vice-president is duly impressed by the professional quality of the broker's report.

Publishing is an expensive, time-consuming operation performed by specialized professionals. Or at least it was until the advent of microcomputer, or **desktop, publishing (DTP)**. Publishing a document by traditional methods requires a writer to write copy; an editor to review the copy for spelling, punctuation, and grammar; a graphic artist to design the document; a typesetter to typeset the text; a proofreader to review galley proofs for errors; and people to operate the printing presses. Today, a user with a mere semblance of artistic ability, a little publishing know-how, and access to a $5,000–$10,000 DTP system can be a publisher.

The potential market for desktop publishing is staggering. Nearly every company needs to produce or hire professionals to produce custom printed matter such as company brochures, catalogs, stationery, price lists, newsletters, financial reports, training manuals, and business cards. DTP systems have already saved the corporate world millions of dollars in professional printing costs. Industry pundits predict that demand for DTP systems will climb steeply for some years to come.

Desktop Publishing Defined

The term *desktop publishing* was coined by Paul Brainard, the entrepreneur who founded Aldus Corporation (developer of PageMaker software). DTP systems have the following characteristics:

They produce high-quality publications with microcomputer technology.

They merge text and graphics on the printed page.

They produce several type fonts (styles of typeface, such as Helvetica or Times Roman) and type sizes (measured in points; a point is $\frac{1}{72}$ inch).

They are affordable.

They can be used by individuals with minimal technical skills.

DTP has its detractors among professional publishers. To some of these people, who have high design and typographic standards, legions of desktop publishers are producing unappealing documents. These professionals are right to a degree. Although DTP systems offer considerable capabilities, the user still needs to acquire some publishing skills to produce attractive, readable publications. Aesthetic considerations, however, have done little to slow the growing use of DTP systems by churches, schools, public relations firms, advertising agencies, and quick-print shops.

Hardware for Desktop Publishing

DTP systems require a computer with high-speed processing power and enough storage capacity to handle large programs and voluminous data. Accordingly, a user who plans on assembling a DTP system should select a computer with at least the power of an AT (a much faster version of the IBM PC)

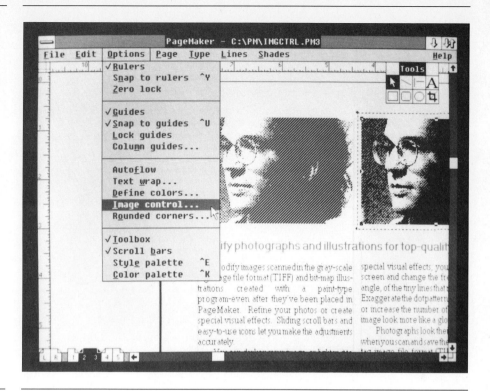

and a minimum of 2 megabytes of RAM. Running a DTP program on the relatively slow PC tends to try the user's patience.

The monitor screen of a DTP system should be sophisticated enough to display both an entire page and a blown-up portion of text (Figure 22.1). This is especially true with DTP programs that provide what-you-see-is-what-you-get, or WYSIWYG (pronounced "wizzy-wig"), capability. WYSIWYG software displays to the screen exactly what a document being worked on would look like if printed.

Other useful additions to a DTP system include a fixed disk, a mouse, a scanner, and a laser printer. A fixed disk's larger storage capacity enables users to piece together publications quickly and easily. Laser printers and scanners are especially helpful in producing publications with high-quality graphics.

Laser Printers

Two laser printers, Apple's LaserWriter and Hewlett-Packard's LaserJet, have set the market's standards for DTP system printers.

Hewlett-Packard LaserJet. In 1985 Hewlett-Packard introduced its LaserJet, the market's first **laser printer**. Quiet in operation and able to print 300 dpi (dots-per-inch) resolution, the LaserJet was heralded as the high-tech replacement for slow, noisy daisy-wheel printers. It could print eight pages of letter-quality text per minute and had two resident fonts, Courier 10 pitch and 16 pitch. The LaserJet's success prompted other computer manufacturers to rush their own laser printers to market. Competitors enticed consumers to buy their machines by offering multiple fonts and type sizes.

In 1987 Hewlett-Packard discontinued its LaserJet and introduced the LaserJet II, which has 512K of memory. Hewlett-Packard made, and most users

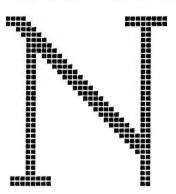

Figure 22.2
An example of a character generated via a bit map. Bit-mapped fonts consist of characters that have been drawn pixel by pixel—like this 12-point *N*—to be printed at a specific resolution, in this case 300 dpi.

purchased, the LaserJet II for printing letter-quality, word processed documents quickly and quietly. However, users quickly discovered that the LaserJet II was an excellent printer for DTP systems.

Both LaserJet printers produce **bit-mapped**, or dot-pattern, **fonts**. Hewlett-Packard wired different styles, sizes, and orientations of Courier characters into the ROM of each machine (Figure 22.2). To print in typefaces other than those residing in the LaserJet's ROM, the user has to download additional fonts into the printer's RAM or plug a special font cartridge into the computer.

Downloading fonts into a printer reduces the amount of RAM the machine can use for printing text and graphics. This is of particular concern with laser printers, which produce an entire page at once and must have all of a page's text in memory before printing. If the LaserJet's RAM is too full to accept an entire page's worth of data from the computer, the printer outputs the text or graphic it has in memory and prints any left-over material on a second page.

A printer with limited RAM also can be overloaded by high-resolution graphics, which are very data-rich. For example, the LaserJet II, with only 512K of memory, is not capable of printing a full-page graphic at 300 dpi—such a piece contains too much information. Only by reducing the LaserJet II's printing resolution to 70–150 dpi (about the quality of a standard dot-matrix printer) will the user be able to print the page.

Hewlett-Packard's printers generate characters with **page control language (PCL)**, a simple language designed to load bit-mapped fonts and graphics into the printer. Characters created in this control language cannot be scaled or manipulated in the printer; the user must perform these operations with the application software. Accordingly, the user's application software must have a special driver for the LaserJet in order to output on the laser printer.

Apple LaserWriter. Shortly after the LaserJet appeared on the market, Apple introduced its LaserWriter. This printer has thirteen resident fonts, 1.5 megabytes of RAM, and can generate high-quality graphics and a wide range of character sizes.

LaserWriter characters vary dramatically from the LaserJet's. Instead of bit-mapped fonts, the Laser-Writer uses mathematical descriptions of the various arcs, circles, and straight lines that make up each character (Figure 22.3). Because it stores characters as mathematical descriptions, the LaserWriter must process a considerable amount of information before printing a page of text or graphics. That is why the LaserWriter has so much RAM. However, Apple's method of producing characters and graphics permits the user to size and rotate material to be printed more easily than does bit-mapping production.

The LaserWriter uses a **page description language (PDL)**, developed by Adobe Systems, Inc., called **PostScript**. This language sends a whole page's

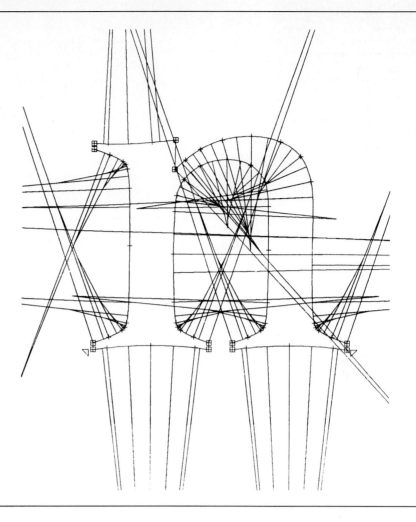

worth of information to the printer at a time, which complements perfectly the full-page output method of laser printers.

The LaserWriter has proved very successful in DTP. In fact, Apple was the first company to market an entire DTP system, which includes the LaserWriter, Macintosh microcomputer, and page-composition software. As a result, many manufacturers have introduced printers that rely on PostScript, which has become a standard PDL for word processors, graphics packages, spreadsheets, and other applications. The LaserWriter (or other PostScript printer) accepts print instructions from any application software that has a PostScript driver—a program that converts the software's instructions into PostScript messages the printer can use. The application software sends document data through a PostScript device driver, which encodes the data into the proper format and routes it to the printer's PostScript interpreter. The printer then builds the document's image into its RAM (Figure 22.4).

Scanners

Scanners are light-sensing devices that digitize (convert into bit-mapped images) paper-based drawings and photographs and store them to a computer file. The user can then resize, rotate, or modify the stored images with a graphics-editor package. Finished images can be inserted into a DTP document to add appeal and information.

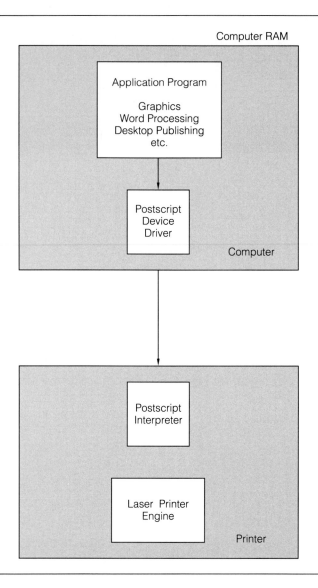

A package like Publisher's Paintbrush by Z-Soft Corporation can be used both to control a scanner during the digitization process and to modify the scanned image. Figure 22.5 depicts a photograph of a Seagate fixed disk. The scanned image of this photograph, created in under two minutes using Publisher's Paintbrush and an AST TurboScan scanner by AST Research, Inc., appears in Figure 22.6.

Most scanners are sold with software that performs the digitizing process. Users also can drive a scanner with an **optical character recognition (OCR)** program, which scans printed material and stores it to a word processing file. OCR software can save a user hours of manually typing in text. However, most OCR software can only read specific fonts; files created by scanning inappropriate type styles will contain a high number of errors.

Scanners have two "reading" modes: **bi-level**, which only scans black and white, and **dither**, which digitizes a range of grays. The user issues the appropriate scanner command on the computer. Bi-level mode works well for line graphics such as found in simple charts. When reading a graphic in bi-level mode, the scanner compares each bit with a value. Bits above the value are rendered in black; those that are below, in white (Figure 22.7).

Figure 22.5
A picture of a Seagate fixed disk about to be scanned. (Courtesy of Seagate)

Figure 22.6
The scanned image of the Seagate fixed disk.

Figure 22.7
A scanned line image.

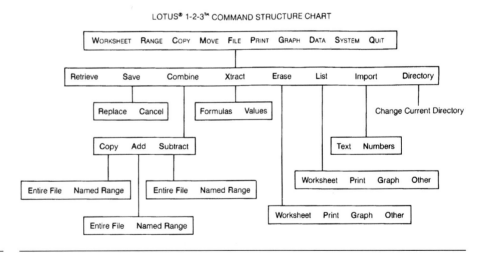

A user must select the dither mode when scanning photographs and other complex graphics composed of grays. In dither mode, a scanner represents grays as patterns of white and black dots, just as newspaper photographs do. The dots give the image a slightly grainy appearance. The poorer a photograph's resolution, the grainier will be its scanned image.

Software for Desktop Publishing

Among the most popular DTP software packages on the market are PageMaker by Aldus Corporation, Xerox Ventura Publisher by Xerox Corporation, GEM Desktop Publisher by Digital Research, and the Office Publisher by Laser Friendly.

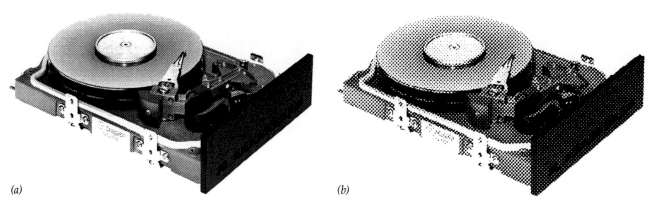

(a)   *(b)*

Figure 22.8
The Seagate fixed-disk photograph (a) at 200 dpi and (b) at 100 dpi resolution.

Most DTP packages are basically page-composition tools that permit users to electronically assemble text and graphics. They offer text- and graphics-formatting commands, rudimentary text editing (for making corrections or typing in phrases), and limited graphic capabilities for embellishing assembled documents. Typically, users don't draft text and graphics on a DTP program but, rather, import them from special application programs.

For example, although text can be typed directly into a DTP file, the user is better off composing copy on a high-end word processor that offers such editing features as thesaurus, spelling checker, and search and replace—features that most DTP packages don't have. Similarly, the user might create needed graphics with a paint program. After storing the text and graphics to a DTP program, the user can call up the material and assemble it to create a document (Figure 22.9). Most DTP programs have a zoom feature with which the user can inspect specific document sections to ensure that they are properly assembled.

Future DTP programs will likely do away with much of the need to import text and graphics. Soon desktop publishers may be able to use DTP packages alone to create all the text and graphics they need for many kinds of documents.

Let's take a brief look at **PageMaker** for the IBM PC. Introduced in 1985 for the Apple Macintosh, PageMaker was the first true WYSIWYG DTP package developed for microcomputers. The WYSIWYG feature, which instantly displays all document changes to the screen, makes PageMaker very user-friendly and is now used by many software manufacturers.

In some non-WYSIWYG DTP packages, such as Fancy Font by SoftCraft, Inc., typed codes replace the mouse and menus for positioning and formatting text. These programs provide at best an approximate preview of how the final document will look. However, they do offer some advantages. For example, they automatically create indexes, footnotes, and tables of contents and are ideal for publications requiring a consistent appearance throughout, such as books. Nevertheless, novice desktop publishers who want an easy-to-learn DTP package and users (such as graphic artists) who need a detailed screen display of a document usually find their needs are better met by WYSIWYG programs.

Document Design

Before laying out text and graphics with a DTP system, the desktop publisher needs to formulate a rough idea of how the finished document should look. This is done in the document-design step, in which the user decides the following:

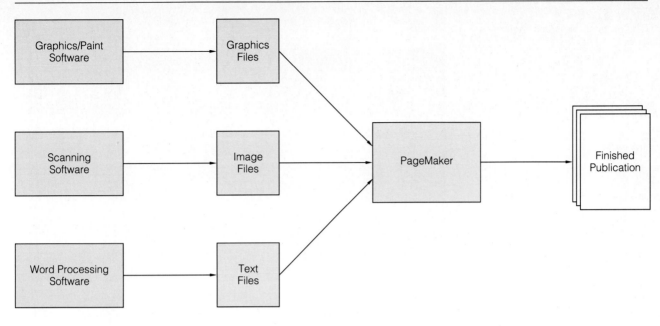

Figure 22.9
The files involved in desktop publishing.

What size paper will be used.

Whether the pages will be single- or double-sided (printed on one side or both sides).

What elements will appear on each page. That is, whether footers, headers, lines between columns, and so forth are required.

How many columns each page will have.

Whether to print the pages in tall-and-narrow (**portrait**) or short-and-wide (**landscape**) format.

What fonts and type sizes to use for headings, captions, and body text.

Desktop publishers can turn to a number of reference books for guidance on document design. One of the most basic design rules is that no more than two fonts should be used to create a document's text—too many type styles will visually confuse the reader. A good way to avoid design problems is to have a professional create a document model. The desktop publisher follows the model's typeface specifications, general layout, and other design characteristics (such as borders and embellishments) but changes the text and graphics as needed.

After formulating a rough idea of what the finished document should look like, the user assembles and manipulates the text and graphics with DTP software. With PageMaker, the screen serves as a drawing board on which the user can organize the document's components (Figure 22.10). This drawing board identifies and displays the document being built.

How much of a PageMaker document can be read at any one time depends on the type of screen the user's DTP system has. A large-screen, or full-page, monitor lets the user read an entire 8½ × 11½–inch page without scrolling. On a standard-size screen, the user has to zoom in on the page to read text—a document displayed in actual size will have its text shown in **"greeked,"** or simulated, form (Figure 22.11).

The PageMaker screen also has a series of pull-down menus containing commands with which the user can manipulate the document's elements. An

Figure 22.10
The parts of the PageMaker screen.

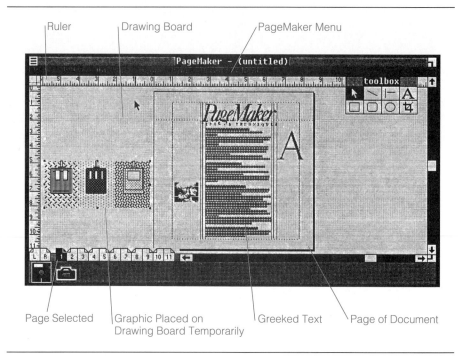

Ruler   Drawing Board   PageMaker Menu

Page Selected   Graphic Placed on Drawing Board Temporarily   Greeked Text   Page of Document

Figure 22.11
A document viewed using the Actual Size command.

on-screen ruler, for measuring and aligning text and graphics, appears at the top and along the left side of the screen. A **toolbox** containing several graphic-design tools sits in the screen's upper right-hand corner. The area around the document is the **pasteboard**. The pasteboard is like the work table surrounding the pages being worked on. Text and graphics may be moved off the page and put on the pasteboard, where they stay until they are needed. Numbers at the bottom of the screen tell what pages are being displayed. Figure 22.12 shows an example of a finished document that was created using PageMaker's tutorial.

Chapter Review

Desktop publishing has had a dramatic impact on all types of organizations. DTP allows users to generate professional-looking documents at a fraction of the cost of traditional publishing methods. DTP systems have the following characteristics: They use microcomputer technology, they offer a variety of

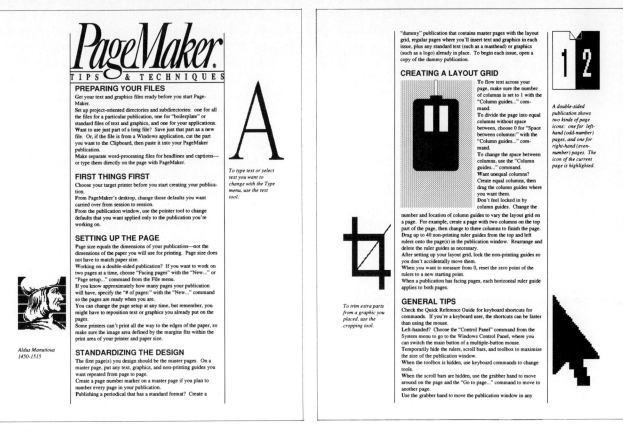

Figure 22.12
This finished document was created with PageMaker's tutorial. (Courtesy of Aldus Corporation)

fonts and type sizes, they merge text and graphics into one document, they are affordable (typical systems cost $5,000–$10,000), and they can be used by individuals who have minimal publishing skills.

Hardware requirements for a DTP system include a high-quality monitor, fixed disk, mouse, laser printer, scanner, and a computer with at least the power of an AT-class machine and 2 megabytes of RAM.

Laser printers come in two classes: those that support PostScript printing and those that do not. Printers that support PostScript define text characters as mathematical formulas. Other printers use a bit-mapping scheme to generate characters. Users can augment the selection of type styles that can be outputted on a bit-mapped printer by loading extra fonts into the machine's RAM.

Users can incorporate line drawings and photographs into a DTP document by digitizing them with a scanner. When driven by optical character recognition (OCR) software, scanners can read paper-based text and store it to a word processing package. A user must set a scanner in dither mode, which renders shades of gray into black-and-white dot patterns, to digitize photographs.

DTP software enables users to combine word processing text files, scanned images, and graphics created with a paint program into a single, high-quality document. The user can manipulate these materials until the document looks just right. Many DTP packages display a document to the screen exactly the way it will look when printed.

Before assembling a document with a DTP package, the user needs to formulate a rough idea of what the document should look like. This entails deciding what size paper to use, how many columns will be on each page, the width of the margins, and so on. A standard publishing design rule is that only two fonts should be used to construct a document's text. To make their work easier and their finished publications more attractive, desktop publishers can base their document's design on a professionally made model.

Key Terms and Concepts

bi-level mode	page control language (PCL)
bit-mapped font	page description language (PDL)
desktop publishing (DTP)	PageMaker
dither mode	pasteboard
greeked text	portrait format
landscape format	PostScript
laser printer	scanner
optical character recognition (OCR)	toolbox

Chapter Quiz

Multiple Choice

1. Which of the following characteristics do *not* apply to desktop publishing?
   a. Ability to use microcomputer hardware
   b. Ability to merge text with graphics
   c. Requires an expert in graphic design
   d. Ability to support multiple fonts and type sizes
   e. All of the above are characteristics of desktop publishing.

2. Which of the following hardware is usually *not* associated with desktop publishing?
   a. Fixed disk
   b. Mouse
   c. Scanner
   d. Laser printer without graphics capability
   e. All of the above are associated with desktop publishing.

3. Which of the following statements about laser printers is false?
   a. Only bit-mapped printers can generate graphics.
   b. A PostScript printer takes less time to generate a page than do other laser printers.
   c. A bit-mapped character is generated using mathematical formulas.
   d. None of the above are false.
   e. All of the above are false.

4. Which of the following statements about PostScript printers is true?
   a. Text cannot be rotated on a page.
   b. A software package generating output must have a PostScript printer driver.
   c. An interpreter to evaluate instructions to the printer is not required.
   d. All of the above are false.
   e. Only b and c are true.

5. What software packages can be used to prepare files for a document?
   a. Paint/draw programs
   b. Word processing programs

    c. Scanning software
    d. All of the above
    e. None of the above

True/False

6. Desktop-publishing packages can be used by people with limited graphic design background.

7. A scanner allows you to scan only a line image or a photograph.

8. PostScript printers allow you to have any size character without loading a new bit map for the characters to be printed.

9. Scanning software many times allows you to control the quality of the scanned image.

10. The pasteboard allows you to temporarily store an image or text.

Answers

1. c 2. d 3. e 4. b 5. d 6. t 7. f 8. t 9. t 10. t

Exercises

1. Define the following terms:
    a. desktop publishing   c. laser printer
    b. bit-mapped font   d. PageMaker

2. The market for desktop publishing is expected to ＿＿＿＿＿＿＿＿ over the next few years.

3. A person with a ＿＿＿＿＿＿＿＿ of skills can use a desktop-publishing system.

4. A ＿＿＿＿＿＿＿＿ is a device which can be used to digitize images.

5. A ＿＿＿＿＿＿＿＿ monitor allows you to see an entire page of a document on the screen at a time.

6. The first laser printers were introduced by the companies ＿＿＿＿＿＿ and ＿＿＿＿＿＿.

7. A character that is described to the printer according to the dots needed to make that character is called a ＿＿＿＿＿＿＿＿ printer.

8. The language that is used to describe a character to a printer via mathematical formulas is called a(n) ＿＿＿＿＿＿＿＿.

9. The LaserWriter uses a language called ＿＿＿＿＿＿＿＿, developed by Adobe Systems, to describe characters.

10. Laser printers print a ＿＿＿＿＿＿＿＿ of text/graphics at a time.

11. A graphics laser printer requires more ＿＿＿＿＿＿＿＿ than does a laser printer that prints only text.

12. The scanner software that is used to read text from a page is called ＿＿＿＿ software.

13. ＿＿＿＿＿＿＿＿ mode is used by a scanner to represent various shades of gray.

14. Various applications packages that can be used to prepare files for processing using PageMaker are

    a.

    b.

    c.

15. Simulated text on a PageMaker screen is called _____ text.

Questions for Thought

1. Prepare a list of applications for which desktop publishing can be used.

2. Compare and contrast the recent releases of PageMaker and Ventura Publisher. Which package would be best suited to your needs?

3. Find an article from one of the microcomputer journals (*Infoworld*, for example) that compares desktop-publishing packages. Which one appears to you to be most useable?

4. Prepare a report that examines the use of fonts as a means of attracting and then holding the user's interest.

5. Prepare a report dealing with the latest technology available for laser printers. How will this new technology affect the area of desktop publishing?

Future Trends

Chapter Objectives

After completing this chapter, you should be able to:

Define artificial intelligence

Discuss the role of expert systems

Discuss the three ways of building an expert system

Discuss the importance of fifth-generation machines

Discuss the impact of changes in communications technology

Discuss the impact of computers on the individual

Artificial Intelligence

The term *artificial intelligence* was coined by John McCarthy for the theme of a 1956 conference held at Dartmouth College. Ever since that conference, the subject of artificial intelligence has produced intense debate in the computer and scientific community over what the term really means. A common definition says **artificial intelligence (AI)** is the attempt to construct computer-based hardware/software systems that think like a human being.

Artificial intelligence is composed of four different research areas:

Natural Languages. These are computer systems that can translate ordinary human commands (natural language) into a code that a computer program can understand and execute.

Robotics. These are machines that move and manipulate objects in the same manner humans do.

Visualization Systems. These are machines that can picture or visualize their environment as humans do.

Expert Systems. These are programs that mimic the decision-making processes of humans who are acquainted intimately with an application.

Developing AI is particularly daunting because scientists do not fully comprehend natural intelligence, that is, how humans think and reason. We don't understand, for instance, why one person can almost instantly intuit the correct solution to a complex problem whereas someone else may take a long time to arrive at a totally different solution. Consider, too, how difficult it would be to program a very human intellectual capacity like common sense, which enables us to act in a reasonable, intelligent fashion and in accordance with social custom.

Natural Language

AI experts design artificial-intelligence systems to interact with humans in natural languages. In human terms, a **natural language** is one that can be used and understood by people on a daily basis, such as Spanish, English, Japanese, German, or Hindi. Applied to computers, it is a language easily understood by both humans and the computer. An example of the latter is CLOUT (Figure 23.1).

Robotics

Computers have proved tremendously successful in manufacturing, aiding in all aspects of the process, including data gathering, information processing, and inventory and production control. Production has been revolutionized by robots, machines that are controlled by microcomputers (Figure 23.2).

Typically, industrial robots are stationary and have a single, jointed arm ending in a gripping device. They are frequently used to work metal in such applications as automobile production and can cost-effectively perform precise, repetitive operations such as welding, painting, or loading and unloading parts.

Vision and Sensing Systems

Vision or sensing systems can discern an object's location, form, size, or color. They also process and interpret images to identify them. Manufacturers employ such systems to sort parts or inspect products for quality control.

Figure 23.1
Examples of a natural-language query processed by CLOUT in an add-in package for RBASE.

```
SHOW ME THE EMPLOYEES

Jones
Adams
Smith
Hunt
Lora

SORT THEM BY NAME

Adams
Hunt
Jones
Lora
Smith

JUST THE ONES WITH GROSS GREATER THAN 260

EMPLOYEE      GROSS
Jones         279.50
Hunt          289.50
```

Figure 23.2
An example of the use of robots in the manufacturing process. (Courtesy of Chrysler Corporation)

The primary item a sensing system needs is a videocamera. A digitizer converts the camera's analog image into digital code, which the software processes in a series of steps designed to identify the image. In the feature-detection step, the computer attempts to detect the edges, corners, and regions of the digitized image. The computer tries to classify these features in general ways in the perceptual step. Finally, the computer performs a pattern-matching step, which identifies the object as a specific entity.

Experts predict the next major step will be providing robots with visual and sensing capabilities (Figure 23.3). Vision systems can use standard TV cameras to scan objects and direct robots. Robots with sensing capabilities

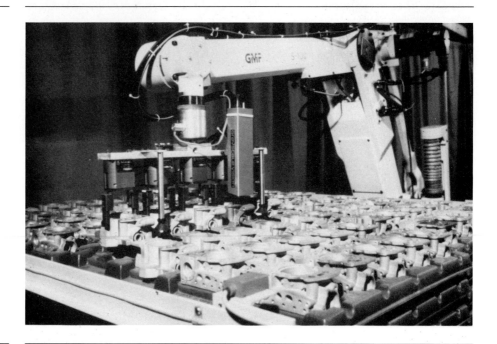

already carry out such dangerous duties as examining nuclear reactor cores
and guarding industrial plants. Sensing robots also are used in quality-control
processes such as inspecting welds for faults.

AI engineers predict robots will eventually assume many of the jobs people dislike—work that is dull, dirty, dangerous, or demeaning.

AI research has had a checkered history. Years after the initial brouhaha
about the potential of AI, researchers in the field still had not designed a system
of real use to the corporate world. One problem that has stymied AI success is
the typical computer's lack of speed and memory. AI researchers also find it
difficult to formulate problems in ways that computers can address.

Expert Systems

One of the first really useful applications of artificial intelligence has been in
the area of expert systems. An **expert system** is software that employs knowledge or rules of action that have been supplied by a human who is considered
an expert in some field. Expert systems represent a small but very marketable
subset of AI. Two major parts of an expert system are the inference engine and
the knowledge base (Figure 23.4).

One of the first applications that AI experts examined using expert systems was the game of chess. AI experts soon discovered it is impossible to
construct a computer fast enough to consider every one of the astronomical
number of moves possible at each turn at play in chess. AI experts solved this
problem by programming chess-playing computers with heuristic expert-
system programs. Heuristics examines the rules which permit a human or
computer to limit the number of alternative actions that need to be considered
in performing a task. The heuristic chess game programs rely on "rules of
thumb" to limit alternatives and "decide" what actions to take. Today, chess
programs can play at a master-player level.

Although decisions made by chess programs cannot be readily applied
to the real world, the research used to develop such programs can be applied

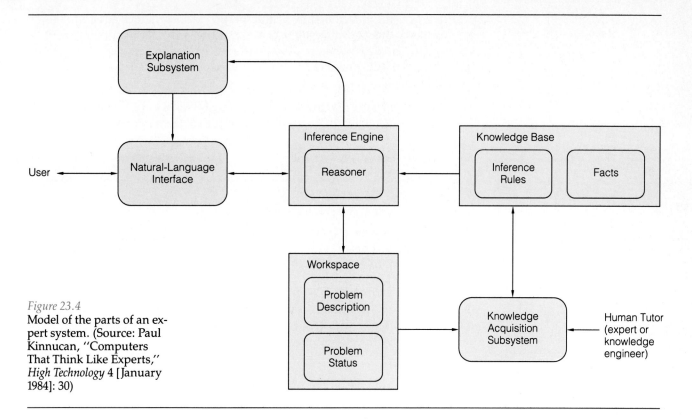

Figure 23.4
Model of the parts of an expert system. (Source: Paul Kinnucan, "Computers That Think Like Experts," *High Technology* 4 [January 1984]: 30)

to decision-making support systems. The goal of these expert-support systems is to provide vast stores of specialized knowledge to which users can refer when making decisions.

This goal is realized in two ways. First, these systems help the user analyze data and problems. Second, they recommend solutions to the user who has limited experience in a field. The program's expert advice actually comes from rules and knowledge provided by fully experienced professionals; this human knowledge is converted into an expert-system program. In effect, a novice can "consult" an expert-system program as if he or she were asking a venerable professional for step-by-step assistance with a problem.

Applications

Expert systems can help businesses in a number of ways. They can preserve knowledge that otherwise may be lost when a key expert in a field retires. They can form a knowledge base that many different employees can access. And they are not subject to such human frailties as boredom, stress, and worry, nor will they panic in a crisis.

Expert systems by their very nature can only be applied to a problem of narrow scope. Examples of successful expert systems include the following:

Delta, developed by General Electric in the early 1980s, is a railroad application that helps maintenance workers identify and correct malfunctions in diesel locomotives.

Dendral, developed at Stanford University, is a chemistry-expert system that estimates the molecular structures of unknown compounds by analyzing mass spectrographs, nuclear magnetic resonance, and other data.

DIPMETER, developed by Schlumberger, Ltd., provides advice to oil drillers when a drilling bit becomes stuck in rock. The company spent more than $20 million to develop the system but expects to quickly recoup the cost because it loses more than $100,000 a day while a drill is inoperative.

Mycin, developed at Stanford University Medical Experimental Computer Facility in the mid-1970s, is a medical-expert system. It diagnoses and prescribes treatments for meningitis and bacteremia infections.

PROSPECTOR was developed for the U.S. Geological Survey as an aid in mineral exploration.

XSEL, developed by Digital Equipment Corporation, assists sales representatives in specifying VAX computer configurations for customers. This program has boosted configuration accuracy from 75 percent to 95 percent and saves Digital $10 million a year.

By some estimates, U.S. corporations use more than a thousand types of expert systems. Applications run the gamut from helping oil companies find oil- and gas-reserve sites to assisting IRS personnel in providing answers to callers who have questions about their taxes.

Obtaining an Expert System

An organization can obtain an expert system in three ways: by purchasing a fully developed system, by purchasing an expert-system shell, and by custom building an expert system.

Purchase. Expert systems require computers with fast processors and sizable memories. At first, AI experts assumed that only mainframe computers would be able to fulfill these requirements. However, today's more powerful micro-computer is fully capable of supporting an expert system.

The corporate world has embraced expert systems not only for their application benefits but also because these benefits are offered in user-friendly programs and at affordable prices. Prices for expert-system packages start as low as $100, and most systems are easy to operate. The popularity of expert systems also stems from the impressive amount of power they put in the hands of the user, who, with minimal software understanding, can obtain expert knowledge to help solve problems.

Expert-System Shells. Although its software may be easy to use, an expert system is tediously complex to construct. Many users ease the task by starting with a software shell—a logically arranged software to which the user writes application rules and knowledge using a natural language. The application-directed statements form the shell's expert data, which the user can later consult to solve problems.

An example of an **expert-system shell** is VP-Expert by Paperback Software. This software package allows the user to represent knowledge in "If-Then" rules. VP-Expert has an inference engine that can process two or more facts, implications, or relationships to form a conclusion. The engine processes data by inserting them forward or backward through the multiple "If-Then" rules written by the user. For example, a doctor may ask his or her VP-Expert system what sort of disease afflicts a patient with edema in one leg, sore joints, and needling pain in one foot. The program inserts these data into its "If-Then" rules to deduce what possible diseases the patient may have.

Building an Expert System. The most expensive way to obtain an expert system is to have one custom built. Only large companies can afford to do this and only for important applications. Custom expert systems are built by knowledge engineers, who use many of the same methods as systems analysts. The knowledge engineer interviews the expert(s), develops the decision rules, and builds the expert system. Performing these steps requires skills in interpersonal communication, psychology, learning theory, and programming. Finally, the knowledge engineer builds the system, using a shell or a programming language such as LISP or PROLOG.

If an application is limited enough, a sophisticated expert system can aid the user in the decision-making process.

Fifth-Generation Computers

Three technologic giants—the United States, Western Europe, and Japan—are vying to be the first to produce and market **fifth-generation computers**. If expectations are realized, this equipment will incorporate many AI features including:

The ability to process data in natural languages. Users will give their instructions to the machine in a humanlike language.

The ability to receive input in vocal, graphic, or document form.

Extremely user-friendly features.

Learning, association, and inference capabilities that enable computers to approach problem solving much like humans do and provide humans considerable decision-making assistance.

Experts predict these future machines will be many times faster than existing hardware (some estimates range up to 10,000 times faster!) and capable of accessing several billion bytes of storage.

One of the major weaknesses of existing hardware is its time-consuming method of processing data. Instructions and data are shunted a piece at a time from main storage to the control unit and then passed back to storage along a single link or bus. Such a design forces the computer to execute one instruction at a time, although it could process several at once (in parallel mode). This drawback is often referred to as the "von Neumann bottleneck" after the father of modern computer architecture (see Chapter 1). Computer engineers hope to resolve this problem by using VLSI (very large-scale integrated) circuitry containing thousands of processors on a single chip. A computer composed of VLSI chips will be able to process numerous instructions in parallel.

Although some of this futuristic hardware is already being produced (see Chapter 1 and the discussion of the "hypercube"), today's software still cannot handle data dependencies. Systems software and applications programs have to be reengineered so that required data are present when needed. When perfected, this technology promises to have a tremendous impact on computer hardware and information-processing systems.

Communications Technology

Until the mid-1980s, there were few links between the communications and computer business sectors. However, this changed dramatically with the introduction of fiber-optic technology and the revamping of government regulations.

Impact of Fiber Optics

Thanks to the introduction of fiber-optic networks by telephone companies, communication between distant computers is rapidly improving. Before the advent of fiber-optic technology, computer-generated digital signals had to be converted into analog signals, transmitted, and reconverted into digital signals at the receiving end. No signal conversion is needed if the transmission is sent over fiber-optic cables, which carry digital signals.

Due to their larger bandwidth, fiber-optic cables can transmit many more bits of information per second than can copper cables. This capability enables users to send such bit-dense transmissions as pictures or graphics.

Changes in Government Regulation

In 1984 a Supreme Court decision forced AT&T to split into several regional, regulated telephone companies. AT&T lost its decades-long monopoly on telephone lines. But the decision also freed AT&T to enter the computer market, and for the first time the distinction between communications companies and computer companies became blurred. IBM and AT&T now compete in both fields. IBM, through ownership in Satellite Business Systems, supplies business with both communication equipment and satellite-communications services.

Impact on the Individual

One of the greatest social impacts produced by computers is the reduced availability of minimal skill jobs. For example, computers have greatly lessened the demand for manufacturing and entry-level clerical workers. On the other hand, available manufacturing and clerical jobs now tend to be more enriching and challenging. This trend is expected to continue.

Jobs requiring computer skills are supplanting many employment positions. One study by Porat showed that more than 50 percent of all jobs deal with the production or dissemination of information.

This increasing emphasis on information processing not only will change what many of us do for a living but also our work habits. In the near future, employees who perform information processing will likely have more say about their working hours. For example, one person may decide to work from 6:00 A.M. to 2:00 P.M., while another person may elect to work from 10:00 A.M. to 6:00 P.M.

Many workers may not have to show up at the office at all, opting instead to work at home and interact with the company by microcomputer in a process known as **telecommuting**. Telecommuting is expected to rise in popularity, but in most professions workers will still need to interact in person to get the job done.

Impact on Hardware

Hardware for fifth-generation computers will be "bigger, faster, but smaller." The phrase means computers will have greater storage capacities, faster processors, and smaller dimensions.

Computers have almost entirely automated the process of computer-chip design. Tasks that used to be performed by software can now be automatically "wired" into a chip. For example, new computers do not need software instructions on how to boot if the information is already wired into the computer's ROM. Eventually, the computer scientist will need only to select and install the right circuits to equip a computer for a particular application.

In a few years, users will find video disks, as exemplified by CD ROM, offered at affordable retail prices. Video disks that can read from, be written to, and erased also will be available, providing the microcomputer user with billions of bytes of secondary storage instead of just millions.

Chapter Review

Artificial intelligence is the attempt to develop computer-based systems that think like human beings. Such systems depend on natural languages for easy communication between the computer and human beings. The history of AI has been checkered by high expectations, disappointments, and some successes.

Expert systems represent the first successful application of AI. An expert system is a software-based system that has been programmed to use knowledge or rules of action formulated by a human expert in a particular field. Expert systems were first designed to provide decision-making support in playing the game of chess. Computer experts used heuristics, which examines rules that reduce the number of alternative actions to be considered, to design these chess-playing computers.

Expert systems have been applied to a number of different areas. One goal of an expert system may be to store the expertise of a key employee who is due to retire. Today, corporations use more than 1,000 different types of expert systems. Many of these are used as extensions of decision-support systems.

There are three ways to obtain an expert system: purchase it, design it with an expert-system shell, or hire a knowledge engineer to custom build it.

Key Terms and Concepts

artificial intelligence (AI)
expert system
expert-system shell

fifth-generation computers
natural language
telecommuting

Chapter Quiz

Multiple Choice

1. Which of the following statements about artificial intelligence is (are) false?
   a. Artificial intelligence has been a success from the initial conference held in 1956.
   b. The basic premise of artificial intelligence is that a machine can be made to behave like a human being.
   c. A hard characteristic to incorporate into artificial intelligence is common sense.
   d. Heuristics involves limiting the number of possible actions.
   e. All of the above are true statements.

2. Expert systems have the following characteristics:
   a. They can be applied to a narrow, well-defined area.
   b. They can be used to assist a decision maker in the decision-making process.
   c. They rely on experts to provide the information that is used to make decisions.
   d. They work best for low-level types of decisions.
   e. All of the above are characteristics of expert systems.

3. Which of the following is not part of an artificial-intelligence research area?
   a. Natural language
   b. Expert systems
   c. Robotics
   d. Touch sensitive
   e. All of the above are part of artificial intelligence.

4. Which of the following allows easy communication with a computer?
   a. Language algorithms
   b. Natural language
   c. Pseudo language
   d. Expert language
   e. None of the above

5. Which of the following has had an impact on communications technology?
   a. The divestiture of AT&T
   b. The digital characteristics of fiber optics
   c. The wide bandwidth of fiber optics
   d. b and c only
   e. All of the above

True/False

6. A knowledge engineer has the skills required to build an expert system from scratch.

7. Expert systems can best be used on small, easy-to-define tasks.

8. The jobs related to information processing are not quickly increasing in number.

9. Fiber optics allows only analog data transmission.

10. Entry-level jobs are becoming more and more technical, requiring computer skills.

Answers

1. a   2. e   3. d   4. b   5. e   6. t   7. t   8. f   9. f   10. t

Exercises

1. The process of trying to make a computer function or act as a human is called the study of _____.

2. The process of examining rules to limit the number of alternative actions is called _____.

3. The ability to communicate with an artificial-intelligence device so that communication between the device and a human can easily occur utilizes a _____ language.

4. A software system that has been programmed to use rules of action that have been supplied by an expert human is called a(n) _____.

5. The expert system _____ is used to diagnose and prescribe treatment for meningitis.

6. The three methods of obtaining an expert system include
   a.

   b.

   c.

7. The four research parts of artificial intelligence are
   a.

   b.

   c.

   d.

8. About _____ percent of employees are involved with processing information.

9. The _____ cable allows both analog and digital data transmission.

10. The company that was most affected by the 1984 communications divestiture decision was _____.

Questions for Thought

1. In what manner should experts in a content area be rewarded for their participation in providing the knowledge necessary for driving an expert system? Should this work be considered to be just part of their job? Should they receive a royalty every time a copy of this expert system is sold?

2. Prepare a report on uses of expert systems and their application to business-related problems.

3. Prepare a report on the impact of the computer on the individual in today's society.

4. Discuss the negative and positive impacts of computer technology on our society. As you carry on your discussion, be sure to keep a list of the positive as well as the negative points.

5. Prepare a report on the current status of the development of fifth-generation computers.

Appendix
A

Instructions for
Using Educational
Versions of Software

Introduction

The diskettes provided by Wadsworth Publishing Company that accompany the textbook *Four Software Tools Plus* contain the educational versions of WordPerfect 4.2, VP-Planner Plus, and dBASE III Plus. **The educational versions differ from the business versions in the following ways:**

WordPerfect 4.2   The characters *WP occasionally appear in a document when it is printed using the training version of WordPerfect. Files size is limited to 50,000 characters; some print commands have been disabled. The Merge feature is not included, and the Help feature shows only the function keys. The Speller and Thesaurus options are limited to the README file contained on the WordPerfect program disk. Otherwise, the training version of WordPerfect contains all of the features of the business edition.

VP-Planner Plus   The spreadsheet contains all of the spreadsheet capabilities except the multidimensional data base ability. The student version allows 64 columns and 256 rows.

dBASE III Plus   The word (demo) appears before the dot prompt. The student version of dBASE III Plus limits a file to 31 records.

IMPORTANT! When you want to leave WordPerfect, always use the proper Exit method. Remove the WordPerfect program disk only when the DOS prompt (A>, B>, C>, or D>) appears on the screen. If you remove the program disk while the computer is running, you can destroy the disk.

If you turn off the computer without properly exiting WordPerfect, unallocated clusters (sectors) are placed on the disk. If you consistently exit WordPerfect improperly, your diskette will eventually fill with these unallocated sectors, and you will receive a disk full error.

Starting
WordPerfect 4.2

If your WordPerfect 4.2 diskette contains DOS, perform the following:

1. Insert the diskette containing WordPerfect 4.2 in disk drive A of the computer (with the label up) and close the door.

2. Either turn the computer on, or, if already on, press the Del key while simultaneously holding down the Ctrl and Alt keys. The "boot" process will now load the operating system into memory.

3. If you want to "date stamp" your files, enter the date and time when you are prompted to do so.

4. In a moment, you should see the system prompt A> on your screen. This indicates that disk drive A is the so-called *default disk*. Change the default drive to B by entering B: and pressing the ENTER key.

5. Type A:WP and press the ENTER key.

6. WordPerfect 4.2 will now be loaded into memory (RAM) and be ready to use. All data files will be stored on the disk in drive B.

7. When you are finished with WordPerfect 4.2 and wish to exit to DOS, issue the Exit command (F7). The B> prompt will then appear.

If your WordPerfect 4.2 diskette does not contain DOS, perform the following:

1. Insert a system diskette—a diskette containing the IBM Personal Computer Disk Operating System (PC-DOS) 2.0 or higher, or a compatible version of MS-DOS—into disk drive A of the computer and close the disk drive door.

2. Turn the computer on. The computer "boot" process will now load the operating system into the computer memory.

3. If you want to "date stamp" your files, enter the date and time when prompted.

4. The system prompt A>, indicating that disk drive A is the default disk, should now appear on your screen. Change the default drive to B by entering B: and press the ENTER key.

5. Remove the system disk from drive A and place the diskette containing WordPerfect 4.2 in its place.

6. Type the letters A:WP and press the ENTER key.

7. WordPerfect 4.2 is now loaded into memory (RAM) and starts to execute.

8. WordPerfect 4.2 is now ready to use. WordPerfect 4.2 automatically saves all files to the diskette in drive B.

9. When you are finished with WordPerfect 4.2 and want to exit to DOS, issue the Exit command (F7). DOS will display the following prompt:

```
Insert disk with COMMAND.COM in drive A and strike
any key when ready
```

Insert any disk that contains the operating system in drive A, close the door, and strike a key; the A> prompt will then appear.

Steps for Using VP-Planner Plus

Note 1: You may wish to configure VP-Planner Plus so that its appearance on the screen emulates Lotus 1-2-3 instead of having the pull-down menus default. This is accomplished by entering the command / Worksheet Global Default Other Screen. The following commands can now be invoked:

Fn Key	Turns the function keys on and off.
Panel-top	Turns the control panel at the top of the screen on and off.
Menu-box	Turns the pull-down menu boxes on and off.
Read-menu	Turns the function key menu in the Control Panel on and off.
Quit	Quits from the Screen menu.

After you have made your selections to configure the screen, execute the Update command to make these changes permanent. Return to Ready mode by executing the Quit command.

Note 2: If you cannot see graphs on the screen with the View command, you must change the hardware video default setting by using the following sequence of commands once VP-Planner Plus is running: / Worksheet Global Default Hardware Video. You can now select the appropriate video display for your computer and execute the Update command to make the change permanent. Return to Ready mode by executing the Quit command.

Note 3: VP-Planner Plus, unless it has been told otherwise, looks for worksheet files on drive A. To change the default location to drive B enter the following

commands: / Worksheet Global Default Directory, Enter B: \
and press the ENTER key. To make this change permanent execute the Update
command; then execute the Quit command to return to Ready mode.

1. Insert a system diskette—a diskette containing the IBM Personal
   Computer Disk Operating System (PC-DOS) 2.0 or higher, or a compatible version of MS-DOS—into disk drive A and close the disk
   drive door. This may be the disk with VP-Planner Plus.

2. Turn the computer on. The computer "boot" process will now load
   the operating system into the computer memory.

3. If you want to "date stamp" your files, enter the date and time when
   prompted.

4. The system prompt A>, indicating that disk drive A is the default
   disk, should now appear on your screen.

5. Remove the system disk from drive A and place the diskette containing VP-Planner Plus in its place.

6. Type the command VPP and press the ENTER key.

7. The VP-Planner Plus Educational copyright notice now appears on
   the screen. Press the ENTER key to start the spreadsheet.

8. VP-Planner Plus is now loaded into memory (RAM) and starts to
   execute.

9. VP-Planner Plus is now ready to use. VP-Planner Plus automatically
   saves all worksheet files to the diskette in drive B.

10. When you are finished with VP-Planner Plus and want to exit to DOS,
    issue the / Quit Exit commands. DOS will display the following
    prompt:

Insert disk with COMMAND.COM in drive A and strike
any key when ready

Insert any disk that contains the operating system in drive A, close
the door, and strike a key; the A> prompt will then appear.

11. *Alternate Method to Finish.* If you want to end the session and you
    have saved your worksheet to disk, remove your diskette(s) from the
    drive(s) and turn off the machine.

Steps for Using
dBASE III Plus

1. Insert a system diskette—a diskette containing the IBM Personal
   Computer Disk Operating System (PC-DOS) 2.0 or higher, or a compatible version of MS-DOS—into disk drive A of the computer and
   close the disk drive door. This may be disk 1 of dBASE III Plus.

2. Turn the computer on. The computer "boot" process will now load
   the operating system into the computer memory.

3. If you want to "date stamp" your files, enter the date and time when
   prompted.

4. The system prompt A>, indicating that disk drive A is the default
   disk, should now appear on your screen.

5. Remove the system disk from drive A and place the sampler 1 diskette containing dBASE III Plus in its place. If your sampler disk 1
   has DOS, omit step 5.

6. Type the command DBASE and press the ENTER key.

7. The first part of dBASE III Plus is now loaded into memory (RAM) and you are prompted to insert sampler disk 2 in drive B and press the ENTER key.

8. dBASE III Plus is now ready to use.

9. When you are finished with dBASE III Plus and want to exit to DOS, issue the `QUIT` command. If you do not enter the `QUIT` command, data in files may be lost. After this has been accomplished, DOS will display the following prompt:

```
Insert disk with COMMAND.COM in drive A and strike any key when ready
```

Insert any disk that contains the operating system in drive A, close the door, and strike a key; the A> prompt will then appear.

Spreadsheet Compatibility

One of the more important concerns for users of 1-2-3 and its work-alikes is the issue of compatibility. The 1-2-3 package itself is not compatible from Release 1A to Release 2. Although the latest version, Release 2.01, has addressed some of these concerns, the problem is compounded slightly when an individual also wishes to use VP-Planner Plus.

This issue is solved simply by avoiding a small number of features in either 1-2-3 Release 2(.01) or VP-Planner Plus that are not supported by either package. Worksheets created by either Release 1A, 2.0, or 2.01 of Lotus 1-2-3 can be read by VP-Planner Plus.

Features of VP-Planner Plus to Avoid

Range column width of zero

Autokey macros

The 1-Custom and 2-Custom format options

The 4(M/D/Y), 5(D/M/Y), 6(Y M D), and T(HH:MM:SS 24-hour time) format options

Multiple windows

Page numbers and row and column numbers from the Other Menu of the Print Menu

The $ (substring search), < (less than), and > (greater than) for data management queries

Features of Release 2(.01) to Avoid

Use of the Hide command (set column width to zero)

Data regression

Data parse

VP-Planner Plus Incompatibilities with Text

The following topics/assignments in this book cannot be accomplished using VP-Planner Plus.

Chapter 9. *p. 234*—Big right and big left pointer positioning commands are not supported.

Chapter 11. *p. 295*—The Column Hide is accomplished in VP-Planner Plus by setting the column to a width of zero (0).

p. 298—There is no password protection in VP-Planner Plus.

p. 302—The Show command is used instead of the Table command to display named ranges. The Show command simply displays the named ranges to the screen. It does not result in cells being used in the worksheet.

Backup Feature of WordPerfect 4.2

WordPerfect 4.2 Set-Up Menu

The **Set-up Menu** is accessed by starting WordPerfect (from DOS) with the command WP/S. The /S tells WordPerfect to display the Start-up Menu rather than going directly to a clear screen.

```
                              Set-up Menu

0 - End Set-up and enter WP
1 - Set Directories or Drivers for Dictionary and Thesaurus Files
2 - Set Initial Settings
3 - Set Screen and Beep Options
4 - Set Backup Options
Selection: _
Press Cancel to ignore changes and return to DOS
```

Option 1 allows you to tell WordPerfect where to find the various dictionary files that it needs for Speller and Thesaurus. If you are using a computer with two disk drives, enter a B: in front of each file. For example, when you are prompted for the location of the first file with LEX.WP, you must change this entry to B:LEX.WP. If you are using a hard disk, make certain that the complete path C:\WP\LEX.WP is entered for each file. If the first file is correct, simply press ENTER until you are returned to the Set-up Menu.

Option 2 allows you to configure WordPerfect to your needs. A menu (see Figure A.1) with options that you can change is displayed on your screen. Each of the options in bold display can be changed by issuing the appropriate commands (found in Appendix B) from the keyboard. (Do not now make any changes to these initial settings; this textbook assumes that the defaults are in effect.)

Option 3 (see Figure A.2) allows you to tailor WordPerfect for your monitor. The menu shown below is displayed. You must either make a change or press ENTER to take the existing value of each selection.

Option 4 allows you to select the appropriate backup option. Upon selection of this option, the screen depicted in Figure A.3 is displayed.

Leave the 0 for the timed backup, but enter a Y for the original backup prompt. Now, when you save a file, a backup will be placed in a file called FILENAME.BK!. From the explanation on the screen, you can see that you do *not* want to use one file name for more than one document, even with different extensions, because this would cause the backups of the various documents to be stored in the same backup file.

Backup Feature of WordPerfect 5.0

Saving your file to disk from time to time can save you a tremendous amount of mental distress and work if something goes wrong. WordPerfect provides two automatic backup facilities to aid people who have difficulty remembering to save documents to disk periodically.

The backup feature of WordPerfect is not a default option. You must specifically tell WordPerfect that you want to use a backup option. Invoking

Figure A.1
The Initial Settings menu invoked from the Set-up Menu.

```
Change Initial Settings


    Press any of the keys listed below to change initial settings


    Key                Initial Settings


Line Format      Tabs, Margins, Spacing Hyphenation, Align Character

Page Format      Page # Pos, Page Length, Top Margin, Page # Col Pos, W/O

Print Format     Pitch, Font, Lines/Inch, Right Just, Underlining, SF Bin #

Print            Printers, Copies, Binding Width

Date             Date Format

Insert/Typeover  Insert/Typeover Mode

Mark Text        Paragraph Number Definition, Table of Authorities Definition

Footnote         Footnote/Endnote Options

Escape           Set N

Screen           Set Auto-rewrite

Text In/Out      Set Insert Document Summary on Save/Exit


Selection: _


Press Enter to return to the Set-up Menu
```

Figure A.2
Various WordPerfect screen and audio options available.

```
    Set Screen Options


        Number of rows: 25

        Number of columns: 80

        Hard return displayed as ascii value: 32

        Display filename on status line? (Y/N) Y


    Set Beep Options


        Beep when search fails? (Y/N) N

        Beep on error? (Y/N) N

        Beep on hyphenation? (Y/N) Y
```

Figure A.3
The backup screen that explains the various Word-Perfect backup options.

```
    Set Timed Backup


    To safeguard against losing large amounts of text in the event of a power or

    machine failure, WordPerfect can automatically backup the document on your

    screen at a chosen time interval and to a chosen drive/directory (see Set-up

    in the WordPerfect Installation pamphlet).  REMEMBER--THIS IS ONLY IN CASE OF

    POWER OR MACHINE FAILURE.  WORDPERFECT DELETES THE TIMED BACKUP FILES WHEN YOU

    EXIT NORMALLY FROM WORDPERFECT.  If you want the document saved as a file you

    need to say 'yes' when you exit normally.



    Number of minutes between each backup: 0




    Set Original Backup


    Wordperfect can rename the last copy of a document when a new version of the

    document is saved.  The old copy has the same file name with an extension of

    ".BK!".  Take note that the files named "letter.1" and "letter.2" have the

    same original backup file name of "letter.bk!".  In this case the latest file

    saved will be backed up.


    Backup the original document? (Y/N) N
```

the backup option, as well as changing defaults, is accomplished by using the WordPerfect Set-up (SHIFT + F1) command.

WordPerfect 5.0 Set-up Menu

The Set-up Menu is accessed by issuing the Set-up (SHIFT + F1) command. Once this command is issued, the menu depicted in Figure A.4 is displayed to your monitor. The options provided here allow you to exercise tremendous control over how WordPerfect displays information on the monitor and how it prints your document on the screen. We will examine only one or two of these options.

Option 1 allows you to select the appropriate Backup option. When you select this option, the screen depicted in Figure A.5 appears on your screen.

Leave the 0 for the timed backup, but take option 2 to change the original document backup entry. Once you have selected this entry, enter a Y to change the default. Now, when you save a file, a backup will be placed in a file called FILENAME.BK!.

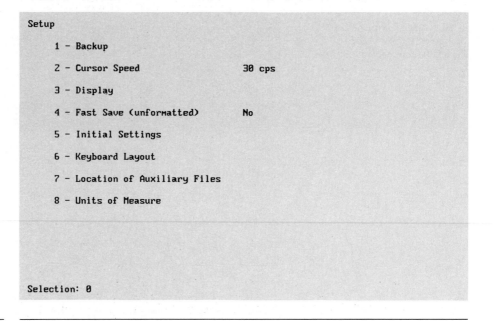

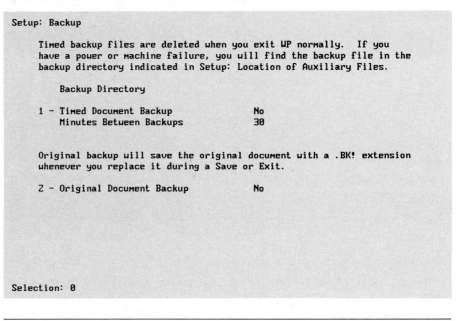

WordPerfect now renames the last copy of a document when a new version of the document is saved. The old copy has the same file name with an
extension of .BK!. Take note that the files named REPORT.1 and REPORT.2 have
the same original backup file name of REPORT.BK!. In this case the latest file
saved will be backed up.

Option 5 allows you to configure WordPerfect to your needs. Option 4 of
this menu (see Figure A.6) allows you to tell WordPerfect which codes to use
each time WordPerfect is started. Any document that is created will automatically have these codes embedded at the beginning of the file.

Figure A.6
The Initial Settings screen of the Set-up Menu used to configure WordPerfect.

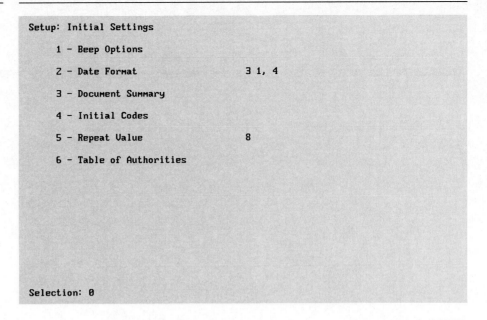

```
Setup: Initial Settings

     1 - Beep Options

     2 - Date Format                       3 1, 4

     3 - Document Summary

     4 - Initial Codes

     5 - Repeat Value                      8

     6 - Table of Authorities




Selection: 0
```

Appendix
B

Software Command
Summaries

WordPerfect 4.2

Command Summary

Advance Line   Shift + F1

Advance Up/Down   Shift + F1

Alignment Character   Shift + F8

Append Block (Block on)   Ctrl + F4

Auto Hyphenation   Shift + F8, 5

Auto Rewrite   Ctrl + F3

Binding Width   Shift + F7, 3

Block   Alt + F4

Block, Cut/Copy (Block on)   Ctrl + F4

Block Protect (Block on)   Alt + F8

Bold   F6

Cancel   F1

Cancel Hyphenation   F1

Cancel Print Jobs   Shift + F7, 4

Case Conversion (Block on)   Shift + F7, 4

Center   Shift + F6

Center Page Top to Bottom   Alt + F8

Change Directory   F5, Enter

Change Print Options   Shift + F7

Colors   Ctrl + F3

Column, Cut/Copy (Block on)   Ctrl + F4

Columns, Text   Alt + F7

Column Display   Alt + F7

Concordance   Alt + F5, 6,5

Conditional End of Page   Alt + F8

Copy   F5, Enter

Create Directory   F5, =

Ctrl/Alt Key Mapping   Ctrl + F3

Date   Shift + F5

Delete   Del

Delete (List Files)   F5, Enter

Delete Directory (List Files)   F5, Enter

Delete to End of Line (EOL)   Ctrl + End

Delete to End of Page (EOP)   Ctrl + PgDn

Delete to Left Word Boundary   Home, Backspace

Delete to Right Word Boundary   Home, Del

Delete Word   Ctrl + Backspace

Display All Print Jobs   Shift + F7, 4

Display Printers and Fonts   Shift + F7, 4

Document Comments   Ctrl + F5

Document Conversion   Ctrl + F5

Document Summary   Ctrl + F5

DOS Text File   Ctrl + F5

Endnote   Ctrl + F7

Exit   F7

Flush Right   Alt + F6

Font   Ctrl + F8

Footnote   Ctrl + F7

Full Text (Print)   Shift + F7

Generate   Alt + F5, 6

Go (Resume Printing)   Alt + F5, 6

Go to DOS   Ctrl + F1

Hard Page   Ctrl + Enter

Hard Return   Enter

Hard Space   Home, Space Bar

Headers or Footers   Alt + F8

Help   F3

Home   Home

Hyphen   -

Hyphenation On/Off   Shift + F8, 5

H-Zone   Shift + F8, 5

Indent (right)   F4

Indent (left and right)   Shift + F4

Index   Alt + F5

Insert Printer Command   Ctrl + F8

Justification On/Off   Ctrl + F8

Line Draw   Ctrl + F3

Line Format   Shift + F8

Line Numbering   Ctrl + F8

Lines per Inch   Ctrl + F8

List Files   F5, Enter

List (Block on)   Alt + F5

Locked Documents   Ctrl + F5

Look   F5, Enter

Macro   Alt + F10

Macro Def   Ctrl + F10

Margin Release   Shift + Tab

Margins   Shift + F8

Mark Text   Alt + F5

Math   Alt + F7

Merge   Ctrl + F9

Merge Codes   Alt + F9

Merge E   Shift + F9

Merge R   F9

Minus Sign   Home, −

Move   Ctrl + F4

Name Search   F5, Enter

New Number (Footnote)   Ctrl + F7

New Page Number   Alt + F8
Number of Copies   Shift + F7, 3
Outline   Alt + F5
Overstrike   Shift + F1
Page Format   Alt + F8
Page Length   Alt + F8
Page Number Column Positions   Alt + F8
Page Number Position   Alt + F8
Page (Print)   Shift + F7
Paragraph Number   Alt + F5
Pitch   Ctrl + F8
Preview a Document   Shift + F7
Print   Shift + F7
Print (List Files)   F5, Enter
Print a Document   Shift + F7, 4
Print Block (Block on)   Shift + F7
Print Format   Ctrl + F8
Printer Control   Shift + F7
Printer Number   Shift + F7, 3
Proportional Spacing   Ctrl + F8, 1
Rectangle, Cut/Copy (Block on)   Ctrl + F4
Redline   Alt + F5
Remove   Alt + F5, 6
Rename   F5, Enter
Replace   Alt + F2
Replace, Extended   Home, Alt + F2
Retrieve   Shift + F10
Retrieve (List Files)   F5, Enter
Retrieve Column (Move)   Ctrl + F4
Retrieve Rectangle (Move)   Ctrl + F4
Retrieve Text (Move)   Ctrl + F4
Reveal Codes   Alt + F3
Rewrite   Ctrl + F3, Ctrl + F3
Rush Print Job   Shift + F7, 4
Save   F10
Screen   Ctrl + F3
Search Backward   Shift + F2
Search Backward Extended   Home, Shift + F2
Search Forward   F2
Search Forward Extended   Home, F2

Select Print Options   Shift + F7, 4
Select Printers   Shift + F7, 4
Sheet Feeder Bin Number   Ctrl + F8
Shell   Ctrl + F1
Short Form Marking   Alt + F5
Soft Hyphen   Ctrl + -
Sort   Ctrl + F9
Sorting Sequences   Ctrl + F9
Spacing   Shift + F8
Spell   Ctrl + F2
Split Screen   Ctrl + F3, 1
Stop Printing   Ctrl + F7, 4
Strikeout (Block on)   Alt + F5
Super/Subscript   Shift + F1
Suppress Page Format   Alt + F8
Switch   Shift + F3
Tab   Tab
Tab Align   Ctrl + F6
Tab Ruler   Ctrl + F3, 1
Table of Authorities (Block on)   Alt + F5
Table of Contents (Block on)   Alt + F5
Tab Set   Shift + F8
Text In (List Files)   F5, Enter
Text In/Out   Ctrl + F5
Text Lines   Alt + F8, 4
Thesaurus   Alt + F1
Time   Shift + F5, 2
Top Margin   Alt + F8
Typeover   Ins
Type Thru   Shift + F7
Undelete   F1
Underline   F8
Underline Style   Ctrl + F8
Widow/Orphan   Alt + F8
Window   Ctrl + F3
Word Count   Ctrl + F2
Word Search   F5, Enter

Cursor Control

Go To   Ctrl + Home (enter page number)

Word Left   Ctrl + Left Arrow

Word Right   Ctrl + Right Arrow

Screen Left   Home, Right Arrow

Screen Right   Home, Left Arrow

Screen Down   +

Screen Up   −

Page Down   PgDn

Page Up   PgUp

Beginning of Text   Home, Home, Up Arrow

End of Text   Home, Home, Down Arrow

Beginning of Line (Text)   Home, Home, Left Arrow

Beginning of Line (Codes)   Home, Home, Home, Left Arrow

End of Line   End of Home, Home, Right Arrow

WordPerfect 5.0

Command Summary

Advance Line   Shift + F8, 4, 1

Alignment Character   Shift + F8, 4, 3

Append Block (Block on)   Ctrl + F4

Auto Hyphenation   Shift + F8, 1, 1

Auto Rewrite   Shift + F1, 3, 1

Binding Width   Shift + F7, B

Block   Alt + F4

Block, Cut/Copy (Block on)   Ctrl + F4

Block Protect (Block on)   Shift + F8

Bold   F6

Cancel   F1

Cancel Hyphenation   F1

Cancel Print Jobs   Shift + F7, 4

Case Conversion (Block on)   Shift + F3

Center   Shift + F6

Center Page Top to Bottom   Shift + F8, 2, 1

Change Directory   F5, Enter

Change Print Options   Shift + F7

Colors   Ctrl + F1, 3, 2

Column, Cut/Copy (Block on)   Ctrl + F4

Columns, Text   Alt + F7

Concordance   Alt + F5, 5, 3

Conditional End of Page   Shift + F8, 4, 2

Copy   F5, Enter, 8

Create Directory   F5, =

Date   Shift + F5

Delete   Del

Delete (List Files)   F5, Enter

Delete Directory (List Files)   F5, Enter, 2

Delete to End of Line (EOL)   Ctrl + End

Delete to End of Page (EOP)   Ctrl + PgDn

Delete to Left Word Boundary   Home, Backspace

Delete to Right Word Boundary   Home, Del

Delete Word   Ctrl + Backspace

Display All Print Jobs   Shift + F7, 4

Display Printers and Fonts   Shift + F8, 3, 1

Document Comments   Ctrl + F5, 5

Document Summary   Shift + F8, 3, 4

DOS Text File   Ctrl + F5, 1, 2

Endnote   Ctrl + F7, 2

Exit   F7

Flush Right   Alt + F6

Font   Ctrl + F8

Footnote   Ctrl + F7

Format   Shift + F8

Full Text (Print)   Shift + F7, 1

Generate   Alt + F5, 6

Go (Resume Printing)   Shift + F7, 4, 4

Go to DOS   Ctrl + F1, 1

Hard Page   Ctrl + Enter

Hard Return   Enter

Hard Space   Home, Space Bar

Headers or Footers   Shift + F8, 2

Help   F3

Home   Home

Hyphen   -

Hyphenation On/Off   Shift + F8, 1, 1

H-Zone   Shift + F8, 1, 2

Indent (right)   F4

Indent (left and right)   Shift + F4

Index   Alt + F5

Justification On/Off   Shift + F8, 1, 3

Line Draw   Ctrl + F3, 2

Line Format   Shift + F8, 1

Line Numbering   Shift + F8, 1, 5

List Files   F5, Enter

List (Block on)   Alt + F5, 2

Look   F5, Enter, 6

Macro   Alt + F10

Macro Def   Ctrl + F10

Margin Release   Shift + Tab

Margins   Shift + F8, 1, 7

Mark Text   Alt + F5

Math   Alt + F7

Merge   Ctrl + F9, 1

Merge Codes   Shift + F9

Minus Sign   Home, –

Move   Ctrl + F4

Name Search   F5, Enter, N

New Number (Footnote)   Ctrl + F7

New Page Number   Shift + F8, 2, 6

Normal Text   Ctrl + F8, 3

Number of Copies   Shift + F7, N

Outline   Shift + F5, 4

Overstrike   Shift + F8, 4, 5

Page Format   Shift + F8, 2

Page Numbering   Shift + F8, 2, 7

Page (Print)   Shift + F7, 2

Paragraph Number   Shift + F5

Preview a Document   Shift + F7, 6

Print   Shift + F7

Print (List Files)   F5, Enter, 4

Print a Document   Shift + F7, 4

Print Block (Block on)   Shift + F7

Printer   Shift + F7, 5

Printer Control   Shift + F7

Rectangle, Cut/Copy (Block on)   Ctrl + F4, R

Redline   Ctrl + F8, 2, 8

Rename   F5, Enter, 3

Replace   Alt + F2

Replace, Extended   Home, Alt + F2

Retrieve   Shift + F10

Retrieve (List Files)   F5, Enter

Retrieve Column (Move)   Ctrl + F4, C

Retrieve Rectangle (Move)   Ctrl + F4, R

Retrieve Text (Move)   Ctrl + F4, T

Reveal Codes   Alt + F3

Rewrite   Ctrl + F3, O

Rush Print Job   Shift + F7, 4, 2

Save   F10

Screen   Ctrl + F3

Search Backward   Shift + F2

Search Backward Extended   Home, Shift + F2

Search Forward   F2

Search Forward Extended   Home, Shift + F2

Select Printers   Shift + F7, 5

Setup   Shift + F1

Shell   Ctrl + F1

Sort   Ctrl + F9, 2

Spacing   Shift + F8, 1, 6

Spell   Ctrl + F2

Split Screen   Ctrl + F3, 1

Stop Printing   Ctrl + F7, 4, 5

Strikeout (Block on)   Ctrl + F8, 2, 9

Super/Subscript   Ctrl + F8, 1

Suppress Page Format   Shift + F8, 2, 9

Switch   Shift + F3

Tab   Tab

Tab Align   Ctrl + F6

Tab Ruler   Shift + F8, 1, 8

Table of Authorities (Block on)   Alt + F5, 5, 4

Table of Contents (Block on)   Alt + F5, 5, 1

Tab Set   Shift + F8, 1, 8

Text In (List Files)   F5, Enter, 5

Text In/Out   Ctrl + F5

Thesaurus   Alt + F1

Time   Shift + F5, 2

Top Margin   Shift + F8, 4, 5

Typeover   Ins

Type Thru   Shift + F7, 5

Undelete   F1

Underline   F8

Underline Style   Shift + F8, 4, 7

Widow/Orphan   Shift + F8, 1, 9

Window   Ctrl + F3

Word Count   Ctrl + F2

Word Search   F5, Enter

Cursor Control

Go To   Ctrl + Home (enter page number

Word Left   Ctrl + Left Arrow

Word Right   Ctrl + Right Arrow

Screen Left   Home, Right Arrow

Screen Right   Home, Left Arrow

Screen Down   +

Screen Up   −

Page Down   PgDn

Page Up   PgUp

Beginning of Text   Home, Home, Up Arrow

End of Text   Home, Home, Down Arrow

Beginning of Line (Text)   Home, Home, Left Arrow

Beginning of Line (Codes)   Home, Home, Home, Left Arrow

End of Line   End of Home, Home, Right Arrow

dBASE III Plus

Command Summary

Conventions

Lower case   User-supplied information

Upper case   Explicit portions of dBASE III Plus commands

[. . .]   Optional portions of dBASE III Plus commands

<. . .>   User-supplied portions of dBASE III Plus commands

<**cstring**>   Character strings

<**ex**>   Valid item or group of items and/or operators

<**exp list**>   List of expressions separated by commas

<**field**>   Record field name

<**field list**>   List of record field names separated by commas

<**file**>   Name of a file to access or create

<**index file**>   Name of an index file to create or access

<**key**>   Portion(s) of a file used to create an index file

<**n**>   Number that dBASE III Plus is to regard as a literal value

<**numeric exp**>   An ⟨exp⟩ whose content is defined as numeric

<**scope**>   Command option that specifies a range of records that dBASE III Plus must treat in executing a command; has three possible values: ALL records in the file; NEXT *n* records in the file; and RECORD *n* (default value varies from command to command)

<**skeleton**>   Allows batch manipulation of files of the same type and/or having matching cstrings in file name

Operators

Logical Operators (in Order of Precedence)

( )   Parentheses for grouping

.NOT.   Logical not

.AND.   Logical and

.OR.   Logical or

$ Substring operator

Arithmetic Operators

( )   Parentheses for grouping

/   Division

*   Multiplication

+   Addition

−   Subtraction

Relational Operators

<   Less than

>   Greater than

=   Equal to

<>   Not equal to

< =   Less than or equal to

> =   Greater than or equal to

String Operator

+ String concatenation

Functions

* Delete indicator identifies record marked for deletion

$(exp,start,length) Substring extracts the specified part of **(exp)** from the given starting position for the given length

DATE( ) Invokes name of the system variable containing the system date

EOF End-of-file function evaluates as a logical true/false whether the last record of the file in use has been processed

STR(exp,length,decimals) String function converts the specified portion of **(exp)** into a character string

TRIM(exp) Trim function removes trailing blanks from a specified string variable

Selected dBASE Commands

APPEND[BLANK] Adds record(s) or blank formatted record(s) to the data base file in use

APPEND FROM ⟨file⟩ Appends data from a data base

ASSIST Activates the Assistant menu

AVERAGE ⟨explist⟩ [WHILE ⟨condition⟩] [FOR ⟨condition⟩] Calculates the arithmetic average for numeric fields

BROWSE [FIELDS ⟨field list] Provides full-screen editing for changing a file

CLEAR Erases the screen

CLEAR ALL Closes all data base files, index files, format files, and relations; releases all memory variables and selects work area one

CONTINUE Continues a LOCATE command

COPY TO <file> STRUCTURE [FIELD <list>] Copies the structure of the file in use into the designated file

COPY TO <file> [FIELD <list>] Copies the file or fields from the file in use to the designated data base file

CREATE [<file>] Starts the creation process for a data base file

CREATE LABEL <.lbl file name> Activates the LABEL menu and enables you to create a label form file

CREATE QUERY <.qry file name> Activates the QUERY menu and enables you to create a filter condition and store it to a .qry file

CREATE REPORT <.frm file name> Activates the REPORT menu and enables you to create a report template and store it to a .frm file

CREATE SCREEN <.scr file name> Activates the SCREEN menu and enables you to create a custom screen format and store it to a .scr file

DELETE [<scope>] [FOR<exp>] Marks record(s) for deletion

DELETE FILE <file> Deletes the specified file

DIR [<drive>] [<path>] Shows the files on the specified drive or path

DISPLAY [<scope>][<field list>][FOR<exp>][OFF]   Displays selected records from the data base file in use

DISPLAY MEMORY   Displays current memory variables

DISPLAY STATUS   Displays current information about active data bases, index files, alternate files, and system parameters

DISPLAY STRUCTURE   Displays the structure of the file in use

EDIT [n]   Starts selective editing of the file in use

EJECT   Sends a form feed to the printer

ERASE <file name>   Deletes the specified file from the directory

FIND <character string>   Positions the record pointer to the first record with an index key that matches the specified character string, which does not have to be delimited

GO or GOTO <n> or TOP, or <BOTTOM>   Positions the pointer at a specific record or place in the file in use

INDEX ON <key> TO <file>   Creates an index file for the file in use

LABEL FORM <.lbl file name> [WHILE <condition>] [FOR <condition.] [TO PRINT]   Prints labels using the indicated label form file

LIST [<scope>][<field list>][FOR <exp>][OFF]   Lists records from the file in use

LIST FILES [ON<disk drive>][LIKE<skeleton>]   Lists files from disk

LIST STRUCTURE   Displays the structure of the file in use

LOCATE [<scope>][FOR<exp>]   Finds the first record that satisfies the specified condition; the CONTINUE command is then used to locate the next record meeting the condition

MODIFY COMMAND <file>   Calls dBASE III's text editor and brings up the designated file for modification

MODIFY LABEL <file name>   Activates the LABEL menu for changing .lbl file parameters

MODIFY QUERY <file name>   Activates the QUERY menu for changing .qry file parameters

MODIFY REPORT <file name>   Activates the REPORT menu for changing .frm report template parameters

MODIFY SCREEN <file name>   Activates the SCREEN menu for changing .scr file parameters

MODIFY STRUCTURE   Allows structural modification of a data base file

PACK   Eliminates records marked for deletion

QUIT   Terminates dBASE III and returns control to the operating system

RECALL [<scope>][FOR<exp>]   Recovers records previously marked for deletion

REINDEX   Rebuilds existing active index files

RENAME <oldfile> TO <newfile>   Enables you to rename a file

REPLACE [<scope>]<field>WITH<exp>[FOR<exp>]   Replaces the value of the specified field of specified records with stated values

REPORT [FORM <filename>][<scope>][FOR<exp>][TO

PRINT] Generates or accesses an existing .FRM file for output of data in a defined format

SEEK <expression> Positions the record pointer to the first record with an index key that matches the specified expression

SELECT <work area/alias> Activates the specified work area for accessing a file

SET See SET commands

SKIP [+ − n] Moves the pointer forward or backward within the file

SORT ON <key> TO <file> [ASCENDING] or [DESCENDING] Creates another data base file, sorted in the order specified by the named key

SORT TO <new file name> ON <field list>[/A][C][/D] Creates an ordered copy of a data base, arranged according to one or more fields

SUM <field list> [TO<membar list>][<scope>][FOR<exp>] Computes and displays the sum of numeric fields

USE <file> [INDEX <file list>] Opens a data base file and (optionally) opens desired index files

ZAP Removes all records from the active data base file

Selected SET Commands

SET commands enable you to redefine the environment in which you are working with dBASE. The default value of each SET command of ON/OFF type is indicated by the order of presentation: OFF/ON indicates that the default is OFF; ON/OFF indicates that the default is ON.

SET BELL ON/OFF ON rings the bell when invalid data are entered or a field boundary is passed; OFF turns off the bell

SET CONFIRM OFF/ON Does not skip to the next field in the full-screen mode

SET DATE TO <MM/DD/YY> Sets or resets the system date

SET DECIMALS TO <expN> Sets the minimum number of decimals displayed in the results of certain operations and functions

SET DEFAULT TO <drive> Commands dBASE III Plus to regard the specified drive as the default drive for all future operations

SET DELETED OFF/ON ON prevents dBASE III Plus from reading/processing any record marked for deletion following a command that has <scope>; OFF allows dBASE III Plus to read all records

SET FILTER TO [FILE <.qry filename>] Causes a data base file to appear to contain only records that meet the specified condition

SET INTENSITY ON/OFF ON enables inverse video or dual intensity to appear during full-screen operations; OFF disables these features

SET MARGIN TO <n> Sets the left-hand margin of printer to <n>

SET MENU ON/OFF Turns menus on or off

Full-Screen Cursor Movement Codes

All Commands

CTRL + X Moves the cursor down to the next field (also CTRL + F)

CTRL + E Moves cursor up to the previous field (also CTRL + A)

CTRL + D Moves cursor ahead one character

CTRL + S   Moves cursor back one character

CTRL + G   Deletes character under cursor

<Rubout> or DEL   Deletes character to left of cursor

CTRL + Y   Blanks out current field to right of cursor

CTRL + V   Toggles between overwrite and insert modes

CTRL + W   Saves changes and returns to command (.) prompt

In Edit Mode

CTRL + U   Toggles the record delete mark on and off

CTRL + C   Writes current record to disk and advances to next record

CTRL + R   Writes current record to disk and backs to previous record

CTRL + Q   Ignores changes to current record and returns to command (.) prompt

CTRL + W   Writes all changes to disk and returns to command (.) prompt

In Browse Mode

CTRL + B   Pans the window right one field

CTRL + Z   Pans the window left one field

In Modify Mode

CTRL + T   Deletes current line and moves all lower lines up

CTRL + N   Inserts new line at cursor position

CTRL + C   Scrolls down one-half page

CTRL + W   Writes all changes onto disk and returns to command (.) prompt

CTRL + Q   Ignores all changes and returns

In Append Mode

ENTER   Terminates APPEND when cursor is in first position of first field

CTRL + W   Writes record to disk and moves to next record

CTRL + Q   Ignores current record and returns to command (.) prompt

Control Key Strokes Operable When dBASE Is Not in Full-Screen Mode

CTRL + P   Toggles printer ON and OFF

CTRL + R   Repeats last executed command

CTRL + X   Clears command line without executing command

CTRL + H   Backspace

CTRL + M   Emulates a carriage return

CTRL + S   Starts/stops CPU operation

Lotus 1-2-3

Command Menus

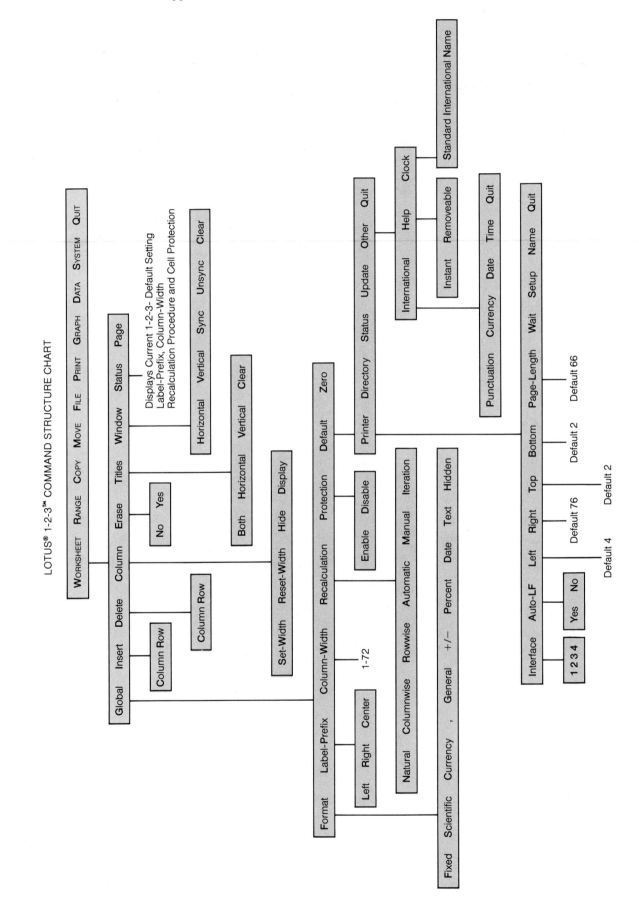

LOTUS® 1-2-3™ COMMAND STRUCTURE CHART

LOTUS® 1-2-3™ COMMAND STRUCTURE CHART

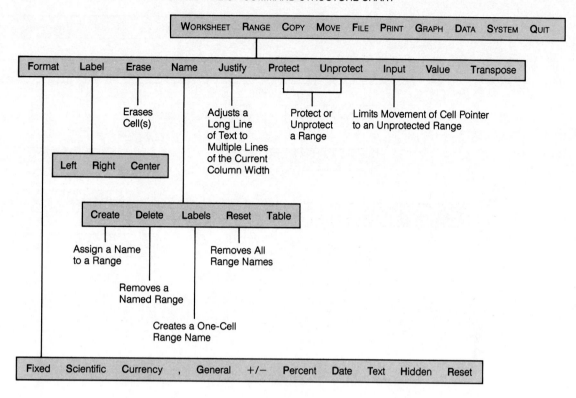

LOTUS® 1-2-3™ COMMAND STRUCTURE CHART

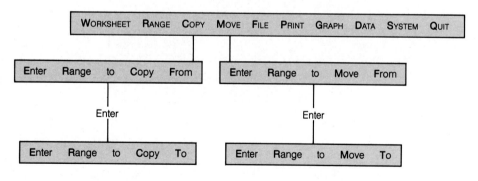

LOTUS® 1-2-3™ COMMAND STRUCTURE CHART

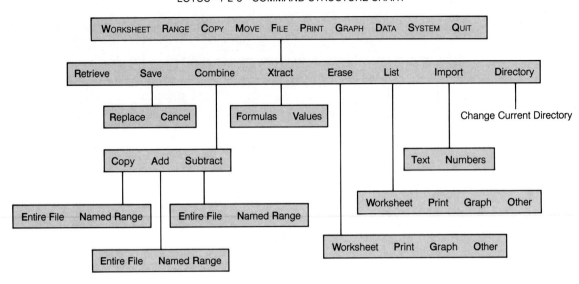

LOTUS® 1-2-3™ COMMAND STRUCTURE CHART

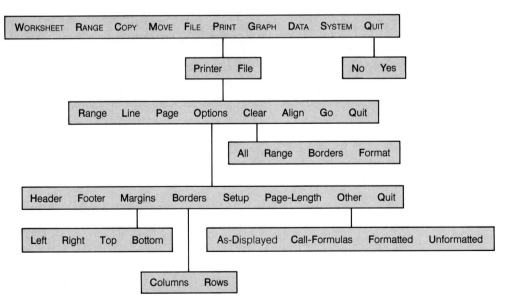

LOTUS® 1-2-3™ COMMAND STRUCTURE CHART

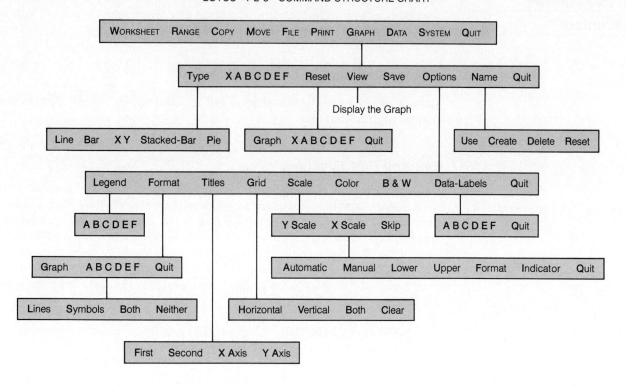

LOTUS® 1-2-3™ COMMAND STRUCTURE CHART

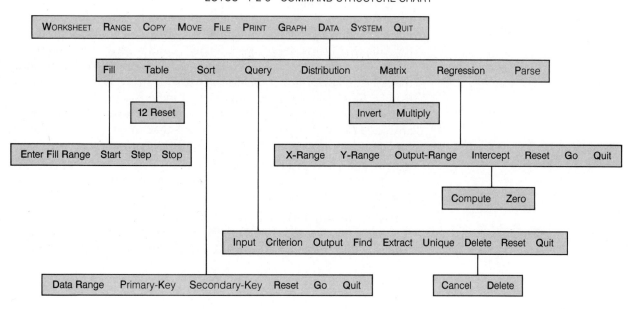

1-2-3 Function Summary

The following summary of 1-2-3 functions lists those most commonly used in a worksheet environment. The functions of a more esoteric nature can be found in the 1-2-3 documentation.

Data Base Functions

These functions are discussed in detail in Chapter 11. Please refer to that chapter for information.

Date and Time Functions

Date functions can generate dates between January 1, 1900 and December 31, 2099. A date function returns a real number with values to the left and right of the decimal point. The value to the left of the decimal point represents a specific day, while the value to the right of the decimal point represents the time of the day. Before a date can be understandable, it must be converted to a format that is readable by a user. This is accomplished via the /Range Format Date series of commands. Once the Date menu is displayed, you may select the desirable format for display.

> **@DATE(YY,MM,DD)** The year (YY) parameter must be a number between 0 (1900) and 199 (2099). A value 88 represents the year 1988, while a value of 103 represents the year 2003. The Month (MM) parameter must be a number from 1 to 12. The Day (DD) parameter must be a number from 1 to 31. Any errors that you make in entering the above parameters results in the value ERR appearing in the cell.
>
> After the date parameter has been entered, a numeric value appears in the cell. This value must now be changed to a readable date format.
>
> Once this function has been entered in a worksheet, other functions like @YEAR, @MONTH, @DAY, and @MOD (determine the day of the week) can be used against that cell.
>
> **@DATEVALUE(datestring)** This function allows you to enter a date string between double quotes and provides you with the numeric value for that date. For example, if you needed to determine the numeric value for the date December 25, 1988, you would enter the function @DATEVALUE("12,25,88") and receive the numeric value 36519. The difference between this function and the @DATE function is that @DATEVALUE function uses a character string as input, while the @DATE function uses three numeric parameters as input.
>
> The date string must be enclosed within double quotes and can be any one of 1-2-3 date formats. This means that any one of the following functions for the example above will return the same value:
>
> @DATEVALUE("25-Dec-88") = 36519
> @DATEVALUE("25-Dec") = 36519 (88 must be the current year.)
> @DATEVALUE("Dec-88") = 36495
>
> **@DAY(date number)** This function returns the day of the month (1 to 31) of the date number. The date number can reference another date function (@DATE, @DATEVALUE, or @NOW) or it can be a cell reference.
>
> @DAY(@DATE(88,12,25)) = 25
> @DAY(A9) returns the day of the month of the date in cell A9.
>
> **@MONTH(date number)** This function returns the month number (1 to 12) of the date number. The date number can reference another

date function (@DATE, @DATEVALUE, or @NOW) or it can refer to a cell reference.

@MONTH(@DATE(12,25,88)) = 12

@YEAR(date number)   This function returns the year number (0 to 199) of the date number. The date number can reference another date function (@DATE, @DATEVALUE, or @NOW) or it can refer to a cell reference containing a date.

@YEAR(@DATE(88,25,88)) = 88

@NOW   This function returns the date value for the current date and time that was entered manually or by the clock calendar feature of your computer when you started your system. If you do not have a clock calendar and did not enter a date, the default value of 01/01/80 is used. This function is many times used to date stamp your worksheet for printing.

@TIME(hr,min,sec)   This function returns the fractional value for the time entered. The parameter values are as follow; the *hr* parameter must be between 0 and 23, the *min* parameter must be between 0 and 59, and the *sec* parameter must be between 0 and 59. If these guidelines are not followed, 1-2-3 displays an ERR message in the cell.

Financial Functions

The 1-2-3 financial functions require you to enter interest rates as percents or decimal fractions. If you enter 17%, 1-2-3 automatically translates that value to .17. You must also express the term and interest rate in the same units of time. If you are dealing with monthly payments, divide the interest rate by 12. If the term is expressed in years, multiply by 12.

@CTERM(int,fv,pv)   This function determines the number of compounding periods it will take an investment of present value *pv* to grow to a future value of *fv*, earning a fixed interest rate *int* per compounding period.

This function uses the formula $\ln(fv/pv)/\ln(1 + int)$ to compute the term:

fv = future value
pv = present value
int = periodic interest rate
ln = natural logarithm

You have just retired and have received a lump sum payment that you wish to invest in a $200,000 CD. The CD pays an interest rate of 11.75% compounded monthly. You are interested in how long it will take to double your investment.

@CTERM(.1175/12,400000,200000) = 71.1

This tells you that it will take 71 months (5.9 years) to double the investment.

@DDB(cost,salvage,life,period)   This function determines the depreciation allowance on an asset for a specified period of time, using the double-declining balance method. The parameters are as follows: *cost* is the amount paid for the asset, *salvage* is the value of the asset at the end of its useful life, *life* is the number of periods for depreciation, and *period* is the time period for which you want to find the depreciation allowance.

This function uses the formula $(bv*2)/n$ to compute the double-declining balance depreciation amount for any period.

bv = book value in this period
n = life of asset

Assume that you have purchased a computer system for $12,500. The useful life is considered to be 4 years, and the salvage value is $1,900. You want to compute the depreciation expense for the second year.

@DDB(12500,1900,4,2) = 3125

This tells you that the depreciation for the second year will be $3,125.

@FV(pmt,int,term)   This function calculates the future value of an investment based on equal payments. The parameters used are as follow: *pmt* is the value that is to be deposited each period, *int* is the periodic interest rate, *term* represents the number of payment periods.

Suppose that you want to provide for the college education of a newborn child. You plan to deposit $1,200 each year into a bank account. The bank is paying 5.75% interest annually. The payment is deposited on the last day of each year. You want to compute the value of the account in 18 years.

@FV(1200,.0575,18) = 36220.45

This tells you that at the end of 18 years you will have $36,220.45 in your bank account.

Computing the future value of an *annuity due* requires the formula @FV(1200,.0575,18)*(1+.0575). This example assumes that you are making the payment of the first day of the year instead of the last day.

@FV(1200,.0575,18)*(1+.0575) = $38,303.12

This tells you that by making the payment on the first day of the year your investment would return an additional $2,082.67 over the ordinary annuity.

@NPV(int,range)   This function computes the present value of a series of future cash flows, discounted at a fixed periodic interest rate. The cash flows are assumed to occur at equal time intervals. The first cash flow, as well as subsequent cash flows, is assumed to occur at the end of the period. The *int* parameter is the periodic interest rate, and the *range* parameter is the range of worksheet cells in which you use to store the series of cash flows.

Assume that the cash flows are $100 per period for 6 periods and that the interest rate is 11%. Your worksheet appears (cells plus their respective values) like the following:

E6   100
E7   100
E8   100
E9   100
E10   100
E11   100

Your NPV function is @NPV(11%,e6.e11), and the value returned is 423.05.

To find the net present value of an investment where you make an initial cash outflow and follow it by a series of inflows, you must factor the initial outflow separately, since it is not affected by the interest. This is accomplished via the +INITIAL+@NPV(rate,range) adaptation of the NPV function.

Assume that your initial outflow for an investment is $5,000. Over the next six years you are to receive flows for the first three years of $1,750 and for the next three years flows of $1,850. The rate of interest is 12%. Your worksheet looks like:

G5	5000	(Initial payment)
G6	12%	(Interest rate)
G7	1750	
G8	1750	
G9	1750	
G10	1850	
G11	1850	
G12	1850	

+G5+@NPV(G7..G13) = 3202.77

@PMT(prin,int,periods)   This function computes the amount of the payment on a loan. Most installment loans are computed like ordinary annuities (payments at the end of the month). The parameters for this function are: *prin* is the principal of the loan, *int* is the periodic interest rate, and *periods* is the number of payment periods.

For example, if you want to take out a mortgage for a home and $95,000 is to be financed at a rate of 10.5% for 20 years, you would use the following formula to calculate your monthly payments.

@PMT(95000,.105/12,20*12) = 948.46

@PV(pmt,int,periods)   This function computes the present value of an investment. It computes the present value based on a series of equal payments, each of amount *pmt*, discounted at periodic interest rate *int*, over the number of periods in *periods*.

Assume that you just won the $6,000,000 Lotto. The payments for the lottery are $300,000 each year for 20 years. Each payment is to be received at the end of the year. You are also given the option of receiving a lump sum payment of $2,700,000 instead of the annuity. You want to find out which option is worth more in today's dollars. You also know that if you were to accept the annual payments you could invest them at an interest rate of 10.25%, compounded annually.

@PV(300000,.1025,20) = 2,511,085

Since 2,511,085 is less than the 2,700,000, the lump sum is worth more in today's dollars.

@SLN(cost,salvage,life)   This function computes the straight-line depreciation of an asset for one period. The straight-line method of depreciation divides the depreciable cost (cost-salvage) over the useful life of an asset.

Assume that you have purchased a computer system for $12,500. The useful life is considered to be 4 years, and the salvage value is $1,900. You want to compute the depreciation expense for the second year.

@SLN(12500,1900,4) = 2,650

This means that $2,650 is the yearly depreciation allowance.

@SYD(cost,salvage,life,period)   This function computes the sum-of-the-years' digits depreciation for a specified period. This method of depreciation accelerates the rate of depreciation so that more depreciation expense occurs in the early life of an asset. The depreciable cost is the cost minus the salvage value. The useful life is the number of periods over which an asset is depreciated.

Assume that you have purchased a computer system for $12,500. The useful life is considered to be 4 years, and the salvage value is $1,900. You want to compute the depreciation expense for the second year.

@SYD(12500,1900,4,2) = 3,180

This means that $3,180 dollars is the depreciation amount for the second year.

@TERM(pmt,int,fv)   This function returns the number of payment periods in the term of an ordinary annuity necessary to accumulate a future value of *fv*, earning a periodic interest rate of *int*. Each payment is equal to the *pmt* parameter.

You are preparing for retirement. You want to know how long it will take to accumulate $250,000 in a bank account. You plan to deposit $3,000 at the end of each year. Interest amounts to 5.75%.

@TERM(3000,.0575,250000) = 31.42

This means that it will take 31.4 years to accumulate $250,000.

Mathematical Functions

@INT(x)   This function returns the integer part of *x*. It truncates *x* at the decimal point. This means that everything to the right of the decimal point is lost.

@INT(75.35) = 75
@INT(75.99) = 75
@INT(@NOW) = only the whole number value is returned

If you want to round, use the @ROUND function.

@MOD(x,y)   This function returns the modulo of the remainder (modulo) of *x/y*. Parameter *x* can be any positive or negative number, while *y* must be a number other than 0. The modulo can also be used to determine the day of the week (the *y* parameter must be 7).

@MOD(15,4) = 3
@MOD(17,5) = 2
@MOD(@DATE(88,12,25),7) = 1

The calendar for 1-2-3 begins on Sunday. This makes Sunday day 1, and every Saturday is day 7.

@ROUND(x,n)   This function rounds a number (*x*) to *n* decimal positions. You can tell 1-2-3 to round on either side of the decimal point. A positive value for *n* rounds to the right of the decimal, while a negative value for *n* rounds to the left of the decimal a power of 10, or position, at a time.

@ROUND(1572.2345,2) = 1572.23
@ROUND(77.89,1) = 77.9
@ROUND(1367.65,-2) = 1400
@ROUND(@PMT(95000,.1025/12,20*12),-1) = 950

@SQRT(x)   This function returns the positive square root of *x*.

@SQRT(144) = 12
@SQRT(14) = 3.741657
@SQRT(-15) = ERR, because *x* is negative

Special Functions

@ERR   This function returns the numeric value ERR. Use this function to force a cell to have the value ERR. All cells containing formulas that reference this cell will also have an ERR. This causes a ripple effect on the worksheet.

`@IF(E3>10000,@ERR,A3*B3)`

If the ERR entry appears, the value in this cell was greater than 10,000; otherwise, the value will be the result of multiplying the contents of cell A3 by the contents of cell B3.

@NA   This function returns the numeric value NA. This means that a number is not available to complete a formula. An NA now appears in this cell as well as any other cells that depend on this formula. This `@NA` function is especially useful when you are constructing a worksheet and are not really certain what data will be involved.

`@IF(E3>10000,@NA,A3*B3)`

If the NA entry appears, the value in this cell was greater than 10,000; otherwise, the value will be the result of multiplying the contents of cell A3 by the contents of cell B3.

Statistical Functions

These functions are discussed in detail in Chapter 10. Please refer to that chapter for information.

String Functions

String functions manipulate a series of characters (strings), allow you to perform calculations on strings, and produce string values. Strings can be alphabetic letters, numbers, or special characters. They must all, however, be preceded by a label prefix.

@LENGTH(string)   This function returns the number of characters in *string*.

`@LENGTH(worksheet)` = 9
`@LENGTH('12345)` = 5
`@LENGTH(12345)` = ERR (not a string)

@PROPER(string)   This function converts the letters in *string* to proper capitalization. This means that the first letter of each word is upper case and all others are lower case.

`@PROPER("FOUR SCORE AND SEVEN YEARS AGO")` = Four Score And Seven Years Ago

@STRING(x,n)   This function converts the numeric value *x* to a string with *n* decimal positions. Rounding takes place automatically to *n* positions.

`@STRING(125,2)` = 125.00
`@STRING(35.6789,2)` = 35.68

@TRIM(string)   This function removes excess blanks from *string*. It removes excess blanks before and after the string, as well as any excessive blanks (more than two) within the string. Each word is still allowed to have one blank between it and the next word.

`@TRIM(" United States ")` = United States

`@TRIM(" Dr . No ")` = Dr. No

@UPPER(string)   This function converts all letters in *string* to upper case.

`@UPPER("usa")` = USA

@VALUE(string)   This function converts the number *string* to its corresponding numeric value. The string can appear as a number (389.65), as a mixed number (23 3/4), or in scientific notation (2.3423E2).

`@VALUE("975")` = 975

`@VALUE(42 1/4)` = 42.25

`@VALUE(E9)` = 15.75 if cell E9 contains 15 3/4.

Figure C.1
A clear screen with the status
line at the bottom.

Doc 1 Pg 1 Ln 1" Pos 1"

WordPerfect Screen (p. 138)

The P g entry gives the current page number. The L n entry gives the current location of the cursor on the page. If line spacing has been set for double spacing (2), this entry will advance ⅓ inch each time the ENTER key is depressed (1 inch, 1.33 inch, 1.66 inch, and so forth). If the line spacing is set for single spacing, these entries are in increments of ⅙ inch (1 inch, 1.16 inch, 1.33 inch, and so forth).

The P o s indicator tells the position of the cursor in inch increments on a line of text and also provides other information. Notice that the P o s indicator in Figure C.1 contains the value of 1" even though the cursor appears to be in the left-most position on the screen. The position displayed on the screen is the lineal position of the cursor in inches on the line in which this character will appear on the printed document. As the cursor is moved, this value changes according to the characters per inch (font size) that have been specified for this document. For example, if ten characters per inch have been specified, this value changes by increments of ¹⁄₁₀ inch (for example, 1.1 inch, 1.2 inch, and 1.3 inch). The various characteristics of the document will be covered later in this appendix.

Line Spacing (p. 152)

Up to this point we have used only single spacing (or whatever your default line spacing was set to). You are allowed to change the spacing of a WordPerfect document in any manner that you wish. You can easily single-, double-, or even triple-space a document. WordPerfect provides this ability through the Format (SHIFT + F8) command. Once you enter this command, the menu depicted in Figure C.2 appears on your screen. This Format Menu allows you to change a number of characteristics about your document. Right now we are interested only in resetting the line spacing. Because this particular option resides under the Line option, we select the Line option of the Format Menu. Note that both the 1 and the L of this option appear in high-intensity video (or the color brown with a color monitor). You can enter either of these characters to get to the Line submenu (depicted in Figure C.3).

Figure C.2

The Format Menu screen appears when you enter the Format (SHIFT + F8) command.

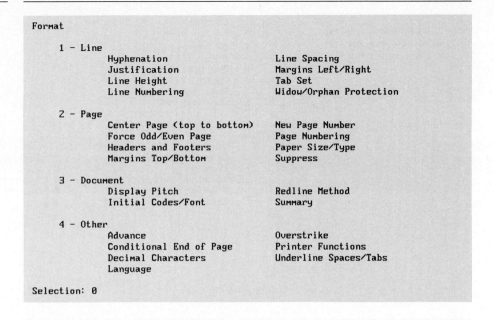

```
Format

     1 - Line
                Hyphenation                 Line Spacing
                Justification               Margins Left/Right
                Line Height                 Tab Set
                Line Numbering              Widow/Orphan Protection

     2 - Page
                Center Page (top to bottom) New Page Number
                Force Odd/Even Page         Page Numbering
                Headers and Footers         Paper Size/Type
                Margins Top/Bottom          Suppress

     3 - Document
                Display Pitch               Redline Method
                Initial Codes/Font          Summary

     4 - Other
                Advance                     Overstrike
                Conditional End of Page     Printer Functions
                Decimal Characters          Underline Spaces/Tabs
                Language

Selection: 0
```

Figure C.3

The Line submenu of the Format command contains the Line Spacing option for resetting the spacing of a document.

```
Format: Line

     1 - Hyphenation                          Off

     2 - Hyphenation Zone - Left              10%
                           Right              4%

     3 - Justification                        No

     4 - Line Height                          Auto

     5 - Line Numbering                       No

     6 - Line Spacing                         2

     7 - Margins - Left                       1"
                   Right                      1"

     8 - Tab Set                              0", every 0.5"

     9 - Widow/Orphan Protection              Yes



Selection: 0
```

You can now change this setting by entering a 4 or an S to change the line spacing. Your cursor now jumps to that option on the screen. Enter a new value for your line spacing, and press the ENTER key when you are finished. Press the ENTER key again to get back to the Format Menu. Press it again to get back to your document.

NOTE You can also use the Cancel (F1) command to back up one menu at a time to return to your document.

Printing the Document (p. 153)

You are now ready to print your INPUT1 document. WordPerfect enables you to print a file that resides either in RAM or on disk; you are not required to save the file before you print. The Print command is evoked by the SHIFT + F7

Figure C.4
The Print Menu is displayed on your screen once you issue the Print command.

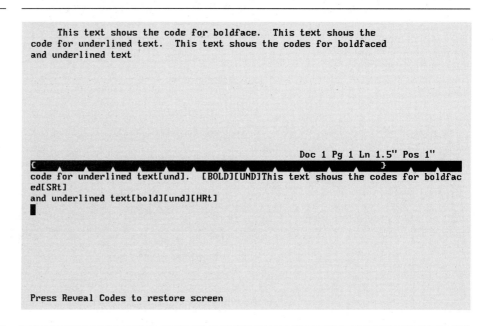

```
Print

    1 - Full Document
    2 - Page
    3 - Document on Disk
    4 - Control Printer
    5 - Type Through
    6 - View Document
    7 - Initialize Printer

Options

    S - Select Printer          HP LaserJet
    B - Binding                 0"
    N - Number of Copies        1
    G - Graphics Quality        Medium
    T - Text Quality            High




Selection: 0
```

Figure C.5
The Reveal Codes screens with WordPerfect 5.0 codes.

```
        This text shows the code for boldface.  This text shows the
code for underlined text.   This text shows the codes for boldfaced
and underlined text




                                         Doc 1 Pg 1 Ln 1.5" Pos 1"
[                                                             }
code for underlined text[und].   [BOLD][UND]This text shows the codes for boldfac
ed[SRt]
and underlined text[bold][und][HRt]



Press Reveal Codes to restore screen
```

keystrokes. Once the Print command has been given, the menu depicted in Figure C.4 is displayed on your screen.

To begin the print operation, depress the 1 or F key. After the * Please Wait * message is displayed on the screen, your document will be printed. Notice that the text on your screen has a ragged right-hand margin and that the printed text has an even right-hand margin (right-justification). This smooth right-hand margin is one of the print defaults of WordPerfect. We'll see later how to turn this off.

WordPerfect Codes

(p. 164)

To exit the Reveal Codes screen, issue another Reveal Codes (Alt + F3) command. If you have a keyboard with twelve function keys, you can also issue a Reveal Codes command by pressing the F11 key. Figure C.5 also shows changes in WordPerfect codes that have occurred from version 4.2 to version 5.0.

Figure C.6
The Print Menu displayed on your screen when the Print (SHIFT + F7) command is issued.

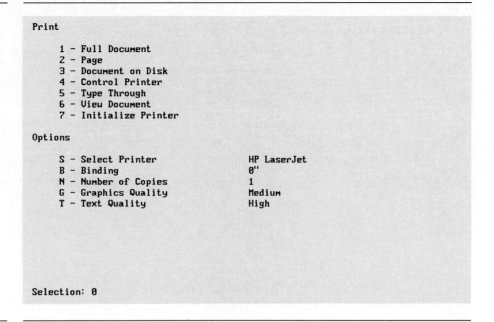

```
Print

    1 - Full Document
    2 - Page
    3 - Document on Disk
    4 - Control Printer
    5 - Type Through
    6 - View Document
    7 - Initialize Printer

Options

    S - Select Printer          HP LaserJet
    B - Binding                 0"
    N - Number of Copies        1
    G - Graphics Quality        Medium
    T - Text Quality            High




Selection: 0
```

Printing Files (p. 165)

Chapter 6 showed you how to print a file with what could be termed the "quick and dirty" method, which assumes that fanfold paper is mounted in the printer. However, you may want your output printed on good single-sheet rag bond paper, or you may not want to print the complete document, or you may want to print only "this" page. The Print (SHIFT + F7) command enables you to give complete printing instructions to WordPerfect.

When WordPerfect prints a file, the character positions line up on the paper in the same fashion that the margins indicated when you are editing the file. Thus, WordPerfect automatically gives you a one-inch left-hand margin on the printed output. This margin can be expanded simply by positioning the paper farther to the left in the printer.

After the Print (SHIFT + F7) command is issued, the Print Menu appears on your screen (see Figure C.6).

Print Option of Print Menu

NOTE WordPerfect usually provides the zero (0) entry of a menu as the default. If you press the ENTER key, you are usually returned to the document or to a higher-order menu.

Option 1. This "quick and dirty" method takes note of all print options that you have previously defined and prints the entire document that resides in RAM accordingly.

Option 2. Only the page on which the cursor resides is printed.

Option 3. This option allows you to tell WordPerfect to print a file that resides on disk. After you enter the file name, press the ENTER key. WordPerfect now wants to know if you wish to print the entire file. If you do, press the ENTER key. If you want to print only selected pages from the file, use the following format:

N	Print only page N
N,M	Print only pages N and M
N-	Print the file beginning at page N

Figure C.7
The Control Printer Menu.

```
Print: Control Printer

Current Job

Job Number:  None                           Page Number:  None
Status:      No print jobs                  Current Copy: None
Message:     None
Paper:       None
Location:    None
Action:      None


Job List

Job  Document              Destination        Print Options




Additional Jobs Not Shown: 0




1 Cancel Job(s); 2 Rush Job; 3 Display Jobs; 4 Go (start printer); 5 Stop: 0
```

N-M	Print pages N through M of the file
-M	Print the document through page M

Option 4. The Control Printer Menu is displayed (see Figure C.7). The entries from this menu allow you to cancel, rush, or display print jobs. You can also see what page is currently being printed.

Option 1 (Cancel Jobs(s)) of the Control Printer Menu allows you to cancel any of the print jobs listed on the Printer Control Menu. After this command has been issued, enter the number of the print job that you wish to cancel. If you wish to cancel all print jobs, type an asterisk (*), then enter a Y to cancel all print jobs.

Option 2 (Rush Job) of the Control Printer Menu permits you to change the priority of a document in the print job list. Only a job found in the print job list can be rushed. This means that you must first submit a job using either option 1 or 3 of the Print Menu (print full document or document on disk). Once you have issued the print command, you can select the Control Printer option and then select the Rush job (2) option. Enter the number of the print job that you want to rush.

WordPerfect now prompts you about when you wish to print this job. If you then select an N, this document will be printed after the current document. If you enter a Y, the interrupted job continues printing until the top of the next page is reached. The new document is then printed. After the rushed document is finished, the interrupted print job is finished.

Option 3 (Display Jobs) of the Control Printer Menu permits you to display a listing of jobs that have been submitted for printing. If WordPerfect cannot display all of the jobs on the screen, a message Additional jobs not shown. appears at the bottom of the menu screen with the number of additional jobs waiting to be printed.

Option 4 (Go) allows you to restart printing if it has been interrupted. Option 5 (Stop) allows you to stop printing if a paper jam or other type of hardware problem occurs.

WordPerfect has its own queuing method for printing files. A queue is another word for a waiting line. Many word processing packages can accept printing instructions for only one document at a time, and before instructions for printing another document can be given, the previous document must be finished. WordPerfect creates a queue (waiting line) of documents to be printed. If printing of the current document is not finished, a document for which you issue the Print command is placed at the end of the waiting line. Any documents nearer the front of the line must print before WordPerfect prints the added document.

Printing multiple files from disk requires that you enter multiple Print commands. For each Print Document on Disk command issued, WordPerfect prompts you for the name of the file and adds that to the queue for later printing. After all of the files that you want to print have been added to the queue, simply press the ENTER key.

Options Portion of Print Menu

The Options portion of the Print Menu is used both to display status information about the selected printer and to change selected print features.

The Select Printer option tells you which printer is currently the active printer. WordPerfect can be configured so that several printers can be used with a single copy of the software. This option is used to select a different printer drive. A listing of printer drivers is displayed on the screen. You select an appropriate printer driver by highlighting the desired driver, using arrow keys to highlight the appropriate printer, and then pressing the ENTER key. The newly selected printer now appears on the Options portion of the Print Menu.

It is important that you have the correct printer specified; otherwise, strange characters will appear on your paper, or the entire document may (maddeningly) be printed with only one line on a sheet of paper.

The Binding option allows you to tell WordPerfect how much space you want text shifted to the right and the left on a page for binding on two-sided copies. This allows room on two-sided documents for punched holes or other types of binding mechanism.

The Number of Copies option allows you to indicate to WordPerfect how many copies of each document it is supposed to print. If a multiple page document is to be printed, the entire document is printed for each copy.

The remaining two options provide you with self-explanatory menus that provide control over the quality of the text and graphics to be printed.

Date Command (p. 169)

The Date command accesses the system date information that you entered and changes it so that it is presented in a format such as January 7, 1990. This command requires that you enter the system date manually or have a clock/calendar in your computer. The Date command, invoked via the SHIFT + F5 keystrokes, displays the following menu (only the date-related portion is illustrated here):

```
1 Date Text; 2 Date Code; 3 Date Format
```

Option 1 inserts the date at the cursor location. Option 2, the Date code, enables you to "date stamp" a document. Then, no matter when you print or retrieve the document, the current date and time will be inserted. For example, if you type a document on January 7, 1989 and then print it two days later, the printout will be dated January 9, 1989.

Figure C.8
The Date Format Menu.

```
Date Format

     Character   Meaning
         1       Day of the Month
         2       Month (number)
         3       Month (word)
         4       Year (all four digits)
         5       Year (last two digits)
         6       Day of the Week (word)
         7       Hour (24-hour clock)
         8       Hour (12-hour clock)
         9       Minute
         0       am / pm
         %       Used before a number, will:
                     Pad numbers less than 10 with a leading zero
                     Output only 3 letters for the month or day of the week


     Examples:  3 1, 4       = December 25, 1984
                %6 %3 1, 4   = Tue Dec 25, 1984
                %2/%1/5 (6)  = 01/01/85 (Tuesday)
                8:90         = 10:55am


Date format: 3 1, 4
```

Option 3 allows you to build your own date format scheme and, to facilitate this process, displays the Format Menu in Figure C.8. Using the options provided in the Date Format Menu, you can indicate to WordPerfect exactly how you want the date and time displayed in your document. WordPerfect does, however, place a limit of twenty-nine characters on the format pattern.

Margin Commands
(p. 170)

The WordPerfect Format (SHIFT + F8) command enables you to reset the right- and left-hand margins by selecting the Line option from that menu. Once the Line Menu is displayed on the screen, you can choose the Margins command to effect your changes. The defaults are a one-inch right- and left-hand margin. If you wish to change the margins, you must indicate the new margin size by entering a change in tenths of an inch. For example, if you wished to change the left-hand margin to an inch-and-a-half, you would enter an M (WordPerfect now places the cursor at the Left margin entry), then enter a margin size of 1.5 and press the ENTER key. (WordPerfect now positions the pointer at the Right margin entry.) If you do not wish to change the right-hand margin, press the ENTER key (see Figure C.9).

The new margins that you set begin at the cursor location; if the cursor is not at the beginning of a line, a [Hrt] is inserted in the text by WordPerfect to place the margins at the beginning of a line.

After you enter a new value for the right-hand margin and press the ENTER key, the new margins are in effect. These margins will remain in effect until new ones are entered. To change the margins for another part of your document, position the cursor at the beginning of a new line and repeat the process. Because embedded codes are used, various margins can be used in different parts of the document without interfering with each other.

Assume that the following text (the Input1 file) is part of a document:

```
A file is a collection of related information. This
information can be in the form of data or
instructions for manipulating that information. In
other words, files can be either data files or
```

Figure C.9
The Line Format Menu after
the left-hand margin is
changed to 1.5".

```
Format: Line

    1 - Hyphenation                        Off

    2 - Hyphenation Zone - Left            10%
                          Right            4%

    3 - Justification                      Yes

    4 - Line Height                        Auto

    5 - Line Numbering                     No

    6 - Line Spacing                       1

    7 - Margins - Left                     1.5"
                  Right                    1"

    8 - Tab Set                            0", every 0.5"

    9 - Widow/Orphan Protection            No


Selection: 0
```

```
program files. You keep track of files on a disk by
their names. Each file name must be unique
(different) from any other file name.
```

Now suppose that you want the left-hand margin to be 2 inches and the right-hand margin to be 1½ inches. You position the cursor to the beginning of the line, issue the Format command (SHIFT + F8), select the Line (L) option to get the Line submenu, enter a 7 or M to select the Margin option, enter a 2 and hit ENTER to change the left-hand margin, and enter a 1.5 and hit ENTER to change the right-hand margin. You should see the following:

```
A file is a collection of related information.
This information can be in the form of data
or instructions for manipulating that
information. In other words, files can be
either data files or program files. You keep
track of files on a disk by their names. Each
file name must be unique (different) from any
other file name.
```

Tabs and Resetting Tabs (p. 173)

Chapter 7 mentioned that each of the triangles beneath the status line on the Reveal Codes screen represents a tab stop. The tab stops in WordPerfect work the same way they do on a typewriter, except that the cursor (rather than the entire carriage) is repositioned to the next tab. The cursor is moved from one tab stop to another by pressing the TAB key.

You may want tab stops at only two or three locations, since one tab stop every half-inch may be too many for a particular application. You can clear all tab stops from the ruler line by entering the Format (SHIFT + F8) command, selecting the Line command from the Format Menu, selecting the Tab Set command, and then entering the Delete to EOL (Ctrl + End) command. Once the Tab command is entered, a screen like that depicted in Figure C.10 appears on your screen. Each L represents one tab stop on the ruler line, and as you

Figure C.10
The Tabs Menu that appears
at the bottom of your screen.

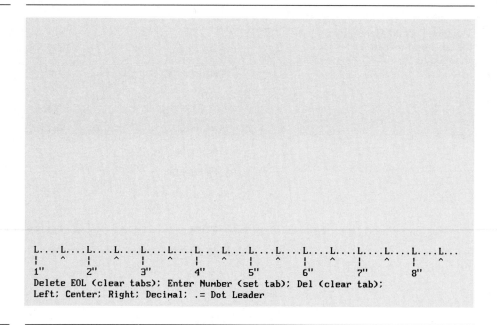

```
L....L....L....L....L....L....L....L....L....L....L....L....L....L....L...
 !    ^   !    ^   !    ^   !    ^   !    ^   !    ^   !    ^   !    ^
 1"       2"       3"       4"       5"       6"       7"       8"
Delete EOL (clear tabs); Enter Number (set tab); Del (clear tab);
Left; Center; Right; Decimal; .= Dot Leader
```

can see, there is one tab stop every half-inch. The menu takes up five lines at the bottom of your screen. The Exit (F7) command is issued when all changes are finished.

To delete all of the tab stops, enter the Delete EOL (Ctrl + End) command. This command is usually executed before the new tab stops are entered, which cuts down on the number of TAB keystrokes. Once the Delete EOL command has been issued, only periods remain on the ruler line. You can now issue the Exit (F7) command to return to your document, or you can create new tab stops. To create new tabs, simply move the cursor to the appropriate location and type t (TAB). An alternative method involves entering the tab location in inches from the keyboard (for example, 2.5 and 4). Assume that you have set tab stops at 2.5 and 4 inches. Now, if you enter the two columns of text below, you will see the following:

```
Men's        125.00
Women's       35.00
Boys'          5.00
Sports       123.50
```

Notice that the columns are oriented toward alphabetic text; that is, the text aligns at the left-hand side of the column, and the numbers do not align on the decimal points.

Aligning columns of numbers is accomplished by using the Tab Align (Ctrl + F6) command. This command lines up text or numbers vertically on a character such as a decimal point. If you wish to change the alignment character, issue the Format (SHIFT + F8) command, take the Other option (4), select the Decimal/Align Character option (see Figure C.11), and enter the new character.

The decimal point (period) is the default alignment character (therefore this command is not needed if you wish to align numbers that contain decimal fractions). You can change this character as often as you wish. For example, if you are dealing with whole numbers and wish to keep track of negative num-

Figure C.11
The Format/Other/Decimal command allows you to change the decimal align character to fit your particular application.

```
Format: Other

     1 - Advance

     2 - Conditional End of Page

     3 - Decimal/Align Character              .
         Thousands' Separator                 ,

     4 - Language                            EN

     5 - Overstrike

     6 - Printer Functions

     7 - Underline - Spaces                  Yes
                     Tabs                    No




Selection: 3
```

bers that are contained in parentheses, your decimal align number would be the right parenthesis. This allows the right parenthesis to appear to the right of any numbers, as in the example below:

```
65,000
 7,000
  (500)
99,567
```

To realign the previous two-column example, each line has to be entered again: Enter the information at the first tab, position the cursor to the second tab by issuing the Tab Align (Ctrl + F6) command, and then enter the numeric text.

```
Men's        125.00
Women's       35.00
Boys'          5.00
Sports       123.50
```

Notice that the numbers align on the decimal point. You also may have noticed that Align char=. appears on your screen as a reminder. Typed text moves to the left until the alignment character is entered (a . in this case) or until the TAB, Tab Align, or ENTER key is pressed. Text typed after the Tab Align command is inserted normally.

You may have noticed that you had difficulty in remembering to enter the Tab Align (Ctrl + F6) command to get the decimal tab stop to work properly. This is a relatively common problem because WordPerfect is using a text tab stop as a decimal tab only when the special command Tab Align is used. You can get around this problem by changing the L of a tab stop on the tab stop ruler line to a D. The D tells WordPerfect that this tab stop is to function as a decimal tab rather than as a text tab. Now, when you are entering numeric text, all that is required is to press the TAB key and the Align char=. message appears at the bottom of the screen when the tab hits this decimal align tab.

You can use the following special characters on a tab stop line to determine how a tab stop operates:

L   Operates as a text tab stop with left-most alignment.

C   Centers text at this tab stop location.

R   Right-justifies text at this tab stop location.

D   Issues a Tab Align command to justify this text according to the decimal tab character.

Block Command
(p. 174)

New WordPerfect Commands
That Use the Block Feature (p. 176)

This command provides you with great flexibility in moving or copying chunks of text and moving them from one place in a document to another. It also allows you to delete the original text, which can consist of a sentence, paragraph, page, or block of text. Using the Move feature of WordPerfect is a two-step process that requires you first to indicate which text is to be moved or copied and then to indicate where the text is to be copied or moved. The Move command, invoked by depressing the Ctrl + F4 keys, displays the following menu:

```
Move 1 Sentence; 2 Paragraph; 3 Page; Retrieve 4: 0
```

The Move (Ctrl + F4) command executes at the current cursor location for a sentence, paragraph, or page of text. After you depress the appropriate numeric key to indicate to WordPerfect the amount of text that you want moved, the affected text is displayed in reverse video (black on white) on your screen and the following menu is displayed:

```
1 Move; 2 Copy; 3 Delete; 4 Append: 0
```

The Move option of the move feature removes the highlighted text from your document and places it in a temporary file.

Figure C.12
WordPerfect 5.0 commands with which you can use the Block command.

```
Bold                    Print
Center                  Replace
Delete                  Save
Font                    Sort
Appearance (All)        Spell
Size (All)              Switch
Format                  Underline
Macro                   Flush Right
Move                    Search
Block
Tabular Column
Rectangle
```

The Copy option leaves the original text in your document but also copies it to a temporary file. The highlighted text returns to regular video and is left unchanged. The copy feature works much as a duplicating machine might, leaving the original intact.

The Delete option removes the marked text from your document without saving it to a temporary file. (This text can, however, be restored via the Undelete command.)

The Append command allows you to take the highlighted text and add it to the end of an existing file on disk. When it is selected, WordPerfect queries you about which file the text is to be added to via the prompt Append to: _. Enter the file name and press the ENTER key; WordPerfect now adds the text to the end of the indicated file.

Retrieving Text. Once you have used a Move or Copy command, WordPerfect provides you with two alternatives for retrieving text. The first method assumes that you are going to immediately retrieve the text at a new location. You now receive a prompt at the bottom of the screen that says Move cursor; press ENTER to retrieve. You now position the cursor to the appropriate location in the document and press the ENTER key. The text is then placed at the cursor location in your document. You can cancel this "immediate move" by issuing the Cancel (F1) command if you wish to perform other tasks and then retrieve the text later.

If you have interrupted the Move command via a Cancel, use the following method of retrieving text. Position the cursor to the place in your document that you want to receive the block. You again issue the Move (Ctrl + F4) command and receive the following menu:

Move: 1 Sentence; 2 Paragraph; 3 Page; 4 Retrieve: 0

The Retrieve portion of the menu is now used. To perform a regular retrieve, press the 4 key. WordPerfect now displays the menu below to ask how you want this text moved:

Retrieve: 1 Block; 2 Tabular Column; 3 Rectangle: 0

Select the Block option (1) and the marked text is copied to the cursor location.

The following example shows how the Move command (move option) is used to move the second sentence to a new position behind the third sentence. The original order is as follows:

This is the first sentence. This is the second sentence. This is the third sentence. This is the fourth sentence.

To mark the second sentence, position the cursor anywhere in that sentence. Enter the Move (Ctrl + F4) command, and the Move Menu is displayed at the bottom of your screen. Select the Sentence option (placing the sentence in reverse video), and then take the Move option. The highlighted text is now deleted from the paragraph and saved to a temporary file, and WordPerfect knows what type of operation is to be performed. After re-forming, the text now appears like that below.

This is the first sentence. This is the third sentence. This is the fourth sentence.

Move the cursor to the T at the beginning of the fourth sentence, and press the ENTER key. The text is now moved and should look like the following:

```
This is the first sentence. This is the third
sentence. This is the second sentence. This is the
fourth sentence.
```

The next example shows the use of the Copy option of the move feature. The same sequence of commands are executed except that the Copy option was selected instead of Move.

Before:

```
This is the first sentence. This is the second
sentence. This is the third sentence. This is the
fourth sentence.
```

After:

```
This is the first sentence. This is the second
sentence. This is the third sentence. This is the
second sentence. This is the fourth sentence.
```

Rectangular Blocks. You may want to move a rectangular or columnar block of text in a highlighted area rather than the entire text. The regular block moves transfer all of the text, from the beginning of the marked area to the end of the marked area, no matter how wide the line or lines are. For rectangular blocks, however, you specify the width of the text block to be moved. The beginning and ending locations of the cursor determine the upper left-hand and lower right-hand corners of the rectangular block of text.

Position the cursor at the upper left-hand corner of the text to be moved. Enter the Block (Alt + F4) command, highlight (the entire lines are highlighted), and place the cursor in the lower right-hand corner. Even though the entire text looks as though it is highlighted, subsequent commands will reduce the area.

After you have highlighted the block, issue the Move (Ctrl + F4) command, and you will receive the Block Move Menu. Select the Rectangle option from the menu depicted below:

```
Move: 1 Block; 2 Tabular Column; 3 Rectangle: 0
```

The area of text denoted by the original upper left-hand and lower right-hand cursor positions is now highlighted on the screen. You now receive the following menu:

```
1 Move; 2 Copy; 3 Delete; 4 Append: 0
```

Only the highlighted text is affected by your choice of operation. All text outside the highlighted area remains unchanged. Now position the cursor to the beginning of the line and press the ENTER key. The column of marked text is now moved.

If you interrupt the move process with a Cancel command, be sure to use the Rectangle option when you retrieve the text; otherwise, the text from the last regular Move command will be restored to the cursor location rather than the text from the rectangle just marked. Also, make certain that there is enough room in the area to receive the block. If there is not enough room, existing text will be moved to the right, and the document will look like a mess.

In the next example, assume that Col1 is to be moved to the right of Col2 below:

```
Col1    Col2
Col1    Col2
Col1    Col2
Col1    Col2
```

In this case, the cursor must be moved under the C of Col1, and the Block (Alt + F4) command is issued. The blocked area is now extended to include the last Col1. Notice that all of the lines in both columns appear in reverse video. Issue the Move (Ctrl + F4) command, and select the Rectangle option. Now only the Col1 is highlighted. Tell WordPerfect to execute a Move command. Your screen will show the following:

```
Col2
Col2
Col2
Col2
```

Now position your cursor to the location that you want to place the text— in this case, to the right of Col2. Press the ENTER key and the text is moved. The following will then appear on your screen:

```
Col2    Col1
Col2    Col1
Col2    Col1
Col2    Col1
```

Redline and Strikeout. These options let you mark text within a document to draw attention to added text or to text that you think should be deleted. The redline feature marks a line(s) of text by placing a vertical bar in the left margin next to any indicated text. You invoke the redline feature by issuing the Font (Ctrl + F8) command and then taking the Appearance option. The following menu is now displayed:

```
1 Bold 2 Undrln 3 Dbl Und 4 Italc 5 Outln 6 Shadw 7 SmCap 8 Redln 9 StkOut: 0
```

Now select the Redline option by depressing the 8 key. You can now enter the text that you desire to be redlined. When you are finished, issue another Font (Ctrl + F8) command, select the Appearance option, and then select Normal (3). On a color monitor, the text will be displayed in red, while a monochrome monitor that has been specially configured for WordPerfect will display the text in some form of shaded video. On a printout, the text will look something like the following:

```
This is an example of a text residing in a paragraph
that has been marked via the redline command.
```

The Strikeout command causes a dash (-) to be printed over every character in a portion of text, indicating that the marked text is not supposed to be there.

To use the Strikeout command, invoke the Block (Alt + F4) command, highlight the desired text, issue the Font (Ctrl + F8) command, take the Appearance option, and choose the Strikeout (9) option. Although the dashes do not appear on the screen, they will appear in the printed document. On a color monitor, the strikeout text appears in green on the monitor.

~~Text marked via the Strikeout command.~~

To remove redline markings and delete all strikeout text, issue the Reveal Codes (Alt + F3) command and remove the codes from your document.

Superscript/Subscript. The superscript or subscript allows you to print a character or a block of characters to be one-third to one-half line above (superscript) or below (subscript) the current line of text. This WordPerfect feature is useful in both scientific and academic environments.

These commands may not be supported (that is, the output cannot always be predicted) on dot-matrix printers, but they are supported by most letter-quality printers. The Superscript/Subscript is accomplished by first including the character(s) in a Block (Alt + F4) command, issuing the Font (Ctrl + F8) command, selecting the Size option, and then taking either option 1 or 2 from the following menu:

```
1 Suprscpt; 2 Subscpt; 3 Fine; 4 Small; 5 Large; 6 Vry Large; 7 Ext Large: 0
```

Once the appropriate command has been issued, the text appears highlighted on the screen, but it does not appear as a subscript or superscript. In order to verify how the text will print, you must issue the Reveal Codes (Alt + F3) command. You turn off subscripting/superscripting by issuing the Font (Ctrl + F8) command and taking the Normal (3) option.

Simple subscript:	A_2
Simple superscript:	2^2
Multiple subscript:	$Chromium_{Dioxide}$
Multiple superscript:	A^{23}

Chapter 8 introduces you to WordPerfect's Format/Print command features that enable you to accent your document with page headings, footings, justified and ragged right-hand margins, and various styles of fonts, among other things.

Format (p. 203)

The Format (SHIFT + F8) command allows you to control how a document is to appear on the screen as well as how it is to be printed on paper. This particular menu (see Figure C.13) contains four submenus: Line, Page, Document, and Other. Together, these submenus provide tremendous flexibility in document design. Once one of these menu options is selected, a new menu appears on your screen. Each of these menus will be discussed in detail here.

Most of the commands in the Format Menu embed codes in your document to perform a desired task. If you want one of these options to affect the entire document, you must first position to the beginning of your document via a Home or Home Up Arrow command. The code for the desired command will now be in effect for the entire document. If you want only an area of the document to be affected, position the cursor to that area of the document and enter the command. From the cursor location on, the document is now affected by this command. You may now have to position the cursor at the end of the area of your document to be affected and then enter a new command to enter the original settings to return the rest of the document to its original settings.

Figure C.13
The Format Menu.

```
Format

    1 - Line
            Hyphenation                    Line Spacing
            Justification                  Margins Left/Right
            Line Height                    Tab Set
            Line Numbering                 Widow/Orphan Protection

    2 - Page
            Center Page (top to bottom)    New Page Number
            Force Odd/Even Page            Page Numbering
            Headers and Footers            Paper Size/Type
            Margins Top/Bottom             Suppress

    3 - Document
            Display Pitch                  Redline Method
            Initial Codes/Font             Summary

    4 - Other
            Advance                        Overstrike
            Conditional End of Page        Printer Functions
            Decimal Characters             Underline Spaces/Tabs
            Language

Selection: 0
```

Figure C.14
The Format Line submenu.

```
Format: Line

    1 - Hyphenation                        Off

    2 - Hyphenation Zone - Left            10%
                          Right            4%

    3 - Justification                      Yes

    4 - Line Height                        Auto

    5 - Line Numbering                     No

    6 - Line Spacing                       1

    7 - Margins - Left                     1"
                  Right                    1"

    8 - Tab Set                            0", every 0.5"

    9 - Widow/Orphan Protection            No




Selection: 0
```

Line

The Line Format Menu (see Figure C.14) contains several menu options that allow you to control line endings, spacing, numbering, grouping, length, and tab settings.

Hyphenation. This option allows you to turn the hyphen help facility of WordPerfect on or off (the default is off). The hyphen help facility allows you to hyphenate words that extend beyond the right-hand margin. If this option is selected, WordPerfect displays the following menu:

```
1 Off;   2 Manual;   3 Auto: 0
```

If manual hyphenation is selected, WordPerfect displays the message Po-sition hyphen; Press ESC on the status line when a word is to be hyphenated along the right-hand margin. If the automatic option (3) is selected, WordPerfect follows internal rules in placing the hyphen.

Hyphenation Zone: Left/Right. WordPerfect offers 10 percent of text line length zone for the left margin and a 4 percent zone line length for the right-hand margin. Generally, the smaller the right-hand margin zone on the right-hand margin, the less space that appears at the end or embedded within a line.

Justification. This option allows you to print the text with spacing added between printed characters to keep an even right-hand margin or to specify that you want a ragged right-hand margin beginning at the cursor location. The default (Yes) enables right justification.

Note that the text on the screen appears with a ragged right-hand margin. If you have not changed this option (the default is Yes), the text will appear with an even right-hand margin when it is printed. You can verify that justification is on by entering the Format (SHIFT + F8) command and then taking the Line option.

Line Height. Line height refers to the amount of space assigned to each line and is measured from the baseline (bottom) of one line to the baseline of the next line. This option is best left on automatic for novice users of WordPerfect.

Line Numbering. This option allows you to print your document so that line numbers appear at the beginning of each line of text. It starts executing at the cursor location and provides you with a number of options. When the command is invoked, WordPerfect displays the menu depicted in Figure C.15. Line numbering can be turned on and off in the document as many times as you desire.

Line Spacing. You are allowed to change the spacing of a WordPerfect document in any manner. You can easily single-, double-, or even triple-space a document by changing this entry to a 1, 2, or 3, respectively. You can also specify line-and-a-half spacing by entering 1.5.

Margins: Left/Right. This option allows you to specify to WordPerfect the length of each of these margins in inches. If a fractional portion of an inch is desired, use decimal fractions. For example, the entry 1.5 results in a margin of 1½ inches.

Tab Set. This option is used to set the tabs within a document. Please refer to the prior discussion on the command.

Widow/Orphan Protection. A widow occurs when only the first line of a paragraph appears at the bottom of a page. An orphan occurs when the last line of a paragraph appears at the top of a page. The Widow/Orphan Protection option allows you to tell WordPerfect to avoid widow and orphan lines throughout a document (if the cursor is at the beginning) or from the cursor location onward. As you can see, the default for this option is No. To use this option, select option 9 and enter a Y. The Widow/Orphan protection is now in effect beginning at the cursor location.

Page

The Page option of the Format Menu (see Figure C.16) provides you with control over how text is to appear on a page, the amount of text that is to appear, paper changes, and headers or footers, as well as page numbering.

Figure C.15
The Line Numbering Menu.

```
Format: Line Numbering

        1 - Count Blank Lines                        Yes

        2 - Number Every n Lines, where n is         1

        3 - Position of Number from Left Edge        0.6"

        4 - Starting Number                          1

        5 - Restart Numbering on Each Page           Yes
```

```
Selection: 0
```

Figure C.16
The Page Format Menu.

```
Format: Page

        1 - Center Page (top to bottom)     No

        2 - Force Odd/Even Page

        3 - Headers

        4 - Footers

        5 - Margins - Top                   1"
                      Bottom                1"

        6 - New Page Number                 1
              (example: 3 or iii)

        7 - Page Numbering                  No page numbering

        8 - Paper Size                      8.5" x 11"
                    Type                    Standard

        9 - Suppress (this page only)
```

```
Selection: 0
```

Center Page (Top to Bottom). This option centers information vertically on the page when the document is printed by inserting the same number of blank lines before and after text; it is used to center short letters of correspondence, figures, or tables on a page. Make certain that you position the cursor at the beginning of the page before entering this command. Only the page on which the code is embedded is centered.

Force Odd/Even Page. This command ensures that a particular page is numbered with an odd or even number. Once this command is issued, the following menu appears on your screen:

```
1 Odd;   2 Even: 0
```

You now enter the appropriate menu selection: 1 for odd or 2 for even.

Headers/Footers. Headers and footers are lines of text printed in the top and bottom margins, respectively. You only need to enter these commands once, at the start of the file, and the headers and/or footers will be repeated in the manner specified. The default is no header or footer. To create a header or footer, first position the cursor to the beginning of the page on which you want the header or footer to start. After you select a Headers or Footers command, the following menu is displayed at the bottom of your screen:

1 Footer A;   2 Footer B: 0

You now respond to the prompt by indicating which header or footer you wish to use. (You can specify up to two headers and/or footers.) WordPerfect now prompts you on how it is to position text on a page via the following menu, which appears at the bottom of your screen:

1 Discontinue: 2 Every Page;   3 Odd Pages;   4 Even Pages;   5 Edit: 0

After you have indicated how you wish this header/footer to appear, WordPerfect clears the screen to allow you to enter the header/footer text. You can use any special feature commands, such as bold, center, underline, or flush right. The status line of the header/footer text entry screen contains the prompt Press EXIT when done, along with the line and position data. When you are finished entering the header or footer (see Figure C.17), simply press the Exit (F7) command.

WordPerfect provides control over printing headers and footers. It prints headers starting at the top margin of the page. It adds .16 inch between the header and the document text.

The last line of a footer is printed at the bottom margin of the printed page. WordPerfect adds .16 inch between the footer and the document text. The footer is never printed in the bottom margin.

If you discover an error in a header or footer line, you must position the cursor on the line in the document holding the [Header/Footer] code. Use the Reveal Codes (Alt + F3) to locate the code, and position your cursor to the right of the code. You are now ready to correct the error. After you issue the Format (SHIFT + F8) command and select the Page option, the Header/Footer Specification Menu is displayed on the screen. Select the appropriate header/footer and tell WordPerfect to edit by taking option 5, the Edit command. The footer is now displayed on the header/footer entry screen. Make any changes and save it using the Exit (F7) command. A HA or FA entry, along with the header/footer, is now displayed to the Format Page Menu.

You may not wish to have a header on the first page of a document, but you may want the footer to print there. In this case, you must place the header code anywhere after the end of the first line of the first page but before the last line of the first page. This results in the header line(s) printing at the top of the second page rather than at the top of the first page.

The ^B (Ctrl + B) command sequence (see Figure C.17) is used to include the page number in a header or footer. For example, the following sequence would result in the header plus the corresponding page number appearing at the top of each page of text in a file:

Four Software Tools Page ^B

The convention just discussed now provides a problem. If you had previously told WordPerfect to print the page number (for example, centered at the

Figure C.17
A sample footer screen.

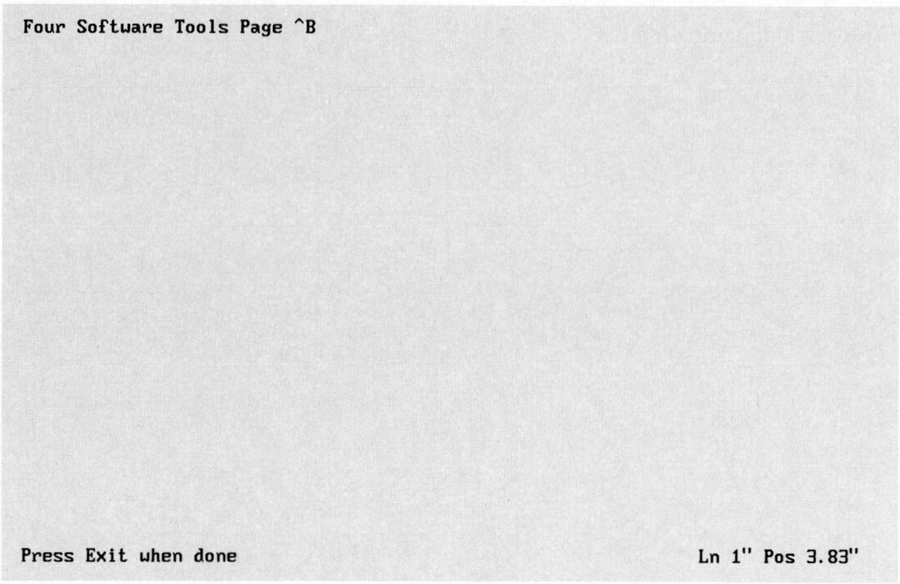

```
Four Software Tools Page ^B




















Press Exit when done                                          Ln 1" Pos 3.83"
```

bottom), it will print the page number twice, once in the header and again at the bottom of each page. You must now tell WordPerfect via the Format (SHIFT + F8) and Page commands not to number the pages.

Margins: Top/Bottom. This option permits you to set new margins at the top and bottom of each page. The default margins are 1 inch.

New Page Number. The page numbering of a document is automatically controlled by WordPerfect. From time to time, however, you may want to alter this automatic numbering. For example, you may be working on a report that is composed of a number of different files—part 1 residing in a file called REPORT1, say, and part 2 residing in a file called REPORT2. Suppose part 1 has ten pages, and you want the two parts to be numbered sequentially. The first page of REPORT2 should then be numbered page 11.

Entering a new page number is a two-step process: (1) enter the new page number, and (2) specify the format of the page number. To accomplish this, place the cursor at the beginning of the REPORT2 file and enter the Format (SHIFT + F8) and Page commands, and then take option 6. Enter the new page number, in this case 11. If you wish to have roman numbering, simply enter the beginning page number as a roman numeral. The Roman option displays numbers as i, ii, iii, iv, and so forth. You can use the Roman option for such things as a preface, foreword, or table of contents.

As soon as you change the page number, the new number appears on the status line. When you print out REPORT1, its pages will be numbered 1 to 10; then when you instruct WordPerfect to print REPORT2, WordPerfect will start the first page of this document with 11 instead of 1. Subsequent pages are numbered consecutively, based on the initial value that you entered.

NOTE When you use page numbers, WordPerfect subtracts the line height of the page number font plus $\frac{1}{6}$ inch from the text space on the page to provide a blank line between the text and the page number. The soft page breaks shown on your screen accurately depict where the printed breaks will occur as long as you do not incorporate headers and footers.

Figure C.18
The Page Numbering Menu.

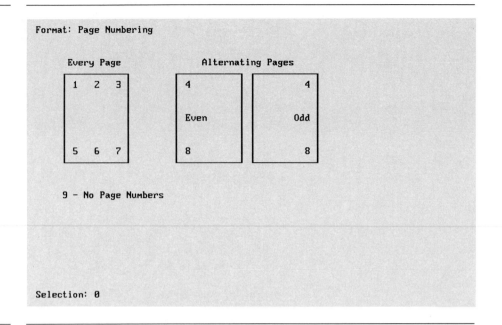

Page Numbering. This option allows you to tell WordPerfect where to place page numbers. The default for this option is no page numbering. When you select this option, a Page Numbering Menu appears on your monitor (see Figure C.18) with the various page numbering options and how they appear when the document is printed. WordPerfect places the page number in the top or bottom margin and subtracts the line height of the page number font plus ⅙ inch from the text space on the page. This means that you get fewer lines of text printed per page. All page numbers are aligned on the margins.

Paper Size/Type. This option permits you to change the size and type of paper that you are using. The default is 8½ × 11 inches. WordPerfect uses this information to keep track of how many lines are to be printed on a page.

Suppress (this page only). This option allows you to turn off any page formatting for this page. You must first position the cursor to the very top of the page and then select this option. The screen depicted in Figure C.19 is then displayed on your screen.

To turn off options 1 and 2, simply enter the option number. To turn off any other options, enter the option number followed by the letter Y (yes).

Document

The Format Document Menu allows you to control the display pitch, change initial WordPerfect settings, determine the redline method, and document a summary within a document.

Display Pitch. This option permits you to control the amount of space that one character occupies on the screen. For novices, this option is best left at the default of automatic.

Initial Settings. This feature lets you display and edit the initial settings for the current document only.

Figure C.19
The Suppress (this page only)
Menu.

```
Format: Suppress (this page only)

    1 - Suppress All Page Numbering, Headers and Footers

    2 - Suppress Headers and Footers

    3 - Print Page Number at Bottom Center    No

    4 - Suppress Page Numbering               No

    5 - Suppress Header A                      No

    6 - Suppress Header B                      No

    7 - Suppress Footer A                      No

    8 - Suppress Footer B                      No




Selection: 0
```

Figure C.20
The Format Document Menu.

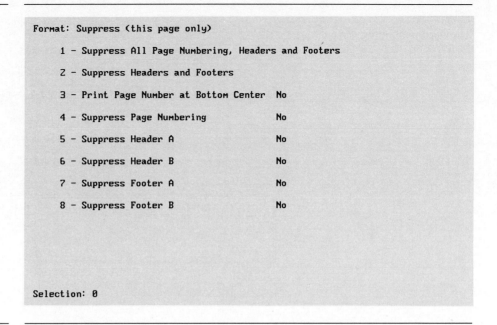

```
Document: Initial Font

* Courier
  Courier Bold
  Courier Bold Oblique
  Courier Oblique
  Helvetica
  Helvetica Bold
  Helvetica Bold Oblique
  Helvetica Narrow
  Helvetica Narrow Bold
  Helvetica Narrow Bold Oblique
  Helvetica Narrow Oblique
  Helvetica Oblique
  ITC Avant Garde Gothic Book
  ITC Avant Garde Gothic Book Oblique
  ITC Avant Garde Gothic Demi
  ITC Avant Garde Gothic Demi Oblique
  ITC Bookman Demi
  ITC Bookman Demi Italic
  ITC Bookman Light
  ITC Bookman Light Italic
  ITC Zapf Chancery Medium Italic

1 Select; N Name search: 1
```

Initial Font. This is the default font selected for your printer. The fonts available are printer dependent. Dot-matrix printers typically have fewer options available than do laser printers. Once this option has been selected, a menu of available fonts is displayed on the screen (see Figure C.20). As you can see from this figure, this printer has many different types of fonts that you can use in a document.

You select the appropriate font by using the arrow keys to highlight that font and press the ENTER key. WordPerfect now asks what point size you wish to use. The larger the point size, the larger the print that appears on paper. (This topic is discussed in detail later.)

Redline Method. This feature, discussed earlier, determines how redline markings are displayed on the printed page. For novices this option is best left to WordPerfect to control.

Figure C.21
The Document Summary
Menu.

```
Document Summary

        System Filename              WORD50AP.P

        Date of Creation             September 26, 1988

    1 - Descriptive Filename         WordPerf50Apndx

    2 - Subject/Account              WordPerfect 5.0 Update

    3 - Author                       Tim Duffy

    4 - Typist                       Tim Duffy

    5 - Comments
       ┌──────────────────────────────────────────────────────────────┐
       │ This file contains the WordPerfect 5.0 Appendix material for the textbook │
       │ Four Software Tools Plus.                                       │
       │                                                                │
       └──────────────────────────────────────────────────────────────┘

Press Exit when done
```

Figure C.22
The Format Other Menu.

```
Format: Other

    1 - Advance

    2 - Conditional End of Page

    3 - Decimal/Align Character          .
        Thousands' Separator             ,

    4 - Language                         EN

    5 - Overstrike

    6 - Printer Functions

    7 - Underline - Spaces               Yes
                    Tabs                 No

Selection: 0
```

Summary. This option allows you to create a document summary for a file (see Figure C.21). The system file name and date of creation are listed. You can also add the author, subject, descriptive file name, and typist. Enter information for each of these items by selecting the appropriate menu item and then enter that data.

Other

The Format Other Menu (see Figure C.22) contains advanced formatting commands. Because your ability to use many of these commands depends on your printer, only the most important commands are covered here.

Advance. This option allows you to position text on the page. The defaults of WordPerfect are sufficient for a novice.

Conditional End of Page. The Conditional End of Page command specifies that, if a page break occurs in the next x lines a hard page break will occur. After entering the command, you must tell WordPerfect how many lines from the cursor location are to be "page-break protected" with the prompt `Number of lines to keep together: _`. This command is useful for protecting tables from page breaks that would otherwise leave half the table at the bottom of one page and place the other half at the top of the next page.

```
Inflation During the 1980s

1980    9.9%
1981    8.5%
1982    6.0%
1983    4.5%
```

In the above example, the cursor is placed at the beginning of the text to be protected. The Format (SHIFT + F8) and Other commands are issued, and the Conditional End of Page command is selected. A 6 is now entered to tell WordPerfect to protect the next six lines from page breaks. This command gives you better control over how page breaks will appear within a document.

Decimal/Align Character. The decimal point (period) is the default alignment character. (Therefore, you do not need this command if you wish to align numbers that contain decimal fractions.) You can change this character as often as you wish. For example, if you are dealing with whole numbers and wish to keep track of negative numbers in parentheses, your decimal align number would be the right parenthesis. This allows the right parenthesis to appear to the right of any numbers, as in the example below:

```
65,000
 7,000
 (500)
99,567
```

If you wish to change the thousands separator from a comma to a right parenthesis, for instance, enter that character after the decimal align character is entered.

Language. This option tells WordPerfect which dictionaries to use. Leave it set at English. This option is useful if you are working on foreign language text and also have the appropriate dictionaries for the new language.

Strikeout. This feature was covered in more detail earlier.

Printer Functions. These advanced features are beyond what beginning WordPerfect users need. Refer to the documentation manual for a discussion of these features.

Underline. This option lets you determine whether or not spaces and tabs are to be underlined. The defaults are Yes for spaces and No for tabs.

Font

WordPerfect's Font Command Menu (see Figure C.23) is used to change your current font and/or change the size, appearance, or color of the text when the document is printed. The manner in which font attributes are displayed on the screen varies with the monitor screen that you are using.

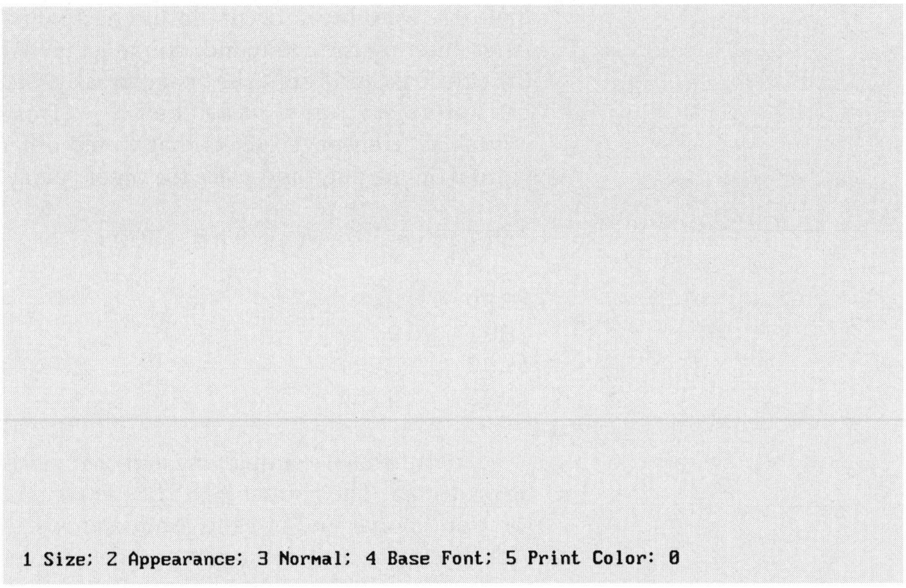

Figure C.23
The Font Menu is displayed at
the bottom of the screen.

```
1 Size; 2 Appearance; 3 Normal; 4 Base Font; 5 Print Color: 0
```

The Font Menu provides you with tremendous flexibility in how your document is to be printed. Various sizes of text can be included in a document using WordPerfect (see Figure C.24 a and b). When using this command, make certain that you have first positioned your cursor where you wish to have the changes start.

When you select a new font size, WordPerfect automatically keeps track of the new line height, character size, and spacing and automatically adjusts all of the spacing increments accordingly. This means that once you have set your margins, you don't have to worry about them even when you are printing larger characters. Page size is also automatically tracked by WordPerfect so that page breaks occur at the correct locations.

When you select this option, be certain that you have the appropriate base font selected. If you want to change the size of the regular type that will appear in your printed document, select option 4 before any other changes are made to the document.

Size. This option determines the amount of space characters are to take up on a line (refer to Figure C.24 a). Once this option is selected, a menu like that depicted below appears at the bottom of your screen:

```
1 Suprscpt; 2 Subscpt; 3 Fine; 4 Small; 5 Large;
6 Vry Large; 7 Ext Large: 0
```

Select the size option that you wish. Any text now selected appears in a specific color or shade based on the type of monitor attached to your computer.

Appearance. The Appearance option deals with the style of text. Once this option is selected, the following menu appears at the bottom of your screen.

```
1 Bold  2 Underln  3 Dbl Und  4 Italc  5 Outln
6 Shadow  7 Sm Cap  8 Redln  9 StkOut: 0
```

Two of these options, Bold and Underline, are available using the F6 and F8 keys, respectively.

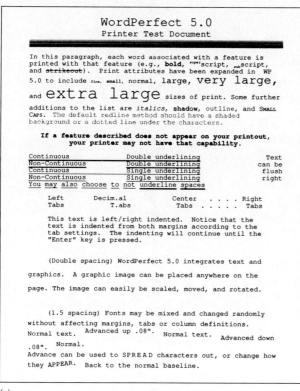

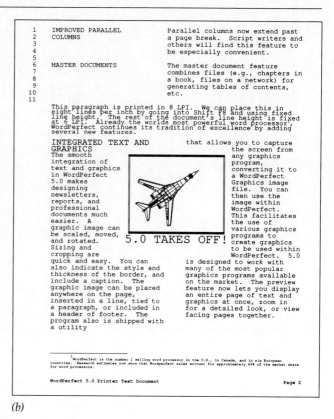

(a)   (b)

Figure C.24
(a) The PRINTER.TST document provides a sample of various font sizes and
(b) an example of how WordPerfect 5.0 can intermix text and graphics.

Normal. The Normal option allows you to cancel any selected font features that have been turned on and return any following text back to the base font.

Base Font. This option lets you select the initial font against which any other font options will be controlled. When this option is selected, menus similar to those depicted in Figure C.20 are displayed. You now select the font as well as the point size to be used as the beginning size.

Print Color. If you have a color printer, this option allows you to control which colors to use in the document; you also determine how these colors will be shaded. Once this option is selected (see Figure C.25), a menu of possible colors is displayed to the screen. If you are using a regular printer, no color is assumed.

Appendix Review

WordPerfect allows you to control how information will appear on the page and provides flexibility in how the document will be printed. Some of the Format commands allow you to control page numbering, centering, page length and the top margin, and the occurrence of widow and orphan lines, as well as insert headers and/or footers and Conditional End of Page commands.

You can obtain other special printing features by using the Font command. Options from this menu allow you to control the pitch and font, underlining style, and size of text to be printed.

Figure C.25
The Print Color Menu.

```
Print Color

                           Primary Color Mixture
                          Red      Green     Blue

         1 - Black        0%       0%        0%
         2 - White        100%     100%      100%
         3 - Red          67%      0%        0%
         4 - Green        0%       67%       0%
         5 - Blue         0%       0%        67%
         6 - Yellow       67%      67%       0%
         7 - Magenta      67%      0%        67%
         8 - Cyan         0%       67%       67%
         9 - Orange       67%      25%       0%
         A - Gray         50%      50%       50%
         N - Brown        67%      33%       0%
         0 - Other

         Current Color    0%       0%        0%




    Selection: 0
```

Key Terms and Concepts

base font	margins
bottom margin	new page number
center page (top to bottom)	numbering style
conditional end of page	page length
decimal/align character	page number position
font	paper size
footer	redline
format	suppress (this page only)
header	top margin
hyphenation	widow/orphan
line spacing	

Appendix Quiz

Multiple Choice

1. Which is the default for page numbering?
   a. Bottom center of every page
   b. No page numbers
   c. Top alternating left and right
   d. None of the above

2. The key sequence for invoking the Format command is:
   a. Ctrl + F8
   b. Ctrl + F7
   c. SHIFT + F8
   d. Ctrl + F8
   e. None of the above

3. Which command is used to avoid widow and orphan lines?
   a. Size
   b. Print
   c. Font
   d. Conditional end of page
   e. None of the above

4. Which of the following command(s) may not work properly on a dot matrix printer?
   a. Headers or Footers
   b. Widows/orphans
   c. Pitch
   d. Size
   e. All will work well.

5. The command(s) used to place one or more lines of text at the top and/or bottom of each page is the:
   a. Conditional Page
   b. Top Margin
   c. Headers or footers
   d. Suppress for current page only

True/False

6. The cursor does not play any role in issuing Format and Font commands.

7. The default file used for receiving output from the Print command is PRINT.TXT.

8. WordPerfect does not allow you to change a header line; rather, you must first delete the header and then re-enter it.

9. WordPerfect allows you to center information both horizontally on a line and vertically on a page.

10. The ^B command is used to include the page number in a header or footer line.

Answers

1. b 2. c 3. e 4. e 5. c 6. f 7. f 8. f 9. t 10. t

Exercises

1. Define or describe each of the following:
   a. font
   b. header line
   c. footer line
   d. conditional end of page
   e. underline style

2. The _____ key sequence invokes the Format command.

3. The _____ key sequence invokes the Font command.

4. The default size for text lines on a page is _____ of an inch.

5. The features invoked using Format and Font commands may not be visible until the document is _____ .

6. Many Format commands must be entered at the _____ of a document.

7. The maximum number of headers and footers that you can specify is _____ .

8. The top margin, unless otherwise specified, takes up _____ of space.

9. The default pitch in WordPerfect is usually _____ cpi.

10. The _____ style of numbering usually appears in a preface.

11. The _____ command allows you to initialize the page counter to a value other than 1 when printing a document.

12. When you specify a page number and print a document, you immediately lose _____ inches of text per page.

13. When you change the page length, the _____ remains unchanged.

14. When printing letters or short memos, the _____ command makes the document appear more balanced.

15. When you are printing a large document, the _____ command is useful in starting the page numbering with a value other than 1.

16. Widow and orphan lines can be avoided by using the _____ command.

17. When _____ is used on a header or footer line, page numbers appear.

18. The column in which the page number is to be printed is _____ reset anytime a margin is changed.

19. The _____ command is used to print large or small characters.

20. The _____ command allows you to print a document with either a smooth or ragged right-hand margin.

Computer Exercises

Below is a summary of the WordPerfect commands covered in this appendix.

Format (SHIFT + F8)	This command allows you to determine how information will appear on each page.
Font (Ctrl + F8)	This command allows you to determine how information will appear on the printed page.

1. Retrieve the BOOKEXER file. If you examine the file, move the cursor to the beginning of the document before starting this exercise.

   a. Tell WordPerfect to center the page number at the bottom of each page. Print the document. Compare this with the printout of this file from Chapter 6. Notice that there are two fewer lines of text per page.

   b. Decrease the top margin by .32 inch. Print the document and compare this to the printout that you generated above.

   c. Turn off page numbering. Create the following header:

      BOOKEXER

      Tell WordPerfect to print this header at the top of each page. Now create a footer that prints the word Page followed by the current page number. Print the document and compare this printout with those from the previous printouts of this file.

   d. At the beginning of the document, tell WordPerfect to turn on widow/orphan protect. Again, print the document.

e. Tell WordPerfect to use 5 as the beginning page number. Use arabic numbers. Print the file. Is the new numbering in effect?

2. Use the Reveal Codes command to examine codes now embedded at the beginning of your document. Identify which code was used for each task above.

3. Clear the screen and load the CH5EX7 letter. Center this letter vertically on the page.

4. Retrieve the CH5EX4 file. Place a conditional end of page to protect the table at the bottom of the page. Print the document.

5. Retrieve the BOOKEXER file. Turn off right-justification and print the document using 12 pitch. Print the document again. Notice that 12 pitch packs more text per line.

6. Print the BOOKEXER file using the following font specifications. Exit without saving the file to disk, after you have printed the document.
   a. For paragraph 1 of page 1 use regular type.
   b. For paragraph 2 of page 1 use Fine size.
   c. For paragraph 3 of page 1 use Small size.
   d. For paragraph 4 of page 1 use Large size.
   e. For paragraph 5 of page 1 use Vry Large.
   f. For paragraph 6 of page 1 use Ext Large.
   g. For paragraph 1 of page 2 use the Base Font.
   h. For paragraph 2 of page 2 use the Shadow.
   i. For paragraph 3 of page 2 use the Outln.

7. Print the BOOKEXER file using 15 pitch. Print and then save the document.

8. Use the Reveal codes command to display the codes from exercise 1e. Delete these codes. Your text should now appear as the original.

9. Print out the BOOKEXER document with each line numbered. Numbering should start over on each page.

10. Print the BOOKEXER file to a file called CH7AEX10. Exit WP and use the More command to view the CH7AEX10 file. It should have the text from the BOOKEXER file.

The language called BASIC (Beginner's All-purpose Symbolic Instruction Code) is a popular programming language that was originally developed at Dartmouth College during the early 1960s and is typically provided as part of the disk operating systems for most microcomputers. The version provided is called Microsoft BASIC, developed by the same firm that has developed MS/PC DOS. This BASIC is usually found on the DOS master disk and must match your version of the disk operating system found on your computer. For example, you cannot run the version of BASIC developed for DOS 2.0 if you are running a 3.0 version of DOS on your computer. Some manufacturers of IBM-compatible machines do not include BASIC on their MS DOS, which they have licensed from Microsoft. In such a situation, you will have to order a copy of BASIC from Microsoft or purchase a copy from a local computer store.

BASIC is also found on computers other than microcomputers, but programs written in that language may not be compatible with the Microsoft BASIC covered in this text. For that matter, versions of BASIC other than Microsoft BASIC used by microcomputers are usually not compatible with one another. This is because BASIC has not been standardized within the computer industry. Although a form of standardized BASIC (ANSI standard) exists, it is extremely limited and cannot perform the tasks typically found in a business transaction processing environment.

To confuse matters even more, Microsoft has developed three different BASICs for MS DOS computers. They have developed a cassette BASIC that resides in ROM of the original IBM PC. This version can only store programs and data on tape cassettes. The disk BASIC is found under the name BASIC.COM and allows you to store data and programs on diskettes. The third version, advanced BASIC, is found under the name BASICA.COM. This version of BASIC allows you to play music and display graphics to your screen. It is this version that is covered in this appendix.

You may wish to copy the BASIC files (files that start with BAS) to another disk. This allows you to store programs to the disk that contains BASIC. That is the convention that is used in this section of the text. If you wish to have BASIC on one disk and save files to another disk, you are required to put the drive identifier in front of the file being saved or run. For example, if you wish to load a file from drive B, you use a command like LOAD "B:FILE1.

Starting BASIC

To start BASICA place the diskette with that program in drive A and enter the command BASICA. Once the program has been loaded into RAM, a screen similar to that of Figure D.1 is displayed on your screen. The top of the screen has the version of BASIC being used (Compaq 3.20 in this example). It also has the copyright dates for Microsoft and, in this case, the company that is the third-party licensee (Compaq).

Notice that a line on the screen states that there are 60,197 bytes free. You may be puzzled by this figure because your computer probably has much more storage than this. The reason that this number does not match the amount of RAM in your machine is that this version of BASIC is designed to recognize only 64K of storage. Even though you have more memory than that, BASIC can only find 64K.

The Ok on the screen is the BASIC prompt. When you see the Ok, that means that BASIC is waiting for you to enter a program statement or to enter a command that it can execute. The bottom line is the menu line for BASIC that corresponds to the tasks that will be performed by pressing a function key. For example, if you press F1, it will list any program statements that you have entered.

Figure D.1
The screen that appears
when BASIC has been
started.

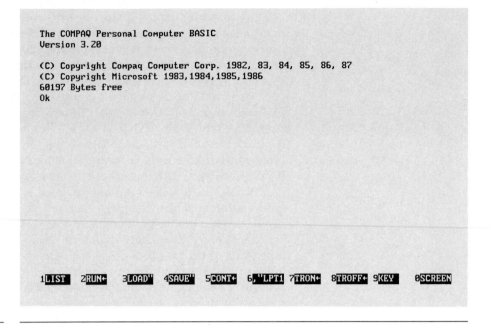

```
The COMPAQ Personal Computer BASIC
Version 3.20

(C) Copyright Compaq Computer Corp. 1982, 83, 84, 85, 86, 87
(C) Copyright Microsoft 1983,1984,1985,1986
60197 Bytes free
Ok
```

```
1LIST  2RUN←  3LOAD"  4SAVE"  5CONT←  6,"LPT1  7TRON←  8TROFF←  9KEY   0SCREEN
```

Leaving BASIC

To leave BASIC, simply enter the command SYSTEM at the Ok prompt. Once the SYSTEM command has been entered, you are returned to DOS.

Writing Programs in BASIC

BASIC uses statements with line numbers to create programs. Each statement is executed in line number order (for example, 10, 20, 30). This means that you can enter new statements between existing statements simply by giving them the appropriate line number (for example, 21, 22, 23). These new statements are then automatically placed in their proper location in the program and executed in line number order. If you give a line the same number as an existing line in the program, the existing instruction is replaced with the new line's instruction.

Editing a BASIC program can be accomplished in the following manner:

Deleting an Instruction. Enter the line number of the instruction to be deleted and press ENTER.

Inserting an Instruction. Give the new instruction a line number between two existing line numbers in the program.

Replacing an Instruction. Enter a new instruction with the same line number of an existing instruction and press ENTER.

Session 1: Entering a Simple Program

The program that you will be entering introduces you to several BASIC commands. These are REM, INPUT, PRINT, RUN, SAVE, FILES, LIST, LLIST, LPRINT, and END. A brief discussion of these commands follows:

REM. REM commands document a program by inserting explanatory remarks about sections of code in a program. The BASIC interpreter does not execute these commands that appear in the program when it is listed to the screen or printed to paper.

INPUT. INPUT commands display a prompt to the user and then accept input from the keyboard. They allow programs to be interactive.

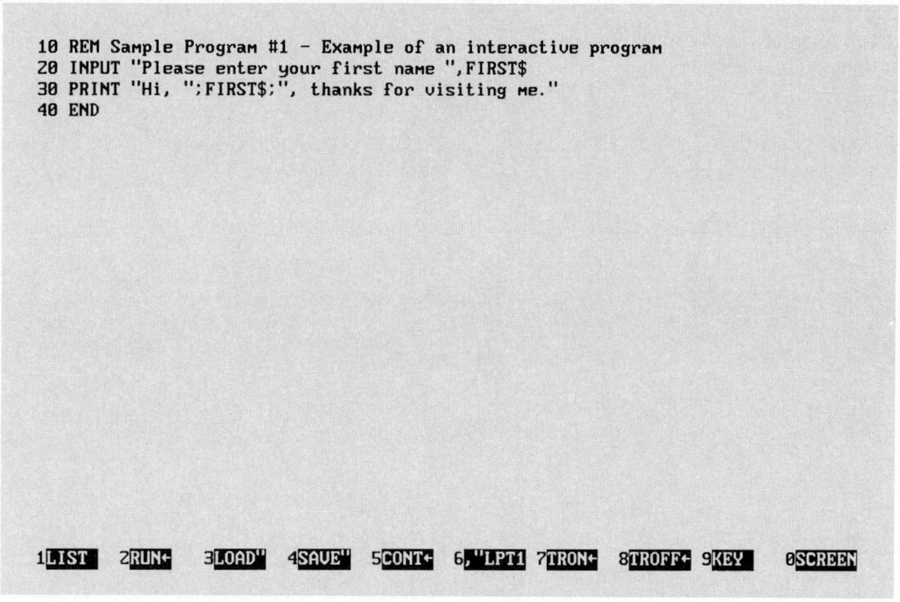

Figure D.2
The entered BASIC program.

```
10 REM Sample Program #1 - Example of an interactive program
20 INPUT "Please enter your first name ",FIRST$
30 PRINT "Hi, ";FIRST$:", thanks for visiting me."
40 END
```

```
1LIST  2RUN←  3LOAD"  4SAVE"  5CONT←  6,"LPT1 7TRON←  8TROFF← 9KEY    0SCREEN
```

PRINT. PRINT commands display information to the screen.

RUN. The RUN command executes a program residing in RAM.

SAVE. The SAVE command saves a program to disk with a .BAS file extension.

FILES. The FILES command displays the names of files residing on the current directory or diskette. The BASIC FILES command is similar to the DOS DIR command.

LIST. The LIST command lists the statements of a BASIC program to the screen of the monitor.

LLIST. The LLIST command lists the statements of a BASIC program to the printer.

LPRINT. The LPRINT command directs the output of a program to the printer instead of to the screen.

END. The END command terminates program execution, closes any files, returns you to command level, and waits for you to enter the next command.

Enter the following program. Be sure to enter the punctuation and spacing exactly as it appears. If you make a mistake, use the BACKSPACE key to correct the error. If you notice an error on a line, reenter that statement (an easier way of correcting mistakes will be covered later).

```
10 REM Sample Program #1 - Example of an interactive program
20 INPUT "Please enter your first name",FIRST$
30 PRINT "Hi,";FIRST$;",thanks for visiting me."
40 END
```

Once you have entered your program, your screen should contain the program statements depicted in Figure D.2. You are now ready to run your program by entering the RUN command. Your program then prompts you to enter your first name (Figure D.3). When you have finished entering your name, press ENTER and you receive the message depicted in Figure D.4. The OK prompt indicates that BASIC is ready to accept another command from the keyboard.

Figure D.3
The prompt for your first name.

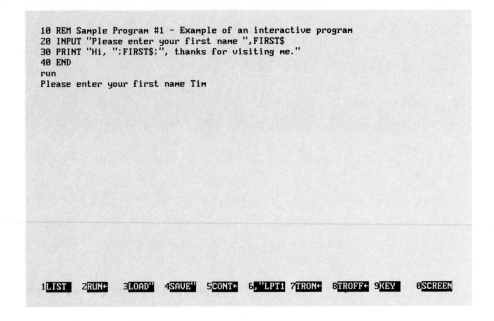

```
10 REM Sample Program #1 - Example of an interactive program
20 INPUT "Please enter your first name ",FIRST$
30 PRINT "Hi, ";FIRST$;", thanks for visiting me."
40 END
run
Please enter your first name Tim
```

1LIST 2RUN◄ 3LOAD" 4SAVE" 5CONT◄ 6,"LPT1 7TRON◄ 8TROFF◄ 9KEY 0SCREEN

Figure D.4
The output of the executed program.

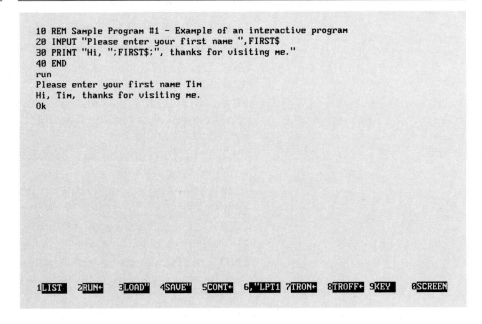

```
10 REM Sample Program #1 - Example of an interactive program
20 INPUT "Please enter your first name ",FIRST$
30 PRINT "Hi, ";FIRST$;", thanks for visiting me."
40 END
run
Please enter your first name Tim
Hi, Tim, thanks for visiting me.
Ok
```

1LIST 2RUN◄ 3LOAD" 4SAVE" 5CONT◄ 6,"LPT1 7TRON◄ 8TROFF◄ 9KEY 0SCREEN

You may wish to list your program to the screen. This is accomplished via the LIST command. The only problem is that the output of the new listing is mixed with the prior output (Figure D.5). BASIC allows you to clear the screen using the Ctrl + Home command. Once the screen is clear, use the LIST command; only the program statements of the LIST command appear on the screen (Figure D.6).

If you want to generate a hard copy of your program listing, use the LLIST command to dump the listing to your printer. BASIC assumes that this output is to be passed to a printer on device LPT#1. The LPRINT command is somewhat like the LLIST command except that output from a BASIC command is sent to the printer instead of the screen.

Once you have entered a BASIC program that properly executes, you will want to save it to disk to use for later execution. This is accomplished via the SAVE command. If you wish to save the file to the default drive, just issue

Figure D.5
Using the LIST command,
the program mixes with prior
output.

```
10 REM Sample Program #1 - Example of an interactive program
20 INPUT "Please enter your first name ",FIRST$
30 PRINT "Hi, ";FIRST$;", thanks for visiting me."
40 END
run
Please enter your first name Tim
Hi, Tim, thanks for visiting me.
Ok
list
10 REM Sample program #1 - Example of an interactive program
20 INPUT "Please enter your first name ",FIRST$
30 PRINT "Hi, ";FIRST$;", thanks for visiting me."
40 END
Ok
```

```
1LIST  2RUN←  3LOAD"  4SAVE"  5CONT←  6,"LPT1 7TRON←  8TROFF← 9KEY    0SCREEN
```

Figure D.6
A cleared screen, using the
Ctrl + Home command fol-
lowed by the LIST command.

```
list
10 REM Sample program #1 - Example of an interactive program
20 INPUT "Please enter your first name ",FIRST$
30 PRINT "Hi, ";FIRST$;", thanks for visiting me."
40 END
Ok
```

```
1LIST  2RUN←  3LOAD"  4SAVE"  5CONT←  6,"LPT1 7TRON←  8TROFF← 9KEY    0SCREEN
```

the SAVE command followed by the file name beginning with a double quote
(for example, SAVE "SAMPLE1). You can save the file to another disk by including the drive identifier in front of the file name (for example, SAVE
"B:SAMPLE1). The SAVE command results in two copies of your file: one in
RAM and one on disk. If a file with the same name already exists on the disk,
it is erased and replaced with the new contents from RAM. The screen does
not display a message about a file already having the same name.

More on Listing a Program

When working with longer programs, you may not want to list the entire
program to the screen via the LIST command. Instead, you may just want to
list parts of the program to the screen, or you may want to generate a printed

Figure D.7
The expanded SAMPLE1
program.

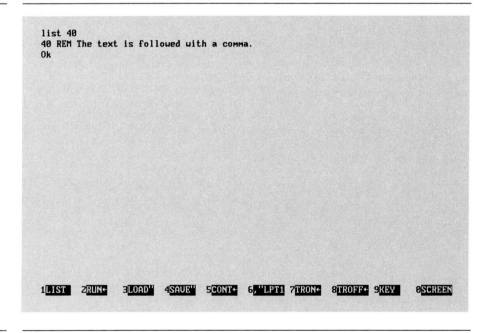

```
list
10 REM Sample program #1 - Example of an interactive program
20 REM INPUT statements are used to display prompts to the user.
30 REM The text displayed is placed between double quotes.
40 REM The text is followed with a comma.
50 REM Any variables that are to receive input from the keybard appear next.
60 REM Since a name with alphabetical characters is to be entered,
70 REM a string variable must be defined to accept this data.
80 REM String variables have a dollar sign ($) following them.
90 REM A variable name can have up to forty characters.
100 REM When you enter your name, it is placed in the variable called FIRST$
110 INPUT "Please enter your first name ",FIRST$
120 PRINT "Hi, "FIRST$;", thanks for visiting me."
130 REM The Print command can be used to combine constant and vairable text.
140 REM Constant text (text that will not change) must be contained between
150 REM double quotes.  Any spacing and punctuation must appear as part of
160 REM this constant text.
170 END
Ok
```

```
1LIST  2RUN←  3LOAD"  4SAVE"  5CONT←  6,"LPT1 7TRON←  8TROFF← 9KEY    0SCREEN
```

Figure D.8
The output of the LIST 40
command.

```
list 40
40 REM The text is followed with a comma.
Ok
```

```
1LIST   2RUN←  3LOAD"  4SAVE"  5CONT←  6,"LPT1 7TRON←  8TROFF← 9KEY    0SCREEN
```

listing of your program to review at your leisure. To illustrate this segment on BASIC, the original SAMPLE1 program has been expanded with some REM statements (Figure D.7).

Listing a Program Statement. Listing a single statement is accomplished by using the LIST command followed by the statement number. For example, Figure D.8 shows the output of the command LIST 40.

Listing a Segment of Code. Listing a code segment—lines 60 through 130, for example—is accomplished by using LIST 60–130. The beginning and ending line must be included in the LIST command. Figure D.9 shows the output of this command.

Figure D.9
Listing a segment of program code via the LIST command.

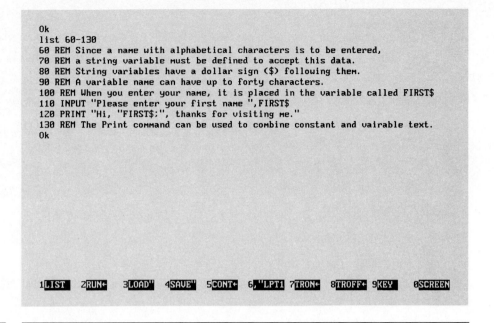

```
Ok
list 60-130
60 REM Since a name with alphabetical characters is to be entered,
70 REM a string variable must be defined to accept this data.
80 REM String variables have a dollar sign ($) following them.
90 REM A variable name can have up to forty characters.
100 REM When you enter your name, it is placed in the variable called FIRST$
110 INPUT "Please enter your first name ",FIRST$
120 PRINT "Hi, "FIRST$;", thanks for visiting me."
130 REM The Print command can be used to combine constant and vairable text.
Ok
```
```
1LIST  2RUN◄  3LOAD"  4SAVE"  5CONT◄  6,"LPT1 7TRON◄  8TROFF◄ 9KEY    0SCREEN
```

Figure D.10
Using the LIST command to indicate the beginning statement number.

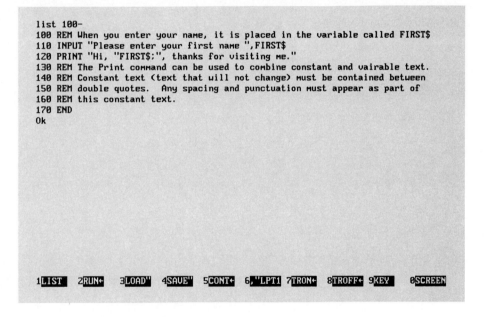

```
list 100-
100 REM When you enter your name, it is placed in the variable called FIRST$
110 INPUT "Please enter your first name ",FIRST$
120 PRINT "Hi, "FIRST$;", thanks for visiting me."
130 REM The Print command can be used to combine constant and vairable text.
140 REM Constant text (text that will not change) must be contained between
150 REM double quotes.  Any spacing and punctuation must appear as part of
160 REM this constant text.
170 END
Ok
```
```
1LIST  2RUN◄  3LOAD"  4SAVE"  5CONT◄  6,"LPT1 7TRON◄  8TROFF◄ 9KEY    0SCREEN
```

List from a Starting Point. You may want to list a program beginning at some line in the program. For example, you want to start listing a program beginning with line 100. This is accomplished by using the LIST 100– command. BASIC interprets the dash as the beginning point and lists all statements beginning with the one indicated (Figure D.10).

List to an End Point. You may want to list a program beginning with the first statement and ending with a given statement. For example, you want to list a program through statement 100. This is accomplished by using the LIST –100. The dash in front of the statement number indicates that this is the last statement to be included in the LIST command (Figure D.11).

Make certain that you have used the SAVE command to save your work to file SAMPLE1.BAS. After you have saved the file, verify that it is on disk by

Figure D.11
Using the LIST command to indicate the ending statement number.

```
list -100
10 REM Sample program #1 - Example of an interactive program
20 REM INPUT statements are used to display prompts to the user.
30 REM The text displayed is placed between double quotes.
40 REM The text is followed with a comma.
50 REM Any variables that are to receive input from the keybard appear next.
60 REM Since a name with alphabetical characters is to be entered,
70 REM a string variable must be defined to accept this data.
80 REM String variables have a dollar sign ($) following them.
90 REM A variable name can have up to forty characters.
100 REM When you enter your name, it is placed in the variable called FIRST$
Ok
```

```
1LIST   2RUN◄   3LOAD"   4SAVE"   5CONT◄   6,"LPT1 7TRON◄ 8TROFF◄ 9KEY      0SCREEN
```

Figure D.12
The FILES command displays the file directory to the screen.

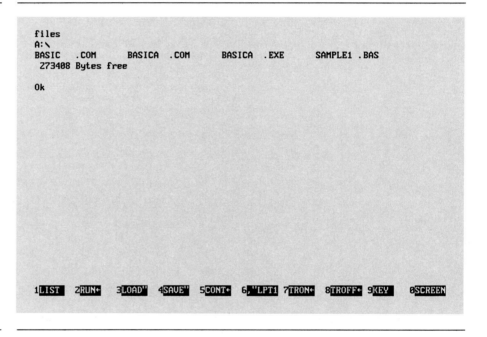

```
files
A:\
BASIC    .COM      BASICA  .COM      BASICA  .EXE      SAMPLE1 .BAS
 273408 Bytes free

Ok
```

```
1LIST   2RUN◄   3LOAD"   4SAVE"   5CONT◄   6,"LPT1 7TRON◄ 8TROFF◄ 9KEY      0SCREEN
```

using the FILES command. The FILES command shows all files that reside on the disk in the default drive (Figure D.12). If you wish to use the FILES command to examine another disk you must include the drive specification after the double quotes. For example, if you want to examine the files contained on drive B, use the command FILES "B:; note that double quotes are required.

To leave BASIC, enter the command SYSTEM and return to DOS.

Exercises

1. Using the following program segment, complete the program so that the output generates "I have 8 chocolate chip cookies." Save this exercise to the file called BASIC1A.

```
10 COOKIES = 8
20 PART1$ = "I have"
```

```
30 PART2$ = "chocolate chip cookies."
```

2. Using one PRINT command, combine the information in the following lines into one PRINT statement. Save this to the file called BASIC1B.

```
10 NUMBER1 = 35.5
20 MESSAGE$ = "is larger than"
30 NUMBER2 = 11.75
```

Session 2: File Commands and Program Editing

File Commands. This session introduces you to the commands LOAD, NEW, KILL, NAME, RENUM, DELETE, and program editing.

LOAD. The LOAD command copies a file from disk to RAM.

NEW. The NEW command deletes the program currently in RAM and clears all variables.

KILL. The KILL command deletes files from the disk.

NAME. The NAME command renames an existing disk file.

RENUM. The RENUM command renumbers the lines of the program.

DELETE. The DELETE command deletes program lines.

LOAD. The LOAD command copies a file from disk to RAM memory. Once the program resides in RAM memory, it can be executed via the RUN command. For example, if you wish to load the file SAMPLE1, the following statement is required:

```
LOAD "SAMPLE1
```

If the file resided on drive B, use the statement LOAD "B:SAMPLE1.

NEW. The NEW command is usually used after a file has been saved to disk. After a SAVE command is used, the original file still resides in RAM. If you wish to start working on another program, you have to get rid of the previous program instructions and variables used by that program via a NEW command. The NEW command erases RAM. Once the NEW command is issued, a LIST command simply results in the display of the Ok prompt signaling that RAM has been cleared.

KILL. The KILL command erases a file from disk. This command requires that both the file name and any extension must be used. If you want to erase the BASIC program file called PROG1, enter the following command:

```
KILL "PROG1.BAS
```

The .BAS is required because BASIC automatically places a .BAS file extension on any program file that is saved using the SAVE command.

NAME. The NAME command changes the name of an existing file on disk. It functions similarly to the RENAME command of DOS. Like its DOS equivalent, NAME requires the original name and the new name. Any file extensions must also be referenced. The file names must be contained within double quotes to indicate to BASIC when one file name ends and another part of the instructions begins. For example, to rename the file PROG1.BAS to PROGRAM1.BAS, the following command is required:

```
NAME "PROG1.BAS" AS "PROGRAM1.BAS"
```

Figure D.13
New statements numbered
1 to 9 to be added to the
SAMPLE1 program.

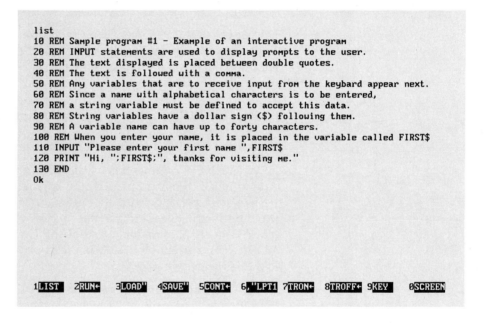

```
1 REM Sample program #1 - Example of an interactive program
2 REM INPUT statements are used to display prompts to the user.
3 REM The text displayed is placed between double quotes.
4 REM The text is followed with a comma.
5 REM Any variables that are to receive input from the keyboard appear next.
6 REM Since a name with alphabetical characters is to be entered,
7 REM a string variable must be defined to accept this data.
8 REM String variables have a dollar sign ($) following them.
9 REM A variable name can have up to forty characters.
10 REM When you enter your name, it is placed in the variable called FIRST$
20 INPUT "Please enter your first name ",FIRST$
30 PRINT "Hi, ";FIRST$;", thanks for visiting me."
40 END
```

1LIST   2RUN←   3LOAD"   4SAVE"   5CONT←   6,"LPT1   7TRON←   8TROFF←   9KEY   0SCREEN

Figure D.14
The renumbered program
listed to the screen.

```
list
10 REM Sample program #1 - Example of an interactive program
20 REM INPUT statements are used to display prompts to the user.
30 REM The text displayed is placed between double quotes.
40 REM The text is followed with a comma.
50 REM Any variables that are to receive input from the keyboard appear next.
60 REM Since a name with alphabetical characters is to be entered,
70 REM a string variable must be defined to accept this data.
80 REM String variables have a dollar sign ($) following them.
90 REM A variable name can have up to forty characters.
100 REM When you enter your name, it is placed in the variable called FIRST$
110 INPUT "Please enter your first name ",FIRST$
120 PRINT "Hi, ";FIRST$;", thanks for visiting me."
130 END
Ok
```

1LIST   2RUN←   3LOAD"   4SAVE"   5CONT←   6,"LPT1   7TRON←   8TROFF←   9KEY   0SCREEN

To verify that a file has been properly renamed, use the FILES command to list the files to the screen.

RENUM. BASIC provides a fair amount of flexibility in renumbering your program. The RENUM command adds new statements to your program by inserting them between existing program statements and then renumbers the program statements. The advantage to this is that if you wish to add more statements than there is room for, simply add as many as you can, issue the RENUM command, and then add more lines. For example, assume that you wish to add some more REM statements to your program SAMPLE1. You insert new statements numbered 1 to 9 like those depicted in Figure D.13. Once these lines have been added, you want to renumber the statements via the RENUM command. When you issue a LIST command, a program like that in Figure D.14 appears on your screen.

Figure D.15
The SAMPLE1.BAS program with all new statements added.

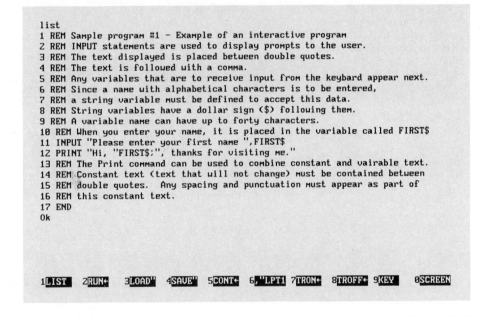

```
list
10 REM Sample program #1 - Example of an interactive program
20 REM INPUT statements are used to display prompts to the user.
30 REM The text displayed is placed between double quotes.
40 REM The text is followed with a comma.
50 REM Any variables that are to receive input from the keyboard appear next.
60 REM Since a name with alphabetical characters is to be entered,
70 REM a string variable must be defined to accept this data.
80 REM String variables have a dollar sign ($) following them.
90 REM A variable name can have up to forty characters.
100 REM When you enter your name, it is placed in the variable called FIRST$
110 INPUT "Please enter your first name ",FIRST$
120 PRINT "Hi, "FIRST$:", thanks for visiting me."
130 REM The Print command can be used to combine constant and vairable text.
140 REM Constant text (text that will not change) must be contained between
150 REM double quotes.  Any spacing and punctuation must appear as part of
160 REM this constant text.
170 END
Ok
```

```
1LIST  2RUN←  3LOAD"  4SAVE"  5CONT←  6,"LPT1 7TRON← 8TROFF← 9KEY    0SCREEN
```

Figure D.16
The renumbered program beginning with 1 by increments of 1.

```
list
1 REM Sample program #1 - Example of an interactive program
2 REM INPUT statements are used to display prompts to the user.
3 REM The text displayed is placed between double quotes.
4 REM The text is followed with a comma.
5 REM Any variables that are to receive input from the keyboard appear next.
6 REM Since a name with alphabetical characters is to be entered,
7 REM a string variable must be defined to accept this data.
8 REM String variables have a dollar sign ($) following them.
9 REM A variable name can have up to forty characters.
10 REM When you enter your name, it is placed in the variable called FIRST$
11 INPUT "Please enter your first name ",FIRST$
12 PRINT "Hi, "FIRST$:", thanks for visiting me."
13 REM The Print command can be used to combine constant and vairable text.
14 REM Constant text (text that will not change) must be contained between
15 REM double quotes.  Any spacing and punctuation must appear as part of
16 REM this constant text.
17 END
Ok
```

```
1LIST  2RUN←  3LOAD"  4SAVE"  5CONT←  6,"LPT1 7TRON← 8TROFF← 9KEY    0SCREEN
```

Add statements to include those listed in Figure D.15. Once you have added these new statements, be sure to issue a RENUM command so that you receive the same line numbers as those in Figure D.15. Once you have finished adding the lines, save the file back to disk using the same name (SAMPLE1).

The RENUM command has the following parts: RENUM BEGVAL, BEGLIN, INCAMT. BEGVAL contains the number to be used in renumbering the lines of the program. BEGLIN is the line number of the first line in the program that you want to start renumbering (the default is the first line in the program). INCAMT is the incremental amount to use from one line to the next (the default value is 10).

For example, if you want the program to be renumbered from 1 in increments of 1, use the command RENUM 1,,1. When you use the LIST command to view the program, you see a listing like that depicted in Figure D.16.

Figure D.17
The renumbered program beginning with 100 by increments of 10.

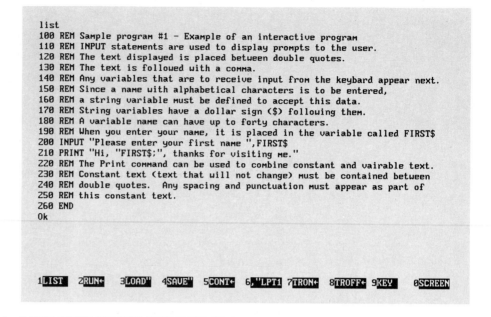

```
list
100 REM Sample program #1 - Example of an interactive program
110 REM INPUT statements are used to display prompts to the user.
120 REM The text displayed is placed between double quotes.
130 REM The text is followed with a comma.
140 REM Any variables that are to receive input from the keyboard appear next.
150 REM Since a name with alphabetical characters is to be entered,
160 REM a string variable must be defined to accept this data.
170 REM String variables have a dollar sign ($) following them.
180 REM A variable name can have up to forty characters.
190 REM When you enter your name, it is placed in the variable called FIRST$
200 INPUT "Please enter your first name ",FIRST$
210 PRINT "Hi, "FIRST$;", thanks for visiting me."
220 REM The Print command can be used to combine constant and vairable text.
230 REM Constant text (text that will not change) must be contained between
240 REM double quotes.  Any spacing and punctuation must appear as part of
250 REM this constant text.
260 END
Ok
```

```
1LIST  2RUN←  3LOAD"  4SAVE"  5CONT←  6,"LPT1  7TRON←  8TROFF←  9KEY     0SCREEN
```

Figure D.18
The renumbered program beginning with 500, starting at statement 170, in increments of 100.

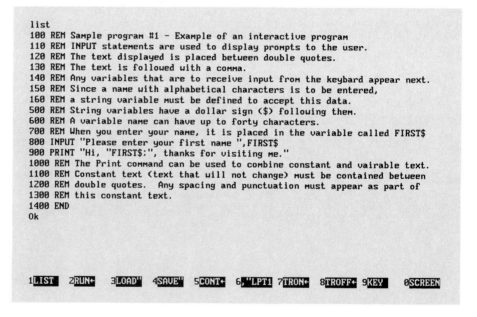

```
list
100 REM Sample program #1 - Example of an interactive program
110 REM INPUT statements are used to display prompts to the user.
120 REM The text displayed is placed between double quotes.
130 REM The text is followed with a comma.
140 REM Any variables that are to receive input from the keyboard appear next.
150 REM Since a name with alphabetical characters is to be entered,
160 REM a string variable must be defined to accept this data.
500 REM String variables have a dollar sign ($) following them.
600 REM A variable name can have up to forty characters.
700 REM When you enter your name, it is placed in the variable called FIRST$
800 INPUT "Please enter your first name ",FIRST$
900 PRINT "Hi, "FIRST$;", thanks for visiting me."
1000 REM The Print command can be used to combine constant and vairable text.
1100 REM Constant text (text that will not change) must be contained between
1200 REM double quotes.  Any spacing and punctuation must appear as part of
1300 REM this constant text.
1400 END
Ok
```

```
1LIST  2RUN←  3LOAD"  4SAVE"  5CONT←  6,"LPT1  7TRON←  8TROFF←  9KEY     0SCREEN
```

If you want to begin with a value of 100 and number by increments of 10, use the command RENUM 100,,10. When you use the LIST command to view the program, you see a listing like that depicted in Figure D.17.

If you want to renumber your program with a beginning value of 500, beginning at current statement 170, in increments of 100, use the command RENUM 500,170,100. The LIST command generates a listing like that depicted in Figure D.18.

DELETE. The DELETE command deletes one or more statements from a BASIC program. Using the DELETE command followed by the statement number can delete a single program statement. A number of DELETE commands and an explanation of each follow:

DELETE 80   Deletes the statement with line number 80 from the program.

DELETE 80-160   Deletes statements 80–160 from the program.

DELETE 80-   Deletes the statements from 80 to the end of the program.

DELETE -80   Deletes all statements up to and including line 80.

Program Editing. You have probably noticed by now that correcting a program statement by reentering the statement number and then retyping the entire line gets to be tedious. An easier method is available, using the full-screen edit mode of Microsoft's BASICA. The advantage of full-screen editing is that you can use the cursor movement keys on the numeric keypad for positioning the cursor to the appropriate part of a BASIC command and then make changes to that command. The full-screen editing commands available in BASIC act similarly to word processing commands and are as follow:

Cursor Positioning Commands

Up Arrow	Moves the cursor up one line.
Down Arrow	Moves the cursor down one line.
Right Arrow	Moves the cursor to the right one character.
Left Arrow	Moves the cursor to the left one character.
Home	Moves the cursor to the upper left-hand corner of the screen.
End	Moves the cursor to the end of the current line.
Ctrl + Right Arrow	Moves the cursor to the right one word.
Ctrl + Left Arrow	Moves the cursor to the left one word.
TAB	Moves the cursor to the next tab stop. A tab stop occurs every eight character positions (1, 9, 17, . . .).

Delete Commands

Del	Deletes the character at the cursor position.
BACKSPACE	Deletes the character to the left of the current cursor location.
Ctrl + End	Erases from the cursor position to the end of the line.
Esc	Erases the entire line at the cursor location.

Mode Command

Ins	The Ins key allows you to switch from overwrite to insert mode. The shape of the cursor identifies the mode. A cursor that looks like an underscore character means that you are in overwrite mode; a cursor that looks like a square box means that you are in insert mode. When you have entered insert mode, any cursor positioning command returns you to overwrite mode.

Other Useful Commands

CLEAR SCREEN. CLEAR SCREEN (Ctrl + Home) clears the screen and is especially useful when the screen is cluttered with commands and the output from those commands.

PAUSE. PAUSE (Ctrl + Num Lock) pauses the scrolling of a program listing or the output of an executing program. A Ctrl + Num Lock pauses the operation that is occurring and freezes the screen until another key is pressed.

INTERRUPT. INTERRUPT (Ctrl + Break) causes any BASIC command that is currently executing to stop. The INTERRUPT command results in the Ok prompt being displayed to the screen.

When you are editing a BASIC program a number of different tools are available for making changes to a program; you can

Add new statements using new statement numbers.

Renumber programs using the RENUM command.

Delete statements using the DELETE command.

Change existing statements by using BASIC's full-screen edit mode.

Exercises

1. Enter the following program (be sure to enter any mistakes) and save it to file BASIC2A.

```
10 REM This program examines the pring command.
20 REM Attempts it to print two lines of string
data.
30 REM It also prints a numeric variabal.
40 REM
50 PART1$="Mary and John have"
60 CARS = 8
70 PART2$="cars between them."
80 Pritn PART1$;CARS;PART2
```

2. After saving the above statements to file BASIC2A, make the following changes. If you are starting a new session use the LOAD command to load the file BASIC1A.
   a. Use the full-screen editing commands to correct the spelling of *print* in statement 10.
   b. Reenter statement 20 to the following: 20 It combines two string variables.
   c. In statement 30 correct the word *variable*.
   d. Delete statement 40.
   e. Renumber the program statements.
   f. Correct the problems in statement 80.
   When you have finished making corrections, save the program to file BASIC2B.

Session 3: Constants and Variable Names

Constants are specific values that are used by BASIC to perform a task. They do not change as the program executes. BASIC has two types of constants: string (sometimes called character) constants and numeric constants. A **string constant** can hold up to 255 characters enclosed in double quotation marks. Examples of string constants are

"Tim Duffy"
"Illinois State University"
"ten"
"1,985.34"

Numeric constants are positive (plus sign is optional) or negative numbers (a number preceded by a minus sign) that are not allowed to have embedded commas. BASIC provides five ways to enter numeric constants. A constant can be an integer or a fixed-point number.

Integer   Integers are whole numbers between −32768 and +32768. Integer constants cannot have decimal points.

Fixed-point   Fixed-point numbers are positive or negative numbers that contain decimal points (sometimes called real numbers).

Variables are areas of storage that are assigned by a programmer to represent values that are used in a program. Like constants, there are two types of variables: numeric and string. A **numeric variable** holds numeric data; a **string variable** can have only a character string value as its contents. When you use a variable, you may set it to an initial value within the program or you may assign it a value as the result of calculations performed when a program instruction executes. The variable type (string or numeric) must match the type of data that is being assigned to it.

When you use a numeric variable before it has been assigned a specific value, BASIC assumes that the variable equals zero. String values are initially assumed to be null, or empty. They have no characters and have a length of zero.

Naming Conventions. A BASIC variable name can be any length, but only the first forty characters are recognized as being part of a variable name. Forty characters is, then, the maximum that can be used effectively. Allowable characters are the letters A–Z, the digits 0–9, and the decimal point. The first character of a variable name must be a letter. Also, you cannot use a BASIC command as a variable name.

Variable Types. A variable's name determines its type (string or numeric). If the variable type is numeric, the name also indicates whether the variable is to hold integer or fixed-point numbers. The following naming conventions are used:

String variables are written with a dollar sign ($) as the last character:

```
N$ = "Monthly Report"
A$ = "Bloomington, Il 61761"
```

The dollar sign indicates to BASIC that whatever is to be held in memory areas N$ or A$ must always be enclosed in double quotes to meet the criteria for string data. The first example translates as "assign the value of Monthly Report to string variable A."

Integer numeric variables are declared by using a percent sign (%) as the last character of the variable name:

```
I% = 2
N% = 100
```

The percent sign indicates that whatever is to be held in that memory variable must be a whole number. If the value to be placed in an integer variable contains digits to the right of the decimal point, they are rounded, and only the whole integer is stored in that memory location.

Figure D.19
Examples of rounding and truncation, using an integer variable as a result field.

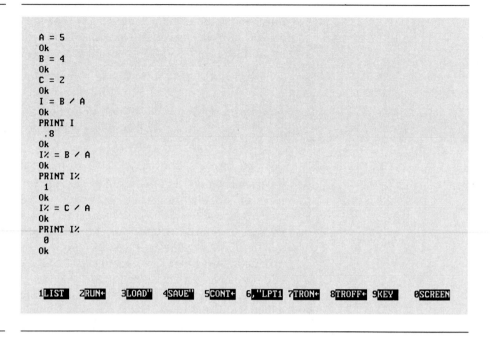

Figure D.19
Examples of rounding and truncation, using an integer variable as a result field.

```
A = 5
Ok
B = 4
Ok
C = 2
Ok
I = B / A
Ok
PRINT I
 .8
Ok
I% = B / A
Ok
PRINT I%
 1
Ok
I% = C / A
Ok
PRINT I%
 0
Ok
```

```
1LIST  2RUN←  3LOAD"  4SAVE"  5CONT←  6,"LPT1 7TRON←  8TROFF← 9KEY   0SCREEN
```

Fixed-point variables are the default of BASIC. If desired, however, you can also use an exclamation mark (!) as the last character:

```
I  = 2.25
I! = 2.25
```

Both of the above statements can be used to define the same variable called I.

The following examples are valid variable names.

```
NAME$
TOTAL!
TOTAL
LINECOUNT%
ACCT21
```

The following are examples of invalid variable names.

LINE COUNT	There is an embedded blank.
%COUNT	The first character is not an alphabetic character.
ACCT#	A special character was used.

The type of numeric storage that you use via a variable name dictates how numeric data are handled by the computer. For example, if you have an integer result field that holds the contents of a calculation, any characters to the right of the decimal point are lost (Figure D.19). When the decimal value to be placed in an integer variable is .5 or greater, it is rounded up. If the value is less than .5, the value to right of the decimal point is truncated.

Assignment Commands and Formulas. Variables can be given an initial value via an assignment command. In an assignment command, the variable name occurs to the left of the equal sign, whereas the value to be placed in the

Figure D.20
Sample program featuring
assignment commands and
demonstrating formulas.

```
10 REM This program introduces you to entering formulas in BASIC
20 REM You first assign values to variables and then include those
30 REM variables in calculations.
40 A = 20
50 B = 30
60 C = 35
70 D = 15
80 E = 75
90 G = A + B + C + D + E
100 H = E / A + C
110 I = E / (A + C)
120 PRINT G,H,I
```

```
1LIST   2RUN◆   3LOAD"   4SAVE"   5CONT◆   6,"LPT1   7TRON◆   8TROFF◆   9KEY      0SCREEN
```

variable appears to the right of the equal sign. The following is an example of
an assignment statement:

```
20 A = 25
```

This statement translates as "assign the value of 25 to variable A."

This type of format is also used in setting up formulas in BASIC. Formulas
in BASIC consist of three parts: numeric variables or constants to be processed
(sometimes called operands); arithmetic operators, which indicate what action
is to be performed; and a variable in which to place the result. The arithmetic
operators for BASIC are the same as those for Lotus 1-2-3:

+	Addition
-	Subtraction
*	Multiplication
/	Division
^	Exponentiation

The order of precedence in BASIC is the same as in Lotus 1-2-3. If you wish to
review this, refer to "Entering Formulas," Chapter 9. The following examples
are valid formulas in BASIC:

```
A = 3 / 4 * 5
C = 5 + B * c
```

Sample Program. Enter the program depicted in Figure D.20. Once you have
entered the program, execute it using the RUN command. Your output should
look like that depicted in Figure D.21. Notice the effect of the parentheses on
the answers generated by statements 110 and 120. As noted in Chapter 9, any
operation that appears within parentheses takes precedence.

Notice also that the output generated by the PRINT command skips between each variable as it prints. This is because BASIC divides a print line into

Figure D.21
The output of the sample
program.

```
10 REM This program introduces you to entering formulas in BASIC
20 REM You first assign values to variables and then include those
30 REM variables in calculations.
40 A = 20
50 B = 30
60 C = 35
70 D = 15
80 E = 75
90 G = A + B + C + D + E
100 H = E / A + C
110 I = E / (A + C)
120 PRINT G,H,I
run
 175            38.75        1.363636
Ok
```

```
1LIST  2RUN←  3LOAD"  4SAVE"  5CONT←  6,"LPT1 7TRON←  8TROFF← 9KEY    0SCREEN
```

Figure D.22
The output using semicolons
in the PRINT command.

```
list
10 REM This program introduces you to entering formulas in BASIC
20 REM You first assign values to variables and then include those
30 REM variables in calculations.
40 A = 20
50 B = 30
60 C = 35
70 D = 15
80 E = 75
90 G = A + B + C + D + E
100 H = E / A + C
110 I = E / (A + C)
120 PRINT G;H;I
Ok
run
 175  38.75  1.363636
Ok
```

```
1LIST  2RUN←  3LOAD"  4SAVE"  5CONT←  6,"LPT1 7TRON←  8TROFF← 9KEY    0SCREEN
```

zones of fourteen spaces. If you want information to be printed without using these zones, you must include a semicolon (;) after the variable. This results in output that is closer together (Figure D.22). Save this program to the file called SAMPLE3.

Exercises

1. Write a program to calculate the area of a rectangle. This program should have two different prompts. The first prompt should request the width of the rectangle, and the second prompt should request the height of the rectangle. Once it has received these two pieces of data, it should print the lines

```
A rectangle that has a height of _____ feet
and a width of _____ feet
has a square footage of _____.
```

Save this program to a file BASIC3A.

2. Write a program that prompts you to enter three grades. After you enter each grade, the program prompts you for the total possible points of each grade. When it has received the three grades, the program should calculate the percentage score. It should print out the total points earned, the total possible points, and the average. Each of these values should be appropriately labeled. The information for the assignments to be entered appears as follows:

Assignment	Received	Possible
First test score	75	95
Second test score	90	100
Third test score	75	80

Save this program to a file BASIC3B.

Session 4: The IF Statement and Looping

IF Statement. The IF statement allows you to embed logic within a BASIC program. You can use an IF statement to check the value contained in a variable and then to perform a task or action based on the contents of that variable. The following is a valid IF statement:

```
130 IF SALES > 1000 THEN COMM = SALES * .1 ELSE COMM = SALES * .05
```

This statement checks to see if the value contained in SALES is greater than 1000. If it is, a 10 percent commission is calculated; otherwise, a 5 percent commission is calculated.

IF statements require relational operators to be used to determine if one variable or constant is less than, equal to, or greater than another. The following are valid relational operators:

Symbol	Explanation
=	Equal to
<	Less than
>	Greater than
<=	Less than, or equal to
>=	Greater than, or equal to
<>	Not equal to

If you need additional information concerning IF statements, refer to "More on Functions" in Chapter 11.

Looping. The loop is an integral part of programming. It allows a program to execute the same set of statements as many times as needed for the application. A loop in BASIC can be provided with an IF statement or via the FOR NEXT command. The following is an example of a loop formed using an IF statement:

```
130 IF I < 10 THEN 30
```

Figure D.23
A FOR NEXT loop.

```
10 M = 20
20 FOR J = 1 TO 10 STEP 2
30 PRINT J;
40 M = M + 10
50 PRINT M
60 NEXT J
RUN
 1   30
 3   40
 5   50
 7   60
 9   70
Ok
```

1**LIST** 2**RUN◄** 3**LOAD"** 4**SAVE"** 5**CONT◄** 6**,"LPT1** 7**TRON◄** 8**TROFF◄** 9**KEY** 0**SCREEN**

This statement checks the value contained in variable I. If that value is less than 10, control is returned to statement 30 in the program, and program execution resumes at that point.

Instead of using IF statements to set up loops, you can also use the FOR NEXT command of BASIC to create a loop. The FOR command is used to indicate to BASIC how many statements are to be included within a loop as well as information to be used in determining how many times to pass through the loop. The NEXT command is the last statement to be contained within the loop. The syntax of the FOR command is:

```
FOR COUNTER = BEGVAL TO MAXVAL STEP INCVAL
```

The COUNTER is a variable that holds the various values as the loop executes. Be sure that you do not have this variable name assigned later in the loop for another purpose. The BEGVAL is the value of the counter when the loop is first encountered. The MAXVAL is the value the counter must have for control to leave the loop, and the INCVAL is the incremental value that is added to the COUNTER each time control passes through the loop. These can be variables or numeric constants. The program depicted in Figure D.23 shows a FOR NEXT loop with a STEP value of 2.

This particular program has statements 20–60 in the loop. Statement 60 (NEXT J) tells BASIC that this is the end of the loop and to return control back to statement 20. BASIC now checks to see if the value contained in J is greater than 10; if it is, control is passed to the statement following statement 60. Once J has a value greater than 10, BASIC tries to pass control to this point in the program and does not encounter a statement. When no statement is present, BASIC assumes that this is the end of the program and execution terminates.

As control is passed through the loop, the current value of J is printed. The semicolon (;) indicates to BASIC that any additional information should also be printed on this line. The next statement (40) adds 10 to the current value contained in M. This statement translates as: "assign M the current contents contained in M plus 10." Statement 50 prints the value of M; because there is no semicolon, BASIC issues a carriage return so that a line feed occurs.

Figure D.24
A BASIC program for calculating the average grade.

```
10 REM This program prompts you to enter a grade and the total possible
20 REM points for that assignment.
30 REM You indicate that you have finished entering grades by entering
40 REM 999 as a grade received.
50 INPUT "Enter the grade received ";GRADE
60 IF GRADE = 999 THEN 110
70 INPUT "Enter the total possible points ";POINTS
80 TOTALGRADE = TOTALGRADE + GRADE
90 TOTALPOSSIBLE = TOTALPOSSIBLE + POINTS
100 GOTO 50
110 AVERAGE = TOTALGRADE / TOTALPOSSIBLE
120 PRINT "TOTAL POINTS RECEIVED IS ";TOTALGRADE;" TOTAL POSSIBLE POINTS ";TOTAL
POSSIBLE;" AVERAGE IS ";AVERAGE
```

```
1LIST  2RUN+  3LOAD"  4SAVE"  5CONT+  6,"LPT1 7TRON+  8TROFF+ 9KEY   0SCREEN
```

The next sample program illustrates the use of a loop using an IF statement (Figure D.24). This program accepts grade information from the keyboard. It prompts you to enter a grade that you have received and the total
points possible for that grade. It then adds these to accumulators. When you
have entered your last grade, you indicate this to BASIC by entering a 999 for a
grade. Upon receiving a value of 999, BASIC prints out your total points, total
possible points, and the average.

Once you have entered the program, execute it and enter the following
grades:

Grade Received	Total Possible Points
23	30
85	95
10	15
90	95
47	50
999	

After you have entered the above grades, the screen should look similar to that
depicted in Figure D.25. Note that the average is .894.

Once you have finished the program, save it to disk under the name
SAMPLE4.

Exercises

1. Load the program BASIC3B. Change it to include IF statements to determine the final letter grade. Be sure and print the letter grade next to the
   average score. Use the following scale to determine the letter grade:

   90 = A

   80 = B

   70 = C

   60 = B

   <60 = F

   Save the altered program to the file BASIC4A.

Figure D.25
Output of the sample pro-
gram depicted in Figure D.24.

```
60 IF GRADE = 999 THEN 110
70 INPUT "Enter the total possible points ";POINTS
80 TOTALGRADE = TOTALGRADE + GRADE
90 TOTALPOSSIBLE = TOTALPOSSIBLE + POINTS
100 GOTO 50
110 AVERAGE = TOTALGRADE / TOTALPOSSIBLE
120 PRINT "TOTAL POINTS RECEIVED IS ";TOTALGRADE;" TOTAL POSSIBLE POINTS ";TOTAL
POSSIBLE;" AVERAGE IS ";AVERAGE
RUN
Enter the grade received ? 23
Enter the total possible points ? 30
Enter the grade received ? 85
Enter the total possible points ? 95
Enter the grade received ? 10
Enter the total possible points ? 15
Enter the grade received ? 90
Enter the total possible points ? 95
Enter the grade received ? 47
Enter the total possible points ? 50
Enter the grade received ? 999
TOTAL POINTS RECEIVED IS  255  TOTAL POSSIBLE POINTS  285  AVERAGE IS  .8947368

Ok

1LIST  2RUN←  3LOAD"  4SAVE"  5CONT←  6,"LPT1  7TRON←  8TROFF←  9KEY  0SCREEN
```

2. Create a program that accepts input about sales by sales representatives,
   calculates the sales commission for each sale, and calculates the total commission. For a sale $1,000 or more, sales reps receive a commission of 15
   percent; if the sale is less than $1,000, the commission is only 7.5 percent.
   A user should be prompted for each sale, which is then entered from the
   keyboard. The following sales have been made by a sales representative.
   The program knows that you have entered the last sale when it encounters a value of 9999.99.

```
Sale 1 - $2,000
Sale 2 - $750
Sale 3 - $1,750
Sale 4 - $200
Sale 5 - $5,234
```

Save this program to the file BASIC4B.

Session 5: READ, DATA, and RESTORE Statements

Up to now, when a program needed data it obtained that data from the person
running the program via interactive processing using the INPUT statement.
That is, the program prompts the user for data, which are then entered at the
keyboard. The program knows that data entering is finished when the user
presses ENTER. Another method of entering information is through batch
processing. In this method, the data to be used by the program is actually a
part of it. This is accomplished with READ and DATA statements.

A READ statement appears in the program with the variables to be supplied with data. The data for a READ command is found in one or more DATA
statements found in a program. The data supplied in a DATA statement must
match the data type required in a READ variable. Each piece of datum must be
separated by a comma.

Figure D.26
A BASIC program that re-
ceives information via READ
and DATA statements.

```
10 REM This program reads a series of grades found in DATA statements.
20 REM It prints each grade after it has been read.
30 REM As each grade is read it is added to a running total.
40 REM When the last grade has been read, it prints the totals and average.
50 REM The following DATA statements contain the data for the READ command.
60 DATA Quiz I,23,30
70 DATA Exam I,85,95
80 DATA Quiz II,10,15
90 DATA Exam II,90,95
100 DATA Exam III,47,50
110 DATA ,999,
120 REM The loop starts here.
130 READ ASSIGNMENT$,GRADE,POINTS
140 IF GRADE = 999 THEN 190
150 TOTALGRADE = TOTALGRADE + GRADE
160 TOTALPOSSIBLE = TOTALPOSSIBLE + POINTS
170 PRINT ASSIGNMENT$,GRADE,POINTS
180 GOTO 130
190 AVERAGE = TOTALGRADE / TOTALPOSSIBLE
200 PRINT "TOTALS",TOTALGRADE, TOTALPOSSIBLE, AVERAGE
```

`1LIST  2RUN←  3LOAD"  4SAVE"  5CONT←  6,"LPT1  7TRON←  8TROFF←  9KEY  0SCREEN`

Figure D.27
Output from the BASIC program using READ and DATA
statements.

```
60 DATA Quiz I,23,30
70 DATA Exam I,85,95
80 DATA Quiz II,10,15
90 DATA Exam II,90,95
100 DATA Exam III,47,50
110 DATA ,999,
120 REM The loop starts here.
130 READ ASSIGNMENT$,GRADE,POINTS
140 IF GRADE = 999 THEN 190
150 TOTALGRADE = TOTALGRADE + GRADE
160 TOTALPOSSIBLE = TOTALPOSSIBLE + POINTS
170 PRINT ASSIGNMENT$,GRADE,POINTS
180 GOTO 130
190 AVERAGE = TOTALGRADE / TOTALPOSSIBLE
200 PRINT "TOTALS",TOTALGRADE, TOTALPOSSIBLE, AVERAGE
run
Quiz I          23              30
Exam I          85              95
Quiz II         10              15
Exam II         90              95
Exam III        47              50
TOTALS          255             285             .8947368
Ok
```

`1LIST  2RUN←  3LOAD"  4SAVE"  5CONT←  6,"LPT1  7TRON←  8TROFF←  9KEY  0SCREEN`

Change SAMPLE4 so that it contains the same statements as those in the program depicted in Figure D.26. In addition, the name of the assignment will be given. As each grade is read, a line will be printed. When all of the grades have been read (a 999 is in the grade-received field), a total line will be printed. Once the program has been entered and any errors fixed, the output generated by the program should appear like that in Figure D.27.

The DATA statements that are used to supply information to the READ statement can appear anywhere in the program. You can have more than one record of information per DATA statement. For example, line 60 of the program in Figure D.28 has two records of information and still executes properly (Figure D.29). Save your program under the name SAMPLE5.

Figure D.28
Statement 60 contains data
for two records.

```
10 REM This program reads a series of grades found in DATA statements.
20 REM It prints each grade after it has been read.
30 REM As each grade is read it is added to a running total.
40 REM When the last grade has been read, it prints the totals and average.
50 REM The following DATA statements contain the data for the READ command.
60 DATA Quiz I,23,30,Homework,5,10
70 DATA Exam I,85,95
80 DATA Quiz II,10,15
90 DATA Exam II,90,95
100 DATA Exam III,47,50
110 DATA ,999,
120 REM The loop starts here.
130 READ ASSIGNMENT$,GRADE,POINTS
140 IF GRADE = 999 THEN 190
150 TOTALGRADE = TOTALGRADE + GRADE
160 TOTALPOSSIBLE = TOTALPOSSIBLE + POINTS
170 PRINT ASSIGNMENT$,GRADE,POINTS
180 GOTO 130
190 AVERAGE = TOTALGRADE / TOTALPOSSIBLE
200 PRINT "TOTALS",TOTALGRADE, TOTALPOSSIBLE, AVERAGE
```

```
1LIST    2RUN+   3LOAD"   4SAVE"   5CONT+   6,"LPT1 7TRON+   8TROFF+ 9KEY    0SCREEN
```

The RESTORE command makes the internal data available to the program again without leaving the program. This means that the first DATA statement's information is again available to the program.

Exercises

1. Write a program that includes a loop and inputs information via READ/DATA commands. This program is to read grade information for a number of individuals and print the average grade for each assignment. A name of "End" signals the end of the data. The individuals and their scores on the assignments are as follows:

Student	Asgn#1	Asgn#2	Asgn#3	Asgn#4	Asgn#5
Randy Simmons	20	25	50	10	5
Sue Ellen Wing	45	49	75	25	15
Helen Capondice	40	42	60	20	12
Ray Trefzger	37	43	63	22	14
Helen Nussbaum	25	39	64	24	15
Bob Seigrest	10	29	44	25	15
End					

Save the completed program to the file BASIC5A.

2. Write a BASIC program to calculate the yearly depreciation expense for five different assets. The yearly depreciation expense is calculated by first subtracting the salvage value from the cost of the asset. This result is then divided by the estimated life of the asset (life in years). Use a FOR/NEXT

Figure D.29
Output of the program
depicted in Figure D.28.

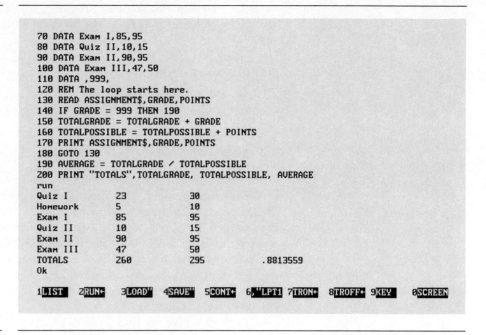

```
70 DATA Exam I,85,95
80 DATA Quiz II,10,15
90 DATA Exam II,90,95
100 DATA Exam III,47,50
110 DATA ,999,
120 REM The loop starts here.
130 READ ASSIGNMENT$,GRADE,POINTS
140 IF GRADE = 999 THEN 190
150 TOTALGRADE = TOTALGRADE + GRADE
160 TOTALPOSSIBLE = TOTALPOSSIBLE + POINTS
170 PRINT ASSIGNMENT$,GRADE,POINTS
180 GOTO 130
190 AVERAGE = TOTALGRADE / TOTALPOSSIBLE
200 PRINT "TOTALS",TOTALGRADE, TOTALPOSSIBLE, AVERAGE
run
Quiz I            23            30
Homework          5             10
Exam I            85            95
Quiz II           10            15
Exam II           90            95
Exam III          47            50
TOTALS            260           295            .8813559
Ok
```

```
1LIST   2RUN←   3LOAD"  4SAVE"  5CONT←  6,"LPT1 7TRON←  8TROFF← 9KEY    0SCREEN
```

loop so that only five assets will be read. A line containing the asset name, cost, salvage value, life, and the yearly depreciation should be printed for each asset. The data to be processed by the program should be placed in DATA statements and appears below:

Asset	Cost	Sal Val	Years
Asset #1	1000	100	10
Asset #2	5000	500	9
Asset #3	15000	1000	14
Asset #4	6000	400	20
Asset #5	400	50	7

Save this program to the file BASIC5B.

Session 6: Advanced Topics

Arrays. An **array** is a grouping of related storage elements/fields that can be referenced under one name. An array is used to store several different values that can then be used repeatedly in a program simply by referring to the area that holds these values. An array can be visualized much the same as a table of values. Arrays are usually created using the DIM statement. The **DIM statement** tells BASIC exactly how many elements or storage areas are to be found in the array. Once the DIM statement is executed by BASIC, it sets all array elements to an initial value of zero for numeric and null for string.

If you use an array without using a DIM statement, the maximum number of storage areas is assumed to be 10. If you try to access more than 10 areas, the screen displays a "Subscript out of range" error message. Even if you are using arrays of less than 10 elements, you should use a DIM statement to define the array because this makes your program more self-documenting.

Assume that you wish to store the gross pay of six different individuals in an array called GROSSPAY. The six values are

Gross pay value #1 = 233.65

Gross pay value #2 = 285.75

Gross pay value #3 = 225.90

Gross pay value #4 = 253.75

Gross pay value #5 = 221.87

Gross pay value #6 = 265.98

We are storing each of the six values of gross pay into one array called GROSS-PAY. Each value stored corresponds to one element of the GROSSPAY array. This element value (position in GROSSPAY) can be referred to as a subscript. For example, the gross pay of the fifth element (occurrence) of our GROSSPAY array is the value 221.87. If we know the position of the value that we want, we can reference that by using the variable name GROSSPAY and the position number (5 in this case). To do so requires that we use a reference like GROSS-PAY(5). This reference informs BASIC that we want the fifth occurrence of the values stored in GROSSPAY.

Let's now take another look at our array called GROSSPAY. The first column contains the value identification. The second column contains the value to be stored. The third column contains the subscript value. The fourth column contains the subscripted values for GROSSPAY.

Value ID	Value	Subscript	Subscript Value
Gross pay value #1 =	233.65	1	GROSSPAY(1)
Gross pay value #2 =	285.75	2	GROSSPAY(2)
Gross pay value #3 =	225.90	3	GROSSPAY(3)
Gross pay value #4 =	253.75	4	GROSSPAY(4)
Gross pay value #5 =	221.87	5	GROSSPAY(5)
Gross pay value #6 =	265.98	6	GROSSPAY(6)

The BASIC program shown in Figure D.30 provides the mechanism for loading the array called GROSSPAY using a FOR/NEXT loop. The data to be used in creating the array are found in a DATA statement. The value of the FOR counter N is used to store each value of PAY in a different GROSSPAY array element. For example, when N has the value of 1, the value 233.65 is stored in GROSSPAY(1). When you execute the program, all that you get is the OK prompt. We have done nothing more than load the array called GROSSPAY with the PAY values read.

Once GROSSPAY has been created and values stored in it, we want to read the values from GROSSPAY, print that value, and print the final total. This is accomplished by adding the statements found in Figure D.31 to our program. Statement 90 prints out the storage element number of this value stored in the GROSSPAY array as well as the value stored in this element. Because J has the value of 7 when the loop terminates, we subtract 1 from it to get the total number of employee gross pay elements processed. When the program is executed, your output should be the same as that depicted in Figure D.32. Save this file under the name SAMPLE6.

PRINT USING. The PRINT USING command controls how strings or numbers are printed by using a specific format to control the print process. The format

Figure D.30

The BASIC program for storing each of the values read from PAY in the array called GROSSPAY.

```
10 DIM GROSSPAY(6)
20 DATA 233.65,285.75,225.90,253.75,221.87,265.98
30 FOR N = 1 TO 6
40 READ PAY
50 GROSSPAY(N) = PAY
60 NEXT N
RUN
Ok
```

```
1LIST  2RUN←  3LOAD"  4SAVE"  5CONT←  6,"LPT1 7TRON←  8TROFF←  9KEY  0SCREEN
```

Figure D.31

The BASIC program for printing the array GROSSPAY and calculating the average gross pay.

```
10 DIM GROSSPAY(6)
20 DATA 233.65,285.75,225.90,253.75,221.87,265.98
30 FOR N = 1 TO 6
40 READ PAY
50 GROSSPAY(N) = PAY
60 NEXT N
70 FOR J = 1 TO 6
80 TOTALGROSS = TOTALGROSS + GROSSPAY(J)
90 PRINT "Gross Pay Value ";J;"is ";GROSSPAY(J)
100 NEXT J
110 EMPLOYEES = J - 1
120 AVERAGE = TOTALGROSS / EMPLOYEES
130 PRINT "Average gross pay is ";AVERAGE
```

```
1LIST   2RUN←   3LOAD"   4SAVE"   5CONT←   6,"LPT1 7TRON←   8TROFF←  9KEY   0SCREEN
```

characters themselves can be included within a PRINT command, or they can be referenced as a variable. The various format control characters are discussed below. Examples of how they work are also included in Figures D.33 and D.34.

String Fields

!	The exclamation point specifies that only the first character in the given string is to be printed.
\ n spaces \	This field specifies that 2 + *n* characters from the string are to be printed. If the backslashes are typed with no spaces, two characters are printed; with one space, three characters are printed, and so forth.

Figure D.32
The output of the GROSSPAY array and the calculated average.

```
10 DIM GROSSPAY(6)
20 DATA 233.65,285.75,225.90,253.75,221.87,265.98
30 FOR N = 1 TO 6
40 READ PAY
50 GROSSPAY(N) = PAY
60 NEXT N
70 FOR J = 1 TO 6
80 TOTALGROSS = TOTALGROSS + GROSSPAY(J)
90 PRINT "Gross Pay Value ";J;"is ";GROSSPAY(J)
100 NEXT J
110 EMPLOYEES = J - 1
120 AVERAGE = TOTALGROSS / EMPLOYEES
130 PRINT "Average gross pay is ";AVERAGE
RUN
Gross Pay Value  1 is  233.65
Gross Pay Value  2 is  285.75
Gross Pay Value  3 is  225.9
Gross Pay Value  4 is  253.75
Gross Pay Value  5 is  221.87
Gross Pay Value  6 is  265.98
Average gross pay is  247.8167
Ok
```

```
1LIST  2RUN←  3LOAD"  4SAVE"  5CONT←  6,"LPT1  7TRON←  8TROFF←  9KEY  0SCREEN
```

Figure D.33
String formats in PRINT USING commands.

```
list
10 REM This program illustrates using string PRINT USING commands.
20 REM The first PRINT command has 15 spaces between the backslashes.
30 REM The second PRINT command has 5 spaces between the backslashes.
40 REM The third PRINT command has no spaces between the backslashes.
50 REM The fourth PRINT command illustrates the use of the ! command.
60 REM The fifth PRINT command issustrates the use of the & command.
70 A$ = "The cat ran up the street."
80 PRINT USING "\               \";A$
90 PRINT USING "\     \";A$
100 PRINT USING "\\";A$
110 PRINT USING "!";A$
120 PRINT USING "&";A$
Ok
run
The cat ran up th
The ca
Th
T
The cat ran up the street.
Ok
```

```
1LIST  2RUN←  3LOAD"  4SAVE"  5CONT←  6,"LPT1  7TRON←  8TROFF←  9KEY  0SCREEN
```

&	The ampersand specifies a variable length string field. When the field is specified with the &, the string is output exactly as input.

Numeric Fields

#	A number sign represents each digit position. Digit positions are always filled. If the number to be printed has few digits than positions specified, the number is right-justified (preceded by spaces) in the field. A decimal point can be inserted at any position in the field. If the format string specifies that a digit

Figure D.34
Numeric formats in PRINT
USING commands.

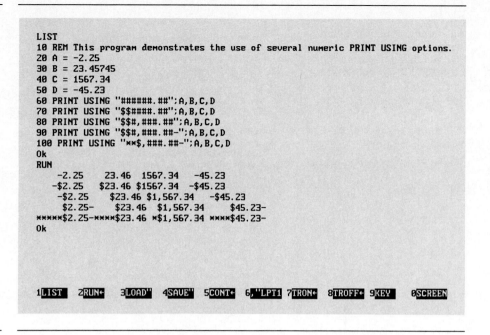

```
LIST
10 REM This program demonstrates the use of several numeric PRINT USING options.
20 A = -2.25
30 B = 23.45745
40 C = 1567.34
50 D = -45.23
60 PRINT USING "######.##";A,B,C,D
70 PRINT USING "$$####.##";A,B,C,D
80 PRINT USING "$$#,###.##";A,B,C,D
90 PRINT USING "$$#,###.##-";A,B,C,D
100 PRINT USING "**$,###.##-";A,B,C,D
Ok
RUN
    -2.25    23.46  1567.34   -45.23
   -$2.25   $23.46 $1567.34  -$45.23
    -$2.25      $23.46 $1,567.34    -$45.23
     $2.25-      $23.46  $1,567.34      $45.23-
*****$2.25-****$23.46 *$1,567.34 ****$45.23-
Ok
```

```
1LIST  2RUN+  3LOAD"  4SAVE"  5CONT+  6,"LPT1 7TRON+  8TROFF+ 9KEY   0SCREEN
```

is to precede the decimal point, the digit will always be printed (as a 0 if necessary). Numbers are rounded as necessary.

+   A plus sign at the beginning or end of the format string causes the sign of the number (plus or minus) to be printed before or after the number.

−   A minus sign at the end of the format field causes negative numbers to be printed with a trailing minus sign.

**   A double asterisk at the beginning of the format string causes leading spaces in the numeric field to be filled with asterisks. The ** also specifies positions for two more digits.

$$ The double dollar sign causes a dollar sign to be printed to the immediate left of the formatted number. The $$ specifies two more digit positions, one of which is the dollar sign. Negative numbers cannot be used unless the minus sign trails to the right.

**$ The **$ at the beginning of a format string combines the effects of the above two symbols. Leading spaces are filled with asterisks, and a dollar sign will be printed before the number. **$ specifies three more digit positions, one of which is the dollar sign.

,   A comma that is to the left of the decimal point in a formatting string causes a comma to be printed to the left of every third digit to the left of the decimal point. A comma that is at the end of the format string is printed as part of the string.

Figure D.35
An example of a format line being stored in a string variable and then referenced in a PRINT USING command.

```
10 REM This program reads payroll information and uses it to calculate gross
20 REM pay.
30 DATA Sam Adams,40,6.5,0
40 DATA Peter Johns,40,4.25,10
50 DATA John Kent,40,6.5,0
60 DATA Mary Hunt,40,6.75,3
70 DATA End,,,
80 A$ = "\              \         ###.##    $##.##   ##.##   $$#,###.##"
90 H1$ = "   Employee Name         Hours   Pay Rate  OvTime    Gross Pay"
100 H2$ = "  Total Gross Pay                                  $$#,###.##"
110 PRINT H1$
120 READ EMPLOYEE$, HOURS, RATE, OVTIME
130 IF EMPLOYEE$ = "End" THEN 190
140 IF OVTIME > 0 THEN OVPAY = RATE × 1.5 × OVTIME ELSE OVPAY = 0
150 GROSS = HOURS × RATE + OVPAY
160 GTGROSS = GTGROSS + GROSS
170 PRINT USING A$;EMPLOYEE$,HOURS,RATE,OVPAY,GROSS
180 GOTO 120
190 PRINT USING H2$;GTGROSS
```

```
1LIST  2RUN←  3LOAD"  4SAVE"  5CONT←  6,"LPT1 7TRON← 8TROFF← 9KEY   0SCREEN
```

Figure D.36
The output of the program using the referenced format lines.

```
50 DATA John Kent,40,6.5,0
60 DATA Mary Hunt,40,6.75,3
70 DATA End,,,
80 A$ = "\              \         ###.##    $##.##   ##.##   $$#,###.##"
90 H1$ = "   Employee Name         Hours   Pay Rate  OvTime    Gross Pay"
100 H2$ = "  Total Gross Pay                                  $$#,###.##"
110 PRINT H1$
120 READ EMPLOYEE$, HOURS, RATE, OVTIME
130 IF EMPLOYEE$ = "End" THEN 190
140 IF OVTIME > 0 THEN OVPAY = RATE × 1.5 × OVTIME ELSE OVPAY = 0
150 GROSS = HOURS × RATE + OVPAY
160 GTGROSS = GTGROSS + GROSS
170 PRINT USING A$;EMPLOYEE$,HOURS,RATE,OVPAY,GROSS
180 GOTO 120
190 PRINT USING H2$;GTGROSS
run
   Employee Name         Hours   Pay Rate  OvTime    Gross Pay
Sam Adams               40.00    $ 6.50    0.00       $260.00
Peter Johns            40.00    $ 4.25   63.75       $233.75
John Kent              40.00    $ 6.50    0.00       $260.00
Mary Hunt              40.00    $ 6.75   30.38       $300.38
  Total Gross Pay                                  $1,054.13
Ok
```

```
1LIST  2RUN←  3LOAD"  4SAVE"  5CONT←  6,"LPT1 7TRON← 8TROFF← 9KEY   0SCREEN
```

One advantage of the PRINT USING command is that you are allowed to place all formats that will be used in printing a line in a string variable. Once the formats have been placed in a string variable, you can refer to that variable in the PRINT USING command and it will be used as the format in printing the line. Figures D.35 and D.36 show an example. Save this program under the name SAMPLEGB.

Reserved Words

Reserved words have a special meaning to BASIC and cannot be used as variable names. They include all BASIC statements, commands, function names, and operator names. You must always separate a reserved word from other commands and/or data by using one or more spaces.

ABS	ERASE	LPRINT	RND
AND	ERDEV	LSET	RSET
ASC	ERDEV$	MERGE	RUN
AUTO	ERL	MID$	SAVE
BEEP	ERR	MKDIR	SCREEN
BLOAD	ERROR	MKD$	SGN
BSAVE	EXP	MKI$	SHELL
CALL	FIELD	MK$$	SIN
CDBL	FILES	MOD	SOUND
CHAIN	FIX	MOTOR	SPACE$
CHDIR	FNxxxxxxx	NAME	SPC(
CHR$	FOR	NEW	SQR
CINT	FRE	NEXT	STEP
CIRCLE	GET	NOT	STICK
CLEAR	GOSUB	OCT$	STOP
CLOSE	GOTO	OFF	STR$
CLS	HEX$	ON	STRIG
COLOR	IF	OPEN	STRING$
COM	IMP	OPTION	SWAP
COMMON	INKEY$	OR	SYSTEM
CONT	INP	OUT	TAB(
COS	INPUT	PAINT	TAN
CSNG	INPUT#	PEEK	THEN
CSRLIN	INPUT$	PEN	TIME$
CVD	INSTR	PLAY	TIMER
CVI	INT	PMAP	TO
CVS	INTER$	POINT	TROFF
DATA	IOCTL	POKE	TRON
DATE$	IOCTL$	POS	USING
DEF	KEY	PRESET	USR
DEFDBL	KEY$	PRINT	VAL
DEFINT	KILL	PRINT#	VARPTR
DEFSNG	LEFT$	PSET	VARPTR$
DEFSTR	LEN	PUT	VIEW
DELETE	LET	RANDOMIZE	WAIT
DIM	LINE	READ	WEND
DRAW	LIST	REM	WHILE
EDIT	LLIST	RENUM	WIDTH
ELSE	LOAD	RESET	WINDOW
END	LOC	RESTORE	WIRTE
ENVIRON	LOCATE	RESUME	WRITE#
ENVIRON$	LOF	RETURN	XOR
EOF	LOG	RIGHT$	
EQV	LPOS	RMDIR	

Selected BASIC Command Summary

ABS(x) Absolute value function that returns the absolute value of the expression x.

$$x = ABS(12 * (-2))$$

ASC(x$) ASCII code function that returns the code for the first character of the string x$.

ATN(x) Arctangent function that returns the arctangent of x.

AUTO[number] [,[increment]]	Generates a line number each time you press ENTER. For example, AUTO automatically inserts a line number each time you press ENTER, whereas AUTO 100,20 generates line numbers 100, 120, 140, and so on.
BEEP	Generates a beep on the computer's speaker. You can also issue a beep via the command PRINT CHR$(7).
CDBL(x)	The double-precision function that converts the numeric expression of x into a double-precision number.
CHDIR path	Changes the current directory to the path specified.
	CHDIR "\" changes the directory to the root directory.
	CHDIR ".." changes to the directory immediately above the current directory.
	CHDIR "C:\BASIC\WORKFILS" changes to the directory WORKFILS found under the directory BASIC.
CHR$(n)	Converts an ASCII code to its character equivalent.
CINT(x)	Converts a formula or numeric constant to an integer.
CIRCLE (x,y),r	Draws an ellipse on the screen with the center at coordinates x and y and a radius of r.
	`CIRCLE(100,70),30`
	The CIRCLE function draws an ellipse at coordinates 100 and 70 with a radius of 45.
CLEAR	Sets all variables used by a program to zero or null without erasing the program.
CLOSE	Closes any files that have been opened for input or output operations.
	`350 CLOSE #1,#2,#3`
	This command closes files 1, 2, and 3.
CLS	Clears the monitor screen and places the cursor at the Home location.
COLOR	Sets the foreground, background, and border colors on the screen.
CONT	Resumes program execution after a Ctrl + Break command has been issued or a STOP or END statement has been issued.
COS(x)	Returns the cosine of x. x is the angle whose cosine is to be calculated.

CSNG(x)	Converts *x* to a single-precision number.
CSRLIN	Returns the vertical coordinate of the cursor.
DATA	Stores the numeric and string constants that are to be accessed by the program's READ statement(s). They can be placed anywhere within the program.
DATE$	Retrieves the system date and places it in a string variable. It can also be used to set the date.

`A$ = DATE$`	Places today's date in A$.
`DATE$ = A$`	Resets today's date to the value contained in A$.

DEF FN	Creates user-defined functions. The format is DEF FNname[(arg[,arg]…)] = expression.
DEFtype	Declares variable types as integer, single-precision, double-precision, or string.

`DEFINT A,B,C`

This declares that any variable name starting with A, B, or C will automatically be integer. This can be overridden using a type declaration character in a name. For example, A$ overrides the above example.

DELETE	Deletes lines from a program.

`DELETE 30`	Deletes line 30 from the program.
`DELETE 30-100`	Deletes lines 30–100 from the program.

DIM	Specifies the size of the array that is being created. If a DIM command is not used, BASIC limits the array size to 10 elements.
DRAW string	Draws an object specified by the defining string.

Un	Move up.
Dn	Move down.
Ln	Move left.
Rn	Move right.
En	Move diagonally up and right.
Fn	Move diagonally down and right.
Gn	Move diagonally down and left.
Hn	Move diagonally up and left.

The *n* represents the number of units to move in this direction.

```
DRAW "R50R50D50L50"
or
I$ = "R50R50D50L50"
DRAW I$
```

EDITline
Displays a line for editing. It functions in the same fashion as the LIST command using full-screen editing.

END
Terminates execution of a program and closes any files that might be open. It can be placed anywhere in a program.

EOF(filenum)
Indicates when the end of a file has been reached. The filenum parameter is the number of the file specified in the OPEN statement.

```
IF FOF(1) THEN END
```

ERASE array
Eliminates arrays from a program.

EXP(x)
Calculates the exponential function of the numeric expression contained in *x*.

FIELD
Allocates space for variables in a random file buffer.

```
FIELD#2, 25 AS CUSTOMER$,
30 AS ADDRESS$
```

This statement allocates storage for the second file that was opened and reserves twenty-five characters for the variable CUSTOMER$ and thirty characters for the variable ADDRESS$.

FILES
Displays a listing of the files in the default or specified drive to the monitor.

FILES Displays the default drive directory to the monitor.

FILES "B: Displays the directory of drive B tc the screen.

FIX(x)
Truncates the numeric constant or variable in *x* to an integer. No rounding occurs when this function is used.

FOR and NEXT
Blocks instructions from being executed until the indicated parameters have been satisfied.

```
FOR COUNTER = BEGVAL TO
ENDVAL,INCVAL
```

COUNTER is the variable that is examined each pass through the loop. BEGVAL is the beginning value to be used by the COUNTER. ENDVAL is the value that, exceeded by the COUNTER, causes the loop to be exited. INCVAL is the value added to the COUNTER each pass through the loop.

FRE(x)

Returns the number of bytes in memory that are not being used by BASIC.

GET

Reads a record from a random file.

```
GET#1,16
```

This command causes the sixteenth record to be read from the first file that was opened.

GOSUBnandRETURN

Branches to the statement (*n*) specified after the GOSUB command. BASIC then begins to sequentially execute commands until it encounters a RETURN command.

```
GOSUB 900
```

This command begins executing the commands beginning at statement 900.

GOTO n

Results in an unconditional branch to the statement with line number *n*.

HEX$(n)

Returns a string that represents the value of the decimal argument *n*.

IF

Provides for decision making within the program. If the condition specified is true, the actions following the THEN are executed. If the condition specified is false, the actions following the ELSE are executed.

INKEY$

Reads a character from the keyboard.

INPUT

Receives input from the keyboard. It can be followed by a string in quotation marks that is used as a prompt to the user.

```
10 INPUT "Enter your
age";AGE
```

This statement displays the "Enter your age" prompt and waits for you to enter a number and press ENTER.

INPUT #

Reads data items from a sequential file and assigns them to variables.

```
20 INPUT
#2,CUSTOMER$,AMOUNT
```

	This statement gets the CUSTOMER string field and the AMOUNT numeric field from file 2.
INPUT$(x)	Returns a string of *n* characters, read from the keyboard or from the file number.
INT(x)	Returns the largest integer that is less than or equal to *x*.
KILL filename	Erases files from disk. This is similar to the DOS ERASE or DEL command.
LEFT$(x$,n)	Returns the left-most *n* characters of x$.
LEN(x$)	Returns the number of characters in x$.
LET	Creates assignments or formulas for use in a BASIC program.
LINE	Draws a line or a box to the monitor.

```
10 SCREEN 1,0
20 LINE (0,0)-(319,199),1
```

These commands result in a cyan box being drawn.

LINE INPUT #	Reads an entire line from a sequential file into a string variable.
LIST	Lists the lines of the program currently in memory to the screen.

LIST	Lists all line numbers.
LIST 30-100	Lists lines 30–100 to the screen.

LLIST	Lists the specified lines to the printer.
LOAD "filename	Loads the specified file into memory.
LOCATE r,c	Positions the cursor to the row column coordinates specified in *r* and *c*.

```
LOCATE 12,40
```

This command positions the cursor to row 12 position 40 on the screen.

LPRINT	Prints data on the printer (LPT#1) and supports all other options that can be used with a PRINT command.
LSET and RSET	Moves data into a random file buffer in preparation for a PUT statement. These commands must follow a FIELD statement for the variables listed in the LSET and RSET commands.
MERGE filename	Merges the lines from an ASCII program file into the program currently in memory.
MID$(x$,n,m)	Returns a portion of the specified string x$. The *m* specifies the length of the character

	string to be returned, whereas the n specifies the beginning character position in x$.
MKDIR path	Creates a directory on the specified drive.
NAME old AS new	Changes the name of a disk file. This command is similar to the RENAME command of DOS.
NEW	Deletes the program currently in memory and clears all variables.
ON ERROR GOTO n	Enables error trapping and specifies the first line to be executed when an error is detected.
ON GOSUB AND ON GOTO	Branches to one of several specified line numbers, depending on the value of an expression.
OPEN	Opens a file for a specified type of operation and as a specific file number. A file can be opened in one of three ways:

OUTPUT	Specifies sequential output mode and erases any existing data in the file.
INPUT	Specifies sequential input mode.
APPEND	Specifies sequential output mode where data is added to the end of the file.

If the mode is omitted, sequential I/O is assumed.

```
OPEN CUSTMAST FOR APPEND
AS #2
```

This statement opens the CUSTMAST file as the second file. It specifies that any data written to the file will be added to the end of the file.

PAINT (x,y),color,boundarycolor	Fills an area on the monitor specified by the x and y coordinates with a selected color. **Color** is the color that is used inside the box, whereas **boundarycolor** is the color number that resides outside the box.
PEEK(n)	Returns the byte read from the indicated memory position n. This value is an integer in the range 0–255.
PLAY string	Plays music specified by the string characters.
POINT(x,y)	Returns the color of the specified coordinates on the screen.

POKE n,m	Writes a byte into a memory location. The *n* is a number in the range of 0–65535 and represents the memory storage location. The *m* is the datum to be written to that location. It must be in the range of 0–255.
POS(n)	Returns the current cursor column position.
PRINT	Displays data to the screen. It can be followed by constant or variable data.
PRINT USING	Determines the format in which data is to be displayed. There are special formats for string and numeric data. The format may be part of the PRINT command or it may reside in a string variable.
PSET(x,y)	Draws a point at the specified coordinates on the screen.
PUT filenum,recnum	Writes a record to the file specified by filenum at the recnum location.

```
PUT#1,16
```

	This command writes to file #1 beginning at record location 16.
RANDOMIZE n	Reseeds the random number generator to the value contained in *n*. The RANDOMIZE command prevents the random number generator from returning the same value each time it is executed.
READ	Reads values from a DATA statement and assigns them to variables.
REM	Puts documentation in the form of explanatory remarks in a program. REM statements are ignored by BASIC when it executes the program.
RENUM	Resequences line numbers in a BASIC program. Any referenced line numbers in the program are changed to reflect any changes that have occurred.

```
RENUM BEGLINE,STARTLINE,INCVAL
```

RESET	Closes all diskette files and clears the system buffer.
RESTORE	Rereads DATA statements from a specified line.
RESUME	Restarts program execution after an error recovery procedure is performed.
RETURN	Returns control to the statement immediately following the GOSUB that initiated the branch to this subroutine.
RIGHT$(s$,n)	Returns the right-most *n* characters of string x$.

RMDIR path	Removes a directory from the specified disk.
RND(x)	Returns a random number between 0 and 1. The x is a numeric expression that affects the returned value.
RUN filename	The RUN command executes the program currently in memory. The RUN filename loads the specified file and executes it.
SAVE "filename	The SAVE command saves a BASIC program file to disk. If a drive other than the default is used, specify the drive identifier after the double quotes. The ASCII parameter can also be used to save a standard ASCII file to disk. For example, SAVE "B:SAMPLE1: ,A saves the file to disk in ASCII format. This file cannot be used in a MERGE command or read by a word processor.
SCREEN n	Sets the resolution of the screen.

	SCREEN 0	Text (40*80 columns)
	SCREEN 1	Medium resolution (320*200 points)
	SCREEN 2	High resolution (640*200 points)

SGN(x)	Returns the sign of the variable x. If x is positive, the returned value is 1. If x is negative, the returned value is -1. If x is zero, the returned value is 0.
SIN(x)	Calculates the trigonometric sine function. The x is the angle in radians.
SOUND freq,dur	Generates sound through the speaker. The first parameter is for the frequency of the sound, whereas the second variable is for the duration of the sound.
SPC(n)	Skips n spaces in a PRINT statement.
SQR(x)	Returns the square root of x.
STOP	Terminates program execution and returns to command level. It does not, however, close any files; you can resume execution via the RESUME command.
STR$(x)	Returns a string value of the numeric expression found in x.
SWAP var1,var2	Exchanges the values of var1 and var2.
SYSTEM	Exits BASIC and returns to DOS.
TAB(n)	Tabs to position n.
TAN(x)	Returns the trigonometric tangent of x. The x is the angle in radians.
TIME$	Sets or retrieves the current time.
TRON and TROFF	Turns on and off program tracing. Tracing is used during debugging and testing.

VAL(x$)	Returns the numerical value of string x$.
WHILE and WEND	Sets up a loop as long as the condition contained in the WHILE statement remains true.

```
While J>0
    statements in loop
WEND
```

WIDTH	Sets the character width of the screen.
WRITE list	This command is similar to the PRINT command except that it places a comma between each item in the list.
WRITE #	Writes output to sequential files. Because commas are required between fields in ASCII files, this is the preferred instruction when writing data to a file.

Many consumers spend a lot of time pondering the idea of purchasing a micro-computer for home use. Over the past few years, microcomputers have become fairly popular Christmas gifts either for children in the family or for the gift givers themselves. A consumer must consider a number of important factors when purchasing a microcomputer for the home. The factors to consider are:

1. The typical computer system
2. Compatibility
3. Special requirements
4. Where to purchase the hardware
5. Software considerations
6. Hidden costs

Typical Computer System Components

The typical microcomputer system comprises four parts:

The microcomputer itself

A storage device

An input device

An output device

The microcomputer contains the internal memory (that portion available to the user), the actual microprocessor, and all the electronic components that are needed to make the device work.

The storage device for the computer stores programs (prewritten instruc-tions to the computer) and data. The common storage medium used today is the diskette. Some computers use cassette tape, but this medium is extremely slow. There are a variety of sizes and types of diskettes on the market. All you must know is whether your computer is capable of recording on one or both sides of the disk and whether the disk is single- or double-density (this determines the quality of the surface). Purchase only that type of disk for your system.

The keyboard is the typical input device for giving instructions to the machine. No two manufacturers seem to make the same type of keyboard. Before you buy a machine, make sure that you try out the keyboard. Nothing can be more discouraging than getting a machine that has the keys arranged in a manner that is different from what you are accustomed to using.

The typical output devices are the monitor and the printer. The monitor is used to output any prompts to the user and for nonessential output that does not have to be saved. When you need information that has to be saved for historical purposes the printer is used. There are a number of different types of monitors and printers. The cost of these devices is typically directly related to the quality of output. The higher the quality of output, the higher the cost of the device.

The Issue of Compatibility

The most important issue to address when purchasing a microcomputer is compatibility. One manufacturer's computer cannot always easily talk with another manufacturer's computer. You must, therefore, decide exactly why you want the machine. At this point, many consumers' purchasing decision be-comes clouded by brand loyalty to some particular machine. This is the worst way to make a purchasing decision.

For example, do you want to take office work home with you? In this case, your machine choice is limited to the types of microcomputer used in the workplace. You do not want to purchase a computer that cannot read information generated by a machine at the office. If you are purchasing a machine for your children, will this machine be able to communicate with the children's computers at school? This allows a child to do work at home and then take it to school. Compatibility with school can be extremely important because many schools have programs that allow students to check out software for home use.

Special Requirements

Today's microcomputers, unlike minicomputers or mainframe computers, do not have many limitations on where they can be placed. They do not have any heat, cooling, or humidity requirements that cannot be easily met within the typical household. Electrical requirements are minimal. You do not need a dedicated electrical circuit for the computer, but you do not also want to put it on the same circuit that already has the refrigerator, microwave, toaster, and coffee maker on it. A voltage–surge protector or lightning arrestor is also a good idea. Voltage–surge devices can cost upward to $100, but a good lightning arrestor (all that is really needed) can be purchased for under $10 at your local hardware store.

A combination of high heat and high humidity might cause the disk unit to develop problems in finding data or programs during the summer months. Many times, this can be remedied simply by turning on the dehumidifier.

The primary problem that many consumers encounter is static electricity. Static electricity, especially during the winter months, can be a real killer for the electronic circuits and chips that reside inside the computer, printers, and disk drives. This problem can easily be resolved by purchasing an antistatic mat, button, or other device that you touch to discharge any built-up static electricity before touching your computer.

Where to Purchase the Machine

There are basically four sources of computers:

Local computer specialty shops

Department/discount stores

Mail order

Used computers

Local computer specialty shops historically have been the primary source of computers for consumers. These shops typically have trained technicians and sales staff who are able to handle most problems that arise. Service on the hardware is usually performed on the premises. These shops typically service only those machines that they sell.

Another source of computers is the department/discount store. Exceptional buys are possible at these locations. The sales staff, depending on the store, may or may not be able to answer questions about the capability of the hardware and/or software. Service on the machines is usually at a location other than where the machine was sold.

Mail-order shops also offer tremendous buys on hardware. The consumer is expected to be fairly knowledgeable about the equipment that they are purchasing. If something goes wrong with the equipment, it must be sent back for repair. Depending on the store, this can take anywhere from one to four weeks. Any questions that you have after the equipment arrives will usually cost a long-distance telephone call.

Used computers can be an exceptional buy. If the system is purchased from an individual, you may be able to purchase a complete system containing both hardware and software for a fraction of the original price. One disadvantage in purchasing such equipment is that the warranty has probably expired, and it might be hard to get the equipment repaired if anything goes wrong with it. Another disadvantage is that the seller may have unreasonable expectations about the value of the old equipment. Used computer stores are also opening in large cities. These stores even provide a warranty for equipment purchased there.

Software Considerations

Once the machine has been purchased, the software (preprogrammed instructions) that allow you to make the machine useful must also be purchased. If you purchase name brand software, you can easily invest one-half the cost of the hardware for programs. There are five basic sources for software:

> Computer/department stores
>
> Mail order
>
> Public-domain software
>
> Shareware
>
> Generic software

Computer and department stores typically stock many types of software packages. It is not uncommon to see literally hundreds of different packages in a store. Unless you purchase a name brand or very popular software, the sales staff may not be able to answer questions that you have about its use. Also expect to pay close to full price for the programs.

Mail-order vendors often have anywhere from a 20 to 60 percent discount on software prices. With such discounts, however, expect almost no support from the vendor. If you have any problems, you will probably have to call the manufacturer of the software.

Public-domain software is software that is available to you for about the cost of a disk. It is not pirated software but software that has been designed and developed possibly for a user's group. Some of this software is excellent, but much of it is a waste. Many times, this type of software is available by joining a local user's group for a specific type of computer.

Shareware is software that is typically available free for evaluation purposes. If, after using the software, you decide that you want to keep it, instructions are included that direct you where to send in a nominal charge for complete documentation and rights to enhancements or updates. A number of good word processing and spreadsheet packages are available in this manner.

Generic software packages combine word processing, spreadsheets, and data base on one diskette. These packages may not have the capabilities of larger, more expensive packages but might be all that's needed for home use.

Hidden Costs

A number of costs are not always considered in making the decision to purchase a home computer. These hidden costs include software, disks, ribbon, paper, and computer furniture. Software, as mentioned previously, can easily reach one-half the cost of the hardware. Other costs include disks. It is not uncommon for a microcomputer owner to have a number of boxes of disks. This cost mounts up when the disks can cost anywhere from $30 to $50 a box (there are ten disks to a box). If you purchase a printer, you will have to buy ribbon and paper for it also. You may also find that the table that you had originally planned to use with the computer is not the right height (typically typing height, or 27 inches from the floor), which necessitates the purchase of a computer table.

Summary

Examining the various options available for purchasing the hardware and software for the home allows a consumer to make a more intelligent purchase decision. Facing the issues of compatibility and special needs of microcomputers allows you to be more comfortable about using the computer and to more completely enjoy the computer later on.

A>: *See* DOS prompt.

ABCDEF commands: Used to specify up to six data ranges to be depicted on a graph.

Absolute addressing: Cell location that does not change in the course of copying a formula to other cells. In a cell marked for absolute address, the formula contains dollar signs.

Absolute range name: Used to give absolute addresses to range names.

Access controls: Protect the computer equipment and facilities.

Acronym: Word formed from letters or syllables in a name or phrase. For example, FORTRAN is an acronym for Formula Translator.

Action line: The first line of the four lines at the bottom of a dBASE III Plus screen. It contains the commands that are entered at the keyboard or built using the menu assisted mode.

Active directory: On a disk device, the last directory that you were in via a CD command. Any files copied to the disk name (with no path specified) get copied to this directory.

Active index: The first index a dBASE user specifies.

Address: (As a noun) number associated with each memory location; (as a verb) to refer to a particular memory location.

Algorithm: A series of steps that manipulates the record key to find a record.

Align command: Tells 1-2-3 to expect the top of a page at this page position.

Alignment character: Entered numeric text moves to the left until this character is entered.

Align option: Resets the top of a page in 1-2-3.

ALL parameter: Lists all the records in a file on the screen.

Alphanumeric: Contraction of the words *alphabetic* and *numeric*. A set of alphanumeric characters usually includes special characters such as the dollar sign and comma.

Alphanumeric keys: Keys with numbers, letters, and special characters that appear on a keyboard device.

Alternate key: Key used to create a second set of function keys in some application programs, to enter the ASCII character code directly from the keyboard, and (together with letters) to enter BASIC commands.

Alt key: Label for the Alternate Key.

Analog signals: Transmission of data via sounds.

#AND#: A logical operator in a 1-2-3 @IF function.

Append command: The WordPerfect option that adds data to the end of a file rather than replacing the file with the indicated data. In dBASE, APPEND enables you to add records at the end of an existing file.

Application program: Precoded set of generalized instructions for the computer, written to accomplish a certain goal. Examples of such programs include a general ledger package, a mailing list program, and PacMan.

Arithmetic/logic unit: Performs the arithmetic operations of addition, subtraction, multiplication, and division and any comparisons required by the program.

Arithmetic operations: Consist of such actions as addition, subtraction, multiplication, and division.

Arrow keys: Keys (down, up, right, and left) found on the numeric keyboard and typically used to move a pointer or cursor.

Artificial intelligence: The attempt to construct computer-based hardware/software systems that think like a human being.

ASCII: Acronym for American Standard Code for Information Interchange (pronounced *ass-key*). Often called USASCII, this code is a standard method of representing a character with a number inside the computer. Knowledge of the code is important only if you write programs.

Assembler: Program that converts the mnemonics and symbols of assembly language into the opcodes and operands of machine language.

Assembly language: Language similar in structure to machine language but made up of mnemonics and symbols. Programs written in assembly language are slightly less difficult to write and understand than programs in machine language.

ASSIGN: The DOS command that allows you to tell DOS to direct read/write requests for one disk drive into read/write requests for another drive.

ASSIGN statement: Used in a CONFIG.SYS file to reassign device names.

Assist Menu: A series of pull-down menus that allows you to use dBASE III PLUS without in-depth knowledge of how dBASE works.

*: A DOS wild card. In a file name or extension, * indicates that any character can occupy that position and any remaining positions in the file name or extension.

Asynchronous protocol: Transmits data a character at a time.

ATTRIB: DOS command that allows you to change the read-only attribute of a file. This determines whether a file can only be read or can be both read and written.

Auto-answer: A feature found in some modems that allows the computer to answer the phone.

Auto-dial: Feature frequently found in modems that enables you to place a call to a specified number without having to dial it yourself.

AUTOEXEC.BAT: File executed by the computer as soon as the boot process is completed. This type of file is used in building a turn-key application that requires very little input from a user before starting.

Automatic Recalculation feature: Enables the worksheet automatically to recalculate itself after any change.

Available memory: Amount of RAM available for use by 1-2-3 in building a worksheet.

BACKSPACE key: Used to erase the last character typed. It is labeled with an arrow that points left.

Backup and recovery: Backup refers to copies made of the data base used to restore (recover) from any disasters. This ensures that no data (or only a minimal amount) are lost.

Backup file: .BK!-extension file that WordPerfect automatically creates as protection against loss of an original file. It can also be an additional copy of an important file created by the user via the DOS Copy command.

Bandwidth: Refers to the grade of transmission media. The wider the bandwidth, the greater the number of bits per second can be transmitted.

Banked memory: Usually two sets of 64K memory used to give a computer a total memory of 128K. Only one set of 64K can be active at a time.

Bar chart: Horizontal or vertical bars that are stacked, floating, or clustered side-by-side.

BASIC: Acronym for Beginners All-Purpose Symbolic Instruction Code, a common, easy-to-learn computer programming language. The advanced version of BASIC is called BASICA. BASIC was developed by Kemeney and Kurtz at Dartmouth College in 1963 and has proved to be the most popular language for personal computers.

Batch file: A file that contains DOS instructions. This file then feeds its DOS commands one at a time to DOS, once the file is invoked.

Batch printing: Prints up to sixteen graph files at one time.

Batch processing: Records grouped together and processed all at once.

Baud rate: Speed at which modems can transmit characters across telephone lines. A 300-baud modem can transmit about thirty characters per second.

Beginning of file (BOF) command: Senses the start of a file in dBASE.

Bell: Sound produced by your computer or line printer, often used by programs to get your attention or to reassure you that computer processing is underway.

Benchmark: A program that approximates the processing demands of a new system's program.

Big Left: The 1-2-3 command (Ctrl + left arrow) that moves you to the left a screen at a time.

Big Right: The 1-2-3 command (Ctrl + right arrow) that moves you to the right a screen at a time.

Bi-level mode: A scanning mode that only scans black and white.

Binary: Number system consisting of two digits, 0 and 1, with each digit in a binary number representing a power of two. Most digital computers are binary. A binary signal is easily expressed by the presence or absence of an electrical current or magnetic field.

Binary notation: The use of 0's and 1's to create characters or numbers upon which the computer then performs operations.

Bit: Binary digit, the smallest amount of information a computer can hold. A single bit specifies a single value of 0 or 1. Bits can be grouped to form larger values. *See* Byte and Nibble.

Bit-mapped font: Text characters that are built using a pattern of dots.

Bit-mapped graphics: A display technology that creates images on a screen via dots generated on the screen.

B&W option: Displays data in black and white.

Black-box concept: Used to break a complex task into simple inputs, process, and outputs.

Block: Designated portion of text, consisting of one or more lines, that is to be copied, moved, or deleted.

Boldface command: Produces darkened text, accomplished by printer striking or printing the same character three or four times.

Boot process: Starting the computer. During the boot process a memory check is performed, the various parts of DOS are loaded, and the date and time are requested.

Boot record: Record that resides on sector 1 of track 0 of a file and contains the program responsible for loading the rest of DOS into the microcomputer.

Bootstrap (boot): Procedure used to get a system running from a cold start. The name comes from the machine's attempts to pull itself off the ground by "tugging on its own bootstraps."

Border: Set of labels for the rows and columns of a worksheet. The columns are labeled with letters, and the rows are labeled with numbers.

Borders option: In Lotus 1-2-3, allows user to specify horizontal or vertical borders to be displayed on each page of a printed report.

BOTTOM: dBASE command that enables you to position the pointer at the end of the file.

Boundary: Defines the limits of a component, the collection of components, or the entire system.

Break: Function for halting the program in progress. Usually the program returns to some higher-level program such as DOS, BASIC, or the main application program, but not all programs have this function. It is invoked by holding the Ctrl key down while pressing Scroll Lock.

Break option: Can be either on or off. Allows user to instruct DOS to check for a control break (Ctrl + Break) when a program requests DOS to perform any tasks.

BROWSE command: Displays a number of records on the screen at one time, enabling you to edit a file quickly in dBASE.

B-tree structure: Structural arrangement that provides the ability to develop indexes that establish the relations for a relational data base file.

Buffers: The DOS command that allows you to determine how much RAM is used for holding information for disk read/write operations. This command is used in the CONFIG.SYS file.

Buffers option: Allows user to determine the number of disk buffers that DOS is to allocate in memory when it starts.

Bug: Error. A hardware bug is a physical or electrical malfunction or design error; a software bug is an error in programming, either in the logic of the program or in typing.

Built-in functions: Processes or formulas that have already been programmed into software such as the spreadsheet package of Lotus 1-2-3.

Bus: Entity that enables the computer to pass information to a peripheral and to receive information from a peripheral.

Bus network: Connects several nodes or computers with a single cable along which computers can send messages in either direction.

Byte: Basic unit of measure of a computer's memory. A byte usually has eight bits, so its value can be from 0 to 255. Each character can be represented by one byte in ASCII.

Cancel option: Used to eliminate errors.

Caps Lock key: Key used to switch the case of letters A through Z on the keyboard. This key does not affect numbers and special characters.

Card: General term for a printed circuit board with electronic components attached. Also called an interface card, a board, a circuit card assembly, and other similar names.

Cartridge: Removable hard disk storage unit that typically holds five or ten megabytes of storage.

Case conversion: WordPerfect command that allows you to change the case of existing text within a document.

CD (compact disk): Stores information via burned-in bubbles using lasers on a disk surface. The storage limit is rated in billions of bytes.

Cell: Intersection point of a row and a column. It is referenced by the cell address COLUMN/ROW.

Center block: Enables user to center a block of text.

Center command: Word processing or spreadsheet command that centers text in a document or cell.

Centering hole: Large hole on a diskette that allows the Mylar plastic disk inside the diskette envelope to center on the capstan for proper rotation.

Center page option: Centers information vertically on the printed page by leaving the same number of blank lines above and below the text.

Central processing unit (CPU): Device in a computer system that contains the arithmetic unit, the control unit, and the main memory. Also referred to as the computer.

Centronics: Standard method of passing information through a parallel data port.

Character: Any graphic symbol that has a specific meaning to people. Letters (both upper- and lower-case), numbers, and various symbols (such as punctuation marks) are all characters.

Character field: Field capable of holding any alphanumeric or special character. In dBASE, such a field can hold up to 254 characters.

Character overprint: Function that enables user to create text using diacritical marks such as tildes. It also creates special effects in printing.

Character pitch: Number of characters printed per horizontal inch of space. Twelve pitch (elite) prints twelve characters per inch; ten pitch (pica) prints ten characters per inch.

? character: Used in dBASE to obtain information displayed on screen.

CHDIR (CD): DOS command that allows you to move to another directory and make that the active directory.

Check Spelling option: Activates PC Works' built-in spelling checker.

Chip: Electronic entity containing one or more semiconductors on a wafer of silicon, within which an integrated circuit is formed.

CHKDSK: DOS command that checks the status of a disk and prepares the status report.

Circular reference: Cell's effect depends on both its contents and the contents of other cells.

Clear command: Functions like the Range Erase of 1-2-3, but in this PC Works' command the range of cells must be highlighted via Extend command before Clear.

Clear option: Allows Lotus 1-2-3 user to return all print options to their default.

Clear screen: Procedure that blanks the screen of all characters. It can be accomplished by pressing the Home key while holding down the Ctrl key.

Clock speed: Measured in millions of cycles per second (megahertz, or MHz), indicates how fast a computer can process information and is a function of the ease with which electricity passes through the CPU.

Closed-bus system: Type of computer system that comes with plugs, called established ports, that accept device cables from the peripheral.

CLS: DOS command that clears the display monitor.

Cluster: Entity composed of two adjacent sectors. Storage is allocated to a file one cluster at a time.

Coaxial cable: The same type of cable often used to connect a television set. Capable of carrying up to ten megabits of data at a time.

COBOL: Acronym for Common Business Oriented Language, a high-level language oriented toward organizational data processing procedures.

Code: Method of representing something in terms of something else. The ASCII code represents characters in terms of binary numbers; the BASIC language represents algorithms in terms of program statements. *Code* also may refer to programs, usually in low-level languages. Invisible command to WordPerfect that tells it how to display or print text.

Cold start: Booting process used to begin operating a computer that has just been turned on.

Color monitor: Display device capable of showing red, green, and blue.

Color option: Displays information in colors preselected by 1-2-3.

Column: Vertical line of text.

Column block: Command that specifies a column of data within a document to copy, move, or delete.

Column Hide command: Enables 1-2-3 user to print certain columns of a worksheet without printing certain embedded columns.

Column Width command: Enables Lotus 1-2-3 user to adjust width of a column.

Combination key: Key that must be used together with another key to perform a task. Combination keys include the Ctrl, Alt, and Shift.

COMMAND.COM: Command processor of DOS, containing built-in functions or subroutines that enable user to copy a file or get a directory listing of a disk.

Command line: Third line of the VP-Planner control panel. It contains the VP-Planner commands that can be issued from the current menu.

Command mode: Often referred to as the dot prompt level. Commands for dBASE are entered from the keyboard rather than assembled from a menu.

Communications packages: Hardware packages that enable you to obtain and/or transmit information over telephone lines.

Compiler: Software that translates a program into machine language. As it performs this translation, it also checks for errors made by the programmer.

Comprehensive Crime Control Act of 1984: Prohibits an unauthorized person from accessing computer records to obtain information protected by the Right to Financial Privacy Act of 1978 or data in the files of a consumer-reporting agency.

Computer: Any device that can receive and store a set of instructions and then act upon those instructions in a predetermined and predictable fashion. The definition implies that both the instructions and the data upon which the instructions act can be changed; a device whose instructions cannot be changed is not a computer.

Computer crime: The commission of unlawful acts by using computer technology.

Computer-generated graphics: Created by converting data into numbers corresponding to screen's width and height coordinates.

Computer system: Has four functional parts: input, processing, storage, and output.

Concatenation: Process of joining two character strings, usually accomplished through use of the + sign.

Concentrator: A multiplexor with built-in circuitry that makes the transmission process more efficient. Also performs rudimentary editing on the data to be transmitted.

Conditional End of Page command: This WordPerfect command specifies that if a page break occurs within a certain number of following lines, a hard page break will occur.

CONFIG.SYS: The file used by DOS after the boot process is finished to further configure your computer system.

Configuration control: Allows only the DBA to make changes to the schema of a data base.

Configured software: Software that has been customized to the specific hardware configuration currently used.

Console log: Devices that record what actions users perform on the machines. These devices even log what tapes were mounted on which drives by the operators, which files the operator altered, and what responses the operator gave to the computer's prompts or instructions.

Constant information: Information that remains the same from one document to the next.

CONTINUE command: Finds the next record in a Locate command search in dBASE.

Control (CTRL) character: Character in the ASCII character set that usually has no graphic representation but serves to control various functions inside the computer.

Control keys: General-purpose keys whose uses include invoking breaks, pauses, system resets, clear screens, print echos, and various edit commands. In instructions, the Control key is often represented as a caret (^).

Control panel: Top three lines on the 1-2-3 worksheet screen, consisting of the status line, entry line, and prompt line.

Control unit: Directs the computer's actions by holding each instruction as it is being executed, decoding that instruction, and then directing the other CPU components on what actions to take.

Coprocessor: Microprocessor chip that is placed in a microcomputer to take the burden of manipulating numbers off the CPU, allowing it to perform other tasks.

Copy command: dBASE and DOS command that copies one or more files onto the current disk or onto another disk. In spreadsheets, it enables you to copy the contents of a cell into one or more other cells; in WordPerfect, it enables you to copy a block of text to another location in a document.

COPY CON: This command copies instructions from the console (keyboard) and creates a file in RAM memory that is saved to disk when the F6 key is pressed followed by the ENTER key.

Copy option: In WordPerfect, leaves original text in user's document while copying it to a temporary file.

CREATE command: dBASE command that enables you to build a data base and describe the fields and the data type of each field. In 1-2-3, saves graph settings of current graph.

Create option: Used to name a range of cells or to redefine the location of the named range.

CREATE REPORT command: Builds a report template on disk containing report format, headings, and fields to be included in report in dBASE.

Criterion range: Area of the worksheet on which you specify the records to be included in an operation.

CRT: Acronym for *cathode ray tube*, meaning any television screen or device containing such a screen.

Ctrl: Key label for the Control key.

Ctrl + Scroll Break keys: Allows Lotus 1-2-3 users to cancel any action taking place and return to the worksheet.

Cursor (pointer): Display screen's special character (__) used to indicate where the next character will be typed, that is, where you are in a file.

Cursor control key: One of the four arrow keys on the numeric key pad used to move the cursor left, right, up, or down on the screen.

Cursor movement: Operation of moving the cursor over the text.

Cut option: In WordPerfect, removes highlighted text from user's document and puts it in a temporary file.

Cylinder: Entity composed of all like-numbered tracks from all recording surfaces of a disk.

Daisy wheel printer: Letter-quality printer that uses a solid-font printing mechanism (the mechanism is shaped like a flower or a thimble).

Data (datum): Information of any kind.

Data base: Collection of data related to one specific type of application. *Data base* is often used synonymously with *file*.

Data base administrator (DBA): An individual appointed by management, who works with users to create, maintain, and safeguard the data found in the data base.

Data base management system (DBMS): Complete set of programs that help users to organize, update, and store records and files in virtually unlimited ways.

Data Base option: Used in PC Works to create a new file.

Data controls: Safeguard data or ensure their proper entry. Batch control slips with control totals and hash totals are examples.

Data-definition language: Used to design the logical structure of the data base. Used to give information such as field name, data type, and size, as well as limit access to these data.

Data dictionary: Contains the meaning of each piece of datum found in the data base; it includes data names, type of data, field size; and describes any interrelationships between this piece of datum with other data items.

Data entry: Process of placing text, values, labels, or formulas into a text document, data file, or worksheet.

Data entry window: The 14- or 23-line by 79-column area of the screen in which you can enter or edit text. Also called *text window*.

Data-flow diagram: Graphical method for documenting systems. A physical data-flow diagram documents the current system, while a logical data-flow diagram is used to document the design of the new system.

Data integrity: Relates to the problem of errors occurring in data that are stored in files.

Data management feature: This Lotus 1-2-3 feature lets users sort, summarize, and extract (make reports) portions of individual records in a file. The entire file is in one worksheet.

Data-manipulation language: Has all the stored routines that allow a user to store, retrieve, change, delete, or sort data or records within the data base.

Data option: Allows 1-2-3 user to specify a range of cells whose contents will be used to label data points of a data range (A-F).

Data Range option: Lets 1-2-3 user mark the area to be sorted.

Data redundancy: The same data are stored in more than one location.

Data security: Classifies user's access rights to data fields.

Data table: 1-2-3 feature that enables you to perform sensitivity analysis on a worksheet easily by asking multiple what-if questions.

Date: Offers Lotus 1-2-3 user a choice of five formats for displaying date (day, month, and/or year).

`DATE` **command:** DOS command that enables you to change the system date.

Date command: WordPerfect command that includes the current date as text within a document.

dBASE II: Relational data base package.

dBASE III: Updated version of dBASE II.

dBASE III Plus: The updated version of dBASE III.

Debug: To find hardware or software faults and eliminate them.

Decision support system (DSS): Provides user-friendly languages or programs that a decision maker can employ to retrieve or store data and perform modeling to solve unstructured problems.

Decision table: Documents in an easily comprehendible, tabular format, numerous conditions and corresponding actions.

Dedicated word processors: *See* Stand-alone word processor.

Default: Original (or initial) setting of a software package.

Default disk drive: Disk drive that is accessed automatically by the microcomputer when a file-oriented command is executed.

Default pitch: Pitch (usually pica) used to print a document unless some other pitch is specified.

Define a Column command: Used in PC Works to add or delete columns.

Define a Row command: Used in adding or deleting rows in PC Works.

`DEL` **(delete) command:** DOS command used to delete one or more files from disk.

Del: Key label for the Delete key.

`DELETE` **command:** dBASE command that enables you to mark a record for later deletion.

Delete command: Used to delete graph settings in memory in 1-2-3.

`DELETE FILE` **command:** Deletes files in dBASE.

Delete indicator: Asterisk (*) that appears in a record when it has been marked for deletion.

Delete key: Used to erase the character to the left of the current cursor position.

Delete option: In WordPerfect, removes marked text in user's document without saving it to a temporary file. In 1-2-3, drops a named range from memory.

Delimiter: Character that indicates to the computer where one part of a command ends and another part begins. Typical delimiters are the space, period, and comma.

Demand report: Used to obtain information that may be needed for a specific problem.

Demodulation: The conversion of analog signals to digital signals.

Design graphics: Helps designers draw with application programs.

Desk checking: Manually traces any data that could be processed through the module.

Desktop organizer: Primarily RAM-resident software package that can include such capabilities as calculators, notepads, automatic dialers, and appointment calendars.

Desktop publishing (DTP): Gives the user typeset quality such as you see in newspapers and textbooks. Also allows you to combine text with pictures.

DEVICE command: Contained in the CONFIG.SYS file that indicates which driver device is to be used for the computer's operation.

Digital signals: Represent the values 0 and 1 by the presence or absence of voltage.

D I R: DOS command that is used to list the files in the directory.

D I R (directory) command: Allows user to obtain lists of files in the directory or of specified files or families of files using wild cards. Used to copy files or families of files, not to copy an entire disk of files to another disk.

Direct access method: Uses algorithms or indexes to locate a record.

Direct conversion: A complete switch from an old system to a new system made at one time.

Directory: Part of a diskette that holds the names of files stored on it. Also contains information about file size, file extensions, their location on diskette, and the dates and times files were created or changed.

Directory (subdirectory): Like a root directory except that it is itself a file and contains DOS housekeeping entries in a regular directory. Does not have the size limitation of the root directory.

DISKCOPY (copy diskette) command: DOS command used to copy a complete disk.

Disk drive: Rectangular box, connected to or situated inside the computer, that reads and writes into diskettes.

Diskette: Square recordlike objects used for storing information from the computer.

Display: (As a noun) any sort of output device for a computer, usually a video screen; (as a verb) to place information on such a screen.

DISPLAY command: Similar to LIST command except only the record at the pointer location is displayed in dBASE.

Distributed data processing (DDP): Distributes and manages resources among several computers or terminals.

Dither mode: Scanning mode that scans shades of grays.

Document file: WordPerfect file that contains embedded codes to tell the monitor how text is to be displayed and to tell the printer how it is to be printed.

DOS: Acronym for Disk Operating System, the program responsible for enabling you to interact with the many parts of a computer system. DOS (pronounced *doss*) is the interface between you and the hardware. To perform system functions, DOS commands are typed on the keyboard, but DOS is actually a collection of programs designed to make it easy to create and manage files, run programs, and use system devices attached to the computer.

DOS editing keys: Allow user to change last DOS command entered.

DOS prompt: Indicates that DOS is ready to receive an instruction. It also tells which drive DOS will try to execute the instruction against, unless told otherwise. Typical DOS prompts are A>, B>, C>, or D>.

Dot-matrix printer: Printer that generates characters by firing seven or nine tiny print heads against a ribbon.

Dot prompt: *See* Command mode.

Double-density disks: Have approximately twice the storage of a single-density disk because they use a higher quality read/write surface on the disks, so that data can be stored in a denser format.

Double-sided disks: Disks on which data can be stored on both surfaces. A double-sided disk has been certified (tested) on both sides.

Double-strike text: Text somewhat darkened by striking or printing each character two times.

Double words: Speller option of WordPerfect can locate and delete unwanted repetition of words (for example, *and and*).

Down arrow: Moves the pointer down one cell position (down one row) in Lotus 1-2-3.

Downloading: Entails receiving a file from another computer.

Dumb terminal: An ASCII terminal that contains no built-in processing powers; it simply sends and receives data.

Dummy, column, row: Used to end a range. This allows user to add another row or column and have that be inside the range specified by a 1-2-3 command referencing that range.

Edit: Process by which the format of data is modified for output by inserting dollar signs, blanks, and so on. Used as a verb, to validate and rearrange input data.

Editing a document: Inserting, deleting, and changing existing text in a word processing text file.

Edit key (F2): Places the contents of a cell on the entry line and on the status line in Lotus 1-2-3.

Edit program: Examines each field of a record to make certain that the appropriate data have been entered.

EGA monitor: Video device capable of presenting clear, vivid graphics. Uses a 640×350 (or more) dot resolution to present crisper, more colorful images. EGA means enhanced graphics adapter.

Electronic funds transfer (EFT): A banking system that electronically records deposits and withdrawals as they occur.

Electronic spreadsheet: Program used to manipulate data that can be expressed in rows and columns.

End key: Used with the Ctrl key to erase characters on the screen from the current cursor position to the end of the line.

End of file (EOF) function: Senses the end of a file in dBASE.

ENTER key: Tells Lotus 1-2-3 that the user has finished typing and wants to send the information to the cell or give 1-2-3 an instruction.

Enter key: Used to tell the computer program that you are finished typing. It is principally used when more than one character is required in the typing input.

Entry line: *See* Input line.

Environmental interaction: Any system that accepts inputs from the environment, processes those inputs, and generates outputs back into the environment.

ERASE command: Used to delete one or more files from disk in DOS.

Ergonomics: The science of adapting work and working conditions to suit the individual worker.

Error message: Message informing you that you typed something the program cannot process or that some other system failure has occurred.

Error message indicator: Brief explanation of what went wrong, appearing in the lower left-hand corner of the worksheet screen.

Esc: Key label for the Escape key.

Escape codes: Special instructions to a printer or computer for processing or displaying data.

Escape key: Key used for general purposes, usually to cause some change in computer processing. In DOS and BASIC, it is used to erase a line of input; in application programs, it is often used to transfer to another section of the program.

Esc key: In Lotus 1-2-3, used to back out of a command sequence, if user is in a menu. If user is entering data in a cell, this key erases anything on the entry line.

Ethics: The study of conduct and moral judgment.

Exception report: Alerts management that an activity or process needs correction.

Execute: To perform the intent of a command or instruction; to run a program or a portion of a program.

Exit command: One of two ways to save a file in WordPerfect.

Expansion board: Printed circuit board that can be inserted into an open bus expansion slot, expanding the computer configuration to include such items as modems and plotters.

Expert system: Software that employs knowledge or rules of action that have been supplied by a person who is considered an expert in some field.

Expert-system shell: Logically arranged software to which the user writes application rules and knowledge using the built-in language.

Extension: One- to three-character portion of a file name. Extensions are typically used to indicate families of files, such as backups (.BK!), regular data base files (.DBF), and indexes (.NDX).

External command: Utility commands that are not part of the COMMAND.COM command processor. They reside on disk as separate files.

External modem: Connects to a microcomputer's serial interface.

Extend command (F8): In PC Works, this command is the equivalent of the Block command in WordPerfect.

Extract: Command used for creating reports from a 1-2-3 data base.

Fair Credit Reporting Act of 1970: Requires credit bureaus and investigatory reporting agencies to let people on whom they maintain records inspect their files.

Feasibility study: Defines a problem and determines whether a solution can be implemented within budget constraints.

Feedback: The process of sampling output to make certain that it is within pre-established limits. Data are then sent back to the system as input.

Fiber optics: A relatively new technology that is replacing copper wires as the dominant message-transmission medium for both telephone and computer networked systems.

Field: Subdivision of a record that holds one piece of data about a transaction.

Fifth-generation computers: Computers that will incorporate many of the concepts of artificial intelligence. These machines will have a natural language, receive voice input, be extremely easy to use, and process data 10,000 times faster than existing computers.

File: Collection of data or programs that serves a single purpose. A file is stored on a diskette and given a name so that you can recall it.

File allocation table (FAT): Entity that keeps track of which sectors belong to which files and of how much available space remains on the diskette (so new files can be created and stored in unused areas of the diskette).

File name: Unique identifier of a file, composed of one to eight characters. If an optional extension is used, there must be a period between the file name and the file-name extension.

File-name extension: One- to three-characters addition to a file name, separated by a period.

File option: Enables user to temporarily leave Works to perform a task in DOS and later return.

FILES command: Allows user to specify the maximum number of files that can be open at any one time.

Fill Down command: Used in PC Works to copy a cell, a row of text, or formulas down a column.

Fill Right command: Used in PC Works to copy a cell, a column of text, or formulas down a column.

Filter program: Program that performs some type of data manipulation on a file, such as sorting or breaking it down into displayable chunks.

F I ND: dBASE command used to locate records in an indexed file, using the index.

Find and replace: Ability of a word processing package to find a character string and replace it with another character string.

Flat-screen monitor: Newer monitors based on state-of-the-art technology that allows manufacturers to dramatically reduce the size of the picture tube.

Flexibility: A system's ability to make changes quickly.

Floppy disk: A term usually applied to 8 inch and 5¼ inch diskettes. The flexible nature of this medium makes the term self-explanatory.

Flush Right command: WordPerfect command that aligns text starting with the right-hand margin rather than the default, left-hand margin.

Font: Character set for printing. Pica, Elite, Helvetica, Courier, and Orator are among the many common fonts.

Font option: Allows 1-2-3 user to select up to two fonts from eleven possible fonts in generating dot matrix output.

Footer: Line of text that appears at the bottom of every page of a document.

Footer option: Enables Lotus 1-2-3 user to enter a line of text to be used as a footing.

FORMAT command: Prepares a disk so that it can be used by the computer. It defines every sector of a diskette, finds and write-protects any tracks having bad sectors, sets up the directory, sets up the File Allocation Table, and puts the boot record program at the beginning of the diskette. *Format* also refers to how data are stored in a worksheet cell, for example, as character or numeric data. In PC Works, changes appearance of numeric cell screen displays.

Format Currency option: Places a dollar sign ($) before each numeric cell entry and commas in large numbers.

Format Date option: Requests user to enter one of five date formats.

Format Fixed option: Displays a fixed number of decimal places (0-15), as specified by user.

Format General option: Suppresses trailing zeros after a decimal point.

Format Hidden option: Allows user to inhibit the display of numbers, formulas, and text in a cell.

Format notation: Refers to the rules that must be followed when entering commands for DOS. These rules are sometimes referred to as syntax.

Format option: Identical to Currency option, except no dollar signs are used. Lets 1-2-3 user change how a specified graph is displayed.

Format Percent option: Displays the numeric entry in a cell as a percentage (%).

Format +/− option: Displays a horizontal bar graph in which the number of symbols is the integer part of the value.

Format Reset option: Enables user to change format of a cell or range of cells back to the global format.

Format Scientific option: Shows data in exponential scientific notation.

Format Text option: Displays a formula in a cell, rather than the results of the formula.

Formatting: Process performed by FORMAT command. *See* FORMAT command.

Formula: Series of characters containing cell references and arithmetic operators for numeric data manipulation.

F O R **parameter:** Limits records included in a report in dBASE.

FORTRAN: Acronym for Formula Translator, a programming language designed for writing problem-solving programs that can be stated as arithmetic procedures.

Fragmented file: Large file whose sectors are not in adjacent locations. Can be stored on a disk in a number of different physical locations.

Front-end processor: A minicomputer that, besides performing general-purpose processing, frees a DDP's mainframe computer from such time-consuming housekeeping tasks as polling terminals for data, synchronizing the message packet, and error checking.

F10 graph key: Used to change data and automatically regraph new data.

Full-duplex transmission: Sends and receives information simultaneously.

Full-screen editing: Editing format that enables you to move about the entire screen using cursor movement keys. This makes changes to a worksheet, document file, or data file much easier.

Fully distributed network: All nodes can communicate directly with each other.

Function call: Enables Lotus 1-2-3 user to name a function.

Function key: One of ten keys (F1–F10) that allows special functions to be entered with a single user keystroke. Computer programs (DOS, BASIC, and so on) use these keys for different purposes.

Function key line: Bottom line on many application software display screens. It identifies the task performed by each function key.

Functions: Formulas or processes built into a software package. These functions save a user a tremendous amount of effort and tedium.

General controls: Regulate access to the computer system.

G O **command:** Can be used interchangeably with GOTO command in dBASE.

Go option: Sends a designated range as output to the printer or named disk file. Also tells 1-2-3 to execute the sort or print a graph.

G O T O**:** dBASE command used to position the pointer at a specific record in a file.

G O T O   B O T T O M **command:** Positions pointer at last record in file in dBASE.

Goto command: A faster way to go directly to the address of a cell in 1-2-3. In dBASE, G O T O can be used interchangeably with G O command.

G O T O   T O P **command:** Positions pointer at first record in file in dBASE.

Global: Spreadsheet command that allows changes entered thereafter to affect the entire worksheet.

Global file-name characters: DOS characters (? and *) that are used to specify a number of files by entering a single command. Also known as *wild cards*.

Graph command: Allows 1-2-3 user to cancel an entire graph.

Graphic display: System used to display graphic items or a collection of such items.

Graphics editor/paint program: Allows you to edit existing computer graphics or to create your own art.

Graphics feature: Allows Lotus 1-2-3 user to display information in the form of a pie chart, bar chart, line, *xy*, or stacked bar chart.

Graph Menu: Offers 1-2-3 users eight options in creating graphs.

Greeked text: Lines displayed to represent text as it will appear in a printed document.

Grid option: Allows 1-2-3 user to choose horizontal and/or vertical lines for display on a graph.

Half-duplex transmission: Sends or receives data, but not both simultaneously.

Handshaking: The number of stop and start bits used for sending and receiving data.

Hanging paragraph: Paragraph in which the first line begins at the left margin and the remaining lines are indented.

Hard copy: Printed document on paper.

Hard disk: Rigid medium for storing computer information, usually rated in megabytes (millions of bytes) of storage capacity.

Hard page break: Convention of word processing packages to show where one page ends another page begins. WordPerfect uses a line of equal signs.

Hard return: Special carriage return recorded in a document when the ENTER key is pressed, usually at the end of a paragraph.

Hard-sectored disk: Disks that have already had their tracks divided into sectors.

Hard space: Space inserted by pressing the Home key plus the spacebar.

Hardware: Physical parts of a computer.

Hardware controls: Incorporated into computers to regulate who can use the machines.

Hardware option: Lets users configure 1-2-3 to the type of print their printers can print and tell 1-2-3 where to find graph and font files.

Hazard controls: Provide provisions in case fire, flood, earthquake, or other disasters threaten a company's computer system.

Header: Line of text that appears at the top of every page of a document.

Header option: Enters one line of text to be used as a heading.

Help facility: Provides on-line information for entering data or instructions for a piece of software.

Help Index option: Provides access to Help feature of PC Works.

Hexadecimal: Number system that uses the ten digits 0 through 9 and the six letters A through F to represent values in base 16. Each hexadecimal digit in a hexadecimal number represents a power of 16.

Hidden: 1-2-3 command used to hide a column so that it does not appear on the screen.

Hidden file: File that exists but does not appear to a user in the file directory. Since it is not visible in the directory, such a file is very difficult to erase mistakenly.

Hierarchical (tree) structure: Structural arrangement in which data elements are linked in multiple levels that graphically resemble an organization chart. Each lower level is owned by an upper level.

High-level language: Language that is more intelligible to humans than it is to machines.

Hi-lo graph: Often used by newspapers to show the high and low selling points of stocks. Emphasizes the range between the highest and lowest values within a category by connecting them with a line.

Home: Upper left-hand corner screen position, where the first printable character can be placed. Also referred to as the initial cursor position.

Home key: Used to send the cursor to the Home position. If used with the Control key, a clear screen results.

IBMBIO.COM: Hidden file in DOS that manages each character that is typed, displayed, printed, received, or sent through any communications adapter.

IBMDOS.COM: Hidden DOS file that handles any information to be passed to disk.

Icon: Symbol used to represent an operation, task, or entity.

`@ IF` **function:** Checks for certain conditions in 1-2-3 and acts on the findings of the check.

Image-Select option: Displays all graph files on the disk in drive B in 1-2-3.

Index: Keeps track of relations in a relational data base environment and provides access to any record in a file.

`INDEX` **command:** Used in dBASE to order information logically within a file without physically reordering the records themselves. Indexes may be single- or multiple-field.

Indicators: Signals that appear in the lower right-hand corner of the work-sheet screen, telling the user which toggle keys are currently activated.

Information: Data that have been processed or manipulated. Gross pay (calculated by multiplying hours worked by pay rate) is an example of information.

Initialization: Process during the boot routine when the computer activates the various peripherals hooked to the computer.

Ink-jet printer: Printer that sprays ink in droplets onto paper to form characters. It is much quieter than a dot matrix or letter-quality printer.

Input controls: Represent some of the most vital controls for they help ensure that the data that users enter into a system are correct.

Input devices: Permit users to input data via the keyboard, mice, scanners, and other devices.

Input line: Second line in the control panel, corresponding to a scratch area. The entry line contains any information you are currently entering for the cell location contained in the status line.

INS: Label for the Insert key.

Insert Chart command: Used to include a graph in a document in PC Works.

Insert key: Used to tell the computer program that you want to insert characters to the left of the cursor. The insert mode continues until you press the key again or until you press another special key (cursor arrows, Del, End), indicating that you want to go on to a different editing operation.

Insert option: The default of WordPerfect.

Instruction: Smallest portion of a program that a computer can execute.

Integrated circuit: Small (less than the size of a fingernail and about as thin) wafer of glassy material (usually silicon) into which an electronic circuit has been etched. A single IC can contain from 10 to 225,000 electronic components.

Integrated data base management system (DBMS): Refers to ability to logically relate one record with another.

Integrated package: Combines a number of applications under one software umbrella. For instance, Lotus 1-2-3 combines spreadsheets, graphing, and data base applications.

Integration: *See* Integrated package.

Interface: Adapter or circuit board containing the electrical components that connect a peripheral with the computer's bus system.

Internal control: Policies and procedures used to safeguard an organization's assets.

Internal DOS command: Part of the COMMAND.COM command processor.

Internal modem: A circuit board that fits into an expansion slot of an open-bus computer.

Internal storage: Provides the ability to store the program being executed, the data operated on, and any intermediate results created by the program.

Interpreter: Program, usually written in machine language, that understands and executes a higher-level language one statement at a time.

Inverse: Command to the computer that tells it to display the characters on the screen as dark characters on a light background instead of the normal display of light on dark.

Justification: Alignment of word processing text flush with the right (and left) margins. This produces straight margins on both the left-hand and right-hand sides of a document.

Key: Data item (field) that identifies a record.

/ Key: Used to invoke the 1-2-3 Main Menu.

Keyboard: System hardware used to input characters, commands, and functions to the computer. The keyboard consists of 83 keys and is organized into three sections: function keys, typewriter keyboard, and numeric key pad.

Keyboard macro: In Lotus 1-2-3, saves keystrokes given alternative meanings by user; a way to avoid repeating sequences of keystrokes.

Kilobyte (K): Abbreviation for the Greek prefix *kilo-*, meaning *thousand*. In computer-related usage, K usually represents the quantity 2^{10}, or 1,024. A kilobyte of storage represents 1,024 bytes.

Label: Alphanumeric information used to identify a portion of a row or column.

LABEL: The DOS command that allows you to create, change, or delete a volume label on a disk.

Label prefix: Tells 1-2-3 whether to left-justify ('), center (`), or right-justify (") text within a cell.

Labels option: Similar to Create option, but range name is taken directly from an adjacent label entry. Aligns labels with data points in 1-2-3.

Landscape format: Text printed on a sheet of paper in 11 × 8⅕ format.

Language: Code that both the programmer and the computer understand. The programmer uses the language to express what is to be done, and the computer understands the language and performs the desired actions.

Language processor: Software that translates a high-level language such as COBOL or BASIC into machine-understandable code.

Laser printer: Printer that uses laser-based technology to form characters on paper via electronic charges and then place toner on the charges to display the characters. The toner is fixed in place by a heat process.

Layout command: Allows PC Works user to change the layout of a worksheet.

LCD (liquid crystal display) monitor: Frequently used on notebook-size portable computers.

Left arrow: Moves the pointer to the left one cell position (to the left one column) in Lotus 1-2-3.

Legend option: Lotus 1-2-3 graph feature used to label sets of data so that a graph can be easily understood.

Letter-quality printer: Printer that generates output of a quality comparable to that produced on a typewriter.

Light pen: Works somewhat like ordinary pen, but it uses light and a computer screen instead of ink and paper to record information.

Line editor: Low-level word processing package that allows you to work on only one line of text at a time.

Line graph: Illustrates lows, highs, and trends with a line or series of lines. Line graphs are ideal for showing trends over time or the distribution of one variable over another.

Line option: Tells the printer to advance the paper one line.

Line spacing: Number of filled and blank lines that are established with each generated line. Double spacing produces one blank line after each generated line.

`LIST` **command:** dBASE command used to display records from a data file contained on disk.

List structure: Structural arrangement containing records that are linked together by pointers.

`LIST STRUCTURE` **command:** Lets dBASE user examine a record structure.

Local area network (LAN): Network used to connect a number of micro-computers to share data or expensive peripheral devices.

`LOCATE` **command:** Used to find data in a sequential file in dBASE.

Lock key: Key used to cause subsequent key operations to be interpreted in a specific manner by the computer. Lock keys are toggle keys; they include Caps, Num, and Scroll.

Logged device: Disk specified to be searched automatically for any needed files.

Logical field: Field capable of holding the values of .T. (true) or .F. (false) or Y (yes) or N (no). Logical fields are always one-byte fields.

Logical operations: Compare one datum with another. This allows a user to determine if the datum is less than, equal to, or greater than another datum.

Logical view: The manner in which a user or an application accesses a data base through a subschema.

Lotus Access System: The first 1-2-3 menu.

Lotus 1-2-3: Popular electronic spreadsheet package.

Lotus worksheet: Contains whatever space is available to the 1-2-3 user for problem solving and includes the cell, pointer, and window.

Lower case: Small letters (a–z).

Low-level language: Language that is more intelligible to machines than to humans.

L/R Indent command: Allows user to indent both left- and right-hand margins.

Machine language: Lowest-level language. Machine language is usually bi-nary; instructions in machine language are single-byte opcodes, sometimes followed by various operands.

Macro: Entity that contains keystroke commands stored for later execution.

Macro key: Enables Lotus 1-2-3 user to give letter keys alternative meanings.

Mag typewriter: Predecessor of the computer, developed by IBM in the 1960s.

Mainframe computer: A large, fast system capable of supporting several hundred input and output devices such as keyboards and monitor screens.

Main logic board: Large printed circuit board at the bottom of the computer.

Management information system (MIS): A formal process using both manual and computerized tools to control information.

Manual recalculation: Functional mode in which a worksheet can only recalculate itself when the F9 key is pressed.

Manual Recalculation option: Allows 1-2-3 user to turn off Automatic Recalculation feature.

Margin: Unused border around a page of a document.

Margin commands: WordPerfect Line Format (SHIFT + F8) command that enables user to reset left and right margins.

Margins option: Allows user to change current margins (left, right, top, and bottom).

Master file: Holds semipermanent summary data about an entity.

Megabyte (meg): One million characters of storage, a quantity usually used as a measure of available storage on a hard disk.

Memory: Another name for internal storage.

Memory location: Smallest subdivision of the memory map to which the computer can refer. Each memory location has a unique address and a certain value.

Menu: List of commands available to anyone using a software package.

Menu-driven mode: The default mode of dBASE III Plus.

Merge: Allows user to combine (merge) a "boiler plate" or template letter with a list of names and addresses, individualizing the letter for each addressee.

Message line: Fourth of the four lines at the bottom of a dBASE III Plus screen. Provides a brief description of a highlighted menu option.

Microchannel: The bus system architecture introduced by IBM for their PS/2 line of computers. This bus system is faster than previous systems and supports multitasking (the ability to run more than one job at a time).

Microcomputer: Computer based on a microprocessor (8-bit or 16-bit) that can execute a single user's program.

Microcomputer information system: Consists of hardware, data/information, software, people, and documentation/procedures.

Microcomputer system: Combined computer, disk drives, monitor, and input and output devices for data processing.

Microprocessor: Integrated circuit that understands and executes machine-language programs.

Microsoft: Company that originally developed PC DOS for IBM (an operating system known, with some minor differences, as MS DOS).

Minicomputer: Smaller, cheaper, and easier to maintain and install than a mainframe but in declining demand because of increasing power of the microcomputer.

Mixed cell address: Address in which the row or column portion (not both) of the cell address can change to reflect a new cell location.

Mixed data multiple-field index: Uses both numeric fields and character fields in dBASE.

MKDIR (MD): The DOS command that allows you to create a subdirectory.

Mnemonic: Any acronym or other symbol used in place of something more difficult to remember.

Mode indicator: Status information that appears in the upper right-hand corner of the 1-2-3 worksheet screen.

Model: Symbolic representation of an entity or process that is difficult to observe.

Modem: Acronym for modulator-demodulator, a device that converts digital computer signals into analog telephone signals (audible sounds that can be sent via telephone) and reverses the procedure at the other end of the line.

Modulation: The conversion of digital signals to analog signals.

Monitor: TV-like device that gives users of microcomputer equipment video feedback about their actions and the computer's actions.

Monochrome monitors: Devices similar to one-color monitors except that monochrome pixels are much closer together, producing clearer characters.

MORE: DOS filter command that displays one screen of data on the monitor at a time.

Motherboard: Another name for the main logic board.

Mouse: Hand-held controller that electronically signals the computer to move the cursor on the display screen. The same movements can be accomplished via the cursor control pad.

Move command: Allows user to cut or copy text and move it from one place in a document to another; also allows for deletions.

Move feature: Relocates cell contents without disturbing other areas of 1-2-3 user's worksheet.

MS DOS: Operating system developed by Microsoft. It is the same as PC DOS except that there is no ROM BASIC provision. Most IBM-compatible computers use this operating system.

Multiple-field index: Combines several fields in index in dBASE.

Multiplexor: A device that routes the output from several terminals or computers into a single channel. This allows one telephone link to carry a transmission that normally would require several such links.

Multipurpose monitor: Capable of handling monochrome, color, and EGA signals.

Multitasking: The ability to run more than one program at one time without interrupting the execution of another program.

Nail down: To indicate beginning of a range of cells in 1-2-3 with a period.

Name option: Enables 1-2-3 user to load graph settings previously saved, reset graph options, and draw graph as specified.

Natural language: A language designed so human beings and machines can interact easily.

Navigation line: The third of the four lines at the bottom of a dBASE III PLUS screen. Provides user with allowable cursor manipulation command options.

.NDX extension: Used to list index files in dBASE.

Nested function: Function that resides inside another function. The innermost function must be executed before any outer ones.

Network structure: Arrangement permitting the connection of data elements in a multidirectional manner. Each mode may thus have several owners.

New page number: This WordPerfect feature enables user to alter automatic page numbering.

NEXT **option:** Displays the next x number of records in a dBASE file.

Nibble: Slang for half a byte (four bits).

Node: A computer or terminal capable of sending and receiving data from other computers or terminals on a network.

`NO FIND` **message:** Displayed when dBASE cannot find request made in `SEEK` command.

Nondocument mode: Operating mode used to create a file that has no control character sequences to provide instructions to the printer. This mode must be selected when you are creating computer programs or building data files.

Nonvolatile memory: Form of storage that does not lose its content when the system's power is turned off. It may take the form of bubble memory, or it may be powered by batteries.

#NOT#: A logical operator in a 1-2-3 `@IF` function.

Number: A numeric value entered in a cell; can be either a constant or a variable.

Numbering style: WordPerfect user can select either Arabic or Roman numerals for page numbers.

Numeric data: Consists of the digits 0 through 9.

Numeric entry: Process of entering numbers into the computer. The numeric key pad can be set into numeric entry mode by using the Num Lock key; after this has been done, numbers and number symbols (decimal, minus, plus) can be entered.

Numeric field: Field that can hold only a number or a decimal point. No alphabetic or special characters can be placed in such a field.

Numeric key pad: Section of the keyboard containing numeric entry and editing keys.

Numeric Lock key: Key used to switch the numeric key pad back and forth between numeric entry and editing.

Num Lock: Label for the Numeric lock key.

Object code: Machine-language code created by the compiler and executed by the computer.

OK option: Loads a selected file in PC Works.

Open-bus system: Contains expansion slots that allow users to expand the system as needed. A peripheral is added to the computer by plugging it into an expansion slot with an interface board.

Open option: Provides access to an existing file in PC Works.

Operating system: Interface between the computer and the user, which provides the user with flexible and manageable control over the resources of the computer.

Operating system prompt: Signal to the user that some type of DOS command or a command to start a program can be entered. The prompt also shows which drive has been specified as the default drive.

Operational decision making: Ensures that employees perform tasks efficiently by measuring their output against preset standards.

Optical character recognition (ORC): Using a scanner driven by the appropriate software that allows text to be read from a typed piece of paper.

Options: Offers 1-2-3 user ten options in designing graphs.

Options Menu: Allows 1-2-3 user to place headings, alter margins and page length, and choose among other options for a printout.

#OR#: A logical operator in a 1-2-3 `@IF` function.

Organization controls: Divide data processing operations among several users so that if fraud is perpetrated there must be collusion among several people.

Orphan: Last line of a paragraph when it appears as the top line of a page.

Other option: Displays 1-2-3 menu of format options.

Outliner: Software that assists you in outlining ideas, goals, or tasks.

Output: Computer-generated data whose destination is the screen, disk, printer, or some other output device.

Output controls: Involve reconciling control totals from one job step to another and scanning the output to make certain that the data were processed correctly. They can also involve delivering output to the authorized individual.

Output devices: Store and present data in forms that can be read by either humans or machines.

Output range: 1-2-3 range that holds any report generated in an Extract operation.

Overstrike command: In WordPerfect, lets user print one character on top of another. Used for placing diacritical marks, as in *à la* and *château*.

PACK command: dBASE command that physically removes any records marked for deletion.

Page: One screen of information on a video display; quantity of memory locations addressable with one byte.

Page break: Mark that shows where one page ends and another begins. In WordPerfect, it is represented by a line of dashes across the screen.

Page control language (PCL): A language designed to load bit-mapped fonts and graphics into a printer.

Page description language (PDL): Creates characters using outline fonts developed from formulas.

Page Down (PgDn) key: Sometimes used to cause text on the screen to move down. Text on the bottom of the screen moves off-screen while text is added at the top.

Page Format command: Enables WordPerfect user to control the appearance of text on the printed page.

Page-length option: Allows WordPerfect and 1-2-3 user to specify the number of printed lines per page.

PageMaker: The first desktop publishing package, developed by Adobe systems.

Page numbering: WordPerfect automatically controls numbering of a document's pages.

Page Number Position option: WordPerfect provides nine alternatives for positioning numbers on pages, such as "top left" and "bottom center."

Page number setting: WordPerfect command used to specify the page number of the first page of a file to be printed. Also resets the page number to a specific value inside a document.

Page option: Advances paper in printer to top of next page.

Page Up (PgUp) key: Sometimes used to cause text on the screen to move up. Text on the top of the screen moves off-screen while text is added at the bottom.

Parallel conversion: Both the new and the old systems operate side-by-side for a period of time.

Parallel interface: Interface arrangement that transmits all nine bits of a character at one time.

Parallel transmission: Sends data one byte at a time.

Parameter: Modifying piece of information that constitutes part of a DOS or dBASE command. It might, for example, indicate which files or fields are to be included in an operation.

Pascal: A language designed for teaching structured programming techniques.

Password: The 1-2-3 feature that allows user to assign a password to a file and then requires user to enter that password before access to that worksheet is allowed.

Pasteboard: The area around a document in desktop publishing.

Path: The complete name for a file, including the complete subdirectory name.

PATH command: Provides the capability to automatically search specified drives or directories if the desired file cannot be found in the active disk or directory.

Pause: Computer function that can be used at any time to temporarily halt the program in use. Pause is invoked by pressing the Num Lock key while holding the Ctrl key down. Pressing any key after a Pause causes the computer to continue from the point of interruption. Pause can also be performed with one hand by pressing the key combination Ctrl + S.

PC (personal computer): Computer equipped with memory, languages, and peripherals, well suited for use in a home, office, or school.

PC Works: An integrated software package capable of spreadsheet and word processing, graphing, data base applications, and intercomputer communications.

Peripheral: Something attached to the computer that is not part of the computer itself. Most peripherals are input and/or output devices.

PgDn: Label for the Page Down key.

PgUp: Label for the Page Up key.

Physical view: The exact manner in which data is stored to devices used in a data base.

Pie chart: Compares the proportional parts of a whole. Useful for comparing component shares with one another and with the combined total.

Pilot conversion: Involves converting only a small portion of the organization to the new system.

Piping: System arrangement that allows a number of different programs to share generated input and output, since the output from one program becomes the input to another. Temporary files are created to achieve this.

Pitch: Refers to the number of characters per inch of a type style.

Pixel: Dot that is turned on or off depending on what character is being displayed on the screen.

Platen: Hard rubber roller that moves the paper in the printer.

Plotter: Device that moves a pen on X and Y axes to draw graphs or pictures. For one of the axes, the paper may move instead of the pen.

@PMT function: Calculates the payment of a loan or mortgage based on principal, interest, and number of periods.

Pointer: Reverse-video bar, sometimes referred to as the cursor. Its width depends on the width of the cell it is referencing. In a data base it is the data item in a record that identifies the storage location of another record that is logically related. It may also indicate the current record being processed. The exact role of the pointer depends on the type of data base structuring technique in use.

Polling: The process of a computer checking to see if there are data at a node location ready for transmission.

Portrait format: Text printed on a regular 8½ × 11 sheet of paper.

PostScript: The PDL language developed by Adobe systems for PageMaker.

Pound sign (#): Used to mark a file for printing in 1-2-3.

Precedence: Order in which calculations are executed.

Predictive report: Used in the planning process to construct "what-if" scenarios.

Presentation graphics: Turn numeric information and data relationships into graphics—charts and graphs.

Press any key to continue: Message often displayed by a program when the computer is waiting for you to do something (read text or load a diskette, for example) and does not know when you will be done. Some keys are generally inactive and do not cause the program to continue when depressed; these include the Alt, Shift, Ctrl, Scroll Lock, Num Lock, and Caps Lock keys.

Primary key: In dBASE, the record number; in sorting, the major sort field.

Primary Key option: Lets 1-2-3 user select the column for sorting the data range.

Primary memory: Internal memory used by the computer for several different functions. It can contain data, program instructions, or intermediate results of calculations.

Primary storage: Short-term memory that is lost when computer is turned off. Holds executing program's instructions, data being processed, and intermediate calculations generated by the program.

PRINT: DOS command used to queue and print disk-based data files.

Print Block command: Allows WordPerfect user to print a portion of a document that is longer than the current page without printing the whole document.

Print command: Enables PC Works or 1-2-3 user to print a whole worksheet or parts (ranges) of it.

Print echo: Function performed by pressing the Print Screen (PrtSc) key while holding the Ctrl key down. Once this key is pressed, whatever is displayed on the screen is printed. The simultaneous printing (screen and printer) continues until the key combination is pressed again. Print echo can also be performed using the key combination Ctrl + P.

Printed circuit board: Sheet of fiberglass or epoxy onto which a thin layer of metal has been applied and then etched to form traces. Electronic components are then attached to the board with molten solder, and thereafter they can exchange electronic signals via the etched traces on the board. Small printed circuit boards are often called cards, especially if they are meant to connect with edge connectors.

Printer: Device used to make a permanent copy of any output.

PrintGraph option: The set of software instructions that allows you to print Lotus 1-2-3 graphs.

Print Menu: Displays these 1-2-3 options: Range, Line, Page, Options, Clear, Align, Go, Quit.

Print Range option: Used to indicate which part of a 1-2-3 worksheet is to be printed.

Print screen: Function produced when the Print Screen (PrtSc) key is pressed while the Shift key is held down. Once this key combination is pressed, the current information on your screen is printed.

Print Screen key: When pressed with the Shift key the screen contents are printed.

Print thimble: Device used by impact letter-quality printers to form characters on paper.

Privacy: The claim of individuals, groups, or institutions to determine for themselves when, how, and to what extent personal information about them is communicated to others.

Privacy Act of 1974: Regulates how the federal government manages information collected on citizens.

Procedural controls: Written instructions for those who operate and maintain a computer system.

Procedures: Written instructions on how to use hardware or software.

Processing controls: Provide evidence that data are being processed properly. A typical example is the control total.

Productivity software: Allows a person to be more productive. These packages include such applications as desktop organizers and outline software.

Program: Set of instructions that tells the computer how to perform a certain task. DOS, BASIC, and the Instructor are all programs.

Program controls: Verify that data are entered and processed properly and that the resulting information is correctly outputted.

Programming language: Special means of providing instructions to the computer to get it to perform a specific task. Examples of programming languages are BASIC, COBOL, Pascal, and FORTRAN.

PROM: Acronym for Programmable Read-Only Memory. A PROM is a ROM whose contents are alterable by electrical means. Information in PROMs does not disappear when the power is turned off. Some PROMs can be erased by ultraviolet light and then reprogrammed.

Prompt line: Last line in the control panel. When a 1-2-3 menu is displayed, it contains a further explanation about a specific command.

Proportional spacing: Including spaces between words to make even right-hand margins.

Protected cell: 1-2-3 cells that cannot be changed by the user. The worksheet has been globally protected by the global protection command.

Protection: In 1-2-3, a way of prohibiting changes on either the entire worksheet or specific cells.

Protocol: Set of rules used for sending or receiving data.

PrtSc: Label for the Print Screen Key.

Pseudocode: Programlike code that does not follow the exact syntax of a language. Used for designing and documenting the logic of a module.

Purpose: Goal of a system.

Query language: A simple, easy-to-learn language used to interface with the data base that allows users to quickly generate needed reports.

Query option: Used to construct a question form in PC Works.

?: A DOS wild card. In a file name or extension, ? indicates that any character can occupy that position.

Queue: A waiting line concept used for printing documents. Any files to be printed are placed at the end of the queue.

Quit: dBASE command that returns user to operating system.

QUIT command: Closes any files that may still be open at end of a dBASE III Plus session. In 1-2-3, returns user to PrintGraph Menu.

Quit option: Tells 1-2-3 to end a print session and returns user to ready mode in the worksheet.

QWERTY: Standard keyboard arrangement, first used with manual typewriters in the early 1900s.

RAM (random access memory): Main memory of a computer. The acronym RAM can be used to refer either to the integrated circuits that make up this type of memory or to the memory itself. The computer can store values in distinct locations in RAM and then recall them, or it can alter and restore them.

RAM-resident program: Means that once the program is loaded into memory, it stays there until either the machine is turned off or you tell it to erase itself.

Random file: Any dBASE file that has an index.

Range: Rectangular or square area of a worksheet.

/Range Format commands: Allow 1-2-3 user to format a specific part of the worksheet.

Range name: Function used to give a specific name to a range of a worksheet; allows user to refer to formulas by meaningful names instead of by cell address only.

/Range Transpose command: Rearranges rows and columns within a range in a 1-2-3 worksheet.

Read process: Transfers data into a computer from a secondary storage device.

Read/write access hole: Oval opening on a diskette that allows the read/write heads to record or access information.

Real-time processing: Updates each master file by processing each transaction as it is entered into a computer and transmits the resulting information back to the user.

Recalculation: Process by which a spreadsheet changes all cell contents affected by a change to any other cell in a worksheet.

RECALL command: dBASE command used to retrieve or unmark records that have been marked for deletion.

Record: Entity that contains information about a specific business happening or transaction.

Receiving cells ("To" range): 1-2-3 cells to which data are copied.

RECNO() function: Used to obtain pointer location from dBASE.

Record key: Data that identify one record from others. Student Social Security numbers serve as record keys in many colleges' sequential files. The file must be searched in sequence; if the desired record is passed, the operator must return to the start of the file and search again.

Record number: Identification used by dBASE as the primary key for a record; the physical location in the file for a given record.

Rectangular block: Enables WordPerfect user to specify the width of the text block to be moved. Also called *columnar block*.

Redirection: System arrangement that allows the IBM PC to accept input from a device other than the keyboard and to send output to a device other than the display screen.

Re-form: WordPerfect feature that automatically readjusts text within existing margins.

Relational structure: Structural arrangement consisting of one or more tables. Data are stored in the form of relations in these tables.

Relative addressing: Automatic changing of cell locations in a copy or move operation to reflect their new locations.

REM: DOS command ignored by DOS and used to insert remarks or prompts to the user.

REN: Abbreviation that can be used for the RENAME command.

RENAME command: Used to rename a disk file in DOS.

Repeating character: Requires 1-2-3 user to use backslash (\) to indicate that a character should repeat.

Replaceable parameters: Used in executing batch files. Pieces of information in a DOS command that might change from one use to the next. Represented by a percent sign (%).

REPLACE command: Used to change several or all records within a data file quickly in dBASE.

Replace command: WordPerfect command used to find a character string and replace that string with another set of characters.

REPORT: dBASE command used to create or access a parameter file modifying how a specific printed report is to be generated.

REPORT FORM command: Generates a report in dBASE; used with report template.

Report generator: Portion of the query language that allows a user to quickly generate reports on paper or video medium.

Report option: Generates reports in PC Works.

Report template: Contains report format, headings, and fields to be included in a report in dBASE.

Reserved tracks: Tracks of disk storage that contain a bad sector and have been set aside so that data cannot be recorded on them.

Reset: Command that usually results in the return of a piece of software to its original default values.

Reset option: Makes 1-2-3 drop from memory all assigned range names. Also selects Reset Menu for graphing.

Reveal Codes command: WordPerfect command used to make visible the hidden codes that control how text is displayed or printed.

Reverse Search command: Allows WordPerfect user to locate a word or phrase by starting at current cursor location and moving toward the beginning of a file.

Revision: The process of making changes to a word processing document.

Right arrow: Moves pointer to the right one cell position (one column) in Lotus 1-2-3.

Right-justification: A smooth, or even, right-hand margin.

Ring network: Joins each computer in the system to two other computers, in opposing directions, forming a circle.

RMDIR (RD): DOS command that allows user to delete a subdirectory.

ROM (read only memory): Memory usually used to hold important programs or data that must be available to the computer when power is first turned on. Information in ROM is placed there during the process of manufacture and is unalterable. Information stored in ROM does not disappear when power is turned off.

Root directory: Main directory of a disk. Subdirectories are created below the root directory on a disk medium.

Root node: Top node of a tree structure.

Row: Horizontal axis on a spreadsheet or document.

Ruler line: Line on the display screen that identifies the location of the right-hand margin, the left-hand margin, and tab stops.

Run: Action of following a sequence of instructions to its completion.

Save Block command: Permits WordPerfect user to save a portion of text to a separate file on disk.

Save command: One of two WordPerfect methods for saving files. This command should be used frequently when user is working on a lengthy document. Used to store graphs in 1-2-3.

Saving files: WordPerfect has two methods for retaining documents—Save command and Exit command.

Save option: Stores files in PC Works.

Scale option: Allows 1-2-3 user to set scaling and format of a graph's X and Y axis.

Scaling: Description of how data values will be displayed on a 1-2-3 graph.

Scanner: Converts text, photographs, and black-and-white graphics into computer-readable form and transfers the information to a computer.

Scatter plot (or XY graph): Two-dimensional graph of points whose coordinates represent values on the X(horizontal) and Y(vertical) axes.

Scheduled report: Generated at set intervals and usually contains a lot of detailed information.

Schema: How data are physically stored in the data base.

Scroll: Function that moves all the text on a display (usually upward) to make room for more (usually at the bottom).

Scrolling: Moving the text under the cursor. The relative position of the cursor does not have to change.

Scroll Lock key: Rarely used in modern programs but intended for use as a Lock-type key, causing displayed text (rather than the cursor) to move when a cursor control key is pressed.

Search command: Enables WordPerfect user to locate the first and all subsequent occurrences of a word or phrase.

Secondary key: Defining key used to order information within the primary key.

Secondary Key option: *See* Secondary key.

Secondary storage: Separate from the central processing unit, it can store data indefinitely—usually on a magnetic disk. Holds most of the data processed by a computer.

Sectors: One part of a track. For the IBM microcomputer, each track is divided into eight or nine sectors of 512 bytes each. This sector holds the data.

Security: Relates to which individuals should have access to which fields of data and the type of access rights that each user should have.

SEEK command: Used to access a random file.

Sending cells ("From" range): 1-2-3 cells that contain data to be copied.

Sensitivity analysis: Procedure used to ask a number of "what-if" questions about the effect of various changes to a worksheet.

Sequential-access method: Stores records in a file in ascending or descending order by record key, data that identify one record from others.

Serial interface: Transmits a byte one bit at a time.

Serial transmission: Sends data one bit at a time.

`SET HEADINGS OFF` **command:** Turns off field headings for a displayed record in dBASE.

Settings option: Offers 1-2-3 user menu of six ways to shape appearance of graphs.

Set-up Menu: Allows WordPerfect user to invoke the backup option and change defaults.

Setup option: Tells printer which escape code to use for printing data.

Set-up string: 1-2-3 feature used to vary the pitch of printed information.

SHIFT key: Used to select the upper-case character on keys that have two characters or to reverse the case of letters A through Z, depending on the status of the CAPS LOCK key.

Simplex transmission: Data can be sent but not received or received but not sent.

Simulation: The process of building a model of a real-life system and examining the impact of changes made to the model enables user to ask "what-if" questions and examine their impact without incurring the real-life costs involved in making such decisions.

Single-field index: A dBASE file ordered by one field only.

Size option: Lets 1-2-3 user specify height and width of graph to be printed.

SKIP command: dBASE command used to move the pointer forward or backward within a data file.

Skip sequential processing: Enables dBASE user to go randomly to a point in a file and then process sequentially from that point.

Slave disk: Has been formatted but does not contain the operating system. You cannot boot the computer by using such a disk.

Soft carriage return: Carriage return accomplished by the word-wrap feature.

Soft page break: The line of dashes that appears in a document to indicate where the page break will occur upon printing the document.

Soft-sectored disk: Has each track divided into sectors during the format process.

Software: Program that gives the hardware something to do.

Software piracy: Illicit duplication of software.

Software virus: An illicit computer program that infects a system and replicates itself destroying data, formatting disks, or sabotaging other operations of the computer.

SORT command: DOS filter command used to sort data files; also the dBASE command used to reorder a data base file physically; also a 1-2-3 command used to resequence part of a worksheet.

Source code: Set of program instructions written in a high-level language.

Source drive: Drive that contains any files to be copied.

Speller: Software that allows user to check the spelling of words in a document.

Spreadsheet: Software package that can manipulate rows and columns of data.

Stand-alone word processor: Computer that does only word processing.

Standard input device: Device that DOS assumes will be used to enter commands or data. Unless otherwise specified, this device is the keyboard.

Standard output device: Device that DOS assumes will be used to receive any output generated by the computer. Unless specified otherwise, this device is the printer.

Standard pitch: Default pitch, usually pica, for most printers.

Star network: Computer nodes radiate like spokes from a central or hub computer.

Status bar: The second of the four lines at the bottom of a dBASE III Plus screen. Gives such information as the file invoked, the default drive, and the option selected from a menu, along with CAPS and INS indicators.

Status line: Top line of the control panel, which displays the cell address, the format of the data, and the cell contents.

Storage: Term that applies to either RAM or external disk memory.

Stored-program concept: Permits the reading of a program into a computer's memory and then executing the program instructions without rewiring the computer.

STR function: Changes numeric fields to character data in dBASE.

Strategic decision making: Includes setting objectives for an organization and devising long-range plans.

Strike-out text: Text produced by placing a dash (–) over each character as it is printed.

String testing: Verifies that interprogram control results in files being transferred properly from one program to the next.

Structure: A method of data base organization.

Structure chart: Depicts in graphic form the system's various modules and their hierarchical relationships.

Structured decisions: Any decisions made via existing procedures.

Structured English: Plain English with certain restrictions, which derive from its structural similarity to program code.

Structured walkthrough: Process of having a number of individuals review a program or worksheet and check it for accuracy, logic, and readability.

Stub testing: Involves designing dummy modules, with a minimum of program code, that allow a programmer to verify that linkage between modules function properly.

Subdirectory: Like a root directory except that it is itself a file and contains DOS housekeeping entries in a regular directory. Does not have the size limitation of the root directory; a subdirectory can expand indefinitely (or until there is no more disk space).

Subroutine: Segment of a program that can be executed by a single call. Performs the same sequence of instructions at many different places in a single program.

Subschema: How data are accessed by a user or an application.

Subscript: Characters printed half a line beneath the current line.

SUM command: Used to total the contents of a field for all records within a file in dBASE.

Supercomputer: The fastest, most expensive computers manufactured. They can run numerous different calculations simultaneously, thereby processing in a minute what would take a personal computer several weeks or months.

Superscript: Characters printed half a line above the current line.

Synchronized: In 1-2-3, the state of having the contents of one or more windows move in a like fashion.

Synchronous protocol: Transmits data in groups of characters, called packets, at fixed quantities and intervals.

Synergism: The concept that the whole is greater than the sum of its parts.

Syntax: Structure of instructions in a language. If you make a mistake in entering an instruction and garble the syntax, the computer sometimes calls this a SYNTAX ERROR.

SYS: DOS command used to place DOS on a disk.

System: The command that allows you to exit a software package to DOS, issue DOS commands, and then return to the software package previously exited. Also a set of interrelated parts that work together to achieve a common goal.

System analysis: Procedure of developing MIS systems that provide managers with the information they need to make decisions.

System analysis report: Describes the present system's problems as well as objectives desired from the new system. Also documents costs and benefits.

System command: Allows 1-2-3 user to run a program or execute a DOS command.

Systems controls: Ensure the proper development of information systems.

System development life cycle (SDLC): A series of formalized steps used in system analysis.

System disk: Disk that has been formatted and has DOS on it. Can be used to boot the system.

System reset: Restarts your computer just like a power on/off when user presses Del key while holding Ctrl and Alt keys down. Three keys are required to ensure that users know what they are doing and to avoid an accidental system reset.

System test: Verifies that the manual and computerized parts of the system function properly.

Tab Align command: Enables WordPerfect user to align columns of numbers.

TAB key: Key used to set automatic spacing for typing input. The TAB key has both a forward and a backward capability.

TAB + SHIFT key: Moves pointer left one screen at a time in 1-2-3.

Tab stops: Points on a line (also called tabs) to which the cursor will position itself whenever the Tab command is issued. Usually represented as marks in the ruler line of WordPerfect.

Table option: Lets 1-2-3 user construct a report containing all range names and their appropriate cell addresses in a worksheet.

Tablet: A flat drawing surface and a pointing tool that functions like a pencil. The tablet turns the pointer's movements into digitized data that can be read by special computer programs. Tablets range from palm- to desktop-size.

Tactical decision making: Implements strategic decision by allocating an organization's resources (personnel, budgeting, production scheduling, and allocation of working capital).

Target drive: Disk to which files will be copied.

Telecommunications: Data communication using communications facilities.

Telecommuting: Workers staying at home and interacting with the company by microcomputer.

Template: Form that contains the prepackaged worksheet instructions needed to perform some type of application. It can be viewed as a piece of application software on which someone has already performed the planning, design, and implementation of the logic involved.

Temporary file: File that is used temporarily in an application. Such a file will have a randomly assigned file extension such as .$$$ or .%%%. When the file is no longer needed, it is erased.

Terminal emulation: Enables a microcomputer to serve as a computer terminal for another system.

Testing: Process by which a program or worksheet is examined and tried out to make certain that it generates the proper results.

Text characters: Letters and numbers, usually in English.

Text window: Twenty-four-line segment of a document that is visible on the standard monitor.

Thermal printer: Uses specially treated paper to "burn" in dots to form characters.

Thesaurus: Software that allows you to obtain synonyms.

TIME command: Used to change the time for the system in DOS.

Timing hole: Small hole to the right of the centering hole on a diskette.

Titles option: 1-2-3 feature used to freeze text on the screen so that it will act as row or column headings.

Toggle key: Key with two states, on and off, that causes subsequent key operations to be processed in a predetermined manner. Toggle keys include the Caps Lock, Num Lock, and Scroll Lock keys.

Token: A control signal passed from one node to the next, indicating which node is allowed to transmit.

Toolbox: An icon-based menu with tools that can be used in desktop publishing.

TOP: dBASE command used to position the pointer at the beginning of a data file.

Top-down coding: The program code for the higher level modules is written and tested before the lower level modules.

Top margin: Default size is one inch or six lines of blank space at the top of a page.

Touch screen: Allows user to enter instructions by touching a menu selection or indicating which text to include in an instruction by tracking through the text with a finger.

Tracks: Concentric circles of storage on a disk's read/write surface on which data are stored.

Traditional approach: File-oriented style of information processing in which a change to a field cannot be made directly to the file.

Transaction file: Contains data about some business action and is by nature transitory. After its information is inputted, the transaction file is discarded.

Transaction log: Contains complete audit trail of all activity of a data base for a given time.

Transaction processing: Processes transactions and outputs the results. The cornerstone for data gathering in an MIS.

Transaction-processing system: Another name for data processing.

TREE command: Allows user to list all directories and subdirectories along with any files that might also be resident in DOS.

TYPE command: Displays file contents on the screen in DOS.

Type option: Allows 1-2-3 user to select one of five types of graph.

Typeover option: Replaces an existing character with the one entered from the keyboard in WordPerfect.

Typewriter keyboard: One of the three main key groupings of a computer system keyboard. It contains the QWERTY typewriter keyboard and some special keys, such as Enter, Backspace, Tab, Esc, and Alt.

Underline command: This WordPerfect command underscores (prints a line under) every character of text and the spaces between words.

Underlined text: Text that has an underscore under every character. Usually underscores are not placed between words.

Unique: 1-2-3 data base command used to get only one record for each data type within a data base file.

Unstructured decisions: Resolve ill-defined or unstructured problems (these are typically made at strategic level).

Unsynchronized: In 1-2-3, the state of having the contents of the windows move independently of each other.

Up arrow: Moves the pointer up one cell position (up one row) in Lotus 1-2-3.

Updating multiple indexes: Automatic process in dBASE for indexes specified after INDEX portion of USE statement.

Uploading: Sends a file from one computer to another computer.

Upper case: Set of upper characters on two-character keys and capital letters (A–Z). Any upper-case character can be typed by holding the Shift key down while pressing the desired key.

USE: dBASE command that makes a file available for manipulation. In 1-2-3, makes stored graphs current.

Variable data: Data that change from one document to the next in a mail merge operation.

VDISK.SYS: The DOS driver file that allows you to create a RAM disk using part of your system's memory.

Vector graphics: A display technology that creates images on the screen via lines or curves.

VER: Command that displays the DOS version number being used.

VGA (video graphics array) monitor: Video adapter introduced by IBM with its PS/2 line of computers. This analog system can display 262,144 different colors or shades of colors.

Video: Anything visual, usually information presented on the face of a cathode ray tube.

View command: Displays currently specified graph in 1-2-3.

Virtual-file allocation: Word processing packages that contain only about six to twelve pages of a document in RAM at one time, saving the remainder on disk.

Virtual word processors: Word processors that enable user to work on a document even when it is longer than the amount of available RAM. Only the needed part of the document is in RAM at any time.

VisiCalc: First spreadsheet introduced for microcomputers.

VOL: DOS command used to display the volume I.D. of a diskette.

Volatile memory: Memory that is erased when the electrical current to the computer is turned off.

Warm start: Booting process used to restart a computer after you have lost control of its language or operating system.

Widow: First line of a paragraph when it occurs at the bottom of a page.

Width command: Used in PC Works to reset the width of a specific worksheet.

Wild cards: Characters that enable you to include a number of files or fields in an operation by using only one command.

Wild card technique: Allows WordPerfect user to search for special character strings.

Window: Displayed portion of a worksheet or document. A window can be split into two or more smaller windows, horizontally or vertically.

Window option: Provides help with commands in PC Works.

WordPerfect: The best-selling word processing package currently on the market.

Word processing: Automated manipulation of text data via a software package that usually provides the ability to create, edit, store, and print documents easily.

Word wrap: Feature that automatically places a word on the next line when it will not fit on the current line.

Works: An integrated software package for small applications that combines word processing, spreadsheets, graphics, data base, and communications under one software umbrella.

Worksheet: Model or representation of reality that is created using a spreadsheet software package. The worksheet is inside the spreadsheet border.

/ Worksheet Global Format option: Allows 1-2-3 user to format an entire worksheet.

Write process: Transfers data out of a computer back to secondary storage.

Write-protected: Diskettes that have been protected from having information stored on them, being altered, or being deleted; this is accomplished by placing a write-protect tab over the small rectangular hole on the side of a diskette.

Write-protect notch: Rectangular notch at upper right-hand edge of some disks. Covering notch with a piece of tape prevents alteration of disk's information, but disk remains readable.

X axis: Horizontal (left-to-right) axis.

X command: Defines range of 1-2-3 worksheet to be used for a graph's horizontal label.

Y axis: Vertical (up-and-down) axis.

Zero command: Enables 1-2-3 user to suppress zeros in numeric cells.

Index

A

ABCDEF commands, 482, 483
Absolute addressing, 312–15
Absolute range name, 315
Access controls, 610–11
Action line, 278
Active directory, 119–20
Active index, 443
Adapter boards, 35
Address. *See* Cells
Algorithms, 15
Align command, 270
Alignment character, 173
ALL parameter, 410
Alphanumeric keys, 26–27, 28
Alt key, 27
American Standard Code for Information
  Interchange (ASCII), 31–32
Analog signals, 517
Angle brackets, 212
APPEND:
  dBASE III Plus, 389, 391, 443
  WordPerfect, 182
Apple LaserWriter, 622–23
A> prompt, 75
Application programs, 64–68, 69–71
Arabic numbers, 204
Arithmetic operations, 4
Arithmetic operators, 235
Arrow keys. *See* Cursor movement,
  Pointer movement
Artificial intelligence, 636
  expert systems, 638–41
  and fifth-generation computers, 641
  hardware, 642–43
  natural languages, 636
  robotics, 636
  vision and sensing systems, 636–38
ASCII code, 31–32
Ashton-Tate, 378, 463–66
ASSIGN, 124
ASSIGN.COM file, 124
Assign statement, 124
Assistant mode, 377–80
Asterisk (*):
  as delete indicator in dBASE III Plus,
    390, 420
  as wild card in DOS, 78
Asynchronous protocol, 520
Atanasoff, John, 6–7
Atanasoff-Berry Computer (ABC), 7
Auto-answering, 67
Auto-dialing, 67
AUTOEXEC.BAT files, 75, 112–14
Automatic recalculation, 315

B

Back arrow, 80
Backslash (\), 275
Back-ups, 46
  control of, 612
  data base, 360
  for hard disks, 49
  WordPerfect, 162–63, 164
Bandwidth, 519
Banked memory, 32
Bar charts, 460, 461, 481
  generating with Lotus 1-2-3, 485–92
  side-by-side, 490
  stacked, 496–498
Barnaby, Bob, 135
BASIC, 63
Batch files, 112–13
  control of, 613
  creating, 113–14
  executing, 114–15
  samples of, 115–16
  substituting data in, 115
Batch mode editing, 147
Batch printing, 504–5
Batch processing, 15–16, 17, 18
Baud rates, 67, 518–19
Beginning of file (BOF), 416
Benchmark, 588
Berry, Clifford, 6–7
Bi-level reading mode, 624
Binary notation, 7–8, 31
  and language processors, 63
  and modems, 67
Binding width option, 167
Bit (binary digit), 13, 31
Bit-mapped fonts, 622
Bit-mapped graphics, 459
Black-box concept, 577
Black boxes, 273–74
Block commands, 174–79
Boards, 34
Boldface command, 168, 174–75
Boot process, 75
Boot record, 74
Borders, 231, 269
Boundary, 575
Brackets ([ ]), 91
  Lotus 1-2-3, 230
  PC Works, 543
  WordPerfect, 165
Brainard, Paul, 620
Break option, 124
Bricklin, Dan, 65, 226
BROWSE, 448–49
Bubble memory, 34

Buffers

Buffers, 124–25
Built-in functions, 236–37
Buses, 34–35
Business software, 71
Bus network, 527, 529
Bytes, 13, 31

C

CAD software, 472–73
CAE software, 472–73
CAM software, 472–73
Caps Lock key, 27
Caret (^), 275
Cartridge hard disk, 49
Case conversion command, 179
Catalog files, 395
Cathode-ray tube (CRT), 40
CD ROM, 49–50, 51
Cells, 65, 225
  formatting, 263–65
  moving, 266–67
  range of, 260
  range names for, 298–304
  sending and receiving, 261–63
Center block, 175
Center command, 167–68, 174–75
Centering hole, 45, 47
Centering text, 205
Center Page option, 205
Central processing unit (CPU), 5–6, 31–33
Centronics, 35
Character overprint, 168–69
Character pitch, 209
Characters:
  in file names, 77–78
  repeating, 275
  wild-card, 181, 202
Character string field, 383
Charting, 553–55
Chart-Master, 463–65, 466
CHDIR (or CD), 119, 122–23
Chip, 26
CHKDSK, 90, 93–94
Circular references, 236, 295–97
Clear option, 270
Clock speed, 32–33
Clones, 36–37
Closed-bus system, 34–35
Clusters, 80, 81
Coaxial cable, 523
COBOL, 63
Codes:
  ASCII, 31–32
  object and source, 63

WordPerfect, 164–65
Cold start, 75
Color monitors, 40
Columns, 225
adding or deleting, 265–66
block commands for, 177–78
changing width of, 274
hiding, 293–95
Comma (,), 263
COMMAND.COM, 74–75
Command-driven modes, 377
Command Processor, 73, 74
Command (syntax), 382
Communications media, 523–24
Communications packages, 67
Compact disk (CD), 49–50, 51
Compatibility, IBM, 36–37
Compilers, 8, 63
Comprehensive Crime Control Act of
1984, 608
Computer crime, 604
characteristics of computer criminals,
606–8
examples of, 604–6
federal laws regarding, 608
Computer-generated graphics, 462. See
also Graphics
Computers, 4
and artificial intelligence, 636–41
and crime, 604–8
data location in, 15
data processing by, 15–16
ethical software development, 608
fifth-generation, 641
history of, 6–9
and individual privacy, 608–10
and literacy, 602
security and controls, 610–13
and the workplace, 602–4
Computer security, 610
documentation, 613
general controls, 610–12
program controls, 612–13
Computer system, 5–6
Concatenation, 439
Concentrators, 524–26
Condition (syntax), 382
Conditional End of Page command, 208
Configuration:
controls, 360
of systems, 124–26
CONFIG.SYS file, 124–26
Console logs, 611
Constant information, 137
CONTINUE, 445
Control block, 126
Control keys, 80
Control panel, 230
Coprocessor, 33
COPY CON, 113–14
Copying:
COPY (DOS), 90, 98–99
Lotus 1-2-3, 261–63
PC Works, 549–51
WordPerfect, 176
Copyright protection, 606
CPU (central processing unit), 5–6, 31–33
Creating:
cell names in Lotus 1-2-3, 299
CREATE (dBASE III Plus), 385
CREATE REPORT (dBASE III Plus),
422–26

Ctrl-Break, 80, 92, 112
Ctrl key, 27
Ctrl-P, 80
Ctrl-S, 80
Cursor movement:
dBASE III Plus, 383, 393–94
Lotus 1-2-3, 231–32
PC Works, 545
WordPerfect, 144–46, 157–58
Cut Option, 176
Cylinder, 80, 81

D

Daisy wheel printers, 42
Dash (-):
Lotus 1-2-3, 306
WordPerfect, 146
Data, 13
controls, 612
conversion of, 516–18
dictionary, 582
entry of, 234–35
entry windows for, 140
as information, 13
integrity of, 350–51
labels, 234–35
Lotus 1-2-3 graphics, 485
management of, 228
numeric, 235
organization of, 15
processing of, 15–16
range option of, 307
redundancy of, 350–51
sorting of, 306–8
substitution of, in batch files, 115
transmission of, 516
Data base management systems, 352, 353.
See also dBASE III Plus, dBASE III
Plus commands
advantages of, 354–55
parts of, 355–59
role of, 352–54
Data bases, 14, 367
administrator for, 359–60
back-up and recovery, 360
building, 367–69
configuration control in, 360
dictionaries, 359
indexes for, 363–66
management of, 68
organization of, 360–67
physical versus logical view of, 354, 355
security of, 360
sequential versus relational
organization in, 367
terminology of, 367–69
transaction log for, 359–60
Data-definition language (DDL), 356–58
Data-flow diagrams, 581
logical, 588, 592
physical, 582–85
Data gathering in system analysis, 580–81
Data-manipulation language (DML), 359
Data-storage hierarchy, 13
Data transmission, 516. See also
Telecommunications
and data conversion, 516–18
direction of, 519–20
protocol modes for, 520
software for, 521

speed of, 518–19
Date arithmetic, 317
Date field, 384
Dating:
DATE (dBASE III Plus), 416
DATE (DOS), 91, 103
Lotus 1-2-3, 233, 264, 274–75, 317
WordPerfect, 169–70
dBASE III Plus, 376. See also dBASE III
Plus commands
activating, 388–91
adding records to files, 391–94
Assistant menu, 377–80
Columns screen, 423–24
communicating in command mode, 382
creating a file, 383–88
cursor control, 393–94
default drive, 382–83
demand reports, 572
editing records, 393–94
exiting, 381–83
file extensions, 394–95
file types, 394–95
full-screen cursor menus, 383, 384
Groups screen, 423
Help facility, 380–81
limitations of, 376–77
modes of, 377
Options screen, 422–23
pointer position commands, 414–16
printing, 426–27
pull-down menu, 61
query language, 354–55, 356
report generator, 356, 358
report template, 422–26
starting, 377
STR function, 442
Substring function ($), 414
dBASE III Plus commands:
access and display, 402–14
APPEND, 389, 391, 443
arrangement, 434–44
ASSIST, 380
BROWSE, 449–50
CONTINUE, 445
CREATE, 385
CREATE REPORT, 422–26
cursor control, 393–94
DATE, 416
DELETE, 419–21, 443
DELETE FILE, 443
DIR, 410, 411
DISPLAY, 409–10, 411
DISPLAY ALL, 410, 411, 446
GO/GOTO, 414
GOTO BOTTOM, 416
GOTO TOP, 415
HELP, 380–81
INDEX, 437–44
LABEL, 394
LIST, 392, 402, 448
LIST field list, 404–5
LIST FILES LIKE, 443
LIST NEXT, 405–6, 407
LIST selected, 408
LIST STRUCTURE, 389, 402–3
LIST WHILE, 406–8
LOCATE, 445
location, 444–49
PACK, 419–21, 443
pointer positioning, 414–16
QUIT, 381–82

dBASE III Plus commands (*continued*)
　RECALL, 420–21
　RECNO( ), 414
　record alteration, 418–22
　REPLACE, 418–19
　REPORT, 356, 358, 380
　REPORT FORM, 426–27
　report generation, 422–28
　RETRIEVE, 392
　SEEK, 445–48
　SET HEADINGS OFF, 445
　SET PRINT, 410
　SET UP, 381
　SKIP, 415, 446–47
　SORT, 434–36
　SUM, 416–17
　UPDATE, 388, 391, 393–94
　USE, 402, 443
DBMS. *See* Data base management
　　systems
Decision-making levels, 570–71
Decision support system (DSS), 573–74
Decision tables, 582–83
Decision types, 571–72
Default disk drives, 76
　setting in dBASE III Plus, 382–83
Delete indicator (*), 390, 420
Deleting:
　columns, 265–66
　DEL (DOS), 102
　DELETE (dBASE III Plus), 419–21, 443
　DELETE (Lotus 1-2-3), 265–66
　DELETE FILE (dBASE III Plus), 443
　WordPerfect, 144, 148–51, 175–76, 299
Delimiters, 92
Demand reports, 572
Demodulation, 517
Dependent word processors, 134–35
Design graphics, 472–73
Desk checking, 589
Desktop organizers, 71
Desktop publishing (DTP), 136, 620
　document design, 626–28
　graphic capabilities of, 459
　hardware, 620–25
　laser printers, 621–23
　PageMaker, 626–28
　scanners, 623–25
　software, 625
DEVICE, 125
Diacritics, 168
Diagram-Master, 466, 467
Dictionaries, 200–203
Digital Equipment Corporation, 9
Digital symbols, 516–17
DIR:
　dBASE III Plus, 410–11
　DOS, 76–77, 90, 99–101
Direct-access method, 15, 18, 19
Directories, 76, 116
　active or current, 119–20
　change, command (CHDIR or CD), 119,
　　122–23
　changing in Lotus 1-2-3, 292–93
　commands for, 117–24
　on disks, 116
　list, command (DIR), 76–77
　make, command (MKDIR or MD),
　　117–19, 123
　PATH command, 121–22
　remove, command (RMDIR or RD), 121,
　　123
　TREE command, 120–21, 123
　use of subdirectories with, 116

Direct system conversion, 594
DISKCOPY, 90, 94–96
Disk drives, 48, 92
Diskettes, 44
　care of, 46–48
　and dBASE III Plus, 377, 382–83
　double-sided, 80–81
　features of, 44–46, 47
　as formatted by DOS, 78–79
　and PC Works, 539
　and WordPerfect, 137–38
Disk full errors, 179–80
Disk operating system. *See* DOS
Disks, 44, 80. *See also* Diskettes, Hard
　　disks
DISPLAY, 409–11, 413
Distributed data processing (DDP), 516
Distributed data processing network, 522
Dither reading mode, 624–25
Documentation, 26, 227
Documents. *See* Files
Dollar sign ($):
　as dBASE III Plus substring function,
　　413
　in Lotus 1-2-3 cell referencing, 313
　as Lotus 1-2-3 currency option, 263
DOS, 73, 90
　boot process, 75
　control keys in, 80–81
　default drive, 76
　directories, 76–77
　disk preparation, 78–79
　editing keys in, 81
　files and file names, 77–78
　5¼″ disk for, 80
　parts of, 73–74
　starting, 75–76
　versions of, 79–80
DOS commands, 90
　ASSIGN, 124
　and batch files, 112–16
　CHDIR (or CD), 119, 122–23
　CHKDSK, 90, 93–94
　COPY, 90, 98–99, 113
　COPY CON, 113–24, 126
　DATE, 91, 103
　DEL, 102
　DEVICE, 125–26
　DIR, 76, 90, 99–101
　directory, 116–24
　disk, 90
　DISKCOPY, 90, 94–96
　ERASE, 90, 101–2, 121
　external and internal, 91
　file, 90–91
　FILES, 126
　FORMAT, 79, 90, 96–98
　format notation for, 91–92
　by function and type, 104–5
　MKDIR (or MD), 117–19, 123
　PATH, 121–22
　RENAME (or REN), 91, 102, 115
　RMDIR (or RD), 121, 123
　summary of, 104
　time, 91
　TIME, 91, 103–4
　TREE, 120–21, 123
　TYPE, 91, 102–3
DOS prompt, 75
DOS text files. *See* Text files
DOS utilities, 91
Dot-matrix printers, 41–42
Dot prompt, 376, 410–13
Double-sided diskettes, 80–81

Double words, 203
Downloading, 521
Drives. *See* Disk drives
Dumb terminal, 521
Dummy columns or rows, 304–6, 307

E

Eckert, J. Presper, Jr., 7, 8
Editing:
　DOS, 81
　EDIT (dBASE III Plus), 393–94
　full-screen, 394
　line, 134
　WordPerfect, 163
Edit program, 15–16
Educational software, 70–71
EDVAC, 7
EGA (enhanced graphics adapter)
　　monitors, 40, 459
Electronic funds transfer (EFT), 609
Electronic mail, 529–30
Electronic spreadsheets, 65–67, 222. *See
　also* Lotus 1-2-3, Spreadsheets
Ellipsis points (. . .), 91
Embedded codes, 164–65
End of file (EOF), 416
Enhanced graphics adapter (EGA)
　　monitors, 40, 459
ENIAC, 7
ENTER key, 27, 80
Entry line, 230
EOF (end of file), 416
Equal sign (=):
　Lotus 1-2-3, 306
　PC Works, 547
　WordPerfect, 146
ERASE, 90, 101–2
Ergonomics, 603–4
Error message, 231
Escape codes, 212
ESC key, 27, 80
Ethics in computer use, 602
　computer crime, 604–8
　computer literacy, 602
　individual privacy, 608–10
　security and control, 610–13
　software development, 608
　workplace aspects, 602–4
Exception reports, 572
Exiting:
　dBASE III Plus, 381–82
　PC Works, 541
　WordPerfect, 142–43, 164
　See also Quit commands
Expansion slots, 34
Expert systems, 638–41
Extend command, 544, 546
Extensions. *See* File-name extensions
External DOS commands, 91
External modem, 517–18

F

Fair Credit Reporting Act of 1970, 610
FAT (file allocation table), 77
Feasibility studies, 578
Feedback, 576–77
Fiber optics, 523, 641–42
Fields, 13–14, 367
　character string, 383
　data base, 367–69

Date, 384
dBASE III Plus, 383–88
  logical, 383
  Memo, 384
  numeric, 383
  and program and data dependency, 351
Fifth-generation computers, 641
File allocation table (FAT), 77
File-name extensions, 77
  .BAT (DOS), 78, 112–14
  .BK! (WordPerfect), 163–64
  .CAT (dBASE III Plus), 395
  .COM (DOS), 78, 113
  .DBF (dBASE III Plus), 383, 394
  .DBT (dBASE III Plus), 394
  .EXE (DOS), 113, 138
  .FMT (dBASE III Plus), 394
  .FRM (dBASE III Plus), 394
  .LBL (dBASE III Plus), 394
  .MEM (dBASE III Plus), 394
  .NDX (dBASE III Plus), 394, 443
  .PIC (Lotus 1-2-3), 480, 483
  .QRY (dBASE III Plus), 395
  .SCR (dBASE III Plus), 395
  .TXT (dBASE III Plus), 394
  .VUE (dBASE III Plus), 395
  .WCM (PC Works), 540
  .WDB (PC Works), 540
  .WKS (PC Works), 540
  .WPS (PC Works), 540
File names. See Naming conventions
Files, 14, 77
  dBASE III Plus, 393–94
  direct-access, 15
  DOS commands for, 90–91, 98–103
  downloading, 521
  FILE (DOS), 126
  fragmented, 93
  hidden, 74
  multiple-field indexes, 439–42
  naming, 77–78
  naming, in dBASE III Plus, 383
  path for, 120
  sequential, 15
  single-field indexes, 437–39
  temporary, 163
  in traditional information processing,
    350–52
  uploading, 521
  worksheet, 292–93
Fill commands, 551
Fixed-disk systems, 539–40
Flat-screen monitors, 40
Flexibility in information processing,
  351–52
Floppy disks, 44. See also Diskettes
Flush right commands, 168
Flystra, Dan, 65, 226
Fonts, 209–10
Footers:
  Lotus 1-2-3, 268–69
  WordPerfect, 206–7
Format files, 394
Format notation, 91–92
Formatting, 45
  DOS, 78–79, 90, 91, 96–98
  Lotus 1-2-3, 265–67, 483
  of pages, 203–9
  PC Works, 551–52
  WordPerfect, 203–9
Formulas:
  entering, 235–36
  operators for, 235
  parentheses and precedence, 235–36

spreadsheet, 225–26
FOR parameter, 426
FORTRAN, 63
Fragmented file, 93
Frankston, Robert, 226
Front-end processor, 526, 527
Full-duplex transmission, 520
Fully distributed network, 527, 529
Function call, 272
Function keys, 27, 28
  DOS, 81
  Lotus 1-2-3, 234
  WordPerfect, 140
Functions:
  Lotus 1-2-3, 272–74, 315–17
  nested, 274

G

General computer controls, 610–12
Gigabytes, 50
Global file-name characters, 78
GO/GOTO, 297, 414
Go option, 270–71, 307
GOTO BOTTOM, 416
GOTO TOP, 415
Graphics, 458
  commands, 480–85
  design, 472
  editor/paint programs, 466–72
  hardware, 458–59
  Lotus 1-2-3, 462, 480–507
  output, 459
  presentation, 460–66
  types of charts and graphs, 461–62
Graphics application packages, 68, 228
Graph menu, 480–85
Graphs:
  bar charts, 461, 485–92, 494, 496–498
  building, 480
  creating, 462
  hi-lo, 462
  legends, 462, 493–94
  line, 461–492
  pie charts, 461, 494–96
  printing, 480, 502–7
  scatter plot, 461–62
  stand-alone packages, 463–66
  titles, 488–89
  types of, 460–62
  XY, 461–62, 498–502
  See also Graphics
"Greeked" form, 627, 629
Grid option, 484

H

Half-duplex transmission, 519
Handshaking, 520
Hanging paragraph, 172
Hard carriage return, 142
Hard disks, 49
  and dBASE III Plus, 377
  and directories, 116
  and Speller, 201–3
  and WordPerfect, 138
Hard page breaks, 146
Hard-sectored disks, 46
Hardware components, 26
  buses, 34–35
  diskettes, 44–48
  hard disks, 49

input devices, 26–30
interfaces, 35
keyboard, 26–27, 28
light pen, 29
microprocessor chips, 36–38
microprocessors, 31–33
monitors, 39–41
mouse, 27, 29
optical disks, 49–51
output devices, 38–44
primary memory, 34
printers, 41–44
processing unit, 30–36
scanner, 28–30
secondary storage devices, 44–51
tablets, 27, 29
touch screens, 30
Hardware controls, 611
Hatch mark (#), 425
Hazard controls, 612
Headers:
  Lotus 1-2-3, 268–69
  WordPerfect, 206–7
Help feature:
  dBASE III Plus, 380–81
  Lotus 1-2-3, 238
  PC Works, 541
  WordPerfect, 140
Hewlett-Packard LaserJet, 621–22
Hidden columns, 293–95
Hidden files, 74–75
Hierarchical (tree) data base structures,
  362–63
High-level languages, 63
Hi-lo graphs, 461, 462
Hit, file search, 445
Home command, 145–46
Hopper, Grace Murray, 8
Horizontal menu, 58–60
Housekeeping, 90
Hypercube, 13

I

IBM, 8, 9
  clones, 37
  compatibles, 36
  word processing, 134
IBMBIO.COM, 74–75
IBMDOS.COM, 74–75
IBM PC DOS. See DOS
Indenting, 171–72
Indexes, 15
  active, 443
  of character data, 383–84
  for data bases, 363–66
  mixed (numeric and character) data,
    442–43
  multiple-field, 439–42
  single-field, 437–39
  updating, 443
Index files, 394
Indicators:
  Lotus 1-2-3, 230–31
  WordPerfect, 139
Information, 13
Information processing, traditional
  approach to, 350–52
Information systems, 574–77
Initialization process, 79
Ink-jet printers, 43
Input controls, 612–13
Input devices, 5, 26

Input devices (*continued*)
  important keys, 27, 28
  light pen, 28, 30
  mouse, 27, 29
  scanners, 28, 30
  tablets, 27, 29
  touch screen, 30
Insert option, 147
Insert Printer command, 212
Ins key, 81
Integrated circuit, 9
Integrated package, 69
Integration, 227
Intel Corp., 9
Intercomputer communication. *See* Telecommunications
Interfaces, 34–35, 575
Internal DOS commands, 91, 117
Internal modem, 517
Internal storage, 4
Interpreters, 63
I/O handler, 73–74
Item, 13–14

J

Justification, 153, 210

K

K (kilobyte), 31
Kapor, Mitch, 226
Keyboards, 26–27, 28
  Lotus 1-2-3, 231–34
Keys:
  in data bases, 367
  primary and secondary, 367–68
  record, 15

L

Label data, 234–35
Label files, 394
Labeling, 299
Labels (spreadsheet), 225
Language processors, 63–64
Language program, 62–64
LAN (local area network), 67, 516, 527–31
Landscape format, 627
Laser printers, 43–44, 621
LCD (liquid crystal display) monitors, 38, 40
Left Indent command, 171–72
Legends, 462, 463, 483
Letter-quality printers, 42, 212
Light pens, 28, 30
Line counter, 271–72
Line editors, 134
Line graphs, 460, 461, 481
Line numbering, 212, 213
Line option, 268
Line spacing, 152–53
Liquid crystal display (LCD) monitors, 38, 40
LIST, 396, 402–9, 448
List Files command, 143–44
LIST FILES LIKE, 443
LIST STRUCTURE, 389, 402–3
List structures of data bases, 361
Local area network (LAN), 67, 516, 527–31

LOCATE, 445
Location, 444–49
Logical data-flow diagram, 588, 592
Logical deletion, 419
Logical fields, 387
Logical operations, 4
Logical operators, 315–16
Logical view of data base, 354, 355
LOGO language, 70
Lotus 1-2-3, 66, 226, 480
  adding rows and columns, 265–66
  addressing, 312–15
  automatic versus manual recalculations, 315
  bar charts, 485–92, 494, 496, 498
  building graphs with, 480
  built-in functions of, 236–37
  copy command, 261–63
  data entry, 234–35
  deleting rows and columns, 265–66
  format, 263–65
  formula entry, 235–36
  functions, 272–75, 315–17
  generating graphs with, 485–502
  graphic displays, 68
  graphing, 462
  graph menu, 480–85
  graph printing, 480, 502–7
  help screens, 238–40
  as integrated package, 69
  keyboard, 231–34
  line graphs, 492–94
  menu structure, 58–59
  moving cell contents, 266–67
  parts of, 227–29
  pie charts, 494–96
  predictive reports, 572–73
  printing, 267–72
  range, 260–61
  range names, 298–306
  sample spreadsheet, 277–83
  sample worksheet, 240–47, 275–77
  saving and retrieving files, 245–48
  screen, 230–31
  sorting, 306–11
  starting, 229
  templates, 226
  titles, 488–89
  windows, 231
  worksheet environment control, 292–298
  worksheet errors, 237
  worksheet navigation, 231–32
  worksheet practice, 317–18
  XY graphs, 481, 498–502
Lotus Access System, 228, 229
Lower-case letters, 32
  ASCII code, 32
  case conversion, 179
  DOS commands for, 91
Low-level languages, 63
L/R Indent command, 172

M

McCarthy, John, 636
Machine language, 62–64
Magnetic disk, 5–6
Mag typewriter, 134
Main Dictionary (LEX.WP), 196
Mainframe computers, 11–12
Main system board, 34

Management-information systems (MIS), 570
  characteristics of, 574–77
  decision-making levels, 570–71
  decision-support systems, 573–74
  decision types, 571–72
  reporting methods, 572–73
  system analysis, 577–94
  versus transaction-processing systems, 573
Manual recalculation, 315
Margin commands, 170–74
Master files, 15
Mauchley, John W., 7, 8
Megabytes (meg), 49
Megahertz (MHz), 32
Memo fields:
  dBASE III Plus, 384
  sorting, 434
Memo files, 394
Memory, 4. *See also* RAM, ROM
  banked, 32
  nonvolatile, 34
  primary, 34
  volatile, 34
Memory files, 394
Menu, 58
  horizontal, 58–60
  vertical, 60–62
Menu-drive modes, 376
Merge feature, 136–37
Message line, 381
MHz (megahertz), 32
Microcomputers, 10, 26
Microprocessors, 9, 31–33
Microsoft, 73, 538
Minicomputers, 9, 11
Minus sign (−):
  Lotus 1-2-3, 235, 264
  WordPerfect, 146
MIS. *See* Management-information systems
Mixed-cell address, 314–15
Mixed data multiple-field index, 441–42
MKDIR (or MD), 117–19, 123
Mode:
  dBASE III Plus, 377
  indicators of, 230–31
Models in MIS, 573
Modems, 67, 68, 517–19
Modulation, 517
Module design, 588–89, 592
Monitors, 6, 38–41
Monochrome monitors, 40
Mother board, 34
Mouse, 27, 29
Move command, 176–77
Move feature, 266–67
MS DOS, 73. *See also* DOS
Multiple-field index, 439–42
Multiplexors, 524–26
Multipurpose monitors, 40

N

Nailing down, 261–62
Naming conventions:
  dBASE III Plus files, 383
  DOS files, 77–78
  Lotus 1-2-3 graphs, 485
  Lotus 1-2-3 ranges, 298–306
Natural language, 636

Navigation line, 379
Nesting, 274
Networks:
    of data bases, 363
    inoperable DOS commands with, 92
    local area, 527–31
    in telecommunications, 522
    topologies, 526–27
Nodes:
    in data bases, 362
    in indexes, 364
NO FIND message, 446
Nonvolatile memory, 34
Number (spreadsheet), 225
Numbering of lines, 212
Numbering style, 204
Numeric data, 235
Numeric fields, 383
Numeric key pad, 27, 28
Num Lock key, 81

O

Object code, 63
Open-architecture design, 37
Open-bus system, 34–35
Operating system prompt, 75
Operating systems, 72. See also DOS
Operational decision making, 570
Operators, arithmetic, 235
Optical character recognition programs, 624
Optical disk (CD ROM), 49–50
Options menu, 268
Organizational controls, 611
Orphans, 146, 208
Outliners, 71–72
Output controls, 613
Output devices, 6, 38
    monitors, 38–41
    plotters, 6, 44, 45
    printers, 41–44
Overstrike command, 168–69

P

PACK, 419–21, 443
Page breaks:
    conditional, 208
    hard, 146
    Lotus 1-2-3, 272
    soft, 146
    WordPerfect, 146
Page control language, 622
Page description language, 622–23
Page Down key, 146
Page Format command, 203
Page Length option, 205
Page Number Position option, 203–204
Page option, 268
Page Up key, 146
Paragraphs, hanging, 172
Parallel interface, 35
Parallel system conversion, 593
Parallel transmission, 519
Parameters, 92
    ALL, 410
    FOR, 426
    replaceable, 115
    WHILE, 406
Parentheses in status line, 230

Pascal, 63
Passwords, 296–97
Pasteboard, 627–28
Path, 120
PATH command, 121–22
Pause (Ctrl-S), 80
PC Paintbrush, 466–72
PC Works, 538
    charting, 553–55
    cursor movement commands, 545
    data bases, 555–60
    editing commands, 546
    exiting, 541
    Extend command, 544–46
    function key names, 545
    Help feature, 541
    integration, 561–63
    pointer movement commands, 548
    spreadsheets, 546–53
    starting, 539–41
    text formatting commands, 545
    word processing, 541–46
Percent sign (%):
    DOS, 115
    Lotus 1-2-3, 264
Periods (.):
    dBASE III Plus, 382
    Lotus 1-2-3, 260–61
Peripheral devices, 34
Personal computers (PCs), 26
Physical data-flow diagrams, 582–85
Physical view of data bases, 354
Pie charts, 461, 482
Pilot system conversion, 594
Piracy, 605–6
Pitch, 209–10
Pixels, 40
Plotters, 6, 44, 45
Plus sign (+):
    Lotus 1-2-3, 235, 264, 547
    PC Works, 547
    WordPerfect, 147
Pointer, 231, 361
Pointer movement:
    dBASE III Plus, 414–16
    Lotus 1-2-3, 231–32
    See also Cursor movement
Polling, 524
Pop-up menu, 61–62
Portability, 38
Portrait format, 627
Ports, 34–35
PostScript, 622–23, 624
Precedence in Lotus 1-2-3, 235–36, 316
Predictive reports, 572–73
Presentation graphics, 460–66
Primary Key option, 307
Primary keys, 367
Primary memory, 34
Primary storage, 5
Print Block command, 176
Printer devices, 6, 41–44
Print Format command, 209–12
PrintGraph, 502–7
Printing:
    dBASE III Plus, 410
    Lotus 1-2-3, 267–72
    PC Works, 552–53
    WordPerfect, 153, 165–67, 209–12
Print Range option, 268
Print thimble, 42
Privacy Act of 1974, 610
Privacy and computers, 608–10

Procedural controls, 612
Procedures, 26. See also Documentation
Processing controls, 613
Processing devices, 30
    buses, 34–35
    interfaces, 35
    microprocessors, 31–34
    primary memory, 34
Processing unit, 30–35
Productivity software, 71–72
Program, 4
Program computer controls, 612–13
Programming languages, 62–64
Program mode, 377
Prompt:
    dot, 376, 410–13
    system, 75
Prompt line, 230
Proportional spacing, 210
Protection of worksheets, 296–97
Protocol, 520
PrtSc key, 27
Pseudocode, 589
Pull-down menu, 61

Q

Query files, 395
Query language, 355–56
Question mark (?):
    dBASE III Plus, 414
    as wild card in DOS, 78
    WordPerfect, 202
Queuing, 167
Quit commands:
    dBASE III Plus, 381–82
    Lotus 1-2-3, 271, 307, 482, 483
    See also Exiting
Quotation marks ("), 234–35, 275
QWERTY keys, 27

R

RAM (random-access memory), 34
RAM disks, 125–26
RAM-resident programs, 61
Random files, 445
Range, 242
    dummy columns or rows, 304–6, 307
    expanding, 324–26
    Lotus 1-2-3, 260–61, 268
    names for, 298–306, 315
    PC Works, 549–50
Range Format command, 263–65
Range Transpose command, 297–298
Read-only memory (ROM), 34
Read process, 5–6
Read/write access hole, 45, 47
Real-time editing, 147
Real-time processing, 16, 19
RECALL, 419–21
Receiving cell, 261
RECNO( ), 414
Record key, 15
Records, 14, 367
Rectangular blocks, 177
Re-form command, 146
Relational structures, 363–67
Relative addressing, 243. See also Absolute addressing
    Lotus 1-2-3, 262, 312–15

REM, 113
RENAME (or REN), 91, 102
Repeating character, 275
REPLACE, 418–19
Replaceable parameters, 115
Replace command, 180–81
REPORT FORM, 426–27
Report Form files, 394
Report generator, 356
Reporting, 559–60
Reporting methods in MIS, 572–73
Report template:
    dBASE III Plus, 422–26
    and indexes, 443–44
Reset option, 299
Reserved tracks, 97
Restoring deleted text, 152
Retrieving files:
    Lotus 1-2-3, 245–47
    WordPerfect, 143–44
RETURN key, 27
Reveal Code, 164–65
Reverse Search command, 180
Revision of text, 136
Right-justification, 153, 210
Ring network, 526–27, 528
RMDIR (or RD), 121, 123
Robotics, 636
ROM (read-only memory), 34
Roman numerals, 204
Root directory, 116
Root node, 364
Rows (spreadsheet), 225, 265–66
Rubinstein, Seymour, 135

S

Saving:
    of blocks, 176
    to disk, 142
    Lotus 1-2-3, 245–47, 483
    WordPerfect, 142–43, 162
Scale option, 484
Scanners, 8, 623–25
Scatter plots, 461–62, 481
Scheduled reports, 572
Schema, 358
Scope (syntax), 381
Screen files, 395
Search and Replace command, 180–81
Secondary Key option, 307
Secondary keys, 367–68
Secondary storage, 5–6
    on compact disks, 49–51
    on diskettes, 44–48
    on hard disks, 48
Sectors, 45, 47
Security of data bases, 360
SEEK, 445–48
Semiconductors, 26
Sending cell, 261
Sequential-access method, 15
Sequential file data processing, 367
Sequential files searching, 445
Serial interface, 35
Serial transmission, 519
SET HEADINGS OFF, 445
Set-up menu, 162
Set Up option, 389
Sheet feeder bins, 212
SHIFT key, 27
SHIFT-PrtSc, 80
Shrink-wrap licenses, 606

Sidekick desktop organizer, 71
Sign-Master, 465, 466
Silicon, 9
Simplex transmission, 519, 520
Simulation with supercomputers, 13
Single-field index, 437–39
SKIP, 417, 446–47
Skip sequential processing, 448
Slash (/):
    dBASE III Plus, 385
    Lotus 1-2-3, 232–33, 274
Slave disk, 98
Soft carriage return, 151
Soft page breaks, 146
Soft-sectored disks, 46
Software components, 26
    application programs, 64–68, 69–71
    integrated, 69
    menus, 58–62
    operating systems, 72–81
    productivity, 71–72
    programming languages, 62–64
    special-use application, 69–71
Software piracy, 605–6
Software viruses, 605
Sorting:
    dBASE III Plus, 434–36
    Lotus 1-2-3, 306–11
    PC Works, 558
Source, the, information package, 67
Source code, 63
Source document, 15
Source drive, 92
Speed:
    of compilers versus interpreters, 64
    of processing, 32–33
Speller, 137, 200–203
Speller Utility (SPELL.EX), 200
Spreadsheets, 222. See also Lotus 1-2-3
    PC Works, 546–53
    problem solving with, 227
    syntax for, 225–26
Stacked bar graph, 482
Stand-alone graphics packages, 463
    Chart-Master, 463–65, 466
    Diagram-Master, 466, 467
    Sign-Master, 466, 468
Standards for serial transmission, 35
Star network, 526, 528
Status bar (or line):
    dBASE III Plus, 378–79
    Lotus 1-2-3, 230
    WordPerfect, 138
Stored-program concept, 7
Strategic decision making, 570
Stress notches, 46, 47
STR function, 442
String testing, 589
Structure chart, 588
Structured decision, 571–72
Structured walk-through, 589
Structure of data base, 369
Stub testing, 589
Subdirectories, 116–24. See also Directories
Subschema, 358
Subscript command, 179
Substring function ($), 413
SUM, 416–17
Supercomputers, 12–13
Superscript command, 179
Supplemental dictionary ({WP}LEX.SUP), 200
Synchronous protocol, 520
Synergism, 574

Syntax, 91
    dBASE III Plus, 382–83
    for spreadsheets, 225–26
System, definition of, 574
System analysis, 577–78
    data gathering, 580–83
    design, 588
    development, 588–92
    hardware for, 588
    implementation, 592–94
    report, 583–88
System command, 292
System-development life cycle, 63
System disk, 97
System reset, 75
Systems controls, 611
System test, 592

T

Tab Align command, 173
Tablets, 27, 29
Tabs, 173–74
Tab stops, 164
Tactical decision making, 570
Target drive, 92
Telecommunications, 516, 641–42
    communication media, 523–24
    concentrators in, 525–26
    data transmission in, 516–21
    front-end processors, 526
    local area networks, 527–31
    multiplexors, 524–25
    networks, 521
    network topologies, 526–27
Telecommuting, 642
Templates (spreadsheet), 226
Temporary files, 163
Terminal emulation, 521
Text files, 394
Text window, 140
Thermal printers, 50
Thesaurus, 137
Think Tank outliner, 71–72, 73
TIME, 91, 103–4
Timing hole, 45, 47
Titles:
    on graphs, 484
    Lotus 1-2-3, 311–12
Token, 527
Toolbox, 627
Topdown coding, 589
Top margin, 206
Touch pads, 30
Touch screens, 30
Tracks, 45, 47
Transaction file, 15
Transaction log, 359–60
Transaction-processing system, 573
Transistors, 8–9
TREE, 120–21, 123
Tree structures, 362–63
TYPE, 91, 102–3
Typeover option, 148
Typewriters:
    keyboards on, 27, 28
    mag, 134

U

Underline command, 168, 175–77, 210
UNIVAC I, 8

Unstructured decision, 572
UPDATE, 388, 391, 393–94
Updated indexes, 443
Uploading, 521
Upper-case letters, 32
    ASCII code, 32
    case conversion of, 179
    and DOS communication, 91
USE, 402
Utility programs, 73, 74

V

Vacuum-tube computers, 8
Variable data, 137
VDISK.SYS, 125
Vector graphics, 459
Vertical menu, 60–62
Video display devices, 40
Video graphics array (VGA) monitors, 40
View commands, 482
View files, 395
Virtual-file allocation, 136
Viruses, 605
VisiCalc, 65–66, 226
Vision and sensing systems, 636–39
Voice recognition units, 31
von Neumann, John, 7

W

Warm start, 75
"What if" alternatives, 222–25
WHILE parameter, 406
Widows, 146, 206
Wild-card characters, 78
    dBASE III Plus, 443
    WordPerfect, 181, 202

Wild-card technique, 181
Winchester disk, 49
Windows:
    Lotus 1-2-3, 231
    text, 140
    WordPerfect, 208
WordPerfect, 67, 136
    Append command, 182
    backing up, 162–63
    block commands, 174–79
    codes, 149, 164–65
    commands, 140
    cursor movement in, 144–46
    deleting text, 148–53
    and diskettes, 137–38
    Disk Full error message, 179–80
    editing, 147
    exiting, 142–43, 162
    file handling, 163–64
    and hard disks, 138
    Help feature, 140
    inserting text, 147–48
    Insert Printer command, 212
    line numbering, 212
    line spacing, 152–53
    List File commands, 143–44
    margins, 170–74
    Merge command, 136–37
    Move command, 176–77
    operating, 140–42
    page breaks, 146
    page formatting, 203–209
    paragraphs, 146, 149–50
    print defaults, 153, 154
    Print Control menu, 165–67
    print formatting, 209–12
    printing, 153
    re-forming, 146
    screens, 138–40
    Search and Replace command, 180–81

Set-up menu, 162
special text entry, 167–69
Speller, 137, 200–203
starting, 137–40
Superscript/subscript, 179
tabs, 173–74
text window, 140
Thesaurus, 137
wild cards, 181, 202
window capabilities, 140
and word processing, 136
Word processing, 67. *See also* WordPerfect
    PC Works, 541–46
    WordPerfect, 134–37
Word wrap, 142
Worksheet Global Format, 263–65
Worksheets, 222–25, 231
WORM storage, 49
Write process, 6
Write-protect notch, 46, 47
WYSIWYG, 621

X

X-axis command, 482
XY graphs, 461–62, 481, 498–502

Y

Y-axis command, 482

Z

Zero command, 292

Internal Commands

CLS	DIR	TYPE
COPY	ERASE	VER
DATE	RENAME	VOL
DEL	TIME	

External Commands

CHKDSK	PRINT
DISKCOPY	SORT
FORMAT	SYS
MORE	

Redirection

<	Specify input other than the keyboard
>	Specify output other than the printer
>>	Specify output other than the printer and add this to the end of an existing line

Copy:

A>COPY fn B:	Copy a file from the default drive to drive B:
A>COPY fna fnb	Copy a file to the same disk under another name
A>COPY B:fn	Copy a file from drive B: to the default
A>COPY B:fn fna	Copy a file from drive B: and place it on the default under a different name

A>Copy *.* B:		Copy all files from a: to b:
A>Copy file? B:		Copy any file beginning with FILE and any character in position 5.

CHKDSK

A>CHKDSK b:	Check the status of the disk in drive B:
A>CHKDSK fn	Check the file, fn, for fragmentation
A>CHKDSK B:*.*	Check all the files on drive B: for fragmentation
A>CHKDSK B:*.*/F	Check drive B: for fragmentation and fix any problems

Format

FORMAT B:	Format the disk in drive B: w/o DOS
FORMAT B:/S	Format the disk in drive B: with DOS
FORMAT B:/V	Format the disk w/o DOS and record a label
FORMAT B:S/V	Format the disk with DOS and record a label

Directory Piping Commands

MORE<filename	Display the contents of filename to the monitor a screen at a time
DIR¦SORT¦MORE	Display the directory in sorted order to the monitor a screen at a time

DIR¦SORT	Sort the directory by file name
DIR¦SORT/ + 10	Sort the directory by file extension
DIR¦SORT/ + 14	Sort the directory by file size
DIR¦SORT/ + 25	Sort the directory by date
DIR¦SORT>DIR1	Sort the directory and place output in file DIR1

WordPerfect

Cursor Movement

GoTo	Ctrl + Home (enter page number)	Screen up	+
Word left	Ctrl + left arrow	Screen down	–
Word right	Ctrl + right arrow	Page up	PgUp
Screen right	Home, right arrow	Page down	PgDn
Screen left	Home, left arrow	Beg. of text	Home, Home, up arrow
		Beg. of line (text)	Home, Home, left arrow
		Beg. of line (codes)	Home, Home, Home, left arrow
		End of line	End or Home, Home, right arrow

WordPerfect

Delete Text

Delete character at cursor	Del	Delete to End of Line	Ctrl + End
Delete character to left of cursor	Backspace	Delete to End of Page	Ctrl + PgDn
Delete to Left Word Boundary	Home, Backspace	Delete (List Files)	F5, Enter
Delete to Right Word Boundary	Home, Del		

WordPerfect

Special Features

Bold	F6	Flush Right	Alt + F6
Center	Shift + F6	Font	Ctrl + F8
Underline	F8	Spacing	Shift + F8
Date	Shift + F5		

Merge Codes

Merge	Ctrl + F9
Merge E	Shift + F9
Merge R	F9
Merge Codes	Alt + F9

WordPerfect

File Commands

Exit	F7
Save	F10
Retrieve	LShift + F10

Search/Replace Commands

Search Forward	F2
Search Backward	Shift + F2
Replace	Alt + F2

Special Commands

Block	Alt + F4
Reveal Codes	Alt + F3
Cancel	F1
Help	F3

Lotus 1-2-3

Arithmetic and Logical Operators

+	Addition	=	Equals	
−	Subtraction	<	Less than	
*	Multiplication	>	Greater than	
/	Division			
^	Exponentiation			

Functions

@COUNT(range)	Number within a range
@SUM(range)	Sum of a range of values
@AVG(range)	Average of a range of values
@MIN(range)	Smallest value
@MAX(range)	Largest value

@STD(range)	Standard deviation
@VAR(range)	Variance
@NOW	Today's numeric value
@DATE(yy,mm,dd)	Get number of a date
@PMT(prn,int,term)	Payment amount

Lotus 1-2-3

Label Prefix

'	Left justify text within a cell
"	Right justify text within a cell
^	Center text within a cell
\	Repeating label

Absolute Cell References

CR	Always come back to the same row and column location (cell).
$CR	The row can change within the address, but the columns must always remain as specified. (Any row in this column)
C$R	The column can change within the address, but the row must remain the same. (Any column in this row)

Lotus 1-2-3

Function Keys

F1 Help	F9 Calc
F2 Edit	F10 Graph
F3 Name	
F4 Abs	
F5 Goto	
F6 Window	
F7 Query	
F8 Table	

Edit Keys

[Backspace]	Delete character to right of cursor
[ESC] or [Ctrl + Break]	Erase entry
right or left arrow	Move cursor one position right or left
[Home]	Position cursor to beginning of line
[Del]	Delete character at cursor
[End]	Position cursor to end of line
[Enter]	Record/save the changes

dBASE

File Commands

Create	Append	Use
Delete File	Edit	Modify
Copy File	Browse	Pack
Display Structure	Index	

Pointer

GOTO #
Skip
Find
Locate

Operators

Arithmetic
+ Addition
− Subtraction
* Multiplication
/ Division

Logical
.OR.
.AND.
.NOT.

Relational
< Less than
> Greater than
= Equal
<> Not equal

<= Less than or equal
>= Greater than or equal

dBASE

Selected Set Commands

Set Bell On/Off — On rings the bell when invalid data are entered or a field boundary is passed. Off turns off the bell.

Set Colon On/Off — On displays colons which delimit or bound input fields: Off hides the colons. (Only dBASE II)

Set Default to ⟨drive⟩ — Commands dBASE to regard the specified drive as the default drive for all future operations.

Set Deleted Off/On — On prevents dBASE from reading/processing any record marked for deletion. Off allows dBASE to read all records.

Set Intensity On/Off — On enables inverse video or dual intensity during full-screen operations. Off disables these features.

Set Margin to ⟨n⟩ — Sets the lefthand margin of printer to ⟨n⟩.

dBASE

Selected Full-Screen Cursor Movement Commands

^X — Moves DOWN to next field
^E — Moves UP to next field
^D — Moves RIGHT one position
^S — Moves LEFT one position
^G — Deletes character at cursor

⟨DEL⟩ — Deletes character to left of cursor
^Y — Blanks out current field
^V — Toggle between overwrite and insert mode
^W — Save changes and return to "•" prompt

Other Common Commands

ESC — Cancel any command and return to "•" prompt
^Q — Ignore any changes and return to "•" prompt
^N — Insert a line at cursor's position (Modify)
^T — Delete current line and move text up (Modify)
^P — Toggle printer On/Off

Function Keys Templates

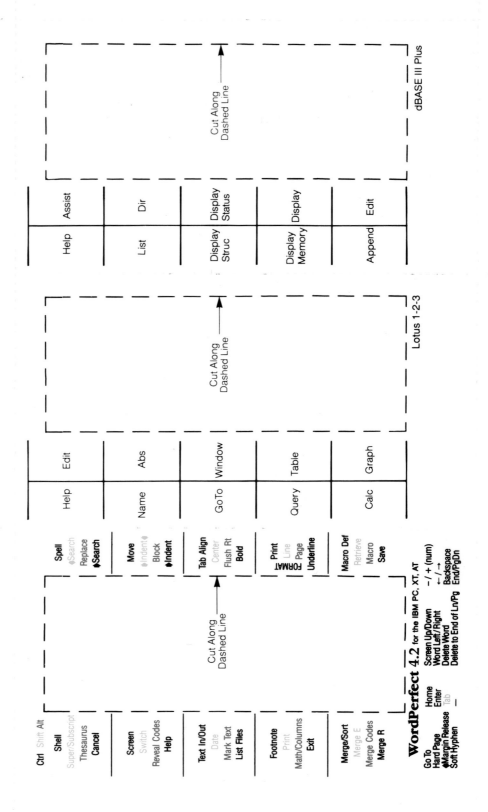

Cut Along Dashed Line

dBASE III Plus

Help	Assist
List	Dir
Display Struc	Display Status
Display Memory	Display
Append	Edit

Cut Along Dashed Line

Lotus 1-2-3

Help	Edit
Name	Abs
GoTo	Window
Query	Table
Calc	Graph

Cut Along Dashed Line

Spell
Search
Replace
Search

Move
Indent
Block
Indent

Tab Align
Center
Flush Rt
Bold

Print
Line
Page
Underline

Macro Def
Retrieve
Macro
Save

Ctrl Shift Alt
Shell
Super/Subscript
Thesaurus
Cancel

Screen
Switch
Reveal Codes
Help

Text In/Out
Date
Mark Text
List Files

Footnote
Print
Math/Columns
Exit

Merge/Sort
Merge E
Merge Codes
Merge R

WordPerfect 4.2 for the IBM PC, XT, AT

GoTo	Home	Screen Up/Down	− / + (num)
Hard Page	Enter	Word Left/Right	← / →
Margin Release	Tab	Delete Word	Backspace
Soft Hyphen	−	Delete to End of Ln/Pg	End/PgDn

Template Format for New IBM Keyboards

WordPerfect 4.2 (IBM Layout)

F1	F2	F3	F4	F5	F6	F7	F8		F9	F10
Shell SUPER/ SUBSCRIPT Thesaurus Cancel	→ Spell ← SEARCH Replace Search →	Screen SWITCH Reveal Codes Help	Move → INDENT ← ↑ Block ↓ → Indent	Ctrl Shift Alt	Text In/Out DATE Mark Text List Files	Tab Align CENTER Flush Right Bold	Footnote PRINT Math/ Columns Exit	Print LINE FORMAT Page Format Underline	Ctrl Shift Alt	Merge/Sort MERGE E Merge Codes Merge R	Macro Def. RETRIEVE TEXT Macro Save Text

Legend: Ctrl + Function Key SHIFT + FUNCTION KEY Alt + Function Key Function Key alone

Lotus 1-2-3

F1	F2	F3	F4		F5	F6	F7	F8		F9	F10
Help	Edit	Name	Abs	/////	GoTo	Window	Query	Table	/////	Calc	Graph

dBASE III Plus

F1	F2	F3	F4		F5	F6	F7	F8		F9	F10
Help	Assist	List	Dir	/////	Display Struc	Display Status	Display Memory	Display	/////	Append	Edit

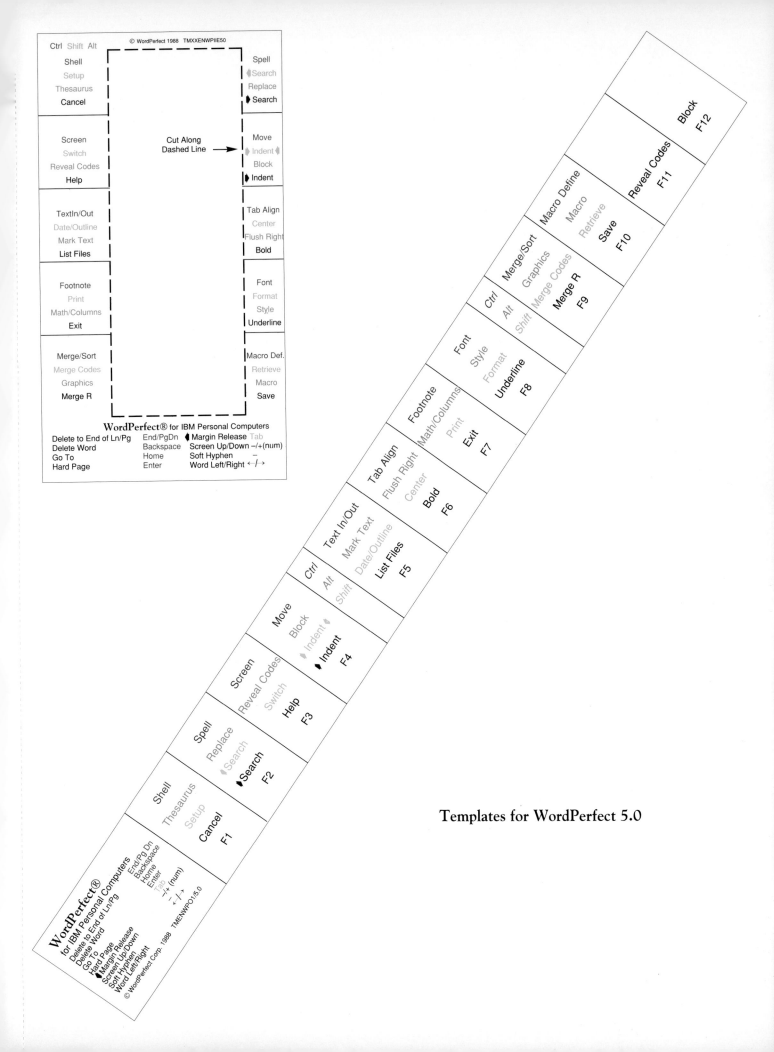

© WordPerfect 1988 TMXXENWPIIE50

Ctrl	Shift	Alt		Spell
Shell				Search
Setup				Replace
Thesaurus				**Search**
Cancel				

Cut Along Dashed Line →

Screen		Move
Switch		Indent
Reveal Codes		Block
Help		**Indent**

TextIn/Out		Tab Align
Date/Outline		Center
Mark Text		Flush Right
List Files		**Bold**

Footnote		Font
Print		Format
Math/Columns		Style
Exit		**Underline**

Merge/Sort		Macro Def.
Merge Codes		Retrieve
Graphics		Macro
Merge R		**Save**

WordPerfect® for IBM Personal Computers

Delete to End of Ln/Pg	End/PgDn	◀ Margin Release Tab
Delete Word	Backspace	Screen Up/Down –/+(num)
Go To	Home	Soft Hyphen –
Hard Page	Enter	Word Left/Right ←/→

Templates for WordPerfect 5.0